THE GOLDEN AGE ILLUSION
Rethinking Postwar Capitalism

A GUILFORD SERIES

Perspectives on Economic Change

Editors

MERIC S. GERTLER
University of Toronto

PETER DICKEN
University of Manchester

**The Golden Age Illusion:
Rethinking Postwar Capitalism**
MICHAEL J. WEBBER and DAVID L. RIGBY

**Work-*Place*:
The Social Regulation of Labor Markets**
JAMIE PECK

**Restructuring for Innovation:
The Remaking of the U.S. Semiconductor Industry**
DAVID P. ANGEL

**Trading Industries, Trading Regions:
International Trade, American Industry,
and Regional Economic Development**
HELZI NOPONEN, JULIE GRAHAM, and ANN R. MARKUSEN, *Editors*

THE GOLDEN AGE ILLUSION

Rethinking Postwar Capitalism

MICHAEL J. WEBBER
DAVID L. RIGBY

THE GUILFORD PRESS
New York   London

© 1996 The Guilford Press
A Division of Guilford Publications, Inc.
72 Spring Street, New York, NY 10012

Marketed and distributed outside North America
by Longman Group UK Limited

Printed in the United States of America

This book is printed on acid-free paper.

Last digit is print number: 9 8 7 6 5 4 3 2 1

Library of Congress Cataloging-in-Publication Data

Webber, Michael John.
     The golden age illusion : rethinking postwar capitalism / Michael
 J. Webber and David L. Rigby
        p.   cm.
     Includes bibliographical references and index.
     ISBN 0-89862-573-4.
     1. Capitalism—History—20th century.   2. Economic history—1945–
 I. Rigby, David L.   II. Title.
 HB501.W465   1996
 330.12′2—dc20   96-2356
                                                           CIP

CONTENTS

LIST OF FIGURES

LIST OF TABLES

PREFACE

I t is sometimes asserted that the turnover times of capital are falling in the modern world. That may be, but the turnover time for this book has been over a decade.

The research project of which this book is a product began in Hamilton, Ontario, in the early 1980s when Simon Foot, David Rigby, and Michael Webber began to work together at McMaster University on analytical and empirical approaches to political economy. That was a time when we, like many others in North America, were seeking to put numbers and formality and—above all—geography into the classical Marxian understanding of economic dynamics. Some of those others have moved on, but we shared a task and encouragement with Trevor Barnes, Kathy Gibson, Julie Graham, and Eric Sheppard in trying to go beyond *The Limits to Capital*.

This book represents an attempt to understand the dynamics of the world capitalist economy over much of the postwar period. It uses the methods and experiences forged during those experiments in Marxian economic geographic dynamics, but it seeks to answer a modern problem: how has the world economy got to its present geographic configuration? The book seeks to use theoretical and methodological tools; but its aim is to understand the real economy. The book also presents a variety of information about the evolution of the economic geography of the world; but it seeks to use that information to inform the development of new theoretical tools.

In the course of our learning about appropriate methods and of a specifically geographic approach to the problems of economic dynamics, we owe large intellectual debts to Trevor Barnes, Simon Foot, David Harvey, and Eric Sheppard. We have been encouraged over the years, rather more generally, by Ruth Fincher, Les King, and Dick Walker. Les King built a department in which rigorous theoretical and empirical research were valued and in which varieties of theoretical position were tolerated.

In addition to our general intellectual debts, we have received a great deal of help from many people. Meric Gertler deserves a large vote of thanks for his detailed comments on the first draft of this book and for the time he spent on the second draft. Both Eric Sheppard and Dick Walker read and provided comments upon several chapters. Bill Anderson provided some of the data used in Chapter 9; Gordon Clark assisted in gaining grants that ended up yielding much of the data about Japan and East Asia in Chapters 8 and 10; Simon Foot's work on the steel industry in Brazil has provided the source of ideas and information used in Chapter 10; Eric Sheppard collaborated in developing the theory of technical change that is stated in Chapter 6; and Sue Tonkin (now Sue White) processed much of the data about Australia that is deployed in Chapter 8. Financial support for the work we report here has been provided by the Australian Research Council, the Canadian Studies Grant Program, the Social Sciences and Humanities Research Council of Canada, the University of California, Los Angeles, and the University of Melbourne. We are grateful to all of these people and institutions for their support: we hope that the result is worth their while.

Some of the research reported in this book has been published in different forms in a number of journals. An earlier version of Chapter 3 was published by *Society and Space*; parts of Chapters 4 and 10 have been published in *Environment and Planning A*; parts of Chapter 6 have also been published with Eric Sheppard in *Environment and Planning A*; some of Chapters 8 and 10 has been published in the *Canadian Geographer* and *Economic Geography*. We are grateful to those journals for their permission to use this material.

We also thank Chase Langford for producing the figures used in the book.

Above all, we wish to express our appreciation for the support and encouragement of Ruth Fincher and Chris Malham.

Michael J. Webber
David L. Rigby

Los Angeles
September 1995

THE GOLDEN AGE ILLUSION
Rethinking Postwar Capitalism

Chapter I

INTRODUCTION

Our own, First World industrial economies seem in disarray. Not only the poorer countries of the Third World but also many middle and higher income countries face huge burdens of debt. In the early 1980s, the government and firms of South Korea owed more than half the nation's gross domestic product (GDP) to foreigners; in 1990 in Gabon, Hungary, and Venezuela, more than two-thirds was owed (World Bank 1985, 1992). In Japan by 1987 cumulative government debt was equal to more than half the gross national product (GNP) and interest on the debt consumed 20% of all government expenditure (Itoh 1990: 187–192).

Unprecedented numbers of people lack work. In Australia in the 1950s and 1960s a 1% unemployment rate was regarded as political suicide for a government; yet the rate of unemployment reached 10% in 1982 and exceeded that in 1992. The unemployment rate in Canada and the USA approached or exceeded 10% some time in the 1980s (OECD 1987b: 135; 1989a: 19).

More and more people are being forced into unstable, part-time, or contractual jobs. In Canada, Japan, and the USA a quarter or more of female employment is part time, in Australia nearly 40%. In Japan some 35% of males and 65% of females in the work force are self-employed, family workers, temporary or day workers, part-time workers, or student workers (OECD 1989a). In the European Community perhaps 10% of all employment is clandestine—on or beyond the fringe of laws and regulations (de Grazia 1984: 14).

The jobs that can be found are commonly in service industries rather than in more traditional forms of production. By 1987, nearly 70% of civilian employment in Canada and the USA was in services and about 60% of that in Australia and Japan (OECD 1989b: 36–37). Some of the jobs are in the burgeoning knowledge industries rather than in sectors that rely on traditional raw materials. The occupations that produce information, process it, distribute it, or provide and maintain infrastructure for it account for more than 40% of all employment in the USA and 30% in Japan (ILO 1984: 179–180).

The large corporations that employ people have become global in reach.

By the 1980s multinational corporations employed some 4 million people in developing countries and perhaps 30 million people worldwide (ILO 1981a: 21; 1981b: 1). In the early 1970s domestic and foreign multinationals employed more than a half of Australia's manufacturing workers, over 70% of those in Canada, and some 40% of those in the USA (ILO 1981b: 6–7). The 500 largest multinationals produce at least 20% of the world's gross product (Dassbach 1989: 2).

And in the midst of this turmoil, increasing numbers of people question the value of growth itself, preferring forms of development that are environmentally sustainable. The growth of Green parties, most spectacularly in West Germany but also in other parts of Europe, indexes this preference. Founded in 1979, the Greens gained over 5.5% of the vote in the 1983 West German election (Rothacher 1984). In their different ways the World Commission on Environment and Development (1987) and Suzuki (1990) also question the desirability of growth. By 1992 the World Bank felt constrained to devote the 1992 issue of its *World Development Report* to explaining how development could be made compatible with environmental values.

Meanwhile, the global economic environment within which our economies flounder has altered out of recognition.

Financial corporations shift billions of dollars daily from one country to another. By 1987 more than $400 billion crossed the world's foreign exchanges each day (Armstrong et al. 1991: 303). In 1981 new bank lending net of loan repayments exceeded $165 billion, nearly five times its 1973 level, and financial flows to developing countries exceeded $170 billion (World Bank 1985: 19, 112). Partly in response, our currencies abruptly alter their value from one day to the next: between 1985 and 1988, the US dollar lost over 35% of its value while the yen gained 40% (Armstrong et al. 1991: 302). In March 1984 the Australian dollar was worth $US0.95; one year later it was worth $US0.65; and three and a half years after that was back to its 1984 value (Daly and Logan 1989: 37).

The rapid increase in production and exports from the newly industrialized countries has posed significant problems for the economies of some developed countries. Exports from developing countries to industrial market economies accounted for 2.5% of world trade in manufactures in 1963 but 4.5% by 1973 and 8.5% by 1984 (World Bank 1987: 135). In 1989 over 30% of the USA's and Japan's imports of manufactures came from developing countries (Dicken 1992: 32).

Farmers in Australia run scared of commodity trade wars between the USA and the European Community. Manufacturers in the developing countries fear protectionism in the USA, the European Community, and Japan. By 1985 the EC had arranged 4 import restraints in the automobile industry, 5 in electronics, and 20 in steel. The industrial market economies, including Japan, subjected a fifth of imports from developing countries to nontariff barriers (World Bank 1987: 140, 142).

The former USSR and eastern Europe are no longer monolithic, closed, command economies. The USSR has broken up into its constituent republics, more or less at odds with each other—all confronted with economic breakdown and bribed by the promise of international loans to use markets rather than commands to allocate resources. Integrating the East German economy with that of West Germany has become an expensive process weighing on the international community. The Czech Republic, Slovakia, Hungary, and Poland are privatizing their state corporations and learning the need to export to pay off their accumulated debts. Yugoslavia, once a promising newly industrializing country (NIC), has fragmented into warring states.

Famine, disease, and disaster yet remain the daily experience of many people in most Third World countries. In 1990, infant mortality rates exceeded 10% in India and many countries of sub-Saharan Africa but were less than 1% in Australia and Japan. The average intake of calories per capita was less than 2500 in the Philippines, India, Peru, and most of sub-Saharan Africa; over 3200 in Australia, Canada, and the USA (World Bank 1992). Sustainable development, national debt, and global integration seem cruel jokes, not central issues, to people at the bottom of the world league. (On their links, though, see George 1988.)

With the disarray has come debate. Once there was tacit agreement that in basically capitalist societies workers had rights to bargain for working conditions, managers had rights to manage, and governments had responsibilities to provide public services and guarantee minimum living conditions. Now that consensus is splintered. From right and left, from representatives of the past and from those who would represent the future, come calls that we must change the way we do things. We must restructure our economies. Americans fear the loss of hegemony. Australians are warned of becoming the white trash of Asia. Canadians are threatened with incorporation into the USA. The Japanese are told to consume more—especially imports—and to work less now that they have caught up with the West. To the right, incentives need to be restored; to the left, equality.

The breakdown of consensus, the radically disparate calls for politically charged action, all are symptoms of restructuring, of attempts to alter the established social and economic relations within a given place. These established relations provide rules, a norm, a framework within which competition between corporations and conflict between sectors, places, and groups can be expressed and controlled. People, corporations, and institutions then generally behave with an understanding of that framework, anticipating that other people, corporations, and institutions will also act with the same kind of understanding. For example, corporations expect that firing a worker for *this* reason will be regarded as acceptable to a union, but *those* working conditions will probably not be; *this* investment will probably work because other corporations will be anticipating *these* forms of economic development; *this* wage claim is probably acceptable because corporations are adjusting costs by increasing efficiency in *these* ways. This is consensus: a set of assumptions within which most people, corporations, and institutions work and plan. Industrial restructuring breaks consensus by changing the relations between class, gender, and ethnic groups, industrial sectors, corporations, and places, so altering global patterns of growth, national industrialization strategies, or local development plans (Webber et al. 1992).

The consensus has broken down for two general reasons. First, it is perceived that earlier strategies have failed to secure the interests of dominant groups in society. That is, when it became accepted that growth in the advanced capitalist countries ran into a profitability crisis after the early 1970s, new sources of growth had to be discovered. Second, restructuring has also been prompted by changes in power relations between groups, sectors, or places. The new authority of Japan and the newly industrializing countries; the power of the finance sector; fluctuations in the strength of workers: all alter power relations as the newly powerful groups, sectors, or places insist that strategies of growth accommodate their interests more explicitly. Either way, a change of strategy will privilege some corporations, sectors, groups, or places and handicap others.

Consensus about strategy has been most commonly built as a national project. The state is the locus of power that determines the form of the market, defines competition between capitals, supervises conflict between classes, and regulates linkages between the nation and the world. The national economy is not independent or freestanding and some fractions of capital have international rather than national ties. Nor is the state autonomous. Yet the nation state is powerful and can express forcefully the interests of dominant sectors. Although national experiences differ, many theories (including core and periphery or international divisions of labor or global capitalism) contend that individual places and industries represent particular instances of a general global pattern of accumulation, from which they deviate to greater or lesser degree: there is a general, global pattern of growth, and individual places exemplify that pattern. However, the processes that couple national strategies into global patterns of growth are obscure: we shall need to investigate some of the processes later. Whatever the links, the success or failure of national plans is not founded solely on global patterns.

The transition from one strategy or pattern of accumulation to another entails bargaining and struggle during restructuring. Nations use economic and industry policy to position firms in the world economy and bargain over rules of trade and finance that govern that economy. Different sectors advance their interests, which are to varying degrees represented by compromises in the strategy. Social groups struggle economically and politically over their shares.

The events of restructuring are real. The world has certainly changed, altering the standing of groups, sectors, corporations, and places; and real responses are being made to those changes. But the extent to which the changes have been recognized publicly differs between places—and depends on the stories told about them. Restructuring involves idealizing the past or other places for history is a tool in the bargaining. We are led to regard the present disarray as a sea change from the world of 30 or 40 years ago. The USA and the USSR were supreme in their respective spheres of influence. We were growing used to low unemployment and to continuous improvements in real wages and living conditions. Mainly, our currencies had relatively fixed values. Under the GATT (General Agreement on Tariffs and Trade) regime, reductions in tariff barriers were regularly negotiated. For people in the Third World, decolonization promised freedom from the shackles of European domination and dependent forms of growth. There was genuine hope that the unemployment of the 1930s and the poverty of the Third World were becoming phenomena of the past. Even the then-dominant philosophy of science—positivism—gave a sense of hope, from the power of reason.

This sense that the world has entered a new epoch is strong. In particular, arguments about restructuring imply that the characteristics of the world's economies now have changed. Then was growth; now is stagnation. Then was full-time, permanent employment (for men, at least); now is unemployment, or part-time and casual jobs. Then was regulated trade and currencies; now is flux and uncertainty. Then was about making real things like food and machines; now is about making symbols and spectacles. A whole host of academic and popular commentators have identified aspects of contemporary life that seem to reflect a division between some (usually ideal) past and a more uncertain and often less than ideal present. Many names have been applied to these distinctions, depending on the phenomena used to characterize the division and the theoretical ground from which the commentators start:

> Fordism–post-Fordism (an idea originating in the so-called French regulation school: see Boyer and Mistral 1978; Lipietz 1986; also Schoenberger 1988)
> Mass production–flexible accumulation (see Dunford 1990; Piore and Sabel 1984; Scott 1988a,b; Storper and Walker 1989)
> Organized capitalism–disorganized capitalism (Lash and Urry 1987)
> The golden age–(the less than golden age?) (Glyn et al. 1990)
> Monopoly capitalism–late capitalism (Mandel 1978)
> National economies–global economy (Dicken 1992); and perhaps the most ambitious distinction of them all
> Modernism—postmodernism (Harvey 1988; Soja 1989)

The idealizations inherent in these distinctions overemphasize the homogeneity of the golden age and tint it too rosily. Unemployment was always high in Canada—well above twice the Australian rate in the 1970s and above even the British rate—and particularly high in the Canadian Maritimes (OECD 1989a: 19). Many black and aboriginal people did not share in the spoils of growth in Australia, Canada, and the USA and were just about totally excluded from Japan. Women's average wages remained low: in the 1970s women workers in manufacturing received 75% of men's pay in Australia and less than half in Japan (ILO 1985: 216). The rate of growth of productivity was lower in the UK than in many other countries of Europe and North America: between 1950 and 1970, labor productivity in Japan rose twice as fast as in the UK; in Germany it rose 1.6 times as fast; and it even rose faster in the USA (Armstrong et al. 1991: 212). There were periodic devaluations of the British pound and French franc. West Germany and Japan were catching up with and then powering ahead of their rivals. The gross fixed capital stock in manufacturing in the Group of Seven (Canada, France, Germany, Italy, Japan, the UK, and the USA) doubled between 1960 and 1973; that same doubling took Japan 5 years and Germany 11 years; it took the UK 28 years (Armstrong et al. 1991: Table A5). And, except in a few places, living standards in the Third World rose only slightly relative to those in Europe and North America. Despite rates of growth of GNP since 1965 well above the US rate, levels of national product per capita in China and India were still less than one-tenth of American levels in 1990 (if measured in international prices; less than one-fiftieth if measured at 1990 exchange rates: World Bank 1992). The golden age was only partly golden: it was more golden in some places than others, for some people than others.

It is also far too easy to generalize unreasonably the present disarray. If the last 20 years have been not even partly golden, they have not been uniformly depressed. The three recessions (1973–1975, 1979–1982, and 1991–1992) have separated years in which growth has approached the rates achieved in the partly golden age. Superimposed on the cycles of production has been a price cycle: after the oil price shocks inflation rose to a peak about 1980 before falling sharply (see Berry 1991). Slow growth also means different things to different countries: whereas France, Germany, Italy, and the UK have experienced rates of capital accumulation in manufacturing of little more than 1% each year in the 1980s, the rate in the USA has been nearly 2%, in Canada 3%, and in Japan over 6% (Armstrong et al. 1991: Table A5). While capital accumulation in Korea and Taiwan has certainly slowed as compared to the 1960s, rates in the 1980s have still approached 10% each year. If times have been hard for some industries in some regions, the last 20 years have also witnessed the remarkable growth of other places and industries. Between 1960 and 1980, manufacturing employment in Orange County, just south of Los Angeles, increased more than fivefold; well over a half of that employment is in a few high-technology sectors connected to the US military and space programs: machinery; electrical and electronic equipment; aircraft, missiles, and space vehicles; instruments (Scott 1988a: 164). In the Los Angeles region, the other rapidly growing sector is finance: employment in finance, insurance, and real estate grew by 60% in the 1960s and 50% in the 1970s (Soja 1989: 198–199). By contrast in the industrial market economies as a group, production of textiles and clothing was static in the 1970s and 1980s while employment in the steel industry has fallen (Dicken 1992: 237, 241). Not all sectors nor all places share the present disarray. If the past was partly golden, the present is only partly tarnished.

Yet there was growth and it was expected to continue. Now those hopes and with them the consensus lie shattered. In retrospect, internal pressures were building in the advanced capitalist countries that must have derailed long-run growth eventually; rates of economic growth in North America were beginning to falter in the late 1960s and with them rates of profit. Nevertheless, by common consensus the outstanding symbol of the break occurred on 17 October 1973, when the ten members of the Organization of Arab Petroleum Exporting Countries announced a plan to cut their collective output of oil by 5% per month for the next 20 months: Gulf crude oil prices rose from $2.70 in early October to $11.65 on 1 January 1974. A less commonly identified symbol of the break occurred on 15 August 1971, when President Richard M. Nixon announced that US dollars would no longer be convertible to gold, thus denying the world a stable reserve currency. The hike in oil prices and the end of the Bretton Woods agreement only symbolize the end of the golden age; they did not cause it. Yet they are symbols of an end that we have collectively taken a long time to recognize.

So the language of restructuring encapsulates the past and other countries in a general parable. In that past golden age we did well; in other places they did better. Depending on taste, the parable might be Fordism, mass production, organized capitalism, a golden age, monopoly capitalism, national economies, or modernism. The parables idealize: the contrasts are overdrawn. Except perhaps for the story of monopoly capitalism, the parables gloss over imperfections of the period of rapid growth: economic cycles, uneven technical change, environmental degradation, the spread of famine, uneven distribution of the spoils of growth, and gender and ethnic inequalities. The major parables also fail to recognize that the end was contained in the period. In the parables are buried the power relations that underpin the construction of a language: class, gender, ethnicity, and nation. Those power relations are reflected in the way in which parables interpret the past, testimony to the deep and widespread reactions to the change in economic fortunes.

Perhaps responding to the political failures as much as to the economic failures of the golden age, many intellectuals have followed G. Deleuze, J. Derrida, and M. Foucault in retreating to a poststructuralist philosophy that stresses the fragmentary, heterogeneous, and plural nature of reality; denies our ability to account objectively for reality; and reduces the subject to an incoherent welter of drives and desires (Callenicos 1989). In a similar repercussion, high school students are reported to find the geography of the modern world "depressing." Other reactions are having an immediate and direct impact on people's lives.

For treasury officials the world over, for bankers national or international, and for the economists who have trained them, the way out of this predicament is straightforward. Let the market set prices. Permit people to respond to income incentives to produce. Free up industries. Remove barriers to trade. Put limits on government spending to reduce national debts and to make more capital available for investment in productive activities. Circumscribe the power of people to demand higher wages and better working conditions, and thus defeat inflation. In Australia reports to the federal government from Garnaut (1989) and the Department of Foreign Affairs and Trade (1992); in Canada studies by the Economic Council of Canada and the Royal Commission on the Economic Union and Development Prospects for Canada (Harris 1985, 1992; McFetridge 1986); in Japan the Maekawa report (1986) and white papers on the economy (EPA annual; MITI annual); and in the USA studies by Accordino (1992) and Feldstein (1988) and selected reports to Congress by the Joint Economic Committee and from the Subcommittee on Economic Goals and International Policy (US Congress: Joint Economic Committee various years): all have adapted the prescriptions of the World Bank and the International Monetary Fund to their national circumstances.

Such proposals rest on the idea that circumstances were good, perhaps more in other places than our own. They claim that we have made mistakes and that our present predicament was created by those mistakes. Prices were manipulated by governments and monopolies. Taxes and regulations reduced incentives. Tariffs protected inefficiency. Government spending crowded out productive investment. Workers became too powerful and demanded too large a share of the surplus. In other words, the benefits that we obtained during the so-called golden age were derived from living beyond our means, from postponing serious economic change: our present so-called disarray is the price of those benefits. Sometimes, our disarray is the price of other people's benefits: some Japanese bureaucrats blame US fiscal and monetary policies for Japan's trade surplus and the subsequent revaluation of the yen in 1985 (Miyazaki 1987: 2–3); and Americans in turn condemn the Japanese and various NICs for unfair trade practices.

To others on the (middle-)left, to whom we are the product of the past rather than the cause of the future, the 1950s and 1960s were a period in which techniques of production and social institutions appropriately cohered in a regime of accumulation. The pieces fit. The regime of the golden age was thus seen as: a macroeconomic structure that guaranteed constant rates of profit by ensuring that real wages rose at the same rate as productivity; a Taylorist system of production in which productivity was raised by dividing and measuring tasks precisely; rules of coordination that made individual decisions consistent with macro-economic principles; and an established international order that raised the salience of economy over international conflict. However, this system began to disintegrate in the late 1960s as productivity growth slowed, real input costs rose, labor markets tightened, and competition from imports intensified. In other accounts, more attention is paid to the problem posed by rising levels of demand for labor.

These ideas have been extended in arguments that the economy is switching toward flexible or post-Fordist, disorganized or global forms of production. The earlier model of production (however identified) during the golden age was underpinned by large, highly capitalized units of production consisting of continuous-flow processes or assembly lines. New flexible production systems permit plants to shift between products or processes quickly and to alter output in the short run without major changes in efficiency: they comprise general purpose machines (often programmable), broader job descriptions, intensification of external economies of scale, faster labor turnover, and use of part-time, temporary, and out work. A spatial shift is occurring as those regions dependent on Fordist industries are deindustrialized, as previously unindustrialized communities are industrialized and as preexisting clusters of flexible producers are reindustrialized. The new, small, specialized, and flexible producers acquire an institutionalized social order to coordinate their activities.

Such interpretations and their prescriptions for change are deeply political. Obviously things are not right: the system is not working as once it did. This is especially clear in small, dependent economies like Australia's or Canada's. But equally obviously the directions in which we are being pushed will work to the benefit of some people and the cost of others. The argument about that direction is conducted in two ways. There is theory: on the one side, as a matter of neoclassical economic logic, market economies work best; on the other, market economies must be supplemented by rules that guarantee their reproducibility. But there is also evidence: look at eastern Europe; see, the past golden age broke down when we did not act appropriately; now our performance is not up to that of country X (commonly, Japan) and we are not acting as they do. This is an argument about the nature of the golden age of the 1950s and 1960s and the reasons why growth seems to have slowed after 1973.

Stories like these that we are told about the past establish the blame for the end of the golden age. Why did it come to an end, if it was so golden? The politics do not allow that the end was inherent; rather, there must have been some cause outside the conditions of the golden age itself. The stories also implicitly allocate the costs of establishing the conditions for a new strategy of accumulation. We now have to change. In that change, some will gain, some will lose. Who will they be? And what price will they have to pay? And will they pay that price now, during the restructuring, or over the long run in a new period of accumulation? Therefore, restructuring entails the claim that if appropriate conditions are established, society will enter a new golden age, with benefits akin to those provided by the previous, idealized, golden age. The claim justifies the cost of instituting the new conditions.

Restructuring proceeds at two levels. At one, competition and conflict establish the capacity of the dominant group to define a growth strategy that satisfies to various degrees the interests of corporations and is accepted by subordinate classes. At the other level, restructuring is justified by claims about an ideal past, the blame for the end of that past, and the nature of an ideal future, if only certain costs are paid. It is politically crucial to understand clearly the central dynamics of growth in the postwar world, to understand what happened and why we are in the present mess.

We therefore seek in this book to comprehend the main features of the history and geography of economic development in the last 40 years. Our aims are to dispel idealized visions of the wonders of that lost world of the golden age and to demonstrate that accumulation faltered for internal, inherent reasons rather than because of external events that can be blamed on others. It is not so much that we made mistakes spending too much, protecting industries, permitting workers to become too powerful, letting the rate of productivity slow; instead, growth would in any rate have slowed, because sustained rapid rates of growth *must* be followed by slower growth and disarray. That fact is an inherent characteristic of our economies. Therefore some of the costs that people are being asked to bear in order to attain the new golden age do not have quite the intellectual basis that is claimed.

The book is organized into distinct topics. The history and our arguments with interpretations of it are contained in Chapters 2 and 3. Chapter 4 describes method. The theoretical tools we need are developed in Chapters 5 through 7: in order, theories of profitability, technical change, and the location of production. Chapters 8, 9, and 10 present the evidence corresponding to the three theoretical chapters. Chapter 11 brings the story together, integrating the theory with the evidence to produce an interpretation of the history and geography of postwar development. While the topics of the book are organized simply enough into discrete chapters, the central arguments run through several chapters.

We begin in Chapter 2 by describing the main features of the evolution of the global economy since about 1950. We examine first rates of economic growth in some countries of the Organization for Economic Cooperation and Development (OECD): some indicators give evidence of a slowdown in some countries. More importantly, growth has essentially taken the form of globalization, the main processes of which are financial integration, the consolidation of production in multinational corporations, and rising levels of trade. These processes have given rise to new patterns of production and trade: the rise of the NICs and Japan, the continued failure of some countries to support their citizens' lives, and new networks of world trade. Finally we outline some of the implications of these changes for the people who work within the advanced industrial economies. We go on in Chapter 3 to survey existing interpretations of these global industrial changes. We argue that interpretations of economic history assume (wrongly) that there exists adequate evidence and theory about the dynamics of the postwar years. The remainder of the book is devoted to developing that theory and presenting the relevant evidence.

To understand the central dynamics of growth in the global economy is not to explain the economic histories of individual countries. Australia's balance of payments problem, Canada's continuing regional disparities, the rapid growth of Japan, the US federal debt: these are not the issue. Rather, the issue is global: has growth become problematic since 1973 and if so why? Our central claim—our major objection to accounts from both the left and the right—

is that *to the extent there has occurred a slowdown, it was inherent in the dynamics of the golden age.* That is, the forms of technical change that sustained the real-wage rises of the 1950s and 1960s also diminished the profitability of production; our present disarray is caused by the continuing lack of profits in production.

Of course, superimposed on this underlying dynamic were accidents, mistakes, and peculiarities of individual countries. Oil prices have gone up and down; wheat prices are as unstable; whereas Ronald Reagan and Margaret Thatcher dominated the English-speaking Northern Hemisphere, the Japanese never embraced such scorched earth policies. Again we emphasize: we are not concerned to demonstrate the logic of particular events. Even less do we claim that a slowdown had to occur in the 1970s. Rather we seek to show that the end of the partly golden age was contained in its dynamic. The end of the period of relatively rapid growth was the product not of mistakes of policy, nor of slower productivity growth, much less of intensified competition from imports, but of the fact that it was a period of rapid growth.

Deriving from the central claim that the 1950s and 1960s were merely partly golden is the argument they were also not an age. To describe a golden age, a regime of accumulation, is to identify an era in which certain features of social life remained constant; after that era and marking its end, some at least of those features changed. The era has a certain homogeneity. We argue against this view: there are important continuities between the 1950s and 1960s on the one hand and the 1970s and 1980s on the other; there were also important changes within the 1950s and 1960s that diminish its apparent homogeneity.

So this is not a book of economic history. It is not a claim about the necessary character of events in particular places or of political responses to those events. It interprets at a global level the perceived slowdown in growth. As such it is as much theoretical as empirical. The perceived global slowdown has been the context for changes in individual countries, a context to which some countries have succumbed but which others have attempted more or less successfully to overcome. The theory of this claim—to the extent there has occurred a slowdown, it was inherent in the dynamics of the golden age— is outlined in Chapter 5; its evidence, in Chapter 8, especially Section 8.1. Throughout, the evidence is derived from two advanced capitalist economies of the core (Japan and the USA) and from two capitalist economies of the semiperiphery (Australia and Canada). Additional evidence is presented about conditions in three NICs: Brazil, South Korea, and Taiwan.

Surrounding and bolstering this central claim are three additional assertions.

There are long-run, persistent profit rate differences between industries and regions (Sections 8.2 and 8.3). The differences are inconsistent with generally received theories of equilibrium, so Chapter 7 explains how and why they arise: profit rates are not necessarily equal at equilibrium. The differences upset usual interpretations of regional change. If a NIC grows faster than the USA does, we commonly reason that production must be more profitable in the NIC than in the USA. Then we seek reasons for the differences in profitability. However, if profit rates can differ at equilibrium, the NIC may grow faster even if production there is less profitable than in the USA. This argument provides scope for examining the relative growth of NICs as matters of state policy rather than of costs of production.

We argue also that *fluctuations in rates of technical change have not caused a slowdown; they mainly reflect a slowdown*. It is sometimes argued that one of the reasons for the apparent slowdown in growth has been diminished rates of technical change (see, for example, Piore and Sable 1984; Lipietz 1986). This argument has the dynamic wrong, at least for the modern period. We construct in Chapter 6 a general theory of technical change from which we can identify different sources of changes in productivity: the adoption of new or copied innovations by individual corporations; the growth and decline of firms that use different techniques; the entry and exit of firms from the market. These sources of productivity change have themselves different causes. Some depend on the rate of innovation; others, on the rate of investment or on market conditions. The evidence in Chapter 9 indicates that market conditions and levels of investment after a slowdown have in turn slowed productivity change.

The export-oriented industrialization of the NICs is blamed by theorists of the French regulation school and of the new international division of labor for some of the ills of the advanced capitalist economies. We argue both that *the perceived slowdown in the advanced economies was one of the factors that permitted the rise of the NICs* and that *the slowdown has in some countries forced an export-oriented strategy*. We have in Chapter 7 identified how economic theory can provide room for state policy. In the examples studied in Chapter 10—Brazil, South Korea, and Taiwan—industrialization has been created by the state in the context of the changing global economy. Such states have exploited conditions in the global economy to their own ends.

These are, if you will, our claims about what has happened. There has been something of a slowdown, at least in some sectors and some places. That slowdown ended for internal reasons, not because of competition from the NICs or the failure of technical change or the rising power of labor. Most existing interpretations of economic history have simply got the dynamic wrong. The errors arise because existing interpretations rely on inadequate theories—theories that are inherently static or comparatively static and that assume economies at equilibrium. Our central methodological contention is therefore that if economic theories are to be useful in interpreting historical geography, they must embody nonequilibrium dynamics. This assertion underpins the theoretical work in Chapters 5, 6, and 7; it is explicit in Chapter 4. There we state and defend empirical applications of the theory of value. Despite all the wavering and waffling about value, the categories employed in the theory of value are consistent and can be measured; to demonstrate this requires a detour into statistics, the nature of equilibrium, and the issue of an auxiliary theory of measurement. In one sense, this methodological claim forms the basis of Chapter 4; in another sense, it provides the means of measuring economic performance and so is justified by the methods and results of the book as a whole.

Chapter 2

THE PARTLY GOLDEN AGE

By 1990, global annual marketed output exceeded $22 trillion. In real terms this was six times the level of 1950. Of course, there were more than twice as many people on the globe in 1990 as there had been in 1950. Even so, on average, they each produced nearly three times as much in 1990 as in 1950. They were also generally trading far more than they used to: the volume of international commodity trade was growing about one and a half times as fast as the volume of output. By 1990, world trade was nearly ten times that of 1950.

These aggregate statistics about growth with globalization conceal two details. Since the early 1970s, the growth of output has slowed: the 20 years after 1950 saw output rise three times; but output only doubled in the 20 years after 1970. Growth rates fluctuate. Furthermore, output has risen much faster in some countries than in others. Japan, West Germany, and the East Asian newly industrializing countries (NICs) have all registered strong gains in output; and the oil-exporting states have benefited from oil price rises. By contrast people in many countries—especially many in Africa—have seen their daily food supply fall. Rates of growth of output are variegated. And with differences in the rates of growth of output have gone differences in the rates of growth of trade.

This chapter identifies the main elements of postwar economic history. First, since the economic process is largely profit oriented, the essential dynamic is growth, though at a fluctuating rate. Secondly, that quantitative expansion has taken the form of globalization. Production processes are increasingly integrated over national boundaries as finance capital shifts around the globe at an ever more rapid pace. Perhaps the most remarked institutional index of globalization is the flowering of transnational (or multinational) corporations. Thirdly, in a world where nations trade only little, the determinants of standards of living are internal: resources, population, and technology. It is the internal balance of these factors that matters. In a global world, though, what matters is the balance of these factors in relation to everywhere else. Globalization forces factories in Australia to compete with those in Zambia. Therefore globalization has transformed patterns of production in the world. Finally, if factories compete globally, labor markets operate to ensure that workers in the USA compete with those in Poland, too. Thus globalization forces changes in the character of jobs in the traditional manufacturing countries: changes to the labor process, to the security of jobs, to the hours of work, to their rates of pay. These changes link the economic process of globalization to changes in social life, especially to gender and ethnic relations within the traditional centers of production.

Some caveats. Globalization means the increasing integration of production, trade, and finance over the surface of the earth. It does not refer simply to internationalization. Nevertheless, given the manner in which data are collected and published, all the indices of integration that we quote measure the links between nations rather than regions. Furthermore, although the economies of regions and nations are (we claim) becoming increasingly integrated, that does not mean either that they are becoming more similar or that regional and national states are becoming irrelevant (Christopherson 1993; Gertler 1992). Our acquaintance with Los Angeles, Toronto, Tokyo, and Melbourne is sufficient to reveal continuing differences even among the advanced capitalist countries. And as we shall argue in Chapter 10, nation-states have still important economic powers (see also Wrigley 1992 for a specific example of the effects of different national regulatory regimes). It is just that everywhere is implicated in everywhere else. Finally, globalization is here understood as an economic process. Yet globalization has cultural dimensions (Peet 1986), and important political changes have also occurred over the last 40 years (Armstrong et al. 1991). These cultural, political, and social changes do bear some relation to globalization as an economic process, though not a determinate one. Except insofar as they bear on the economic process, cultural, political, and social changes will be ignored here, for they would require far more than this book to work out.

2.1 THE MAIN GAME: GROWTH

Growth can be measured in two main ways. The measure that is of most relevance to consumers is welfare—commonly indexed by gross national product (GNP) or gross domestic product (GDP) per capita. More relevant to producers is capital accumulation—the rate at which the stock of capital available for production is enlarged. Here we examine changes in both measures. We try to be careful, however, for the characteristics of the growth of output have been long debated.

The basic record of growth of output is contained in Figure 2.1. There are large year-to-year fluctuations in rates of growth of GDP. Until the early 1970s, growth rates averaged nearly 5% per year in the OECD as a whole; there were downturns in 1954, 1957, 1967, and 1970, but rates of growth were reasonably well maintained throughout the 1950s and 1960s. However, there have since occurred three OECD-wide recessions—in 1974/75 (the oil

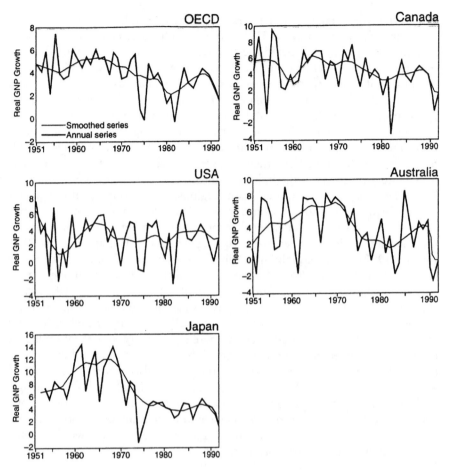

FIGURE 2.1. Annual average percentage rate of growth of real GDP, 1951–1992. OECD data for 1951–1960 are the unweighted averages of the rates of growth of Australia, Canada, Japan and the USA. The smoothing function is a Cleveland LOWESS smoother. *Source*: OECD, various years.

price effect), in 1982, and in 1991/92—and in general the graph gives the impression that growth has been slower since 1973 than it was earlier.

The histories of individual countries are not especially similar, at least at this level of detail (Table 2.1). Average annual rates of growth of GDP (nearly 7%) are far higher in Japan than in the other three countries. Equally, Canada's average rate of growth has been above that in the USA; Australia's performance lies between these two extremes, near the OECD average. While the rates of growth of individual countries are more volatile than that of the OECD as a whole, growth in the USA has been especially variable. And, in detail, the individual histories are not well correlated: the records of the USA

TABLE 2.1. Characteristics of economic growth, 1951–1992

Characteristic	OECD	USA	Japan	Canada	Australia
Lowest rate	-0.30	-2.50	-1.20	-3.30	-0.80
Highest rate	7.49	7.78	14.29	9.53	7.37
Mean rate	3.82	3.02	6.71	4.12	3.78
SD	1.79	2.63	3.69	2.74	2.30
Coefficient of variance	0.47	0.87	0.55	0.67	0.61

	Comparisons of Growth Rates				
Pairs compared	Mean difference	SD of difference	t statistic	Probability	Correlation
OECD/USA	0.79	1.81	2.80	0.008	+0.74
OECD/Japan	–2.80	3.42	–5.18	0.000	+0.38
OECD/Canada	–0.38	1.88	–1.29	0.206	+0.72
OECD/Australia	0.00	2.07	0.00	0.999	+0.52
USA/Japan	–3.59	4.23	–5.36	0.000	+0.14
USA/Canada	–1.10	2.36	–3.01	0.004	+0.61
USA/Australia	–0.76	3.00	–1.64	0.109	+0.26
Japan/Canada	2.36	4.21	3.55	0.001	+0.13
Japan/Australia	2.77	3.69	4.75	0.000	+0.30
Canada/Australia	0.34	2.93	0.75	0.458	+0.34

Notes: The mean difference is negative if the average rate of growth in the first-named country is less than that in the second.

Probability denotes the chance of observing a *t*-value at least as large as that measured. Tests are paired, two-tailed, *t*-tests. There are 42 years of data, except in the case of the OECD (41) and Japan (40).

Source: Computations on data in Figure 2.1.

and Canada are reasonably correlated; but no other pair of countries exhibits correlations of over 0.35. Thus, Japan and Australia escaped the recession of 1954; Japan was unaffected in 1957; Australia and Japan did not suffer the effects of the downturn in 1967 or in 1970; the effects of the 1974/75 recession were less sharp in Canada and Australia than in the USA and Japan; Japan largely escaped the recession of 1982 and entered the 1991/92 recession late. The sense of a global golden age is not well established by these data.

Three general claims have been made about such series of growth rates. First, it is claimed that there are short cycles of 7–11 years, called Juglar cycles. Secondly, Kuznets (1930, 1966) has produced evidence of growth cycles of production, superimposed on the Juglars and averaging nearly 25 years in length. This evidence has been supported more recently by Solomou (1989) and Gerster (1989), who both claim that data indicate the existence of long waves of 20–30 years in many countries in the nineteenth and twentieth centuries. Berry (1991) contains similar evidence for the USA. He demonstrates that in the USA there were peaks of real GNP per capita growth rates in 1938, 1973, and (he says) in 1987; there were troughs in 1954 and 1981. A third group, including

Glyn et al. (1990), Itoh (1990), Lipietz (1986), and Mandel (1978), argue that the postwar years can be divided into two intervals: the first a golden age to 1973, and the second a period of slow growth since then.

We need to sort these claims out. The existence of Juglar and Kuznets cycles makes it difficult to compare rates of growth over long periods. For example, it is common to compare long-run average rates of growth for the years up to and since 1973. But this is not to compare like with like: the first period may begin at a peak and end during a recession, whereas the latter may start at a recession and end at a peak. Thus long-period comparisons need to be standardized to coincide with growth cycles. In particular, growth rates need to be measured from peak to peak or trough to trough, or averaged over entire cycles, because variable length cycles are not entirely removed by filters of fixed length. To make our interpretation robust we have used a variety of techniques.

The data on annual rates of growth of GDP were first smoothed so that year-to-year fluctuations are removed and the main trends revealed (Figure 2.1). In the OECD as a whole the early 1950s were a period of slowly falling rates of growth, which then recovered to average around 5% per annum until the mid-1960s. Since then rates of growth of GDP declined to a low of about 2% in 1981. The brief (and weak) recovery to the late 1980s was snuffed out by the recession of 1991/92. There is little evidence of Juglar cycles here; and while the two minima of 1956 and 1981 agree with the Kuznets timing, the second corresponds to a far lower rate of growth than the first (and the fact that the series starts in 1950 makes the first minimum suspect). Nor for that matter is there much evidence of a golden age: only in the period 1961–1966 were growth rates high and stable. Perhaps one of the reasons for this inconclusive evidence is the fact that the OECD series averages the performance of individual countries whose records are quite different.

The first half of the 1950s was quite different in the four countries. In the USA rates of growth were falling sharply, in Canada more slowly; in Australia and Japan growth rates initially rose. However, after 1959 the four histories moved in parallel: rising to peak rates of growth between 1964 and 1968 and falling back to the trough in 1981 or 1982. Again though the details are quite different. Rates of growth in Japan fell sharply after 1968. They fell in the USA after 1965 to a prolonged trough that lasted essentially from 1969 until the mid-1990s (with only a short and limited recovery between 1976 and 1979). Australia's rate of growth peaked in 1969, but was then low between 1976 and 1982. In Canada rates of growth remained relatively high until 1972 (though with a dip in 1968/69) and then fell slowly to 1981. There are varying signs of recovery after 1981—weak in Canada, Japan, and the USA, somewhat stronger in Australia. The recession of 1991/92 brought trend rates of growth down to their postboom lows in all four countries. These differences in history, even after smoothing, are reflected in low correlations between the histories of the individual countries: only the correlations between smoothed rates of GDP growth in Australia, Canada, and Japan exceed 0.55.

Until the recession of 1991/92, this history had corresponded to the basic

Kuznets timing with little evidence, except perhaps in Canada, of Juglar rhythms. On these data the golden age characterization does not do well. If we define a golden age as a period of rising and then of sustained high rates of growth (after smoothing), the golden age in the individual countries is as follows:

USA	1957–1965
Japan	1957–1968
Canada	1960–1965
Australia	1958–1970

In North America, the golden age was particularly short, ending before the mid-1960s; only in Australia and Japan did it extend to the end of the 1960s.

Another way of examining the data is to identify the extremes. From the original series it is possible to catalog those years in which rates of growth exceeded the average by more than 1 SD (booms) or fell below the average by more than 1 SD (busts). The sequence of booms and busts is striking (Table 2.2). After confusion in the early 1950s, when booms and busts alternated rapidly, the years from 1955 through 1973 contained almost only boom years—26 booms and only 4 busts in the four countries. By contrast since 1974 there have been only 2 booms but 18 busts in the four countries. This is a highly significant contrast. Here is little evidence of cycles of boom and bust; instead there was a phase mainly of rapid growth followed by a period of mainly slow or negative growth—the golden age hypothesis.

TABLE 2.2. Years of boom and bust: output

	1950s	1960s	1970s	1980s	1990s
	0123456789	0123456789	0123456789	0123456789	0123
Booms:					
OECD	. . 3 . 5 . . . 9	. . . . 4 . . . 8 .	. . . 3	. . . .	. .
USA	1 . . . 5 . . . 9	. . . . . 5 6 . . .	. . . .	. . . . 4	. . .
Japan	. . . .	0 1 . 3 4 . 6 7 8 9	. . . .	. . . .	. . .
Canada	. 2 . . 5 6 . . .	. . . . . 5 6 . . .	. 1 . 3	. . . .	. . .
Australia	. . 3 . . . . 8 .	. . 2 3 4 . . 7 . 9	0	. . . . 4	. . .
Busts:					
OECD	. . . .	. . . .	. . . . 4 5	0 1 2	. 1
USA	. . . 4 . 6 . 8 .	. . . .	0 . . . 4 5	. . 2	. 1 .
Japan	. . . .	. . . .	. . . . 4 5	. . 2 . . . 6 . . .	. . 2
Canada	. . . 4	. 1	. . . .	. . 2	0 1 2
Australia	. 2	. 1	. . . . 7 . .	. . 2 3	0 1 .

Note: The numbers in the table indicate the year in which there was a boom or bust; thus, from the first row, 1953, 1955, 1959, 1964, 1968, and 1973 were booms in the OECD. A Fisher exact test on the frequency of booms and busts in 1955–1973 and 1974–1992 gives $p = 0.000$.

Source: Calculations on data in Figure 2.1 and Table 2.1.

With all this in mind, we compare average rates of growth for two different periodizations (Table 2.3). The upper portion of this table compares mean
rates of growth for the intervals 1951–1973 and 1974–1992. In each country
and in the OECD as a whole the average annual rate of growth was higher in
the former period than in the latter. However, in the USA this difference is not
significant. But this comparison is unfair, for the two intervals start and end
at different points in the business cycle. The lower portion of Table 2.3 compares rates of growth for two intervals that both start and end with busts (see
Table 2.2). In the OECD as a whole and in Japan average annual rates of
growth of GDP were at least twice as high in 1954–1974 as in 1975–1991.
However, the differences between average rates of growth in Australia and
Canada are smaller and in the USA are not significant—though in the expected direction.

So what are we to make of these histories of growth of output? First,
there is little sense of global cohesion: the individual histories are similar only
at the most gross level. Secondly, there is some evidence, though not especially strong, of a Kuznets cycle with troughs in the mid-1950s and in 1981.
However, this interpretation is much weakened by the recession of 1991/92.
There is limited evidence of Juglar cycles. Thirdly, there is some sense that after fluctuations in the early 1950s, the period 1954–1973 contained more
good years than did the interval that followed. Fourthly, though, the evidence
for a golden age is weak, especially in North America—the years of sustained
rapid growth were short and not significantly more rapid than the years of
decline. The USA would seem to be exactly not the example to choose to
make a golden age argument. Finally, the overwhelming impression from the
smoothed data is that there was a boom from the late 1950s to the mid-
1960s, followed by a long decline to 1981—but with individual deviations.

The history of rates of capital accumulation is equally complex (Figure
2.2; Table 2.4). The history of capital formation in the OECD parallels that of
the growth of GDP. After 1951 levels of gross fixed capital formation rose

TABLE 2.3. Characteristics of periods of growth

Characteristic	OECD	USA	Japan	Canada	Australia
Periodization A:					
1951–1973 average rate	4.85	3.49	9.29	5.20	4.65
1974–1992 average rate	2.51	2.46	3.86	2.82	2.72
Probability	0.00	0.21	0.00	0.00	0.01
Periodization B:					
1954–1974 average rate	4.65	3.00	8.88	5.04	4.79
1975–1991 average rate	2.61	2.63	4.31	2.85	2.82
Probability	0.00	0.67	0.00	0.01	0.01

Note: Probabilities are from pooled variance, independent sample, two-tailed *t*-tests.
Source: Calculations on data in Figure 2.1.

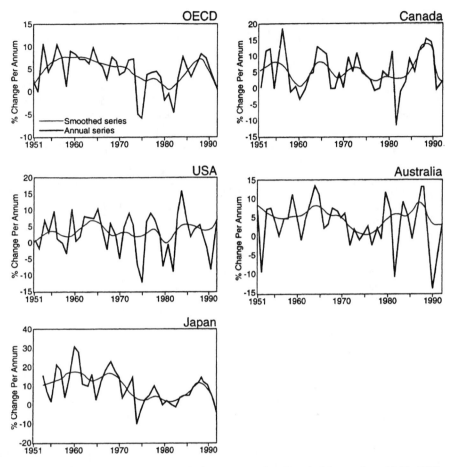

FIGURE 2.2. Annual percentage change in gross fixed capital formation, 1951–1992. *Source:* see Figure 2.1.

rapidly at rates of 7% per annum or more. A long decline set in after 1960 culminating in the two recessions of 1974/75 and 1980–1982, during which gross fixed capital formation was declining. There was a recovery from 1982 until the recession of 1991/92.

Again though, these histories are not well correlated even after the tremendous year-to-year fluctuations have been smoothed. Capital formation has increased more rapidly in Japan than in the other three countries. While the average increase in capital formation has been greater in Canada and less in the USA, the differences in rates of increase between Australia, Canada, and the USA are not significant. The correlations between rates of increase of capital formation in the four countries nowhere exceed 0.5. The USA exhibits only a brief interval in the early 1960s when there was anything approaching

TABLE 2.4. Gross domestic capital formation, 1951–1992

Characteristic	OECD	USA	Japan	Canada	Australia
Lowest rate	−5.66	−11.89	−9.41	−10.99	−10.58
Highest rate	11.06	15.88	30.73	18.27	13.00
Mean rate	4.81	2.61	9.40	4.52	3.16
SD	4.03	5.98	8.42	5.90	5.76
Coefficient of variance	0.84	2.29	0.90	1.30	1.82

	Comparisons of Growth Rates				
Pairs compared	Mean difference	SD of difference	t statistic	Probability	Correlation
OECD/USA	2.29	4.51	3.25	0.00	0.66
OECD/Japan	−4.68	6.39	−4.58	0.00	0.67
OECD/Canada	−0.15	5.86	−0.17	0.87	0.35
OECD/Australia	1.57	5.49	1.83	0.08	0.42
USA/Japan	−6.62	9.58	−4.37	0.00	0.16
USA/Canada	−1.91	7.31	−1.69	0.10	0.24
USA/Australia	−0.55	6.31	−0.57	0.57	0.42
Japan/Canada	4.96	9.88	2.86	0.01	0.08
Japan/Australia	6.02	9.03	4.21	0.00	0.21
Canada/Australia	1.36	6.83	1.29	0.21	0.31

Notes: The mean difference is negative if the average rate of growth of gross fixed capital formation in the first-named country is less than that in the second.

Probability denotes the chance of observing a t-value at least as large as that measured. Tests are pooled variance, paired, two-tailed t-tests. There are 42 years of data, except in the case of the OECD (41) and Japan (40).

Source: Computations on data in Figure 2.2.

a boom of capital formation. Gross fixed capital formation in Canada has been unlike that in any other country: the history has been strongly cyclic, with low points in 1958–1960, 1968/69, 1977/78, and 1982 before the severe drop in capital formation since 1989. In Japan capital formation proceeded rapidly until 1968 but then fell away to the low of 1982, before recovering briefly between 1985 and 1990. The history of Australian capital formation reveals a boom to 1964 followed by a decline to the long investment depression in the 1970s, since when capital formation generally recovered until 1988. This gives even less evidence of a pattern of long boom followed by a bust than do the GDP data.

There are, however, distinct patterns of boom and bust in the histories of capital formation (Table 2.5). Between 1955 and 1973 there were 19 years of boom and only 3 years of bust in the four countries; since 1974 there have been 7 years of boom and 17 years of bust. (As before, years of boom are those in which the increase in gross fixed capital formation exceeds the average increase by more than 1 SD; years of bust are those in which the increase in capital formation falls below the average by more than 1 SD.) This is the sort of history that would be expected of a long boom pattern of growth.

TABLE 2.5. Years of boom and bust: capital formation

	1950s	1960s	1970s	1980s	1990s
	0123456789	0123456789	0123456789	0123456789	0123
Booms:					
OECD	..3..6..9	....4.....	....	89	..
USA	....5...9	.....5....	..2....7..	...34.....	...
Japan	...67..	01.....789	....	....	...
Canada	.23..6...	...456...	...3......	.1.....7..	...
Australia	9	...45....	....	0...4.....	...
Busts:					
OECD	.2.......	....	....45....	012.......	..
USA	....	....	0...45....	0.2.......	.1.
Japan	....	....	....45....	0.23......	..2
Canada	....	0.........	....	..2.......	01.
Australia	.2.......	....	....	..2.......	01.

Note: The numbers in the table indicate the years of boom or bust; so there were booms in the OECD in 1953, 1956, 1959, and 1964. A Fisher exact test on the frequency of booms and busts in 1955–1973 and 1974–1992 gives $p = 0.001$.
Source: Calculations on data in Figure 2.2 and Table 2.4.

In general capital formation increased more rapidly in the years until 1973 than in the years since (Table 2.6). However, only in the OECD as a whole and in Japan were these observed differences sufficiently marked to be significant. Given the very high variability of rates of gross domestic capital formation, the differences in rates of capital formation between the intervals are not significant in Australia, Canada, and the USA.

Gross fixed capital formation includes various expenditures: residential construction, nonresidential construction, plant and machinery, and land. It includes expenditures in manufacturing, agriculture, and other industries. Only some of these elements of capital formation measure the increase of business capital. Comparable data about these various components of gross fixed capital formation are not readily available. Still some calculations have been made of the rate of increase of the gross stock of fixed capital in manufacturing; of the rate of increase of gross fixed capital formation in manufacturing; of the rate of increase of non-construction-related gross fixed capital formation; and of the rate of increase of gross machinery and equipment capital formation. None of these data alter the general conclusion: there has been a general tendency for rates of increase of gross fixed capital formation to fall off since 1974, but this fall has not been significant (except in Japan). The only surprising feature of these data is that the share of gross fixed capital formation that is accounted for by construction has been falling in Australia, Canada, and the USA.

In the OECD as a whole and in the four individual countries, there was a boom in the mid-1960s. It is visible both in rates of growth of GDP and in

TABLE 2.6. Characteristics of periods of capital formation

Characteristic	OECD	USA	Japan	Canada	Australia
Periodization A:					
1951–1973 average rate	6.16	3.77	14.38	5.71	4.69
1974–1992 average rate	3.09	1.22	3.91	3.08	1.32
Probability	0.01	0.17	0.00	0.15	0.06
Periodization B:					
1954–1974 average rate	5.90	3.57	13.20	5.35	4.87
1975–1991 average rate	3.55	1.38	4.98	3.21	1.53
Probability	0.07	0.28	0.00	0.27	0.07

Note: Probabilities are from independent sample, pooled variance, two-tailed *t*-tests.
Source: Calculations on data in Figure 2.2.

rates of increase of gross fixed capital formation. However, this boom is of different lengths in different countries and was especially short in North America. It was followed by a long decline to the bust of 1974 and after brief recoveries, the more serious busts of 1981/82 and 1991/92. Even so, differences in the rates of growth in the earlier and later periods are sometimes not significant. The details of growth in the four countries are quite different and provide little support for the notion of a global long boom.

While there may be cycles in rates of growth of output there have been secular trends in the relative significance of manufacturing within the industrial economies (Figure 2.3). In the OECD as a whole manufacturing accounted for an increasing share of civilian employment until 1970; manufacturers then employed 27.6% of all people in work (and produced about one-third of all output). The proportion of employment has since steadily declined to less than 22% after 1983 and is now about 20%. In Japan in the 1960s the share of employment in manufacturing was still growing, peaking at 27.4% in 1973. Since then the share of employment accounted for by manufacturing declined slightly to 25% but has hardly changed since the late 1970s. Similarly, the share of manufacturing in GDP has fallen slightly—from 34% in 1965 to 29% in 1990 (World Bank 1992). By contrast, in Australia, Canada, and the USA manufacturers have employed a diminishing share of the civilian labor force since at least the mid-1960s, now less than 17.5%. The share of manufacturing in the GDP of the three countries has also fallen, from 26% to 28% in the mid-1960s to 20% or so by the mid-1970s; in the USA the share of manufacturing in production has since stabilized, but in Australia and Canada it has continued to fall, to about 16% by the early 1990s. The decline of manufacturing employment in Australia has been particularly sharp: of the four countries Australia had the greatest proportion of employment in manufacturing in 1960, but by 1987 it had the smallest.

Three central facts stand out in this history of the OECD and some of its member countries. (1) Growth rates of output and of capital formation have

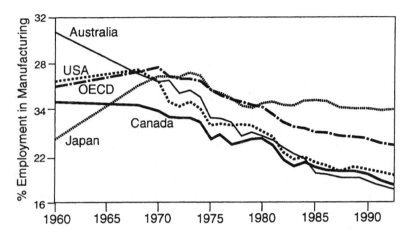

FIGURE 2.3. Proportion of civilian employment in manufacturing. *Source*: OECD, 1990.

fluctuated in a cyclic fashion since 1950. (2) Nevertheless there is some evidence that growth has slowed from a short boom in the early to mid-1960s and particularly since 1973. We insist: there was a short boom, which was over by the mid-1960s in North America and by the late 1960s in Australia and Japan. (3) Superimposed on these fluctuations have been secular changes in industrial structure. These are not isolated facts; they are related both to each other and to other aspects of the economic history of the postwar world.

2.2 THE FORM: GLOBALIZATION

Among these other aspects perhaps the key is globalization, the increasing integration of production over most of the surface of the earth. This process puts firms in one country in competition with those in others and appears to pit workers in different parts of the world against each other. Globalization has many facets. Here we focus on three: the globalization of money markets through financial deregulation; the development of multinationals, a principal means by which global production is integrated; and trade, the most obvious expression of global production.

2.2.1 Finance

The world of finance is now completely different from that of 1970. Money and flows of currency, commercial paper, bonds, and equities between the countries of the world now tie us all together in a manner that would have been impossible to foresee even 20 years ago. In this sense the economic system of the years since 1973 is quite different from that of the 1960s. Yet the seeds of the global financial system were sown in the 1950s and 1960s. They were apparent in the development of the technologies that have made global finance possible—international telecommunication networks and computers especially. Without these developments finance could not have changed so. Yet the global financial system has also emerged from the unequal developments of the 1950s and 1960s: the US trade surpluses of the early postwar years, the growth of trade surpluses in Japan and West Germany, the increasing dependence on oil and therefore on OPEC (the Organization of Petroleum Exporting Countries), and the slowdown of growth after the mid-1960s in the advanced industrial countries. All of these have both provided the money for investment and ensured that much of it would be invested in new forms and new places.

The origins of global finance had been developed much earlier. By the late Middle Ages Italian merchant bankers had established branches throughout Europe, promoting trade by discounting bills of exchange and trading in currency and precious metals. In the mid-sixteenth century primitive equity markets existed in some European capitals and international money market centers operated in Antwerp and Lyons (Park and Zwick 1985; Jones 1990). Multinational banking on a large scale, however, originated in nineteenth-century Britain (Jones 1990; Walmsley 1991) when overseas branches of British banks began to compete with merchant banks in financing the growing volume of international trade. London emerged as the capital of international finance. Flush with capital from Britain's manufacturing success and its domination of global trade, British banks funded the post-Napoleonic reconstruction of France, Russia, and other European nations. In the three decades before the outbreak of World War I, short-term sterling loans increasingly replaced bills of exchange, financing about 60% of world trade. Britain remained the world's leading creditor nation, exporting about 40% of its domestic savings (Walter 1991). The international demand for sterling maintained Britain's balance of payments surplus despite the decline of its manufacturing.

The machinery of private international finance spent the interwar years in cold storage (Hirsch and Oppenheimer 1977). The international banking system effectively collapsed with the resurgence of economic nationalism and increasingly protectionist trade policies during the Great Depression, which saw global exports shrink from $33 billion in 1928 to $13 billion by 1932 (Moffitt 1983).

The gold standard was seen by many as having compounded the Great Depression by imposing too harsh a financial discipline on governments to maintain external equilibrium in their balance of payments (Hallwood and MacDonald 1986). Yet few nations were willing to relinquish all ties with gold as the world sought a new framework for international trade and finance at the end of World War II. The Bretton Woods Agreement of July 1944 established a flexible gold standard. Par values of currencies were set, and central banks were to intervene in the foreign exchange market to keep the exchange rate within 1% of the par value. To counter the strictures of a pure gold standard, Bretton Woods allowed nations to remedy "fundamental disequilibrium" in balance of payments by borrowing from new international organizations such as the International Monetary Fund (IMF) and the World Bank [officially called the International Bank for Reconstruction and Development (IBRD)] or by adjusting par values.

Since the dollar was the only convertible currency at the end of World War II, Bretton Woods effectively made the dollar equal to gold. Linking the dollar and gold was a boon to trade and the emerging postwar international financial system. Dollars could be produced more easily than gold, and thus international liquidity accelerated more rapidly than under a pure gold standard. Furthermore, unlike gold, dollar reserves could be invested to earn interest.

The basic principles of the Bretton Woods system were strained almost immediately. The lend-lease program of the USA and Canada ended, and European war debt and payments deficits threatened deflation. In 1946 the US trade balance with Europe ran a surplus of $1.65 billion (Millward 1977). The IMF and World Bank were too small to fund the European recovery. In part a reaction to growing US–Soviet tensions, the Marshall Plan's huge financial assistance eased Europe's shortage of dollars and contributed the necessary spur to growth. Between 1948 and 1952 the Marshall Plan provided over $12 billion of loans to Europe and Japan while the IMF spent less than $3 billion on European reconstruction (Moffitt 1983; Fraser 1987).

In the 1950s the growth of international financial flows was moderate. Each year, world production grew by about 4%, world trade accelerated by almost 6%, and the volume of international reserves increased by about 2.2% (Walter 1991). Much of the growth of international money that did occur was financed by the US balance of payments deficits (the USA was running a trade surplus but a balance of payments deficit). Moffitt (1983) estimates that of $8.5 billion in international money created during the 1950s, $7 billion was financed through US balance of payments deficits.

Growing foreign competition began to press the US economy in the late 1950s. Between 1950 and 1957 the US balance of payments deficit averaged some $770 million a year. In 1958/59 it increased to $3.2 billion as the trade surplus deteriorated from almost $5.5 billion in the mid-1950s to $3.3 billion in 1958 and only $1 billion in 1959 (Walter 1991), and the deficit worsened in the 1960s. The instability of the gold–dollar system was buoyed by the decline of US manufacturing relative to that of West Germany and Japan and by the onset of the Vietnam War, while the growing volume of dollars financing international trade had outstripped the volume of gold produced, raising doubts about the convertibility of the dollar.

Attempts by the US government to reduce the balance of payments deficit and to prevent the massive outflow of private capital contributed to the growth of the Eurocurrency market, perhaps the most innovative development of the postwar international financial system. The Eurodollar market was born in the late 1950s when the British government restricted the use of sterling by nonresidents to finance trade. This move prompted British banks to substitute dollars for sterling in an "offshore" dollar market. The US deficit fueled the growth of the Eurodollar market as European and US banks sought to replace the increasingly regulated US bond market with a European alternative. US banks set up foreign branches, especially in Europe: Park and Zwick (1985) report that in 1960 13 US banks controlled 211 foreign branches; by 1970 79 banks managed 532 foreign branches. In 1965 US banks held $377 billion in domestic loans and $9 billion in foreign branch loans; by 1976 assets in foreign branches had risen more than 20 times while domestic assets merely tripled (Moffitt 1983). After 1958 the Eurodollar market grew at an annual average rate of over 20%: by 1983 the net size of the Eurodollar market (gross liabilities less interbank loans) was approximately $760 billion (Hallwood and MacDonald 1986). The Euromarket has transformed global finance, creating a single global money market free of most government regulation. In the 1960s and 1970s international bank lending was growing at 25% per annum, over three times as fast as world trade and nearly five times as fast as global production (Moffitt 1983).

Relatively high European interest rates, inflation, and a deteriorating current account surplus fanned by the Vietnam War caused mounting pressure on the dollar in the late 1960s and early 1970s. Concern about the convertibility of dollars for gold increased, and US gold reserves declined steadily as foreign governments exchanged their growing surpluses of dollars for gold. Convertibility of the dollar was suspended in 1968. By the time the USA posted its first postwar trade deficit in 1971 it was clear that the international financial system was pegged to an overvalued dollar. There had been a huge expansion of US foreign direct investment in the early 1970s as foreign capital was purchased at bargain prices with an inflated dollar. Domestic monetary policy in the USA, as most everywhere else, was less and less able to control the international financial environment. The official end of the fixed-exchange Bretton Woods system came with the Nixon shock of 1971 when the "gold window" was closed (Fryer 1987).

The demise of Bretton Woods intensified conflict between public institutions and the private market over the control of international finance. The private market won the war in a series of battles over fixed versus floating exchange rates in the early 1970s. The Smithsonian Agreement of December 1971 saw the gold standard dismantled and most international currencies repegged to a devalued dollar. Several European countries had by this time decided to float their currencies, most importantly West Germany. The new more flexible peg did not last long. After private speculation against sterling in 1972, the Bank of England yielded to market pressure and let sterling float (Moffitt 1983). Once sterling floated international pressure returned to the dollar. In 1972 the US trade deficit increased again, reaching $6.5 billion, of which $4 billion resulted from trade with Japan alone (Fraser 1987). The US deficits were balanced by enormous increases in foreign exchange reserves in Japan and West Germany, which rose from $5.3 billion in 1969 to $25.3 billion in 1973 (Tew 1985). In 1973 the dollar peg was abandoned.

The late 1960s and early 1970s witnessed uncertainty over the future of the dollar as the dominant world currency. As the unregulated Euromarket grew and as new modes of telecommunication increased the amount of information about global finance and the ease of international financial trading, so currency trading exploded in the early 1970s, destabilizing money markets. The dollar standard wilted when multinational corporations, international banks, and private investors realized the profits to be made in money market trade. Turnover in the world's foreign exchange markets, chiefly the Euromarket, increased from less than $25 billion a day in 1970 to over $100 billion a day in 1973 (Moffitt 1983).

It was anticipated that floating exchange rates might induce competitive currency devaluations and global recession. These fears were forgotten in October 1973 when OPEC reduced production and quadrupled the price of crude oil. The devaluation of the dollar had decreased the real price of oil and upset the Tehran Agreement of 1971 that mandated modest annual increases in oil prices through 1975. Since oil transactions were largely carried out in dollars, their dollar surplus provided a cushion to most oil importers against the price increases. Even so, the magnitude of the increase posed problems of financing oil imports. The oil exporters' trade balances rose from $19 billion in 1973 to $84 billion in 1974 and again from $44 billion in 1978 to $160 billion in 1980, and their current account balances moved similarly (Bank of England *Quarterly Bulletin* June 1980; see also Hoogvelt 1982).

Fortunately for the oil importers the oil-producing nations lacked the economic infrastructure to absorb and invest their rapidly expanding trade surplus. The growing reserves of petrodollars were thus recycled largely in OECD accounts, often providing the loans needed to pay for oil imports. Tew (1985) shows how the petrodollars were recycled: bank deposits $147 billion; US/UK government securities $28 billion; finance to IMF/IBRD $14 billion; financial support to developing countries $47 billion; other $81 billion.

The breakdown of the Bretton Woods system was merely the beginning of two decades of global financial reform contested by the private market and by government and other public institutions. The private market triumphed, riding a wave of growth in international capital flows. In 1986 the value of world trade was a little over $2.3 trillion (Bryan 1987) while the London Eurodollar market had a turnover of $75 trillion a year (Walter 1991). Annual transactions in the London Eurodollar market represented six times the value of world trade in 1979, expanding to twenty-five times by 1986 (Drucker 1986). The dominance of the private capital market over central banks is illustrated by the fact that at the end of 1989 the stock of outstanding international bonds totaled $1.25 trillion and international interbank deposits amounted to a further $3.5 trillion (BIS August 1990), six times the total foreign exchange reserves of central banks (Walter 1991). Daily trade in the foreign exchange markets of

London, New York, and Tokyo combined was around $431 billion in 1989 (Bank of England *Quarterly Bulletin* November 1989). It is easy to see why national governments run scared of currency speculators.

The volume of capital flows is not the only distinguishing feature of the global financial system. Innovations have refashioned the world of finance during the 1980s, creating new financial instruments, techniques, and markets. The new instruments of finance attempt to separate the risks and characteristics of existing financial tools and reassemble them in new combinations (Harrington, 1992; Llewellyn 1980; Thrift and Leyshon 1988). The unbundling of financial products has raised competition between different types of financial institution. Divisions between commercial, savings, and merchant banks have steadily declined. Perhaps more important has been the blurring of traditional demarcations between banking and security dealing, as bank assets are increasingly securitized and as markets in short- and medium-term paper expand (A. Hamilton 1986). Banks and securities houses have diversified through the 1980s into new functions (capital markets, securities trading, and corporate finance) and into new locations (aiming to operate in the three major financial centers of London, New York, and Tokyo) (Bingham 1985; A. Hamilton 1986; Thrift and Leyshon 1988).

The causes of the global financial boom of the 1980s are many. Here we focus on just three.

First, financial activities have been revolutionized by new technologies, particularly telecommunications and information processing equipment. Huertas (1990) estimates that the real cost of recording, transmitting, and processing information has fallen more than 95% since the mid-1960s. The ease and relatively low cost of transferring information has heightened the sensitivity of institutions and private investors to differences in risks and yields on assets in different markets. It has also increased the instability of global financial markets.

Second, the removal of restrictions on capital flows and deregulation of capital markets, has also aided the growth of the global financial system. Deregulation has removed interest rate limits, aided the creation and development of money markets for commercial paper and treasury bills, eased reserve requirements and credit controls on banks and other deposit taking institutions, opened stock exchanges to foreign companies, removed exchange and capital controls, and encouraged financial concerns to widen their range of activities (A. Hamilton 1986; Khoury 1990). In the USA restrictions on capital flows were abolished in 1974, all restrictions on interest rates had been dropped by 1986, banking regulations were steadily relaxed through the 1970s, and in 1981 banks were permitted to offer international banking facilities within the USA. The New York Stock Exchange abolished fixed commissions on securities transactions in 1975. In the UK the "Big Bang" of October 1986 ended the fixed commission rate structure on the London Stock Exchange and saw restrictions on foreign ownership of stock exchange members scrapped, ushering in a spate of takeovers and mergers involving foreign financial institutions as most barriers between banks and securities houses were removed. In Japan deregulation has occurred more slowly than in most other OECD nations. Deregulation really began with the oil crisis in 1973 when Japanese government borrowing squeezed local markets: the securities market developed to aid firms tap financial markets directly. In 1980 the Revised Foreign Exchange and Foreign Trade Law relaxed foreign exchange controls and permitted Japanese life insurance and pension funds to invest up to 30% of their assets overseas (Khoury 1990). Net outflows of these capital reserves largely funded the US government deficits of the Reagan administration. During the 1980s restrictions on banking and securities operations were eased and foreign banks and securities houses entered Japanese markets.

The general deceleration of manufacturing growth since the early 1970s coupled with increased global liquidity resulting from the oil shocks and the growing surpluses of West Germany and Japan has been the third factor prompting global financial change. Declining rates of profit and growth in manufacturing mean that accumulated funds could no longer be reinvested in manufacturing at rates competitive with financial markets. At the same time the petrodollar surpluses of OPEC nations (over $460 billion between 1973 and 1982) and the expanding current surpluses of West Germany and Japan ($75 billion per annum between 1982 and 1989) were flooding the world with capital seeking new investment opportunities (Walter 1991). Many of these funds were channeled through international deposit markets to the non-oil-producing developing countries in the form of syndicated bank loans during the 1970s, and through the 1980s were used to finance the US current account deficit. Financial deregulation has both reflected the need to recycle the surpluses and permitted banks, flush with petrodollars and Eurodollars, to range over the world.

The emergence of the new global financial system has profoundly affected the global economy, reshaping the interaction of production, trade, and finance and helping produce new economic geographies. Production, trade, and capital flows have become uncoupled. During the Bretton Woods regime, when exchange rates were fixed, there was little currency speculation and capital flows in the form of reserve currencies and gold indicated a nation's current production and trade position. Now only 20 years after Bretton Woods' demise, 90% of foreign exchange flows are unrelated to current account positions and the strength of a currency no longer measures a nation's trade balance or current account. Thus, between 1971 and 1980 the US dollar depreciated 25% against a trade-weighted index of foreign currencies, whereas between 1980 and 1985 the US dollar rose by 67% against a share-weighted average of other OECD countries (Destler and Henning 1990). The rising dollar did not parallel improvements in trade: the US trade balance deteriorated from −$22.4 billion in 1980 to −$158.2 billion in 1987. To fund deficit spending, the strength of the dollar was bolstered by the Reagan administration at the cost of raising US real interest rates. After 1983 the USA became the largest debtor nation in the world.

Not only does the world of finance now move to its own beat, it increasingly dictates the rhythm of economic activity. Improvements in communications and deregulation of financial markets have boosted the sensitivity of capital nowadays to differences in expectations, risks, and returns, reducing national financial independence and inciting volatility in financial markets. The size of private capital flows also hampers the ability of governments to control their domestic economic programs. Responding to inflation and growing deficits, interest rates in the USA fluctuated wildly during the first half of the 1980s. From a 1–2% real interest rate on 3-month Treasury bills in 1979/80, rates climbed to 9% in 1982 and fell back to 4–5% within a year. Between 1933 and 1949 in the USA the average monthly change in short-term interest rates was 0.03%; in the 1950s, it was 0.07%; but between 1980 and 1982, it was 1.72% (Daly and Logan 1989: 110). In exchange markets the volatility of currency movements and the effects of speculative trading have equally dramatic effects. Between 6 and 20 February 1985 the Australian dollar fell from $US0.83 to less than $US0.70. More recent exchange rate swings in the European Community threaten the existence of the European Monetary Union (EMU): Italy was forced to devalue the lira by 7% during September 1992; in spite of support by the Bank of England, the pound fell by almost 10% against the mark in just 4 days: in Sweden the base lending rate was increased by 59 points between September 8 and 9, on September 14 it fell 55 points, and on September 16 it climbed 480 points to a rate of 500% overnight (*The Economist,* September 26–October 2, 1992).

The developing nations are also the victims of this volatility in financial markets. Their debt crisis directly reflects the interest rate hikes announced in the USA in the early 1980s, but the roots of this crisis lay in the oil price rises of the 1970s and the recycling of petrodollar funds through commercial banks. Able to borrow increasingly freely on bloated international capital markets, the non-oil-producing developing countries postponed paying for expensive energy. Real interest rates were often negative in the 1970s, and the terms of trade for many developing nations were improving (de Vries 1990). Unfortunately the bubble burst in the early 1980s as shifts in US financial policy sent interest rates soaring and with them service payments on Third World debt, most of which was denominated in US dollars at floating interest rates. Third World export earnings also collapsed during the recession of 1982, and interest burdens became unmanageable for most countries. In 1967 the debt of developing countries was $35.7 billion, of which 33% was from private creditors; by 1976 the debt had reached $168.8 billion and 52% was private; and in 1984 long-term debt exceeded $700 billion, of which 62% was private (World Bank 1977; OECD 1985). By 1987 the long-term debt of developing countries was nearly $1 trillion; equal to 42% of their GNP (World Bank 1989). The interest payments of developing countries as a whole cost more than 10% of their exports by the mid-1980s (World Bank 1987): Brazil and Mexico were then paying more than half their export earnings in debt service charges (OECD 1985).

In a sense deregulation and the development of the global financial system has been a means of shifting the OPEC and other trade surpluses to the developing countries (and to such developed countries as Australia and the USA). The effects of the new system though are felt everywhere, in the developed as well as in the developing countries. Global finance has been one means by which the system of production has become increasingly integrated.

2.2.2 Multinationals

The development of global enterprises implies a shift from arm's-length international trade toward international production and trade within corporations (Hoogvelt 1982). While transnational production appears to date from the mid-nineteenth century, the annual rate of formation of overseas manufacturing subsidiaries by large transnational corporations rose dramatically after the mid-1950s (Vaupel and Curhan 1973). Perhaps 20% of total world production is now performed by transnational corporations. The four largest transnational corporations have a combined turnover greater than the total GNP of Africa. From less than $26 billion in 1938, it is estimated that the stock of accumulated foreign direct investment had reached nearly $70 billion in 1960, $172 billion in 1971, and nearly $400 billion in 1978 (Dunning 1983: 87). By the early 1970s, the 400 largest multinational corporations employed some 30 million people worldwide (ILO 1981a,b). Though a falling share of all international financial flows, foreign direct investment has been transforming global production systems.

Initially, transnational corporations were vehicles for foreign private direct investment. In a bid for control many Third World countries in the 1960s demanded an equity stake in such investments. So transnational corporations devised a system of control that does not require ownership of capital but formal ownership of the product (via patents), the power from which permitted firms to specify production and marketing arrangements. As this practice has come under scrutiny, so corporations are shifting to a control based on ownership of the technical properties of the product: by differentiating their machinery, processes, and product, transnational corporations can preserve supply, servicing, and maintenance linkages (Grimwade 1989: 240–256). After all, the purpose is only to appropriate the surplus: with ownership of capital in corporations like Ford and General Motors, that meant simply transfer of profits; later—to such corporations as Coca-Cola, McDonald's, and Nike—this became royalties, interest, transfer prices, management costs, and servicing charges (Hoogvelt 1982). Many of the ventures of transnational corporations therefore no longer include much or all equity: joint ventures, management agreements and service contracts, licensing and franchise arrangements, production-sharing agreements, and subcontracting can all replace equity. This makes data collection difficult. But it also separates ownership and control. Furthermore, the process indicates why foreign direct investment has been diminishing in relative significance while the role of banks has increased (to provide infrastructure investment and loans to Third World corporations that establish production processes for transnational corporations). Even so, evidence of the growing significance of transnational corporations is clear.

An increasing proportion of world trade occurs within transnational corporations, that is, from one branch or plant of a corporation to another branch in a different country. In 1970, more than a quarter of US manufactured exports were sold by multinational corporations to a majority-owned foreign affiliate (Lall 1978). In 1977, 48.4% of US imports were bought by corporations that were related by ownership to the selling firm (Helleiner and Lavergne 1979). The ratio of sales by foreign affiliates to total sales in a sample of corporations rose from about 30% in 1971 to about 40% in 1980 (UNCTNC 1983). Some 40% of world trade now occurs within a corporation, and to that extent trade is not necessarily subject to market prices (Lall 1980). Transfer pricing is significant, and there are important reasons to do it (different tax rates on profits, price controls, import duties that exceed effective price controls, and fluctuating exchange rates). Lall also provides evidence of differential pricing from the pharmaceutical industry in Colombia.

Almost all foreign direct investment originates in the developed world. In 1978 the USA alone provided 41.4% of the total stock of accumulated foreign direct investment; Japan, 6.8%; and Canada, 3.5% (Dunning 1983). A mere 3.2% derived from developing countries. Only eight countries—the USA, the UK, Japan, Switzerland, the Netherlands, West Germany, Canada, and France—accounted for all but 9% of the stock of foreign direct capital (Dunning and Cantwell 1987: 813). By 1983 the share of Japan had risen to over 10% and that of Canada to nearly 5%, while that of the USA had fallen to 38.4%.

Nor is the Third World as a whole an important host to transnational corporations. In 1960 the Third World received about one-half of all foreign direct investment, but this had fallen to one-quarter by 1974 (Hoogvelt 1982). Other estimates indicate that whereas developing countries contained over a half of the stock of foreign direct investment before World War II, that had fallen to about one-third by 1960; since then it has declined to 27% (Dunning 1983). Although these estimates differ in the precise proportions, both indicate that the proportion of foreign direct investment that is contained in developing countries has been falling. Thus much investment has been in other advanced countries: by 1978 the USA and Canada each had over 10% of the total and New Zealand, South Africa, and Australia nearly 7%. By 1983 the US share had risen to 25.4%, and that of such developing countries as Brazil (4.3%), Mexico (2.8%), and Malaysia (1.5%) was growing rapidly (Dunning and Cantwell 1987: 814). The destination of foreign direct investment differs by country of origin. For the UK and USA in 1971 over 80% of foreign direct investment was located in other developed countries; for West Germany, over 72%. By contrast Japanese transnational corporations' manufacturing investment is located primarily in Asia (35%), North America (23%), and Latin America (20%) (Dicken 1992).

Within the Third World the stock of foreign direct capital is unevenly distributed. In 1982, $19.3 billion was located in Africa; of this Egypt, Nigeria, and Zimbabwe held more than half. Some $26.3 billion was invested in Asian developing countries, notably Hong Kong, Indonesia, Malaysia, and to a lesser extent China, South Korea, the Philippines, and Thailand. Of Latin America's $68.6 billion of foreign direct capital stock, Brazil accounted for a third, Mexico a fifth, and Argentino and Venezuela 10% each. There was $13.3 billion of foreign direct capital in Saudi Arabia (Dunning and Cantwell 1987: 800–801). Foreign direct investment in the Third World is highly selective.

Transnational corporations have become a means of industrialization in at least some NICs. As such they transfer technology and affect local industrial development. Transnational corporations have been criticized as being inappropriate means of transferring technologies to the Third World (often in whole bundles) or as transferring only low-skilled activities (Hymer 1975). It has also been claimed that transnational corporations provide few linkages to encourage further development (Lall 1980), though there is evidence of indirect transfers of technical knowledge from transnational enterprises to domestic firms in Mexico (Blomström and Persson 1983).

The sectoral distribution of foreign direct investment is, like the geographic distribution, uneven. Overall transnational corporations are especially involved in the following industrial activities: (i) technologically advanced sectors (pharmaceuticals, computers, scientific instruments, electronics, synthetic fibers); (ii) large-volume, medium-technology, consumer goods industries (motor vehicles, tires, televisions, refrigerators); (iii) mass-produced branded consumer goods (cigarettes, soft drinks, toilet preparations, breakfast cereals) (Stopford et al. 1981).

Perhaps the symbol of globalization in the 1950s and 1960s, transnational corporations have seemed to take second place to the international activities of banks and other financial institutions in the 1970s and 1980s. Nevertheless transnational corporations have invested ever larger sums in a few developing countries as well as engaging in an increasing variety of nonequity forms of international production. Just as the growth of "free-range banking" (the phrase is from Daly and Logan 1989) has restricted the power of the nation-state to control fiscal and monetary policy, so the control of world production and trade by corporations that operate in many countries is making economic and trade policy more difficult.

2.2.3 Trade

Throughout the postwar years the volume of world trade (corrected for price changes) has grown consistently. Only in 1974/75 and 1981/82 did the volume of all trade fall (Figure 2.4). By 1991 the volume of world trade was over five and a half times greater than it had been in 1960, representing an average annual rate of increase of 5.8%. The increase in trade of manufactures has been especially spectacular; its volume has increased at an average annual rate of 7.3%. By contrast, trade in mineral and agricultural commodities has been growing at average rates of only 2.9% and 3.4% each year. Indeed, in 1991 the volume of minerals exported was hardly greater than it had been in 1973. As a consequence manufactures in 1985 accounted for 62.3% of commodity trade and food accounted for 10.4%, compared to 44.7% and 21.9%, respectively, in 1955 (Grimwade 1989: 58).

Trade has been growing faster than world production (Figure 2.5; see also World Bank 1987). By 1991 the volume of world trade as a proportion of the volume of world output was 1.7 times greater than it had been in 1960. The 4.1% average annual increase in the volume of world output was matched by a 5.9% increase in the volume of trade. Similarly the 5.1% average annual increase in the volume of output of manufactured commodities generated a 7.5% average annual increase in trade. The exports of agricultural products grew faster than output too. And even in relatively insular countries trade has become of increasing significance: in the USA exports were 11.5% of output in 1960 but 25.3% in 1979; in Japan the proportion rose from 18.8% to 29.2%. Production and consumption are becoming increasingly integrated across national boundaries, becoming global.

This growth in trade has been underpinned by reductions in the barriers to trade. On the one hand, the real costs of transport have fallen; as transport costs fall in comparison to other costs of production, it becomes relatively more profitable to seek locations at which production is cheap (for example, places where labor or land are cheap or where technology is especially well developed), rather than locations at which the costs of transport are low. On

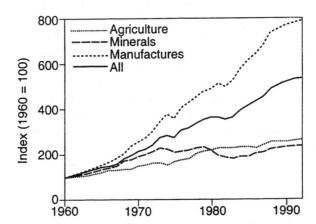

FIGURE 2.4. The volume of global exports, 1960–1992. Minerals include fuels and nonferrous metals. *Source*: GATT, International Trade (annual). Geneva: General Agreement on tarrifs and Trade.

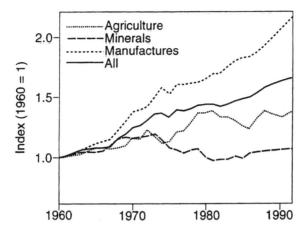

FIGURE 2.5. Index values of the ratio of the volume of world trade to the volume of world output, 1960–1992. See Figure 2.4.

the other hand, tariff and nontariff barriers to trade have progressively been removed over the past 40 years. Free trade associations and customs unions, such as the Central American Common Market, The European Community (EC), the European Free Trade Association (EFTA), the Latin American Free Trade Area, and more recently the North American Free Trade Agreement (NAFTA), have reduced barriers to trade between their member states. GATT also has sponsored a series of trade negotiations: 1947 in Geneva; 1949 in Annecy; 1950/51 in Torquay; 1955/56 in Geneva; 1960–1962 in Geneva (the Dillon round); 1964–1967 (the Kennedy round); 1973–1979 (the Tokyo round); and most recently the Uruguay round. The biggest cuts in tariffs occurred in the first and sixth rounds (Grimwade 1989: 30–36).

Yet the expansion of trade has not occurred at a uniform pace nor at the same rate in the four countries (Figures 2.6 and 2.7). Globally, exports grew at a relatively constant rate from the mid-1950s until the early 1970s. Exports boomed in the early 1970s, culminating in the remarkable expansion of 1973 and 1974, when exports grew by over 75%. The boom was followed immediately by the post-OPEC crash and a decade of falling rates of growth of exports. By the early 1980s the value of exports was declining; only since the mid-1980s has the value of exports begun to rise once again. With wide annual fluctuations about the general trend the postwar history of the growth of exports seems to reflect a cyclical rather than a long boom pattern: a period of slow growth to 1970, a boom in the early 1970s, a depression in the early 1980s, a recovery to the late 1980s, and some signs of perhaps another decline in rates of growth in the early 1990s. Whereas exports were growing at 10.2% annually until 1974, they have grown at only 4.5% annually since then (Table 2.7).

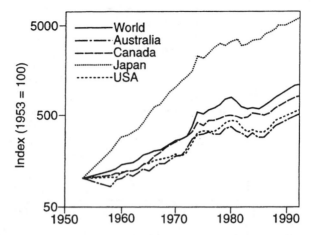

FIGURE 2.6. Index of the value of exports, 1953–1992. The data are expressed in billions of $US; they have been reduced to 1986 dollars using the US consumer price index and then converted to an index number. The data thus reflect changes in the volumes of exports and changes in the value of the $US to other major trading currencies. The vertical axis is logarithmic. *Source*: IMF (annual), *Direction of Trade Statistics Yearbook*, Washington, DC: International Monetary Fund (for 1958–1992); and UN-DESA (annual), *Yearbook of International Trade Statistics*, New York: United Nations Department of Economic and Social Affairs (for 1953 and 1958).

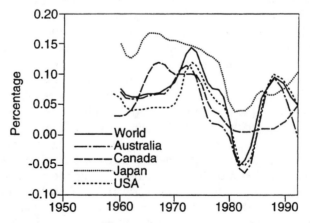

FIGURE 2.7. Annual rate of growth of exports, 1960–1992. See Figure 2.6.

TABLE 2.7. The slowdown of world exports, 1958–1992

| Country | Average rate of growth | | t statistic (pooled variance) | Probability |
	1958–1974	1974–1992		
World	10.21	4.50	1.87	0.07
USA	7.76	4.30	1.04	0.31
Japan	16.36	6.20	3.43	0.00
Canada	8.94	3.40	2.38	0.02
Australia	9.03	3.50	1.66	0.11

Notes: Probability denotes the chance of observing a *t*-value at least as large as that measured. Tests are paired, two-tailed, pooled variance *t*-tests. There are 16 observations in the first period and 18 in the second.
Source: Calculations on data from Figure 2.6.

The histories of individual countries have followed this general pattern more or less closely (see also Table 2.8). Japan's exports have of course grown faster than those of the world as a whole and faster than those of Australia, Canada, and the USA. By contrast exports from Australia, Canada, and the USA have grown about 1% per annum more slowly than those of the world as a whole. The rates of growth of exports of all countries are correlated: when exports from one grow, so do those from others. In all four countries exports have grown more slowly since 1974 than before then (Table 2.7), though the slowdown is not statistically significant in the USA and Australia. Seemingly there is some consistency about the slowdown.

TABLE 2.8. Comparison of rates of growth of exports, 1958–1992

Pairs compared	Mean difference	SD of difference	t statistic	Probability	Correlation
World/USA	0.013	0.050	1.464	0.153	+0.861
World/Japan	−0.038	0.079	−2.815	0.008	+0.666
World/Canada	0.012	0.070	0.978	0.335	+0.664
World/Australia	0.011	0.088	0.708	0.484	+0.582
USA/Japan	−0.051	0.100	−2.961	0.006	+0.489
USA/Canada	−0.001	0.076	−0.070	0.945	+0.638
USA/Australia	−0.002	0.083	−0.140	0.890	+0.647
Japan/Canada	0.050	0.080	3.643	0.001	+0.611
Japan/Australia	0.049	0.129	2.203	0.035	+0.160
Canada/Australia	−0.001	0.086	−0.073	0.942	+0.536

Notes: The mean difference is negative if the average rate of growth of exports in the first-named country is less than that in the second. Probability denotes the chance of observing a *t*-value at least as large as that measured. Tests are paired, two-tailed *t*-tests. There are 34 observations.
Source: Calculations on data from Figure 2.6.

2.3 THE OUTCOME: PATTERNS OF PRODUCTION AND TRADE

Growth and globalization have gone hand in hand. As they have, the geography of production and trade has changed dramatically.

2.3.1 NICs, IMEs, and Japan

By the end of the 1960s it was being observed that there was some variation in the economic performance of the developing countries (Hoogvelt 1982). Since the quadrupling of oil prices in 1973/74, a great divide has become apparent between Third World countries on the basis of those that have resources (oil or other scarce minerals) or industrial markets and those that do not. The countries of the Third World are conventionally classified into the following categories:

1. A low income group with per capita incomes less than $400 in 1985
2. The capital surplus oil exporters (such as Iran, Iraq, Saudi Arabia, Libya, and Kuwait)
3. The middle income countries, of which a subset are—
4. The middle income newly industrializing countries

(The classification of oil exporters has changed regularly in the 1980s.)

The middle income NICs are themselves diverse. At the end of the 1970s, they were identified by both the OECD and the World Bank. The OECD (1979: 19) definition includes countries that (i) are rapidly penetrating the world market for manufactures; (ii) have a rising share of industrial employment; and (iii) are increasing real GDP per capita faster than the industrial countries. The World Bank (1977) included middle income countries in which manufacturing accounts for at least 20% of GDP. These are the following:

1. Those Latin American countries that had started the process of industrialization some time ago (Brazil and Mexico according to the OECD, plus Argentina and Colombia according to the World Bank)
2. The East Asian exporters (Singapore, South Korea, Hong Kong, and Taiwan for the OECD, plus Malaysia and the Philippines according to the World Bank)
3. Some countries in southern Europe (Spain, Portugal, the former Yugoslavia, and Greece according to the OECD, plus Turkey according to the World Bank)
4. South Africa, according to the World Bank

It seems that Argentina can no longer be included in the group of NICs and that Malaysia may not yet belong to it (Table 2.9). Presumably, too, some of the republics of the former Yugoslavia are no longer included in the group.

TABLE 2.9. Growth of NICs

Country	GNP/person 1991 ($US)	Real Growth (%pa)		Growth of manufactured output (%pa)			Mfg/GDP	
		1965–1985	1980–1991	1960–1970	1970–1979	1980–1991	1987	1991
Hong Kong	13,430	6.1	5.6	—	6.1	—	0.22	0.17
Singapore	14,210	7.6	5.3	13.0	9.3	7.0	0.29	0.29
Spain	12,450	2.6	2.8	9.7	6.6	0.4[b]	0.27	—
Taiwan	7,761	8.4	6.7	14.0	12.7	10.2	0.40	0.32
Portugal	5,930	3.3	3.1	8.9	4.6	—	—	—
South Korea	6,330	6.6	8.7	17.6	17.8	12.4	0.30	0.28
Yugoslavia	2,480[a]	4.1	—	5.7	7.6	—	—	—
Argentina	2,790	0.2	-1.5	5.7	1.9	0.0[b]	0.31	—
Brazil	2,940	4.3	0.5	—	10.9	1.7	0.28	0.26
Mexico	3,030	2.7	-0.5	9.4	6.4	1.8	0.25	0.22
Malaysia	2,520	4.4	2.9	—	12.4	9.6	—	—
Turkey	1,780	2.6	2.9	10.9	8.7	7.2	0.26	0.24
IMEs	21,050	2.4	2.9	6.2	3.0	3.02	—	—

Notes: Gross national product (GNP) per person is measured in 1991 $US.

Real growth is the average annual percentage rate of growth of gross national product per person, discounted for inflation.

Growth of manufactured output is average annual percentage rate of growth of output, discounted for inflation. The IMEs (industrial market economies) are the OECD countries less Greece, Portugal, and Turkey (by 1989 Hong Kong, Singapore and Spain were included in this group).

[a]1987.

[b]1980–1987.

Sources: World Bank (1981, 1987, 1989, 1992). Data for Taiwan are drawn from Directorate General of the Budget, Accounting and Statistics (annual) *Statistical Yearbook of the Republic of China* Taipei.

Throughout the 1960s and the 1970s the NICs were clearly outperforming the industrial market economies. Their rates of growth of GNP per capita all exceeded the average for the industrial market economies (IMEs). In Hong Kong, Singapore, South Korea, and Taiwan output per person was doubling every decade or so. In addition the output of manufactures in the NICs was growing more rapidly than in the IMEs: in the 1970s except in Portugal manufactured output was growing at least twice as fast in the NICs as in the IMEs. Spectacular rates of growth were recorded by Taiwan, South Korea, and Singapore. Between 1965 and 1985 the middle income countries as a group recorded an average annual real rate of increase of manufactured output of 6.6% per annum compared to 3.8% in the IMEs. Accordingly their share of the world's manufactured output rose from 7% to 11.2%, whereas that of the IMEs fell from 85.4% to 81.6% (World Bank 1987). A new set of industrial producers had entered the global scene.

The 1980s have been much less kind to the NICs. Only Singapore, South

Korea, Taiwan, Malaysia, and Turkey have maintained anything like their earlier exceptionalism—and even their rate of growth of manufactured output has been reduced. In part this slowdown reflects the global slowdown; but most NICs are no longer outperforming the IMEs as a group. Growth has become more selective. By the mid-1980s export-led growth in the NICs was declining as cost advantages were eroded by technical change, changing currency values, the collapse of raw material prices, the costs of foreign debt, and changes in the restructuring strategies of transnational corporations (Fagan and Rich 1986).

As the NICs have grabbed an increasing share of world industrial production, they have also broadened the range of products they make (Table 2.10). Resource-based products have never accounted for anything but a small proportion of industrial output in developing countries (most resource products are exported without processing), and that proportion is declining. Among the NICs only in Malaysia, Mexico, and Argentina did food and agricultural products account for over one-fifth of the value added by manufacturing in 1986. Also declining is the share of exports taken by traditional labor-intensive manufactures like textiles and clothing. These now account for less than one-third of the exports of developing countries. Only in Hong Kong (39%), Portugal (29%), South Korea (22%), and Turkey (37%) did textiles, clothing, and footwear account for over one-fifth of the value added

TABLE 2.10. Composition of exports of NICs

Economy	Primary commodities		Textiles & clothing		Machinery & transport equipment		Other manufactures	
	1965	1990	1965	1990	1965	1990	1965	1990
Hong Kong	6	4	52	39	7	23	35	34
Singapore	65	27	6	5	10	48	18	20
Spain	60	24	6	4	10	39	23	33
Taiwan								
Portugal	38	19	24	29	3	19	34	32
South Korea	40	7	27	22	3	37	29	35
Yugoslavia	43	21	8	7	24	30	25	42
Argentina	94	65	0	3	1	7	5	26
Brazil	92	47	1	3	2	18	6	32
Mexico	84	56	3	2	1	25	12	17
Malaysia	94	65	0	3	1	7	5	26
Turkey	98	32	1	37	0	7	1	24

Note: Numbers are percentages of total exports by value in each category. The categories follow the Standard Industrial and Trade Classification (SITC): primary commodities include food, fuels, and other primary commodities (SITC Sections 0, 1, 2, 3, and 4 together with nonferrous metals from Division 68); textiles and clothing are a manufactured category (Division 65 and 84); machinery and transport equipment are the commodities in SITC Section 7; other manufactures are the commodities in Sections 5, 6, 8, and 9 less Divisions 65, 68, and 84.
Source: World Bank (1992).

by manufacturing in 1990. The major growth in exports has occurred in nontraditional products that in the past have been associated with the industrial countries of Europe and North America: electrical and nonelectrical machinery, transport equipment, chemicals, and iron and steel. In 1990, 48% of the value added in manufacturing in Singapore derived from the machinery and transport sectors; 39% in Spain; 37% in South Korea; and 30% in the former Yugoslavia.

The other major locational change that has occurred in the postwar world has been the shift in the balance of economic power between Japan and the other members of the industrial club. This shift is attested by various indicators. Between 1960 and 1973 Japan's average rate of growth of GDP exceeded 13% per annum, more than twice the OECD average (6.1%, which itself includes Japan's contribution). Figure 2.8 illustrates the change in quantity of manufactured goods produced by the four countries. Japan's value added in manufacturing quadrupled between 1960 and 1970 and between 1968 and 1988; that in North America rose only one and a half times to 1970 and again to 1988. Manufacturing value added in Australia has grown very slowly: from an index value of 100 in 1968 it had reached barely 130 in 1985, only a little above its 1973 value, and was little over 160 in 1991.

Thus, the share of world manufactured output produced in the USA fell from 40.3% in 1963 to 29.4% in 1980; that of Canada from 3.0% to 2.4%. By contrast the share of Japan rose from 5.5% to 15.7% and that of West Germany from 9.7% to 12.4%. As the UK lost share, France and Italy gained share (Dicken 1992: 28).

These changes in the location of production are exemplified by the steel industry (Foot 1986). Just over 150 million tons of raw steel was produced in the USA in 1973. By 1982 output had fallen to 74.5 million tons. Between

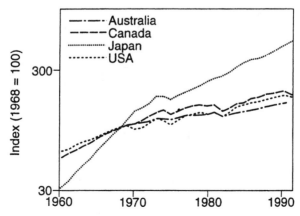

FIGURE 2.8. Index of value added in manufacturing. *Source*: OECD, various years.

1973 and 1983 the labor force was cut from 509,000 to 243,000, and between 1982 and 1984 steel companies lost $5.8 billion (American Iron and Steel Institute *Statistical Yearbook*). These figures demonstrate a recent crisis in the steel industry, a crisis not atypical of other industries in the USA (Bluestone and Harrison, 1982).

However, rapid contraction is not characteristic of world steel production as a whole. The pattern of world steel output has changed (Table 2.11). While US steel industry output shrank by 50%, world output (market economies only (fell by only 19%. The decline in US steel output alone accounted for 74% of the decline in world output. In some already industrialized countries the decay presents a similarly gloomy picture (the UK being the most notable with a decline in output from 29.5 to 12.4 million tons of raw steel between 1973 and 1980). In Japan the steel industry was hit especially hard by the downturn after 1974; since then output has fluctuated with little apparent trend. In some developing countries steel output has expanded. The South Koreans did not start producing steel in integrated mills until 1970; yet output had reached 16 million tons by 1986. In Brazil output has almost tripled from 7.9 million tons in 1973 to just over 20 million tons in 1984. The US share of world output in steel fell from almost 28%, in 1973 to only 17% in 1982, while the share supplied by developing countries grew from 7% to over 17%.

TABLE 2.11. World raw steel output, 1973–1992

Country or area	1973	1975	1977	1980	1982	1984	1986	1988	1990	1992
USA & Canada	166	131	140	129	87	108	97	116	112	108
Western Europe	198	171	171	178	159	173	162	181	180	174
Australia & New Zealand	9	9	8	9	7	7	8	8	8	8
Japan	132	113	113	123	110	116	108	117	122	108
All developed countries	504	423	433	439	363	405	376	421	422	399
Latin America	18	21	24	32	30	37	42	47	43	46
Brazil	8	9	12	17	14	20	23	27	23	26
Africa	7	9	9	12	11	11	12	13	14	15
Middle East	2	1	2	3	3	4	5	6	4	6
Asia	11	14	19	27	32	35	40	52	61	72
South Korea	1	2	5	9	13	14	16	21	26	31
Taiwan	1	1	2	5	5	6	6	9	11	12
All developing countries	38	44	54	74	76	86	98	118	122	139
Total market economies	541	467	487	513	439	491	468	539	544	537

Note: Data are in millions of short tons.
Source: American Iron and Steel Institute various years *Annual statistical report*.

2.3.2 The Losers

At the other end of the scale are the people who have lost out in the global game. They are the people who lead short, hungry lives.

In 1979 some 200 million people lived in the ten poorest countries on earth (World Bank 1981). These countries were Cambodia, Laos, Bhutan, Bangladesh, Chad, Ethiopia, Nepal, Somalia, Mali, and Myanmar (formerly Burma). Each of them averaged less than $160 of GNP per head, worth maybe $300 in today's money. In four of these countries—Bhutan, Bangladesh, Chad, and Somalia—GNP per head had been falling consistently since 1960. In none of them had GNP per head risen faster than 1% per year (compared to about 3.5% per year for the world as a whole). The adult literacy rate was less than 30%, except in Somalia (60%) and Myanmar (67%). Life expectancy at birth was less than 50 years, except in Myanmar (54 years).

To people this poor the major material concern is food. On average, the ten countries perform poorly (Table 2.12). No country supplied on average more than 2500 calories per head in 1965, and only Laos did so in 1989. In none of the countries did food production per head increase in the 1970s (food production per person fell by over 15% in Somalia and Ethiopia and by about 10% in Bangladesh, Chad, Nepal, and Mali), and it has been decreasing in Ethiopia and Nepal in the 1980s as well. In 1989 Chad, Ethiopia, and Somalia supplied less than 2000 calories per head; other countries—not among the world's ten poorest—that failed to supply this amount of food were Mozambique (1595 calories per person), Rwanda, Sierra Leone, the Central African Republic, Haiti, Ghana, and Guinea. [Recommended nutritional levels depend on gender, age, weight, environment, health, and workload; recommended levels for 56 kg adult males undertaking moderate work are 3000 calories per head; the needs of women are normally lower (see Dreze and Sen 1989: 35–45).]

Estimates of changes in the numbers of people who are undernourished vary widely. Partly the variations reflect assumptions about the amount of food needed under different circumstances; partly they reflect different standards—amounts needed to prevent stunted growth and serious risks to health as compared to amounts needed to permit an active working life and intellectual development. One set of consistent estimates has been produced by the Food and Agriculture Organization (see Grigg 1986: 50). The FAO estimates that the number of people receiving less than the minimum requirement (1.2 times the basal metabolic rate) has been about 550 million since about 1950 (though with a jump to 650 million in the early 1960s). Whereas these 550 million people represented about 34% of the population of developing countries in 1950, they make up about 17% of their population now. A World Bank (1987: 17) estimate for 1980 is 730 million; other estimates have commonly ranged up to a billion people and some to 3 billion people (Grigg

TABLE 2.12. Food supply in poor countries

Country	Calories per person, 1965	Food production per person		Calories per person, 1989
		1978/1970	1989/1980	
Kampuchea	2276	—	1.65	2166
Laos	1956	0.87	1.14	2630
Bhutan	—	1.00	0.93	—
Bangladesh	1972	0.92	0.96	2021
Chad	2399	0.91	0.85	1743
Ethiopia	1824	0.84	0.84	1667
Nepal	1901	0.88	1.15	2077
Somalia	2167	0.85	0.94	1906
Mali	1859	0.88	0.97	2314
Burma	1917	0.97	0.93	2440
All low income countries	1993	1.05	1.19	2406
Middle income countries	2463	1.07	1.02	2860
High income countries	3083	1.10	1.00	3409

Notes: The two outer columns of data indicate the calorie supply per person. The two inner columns contain indexes of food production per person. The food production indexes are calculated from average production data for three years at the beginning and end of the period: 1969–1971, 1979–1981, and 1988–1990. They indicate how many calories were available per person at the end as compared to the beginning of the period.
Source: World Bank (1981, 1992).

1986: 6). The world has been able to do little to reduce the numbers of people who are in extreme poverty despite all the impressive growth figures quoted in this chapter.

Quite apart from the obvious class attributes associated with such deprivation there are strong gender distinctions too (Dreze and Sen 1989: 46–61). There is anecdotal evidence about inequalities in the distribution of food within households and better evidence of gender inequalities in access to health care and parental attention. These inequalities produce remarkable variations in the proportion of a population that is male or female. In North America and Europe there are 1.05 females for every male, and in sub-Saharan Africa 1.02. Yet in China, Bangladesh, India, and Pakistan the ratio is less than 0.94. Dreze and Sen (1989: 52) calculate that 13% of the female population of Pakistan is "missing": there would need to be that many more females to raise the female/male ratio to sub-Saharan African levels. These data seem to provide evidence of gender inequalities in access to the resources needed to survive.

2.3.3 The Network of World Trade

As some regions have grown and others have declined relatively, the pattern of world trade has altered too.

If the rate of growth of production in the NICs has been high, that of exports has been nothing short of spectacular (Table 2.13). Between 1965 and 1985 manufacturing production in the middle income developing countries grew at 6.6% per annum (compared to 3.8% in the industrialized market economies and 4.5% in all market economies). However, their exports grew by 13.8% per annum (compared to 6.8% among the IMEs and 7.4% in all market economies). That is, exports from the middle income countries were doubling every 5 years or so. Production in the middle income countries has become increasingly export oriented: whereas in 1960 and again in 1973 the middle income countries accounted for a smaller share of world trade than of production, by 1985 their share of world trade was much larger than their share of world production.

Among the NICs, rates of growth of trade have been even greater (Table 2.14). In South Korea since 1960 exports have been increasing in real terms at 20% each year; in Taiwan they have grown at about the same pace. In Hong Kong and Spain exports have been rising at nearly 10% a year. In every country except the former Yugoslavia the rate of growth of exports has exceeded the rate of growth of exports from the IMEs in at least one of the intervals. Rates of growth of imports have been correspondingly high. However, in Yugoslavia and Argentina, imports fell in the 1980s. In virtually all the NICs merchandise exports have been growing more rapidly than imports for most of the period since 1960. This means that the net trade imbalance in services and the net outflow of capital has been growing since the 1960s, particularly in the 1980s. It also means—since the bulk of world trade is among the IMEs and NICs—that the industrial economies' balance of commodity trade is becoming less positive. We shall see evidence of this below.

TABLE 2.13. Growth of production and exports of manufactures

Country group	Production				Exports				
	Share 1965	Growth 1965–1973	Growth 1973–1985	Share 1985	Share 1965	Growth 1960–1973	Growth 1973–1985	Share 1985	Share 1991
IMEs	85.4	5.3	3.0	81.6	92.5	10.6	4.4	82.3	78.6
Low income	7.5	8.9	7.9	6.9	2.3	2.4	8.7	2.1	2.1
Middle income	7.0	9.1	5.0	11.2	5.0	14.9	12.9	15.3	19.0
High income oil	0.1	5.8	3.5	0.3	0.2	10.7	5.3	0.3	0.3

Notes: "Share" is share of manufactured output of market economies. "Growth" is annual average percentage rate of growth in real terms.
Source: World Bank (1987: 47); the 1991 data are estimated from GATT (1993) *International Trade*. Geneva: General Agreement on Tariffs and Trade.

TABLE 2.14. Growth of trade in NICs

Country	Annual average rate of growth (% pa)						Share of exports to IMEs	
	Exports			Imports				
	1960–1970	1970–1979	1980–1991	1960–1970	1970–1979	1980–1991	1965	1985
Hong Kong	12.7	8.3	4.4	9.2	8.4	11.3	67	54
Singapore	4.2	11.0	8.9	5.9	8.0	7.2	28	47
Spain	11.5	10.8	7.5	18.5	3.4	9.4	73	66
Taiwan	21.3	21.6	10.0	14.4	20.1	8.9	—	68
Portugal	9.6	-0.3	11.1	14.2	3.3	10.0	65	85
South Korea	34.1	25.7	12.2	20.5	13.5	11.1	75	69
Yugoslavia	7.7	4.7	-1.2	8.8	5.0	-1.2	40	33
Argentina	3.4	10.7	2.1	0.3	—	-5.5	67	43
Brazil	5.1	7.0	4.3	4.9	5.6	0.8	77	62
Mexico	2.8	10.9	3.5	6.4	5.0	2.2	82	86
Malaysia	5.8	6.5	10.9	2.3	6.2	7.2	56	52
Turkey	—	1.7	7.2	—	3.3	7.4	71	51
IMEs	8.4	5.9	4.1	9.3	4.5	5.1	70	71

Notes: Data refer to merchandise exports.
Sources: World Bank (1987, 1989, 1993). Data for Taiwan between 1980 and 1991 are drawn from Directorate General of the Budget, Accounting and Statistics (annual) *Statistical Yearbook of the Republic of China* Taipei.

The nature of the commodities exported by the NICs has been changing too. In 1963 the NICs accounted for over 5% of total imports into the OECD of clothing (17%); leather, footwear, and travel goods (7%); wood and cork manufactures (12%); and textiles (6%). By 1979 this list had broadened and changed: clothing (38%); leather, footwear, and travel goods (29%); wood and cork manufactures (27%); electrical machinery (16%); textiles (12%); miscellaneous (11%); rubber manufactures (9%); metal manufactures (9%); and iron and steel (6%) (Dicken 1992).

In the 1960s the great bulk of the exports of the NICs were destined for the IMEs. The only major exception to this rule was Singapore. By the mid-1980s, though, both the differences in dependence between individual NICs and their overall degree of dependence on IMEs had fallen. By 1985 only Portugal and Mexico exported more than 70% of their merchandise to the IMEs: as a group the NICs depended on industrial economies' markets even less than did the IMEs themselves.

These changes are reflected in the changing network of world trade (Figure 2.9). The rise in the share of world exports contributed by Japan and the NICs is especially evident (a combined share of 10% in 1960; a share of nearly 33% by 1988), as is the corresponding decline in the shares contributed by

Europe and North America (nearly a half of all exports in 1960; only 30% in 1988). Even more dramatic has been the decline in the share of world exports that originates in the other developing countries: they provided over 20% of world exports in 1960—about as much as North America—but only 10% in 1988. The isolation of the centrally planned economies has persisted through the 30 years: North America, Japan, the NICs, and the oil economies have small trade links with the centrally planned economies.

The direction of trade has changed too. In 1960 the main flows and surpluses identified a pattern in which North America exported to Europe, Japan, and other countries; Japan exported to Europe; and Europe exported to other countries (as shown in the chart below).

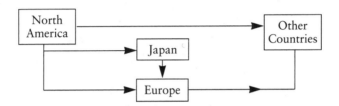

By 1988 the pattern of flows and surpluses had changed to one in which Japan exported to the NICs and to North America; the NICs exported to Europe and North America; and Europe exported to North America (as the chart below shows).

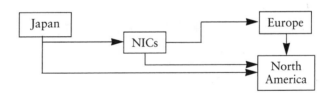

The pace of change in the network of world trade seems to have quickened since the early 1970s. Whereas the correlation between the flow volumes of 1960 and those of 1973 is $r = +0.94$, that between the volumes of 1973 and 1988 is only $r = +0.78$ (calculated on the proportions of all world exports that occur between the seven major trading groups represented in Figure 2.9). One way of measuring the changes in the overall network of trade from one period to the next is to estimate a model of the change. Let T_{ij}^k denote the proportion of world exports that are sold from bloc i to bloc j in year k ($i, j = 1, 2, \ldots, 7$). For each $k \Sigma_{ij} T_{ij} = 1$. Now denote the proportion of world exports that originate in block i by O_i; evidently, $O_i = \Sigma_j T_{ij}$; similarly let the proportion of world exports that are bought by block j be

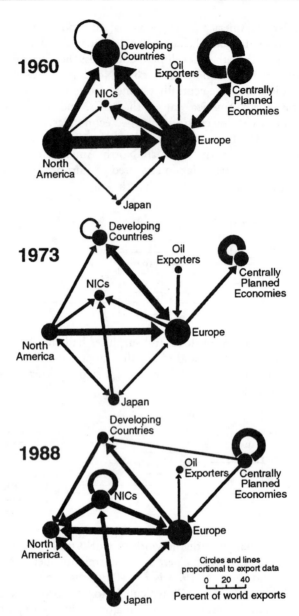

FIGURE 2.9. The network of world trade: upper—1960; middle—1973; lower—1988. Circles have diameters proportional to total exports of the region indicated; lines have widths proportional to exports of the larger trading partners; arrows indicate the balance of trade, if the difference in exports exceeds 0.2% of world trade. Trade within North America and within Europe is excluded from the calculations. Only flows that exceed 1.7% of total world exports are represented. Exports from the NICs to other developing economies are estimated. The regions are: North America = Canada + USA; Europe = Australia, New Zealand, South Africa + Europe (excluding the countries noted below); Centrally planned economies = USSR + Eastern Europe +

D_j, with $D_j = \Sigma_i T_{ij}$. In order of increasing complexity, three models of trade are as follows:

Model 1. $T_{ij}^k = \alpha$, for α = a constant.

Model 2. $T_{ij}^k = \alpha O_i D_j$.

Model 3. $T_{ij}^{k'} = \alpha O_i D_j (T_{ij}^k)^\beta$,

where k' is the period that follows period k.

The three models are most probable distributions of trade under different information. Model 1 arises when there is no information about trade except its existence. It predicts that all trade flows are equal. Model 2 is the most probable distribution of trade when all that is known are the total exports and total imports of each region. It predicts that trade between any pair of blocs is proportional to the total exports of one bloc and the total imports of the other. Model 3 modifies that distribution to reflect information about the previous period's pattern of trade. The parameter β measures the importance of the previous trade pattern in predicting the current pattern. The models have all been estimated from the 7 × 7 trade network, except that flows within North America and within Europe have been ignored and there is no international trade within Japan (so there are 46 trade flows). The models were estimated by nonlinear methods (using simplex search) so as to minimize the sum of the deviations between the actual and the estimated flows, that is, to minimize the loss function

$$L = \Sigma_{ij} |T_{ij} - T_{ijest}|.$$

The change in L from Model 2 to Model 3 provides information about the similarity of the present pattern of trade to the previous pattern.

The losses are all quite high (Table 2.15). Model 1 as expected is quite hopeless: 35–40% of world trade would have to be redirected before its predictions would correspond to reality. Model 2 is better: 20–25% of trade needs to be redirected before its predictions would correspond to the actual flows. But even in Model 3 some 15% of world trade would have to be redirected for the actual pattern to correspond to the predicted pattern. That is,

China and other centrally planned economies in Asia; the NICs are Singapore, and Taiwan from Asia + Brazil and Mexico from Latin America; the oil exporters are represented by the non-African Middle East (OPEC's exports are now about 30% larger than those from the Middle East); developing countries are all the rest. The classification is adapted from GATT and is the same for all three years. *Source*: GATT (annual), *International Trade*, Geneva: General Agreement on Tariffs and Trade and IMF (annual); *Direction of Trade Statistics Yearbook*, Washinton, DC: International Monetary Fund.

TABLE 2.15. Value of the loss function, 1960, 1973, and 1988

Year	Value of the loss function L			Percentage reduction in L	
	Model 1	Model 2	Model 3	2 compare 1	3 compare 2
1960	.8371	.5585	—	.333	—
1973	.6999	.4540	.3004	.351	.338
1988	.7238	.4187	.3188	.422	.239

the pattern of trade links is specific to the partners: some links are stronger than expected; others weaker. As compared to Model 2, Model 3 provides a 33.8% improvement in predictions of trade flows in 1973 but only a 23.9% improvement in 1988. The 1988 pattern of world trade reflects the historical situation of 1973 rather less well than the 1973 pattern reflects the situation in 1960. In sum, most of the change in the network of world trade between 1960 and 1988 occurred after 1973.

2.4 LABOR MARKET CHANGES

These changes in the global system of production and distribution have major implications for the labor markets of the IMEs. Three are particularly significant: growing levels of unemployment; growing levels of female employment; and changes in the nature of jobs, from regular full-time to part-time and casual work.

Rates of economic growth have apparently slowed since the early 1970s, though the difference between the so-called boom years of the 1950s and 1960s and the slump of the 1970s and 1980s is not as sharp as sometimes thought. Nevertheless that difference in growth rates has been sufficient to cause a rapid and sustained increase in unemployment in the advanced capitalist economies. Unemployment rates have grown uniformly in the OECD since the mid-1960s (Figure 2.10; Table 2.16). In the OECD as a whole, male unemployment rates were less than 3% until 1974. Then there was a jump to rates of 4–4.5% through the remainder of the 1970s. Between 1980 and 1982 unemployment rates again jumped to over 7%, and yet again in 1991/92. Since 1970, each recession seems to have pushed unemployment rates to new highs for which the subsequent recoveries have been unable to compensate.

Average levels of unemployment differ between the countries and by gender. (These differences reflect not only differences in economic performance but also in the legal definition of unemployment, particularly of that of married women.) Canada has had the worst unemployment record throughout the period, generally 1.5 times the OECD average; with Australia, it also

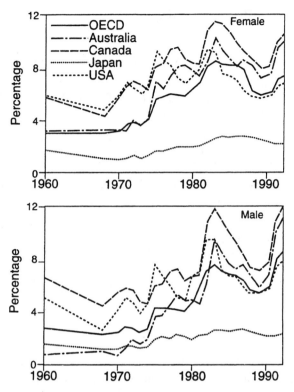

FIGURE 2.10. Unemployment rates by gender. *Source*: OECD, various years.

seems to exhibit the greatest sensitivity to fluctuations. The US rate was initially similar to the Canadian rate but has been well below it since the late 1970s. Even so, US rates of unemployment have exceeded the OECD average. Until 1971 the Australian and Japanese unemployment rates were similar, near or below 1%. However, after 1973 the Australian unemployment rate has grown sharply and has generally exceeded the OECD average since the mid-1970s. By contrast, the Japanese rate has remained relatively low (a half or less of the OECD average)—though it has shown the same tendency to grow as the rates of other countries. Female unemployment rates are generally 0.5–1% above the male rates for the same year. In Japan female unemployment rates are close to those of males; by contrast in Australia female unemployment rates are much higher than those of males.

Until recently working for wages was for women temporary and discontinuous, to be undertaken only when household duties were light or there was a national emergency (Hagen and Jensen 1988). More and more women are now entering the labor force, and their participation is more permanent: the

TABLE 2.16. Unemployment rates, 1960–1992

		OECD		USA		Japan		Canada		Australia	
Period		Male	Fem.	Male	Fem.	Male	Fem.	Male	Fem.	Male	Fem.
1960–1992	Mean	4.99	5.90	6.10	6.98	2.06	1.97	7.70	8.46	5.15	6.87
	SD	1.88	1.81	1.65	1.27	0.50	0.58	2.30	1.88	3.05	2.33
1960-1974	Mean	2.67	3.49	4.40	6.11	1.39	1.23	5.40	6.09	1.34	3.50
	SD	0.24	0.38	0.88	0.71	0.16	0.24	0.75	0.91	0.47	0.38
1975-1992	Mean	5.72	7.05	6.76	7.32	2.33	2.26	8.54	9.44	6.63	8.18
	SD	1.39	1.19	1.39	1.29	0.28	0.38	2.10	1.26	2.18	1.07

Note: Data are available only for the years indicated on Figure 2.10. There are 7 data points in the first interval and 18 in the second (only 16 in Canada). For all 5 areas and both genders the mean rate of unemployment is significantly higher in the second period that in the first (pooled variance, two-tailed t-test, $p < 0.05$).

When the 10 average rates of unemployment over 1960–1987 (5 areas and 2 genders) are compared, all pairs of differences are statistically significant except for the following: F Australia–F USA; F USA–M Canada; M OECD–M Australia; F OECD–M USA; M Australia–M USA (paired sample, pooled variance, two-tailed t-test, $p < 0.05$).
Source: Computations on OECD (1989a); also OECD (1993a) *Economic Surveys 1992–1993* (Paris: OECD), for Australia, Canada, Japan, and the USA; OECD (1993b) *Labour Force Statistics 1971–1991* (Paris: OECD).

labor force has been growing more female. In the OECD as a whole the proportion of the labor force that is female has grown from 33% to over 40% between 1960 and 1992 (Figure 2.11). These proportions correspond to increases in the female participation rate from about 40% to about 56% and decreases in the male participation rate from over 90% to about 83% (Beechey and Perkins 1987: 11, 42). Male participation rates have fallen as increasing proportions of youths stay later in education and as more people in

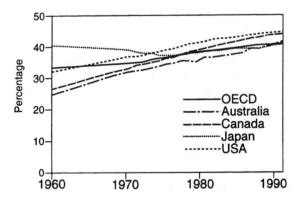

FIGURE 2.11. Proportion of the labor force that is female. *Source*: OECD, varous years.

their late fifties and early sixties retire early (there must have been similar effects on female participation rates, but they have been swamped by other changes).

But the four countries show quite different histories. The Australian proportion has been below the OECD average, rising from 25% in 1960 to catch up with the OECD in 1990. In Canada the proportion of the labor force that is female started at about the same level as in Australia but has since risen more rapidly, to approach the proportion in the USA (45.2%). In Japan two different trends have occurred. Until 1975 a decreasing proportion of the labor force was female: the proportion fell from 40.7% to 37.3%. Since then, though, there has been a slow reversal of this trend, and by 1991 the proportion in Japan had reached 40.8%, slightly below the OECD average. This history apparently reflects two opposed processes: a decline in agricultural employment on the one hand (where women have traditionally made up a high proportion of the labor force), and a rise in industrial-urban employment on the other (where participation rates have been rising) (Saso 1990).

The paradox is that women's increasing commitment to the paid labor force has not wrought much improvement in their occupational status as compared to men. In Canada and the USA there is a gap in earnings between women and men: women are concentrated in low-pay occupations and industries and have historically received less education than men (Bakker 1988). Gender segregation of the workforce in Japan appears from the statistics to be relatively low in comparison to that in other OECD countries. In part this arises from the employment of large numbers of men and women in agriculture and informal family businesses; but this spread of women across industries and occupations conceals a pronounced vertical segregation (Saso 1990: 51–85): though women made up 40% of the workforce in 1987, only 7.3% of managers were female. In Australia levels of both industrial and occupational segregation by gender are high and show little sign of declining: within manufacturing only clerical jobs (already dominated by women), sales positions, and professional occupations were being feminized (Webber et al. 1990). In the mid-1970s on average women in paid work earned 54% of the wage of the average male; of the difference in earnings 29.3% was accounted for by the fact that women worked fewer hours and were younger and less educated than their male counterparts; 34.2% was accounted for by differences in returns to age and education; and 36.5% reflected a flat difference in earnings between males and females (Haig 1982).

Those increasing proportions of women who are seeking paid work are entering a labor market that is changing rapidly. Forms of employment other than the standard of full-time, permanent jobs are becoming more common. There are varieties of these forms of nonstandard employment including part-time jobs, temporary employment agencies, fixed-term contracts, self-employment, concealed employment, casual employment, and such novelties as employee leasing (OECD 1991). There are three main forms of nonstandard employment, though the quality of job (number of hours, permanence, working conditions) varies widely within each form.

One of the most common is part-time work. In the USA since 1973 about a quarter of all new jobs have been part-time; part-timers now represent a sixth of all workers (Christopherson 1990)—about a quarter of women and a tenth of men. These proportions have not changed greatly over the past 20 years (Figure 2.12). Rates of part-time work in Canada have gradually risen toward US levels, particularly in the late 1970s. In Australia in 1993 one in twelve male employees were working part-time but over 40% of female employees: these rates have been rising throughout the 1970s and 1980s. Japan's rates of part-time employment are lower than in other countries, but they too have been rising (Beechey and Perkins 1987: 43). Except in the USA, part-time work has evidently been on the increase since the mid-1970s at least—and especially among women. Nowhere has part-time employment made a large contribution to the growth of employment of males, except recently in Australia.

Some part-time work is involuntary: people would prefer to work more hours or normally do work full-time but have been stood down for part of the week. Involuntary part-time work is more common among males than among females: for example, in Australia in 1989 30% of male part-timers but only 16% of female part-timers would prefer to work more hours; in

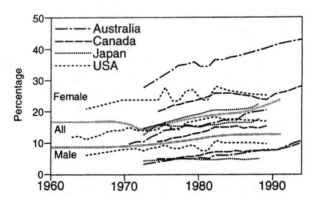

FIGURE 2.12. Proportion of work that is part-time by gender. For each country, the graph inicates the proportion of females, males, and all workers that are employed part-time. In every country, the proportion of female part-time workers exceeds the proportion of all part-time workers, which in turn exceeds the proportion of male part-time workers. *Source*: For Australia, ABS, *Labour Force Survey*, Canberra; for Canada, Statistics Canada, *Historical Labour Force Statistics*, Ottawa; for Japan, OECD, *Employment Outlook*, Paris; for the USA, US Bureau of the Census, *Statistical Abstract of the United States*, Washington, DC.

Canada the comparable proportions are 43% and 30%; in Japan 38% and 20%; in the USA 28% and 17%. There is some evidence that involuntary part-time work is increasing: in Australia involuntary part-time work accounted for about 20% of male part-time employment in the late 1970s, but during the 1980s that share rose to between 25% and 30%; among females the share of involuntary part-time work rose from 9% in 1977 to 15% in 1983–1989.

Another common form of nonstandard employment is temporary or casual work (temporary from the point of view of the employee). In the USA there were 340,000 temporary jobs at any one time in 1978 but 944,000 in 1987 (Christopherson 1990). In Australia in 1990 27.7% of female employees were casual and 16.2% of males; the male casuals were about equally divided between full-timers and part-timers, but the female casuals were 88% part-timers (Burgess and Campbell 1992). In Japan nearly 20% of females but only 5% of males are casual or temporary workers: the proportion of females who are temporary or casual employees rose sharply in the 1970s and early 1980s but has since stabilized. In both Japan and the USA about two-thirds of temporary workers are women (OECD 1987a: 37).

The other major form of nonstandard employment is self-employment (Figure 2.13). In Australia nonemployees rose from 14% of the workforce in 1971 to 16% in 1977 but since then have remained a slowly falling share of

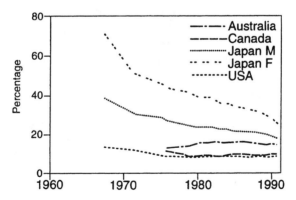

FIGURE 2.13. Casual and self-employment: (a) self-employment in Japan and the USA; (b) casual and temporary employment in Japan. In Japan and the USA self employed persons include own-account workers and those with employees. In Japan self employed persons include family workers. In both cases farmers are included. Casual and temporary employment is measured as the proportion of all employees (self employed and family workers are excluded from all employment) who are defined as casual employees or day laborers. *Source*: For Japan, Economic Planning Agency *Japan Statistical Yearbook* Tokyo; for the USA, US Bureau of the Census *Statistical Abstract of the United States* Washington DC.

the workforce (Burgess and Campbell 1992). In the USA 8–9% of the work-force may be self-employed (Christopherson 1990; see also Figure 2.13); the proportions in Canada are slightly higher. Japanese women have long been self-employed or working in family businesses (often on farms): as a propor-tion of women in the labor force, self-employees accounted for 15.8% in 1960 but only 12.0% in 1987; women working in family businesses were 43.4% in 1960 but 19.3% in 1987 (Saso 1990: 30). In all four countries, about a third of the self-employed are female (OECD 1991). Unlike part-time or temporary employment there is little evidence that self-employment is growing in significance, even if allowance is made for the decline of family farming.

Evidently nonstandard employment is a matter primarily of gender [even if wage inequality may be increasingly a matter of class rather than gender (McDowell 1991)]. There are males who are part-time and/or temporary workers, but they form a relatively small proportion of the workforce. In Australia, for example, full-time permanent workers made up nearly 90% of male employees but less than 60% of female employees (Burgess and Camp-bell 1992). Women made up 70% of all those who were part-time and/or ca-sual. This development of a female nonstandard workforce depends on three trends in labor demand: first, the rise of industries that rely on part-time or casual jobs (such as retailing and some services); secondly, the increasing at-tempt of firms to control labor costs by tailoring hiring to labor needs (some-times, but erroneously, called flexibility); thirdly, the attempt by firms to de-sign jobs for particular sections of the labor pool (particularly women who bear the main responsibility for child care and housekeeping). And it depends on trends in the supply of labor: first, those forces that prompt women to seek paid work and, second, those social characteristics (particularly the household division of labor) that make part-time or temporary work rela-tively more attractive for women than for men (Jamieson and Webber 1991). The fact that the part-time employment of females has increased most in those countries (Australia, Norway, and Sweden) in which it was highest in 1973 suggests that the employment and household arrangements that cater to and encourage part-time work by women are culturally specific (OECD 1989a).

2.5 CONCLUSION: AGENDA

So the world economy has grown and changed since 1950. It is six times big-ger than it was; it is more integrated as countries are more closely bound to-gether by financial and trade links and by the operations of transnational cor-porations. And it has changed: different economic activities are emerging; Japan and the NICs have emerged as major players in the world economy;

several developing countries have proved unable to support their citizens' lives; women's contribution to paid employment has expanded, though often within nonstandard forms of employment.

Evidence about the pace of change is, however, ambiguous. As a means of assessing the "golden age" and "long boom" hypotheses, we try first to summarize the evidence that has been assembled in this chapter.

First, as to the rate of growth of output (GDP), Figure 2.1 and Tables 2.1 through 2.3 support the following conclusions:

1. The rate of growth of output has been lower in the advanced industrial countries since 1974 than until then, though not in the USA.

2. There are significant differences between the advanced industrial countries in terms of their average rate of growth of output and the timing of fluctuations in that rate of growth.

3. Periods of rising and sustained rates of growth of output (after smoothing to reduce year-to-year fluctuations) are quite short, especially in North America, as shown in the accompanying tabulation.

	Last bust before boom	Boom	First bust after boom
OECD	(1954)	1958–1966	1974
USA	1956	1957–1965	1970
Japan	(1954)	1957–1968	1974
Canada	1954	1960–1965	1982
Australia	1961	1958–1970	1977

(The "boom" is the period of rising and sustained (smoothed) rates of growth of GDP. In the OECD and Japan there was no bust prior to the onset of the boom; 1954 is the year of slowest growth there.)

Figure 2.2 and Tables 2.4 through 2.6 contain comparable evidence about the rate of increase in gross domestic capital formation. They indicate that—

4. Rates of growth of gross domestic capital formation have generally not been significantly lower since 1974 than until then—except in Japan.

5. There are significant differences between the advanced industrial countries in terms of their average rate of growth of gross domestic capital formation and the timing of fluctuations in that rate of growth.

6. Periods of rising and sustained rates of growth of gross domestic capital formation (after smoothing to reduce year-to-year fluctuations) are very short and generally preceded the booms in rates of growth of output, as shown in the tabulation.

	Last bust *before boom*	*Boom*	*First bust* *after boom*
OECD	1952	1952–1959	1974
USA	(1958)	1959–1964	1970
Japan	1955	1953–1960	1974
Canada	1960	1961–1965	1982
Australia	1952	1960–1964	1982

(The "boom" is the period of rising and sustained (smoothed) rates of growth of gross domestic capital formation. In the USA there was no bust prior to the onset of the boom; 1958 is the year of slowest growth there.)

Fluctuations in rates of growth of gross domestic capital formation in general give evidence of short cyclical movements rather than of long boom-and-bust cycles.

Figures 2.4 through 2.7 and 2.9 and Tables 2.7 and 2.15 describe some aspects of the growth of exports from the countries of the world. They suggest that—

7. Rates of growth of exports from all countries and from a selection of advanced industrial countries are lower since 1974 than until then, though not significantly so (except in Canada and Japan).

8. Apart from those two countries, rates of growth of exports have been dominated by cycles: a long, slow acceleration in the 1960s leading to a boom in the early 1970s, followed quickly by the slump in the early 1980s and then by a miniboom in the late 1980s.

9. There are significant differences between the advanced industrial countries in terms of their average rate of growth of exports and the timing of fluctuations in that rate of growth.

10. The pace of change in the geography of world trade has been quicker since 1974 than before it.

Figures 2.3 and 2.8 and Table 2.11 provide evidence about the growth of the manufacturing sector in Australia, Canada, Japan, and the USA. These data indicate that—

11. Rates of growth of value added by manufacturing have been lower since 1974 than before then, though not significantly so in Australia and the USA.

12. In Japan the rate of growth of value added in manufacturing slowed dramatically after 1970; in North America and Australia, the rate of growth slowed in 1969—1971, 1974/75 (1974–1977 in Australia), 1979–1982 (1980–1983 in Australia), and 1991.

13. There are significant differences between the advanced industrial countries in terms of their average rate of growth of value added from manufacturing.

Figures 2.10 through 2.13 and Table 2.16 provide data about changes in the labor markets of the four advanced industrial countries. They indicate that—

14. There has been a gradual increase in the proportion of the workforce that is female, a general increase in the share of all jobs that are part-time, and a continued reduction in self-employment. However, the available data do not indicate that any of these trends have accelerated or decelerated in the early 1970s.

15. Rates of unemployment have been significantly higher since 1974 than before, in all four countries.

16. There are significant differences between the advanced industrial countries in terms of their average rate of unemployment.

17. The rate of unemployment is highly cyclical: it has trended upward since 1973, with short recovery phases in the late 1970s and the late 1980s.

Tables 2.9 through 2.14 provide evidence about growth rates in some Third World countries and in some sectors. They indicate that—

18. Rates of growth of production in middle income countries as a group have slowed since the mid-1970s, even though the rate of growth of exports has not. Some countries are growing more rapidly (or as rapidly) in the 1980s than before.

19. In the low income countries, food supply per person has increased more rapidly in the 1980s than in the 1970s.

Other data about the development of global finance markets and multinationals are far too skimpy to permit conclusions to be drawn about rates of change. They suffice, though, to demonstrate that global forms of production and exchange are growing apace. The pace of change in the geography of world trade is apparently increasing.

Evidently there has been a general reduction in the pace of growth. This is true of GDP (conclusion 1, but not in the USA), gross domestic capital formation in Japan (conclusion 4), exports from Canada and Japan (conclusion 7), value added in manufacturing in Canada and Japan (conclusion 11), and production in most middle income countries (conclusion 18). As a consequence rates of unemployment have been higher recently than they were earlier (conclusion 15).

There are wide differences between countries in the pace of their growth and in the timing of fluctuations in growth (conclusions 2, 5, 9, 13, and 16). The degree to which the pace of growth has slowed varies too between countries: in Japan and Canada growth has slowed most perceptibly; in Australia and the USA, to a lesser extent. In some middle income countries earlier growth rates have been maintained or surpassed in the 1980s (conclusion 18). In low income countries, food supply improved more rapidly in the 1980s than in the 1970s (conclusion 19).

In some of the series, fluctuations are dominated by shorter cycles rather than by a long-period boom-and-bust sequence. This is true of gross domestic capital formation (conclusion 6), of exports (conclusion 8), and to some extent of value added in manufacturing (conclusion 12). There is some evidence of a short boom followed by a long bust in GDP (conclusion 3); the boom was especially short in North America. The sequences of rates of unemployment combine highly cyclical features with a post-1974 upward trend (conclusion 17).

The point of break between a period of faster growth and a period of slower growth is not, however, easy to find. Smoothed rates of growth of GDP began to slow between 1965 and 1970, but the first busts after that short boom did not occur until 1970 (USA), 1974 (Japan and the OECD), 1977 (Australia), and even 1982 (Canada). Similarly the short booms in gross domestic capital formation began to falter between 1960 and 1965, though the first busts were delayed until 1970 (USA), 1974 (Japan and the OECD), and 1982 (Australia and Canada). Except in Canada, rates of growth of exports tended to decline continuously from the peak in 1973 to the trough in 1982. The rates of growth of value added in manufacturing began to slow dramatically after 1970 in Japan but after 1969 in North America and Australia. Rates of unemployment had begun to rise by 1970.

The OPEC price rises at the end of 1973 do not, therefore, separate postwar history into two distinct periods—a golden age and a not-so-golden age, or a long boom and a long bust. It seems more accurate to think of a slowdown in rates of growth in the advanced industrial countries—especially in Canada and Japan—with a very short period of rapid growth that soon gave way to a slide into the minor bust of 1974 and the much more serious affairs of 1982 and 1991. The timing of these phases is different in different countries. Outside the advanced industrial countries the pace of growth has increased in some countries and, if anything, the pace of change in the organization of the world economy has quickened.

The phases merge. After all, some of the characteristics of the two intervals are not all that different: the rates of economic growth of some middle income countries, for example. Furthermore changes that have become obvious since 1973 can be traced to earlier characteristics—for example, the technical changes and the emerging trade surpluses that made global finance possible. Indeed the pick up in the pace of change originates in part in the slowdown in growth. Now we do not want to argue that the globalization of finance, growth of trade and multinationals, emergence of NICs and changes in labor markets are all directly and immediately caused by the fact that economic growth has slowed. Yet we do think that they are linked. So the history that we have described is not merely a background to the theory and evidence we present—it also reflects those processes we theorize. We turn now to analyze existing interpretations of postwar economic history and geography, focusing especially on the slowing of growth.

Chapter 3

COMPETING THEORIES OF POSTWAR GROWTH AND CHANGE

What on earth is going on? What happened to cause growth to slow, internationalization, changed patterns of production, and altered conditions of work? Did the stability conditions for mass production fall apart? Was mass production undermined by workers' revolt and productivity slowdowns? Was organized capitalism disorganized? Was this another Krondatieff down phase? Was monopoly capitalism in transition? Is this merely another crisis of capitalism? These suggestions not only offer explanations or interpretations of the economic events of the postwar years; they also provide a guide to the changes now underway and a prognosis about the type of economy to which we are in transit.

So the transition has spawned attempts to characterize the present and potential form of economic life. Notions like post-Fordism, flexible production, and flexible accumulation are widely used. They arise in detailed studies of industrial location (e.g. Scott and Storper 1987) and urbanization (Scott 1988a) as well as more general analyses of the postmodern condition (Harvey 1988; Soja 1989). They are found in disciplines from sociology (Lever-Tracy 1988) and industrial relations (Hyman 1988) to economics (e.g. Lipietz 1986). At least in Australia, such notions are also widely deployed in public debates about industrial policy (ACTU 1987; Bramble 1988); they thus affect attitudes to the transition.

However, concepts like post-Fordism, flexible production, and flexible accumulation are interpretations of the present rather than descriptions of it. They are interpretive in two senses. First, they rely upon a particular theory of history—and especially upon a particular periodization of history. Secondly, the process of assigning one name to a whole set of concrete, on-the-ground changes implies that those changes are all related in some way. Thus, particular, concrete changes—the incorporation of women, immigrants, and new Third World countries, the growth of part-time labor, the use of information technology, and the like—are interpreted in different ways by different theories. But the significance of such changes lies precisely in their interpretation, for it is the interpretation that provides the foundation for political action: different theorizations of the contemporary transition imply different political responses to it.

This chapter analyzes critically some periodizations that have provided the bases of such interpretations. What are the objects of analysis? What variables determine the character of the periods identified? Do periods have characteristic spaces? What are the processes of transition between periods? Why did the previous period end? (Why are we now in a transition?) Which characteristics are cause and which effect? What are the crucial contrasts between the different periodizations, and therefore what general kinds of evidence can distinguish between their stories? Our point is to identify the kinds of theory and evidence that are needed to make sense of the history described in Chapter 2.

These are questions in economic history. They concern theories about what happened. As such, they are not questions about crisis theory—the theory that asks why the profitability of production declines and how that decline affects social life (e.g., see Bowles et al. 1986; Devine 1983; Weeks 1981). Obviously, these are not completely separate questions: crisis theory informs people's interrogation of economic history, while the data from that history influence our regard for different versions of crisis theory. But we start from economic history, which is messier and fuzzier than crisis theory.

We examine the statements of specified texts. For example, one group of theories is that due to the "French regulation school"; but rather than trying to describe the whole body of thought produced by that school—with the varying emphases of its members and its change over time (compare, for example, Aglietta 1979; Boyer and Mistral 1978; Lipietz 1979, 1986)—we analyze two papers by a single author (Lipietz). In this way, the analysis can be more precise. Where there is choice, we have chosen the most forthright and accessible statements of the authors for analysis.

Several of the texts to be analyzed are not merely about economic life, nor about production only. Lash and Urry (1987), for example, interweave cultural and political history in their account of the organization and subsequent disorganization of capitalism. However, this chapter concentrates on changes in the organization of economic life and especially examines production. Other issues—finance, the state, and culture—intrude only where strictly necessary. In some cases, the result only partially describes the authors' claims. This strategy should not be taken to imply a belief that economic life dominates other aspects of society, nor that it is strictly separable.

The chapter has six sections. The first briefly recounts the theories to be analyzed. The logic of periodization is examined in Section 3.2, which describes the objects of analysis, the character of periods, their characteristic spaces, and the processes of transition between periods. Section 3.3 contrasts the theories' explanations of the end of the previous period. Which character-

istics are interpreted as cause and which as effect? The main contrasts between the different periodizations are stated in Section 3.4, together with the
sort of evidence that can be used to evaluate them. Section 3.5 summarizes
the argument by returning to the issue of interpreting the present, arguing
that the concept of flexibility misinterprets the changes that are now occurring in economic life. Finally, Section 3.6 starts on the way to some more positive conclusions by establishing what is meant by such entities as "economy"
and "capitalist economy." It begins to delimit the scope of the theoretical and
empirical investigations that are possible in this book.

3.1 CHOICE OF THEORIES TO ANALYZE

The following interpretations have been analyzed: Freeman and Perez (1988),
Gibson and Horvath (1983; see also Graham et al. 1988), Lash and Urry
(1987), Lipietz (1986; see also Leborgne and Lipietz 1988), Mandel (1978),
and Piore and Sabel (1984). Many theories could have been chosen for analysis. We have excluded those that are focused on a single country; thus, the
concept of "social structures of accumulation" (Gordon et al. 1982) is omitted. We have excluded other presentations of the same authors, as complicat-
ing the statement of their views. We have also omitted other theories with a
similar theme. Thus, other "regulationists" are omitted, Lipietz being preferred as the one most commonly cited. So also are others who belong to the
"technological school" (e.g., Kleinknecht 1987; Mensch 1979), Freeman and
Perez being preferred as the more well known. Otherwise, the range of theories is wide: from technological through social, from left through right.

All these theorists agree that economic, social, and political conditions in
the late 1970s and 1980s were different in many advanced industrial
economies than they were in the 1950s and 1960s. They agree over many of
the changes that have occurred, but they do differ over the causes of those
changes. In this section we describe the theses that are being advanced.

Freeman and Perez (1988) study Kondratieff waves. These are regular
fluctuations in economic life, with a period of 45–60 years. According to the
Kondratieff timing, four complete cycles of sustained growth and depression
have paced capitalist development since the industrial revolution, with major
boom periods in the late 1770s and 1780s; through the 1840s; from the late
1890s until the outbreak of World War I; and from the late 1930s through the
mid–1960s. These upswing phases are purportedly separated (and succeeded)
by phases when growth has been slow. There is evidence that these alternating
phases exist—in time series of world industrial production and of GNPs of
the USA and several European countries (see Freeman and Perez 1988:
50–57; Kleinknecht 1987: 19–51; but contrast the far more skeptical view offered by Berry 1991).

Freeman and Perez (1988) view long waves as periods of accordance and
discordance between new technology systems and socio-institutional frame-

works. Their "techno-economic paradigms" are more than simply clusters of radical and incremental innovations [the essential motor of upswings according to Kleinknecht (1987) and Mensch (1979)], demanding entirely new systems of social management that complement the essence of emerging technologies. New techno-economic paradigms are claimed to develop during the downswing phases of Kondratieff cycles, when established key factors of production and related innovations yield diminishing returns and limit increases in productivity and profitable investment. Only under these conditions are the high costs and risks of finding and developing new technologies justified. Freeman and Perez view depressions as periods of "structural adjustment" when the existing social and institutional regime is adapting to the major new technologies. The depth of downturns is related to the degree of mismatch between the emerging technologies and the old socio-institutional framework. The clustering of radical innovations in new technology systems is seen as the springboard for growth as new industries emerge and technology is diffused throughout the economy. Once a match between technology and regulatory infrastructure has been found, a relatively stable pattern of long-term investment opportunities is thought to emerge as the new techno-economic paradigm is consolidated throughout the economy.

Mandel (1978) also uses Kondratieff waves as the empirical foundation of his study. He describes a recent phase that began during World War II in the USA and after it elsewhere. The period of rapid accumulation began after wages had been suppressed and the rate of surplus value was therefore high. Initially investment and new technology was directed to the production of arms and raw materials. Technological rents became the primary source of surplus profits, leading to a high rate of innovation and a reduced turnover time of fixed capital. (Unlike Freeman and Perez, Mandel does not claim that earlier upswings were also caused by the development of new techno-economic paradigms.) These conditions provided an expanded market for the extended reproduction of capital.

However, as that technical revolution spread through the economy, it raised the organic composition of capital. By the mid-1960s, the reserve armies of labor in western Europe and the USA had been used up, so the rate of surplus value could no longer be increased. Therefore the rate of profit began to fall and the desired rate of accumulation of capital declined (capital had been overaccumulated). Since the late 1960s, the rate of accumulation has remained low, as capital "waits" for the rate of profit to be raised once more. Such a rise would require a fall in the organic composition of capital; an increase in the rate of surplus value; a fall in the price of constant capital; or a fall in turnover time. However, since Mandel was writing in the early 1970s, he does not have an explanation for what has happened since then.

To Piore and Sabel (1984), the problem is a purely technical one. The 1950s and 1960s were a period of mass production (the apogee of a system established in the nineteenth century). In a mass production economy, firms must stabilize their own markets in order to achieve economies of mass production and there must exist institutions that match aggregate supply and aggregate demand, since prices can no longer perform this function. The central mechanism that performed this role in the USA and many other industrial economies was wage contract bargaining, which worked so that the increase in wages equaled the economy-wide increase in productivity plus the rate of inflation. In such a system, an inflationary shock is perpetuated through subsequent wage increases; such a shock was avoided in the 1950s and 1960s by off-farm migration, raw material stockpiles and imports, and government interventions.

Piore and Sabel provide two explanations of the collapse of this system. They are not contradictory, though the authors present them separately.

The first tale is one of accidents and mistakes. The 1970s witnessed three inflationary shocks: increasing labor shortages, the wheat shortage and oil price rise of 1973, and the oil price rise of 1979. These destroyed the regulation of inflation. But the floating of exchange rates in 1972 discouraged investment in comparison with speculation; the increasing emphasis on deflationary policies after the mid-1970s also discouraged investment. The consequence was a period of slow growth, small increases in productivity, and rising unemployment.

The second tale emphasizes the inherent limitations of the system whereby mass production was regulated. First, domestic markets became saturated for mass-produced consumer goods, leading to increasing trade between the industrial countries. The mass production economy thus became international. But there was no international mechanism that regulated demand and supply. Therefore, at some point a shortfall in demand had to occur (as it had in unregulated national economies, to cause the Great Depression). Secondly, the actual shortfall that occurred was caused by the saturation of markets and by competition from the NICs (which reduced imports and expanded their exports of industrial commodities). This is a classic underconsumption explanation.

In both explanations demand has failed. In the first tale, demand failed because of accidents and mistaken policies. In the second, markets became saturated. The failure of demand has reduced investment and so limited the growth in productivity from mass production, also prompting firms to seek market niches through product specialization. Both phenomena have tended to increase the competitiveness of craft production in comparison with mass production. Flexible specialization has become a strategy by which firms react to changing cost and product market conditions. The crisis of regulation has become an industrial divide.

Gibson and Horvath (1983; see also Graham et al. 1988) describe the change as one between monopoly and global capitalism. The change involves more advanced automation and robotics, a neo-Fordist rather than Fordist labor process, and a shift from segmented to peripheralized labor. It is characterized by global rather than national corporations and by the internationalization of productive rather than just money capital. Graham et al. regard the change as occurring sector by sector rather than in the economy as a whole.

The basic cause of the crisis and the change in variant that is now occurring is a fall in the rate of profit enjoyed by monopoly capitalism. (The reason for this fall is not specified.) The diminution of the rate of profit implies increased competition between firms and enhanced selection of successful firms. Structural change is therefore concentrated in a short period rather than occurring more generally.

Lash and Urry (1987) describe organized capitalism as a set of conditions rather than a system that solves a specific set of problems. Organized capitalism involves centrally the formation of large groupings of industrial capital, financial capital, workers, and the state—together with the linkages between them. It is also a system of specialization: separation of ownership and control; distinctive national overseas markets; concentration of capitalist social relations within a few sectors and states; regional specialization; large industrial cities. Organized capitalism is an economy of the large and the specialized, institutionally linked.

A number of interconnected developments have disorganized Western capitalist societies, involving industrial, financial, and political changes. The political changes essentially concern class voting patterns, new social movements, the character of working class communities, and the structural significance of the welfare state; they are ignored in this account of economic changes.

The basic industrial change is the internationalization of production, caused by the breakup of empires, improvements in transport and communications, falling rates of profit, and international financial speculation. This has reduced the ability of corporations to control their markets as it has reduced the ability of states to regulate their national economies. The mass markets for standardized products have broken down, and craft production has become more important because of advances in microelectronics, rejection of mass consumption patterns, and failure to compete on price with the Third World.

The role of banks and money is also crucial. Banks have become international, using the funds accumulated in the oil surpluses after 1973. The deregulation of the international exchange system, the internationalization of production, and more widespread industrialization have provided the incentive for banks to become international operators. Banks now have their own concerns separate from industry, and they no longer play a national role. Their trade in money is destabilizing.

With this disorganization, corporatism is dissolving. (Corporatism is a system in which the following features stand out: there are organized interests of employers and workers, these interests being represented by national organizations; there are resources to mobilize these interests; the state is modernized; and the organizations control their members in return for power within the state apparatus. Labor may or may not be included in these arrangements.) The crisis of corporatism stems from: the internationalization of the world economy, which dislocates the national project of corporatism; the decreasing significance of those workers—in mass production—who were at the heart of the bargain; the decline in collective identity of the national working class; and the oil crises, which curtailed real-wage rises.

Lipietz' account (1986; see also Leborgne and Lipietz 1988) is much more straightforward—and less comprehensive. Capitalist history is conceived as a series of regimes of accumulation: the 1950s and 1960s were a period of Fordist accumulation. Technically, Fordism is characterized by the attempt to standardize the production of goods and to separate conception from execution. As a regime of accumulation, productivity increases were equal to increases in fixed capital per worker and output increases were matched by increases in consumption. And as a mode of regulation, wage and price setting encouraged productivity growth and the state encouraged consumption.

However, by the late 1960s, the rate of productivity increase fell. This fall was due to a (naturally) reduced rate of learning by doing and to the effects of excluding workers from contributing to productivity. Therefore the capital/output ratio began to increase and so the rate of profit fell. Firms reacted by internationalizing production (made more profitable as wages in the industrial economies were growing in relation to those in the NICs) and the state by austerity. So arose the crisis of employment and therefore of demand.

3.2 WHY PERIODS?

In this section begins the analysis of the six competing theories. What are their objects of analysis? What variables determine the character of the periods that they identify? Do periods have characteristic spaces? What are the processes of transition between periods?

3.2.1 Objects of Analysis

While all six theoretical approaches agree that the 1970s and 1980s form in some sense a period of crisis, different from the earlier postwar years, the authors nevertheless are analyzing different objects (Table 3.1). At the most specific level, Piore and Sabel are describing changes in technology and the operation of markets (or, slightly differently expressed, in the labor process and the organization of firms). Similarly, Freeman and Perez discuss the decline in productivity and the instability of investment behavior concomitant with the change from one technological regime to another and the emergence of new key growth industries. By contrast, Gibson and Horvath investigate changes in the process of production as a whole, deriving variants of the mode of production. Lipietz, on the other hand, is more comprehensive, examining also

TABLE 3.1. Objects of analysis

Authors	Object of analysis	Kind of fluctuation
Freeman and Perez	Technology	Cycle (see text)
Piore and Sabel	Technology	Period
Gibson and Horvath	(Variant of) mode of production	Period
Lipietz	Accumulation	Period
Mandel	Accumulation	Wave
Lash and Urry	Social formation	Period

the social conditions that foster accumulation. With somewhat different emphases, here too is the work of Mandel. Thus, Lipietz and Mandel are examining the process of accumulation, introducing other aspects of social life as necessary to understand that. At the most comprehensive (and concrete) level, Lash and Urry examine changes in the social formation: in the whole gamut of economic, social, and political changes that are visible in modern (postmodern?) life.

The six texts also identify different kinds of fluctuations, as described in Table 3.1. Piore and Sabel, Gibson and Horvath, Lipietz, and Lash and Urry all have some sense of defined periods. By a "period" is meant an interval that shares some common characteristics, during which some features of social life are relatively constant: the technology, the variant of the mode of production, the process of accumulation, and the social formation, respectively. A period is followed by a time of transition, during which the conditions of the succeeding period are established. Freeman and Perez describe a long "cycle": successive intervals of faster and slower growth, determined by endogenous economic forces. In this tale, fast growth must be succeeded by slow growth, and slow growth by fast growth—because growth rates affect the timing of the introduction of new "techno-economic paradigms," which themselves force the pace of growth by introducing clusters of innovations and related organizational systems. Mandel identifies a "wave," a time of relatively fast accumulation and a succeeding time of slower accumulation. In contrast to Freeman and Perez, however, Mandel does not suppose that a period of slow growth must be followed by one of faster growth, nor that the mechanism that promotes growth is the same in all upswings. Thus, the term "phase" must now be used to refer to an interval that may be a period, a cycle, or a wave.

Most of the theorists assign a particularly significant role to some leading industries. Piore and Sabel and also Lash and Urry identify large-scale, monopolized industries as giving character to a period. And Lipietz calls certain industries "hegemonic"—important not only by virtue of their quantitative links to the rest of the economy but also in the sense of providing a model for change in other industries. In these three theories, particular industries characterize particular periods. Mandel claims that new, technically sophisticated industries (e.g., transport and chemicals since the war) that incorporate radical technologies lead the rest of the economy into an upswing, but he does not characterize the phase. Freeman and Perez identify key "carrier branches," or industries that herald the dominant technology of each cycle, and they note the main forms of firm organization and competition. Gibson and Horvath are different again in that they presume that different variants of capitalism can characterize different sectors at the same time: these are periods for each sector, rather than the whole economy.

3.2.2 Nature of Phase

What determines the character of a phase? That is, what are the variables whose values lead one to identify one phase rather than another? The identifying characteristics of phases differ widely between the six theories (Table 3.2).

For Piore and Sabel, the central issue is technology. A period of mass production was established in the mid- to late nineteenth century and lasted until about 1970. We are now in a transition to a period of flexible, smaller scale production. The manner in which demand is regulated is secondary, and changes over subperiods. They identify the longest period. Correspondingly, their account of history glosses over many of the changes that are identified by the other authors.

TABLE 3.2. Nature of Periodization

Author	Name of phase	Determinants of character of phase	When established
Piore and Sabel	Mass production	Main: Technology Secondary: Demand regulation	Mid- to late 19th century to 1940s
Gibson and Horvath	Monopoly capitalism	Form of exploitation Form of competition	Early 20th century; depends on sector
Lash and Urry	Organized capitalism	Specialization/size Corporatism Bank/industry links	Varies by country— late 19th to early 20th centuries
Freeman and Perez	Fordist mass production 4th Kondratieff	Leading industries and technology	1930s
Lipietz	Fordism	Technology Mode of regulation Regime of accumulation	1940s
Mandel	Late capitalism	Search for surplus profits	1940s

Gibson and Horvath and Lash and Urry have a common focus on the pattern of ownership of corporations and the competition between them. For example, both regard the monopoly form of capitalism as an identifying characteristic of the phase that was initiated early in this century. However, whereas Gibson and Horvath are concerned only with the mode of production (and so identify different phases in different industries), Lash and Urry investigate the social formation (and so generalize their characteristics over the economy as a whole).

Freeman and Perez, Lipietz, and Mandel identify phases that start in the late 1930s and 1940s, since for all of them the establishment of the conditions for rapid accumulation is significant. Other aspects of their characterization are quite different. For Freeman and Perez, to the extent that a cycle has a "character," it is that of its leading industries, the technology on which they rest, and—to a lesser extent—on the institutions that regulate demand. For Mandel, waves can be differentiated by the source of surplus profit that is exploited to produce the upswing. In contrast, Lipietz ascribes a "character" to each phase, depending on technology, mode of regulation, and regime of accumulation.

3.2.3 The Phases of Space

The degree to which society and space are thought to be integrated differs markedly between the six theories. In some (Freeman and Perez; Gibson and Horvath), spatial structure is hardly discussed. In some (Piore and Sabel; Lipietz), the implications of a change in phase for a change in space have been described. In the others (Lash and Urry; Mandel), space plays a more central role in social change.

In neither Piore and Sabel nor Lipietz does space play a central role in determining the character of a phase or the change of phase. Rather, some of the implications of the phase for spatial structure have been described. To Piore and Sabel, for example, the 1970s and 1980s have witnessed the end of a period of large-scale industry and the emergence of small-scale, flexible production; associated with this has been a shift from a search for internal economies of plants to a search for external economies and a concomitant shift from isolated, large plants to specialized industrial districts (Storper and Scott 1988). Equally, one aspect of demand management in the Fordist period was, according to Lipietz, the suburbanization of population in the major cities, with its associated privatization of consumption (see also Walker 1981).

To Lash and Urry, space is more completely integrated in the characterization of a phase. Two aspects of this integration can be noted here. First, the period of organized capitalism was one of big industry—large plants, monopoly ownership—located in large cities with large, homogeneous workforces. Disorganization is a process in which smaller plants, smaller cities, smaller and more differentiated workforces become viable again. Secondly, organized capitalism was also a period in which national territories were effectively integrated by strong states: one of the elements of the breakdown of organized into disorganized capitalism has been the weakening of the power of states as the global economy has emerged more powerfully. Such claims more closely integrate space and phase than do Lipietz or Piore and Sabel.

Even more closely does Mandel integrate time and space. To Mandel, the search for surplus profits is essentially a matter of exploiting uneven development. In earlier waves, that uneven development had been spatial: first, differences in development between town and country; later, differences in levels of development between countries of the core and of the periphery. In the latest wave (the upswing that began in the 1940s), the uneven development has been sectoral: firms have exploited differences in the development of techniques. Thus, the role of space in providing the source of surplus profits has diminished in this period. To Mandel, then, space is not merely an element of the description of a phase but also an element of the process.

3.2.4 The Process of Transition

The six texts propound quite different theories about the process of change between phases (Table 3.3) that combine several separate ideas. The latest phase came to an end either because the conditions for stability broke down (Lash and Urry; Lipietz; Piore and Sabel) or because the rate of profit fell (Freeman and Perez; Gibson and Horvath; Mandel). According to Piore and Sabel as well as Lipietz, the present is a phase of enhanced experimentation; similarly, Gibson and Horvath describe a phase of enhanced competition, implying increased rates of selection, while Freeman and Perez argue that in phases of slow growth firms seek more radical (technology-based) solutions to the problem of declining productivity growth and the lack of profitable investment opportunities. In these ideas, there is a process of experimental search for new solutions to the problems posed by the failure of the previous phase, and a selection of one or more of those solutions, depending on: the power of owners of technology (Piore and Sabel); the struggle between labor and capital and the ability of the solution to provide a basis for smooth accumulation (Lipietz); or the profitability of the experimenting firms (Gibson and Horvath). By contrast, Mandel does not describe a general process; rather, he describes the necessary outcome of that process—a fall in the organic composition of capital, a rise in the rate of surplus value, a fall in the price of constant capital, or a fall in the turnover time. The history of one transition between waves is particular to that transition.

Thus there exist two somewhat different stories. (1) Either stability conditions failed or rates of profit fell. (Of course, the failure of stability conditions may also imply that the rate of profit fell.) Whatever the cause, however,

TABLE 3.3. How are phases started and ended?

Author	Cause of end of period	Process of change	Determinant of outcome
Lash and Urry		No process or determinant specified	
Piore and Sabel	Stability conditions break down	EXPERIMENTATION (competition) → rapid selection (radical innovations)	Power of owners of technology
Lipietz			Labor/capital compromise Stability condition Macroeconomic
Gibson and Horvath	FROP (this time)		Structural change
Freeman and Perez	Fall in productivity		Higher profits Upswing
Mandel	FROP (ultimate limit)	Fall in OCC or Rise in S/V or Fall in price C or Fall in turnover time	

Note: FROP=falling rate of profit; OCC = organic composition of capital—the ratio of the value of capital (plant, equipment, and purchased inputs) to the (capitalized) value of labor power employed in production; S/V = rate of surplus value—approximately, the share of the surplus in value added; C = constant capital (plant, equipment, and purchased inputs other than labor power).

the response is more experimentation, competition, or receptiveness to radical ideas. The characteristics of the next phase are selected during this phase of uncertainty. (2) The only dissident from this tale is Mandel, who is less concerned with the process of change than with its necessary outcome.

The answers to the question about the origins of phases thus fall into three groups. Piore and Sabel, Lipietz, and Lash and Urry regard historical periods as times of relatively constant conditions, held together by stability conditions. When those conditions fail, the period comes to an end, and a process of transition is set in train during which new conditions for stability are sought. Gibson and Horvath also identify periods as times of constancy (for sectors) but do not identify why they come to an end (though they do describe a process of transition). The views of Freeman and Perez and of Mandel are quite different: their phases are cycles or waves, alternating intervals of relatively fast and relatively slow accumulation. For Freeman and Perez, the effectiveness of innovations and their institutional regulation determine the rate of growth. Each Kondratieff wave has characteristic industries and modes of regulation. Short phases of sustained growth thus exhibit some characteristics of a period. When productivity growth associated with one technological system falters, clusters of radically new competing technologies are introduced to the economy in search of superprofits. According to Mandel, the pace of accumulation increases as new sources of exploitation—new workers, new technologies, and new markets—are incorporated into the capitalist mode of production. Accumulation will eventually decline, however, as the struggle for sources of surplus profits eventually runs against the limits posed to the rate of profit by widening technical change.

3.3 WHY DID ACCUMULATION CEASE?

The different answers provided to this question by the theories are illustrated in Figures 3.1 through 3.5, which interpret the arguments of the texts. The argument of Lash and Urry, in particular, has been given a cause-and-effect form that is much stronger than their description. Since Gibson and Horvath do not explain the falling rate of profit, their account is omitted.

Mandel (Figure 3.1) presents a classic argument about the rate of profit falling through technical change, explaining the failure of firms to raise the rate of surplus value through an exhaustion of the reserve army of labor. [(The abbreviated diagram in Figure 3.1 is greatly expanded in Mandel's *Late Capitalism* (1978).] The slowdown in the rate of growth of productivity is a consequence of the fact that the fall in the rate of profit limited op-

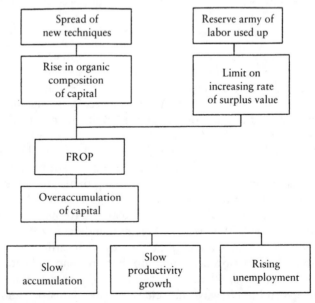

FIGURE 3.1. Mandel's theory (1978) of the end of the phase.

portunities for the profitable accumulation of capital. (Mandel, writing earlier than the others, offers less information about the current transition than they do.)

Piore and Sabel (Figure 3.2) offer a pair of explanations that revolve around underconsumption. Either because of inflationary accidents and policy mistakes or because of market saturation and international competition from the NICs, demand has failed. The falls in the rate of profit and the rate of productivity growth are consequences of that failure. Unlike Mandel, Piore and Sabel regard underconsumption as a cause; like Mandel, they regard the slowdown in productivity growth as a consequence.

Similar sets of factors are adduced by Lipietz (Figure 3.3), though in a different causal order and in different combination. Lipietz looks to slower productivity growth in the context of a fixed pattern of wage rises to explain the falling rate of profit. Slower productivity growth is now a cause. The reduced rate of profit is then linked (as a consequence) to slower accumulation by the internationalization of production and austerity policies. This is a quite different story to that of either Mandel or Piore and Sabel.

Freeman and Perez (see also Freeman et al. 1982) likewise explain the slowdown in terms of a reduced rate of productivity growth (Figure 3.4). However, they regard the productivity slowdown as a matter of the nature of

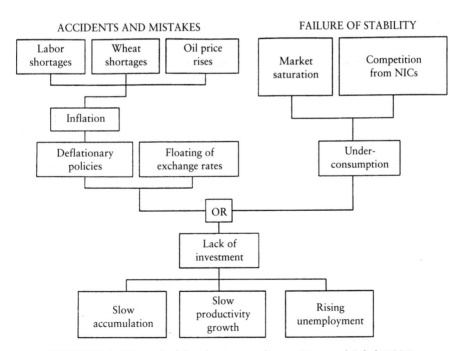

FIGURE 3.2. The end of the phase, according to Piore and Sabel (1984).

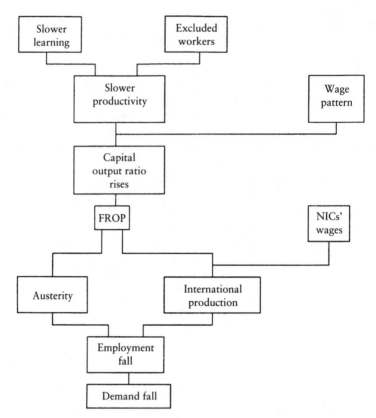

FIGURE 3.3. Lipietz's explanation (1986) of the end of the phase.

the innovation process. Once products have been developed (in radical, product innovations) they become standardized; thus the pattern of technical change shifts over time through a life cycle from product innovation to process innovation. As new industries and technologies mature, competition intensifies pressure on input costs so that economies of scale become increasingly important. Increasing standardization and rising capital intensity of production follow from attempts to reduce costs, especially labor costs that are relatively high following a lengthy period of full employment. But as more and more process innovations are introduced, they become increasingly subject to diminishing returns, yielding progressively smaller improvements in productivity and generating diminishing increases in demand. As the growth of demand falls, industries—especially the capital goods industries—find themselves with overcapacity. And it is this overcapacity together with the productivity slowdown that explain the reduction in profitability.

Lash and Urry (Figure 3.5) provide the most complex explanation,

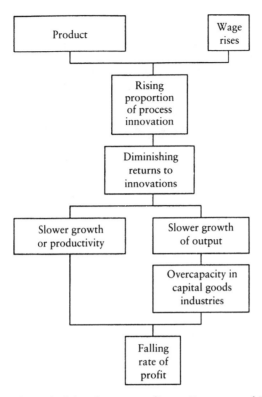

FIGURE 3.4. The end of the phase, according to Freeman and Perez (1988).

though their explanandum is also the most complex. They do not explain the falling rate of profit (nor do Gibson and Horvath) but do describe a set of changes in technology, consumer tastes, and economic policies that have led to the break up of mass markets, the internationalization of production, and the decreasing control of corporations over domestic markets and states over domestic economies. Their description has much less sense of cause and effect than the others.

An explanation of the falling rate of accumulation during the 1970s thus centers in these theories on the following factors: rising organic composition of capital; rising power of labor and wage patterns; inflationary shocks (especially involving oil and wheat); deflationary policies; deregulation of financial and exchange markets; market saturation; competition from the NICs; slower productivity change; changing patterns of innovation; internationalization of production; exogenous changes in consumer taste; technical changes in microelectronics, transport, and communications. Are these factors exhaustive? And how are they to be assembled?

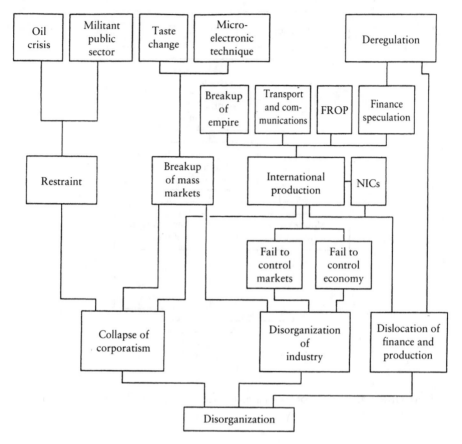

FIGURE 3.5. The end of the phase, according to Lash and Urry (1987).

3.4 SOME ISSUES

Let us turn, then, to consider more precisely the distinguishing characteristics of the theories. It is beyond our scope to reexamine in detail the economic history described by the theories—the timing of changes, the evidence, the logic. Rather, in this section we seek to demonstrate the methods and evidence that may be used to evaluate the theories.

3.4.1 Distinguishing Causes

It is agreed by most of the theorists and many commentators that the changes listed have indeed occurred in the 1970s and 1980s. But which are cause and which are consequence? It is insufficient to demonstrate that changes in productivity or wages or regulation have occurred. Rather, we need to demonstrate that some factors are more clearly cause and others more clearly consequence.

Thus, it is generally agreed that the growth of productivity has slowed in the 1970s and 1980s (BIE 1985). But is the productivity slowdown a cause (as Lipietz and also Freeman and Perez maintain) or a consequence (as in the accounts of Piore and Sabel and of Mandel) of the slower rate of accumulation? We largely lack the conceptual apparatus to answer this question, for there does not exist a good theory to explain the pace and direction of technical change. To what extent do changes in technique depend on the rate of investment, the degree of competition, and the supply of innovations? How does the direction of technical change respond to price changes of inputs? Since we even lack good empirical measures of the pace and direction of technical change that do not depend on neoclassical economic theory, there has been little attention given to measuring the importance of these determinants of technical change. There is therefore no empirical basis yet for distinguishing the different accounts of the role of productivity change.

Again, how are the capital/output ratio, wage increases, the failure of demand, and technical change to be related to the falling rate of profit? (And how, conversely, does a fall in the rate of profit translate into a failure of demand?) This is a classic problem of macroeconomic dynamics. Again, the technical apparatus of theory is inadequate to permit a good characterization of the problem, for despite all the effort that has been put into the theory of the falling rate of profit, formal dynamic models do not relate all these variables. There simply does not exist a formal, dynamic, macroeconomic model in which all these variables are internally related to each other and to the rate of accumulation.

What has been the role in the recent development of capitalist history of the internationalization of production? This process has several components: increasing trade between "Western" (advanced industrial) economies; increasing rates of international investment (and a change in the form of that investment to finance rather than direct forms); the rise of the NICs. Only recently have attempts been made to theorize international capital (e.g., Bryan 1987). To what extent is the rise of the NICs autonomous and to what extent explained by a falling rate of profit in the "Western economies" and relative wage levels? [Corbridge (1986) introduces some of these debates; see also Hamilton (1983) and Webber and Foot (1988).] And what was the effect of the accident of the OPEC surplus and the policy "mistake" of deregulating exchange rates and international capital movements (see Daly and Logan 1989)?

The role of the NICs raises a more general question. To what extent is the present period one of a global crisis of capitalism and to what extent a regional crisis (of North America and western Europe)? What are global rates of capital accumulation—measured so as to reflect the spatial and sectoral expansion of capital into new regions and types of production? What are global rates of profit? We know something of the history of rates of profit and accumulation in individual countries and even in sets of countries, but we know little of the rate of expansion of capital into regions and sectors previously uncapitalized.

Even more generally, what has been the role of space in the development of phases? The detailed integration of the histories and spatial structure has yet to be worked out: even Soja (1989) only sketches a preliminary account that skates over the differences between the authors. Do phases really have characteristic spaces? Furthermore, half of the socio-spatial dialectic, the effect of space on society, is generally ignored. Apart from the account in Mandel, which Soja applauds without embellishing, there exists no account of the influence of space on the character of or the change in phase. Indeed, it would seem that all the accounts (except Mandel's) require major modification before a complete integration of phase and space is possible.

It appears, then, that we lack the evidence with which to distinguish the explanations adduced by the various theories. What is needed is an appropriate body of theory to demonstrate how various factors are related to the rate of profit, to identify measures that can distinguish between the accounts, and to evaluate their treatment of space. Much of this book is devoted to developing appropriate theories for this evaluation and to illustrating the evidence to which they give rise. However, there do exist other tests that can be applied to the six theories.

3.4.2 Existence of Periods

One of these tests concerns the existence of periods. Was there a period? How widespread (hegemonic) were the techniques of production? How general were the social and economic controls that have been adduced to explain the rapid postwar growth? Are all the phenomena that characterize these periods correlated as they change? That is, were the times a system?

The first fact is that there have indeed occurred alternating phases of faster and slower growth. Although the existence of Kondratieff waves has long been disputed or relegated only to the price sphere (van Duijn 1977; Glismann et al. 1984; Cleary and Hobbs 1984), there is evidence that such phases have occurred in world industrial production as well as in the production of many individual countries since at least the turn of the century (Kleinknecht 1987; but see Berry 1991). The latest phase of rapid growth is 1939–1974, since when we have been in a phase of slower growth (Chapter 2).

The second fact is that there is widespread divergence between the experiences of different industries during any one phase. Freeman and Perez (1988) point to different growth and innovation histories of different industries, while Graham et al. (1988) have clearly demonstrated that the transitions from one variant of the mode of production to another occur at quite different times in different industries. Given this evidence, it is difficult to accept the notion of a hegemonic variant of the mode of production in any except a quantitative sense (as growth industries).

The third fact is that there is widespread divergence between the experiences of different places during any one phase (Chapter 2). Freeman and Perez (1988) indicate the different experiences of the advanced industrialized nations and the developing economies of the world in accommodating a fifth Kondratieff upswing driven by information technology. Both Piore and Sabel (1984) and Lash and Urry (1987) illustrate how the French economy evolved in the nineteenth and early twentieth centuries in quite a different fashion from the German. And there is a host of evidence about different regional experiences (e.g., Clark et al. 1986; Massey 1984; Massey and Meegan 1982; Rodwin and Sazanami 1989; Stilwell 1980). It remains to be demonstrated that these different experiences are consistent with the concept of a coherent period.

The fourth fact is that there is little evidence of a period in the quantitative indicators of economic growth. Kleinknecht's (1987) data clearly indicate cycles rather than periods. Reati (1986), Webber and Rigby (1986), and Dumenil et al. (1987) have demonstrated that the German and North American economies were characterized by steady falls in profitability after the early 1950s rather than by relatively constant rates of profitability followed by a decline. The data presented in Chapter 2 are consistent with this evidence. Other key indicators—composition of capital, real wages, productivity (and the wage/productivity ratio)—also shifted throughout the phase rather than at the end of it.

One conclusion that can be drawn from these facts is that there is evidence of the existence of waves or cycles but not of the existence of periods. Theorists of periods either have to adapt their theories to explain waves or cycles or have to explain how these four facts are consistent with the concept of a period. For the moment, we should cease using language (of periods) that implies that conditions are for a time constant and then change. Furthermore, we should cease to look for evidence of a new period, but rather seek evidence of upswings in profits and accumulation and of actions to ensure those upswings.

3.4.3 Current Changes

It is possible also to evaluate the theories' capacity to interpret evidence about changes now occurring.

A variety of changes have been observed both within production and in the geography of production. Within production, these include the following: multitasking, worker involvement, part-time labor, and education; use of the machinery of information technology; new materials and combinations of materials, and just-in-time flow systems; new divisions of labor; and faster communications (Sayer and Walker 1992; Walker 1989). The relation between production and finance is also shifting (Daly and Logan 1989). The space of production is changing too. Some new industrial spaces are being created (Castells and Hall 1994; Scott 1988b; Storper and Scott 1988), though such expansion is hardly a novel feature of capitalism. Equally, however, deep changes in the organization of production are occurring in old industrial regions (Hudson 1989). In some sectors and countries, mass production has virtually collapsed (e.g., electronics and domestic appliances in the USA) but in others is being revitalized (e.g., steel and auto production in South Korea).

These phenomena can be understood in three main ways. They may be regarded as unrelated, in which case it is happenstance that they occur at the same time. They may be regarded as the outcomes of a series of experiments, a search for a "new way forward." Or they may be regarded as interconnected, reflecting in some way the emergence of a new phase. Only in this last case would it be correct to give the whole assemblage of changes a common name. The various theories take different positions in this spectrum.

As far as Piore and Sabel are concerned, the only feasible way forward is through flexible production. The only changes that are in the long run viable are those that augment flexibility. The others are mutations that will fail: their occurrence is happenstance. This is an approach that dismisses the notion that the variety of experiences may be a central feature of the times. Piore and Sabel emphasize a single characteristic (flexibility) rather than the whole variety of changes that are occurring—and rather than linkages between flexibility in one place or sector and other forms of production in other places or sectors.

To Leborgne and Lipietz (1988), the different models that are being thrown up now represent a series of experiments; presumably one will emerge as hegemonic, but not necessarily during this century. Again, a single emerging characteristic is emphasized rather than a variety or a link between different characteristics in places or sectors. Unlike Piore and Sabel, however, Leborgne and Lipietz do not predict exactly what the successful model will be.

To Freeman and Perez, a series of innovations is occurring—especially in information technology, but also in management science—that will provide the basis for the next upswing. The other changes are happenstance. This does seem to omit a good deal of struggle over politics and welfare.

For Mandel, the essential feature of the current phase is that the basis for a new phase of accumulation is being laid by the search for a new source of surplus profit. The particular events that comprise this search may include changes not only within the traditional foci of Western economies but also the rush of Western firms to exploit new opportunities in eastern Europe and innovation and investment in environmental management. Interestingly, if these sources of surplus profit turn out to be significant, the exploitation of space will again form the basis for an upswing in profitability and accumulation.

3.5 THE FUTURE

How, then, can we tell what our present time of transition is all about?

As is generally true, data do not precisely distinguish the various theories. The issues pose not only empirical questions—though they certainly do pose such questions—but also ask theoretical questions, for the assemblage of cause and effect must depend too on theoretical knowledge. However, they ask questions that our theoretical and empirical tools are so far largely inadequate to answer.

The empirical observations do, however, sharpen the differences between the theories. It seems more reasonable to think of phases in terms of waves or cycles rather than of periods. This necessitates recasting the terms of the theories of Piore and Sabel, Lipietz, and Lash and Urry. It also seems that Piore and Sabel and Lipietz have to dismiss many of the changes that are now occurring as irrelevant to the future (because they will become failed experiments). For Freeman and Perez also, the current crisis involves a search for new social and political solutions to complement recent developments in computers and telecommunications technology. While the institutional structure of the future is uncertain, its base in information technology is secure. For Mandel, the present is a time of search for super-profits potentially through renewed exploitation of spatial differences.

If the issue is simply one of finding an appropriate mode of accumulation about which labor and capital can compromise and which satisfies the required conditions for stability and growth, then it is straightforward to evaluate alternatives, as Lipietz does. The new mode must encourage productivity change and ensure a pattern of wage increases to maintain profitability while saving (at least sufficient of) the domestic market from competition from the NICs. It is possible to see in this prescription a compromise in which both labor (in the "Western economies" at least) and capital are better off by finding such a mode. A similar compromise can be seen to emerge from the analysis of Piore and Sabel. It is well known that one of the options prescribed from this position is flexible production, linked by Lipietz with a degree of flexibility in the labor contract.

For Mandel, by contrast, the issue is more stark. Capitalists must search—or the state on their behalf must search—for solutions to the problems of profitability that they face. These solutions involve struggles against labor, either to reduce the value of labor power or increase the intensity of work, or to alter conditions of production in some region or sector. Firms may well be seeking "flexible" methods, but these methods are a means of reducing labor costs, the organic composition of capital, the price of constant capital, or the turnover time. They are not a means of ensuring new conditions of stability. Furthermore, elements of the solution to the problem of profitability may involve changes outside the traditional capitalist economy: eastern Europe and environmental management.

And this, it seems, is the heart of the current dilemma. Is the search for flexibility of production systems and wage contracts a matter of reestablishing conditions for stability? Or is it a matter of using flexible methods and social relations to reestablish the conditions for profitable accumulation (lower labor costs, reduced organic composition of capital, cheaper constant capital, reduced turnover time)? The terms *flexible production* and *flexible accumulation* imply the former; but there is little evidence that this is indeed the cause of the transition in progress.

Despite the lack of evidence with which to evaluate causes, several conclusions can be drawn. There is evidence of waves or cycles rather than periods of constant characteristics. We should talk of phases or waves rather than periods. There is evidence that "flexibility" interprets only part of the changes now occurring in production and space. We should cease using the interpreted term *flexibility* to refer to concrete changes (such as a shift to part-time labor) that may better be interpreted differently. And we should consider how to theorize all the changes that are occurring rather than simply identifying a small number as significant. There is also evidence that an integration of society and space has as yet been achieved only in Mandel's theory.

3.6 DIRECTIONS FOR ANALYSIS

This chapter has asked some questions of recent historical economic geography. It has argued that interpretations of history are divided and many of the facts that could help decide between the interpretations are unclear. To sharpen the ability of evidence to discriminate, some new theoretical tools must be developed. That is, the questions posed by historical economic geography ask for more evidence; in turn that evidence must rest on a proper theoretical footing. The tools now available are inadequate to the task posed by history.

The job of this book is to describe both the new theoretical tools and the evidence to which they give rise. Three of those tools are presented: a formal, dynamic theory of demand and profitability in the context of changes in productivity; a formal theory of technical change; and a theory of internationalization. In turn, we present some of the evidence which those theories permit concerning profitability, technical change, and the growth of the NICs. The book, then, is about the economic-geographic dynamics of capitalist societies. It is not about the economic-geographic histories of individual countries. Theorized or interpreted histories, like those reviewed in this chapter, are underpinned by an understanding of capitalist dynamics. We seek to expand that understanding.

But what sort of entity is it that exhibits "capitalist dynamics"? What entity (or entities) have exhibited problematic growth since the early 1970s? This section outlines our answer to these questions.

The first analytical focus of this book is the economy. More precisely, it is the economy of capitalist producers. (Chapter 4 describes in more detail what an economy of capitalist producers looks like and identifies methods whereby its performance may be measured.) This decision sets the level of abstraction employed in theory and measurement. So we ignore the accidents, mistakes, and peculiarities of individual countries: we do not demonstrate the logic of particular events. We do seek to show that the end of the partly golden age was contained in its own, internal dynamic. The focus also implies that the problems of growth have become general across all (or virtually all) particular nation-states.

So Chapters 5 and 6 concern abstract capitalist production systems. These systems are analyzed in a manner quite separate from the characteristics of particular societies in which they might be embedded (indeed the entire concept of society is irrelevant to this analysis). The data foreshadowed by these theories are presented in Chapters 8 and 9. Given the vagaries of data collection systems and the different methods employed by each nation-state, these data are organized in terms of national economies (and sometimes for politically defined regions within those countries). Interested as individual readers might be in the evolution of "their" economy, the point of these data is not to understand the particularities of each national economy but to illustrate the degree of commonality of experience and the extent of the differences in experience.

Of course, capitalist production has a social basis. The economy is not something separate from (or prior to) society. This is true historically: primitive accumulation in western Europe was a process in which force and legal instruments were used to render societies of independent artisans into atomized individuals who owned only their labor power. A similar history has more recently been repeated in the NICs, where state actions have created new capitalist economies. (Some of this history is recounted in Chapter 10.) But equally in contemporary capitalism, capitalist production continues to rest on social supports. Households produce: especially, they produce labor power—a crucial commodity for capitalist production. Legal and property relations underpin corporate behavior and labor markets. Infrastructures, both social and physical, are largely produced outside the capitalist production system, despite the mania for privatization in the English-speaking world. In some ways states have acted to protect the interests of workers: minimum wages, employment, and health standards are usual. And in other ways states have acted to protect (or at least regulate) the interests of capitalist producers: tariff and nontariff barriers, regulations, subsidies, and trade policies are everywhere to be found. Were societies not important, capitalism would everywhere be the same. That is, the so-called economic base has itself crucial noneconomic conditions of existence: money, law, and the state, for example (Jessop 1990: 81–85).

All this is true. Yet, even though the capitalist economy has crucial noneconomic conditions of existence, its internal dynamic centers on the activities of productive capital. Despite all the supports of the economy from law and the state and despite household production of labor power, the central motor is capital accumulation, itself primarily determined by the organization of the capitalist economy. And that organization occurs through the market, which coordinates the different moments of the circuit of capital. Even labor power is exploited largely through market relations rather than through noneconomic forms of coercion (Jessop 1990: 81–85).

Nor for that matter is capitalist production the only form of production in advanced capitalist countries. There are other producers. Households produce perhaps as much again as the measured GNP. Independent commodity production—in retailing, agriculture, fishing, the law, and other professions—shows no sign of withering into insignificance. The state produces too: infrastructure and sometimes commodities for sale in the market. These forms of production are all implicated in capitalist production (they trade with and may be dominated economically by capitalist producers), but the social relations within such places of production are not capitalist. There are also increasingly important realms of nonproductive activities. Perhaps the most important of these is finance, an industry that seems to have taken on a life all its own in rendering the world global. What has happened to the scale, reach, and organization of the various parts of the finance industry has altered phenomena as disparate as how we now view the world (as a global economy) and how we build the downtown office blocks of our cities.

Again, agreed. As to noncapitalist forms of production, we plead both that they require serious and separate investigation and that they are less important in understanding the global slowdown than is capitalist production. This is perhaps less contentious than the second part of the claim: capitalist economic processes are understood firstly by the activities of productive capital and only secondarily by the circuits of money or commodity capital. We will claim, like others before us, that some of the impetus to these developments has been changes within capitalist production—in the prospects for profitable capital accumulation.

Moreover, the whole world is not capitalist. It is a travesty that removes virtually all meaning from the word to call such societies as present-day China, or Cuba, or Laos, or Rwanda, or Ukraine capitalist. Some production in virtually all societies is now capitalist. (But much production in the advanced capitalist societies is not capitalist.) In some societies, such as China, capitalist production may be hegemonic in the sense that it is the form of production which the state most seeks to encourage. In others, such as Laos, capitalist forms of production are regarded much more circumspectly.

We do not claim, then, that the world is capitalist. We claim only that the parts of the world we are analyzing contain large capitalist production sectors. The economies of North America and western Europe, Japan, and the former dominions have been organized with capitalist production throughout the postwar years. Other economies, notably the NICs, have developed capitalist production sectors only during this period. Indeed, one of the central issues to which we shall return in Chapters 7 and 10 concerns the colonization by capitalist producers of societies that formerly lay largely outside the formal sphere of capitalist forms of production. This is an issue of the relationship between capital accumulation and the organization of space.

Nor, finally, do all the social divisions that matter in our societies originate in production. Class originates in production, and its forms in our societies originate in capitalist production. But production is not the source of gender, sexual orientation, ethnicity, age, and other distinctions that form the basis for so many other arenas of oppression in modern life (McLennan 1984). The technical division of labor may be developed in some ways in order to exploit these distinctions; and their existence is not unrelated to the specific forms taken by capitalist social relations in some societies (Sayer and Walker 1992).

We claim simply that to understand the dynamics of capitalist production it is not necessary to understand these other forms of oppression. (Indeed it is problematic whether Marxist understandings of the nature of capitalist production can comprehend the whole variety of oppression.)

This book therefore analyzes first an economy of capitalist producers. Many important aspects of social life are thereby excluded from view, including noncapitalist forms of production and nonclass forms of oppression. Important as these are in understanding the totality of social life, they are not our problematic. Rather we are concerned with another important aspect of modern social life: difficulties in maintaining rates of capital accumulation since the early 1970s. And we claim that an initial approach to that problematic can be made by examining the dynamics of capitalist production systems, ignoring both the social supports of those systems and the societies that lie outside the sphere of capitalist production relations. Our deep (and unexamined) claim is that to understand the dynamics of capitalist production in the advanced capitalist countries (and in the countries that aspire to that status) is the first step along the road to understanding global economic geographies.

This is not to argue that the sort of abstract economic-geographic dynamics that we examine cause the events of daily life. The prices of individual commodities change in their own idiosyncratic ways. Politicians in individual countries develop their own policies. The strategic directions taken by individual corporations differ widely. The relations between ethnic groups, men and women, age groups, and other forms of "difference" are quite dissimilar in the various national spaces. These characteristics and events have multiple causes at a variety of levels:

> Theoretically, every event in the world is conditioned by every other event in the world. . . . Practically, then, any event is the result of a number of causal chains intersecting at some point in time/space. The event is caused, but nevertheless not determined; rather it is contingent on the indispensable, but fortuitous intersection in time/space of multiple chains of causation (Lukerman 1965: 130).

In another language, Jessop (1982: 212–213) observes the contingent necessity of what happens: various causal chains intersect in specific events. The capitalist production system interacts with a variety of social forces, evolving together and reciprocally adapting to cause and be caused by the events of everyday life. Nevertheless one element—indeed, one important element—in the multiple causal chains that intersect to produce those events is precisely the abstract economic-geographic dynamics.

This argument raises questions about the actors within the abstract capitalist economic system. One pair of actors consists of the abstract persons who fill the roles of capitalist and worker. Just as we have abstracted from those parts of society that do not lie within the sphere of capitalist production, so we abstract from those aspects of people's lives that are not concerned with their roles within capitalist production. The actors within this system are not whole people but those aspects of those people who occupy positions within the class structure of capitalist production. This method does not imply that other parts of daily life are caused by roles in capitalist production: real lives are multiply determined. It does imply that people's class position is a determinant of the kind of daily life they enjoy.

At the level of our abstract capitalist economic system there is no role for a state. The central core of capitalist production is closed or autonomous. A capitalist production system may have been set up with the assistance of a state; it may need too the continuing support of a state. But the operation and social relations of an abstract capitalist economic system are fundamentally outside the realm of the state. That is, there is no general theory of the state. There are no inevitable or logical economic functions which the state comes into existence to serve: all states are not necessarily solely instruments of class oppression; the role of the state is not simply one of facilitating capitalist interests.

Perhaps we should indicate what we mean by the state. The state is a set of institutions, not a coherent whole (unless made so in a specific managerial project) and not an autonomous subject (Jessop 1990: 117–118). The recognizably distinct institutions that constitute the state make rules, control, guide, and regulate behavior: they monopolize legal power and supposedly exercise that power equally over all the individuals in the sovereign territory (Dunleavy and O'Leary 1987: 1–4). The state's apparatuses are specialized institutions that have their own projects (or at least reflect the projects of their officials). These projects both influence and reflect the balance of forces within a sovereign territory: the forces may include class power (and indeed the power of different fractions of classes), but they also include pressures that arise from other states, from other forms of production, and from people's responses to other kinds of oppression.

States, then, are tied to specific places. So knowledge of the forms of the state and the logic of state policies—and even of the details of those policies—is required if we are to understand what happened in Japan as compared to what happened in the USA or in Canada as compared to Australia. Furthermore if we are to comprehend the spatial extension of capitalist production then state action must be understood: globalization as a specific process has taken forms that have been aided and directed by states' policies.

We analyze abstract capitalist production economies in Chapters 4, 5, and 6 and provide relevant empirical information in Chapters 8 and 9. Therefore in those chapters the influence of states is largely ignored. However, Chapter 7 comes down to the use of space, at least as a system of regions or nations; and Chapter 10 focuses on one feature of the organization of the global economy—the rise of the NICs. Therefore once we come to theorize about particular regions or groups of countries and when we come to explain the spatial organization of the global economy, we must introduce the state. The changing uses of space by capitalist producers—the phases of space—are mediated by the system of states. For whatever may be argued about the openness of national boundaries and the countervailing power of transnational corporations, the distance-shrinking properties of modern machines of war, and the assertion of power by cultural minorities (Beetham 1984), by far the most significant territorial unit within which capitalist production is organized remains the nation-state (see also Dicken 1992). Most importantly, the nation-state—and confederations of states like the European Union—may well be the only institution that can possibly compete with the power of transnational corporations.

Whatever the pressures on them and their degree of freedom of action, states seem to perform two broad categories of projects, two general kinds of accumulation strategies (Jessop 1990: 199–210). Some strategies are *plan rational* (Johnson 1982); such states are sometimes called development states. Other strategies are *market rational* (again the term comes from Johnson); such states are concerned to regulate markets. Within the nation-state lie the powers that determine the form of the market, define competition between capitals, supervise conflict between classes, and regulate linkages between the nation and the world. In Porter's (1990) terms, the nation-state is the source of the skills and technology that underpin competitive advantage. Naturally, superimposed on the specific actions or policies used to implement these strategies (see Dicken 1992; also Chapter 10) the state performs ideological tasks, particularly to convince people and other actors of the importance of the strategies that are being followed.

So the general framework within which we approach the spatial organization of capitalist production is that of an interaction between the purposes and goals of capitalist producers and the purposes and goals of states. Like any specific characteristics and events, the concrete histories of the expansion of capitalist production within particular territories or of the relations between capitalist producers in different territories are the product of multiple chains of causation, many of which lie outside the dynamics of the capitalist economy. Likewise the actions of states: these are determined by many pressures and by a variety of goals. So our approach has been to identify how the dynamics of a capitalist economy generate one or more preferred geographies and then to comprehend the manner in which particular states have grasped those preferences and modified them. The industrialization of the NICs—the spread of capitalist forms of production, exchange, and finance to other regions of the world—and globalization—the integration of those regions in a spatially extensive network of production, exchange, and finance—have not been on the terms of (the abstract) capitalist producers but have also reflected goals articulated by states. This dynamics of two interacting systems is, like the dynamics of the capitalist economy, abstract: it is not an explanation of what happened, but one of the (many) causes of that history. This interacting system does not comprise what Mandel (1978) calls fused capitals [i.e., transnational corporations that are without dominant national ownership or control so that critical differences according to nationality disappear (see Elson 1984)]. Perhaps, as Mandel argues, transnational corporations that because of the internationalization of production are indifferent to the state, are also likely to find that the state is indifferent to them. States and nationality remain of critical importance in understanding the global economic geography of capitalist production, an effect quite different from that identified by world system theory (see Dale 1984).

So the history sketched in Chapter 2 has inspired this book. However, we have taken two steps back from that history. The first step has been away from the details of actual events to the kinds of interpretation that have been analyzed in this chapter—toward generalized, theorized histories. But those existing theorized histories are inadequate, for the evidence that would discriminate between them is largely missing and, we would argue, the theory that underpins them is imperfect. So the second step back from actual events has been toward theory, in particular to theory about the dynamics of capitalist economies. Armed with that theory and the evidence to which it gives rise, we return in Chapter 11 to theorized history. But we cannot return to the actuality of history, for we do not understand the dynamics of all the other elements besides capitalist production that make up real societies: their events have multiple causalities of which the dynamics of capitalist economies are only one.

Chapter 4

THE LABOR THEORY OF VALUE AND EXPECTED PRICES

W hat is the evidence by which the various explanations of the contemporary transition are to be evaluated? Our tasks in this book are to develop theories of technical change, profitability, and interregional investment. Those theories in turn provide the means of measuring changes in the postwar world so that the narratives described in Chapter 3 can be rated. Yet theories and measurements depend on more basic principles.

This chapter aims to define the central categories of production and value and to show how to measure them. The theory of value has a long but not always distinguished history. We build on the history. Two central principles have guided that building. First, if the categories of production and value are to be of any use, they must be measurable. There is no point in a theory that does not support any empirical observation at all; furthermore, theories that purport to be about quantifiable concepts like value must support empirical measurement. At a minimum, therefore, the definitions have to be precise and mathematically exact. This principle guides Section 4.1. Secondly, if the categories of production and value are to be useful, they must correspond to what we take to be the structure of reality. Of course, theoretical categories have to be generalized and abstract, otherwise they would simply reproduce reality. But that does not mean that the categories can be derived from assumptions that are regarded as wrong. So the definitions must rest on an understanding of production that corresponds to the way in which capitalist systems are thought to work. Convenience—even mathematical convenience—does not provide good grounds on which to identify categories. This principle is important in Section 4.2.

The principles take us to some important theoretical claims. Existing theories of production and value rely on the notion of equilibrium. [This is an observation that is also true of theories of the falling rate of profit (FROP), theories of technical change, and theories of interregional investment: it will therefore arise again in each of the next three chapters.] Indeed the entire idea

of "the price" reflects the deeply ingrained equilibrium thinking that all instances of a commodity are offered for sale at the same price. Similarly, the
idea of "prices of production" refers to those prices that firms would charge if
they all earned an equal rate of profit. This is what we have referred to as a
wrong assumption: all economies are off equilibrium all the time. Instances of
a commodity—sold in this shop or that, in this city or that—do not normally
command the same price. The demand and supply of commodities differ geographically and vary historically; wages depend on the demand and supply of
labor but also on historical and geographic conditioning; capital is under- or
oversupplied.

The concept of prices of production is therefore not an empirical category. Such prices never exist. If we abandon the notion that firms all earn the
same rate of profit and that all instances of a commodity are sold at the same
price, the tools of probability theory can be used to investigate the average
and variance of the prices at which a commodity is sold. We follow Farjoun
and Machover (1983) in moving to the concepts of *expected prices* and *expected rates of profit*. The transformation problem can now be ignored. Aggregate rates of profit are the same in the value and the expected price calculus. Models, whether written in terms of values or expected prices, can be
directly related to empirical observations that are made in the price sphere.

It is not necessary to redefine value in the same way (Section 4.1). The
concept that value expands is a natural one; if the concept is used, value must
be measurable. But if value is to expand in production, all the inputs (including labor power) and all the outputs must be valued. That is, the value of a
thing can only be measured if it was produced for sale by commodity labor
power; value is therefore a category restricted to capitalist production. Value
is a universal standard of commodities, required for historical, comparative
research. Indeed, it is an objective standard, for objectivity is enforced by the
market.

Value is by definition an average of conditions in different factories and
is unaffected by differences between factories. To be measurable, value must
be defined as the quantity of productive labor power invested in an article under socially normal conditions of production and using labor of average skill
and intensity, no matter what the concrete form of that labor. Here—

1. "Socially normal" means the average of the techniques that actually
   exist.
2. The value created by 1 hour of labor power of a person of average
   skill must be the same as that of any other person of average skill no
   matter what the concrete form of their labor.
3. Skilled laborers produce more value per hour than do unskilled laborers because they produce more commodities per hour.
4. Productive labor power is labor power that creates use values that are
   in the commodity form, that has the commodity form, and that is exploited.

The measure of value, then, is the average productive labor content of an article: no arbitrary assumptions—just what is, we think. These are interlinked elements of a definition of value that is measurable and consistent with the theory of capital.

Given these definitions, the usual theoretical device is to propose to measure value from data in input–output tables and from information about the inputs of productive labor in each industry (Morishima 1973). But the mathematics of this device works only if each industry uses only one technique of production; each industry produces only one commodity; all labor is the same quality, unskilled; there is no fixed capital; all commodities take the same length of time to produce; all purchases by firms are made on the same day, and all sales are made on another, later day; there are constant returns to scale. These assumptions are all wrong in the sense that they do not correspond to the way production actually is organized. Therefore measurements that use this mathematical procedure make mistakes. Worse, some neo-Ricardians (like Steedman 1977) claim that if these assumptions are relaxed then the measure of value produces odd results (for example, negative values: making the theory of value about as odd as a theory that predicts negative prices).

So Section 4.2 is devoted to explaining how to measure values properly. The assumptions become irrelevant (and Steedman's criticism wrong). The explanation is inherently statistical, relying on definitions that are the averages of actual instances. Thus a unit of socially necessary labor power of average skill and intensity is a unit that produces the average quantity of value. Then the expected (average) quantity of value created in an industry equals the quantity of productive labor power supplied to that industry. Adjustments for different techniques, joint production, different kinds of labor, fixed capital, different lengths of production times, and varying purchase and sales dates are all straightforward after these definitions.

All of this makes for much simplified empirical work. Expected prices are just the amounts paid divided by the quantity sold; no theoretical equilibrium price has to be computed. Profit rates computed in terms of prices are profit rates in the value calculus: no transformation is needed. Labor values are simply average labor inputs per unit of output (including, of course, the contribution of plant and equipment). These calculations can all be made without input–output tables; therefore they can be readily repeated for many places and many times.

From these initial calculations follow other variables of interest. Technical and value compositions of capital can be defined precisely. So can rates of exploitation. It follows that the historical conundrum about the relative effects of changes in the value composition of capital and in the rate of exploitation on the rate of profit can be investigated empirically. The turnover time of capital is readily assessed. So too are the average capital and labor input coefficients: this means that technical change can be measured directly without detouring through the limiting assumptions and errors of neoclassical measures of total factor productivity. That is, the theoretical innovations inspired by Farjoun and Machover (1983) and outlined in this chapter permit the empirical work in this book to address directly some of the central questions that were posed in Chapter 3: the history of the rate of profit and the reasons for its (presumed) fall; the history of technical change and its effect on the rate of profit.

The chapter is methodological and theoretical, establishing the claim that there exist methods of confronting theoretical categories with empirical information. The chapter (particularly Section 4.2) is inherently mathematical, for part of our claim is that debates about the theory of value and its empirical usefulness have been fueled by imprecise thought. Some readers may be happy to accept this summary of the categories we use in Chapters 5 through 7 and the measurements we make in Chapters 8 through 10: they can skip this chapter if they like. Others may have their curiosity whettened: the chapter does, we think, clarify the theory of value.

4.1 PRODUCTION AND VALUE

If the principal problem of economics is to explain how an economy works, that is, how labor is allocated to particular tasks, the central tool is the theory of value. This theory explains how and why commodities are valued and relates the value of each commodity to its price. The theory of value is one of the most complex and contentious aspects of economic theory [Harvey (1982: 1–38) briefly introduces this theory]. At the risk of oversimplifying, three main lines of contention in the theory of value can be described.

One group claims that the theory of value is a theory about relative prices and that value itself is the embodied labor content of commodities. Such people have been called neo-Ricardians; typical representatives are Hodgson (1981, 1982) and Steedman (1977), whose method follows the pioneering work of Sraffa (1960). Neo-Ricardians make two additional claims: first, since prices can be computed directly from the material conditions of production, the detour via labor values is unnecessary; secondly, there are internal inconsistencies in the theory of value that give rise to perverse results.

A second group claims that the theory of value is not a quantitative theory at all but a qualitative theory that explains how and why labor under capitalism assumes the form that it does. Elson (1979), Wright (1981), and Harvey (1982) all espouse this position. For some, such as Wright, this claim represents a retreat from the third position: that the theory of value has both qualitative and quantitative functions.

We argue the third claim: that value theory has both quantitative and qualitative aspects. The argument is made by Rubin (1972), Sweezy (1970), and Desai (1979); for a similar argument in a different direction see Itoh (1980: 47–79). By this third claim the irrelevancy argument of the neo-Ricardians is avoided but the inconsistency argument remains. The argument proceeds through three stages: first, a review of the theory of value as a whole;

secondly, a statement of the quantitative aspect of the theory; and, finally, a defense of that quantitative aspect against the neo-Ricardian argument of inconsistency. This section (4.1) comprises the review of the theory, whereas Section 4.2 states and defends the quantitative aspects of the theory.

4.1.1 The Theory of Value: Basic Argument

The wealth of capitalist societies appears as an accumulation of commodities. A commodity is a thing produced by human labor for exchange; it has three interrelated characteristics. It is first an object that satisfies human needs; this usefulness makes it a use value. Secondly, a commodity has an exchange value (the ratio in which it exchanges with another); since a commodity can exchange with many others it has many exchange values. The exchange value of a commodity with money is called its price. So the exchange of commodities expresses something equal between them; or rather their exchange value is the phenomenal form of something contained within them. This common something is the fact that they are products of human labor: not of particular, concrete kinds of labor, but of labor in the abstract, labor as labor. Apart from their useful characteristics, then, commodities are thirdly congelations of human labor power and in this respect they are simply values.

A commodity has value because labor is embodied in it. The magnitude of value must therefore be measured by the quantity of value-creating substance (labor) contained in it: this quantity is labor time, socially necessary under normal conditions and skills. Commodities in which equal quantities of labor time are embodied have equal value. Alternatively expressed, the value of a commodity varies directly as the quantity and inversely as the productivity of the labor embodied in it. Some use values such as clean air have no value; some useful products of labor such as the dinner we cook tonight are not commodities; and useless things contain no useful labor even if they are produced.

Objects are commodities because they are both use values and depositories of value. Use value is a material attribute of commodities, whereas value is a social characteristic, acquired only insofar as commodities are expressions of human labor. So value is manifest only in exchange; that is, exchange value is the form in which value appears. Exchange is also the means whereby the value of commodities is objectified.

Just as commodities have a dual character, so does labor. Useful labors differ qualitatively: the different kinds of labor reflect the division of labor without which there could be no commodities. In addition commodities as values are also objective expressions of essentially identical labor. This labor is the expenditure of simple labor power which exists in every ordinary person; in a particular society it is given. Skilled labor is merely simple labor multiplied, the proportions being established by a hidden social process.

The exchange of two commodities, even indirectly through the medium of money, implies that the labor embodied in the one is equated to the labor embodied in the other. The different kinds of concrete labor are thus reduced to their common property of being labor. This is abstract labor. Just as use value is the material property of commodities and value their social property, so concrete labor is the material and individual aspect of useful labor whereas abstract labor is its social aspect, the qualitative equivalence imposed by the fact that commodities can be exchanged. Abstract labor is not a common property of concrete labors but a different way of regarding them (Kay 1979).

The complexity and subtlety of commodities does not result from their being use values nor from their being products of labor, but from the commodity form itself. By this form the equality of different kinds of labor is expressed in their products being values, the expenditure of labor power is measured as the value of products, and the relations between producers take the form of a social relationship between commodities. Thus the social character of labor is only revealed in exchange; labor is first performed as private labor and transformed into social labor by the sale of its product (de Vroey 1981).

This argument summarizes the way we understand Chapter 1 of Marx's *Capital* (1967). There exist many views about Marx's argument. We make no attempt to summarize this debate; we do though describe the main issues that affect the quantitative aspects of the theory of value. To what kinds of production does the theory of value apply? Why is labor the standard of commodities in that production? What is the meaning of socially necessary labor? How is skilled labor reduced to simple labor? How are different concrete labors compared? And what kinds of labor produce value?

4.1.2 Capitalist Production

The first question concerns the scope of the theory of value. Neither neo-Ricardians nor subjective preference theorists regard production and exchange as social and material processes. [Cole et al. (1983) summarize these theories of economics.] According to neo-Ricardians, price is fixed by the material conditions of production. Subjective preference theorists believe that prices are set in the market by supply and demand; in equilibrium prices reflect both the subjective wants of consumers and the material conditions of production. To this extent neo-Ricardian and subjective preference theories are ahistorical: their theories of price do not depend on the structure of society. Marxists regard the theory of value as historically specific.

A society in which commodity production and exchange are generalized is necessarily a capitalist society (Harvey 1982: 1–38). Capital is self-expanding value: capital is defined by what it does. Now value is a property of some kinds of things such as stereo receivers, lettuce plants, and concerts: it is the property that these things acquire by virtue of their being products of human labor. But if value is to expand it must be measurable; it must also be objectively measurable. This measure is the quantity of socially necessary abstract labor expended (taken to include the value of tools and materials used by labor) in production. The objectivity of the measure is ensured by valuing produced things by the socially normal method of production, that is, by the average amount of labor expended. (A real process, competition, ensures this socially normal valuation.) Furthermore, if value is to expand, value must persist; things must store value. But a thing can only store value if, during or after its production, someone wants it: if no one wants the thing, the labor that made it was wasted. Value is a property of some kinds of produced use values.

There exist different kinds of use values. The fresh air on the west coast of Vancouver Island is certainly a utility; but it is not produced and so stores no value. The pie that was baked for dinner last night was a utility for the family (at least they said so). Since this pie was not marketed in competition with the pies produced by others there can be no objective measure of its value even though someone labored to make it. So a primary distinction exists between marketed and nonmarketed produced use values: the former, called commodities, have an objectively measured value; the latter do not. Commodities then are those things that store objective value: value is a property of some kinds of commodities.

A commodity is a thing that stores objective value. The empirical basis for this definition is the fact that a commodity is produced for the market, so its production process must in the long run satisfy social norms; by contrast one can take several hours to make an apple pie without contravening any market rules. Another characteristic of a commodity follows: it must be capable of storing value for the entire period between its production and the validation of that value on the market but not necessarily any longer. All things that are bought and sold evidently meet this criterion: therefore the set of commodities includes all marketed, produced use values, for these are all capable of storing objective value. Services like a concert and a haircut are therefore commodities as much as stereo receivers. Finally the source of the usefulness of a commodity is irrelevant, as is the market on which it is sold: if the thing is useful to someone, it has the capacity to store value. It is irrelevant to inquire about the nature of usefulness, just as a person's "real need" for a commodity is irrelevant and not measurable. A commodity can be objectively valued provided that it is useful to someone and validated on a market. An advertisement sold to a client is a commodity; the transport and storage of goods are commodities if they are desired by someone and objectively valued on a market.

Another type of commodity is produced by households: labor power—the capacity of laborers to work. This capacity is produced by human labor in the household. It is a use value, for it has utility to employers. Some forms of labor power are objectively valued on the market. Thus some labor power is a commodity and its value is the value of the labor power that is socially necessary to produce it. Only some kinds of work use commodity labor power. In particular commodity labor power is the capacity to work that is objectively valued on the market: the man down the street who makes and sells hand-made shoes or the potter who exhibits her work in the local cooperative gallery do not use commodity labor power in their work, for their labor power is not objectively valued on the market even though the commodities they produce are objectively valued. Equally the housework of a person and partner who collectively produce their labor power for sale on the market is not commodity labor power. So there exist two kinds of labor power: commodity labor power, objectively valued on the market, and noncommodity labor power, not itself objectively valued even though the things it produces might be.

So far we have put forward three major definitions—of capital, value, and commodity. These definitions are linked. Because capital is self-expanding value, value must be objectively measurable. The measurement is made by the market in capitalist societies. We must therefore distinguish things that store value (commodities) from those that do not. One definition cannot be altered without altering the others. The definitions are mutually consistent. We have also considered what items belong to these categories. Armed with these definitions we can examine the process of production in capitalism.

Production is first a process of creating use values, of making things that some people want. Some production creates things that are not commodities—baking an apple pie for dinner. Other processes create commodities: some household labor creates commodity labor power, the potter creates a bowl, the transit company produces bus rides, and the factory makes earth-moving equipment. So the first distinction, arising from the earlier definitions, is between commodity production and noncommodity production. Since noncommodity production does not produce things that store value it does not use capital. By contrast, commodity production does produce things that store value.

Subsistence farmers, even if they sell part of their product, are noncommodity producers. Their subsistence mode of production has the form

$$\text{means of production} + \text{labor} \rightarrow \text{products.}$$

Farmers must labor enough to reproduce their family. Their effort to economize applies to the entire process of family reproduction, not just to production for exchange. Subsistence farmers economize on labor time. Their goal is to maximize total output subject to the constraints imposed by the availability of land and family labor. So a machine that economizes on labor without increasing output per hectare would not be adopted by such farmers unless the labor they had saved could be used in other lines of production (by acquiring more land or working off the farm).

Some commodities are produced with noncommodity labor power. Labor power itself is like this; so also are the things made by independent producers who sell their commodity but not their labor power on the market. Such production has the following form: starting with a sum of money M, the producer buys raw materials and equipment C and keeps herself alive so that she can labor (L) to make the bowl C_1 which is sold for M_1. Thus,

$$M \rightarrow \begin{bmatrix} C \\ L \end{bmatrix} \rightarrow C_1 \rightarrow M_1.$$

Is $M_1 > M$? Possibly but not necessarily: the process can certainly operate with $M_1 = M$. The production process itself is the central transformation:

$$\begin{bmatrix} C \\ L \end{bmatrix} \rightarrow C_1.$$

Is value created in this process? We do not know: while C and C_1 are valued objectively on the market (they are commodities), the labor power is not a commodity and so has no objective value. Hence C and L are not commensurate and the value of inputs cannot be compared to the value of outputs; M and M_1 are money stores of value, but they are not capital, for they are not value that is necessarily self-expanding. This form of production is called independent commodity production.

Independent commodity producers face a different problem from that of subsistence farmers. They buy some means of production, so these means must be replaced in the money form: hence price must cover money costs. Labor is not paid a wage and so does not have to be replaced by money. The goal of such producers is to maximize their income subject to the constraints imposed by the available means of production and labor time. This income is notionally split in some accounting systems into a reward for labor (imputed according to a prevailing wage) and a surplus (reward for entrepreneurship). This is merely a notional distinction: the producers simply earn an income.

Now consider commodity production that uses commodity labor power. Since the labor power used in this process is objectively valued, C and L are commensurate both with each other and with C_1. Hence we know whether or not $C_1 > C + L$ and we know whether $M_1 > M$. Sometimes $M_1 < M$, but if production continues to lose money in this fashion it eventually must cease for the initial outlay is gradually frittered away. Therefore in general $M_1 > M$: the value of outputs is at least as great as the value of inputs. Potentially M is capital for it is nondecreasing value. If the goal of production is to make M_1 larger than M then the money is capital, self-expanding value, and the production is called capitalist production. That is, capitalist production is production that starts with capital; it is the process of the self-expansion of value; it is commodity production that uses the commodity labor power. These are equivalent definitions.

Capitalist production is organized by owners of money who buy raw materials, plant, and equipment (means of production) and hire labor to produce commodities for sale at a profit. The purpose of production is profit; the method of obtaining profit is commodity production. Capitalist production is performed by laborers, people who own no means of production yet survive by selling the one commodity they control: labor power, the capacity for labor. The use value of labor power is its capacity to produce a surplus; its exchange (price) is the wage; and its value arises from the fact that it is produced by labor for exchange. The magnitude of the value of labor power is the quantity of socially necessary labor time required to reproduce it. The value of labor power is determined before and independently of the production process to which that labor contributes; by contrast, in subjective preference theory the wage is determined in production by the marginal productivity of labor.

Capitalist producers face a different problem from those of independent commodity producers and subsistence farmers. Their means of production and labor power are bought in the market, and therefore the price must cover all costs. The goal of capitalist production is to maximize profit subject to the constraint that purchased inputs (all inputs) cost no more than available capital. Now inputs can be freely substituted according to the available technologies subject to the capital constraint. Capitalist producers do not have to worry whether the labor they replace with machinery can find alternative employment.

In its most abstract form the capitalist mode of production corresponds to a society of two classes. One class consists of capitalists who together monopolize the means of production. Capitalists are agents of a process: the self-expansion of capital—the advance of money to produce a surplus. So capital is not to be understood as money per se, nor even as a stock of use values (these represent wealth), but rather as a social relation, an instrument tying one class to another (Harvey 1982: 20–21). The other class comprises free laborers—free in the senses that they own no means of production and that their only ties to capitalists are those of contract (equally exchanging labor power for its value).

Other kinds of production exist even in capitalist societies. These forms of production generate additional classes. Independent commodity production is the production of commodities without hired labor: the person who organizes production and owns the means of production also does the work. Family farmers, independent fishermen, artists, and people in private, professional practice are independent commodity producers. Another mode is subsistence production: objects are produced for a producer's own consumption rather than for a market. Still this book is concerned only with capitalist production of commodities. No attention is paid to the fact that some items (such as land) are not themselves entirely products of human labor [Harvey (1982: 330–372) and Sheppard and Barnes (1990) discuss the theory of rent]. The fact of noncapitalist production is ignored (but see Sayer and Walker 1992). This limitation reflects our view that production in advanced capitalist countries is dominated by capitalist production and our empirical focus on manufacturing activity, which in those countries is almost entirely capitalist.

Value is a category of the capitalist mode of production. In this mode the private labor of individuals is not directly social (not consciously organized by society) but is rendered so by the exchange of products as commodities (de

Vroey 1981). The labor theory of value explains the socialization of private labor by analyzing how concrete labor becomes abstract (Weeks 1981: 11–12, 27–49). Thus to the criticism of Samuelson (1957) and Steedman (1977) that value is an unnecessary detour on the road to explaining price we reply: first, that value is a historically specific phenomenon, unlike price; secondly, that the labor theory of value is concerned with explaining more than just price formation in capitalism—it is also concerned with the manner in which labor is represented under capitalism (Elson 1979). The usefulness of analyzing different modes of production separately has been illustrated using examples from Weeks (1981: 27–49).

Different modes of production impose different goals on producers. As the goals of production differ, so do decisions about choice of technique. Subsistence producers may fail to adopt new techniques of production that would be efficient for capitalists, not so much because they are indolent or lack entrepreneurship as because there may be no alternative uses for the labor that would be displaced. It is not sufficient to analyze production merely as a material process without examining also the social structure of that production. The labor theory of value attempts to analyze the social structure of production (and exchange) under capitalism.

4.1.3 Labor as the Standard of Commodities

Marx argued that since commodities are exchanged, they possess a common property, namely, they are products of labor. One of Marx's earliest critics, Bohm-Bawerk (1975) pointed out that commodities have other common properties: they contain inputs of energy, they can be possessed by individuals, and they are scarce. Why should labor be taken as the common property of commodities and as their standard? Farjoun and Machover (1983: 84–100) have clarified the answers to this question.

The first answer is that the concern of economics is social labor, the productive activity of human beings. Economics is not about the allocation of energy (or any other commodity) to different processes; nor is it about the laws of possession; much less is it about the allocation of scarce resources to achieve given ends. Rather, the subject matter of economics is the social processes by which social labor is organized and performed and the output of this labor distributed (Farjoun and Machover 1983: 85; Shaikh 1982: 70). So a concern with the production and exchange of commodities is mainly a concern with the production and exchange of things that embody labor; the appropriate standard of commodities is then the labor time embodied in them.

The second answer is that labor power is the only commodity that must be embodied in every other commodity (Farjoun and Machover 1983: 88–90). Capitalism could exist without iron or oil or any other specific use value. By contrast labor power as a commodity is essential to capitalist production and exists only under capitalism. Labor power is also a commodity that is produced without capital and sold without profit; all other commodities are normally produced with capital and for profit. So suppose that two systems of accounting are set up: one in which commodities are evaluated and profits measured in prices, and one in which commodities are evaluated and profits measured in units of labor content. Labor content is the only standard on which all and only those sectors that are in principle profit making in the price sphere are also profit making in the standard (labor content) sphere (Farjoun and Machover 1983: 90–93).

Related to this is the third fact: labor content is an invariable measure of commodities (Farjoun and Machover 1983: 93–96). Suppose that we compare two different economies at two different times. It is impossible to make this comparison exact in price terms since there exists no common basket of commodities to establish relative price levels (to translate nominal prices into "real" prices). In fact the comparison cannot be conducted in terms of any commodity except labor power: only labor power is universal in capitalism.

So if there is to be a standard of value against which to compare price and which regulates price, it must be socially necessary, abstract labor content. The claim that value regulates price does not imply that commodities are exchanged according to the socially necessary labor time embodied within them; however, the precise meaning of the notion of "regulation" must await a more careful discussion of price in Section 4.2.

4.1.4 Social Necessity of Labor

Neo-Ricardians and Marxists interpret differently the measure of the labor content of commodities. The labor content of a commodity is the quantity of labor time that is applied to its manufacture plus the labor time of the plant, equipment, and raw materials used up. This measure is determined entirely within production. The magnitude of value is different: it is the quantity of socially necessary abstract labor contained in a commodity. Several principles enter this definition.

The first question concerns the meaning of social necessity. A commodity, sugar say, is produced by various techniques: each factory uses different machines of different ages, different mixes of skilled and unskilled labor, different numbers of people per machine, and different numbers of managers per laborer. These differences mean that the labor content of the sugar produced by one factory is different from that produced by another. What then is meant by the notion of the socially necessary labor content of sugar? Two general answers have been proposed to this question.

One claims that socially necessary labor content is calculated from the best practice norm: the labor content of the sugar produced by the most efficient factory. Thus Morishima and Catephores (1978) claim that the labor content of commodities should be computed from a program that optimizes the production of the required bundle of commodities subject to constraints on the availability of labor and capital. The labor content of a commodity is measured in this scheme as the hours of labor directly and indirectly required to produce it if the optimum available technique were used: the optimum technique is that which minimizes labor content.

Alternatively social necessity means the average of the techniques actually in use in the place and at the time being investigated. Accordingly more labor is invested per unit of value in inefficient factories than in efficient ones. Competition is therefore likely to force capitalists to adopt techniques that are close to the best practice: the average actual technique may be similar to the optimal technique. [Farjoun and Machover (1983) assume that production techniques are actually the same for all plants within an industry.] However, there has been little analysis of the circumstances under which this process occurs. There are also known to exist large differences in techniques of production between different countries [see the discussion of the steel industry in Foot (1986)].

Since actual techniques are not optimal the measure proposed by Morishima and Catephores (1978) is not real. Their measure of labor content is a product of the mind rather than a real category that actually exists. Values computed from actual labor times reflect the actual operation of the economy, whereas optimal values are fictitious, computed from least labor times (Fine and Harris 1979). Therefore the measure adopted here is the industry-wide average of the labor content of commodities.

The qualifier "socially necessary" implies not only that techniques of production are socially necessary but also that the commodities produced are socially necessary. "Social necessity" connotes "required by actual capitalist societies" rather than "required by ideal, rational societies." One criterion of a socially necessary commodity is that it can find a buyer on the market. As de Vroey (1981) has argued, the creation of value is not simply a technical process of production but refers to the validation of labor on the market: if no sale is made, no value is created. More generally, socially necessary production must also reproduce capitalist class relations: maintain capital and reproduce labor. Capitalist production is not simply about producing commodities but also about maintaining the capitalist production system. The labor that performs these tasks is labor of reproduction rather than labor of production.

In sum the socially necessary labor content of a commodity is its industry-wide average labor content. The labor expended upon unsold commodities is excluded. This is a narrow definition of the labor employed in productive activities (see also Section 4.1.7). A commodity has also to carry its share of the costs of reproduction: a share (proportional to the total capital of the industry) of the total labor expended in reproducing capitalist class relations is added to the labor directly expended within the industry. (The share of the costs of reproduction is excluded from most calculations made in this book: the costs of reproduction must be calculated over the entire economy rather than simply one sector like manufacturing.)

4.1.5 Skilled Labor

The labor actually performed by individuals is concrete labor involving different tasks and skills. Yet commodities are valued according to their socially
necessary *abstract* labor content. Given different kinds of labor and skills,
how can commodities be valued? There are three different issues here: first,
the existence of different wages for different jobs or for the same job in different industries and places; secondly, the reduction of skilled to simple labor;
and, thirdly, the process whereby different concrete labors are compared (this
third issue is discussed in Section 4.1.6).

The determination of wages is, like the determination of prices, a matter
of complex and detailed variation between jobs, industries, and historico-geo-
graphic contexts. The wage is a price, the form of exchange value of the commodity labor power. It is not the value of labor power, but like other prices
the monetary expression of value. Therefore wage differences will be briefly
considered when prices are analyzed.

The reduction of skilled to simple labor is a more complex problem:
what are the relative values of two commodities if one contains 1 hour of simple labor and the other contains 1 hour of skilled labor? Marx merely remarked that skilled labor is simple labor multiplied and that skilled labor is
reduced to simple labor by an obvious social process. What is this process,
and what are the relative value creating capacities of skilled and simple labor?

A real, historical process reduces skilled to simple labor (Desai 1979:
20). This process converts people with craft skills into a proletariat divorced
from their means of production: people with monopolizable skills in different
jobs are reduced to common, homogeneous, undifferentiated labor. Thus Desai identifies the formation of simple labor as the homogenization of labor;
this specifically capitalist process is analyzed by Braverman (1974). However,
this view is too simple (Harvey 1982: 98–136). In the first place deskilling
and homogenization in one sphere (workers' jobs) require new skills in another sphere (producing and operating numerically controlled machinery). In the
second place while monopolizable skills are being eliminated under capitalism, a new skill is being created: adaptability, the ability to change jobs and
acquire new, temporary "skills." Despite the homogenization of labor described by Desai and recognized by Harvey there remain differences in skill
between laborers. If value is to be measured, these differences must be accounted for.

Skilled laborers produce more physical units of a commodity (or higher
quality commodities) per unit of their time than do unskilled laborers in the
same job. Hilferding (1919) argued that skilled labor is physically productive
because "capital" is invested in training. Sweezy (1970) and Rowthorn
(1974) follow Hilferding: the extra value created by skilled labor represents
the socially necessary labor spent in acquiring skill. So skilled labor simultaneously expends the skilled worker's own labor and a share of the past labor
that was needed to acquire the skill. If each hour of a skilled laborer's time in-

corporates also an hour of past training, then a commodity that embodies 1 hour of skilled labor has a value of 2 whereas the commodity that embodies 1 hour of simple labor has a value of 1.

Both David Harvey (1982: 57–61) and Philip Harvey (1985) observe problems in Hilferding's approach. First, it introduces a version of human capital theory that is quite contrary to the general theme of Marxist theory. Secondly, whereas the value creating capacity of unskilled labor is presumed to be given for a particular society independent of the labor required for its reproduction, the value created by skilled labor does seem to depend on the labor required to produce it. (It was one of Marx's central observations that the value of labor power is different from the value created by labor.) Thirdly, Hilferding's method presumes that skill is labor preserving rather than labor saving: the past labor embodied in skilled labor is transferred to the product in an amount equal to its added productivity.

The issue has a simple solution. Consider a single industry producing a commodity. The unit of labor power is labor of average intensity and skill. One hour of this labor expended in production adds 1 unit to the value of the commodity. Suppose that on average 75% of labor power is unskilled and 25% skilled; then the unit of labor power is 0.75 unskilled + 0.25 skilled. If unskilled labor produces 1 unit of commodity and skilled labor produces 2, each unit of labor power produces $0.75 \times 1 + 0.25 \times 2 = 1.25$ units of commodity: a unit of commodity has the value $1/1.25 = 0.8$. A factory that uses only unskilled laborers produces 1 unit per hour of labor: 0.8 units of value per hour of labor. A factory that uses only skilled labor produces 2 units per hour of labor: 1.6 units of value per hour of labor. The ratio of the value created by unskilled labor to that created by skilled labor is equal to the ratio of the physical output per hour of the two kinds of labor.

This solution has an important empirical implication. The example corresponds to an economy in which 10 million units of commodity are produced using 8 million hours of labor, 6 million of which are unskilled. The unit value of a commodity is 8 million/10 million = 0.8 hours per ton. The correct (adjusted for skills) labor content of commodities is obtained by dividing the hours of labor input by the quantity produced: it is simply not necessary to know how many skilled and unskilled laborers there are, nor to know their relative physical productivity.

Suppose that social conditions change: the 8 million hours of labor now include only 1 million hours of skilled labor. If technical conditions of production do not change, this labor power produces (2×1 million + 1×7 million) = 9 million units of commodity. The unit value of a commodity is now $8/9 = 0.89$ hours per ton. If no other changes raise output per hour, deskilling in society as a whole raises the value of commodities.

The problem is more complex if several industries are analyzed. Consider auto production and brewing. The industries produce different products, cars and beer; they employ different ratios of skilled and unskilled labor; and the meaning (degree of training and relative productivity) of skilled and unskilled labor differ. It is impossible to measure the relative value creating capacities of the different kinds of labor by referring to the value of those labor powers: that was Hilferding's error. Nor is it possible to compare the average physical productivity of labor in the two industries: how many beers equal one car? This issue is the problem of heterogeneous labor.

4.1.6 Heterogeneous Labor

The most ambitious attempt to solve the problem is found in Krause's *Division of Labor* (1982). Krause provides many insights into the mathematical structure of exchange and of money as a means of circulation. Most useful is his discussion of abstract labor (Krause 1982: 79–95). Given a two-commodity system that has two kinds of concrete labor, what are the relative values of the two commodities?

Suppose that the two commodities are tractors and food. Tractors are produced by industrial workers using tractors and food. Food is produced by capitalist farmers using tractors and food. The net output of tractors (tractors produced less tractor inputs) depends on inputs of food and industrial labor; the net output of food depends on inputs of tractors and farming labor. For example,

$$3 \text{ food} + 2 \text{ industrial labor} \rightarrow 10 \text{ tractors}$$

$$1 \text{ tractor} + 1 \text{ farming labor} \rightarrow 1 \text{ food.}$$

Substitute the second relation in the first:

$$3(1 \text{ tractor} + 1 \text{ farming labor}) + 2 \text{ industrial labor} \rightarrow 10 \text{ tractors,}$$

or

$$3 \text{ farming labor} + 2 \text{ industrial labor} \rightarrow 7 \text{ tractors.}$$

Equally,

$$1(0.3 \text{ food} + 0.2 \text{ industrial labor}) + 1 \text{ farming labor} \rightarrow 1 \text{ food,}$$

or

$$0.2 \text{ industrial labor} + 1 \text{ farming labor} \rightarrow 0.7 \text{ food.}$$

Thus commodities are equivalent to bundles of concrete labors: a tractor is the bundle (3/7, 2/7) and a unit of food is the bundle (2/7, 10/7) of the concrete labors (industrial labor, farming labor).

Suppose that the price of tractors is p_t and the price of food p_f. Tractors and food can be exchanged: $1/p_t$ tractors buys $1/p_f$ food. This exchange equates the two bundles of concrete labors:

$$p_t^{-1}(3/7, 2/7) \leftrightarrow p_f^{-1}(2/7, 10/7).$$

(The symbol $\leftrightarrow$ denotes the fact that the two bundles of concrete labors are equated, not that they are mathematically equal.) Therefore

$(3p_t^{-1} - 2p_f^{-1})$ industrial labor $\leftrightarrow (-2p_t^{-1} + 10p_f^{-1})$ farming labor,

from which it follows that 1 unit of industrial labor is equated with

$$A = \frac{-2p_t^{-1} + 10p_f^{-1}}{3p_t^{-1} - 2p_f^{-1}} \text{ units of farming labor.}$$

Krause argues that the ratio A is the coefficient that reduces farming labor to industrial labor via the market: it is the abstract labor coefficient.

This argument has an interesting implication. By the definition of A it follows that

$$\frac{p_t}{p_f} = \frac{3A + 2}{2A + 10},$$

which is precisely the ratio of the labor contents of the two commodities, measured in units of farming labor. The ratio of the values of commodities equals the ratio of their prices.

This implication arises from a feature of the coefficient that reduces one type of labor to another. By definition A, the abstract labor coefficient, depends on the structure of prices. As market prices change, so does the abstract labor coefficient; this is a matter of definition rather than of conclusion. But if the abstract labor coefficient depends on prices, so too do the relative values of commodities (also by definition rather than by conclusion). Krause assumes that abstract labor coefficients and so commodity values depend on prices.

Different kinds of labor work in different industries. Since both the labor and the products of the industries differ, either the labor or its products must be equated. Krause proposed that the concrete labors be compared by equating the products of the two industries in proportions that reflect prices. An alternative equates the concrete labors of the two industries, so that products are compared as bundles of equated labor. Now the concrete labors of the two industries are equated in proportions that reflect the wage structure (if auto workers are paid $10 per hour and brewery workers $8, the abstract labor coefficient that reduces auto labor to brewing labor is 10/8 = 1.25). This also implies that abstract labor coefficients and therefore values depend upon prices (wages). However the concrete labors of the two industries could be equated directly: the value-creating capacity of labor power of average intensity and skill in one industry equals that in another industry. (This is not to say that the value of labor power is the same in the two industries.)

Methods of valuing commodities when labor is heterogeneous thus fall into two groups. Either the reduction of concrete to abstract labor depends on prices (the prices of commodities or the wages of laborers) or the reduction is obtained directly by equating the value-creating capacity of the average labor power in different industries. A reduction that depends on the price structure suffers from two defects.

First prices fluctuate. Some changes in price flow from changes in production conditions: new techniques are used or more distant ore is extracted. But some price shifts reflect market circumstances and are unrelated to production conditions: changes in the strength of OPEC move the price of oil. Other price shifts are driven by expectations: demand may rise now if buyers expect future price increases. As prices fluctuate, so do values; in particular values fluctuate not simply because of shifts in production conditions but also because of changes or anticipated changes in market conditions. This result of Krause's scheme is contrary to the spirit of the definition of value as arising in production but expressed in the market.

The second weakness of a reduction through prices is that it is impossible to compare one society at different times or to compare two noninteracting societies. Krause's scheme reduces the various concrete labors in Canada in 1985 to Canadian brewing labor of 1985. It reduces the various concrete labors in Canada in 1984 to Canadian brewing labor of 1984. Values of output can therefore be computed in 1984 and 1985 using as basis Canadian brewing labor of 1984 and 1985, respectively. But Canadian brewing labor of 1984 is not the same as that of 1985, and since 1984 commodities are not exchanged for 1985 commodities, 1984 brewing labor cannot be reduced to 1985 brewing labor. So the values of output in the two years cannot be compared in Krause's scheme: history is precluded.

The only way of reducing concrete labors to abstract labor is therefore direct. Labor power of average intensity and skill has the same value creating capacity no matter what industry it is applied to. Labor power of average intensity and skill in Canada in 1985 has the same value-creating capacity as labor power of average intensity and skill in any other country or any other year even if the average intensity or skill has changed in the meantime. Krause (1982: 97–101) complained that the stipulation that different concrete labors are homogeneous is dogma within the labor theory of value; actually, it is a prerequisite of historical and national comparisons.

4.1.7 Productive Labor

Different concrete labors have the same value-creating capacity: they represent labor as labor. But do all types of labor actually add value? This question has spawned debate about productive and unproductive labor. It is widely agreed that productive labor has at least two attributes. In any mode of production, productive labor produces use values. Under capitalism productive labor satisfies an additional criterion: that laborer alone is productive who produces surplus value for the capitalist and who thus works for the self-expansion of capital (Marx 1967: Chap. 16). But beyond this statement there is wide dispute.

One aspect of disagreement concerns "use value," or useful effect of labor. Baran (1957: 32) defines productive labor as creating goods and services that would be required in a rationally ordered society; on the other hand, unproductive labor "consists of all labor resulting in the output of goods and services the demand for which is attributable to the specific conditions and relationships of the capitalist system, and which would be absent in a rationally ordered society." Thus unproductive labor may be necessary for the existence of capitalism. Hunt (1979) approves of Baran's distinction, but O'Connor (1973) and Tarbuck (1984) do not.

Baran's argument is important. A moral case does need to be made against waste and irrationality in capitalism. Yet the argument cannot support a distinction between productive and unproductive labor in capitalism for it proposes an idealist criterion, a personal evaluation, rather than a real description. Baran's moral evaluation must derive from rather than generate a definition of productiveness. Since rationality is a theoretical criterion Baran implies that productiveness stems from a theoretical evaluation of society; really though, productiveness is an objective characteristic of a person's labor. In any case we cannot know what a rational society would need: One car per household? What kinds of housing? Which of the commodities of possessive individualism?

One of the clearest disagreements about productive labor concerns the definition of commodities. Some such as Poulantzas (1975) and Tarbuck (1984) regard commodities as material depositories of utility. Tarbuck, for example, quotes Marx's (1967) statement that "a commodity is, in the first place an object outside use." Others such as Carchedi (1975), Meiksins (1981), and Wright (1979) take a much broader view of commodities. O'-Connor (1973) considers transport, storage, and packaging activities within the sphere of circulation to be productive; Meiksins (1981) quotes Marx's example of the "teaching factory" to argue that service labor can be productive. Hunt (1979) raises a more difficult issue. Consider the production of a film clip to advertise a product on television. Advertising is widely regarded as unproductive. Yet is not the film a use value and cannot the people who make the film be forced to produce surplus value? So is the production of advertising material regarded as unproductive because of Baran's irrationality criterion? Or is filmmaking productive and only the showing of the film unproductive?

A third source of contention concerns luxuries. To Baran (1957) luxuries are by definition irrational, so the labor expended in making them is unproductive. Tarbuck (1984: 97) argues in a similar vein: from the point of view of total social capital, luxury production is merely a form of consumption of revenue and its product cannot be transformed into capital. Carchedi (1975) takes the opposite position: the cause of an object's utility is irrelevant, for so long as it is useful to someone it is a use value. (Although Baran's argument has been shown to be idealistic, the difference between Tarbuck and Carchedi is substantial.)

These three disagreements concern the nature of use values. To some, use values must be required in a rational society or must be material or must be purchased by workers. To others, the nature of the use value is unimportant so long as someone has a use for it. We rely on Section 4.1.2: a commodity is something that stores value—its material form and the source of its demand are irrelevant. By contrast the remaining arguments concern the type of labor that is productive.

In capitalism the work process has been so divided that few workers now make a use value themselves: most perform only one task of the many that are needed to produce a use value. So the notion of productive labor is commonly expanded to include those workers who collectively produce a use value and collectively produce surplus value (Gough 1972: 54). How large is this collective? After quoting Marx (1967: Vol. I, 156–157) to the effect that "included among these productive workers, of course, are those who contribute in one way or another to the production of the commodity, from the actual operative to the manager or engineer (as distinct from the capitalist)" Gough (1972: 55) continues: "This would suggest the inclusion nowadays of large numbers of scientists, technologists, technicians and engineers, plus substantial sections of management and white collar workers . . . ."

The concept of the collective worker has spawned a large literature on the class position of managers (Carchedi 1975; Poulantzas 1975; Wright 1979). Insofar as they coordinate and unify production, managers are necessary and so members of the production working class. Thus they produce surplus value. Yet the same managers also control and supervise direct workers and in this capacity act as agents of owners and capital; to use Carchedi's phrase, they are performing the global function of capital. Again Baran's (1957) concern about the labor necessary in a rationally ordered society seems to have surfaced. In large measure the two roles played by managers correspond to labor that is necessary in a rational society (to coordinate production) and labor that is needed only because of the irrational form of capitalist commodity production (to control and supervise labor). This argument in favor of including some managers, engineers, technologists, and scientists among the collectively productive (along with direct workers) must be rejected, for it evaluates jobs idealistically rather than really defining them. The question is whether managers, engineers, and scientists are part of the collective, productive labor. Do they collectively produce use values and create surplus value? Or are they simply an element of the infrastructure that is necessary to create surplus value?

Another disagreement concerns exploited workers. Narrowly defined, exploited workers produce surplus value for their capitalist employers. O'Connor (1973) refers to another group of workers, the oppressed, who contribute surplus labor (work more hours than they are paid for) but whose surplus labor is not in the form of value. There is disagreement about the significance of the difference between being exploited and being oppressed. Gough (1972) and Meiksins (1981) are skeptical. Gough claims that the distinction between productive and unproductive labor rests on an ambiguity: the necessity of the use value is ignored, while the necessity of the labor used to produce it is emphasized. In particular the growth of state expenditures, of the number of commercial and service workers, and of "unnecessary" consumer goods all put a strain on this tenuous distinction (Gough 1972: 61–62). Meiksins (1981: 39) argues that whether a laborer is exploited or oppressed makes little difference, for the one can be doing precisely the same job as the other.

A persistent current in the debate about productive labor concerns the relationship between productiveness and necessity. Baran (1957) raised the issue in a form that has been employed in arguments about the productiveness of the sphere of circulation and about the size of the collective that produces surplus value. But the concept of necessary labor has been used in a different sense. Hunt (1979) in particular argues that whether labor is necessary for the maintenance of the capitalist mode of production is more important than whether it produces surplus value. He observes, first, that advertisers may be more useful than producers of luxury goods; secondly, government workers who reproduce the existing system of social relations may be more important in creating and realizing profits than are some direct production workers; thirdly, those who labor to produce guns represent just as much a drain on social resources as do those who control and supervise. In the same spirit one might ask why reproductive labor in the home is unproductive. These arguments, like those of Gough, really claim that the definition of productive labor fails an empirical test, for it does not explain why some important jobs exist and grow in capitalism. Two questions follow: What is the explanatory power of the tendencies that can be deduced from the definition of productive labor? And if Hunt and Gough are correct, what definition (possibly in addition to productive labor) is needed to explain these new phenomena? We need to draw on the analysis of capitalist production in Section 4.1.2.

Capital is self-expanding value. Capitalist production therefore has the form

$$M \to \begin{bmatrix} C \\ L \end{bmatrix} \to C_1 \to M_1.$$

Call the surplus the difference between the value stored in M_1 and the value stored in M:

$$S = V_{M_1} - V_M.$$

The value of C_1, V_{M_1}, is the value of the commodity input (V_C) plus the labor time used up (L). The value of input is V_C plus the value of labor power V_L. Therefore,

$$V_{M_1} = V_C + L,$$

$$V_M \leq V_C + V_L,$$

and

$$S = L - V_L.$$

That is, value is expanded if and only if the amount of labor time exceeds the value of labor power. Since capital is self expanding value the basis for capital is labor for which the time worked exceeds the value of labor power. Such labor is productive.

Productive labor, then, is labor that creates surplus: the quantity of labor power sold (the time worked) exceeds its value—that is, exceeds the value of the labor time required to produce it. This definition, however, excludes the cost of reproducing capitalist social relations. Other characteristics of productive labor follow. Productive labor works in *capitalist commodity production:* "capitalist," for production uses commodity labor power in the self-expansion of value; "commodity," since the use values are objectively valued on the market; and "production," in the sense that the use values are created. The definition is one of a series of linked definitions that describe some operations of capitalist society: it cannot be altered without affecting the other definitions—indeed, without altering the entire concept of capitalist society. In this respect the definition of productive labor is an integral ingredient of a vision of society: it is evaluated empirically largely by evaluating the theory as a whole.

Production, we have said, is the process of making use values, of performing effects that have utility for some people. Two questions remain. First, is it possible to create value without producing use values? Nonuse values can be created, but they cannot store objective value since they cannot be marketed: no one wants them. So producing nonuse values cannot create value. The consumption of a use value outside production (including the production of labor power) leaves nothing to be marketed and so cannot create value. And finally the exchange of use values cannot create value either, for mere transfer of ownership cannot of itself affect the objective market valuation of a use value. Thus creating value inherently depends on producing use values, though use values can be produced without creating value. Secondly, what are the activities that constitute production? Production has been defined, but the set of activities that actually produces use values has yet to be delimited empirically.

We repeat: productive labor is labor that produces surplus value. This definition has now to be applied to concrete and changing reality to distinguish empirically the categories of labor that are productive from those that are not. The theory of production (Section 4.1.2) suggests tests—labor is productive if all the following criteria are met:

1. It creates use values (we exclude labor that makes transactions or facilitates production).
2. The use values are in the commodity form (we exclude much household and government labor).
3. The labor power employed has the commodity form (we exclude all household labor and independent commodity producers).
4. The labor is exploited (we exclude noncapitalist production and non-exploited workers).

The tests of the productiveness of labor concern its social function not its concrete content. One's labor in baking a pie has the same concrete content as the labor of a baker in town. Yet the function of the two labors is different: one's own labor is directed at producing a use value; the baker's labor is intended to produce surplus value for the baking company, and the manufacture of a pie is only a means to that end.

It is now an empirical matter to determine whether a given act constitutes productive labor. Although the principles of the definition can be laid out theoretically, there remains the empirical issue of judging the productiveness of particular concrete tasks. In practice this task has proved difficult because much unproductive labor takes place in the same circumstances as productive labor. For example, the form of operation of a real estate corporation is similar to that of a clothing factory (both own plant, purchase raw materials, and hire wage labor).

An interesting feature emerges when the concrete character of productive labor is tabulated. The types of labor identified by this definition are correlated with the types identified by some of the other definitions. Baran's (1956) definition of unproductive labor as the labor needed only because capitalism is irrational and O'Connor's (1973) notion of the productiveness of necessary service labor both find echoes in the lists of concrete labor included in our definition. This does not mean that their definitions are correct—only that they are correlated with our definition. Similarly Marx seems to have maintained two definitions of productive labor (Hunt 1979): one that essentially corresponds to our definition, and one that identifies necessary labor. However, the correlation is not perfect: we exclude facilitating labor, unlike Carchedi (1975) and Wright (1979).

4.1.8 Conclusion

We do not deny that value plays a qualitative role in the theory of capital but argue that it also has a quantitative function. It is possible now to deduce how value must be measured to be consistent with the theory of capital.

Capital is self-expanding value. Therefore value must in principle be measurable; otherwise it is not possible to discuss its expansion. So the value of outputs from production must be compared with the value of inputs. But in noncapitalist production (that does not produce commodities by commodity labor power) not all inputs can be valued. Therefore value is a category restricted to capitalist production: whereas it is possible to measure the concrete labor content of anything produced by any mode of production, the value of a thing can only be measured if it was produced for sale by commodity labor power.

Value is then a standard of commodities. It is an objective standard, the objectivity being enforced by the market. It is the only possible universal standard (across all capitalist forms of production) that permits the prices of different commodities or commodities produced in different places to be compared. We can speak of the price of cars as $3 per unit of value and the price of microcomputers as $4.50 per unit of value, rather than $8795 per ton and $435,768 per ton, respectively. How do prices and values compare?

To be measurable, value must be measured as the quantity of labor power invested in an article under socially normal (average) conditions of production by labor of average skill and intensity. The value created by 1 hour of labor power of a person of average skill must be the same as that of any other person of average skill no matter what the concrete form of their labor. This is not a matter of dogma but of necessity if the measure of value is to be logically independent of price. Skilled laborers produce more value per hour than do unskilled laborers because they produce more commodities per hour.

This definition of the measure of value is dictated by the definitions of capital and capitalist production and by the requirement of objective measurability. We now must make the definition more precise, demonstrate that the definition is consistent with other requirements (such as positivity), and indicate how to measure value in practice.

4.2 QUANTITATIVE REPRESENTATION OF VALUE

The magnitude of value of a commodity, we have claimed, equals the quantity of labor power socially necessary to produce it. The labor power is supplied by productive labor of average skill employed under conditions of normal intensity. The labor embodied in commodities used up in production is included as well as that directly employed in production.

Consider then the capitalist production of commodities. Let $\mathbf{A}$ be a $n \times n$ matrix of input–output coefficients such that a_{ij} denotes the quantity of commodity i required to produce 1 unit of commodity j. Let $\mathbf{l}$ be a $n \times 1$ vector of direct labor coefficients, such that l_i denotes the quantity of productive labor power socially necessary to produce 1 unit of commodity i. And let $\boldsymbol{\lambda}$ be a $n \times 1$ vector of commodity values, such that λ_i denotes the value of commodity i. So, for each commodity i,

$$\lambda_i = a_{1i}\lambda_1 + a_{2i}\lambda_2 + \cdots + a_{ni}\lambda_n + l_i,$$

or, more compactly,

$$\lambda' = \lambda' A + l'. \tag{4.1}$$

Equation (4.1) is Morishima's (1973) definition of the magnitude of the value of commodities.

Equation (4.1) is imprecise. What exactly is the meaning of average skill, of normal intensity, or of social necessity? Verbal definitions of these terms have been offered in Section 4.1, but the numbers in equation (4.1) must be specified in formal mathematical terms. The equation also skates over commodities and industries: How are they defined? And what is the relation between them?

The equation suffers another defect. Morishima states that equation (4.1) correctly measures values only if—

1. Each industry uses one and only one technique of production: there is no choice of technique so each commodity is produced by only one industry.
2. Each industry produces one and only one commodity: without joint production, industries correspond one-to-one with commodities.
3. There are no primary factors of production except homogeneous, unskilled labor.
4. There are no fixed capital commodities: all inputs are entirely used up in one production period.
5. All commodities have the same period of production (a year say).
6. Production processes are all point input–point output: inputs are all bought on one day and outputs are all realized on one day, a year later.

Abraham-Frois and Berribi (1979) claim also that equation (4.1) is correct only if—

7. There are constant returns to scale.

These assumptions are all wrong: they bear no correspondence to the real world. If equation (4.1) is valid only when the assumptions hold, then the quantitative theory of value must be reformulated.

Otherwise measurements will be inaccurate. For example, commodities have different periods of production and processes are not point input–point output. Therefore actual input–output tables (which reflect these facts) do not conform to assumptions 5 and 6, above, and cannot be used in equation (4.1) to calculate values. Some measures of the rate of profit (Wolff 1979; Sharpe 1982) assume that conditions 5 and 6 are satisfied by the data; so they are inaccurate. Accurate measurement demands an exact theory of the measure of value.

Theoretical troubles are also raised by the conditions. One neo-Ricardian critique of the theory of value rests on Steedman's (1977) claim that if there is fixed capital, choice of technique, or joint production, values need not be positive: then positive inputs of labor power might produce negative values, contrary to the spirit of the definition of value in Section 4.1. The claim has been widely accepted (for example, by Morishima 1973; Abraham-Frois and Berribi 1979; Krause 1982; and Harvey 1982).

A general theory of the measure of value must relax these assumptions, show that they are unimportant, or explain that equation (4.1) does not need them. It must also make precise the definitions that underlie equation (4.1). These are the tasks of this section. We begin by defining social necessity, average intensity, and normal skill statistically. Next we examine assumptions 1–7 and reveal how to measure values even if they are not met: the criticisms of Steedman are misplaced. Measures of performance are then reviewed and costs of production are distinguished from capital advanced so that values and profit rates can be measured accurately. The final subsection relates values and prices.

4.2.1 Social Necessity

Consider a standard period. This period is sufficiently short that conditions within the period are reasonably assumed to be constant and yet sufficiently long that a large sample of events occurs. In deference to the way in which many data are collected this period is called a year.

During the period a set of capitalist commodity-producing plants operate. A plant is the smallest operating and accounting unit of firms. The number of plants is finite and constant throughout this period. The plants are numbered $1, 2, \ldots, M$, and the mth plant is denoted by P_m.

Workers sell labor power to plants. The unit of labor power is an hour. It is possible to list every unit of productive (commodity) labor power sold during the period; suppose that there are n_l such units. The plant to which each unit is sold is identified; if the ith unit of labor power is sold to plant P_m, we write $l_i \rightarrow P_m$. The units of labor power are of different skills and intensities and have different concrete forms. So the different units of labor power produce different quantities of value. We denote by v_i the value produced by the ith unit of labor power.

Thus a unit of socially necessary labor power of average skill and intensity is a unit l_j for which

$$v_j = \frac{\sum_{i=1}^{n_l} v_i}{n_l} = 1.$$

A unit of socially necessary labor power of average skill and intensity is a unit that produces the average quantity of value; to fix standards this average quantity is set to 1.

It follows that the total value produced by workers during the standard period is

$$\sum_{i=1}^{n_l} v_i = n_l.$$

The total value produced equals the total quantity of labor power sold in the period. It follows that the average quantity of value produced per unit of labor power is 1:

$$E(V) = 1.$$

During the period each plant uses up certain quantities of commodities to produce other commodities. Plant P_m uses quantities $(b_{1m}, b_{2m}, \ldots, b_{nm})$ of commodities $1, 2, \ldots, n$. These are quantities used, not quantities bought: the difference is that between opening and closing stocks. In the same period the plant produces quantities $(b^*_{m1}, b^*_{m2}, \ldots, b^*_{mn})$ of the commodities. The quantities are all measured in physical units, such as tonnes (metric tons). In keeping with the spirit of Morishima's (1973) treatment it is temporarily assumed that there is no fixed capital.

Suppose, following Morishima, that during a standard period each plant produces only one kind of commodity: only one of the numbers $b^*_{m1}, b^*_{m2}, \ldots,$ b^*_{mn} is greater than zero. So plants can be classified according to the commodity they produce: if plant P_m produces commodity C_n, we write $P_m \to C_n$, and we say that plant P_m belongs to industry n. For each commodity C_k, we compute the total quantity produced by all the plants during the standard period: it is

$$a_k = \sum_{P_m \to C_k} b^*_{mk}.$$

Furthermore the total quantity of input commodities used by the plants that produce each commodity C_k during the period is

$$(a^*_{1k}, a^*_{2k}, \ldots, a^*_{nk}) = \sum_{P_m \to C_k} (b_{1m}, b_{2m}, \ldots, b_{nm}).$$

Thus, for each commodity C_k, the input–output coefficients of equation (4.1) are defined as

$$(a_{1k}, a_{2k}, \ldots, a_{nk}) = (a^*_{1k}, a^*_{2k}, \ldots, a^*_{nk})/a_k.$$

The total quantity of value produced and stored in the output of commodity C_k during the standard period is

$$\sum_{P_m \to C_k} \sum_{l_i \to P_m} v_i.$$

This value is produced by all the units of labor power that are sold to each plant producing commodity C_k.

Assume that the units of labor power supplied to industry k constitute a random sample of all existing units of labor power. It follows that the expected value produced by the labor power supplied to industry k is

$$E_k(V) = 1,$$

the same as the average value contributed by each unit of labor power in the economy as a whole and the same as the value created by a socially necessary unit of labor power of average intensity and skill. Therefore the expected quantity of value created in industry k equals the quantity of labor power supplied: $a_k l_k$. Thus the expected number of hours of socially necessary labor power of average intensity and skill required to produce a unit of commodity k is l_k.

It is useful to know how accurate this expectation is. The quantities of value created by the units of labor power are $v_1, v_2, \ldots, v_n$, instances of the random variable V. The mean of this random variable is 1. Suppose that it has standard deviation s. The expected value created by the labor power contributed to industry k is

$$E_k(V) = 1$$

provided that the industry randomly samples labor power. Suppose that the industry is "large"; then the standard deviation of that mean is

$$s_k(V) = s/\sqrt{a_k l_k}.$$

The implications of this result are important. Suppose that $s = 0.2$. Then virtually all units of labor power create value in the range $(0, 2)$. If $a_k l_k = 1,000,000$ (the industry buys 1 million units of labor power during the standard period), then

$$s_k(V) = 0.2/1000 = 0.0002.$$

The mean value created by virtually all samples of 1 million units of labor power therefore lies in the range $(0.999, 1.001)$. Therefore, the error in assuming that the actual value created per unit of labor power equals the expected value created is virtually always less than 0.1%. For all practical purposes the error made by assuming that the value created in an industry equals the number of units of labor power employed by that industry is negligible.

This section has made explicit the basis for measuring the value of commodities. An economy is a set of plants operating during a standard period. The commodities used by the plants (including labor power) and their outputs are recorded. The labor power is heterogeneous. A unit of socially necessary labor power of average intensity and skill is defined as one that produces value equal to 1 unit. Three assumptions are made: first, that economic conditions remain constant within the standard period; secondly, that each plant produces only one commodity; and, thirdly, that each industry buys a random sample of the units of labor power offered for sale. Then the *expected* value of the commodities produced during the standard period is

$$\lambda' = \lambda'A + l' \qquad\qquad (4.2)$$

where l denotes the number of hours of productive labor power purchased by industries. If industries are large, there is virtually no error in assuming that the actual value of commodities equals their expected value. This description of commodity values is more precise than that of Morishima. The price of this care is that λ no longer denotes the actual value of commodities but only their expected value.

4.2.2 The Assumptions

Now contemplate more carefully the assumptions made by Morishima (1973) and Abraham-Frois and Berribi (1979). We seek a model of a capitalist commodity-producing economy in which commodities can be valued correctly: there is little point in a model of values that is as severely limited as is equation (4.1) by conditions 1 through 7. We begin in Section 4.2.2.1 by examining the minor assumptions (3, 5, 6, and 7) and then discuss choice of technique (Section 4.2.2.2), joint production (Section 4.2.2.3), and fixed capital (Section 4.2.2.4). Section 4.2.2.5 shows that even when the conditions are not met, values can be measured and satisfy criteria of consistency.

4.2.2.1 Preliminary Assumptions

Conditions 3, 5, 6, and 7 are straightforward and the modifications they impose are minor.

Condition 3 demands that the only primary factor of production is homogeneous, unskilled labor, or (more correctly) homogeneous, unskilled labor is the only value-creating factor. The statement has two parts. First, labor is the only value-creating factor: it is impossible to dispense with this claim. Secondly, all labor power is of the same quality, homogeneous and unskilled. Section 4.2.1 has shown how to generalize this assumption: labor power may be heterogeneous, of varying skill and intensity, and of different concrete forms, but so long as industries sample from labor powers randomly equation (4.2) measures the expected values of commodities. Condition 3 can thus be replaced by the assumption that industries sample randomly from the labor powers sold during the standard period.

Condition 5 requires all commodities to have the same period of production. This condition has two parts. On the one hand, differences in the period of production affect the time for which capital has to be advanced before returning a profit: $1000 profit after 6 months is a different rate of return from $1000 profit after 1 year. So differences in the length of the period of production must be recognized carefully when the performance of industries is measured (see Section 4.2.3). On the other hand, do variations in the period of production affect the expected values of commodities that were defined in equation (4.2)?

Consider first industries whose period of production is unrelated to the timing of the standard period. If the standard period is a year, these industries are not affected by the passage of the seasons. Suppose that industry k is such an industry and that its period of production is t_k days. Plants $P_1, P_2, \ldots, P_n$ belong to this industry. Since the period of production is unrelated to the standard period, suppose that plant P_i's first whole period of production in a year begins on the $(d_i + 1)$th day of the standard period; D is a random variable. The first d_i days of the year are devoted to finishing production that began the year before with $0 \le d_i < t_k$. For simplicity assume that each plant uses the same technology (A) and produces the same quantity (1 unit) in each period. All inputs are bought on the first day of the production process, and all outputs are sold on the last day. How much is produced and what inputs are used?

Denote by s_k the integer part of $[365/t_k]$; every plant begins and ends at least s_k production periods in a year. If $t_k > 365$, then $s_k = 0$. Denote $r_k = [365/t_k] - s_k$; r_k is the remainder left over after dividing t_k into 365. Of all the possible arrangements of production periods within a year, a proportion $p_k = r_k/t_k$ have $1 + s_k$ starts or ends in a year while $1 - p_k$ have s_k starts or ends in a year. Since production periods are arranged randomly within the year, the expected number of production starts and ends within a year is

$$p_k = (1 + s_k) + (1 - p_k) s_k = 365/t_k.$$

It follows that the expected quantity produced is $365/t_k$ and that the expected quantity of inputs used up is

$$[365/t_k] (a_{1k}, a_{2k}, \ldots, a_{nk}).$$

No matter what the length of the production period the coefficient matrix **A** measures the expected quantity of inputs used to produce 1 unit of each commodity.

The matter is more complex if the production periods within an industry depend on the standard period. In practice, if the standard period is a year, seasonal industries exhibit such dependence: agriculture, fishing, forestry, and building are all seasonal. The high demand for consumer goods at Christmas also imposes seasonality on many production processes. Such dependence invalidates the statistics of the previous paragraph. Suppose, for example, that an industry produces commodities sold only in December. The production period lasts 365 days and the standard period starts on 1 February. Then in one standard period the following transactions are recorded: sales are made in December, and in January purchases are made for the next production period. The quantity of inputs is determined by the demand for the next standard period, whereas sales are produced using inputs purchased in the previous standard period. The measured ratio of inputs to output (**A**) confounds next period's inputs with this period's output and thus does not reflect the technology used to produce this period's output.

There is then a relation between the accuracy of equation (4.2) and the length of periods of production. However, (4.2) measures the expected value of commodities provided that each industry's production periods begin at times that are unrelated to the beginning of the standard period. If industries are "large," the expected value determined by equation (4.2) is virtually certain to be close to the actual value.

Condition 6 requires that production processes be point input–point output: purchases are all made on day 1 of the production period, and sales are all realized t_k days later. The spread of purchases over the production period implies that some capital does not have to be invested immediately that the production period begins, and this certainly affects measures of performance. However, equation (4.2) simply relates total inputs to total output and remains valid whenever purchases or sales are made within the production period.

Equally condition 7 (constant returns to scale) is not actually required. Equation (4.2) provides an *ex post* expected valuation of commodities by describing what the actual state of affairs was over a standard period. It does not prescribe what will happen in any other standard period; much less does it imply the restrictive assumption that doubling inputs doubles outputs. Equation (4.2) presumes that the actual level of inputs and output is represented by a point in $n \times n$ Euclidean space but not that there is any particular functional relationship between inputs and output. Equation (4.2) describes a point not a production function.

So these conditions are relatively minor. Still most debate has focused on conditions 1, 2, and 4: there are no fixed capital goods, no joint products, and no choices of technique. These conditions are related because von Neumann's (1945) method of accounting treats fixed capital goods as joint products and regards processes that use capital goods of different ages as different techniques (Steedman 1977; Morishima and Catephores 1978). A process that uses fixed capital good Y to produce output Z is said to produce a joint product (Z and one-year-old Y), and the process is regarded as different from that which produces Z and two-year-old Y. This method of accounting appears to destroy some crucial aspects of value theory: both Steedman (1977) and Morishima (1973) claim that the values of commodities may be negative even if processes are productive and that a positive rate of exploitation is no longer necessary and sufficient for a positive rate of profit (see also Fine and Harris 1979). Therefore we must examine these conditions.

4.2.2.2 Choice of Technique

Suppose that there are two ways of producing a commodity. The calculated value of the commodity may depend on the way in which it is produced. In practice each commodity is produced by a host of techniques, all more or less different, for lack of information or capital prevents capitalists from adopting the most profitable technique available. This fact is well known and is easily solved. The magnitude of the expected value of a commodity produced by the plants in an industry is defined as the expected labor time required in production—that is, the average labor time actually needed. This is how the matrix A and the vector l are computed: as an average over all producers weighted by their output levels.

Thus the input vector for plant P_m, $(b_{1m}, b_{2m}, \ldots, b_{nm})$, is an instance of a random variable. The input–output coefficients for the plants of industry k that produce commodity C_k are the average of these input vectors:

$$(a_{1k}, a_{2k}, \ldots, a_{nk}) = \sum_{P_m \to C_k} \frac{\sum_{P_m \to C_k} (b_{1m}, b_{2m}, \ldots, b_{nm})}{b^*_{mk}},$$

where b^*_{mk} is the output of commodity C_k from plant P_m. A similar definition holds for l.

Himmelweit and Mohun (1981: 257–258) have objected to this solution to the problem of choice of technique on two grounds. First, it requires large amounts of data not only about methods of production but also about the extent of their use. The solution does indeed require lots of data, yet it is precisely the way in which input–output tables are actually constructed. Secondly, the expected values computed according to this definition are descriptive statistics stripped of analytical content. We argue that expected values computed from this formula reflect the actual performance of the economy and it is precisely this reality that makes them useful in analyzing what has happened. Equation (4.2) describes the characteristics of industries; it cannot be used to analyze the production decisions of individual plants.

4.2.2.3 Joint Production

There exist many instances of joint production. Wool and mutton are technically joint (the one cannot be produced without the other), whereas washing machines and dryers are contingently joint (they are typically produced together but not because of natural necessity). The existence of joint production raises two issues: first, the possibility that values may be negative; secondly, the valuation of the individual products that are produced jointly.

Steedman (1975) uses an example to demonstrate that values may be negative when products are joint. Suppose that there are two processes. The first uses 1 hour of labor power and 5 tons of commodity one to produce 6 tons of commodity one and 1 ton of commodity two. The second uses 1 hour of labor power and 10 tons of commodity two to produce 3 tons of commodity one and 12 tons of commodity two. The values of commodities are computed from

$$[\lambda_1 \, \lambda_2] \begin{bmatrix} 6 & 3 \\ 1 & 12 \end{bmatrix} = [\lambda_1 \, \lambda_2] \begin{bmatrix} 5 & 0 \\ 0 & 10 \end{bmatrix} + [1 \ 1]. \tag{4.3}$$

As Steedman shows $\lambda_1 = -1$, $\lambda_2 = 2$. The system generates negative values and, for some wage levels, negative rates of surplus value but positive rates of profit. These are undesirable outcomes: if labor power produces a commodity and if the standard of value of commodities is the labor power used to produce them, it is unreasonable that values can be negative; and if negative rates of surplus value can coexist with positive rates of profit, there is doubt about the proposition that profit originates in exploitation (the existence of which implies a positive rate of surplus value).

However, this example should be analyzed more thoroughly before Steedman's (and Morishima and Catephores' 1978: 30–38) conclusions are accepted. Equation (4.3) can be written in terms of net output as

$$[\lambda_1 \, \lambda_2] \begin{bmatrix} 1 & 3 \\ 1 & 2 \end{bmatrix} = [1 \ 1],$$

and in turn this equation can be generalized as

$$[\lambda_1 \, \lambda_2] \begin{bmatrix} b_{11} & b_{12} \\ b_{21} & b_{22} \end{bmatrix} = [1 \ 1]. \tag{4.4}$$

In equation (4.4), b_{11} and b_{21} denote the net output of a unit of labor power applied to process one while b_{12} and b_{22} denote the net output of a unit of labor power applied to process two.

Equation (4.4) has a nontrivial solution if and only if

$$b_{11}b_{22} - b_{12}b_{21} \neq 0.$$

Suppose that this condition holds. Then the solution is

$$[\lambda_1 \, \lambda_2] = \frac{1}{b_{11}b_{22} - b_{12}b_{21}} [1 \ 1] \begin{bmatrix} b_{22} & -b_{12} \\ -b_{21} & b_{11} \end{bmatrix}.$$

Clearly λ_1 and λ_2 are both positive if and only if

$$\lambda_1 = \frac{b_{22} - b_{21}}{b_{11}b_{22} - b_{12}b_{21}} > 0 \quad \text{and} \quad \lambda_2 = \frac{b_{11} - b_{12}}{b_{11}b_{22} - b_{12}b_{21}} > 0.$$

It follows that both λ_1 and λ_2 are positive if and only if either

$$b_{22} > b_{21} \quad \text{and} \quad b_{11} > b_{12} \quad \text{or} \quad b_{22} < b_{21} \quad \text{and} \quad b_{11} < b_{12}. \quad (4.5)$$

The meaning of condition (4.5) is clear when the productiveness of the two processes is compared. A process is technically more productive than another if it produces more net output of both commodities than the other. If a process is technically less productive than another, it cannot be as profitable to operate that process no matter what the relative prices of commodities. Neither process is technically more productive than the other if

$$b_{11} > b_{12} b_{21} < b_{22} \quad \text{or} \quad b_{11} < b_{12} b_{21} > b_{22}.$$

To see this, consider equation (4.4). If both $b_{11} > b_{12}$ and $b_{21} > b_{22}$, then process one produces more of both commodities than does process two. Equally, if both $b_{11} < b_{12}$ and $b_{21} < b_{22}$, then process one produces less of both commodities than does process two. But these are precisely conditions (4.5). That is to say, we have proved the following fact: if neither process is technically more productive than the other, both values are positive; if one process is technically more productive than the other, one value is negative.

The claim that joint production may cause values to be negative is thus not serious. It is not joint production that causes values to be negative but the fact that one process is technically less productive than another. Even if production is joint, values will not be negative provided that neither process is technically more productive than the other. A negative value means that more net output of both commodities can be obtained by using the more efficient process alone rather than in combination with the less efficient process. In practice capitalists may employ such inefficient techniques, at least temporarily: new techniques may not have been adopted by all producers yet, capacity constraints may exist, or accidents may disrupt production. But that issue concerns choice of technique not joint production.

Still we must generalize the description of an economic system to recognize that plants may produce several commodities. In Section 4.1 a plant was said to belong to industry k if it produced commodity C_k. From the set of commodities, $C_1, C_2, \ldots, C_n$, construct a set of composite commodities, $c_1, c_2, \ldots, c_N$, as the set of commodities taken one at a time, the set of commodities taken two at a time, the set of commodities taken three at a time, and so forth; from this set are deleted those composite commodities that are not in fact produced. An industry k consists of the plants that produce the same composite commodity c_k. The plants in industry k all produce the same commodities but not necessarily in the same relative quantities. These definitions accord with a comment of Fine and Harris (1979).

Von Neumann's (1945) method of representing commodity accounts identifies the simple commodities purchased and produced by each industry. Let $\mathbf{B}_{n \times N}$ denote the commodities produced by each industry, such that b_{ij}

represents the quantity of simple commodity i produced by industry j; and let $A_{n \times N}$ denote the commodities purchased by each industry; $\lambda_{n \times 1}$ is a vector of commodity values, and $l_{N \times 1}$ is a vector of labor inputs into each industry. The value equation is

$$\lambda'B = \lambda'A + l'. \tag{4.6}$$

Unfortunately (4.6) consists of N equations in n unknowns: N may be larger than n (commodities are produced in lots of different combinations) or less than n (there are fewer commodities than industries). So commodity values cannot be uniquely or consistently identified from this equation, a mathematical effect of the fact that jointly produced commodities cannot be separately valued. This is a real limitation upon the valuation of commodities.

Therefore production processes must be accounted for on the basis of transactions between industries, which are also transactions between composite commodities. Suppose that there exists a weight $W_{n \times N}$ such that $w_{ij} \geq 0$ denotes the relative contribution of commodity i to the output of industry j. The total output of industry i is

$$a_j = \sum_{i=1}^{n} a_{ij} w_{ij}.$$

This weighting function, together with the understanding that an industry consists of all plants that produce the same composite commodity, allows us to continue to use equation (4.2) to calculate expected values.

Two weighting functions are commonly used. In some industries $w_{ij} = 1$ for all i. For example, in the steel industry the output of plants is often measured as the total tonnage of steel products, implicitly equating a ton of slab and a ton of tubes. More commonly the different commodities produced by an industry are aggregated by price. The unit of output of (say) agriculture is a dollar's worth of agricultural output. This implies not that prices determine the values produced by industries but rather that prices provide a common basis for measuring the different commodities produced by industries and so offer a means of computing the unit values of industries' output.

4.2.2.4 Fixed Capital

Fixed capital is capital that transfers only part of its value to output in a production period. It is capital employed in production rather than used up in production. Therefore fixed capital transfers part of its value to the output commodity without becoming a physical part of that commodity. By contrast circulating constant capital physically becomes a part of the commodity produced.

In von Neumann accounting fixed capital is treated as a special case of joint production. A partly used machine is regarded as one of the outputs of the production process. If machines of different vintages are distinct products and the processes using them are separate processes, capital commodities may have negative values—though if the system is productive, both circulating capital and new fixed capital are positively valued. Examples are provided by Morishima (1973) and Steedman (1977).

Morishima (1973: 182–183) discusses the following example. Crops and machines are produced; machines last two production periods; crops use crops, labor power, and machines as inputs; machines are made from crops and labor power. There are three processes: one produces crops (and old machines) using new machines, one produces crops using old machines, and the third produces machines. The von Neumann equations are

$$[\lambda_1\ \lambda_2\ \lambda_3] \begin{bmatrix} 1 & 1 & 0 \\ 0 & 0 & 1 \\ 0.5 & 0 & 1 \end{bmatrix} = [\lambda_1\ \lambda_2\ \lambda_3] \begin{bmatrix} 0.7 & 0.5 & 0 \\ 0.9 & 0 & 0.5 \\ 0.2 & 0 & 0 \end{bmatrix} + [1\ 1\ 0.5],$$

where λ_1, λ_2, and λ_3 denote the values of crops, new machines, and old machines, respectively. The solution is

$$\lambda_1 = 7.5; \qquad \lambda_2 = 2.0; \qquad \lambda_3 = -0.5.$$

This example violates several principles of accounting. First, it treats old machines as commodities on a par with crops or new machines. In fact old machines are not "produced" for sale at all and therefore are not commodities. Secondly, the example makes the relative value of new and old machines depend on their relative productivity (that is on their value in use) not on the way in which they are produced: actually value depends on the characteristics of production not on the usefulness of the commodity. Thirdly, Morishima and von Neumann have measured the value of fixed capital from the methods that were used to make it. Actually value is measured from the production methods that are now used to produce fixed capital: every time a technical change occurs in the capital goods sector the value of old fixed capital falls as well as the value of new fixed capital. (This counters the tendency for the rate of profit to fall.)

Processes one and two are merely different techniques used in the same industry. They must therefore be aggregated in order to determine socially necessary labor times. If processes one and two are employed in proportions α and $1 - \alpha$, respectively, Morishima's equations become

$$[\lambda_1\ \lambda_3] = [\lambda_1\ \lambda_3] \begin{bmatrix} (0.9 - 0.2\alpha) & 0.2 \\ 0.2(1 - \alpha) & 0 \end{bmatrix} + [1\ 0.5]$$

since old and new machines are valued equally. The equations have the solution

$$\lambda_1 = [1.25 - 0.25\alpha]/0.3\alpha$$
$$\lambda_3 = [0.25 + 0.1\alpha]/0.3\alpha.$$

(If $\alpha = 0.5$, then $\lambda_1 = 7.5$ and $\lambda_3 = 2.0$.) Provided that the economy is productive, this accounting generates positive values.

4.2.2.5 Measuring Values

It remains to assemble these ideas to generalize equation (4.2). The definitions provide a basis for a generalized theory of value magnitudes.

An industry k consists of the plants that produce composite commodity c_k; there are N industries. Industries are defined in terms of their output of commodities not in terms of their techniques of production. Old fixed capital is not an output commodity. The individual commodities that make up a single composite commodity are weighted in a fashion that provides a common basis for measuring each individual commodity. Industry k produces quantity a_k of the composite commodity c_k. The quantity a_k is measured in tons or bushels if c_k is a simple commodity or in units of dollars if it is a composite commodity.

For each composite commodity c_k (or industry k) the input–output coefficients are

$$(a_{1k}, a_{2k}, \ldots, a_{Nk}) = (a^*_{1k}, a^*_{2k}, \ldots, a^*_{Nk})/a_k,$$

where a^*_{jk} denotes the total quantity of composite commodity c_j used by plants in industry k in the standard period. The expected number of hours of socially necessary labor power of average intensity and skill needed to produce 1 unit of composite commodity c_k is l_k, the quantity of labor power supplied to the industry k divided by its output.

The nonnegative matrix $F^*_{N \times N}$ records the total fixed constant capital in place during the year; f^*_{jk} denotes the quantity of industry j's products used as fixed constant capital by industry k. Define $F_{N \times N}$ by

$$f_{jk} = f^*_{jk}/a_k.$$

Here F denotes the fixed constant capital per unit of output. Another matrix $T_{N \times N}$ records the service life of each fixed constant capital item in each industry, T being fixed by social practice in the same way as the other coefficients defined here; f_{jk}/t_{jk} is the quantity of fixed constant capital from industry j used up by industry k per year per unit of output.

The terms A, l, F, and T are real, socially necessary quantities. They reflect the actual performance of an economy in the period. This performance is not exogenous but determined by the state of technology, availability of capital and labor, and social relations between capital and labor. It is not claimed

that the same coefficient matrices would characterize the economy if output
levels were changed.

The expected unit value of each industry's output is

$$\lambda' = \lambda'(A + f_{jk}/t_{jk}) + 1'. \qquad (4.7)$$

Equation (4.7) generalizes equation (4.2). It assumes that economic conditions remain constant during the standard period, each industry buys a random sample of the units of labor power sold during the period, and production periods are not related to the standard period. The matrix

$$C = A + f_{jk}/t_{jk}$$

is not a matrix of capital inputs but a matrix of current inputs: circulating
constant capital plus fixed capital used up. If all periods of production equal
1 year and if all industries are point input–point output, current inputs equal
capital inputs. In general, however, $\lambda'C$ is a vector of constant current inputs,
the cost in values of production. Furthermore the contribution of fixed capital
to the value of output is measured at its current not its historic value and is
prorated over the service life of that fixed capital.

In equation (4.7) there is no choice of technique problem because A and
F record industry–industry transactions. Commodities may be jointly produced. Some output is employed as fixed capital. Industries do not all have
the same period of production, nor are all processes point input–point output.
Equation (4.7) thus generalizes equation (4.2).

By definition

$$A \geq 0; \qquad f_{jk}/t_{jk} \geq 0; \qquad 1 \geq 0.$$

Hence, $C \geq 0$. Equation (4.7) has the solution

$$\lambda' = 1'(I - C)^{-1}. \qquad (4.8)$$

Furthermore the solution satisfies $\lambda \geq 0$ provided that

$$(I - C)^{-1} \geq 0.$$

Such a solution exists if there exists a vector of outputs $x \geq 0$ such that

$$x'(I - C) \geq 0. \qquad (4.9)$$

But $x'(I - C) = x' - x'C$, where x is the vector of outputs and $x'C$ is the vector
of total nonlabor inputs. Hence $x'(I - C)$ is the net output of the economy and
condition (4.9) is simply the condition that the economy be productive.

Thus equation (4.7) is a general description of an economy subject only to the stated assumptions. The resulting solution (4.8) exists and is nonnegative provided that the economy is productive. This premise is not trivial, for it requires that each industry be productive each year. While industries need not be productive in the short run, the net output of each industry must be positive in the long run; otherwise the industry's products would gradually disappear. The debate about negative values and negative rates of surplus value has largely followed the twin red herrings of von Neumann accounting and examples based upon technically unproductive industries.

4.2.3 Measures of Performance

Morishima's assumptions 5 and 6 require that all commodities have the same period of production and that all processes are point input–point output. These assumptions do not affect the way in which the values of commodities are determined, but they are crucial in measuring the performance of an economy. In this section the assumptions are explained and appropriate measures of performance are described that relax them.

4.2.3.1 Variable Periods of Production

Consider an industry k in which the period of production is t_k days and which has $T_k = 365/t_k$ periods of production per year. The "period of production" coincides with Marx's (1967: Vol. II, 155) turnover time, comprising the period of production and the period of circulation: the turnover time of capital is the length of time between its first advance and its return as money after production and realization. For the entire production process the turnover time is the average of the turnover times of each capital [Marx (1967: Vol. II, 183–188) shows how to compute this average].

The firm begins with capital C, which is increased to C + c after t_k days. If there is no accumulation during the year, the C capital is reinvested and another C + c recouped. In one year C capital is advanced, T_kC cost of production is incurred and $T_k c$ surplus is created. So the capital advanced for production in 1 year does not equal the cost of production for that year. The cost of production is T_k times the capital advanced. Therefore the performance of an economy can be measured in two ways: the rate of profit on capital advanced ($T_k c/C$) or the rate of profit on costs of production ($T_k C/T_k c = c/C$). Only if the periods of production in each industry are the same are the two measures proportional. That this distinction is novel in value theory is surprising in the light of Marx's (1967: Vol. II, 293–308) clear understanding of the problem and its solution.

In practice many attempts to measure values, rates of profit, and rates of exploitation assume that the period of production of all industries equals 1 year (see Wolff 1979; Sharpe 1982; Webber and Foot 1984). Implicitly they measure the rate of profit on costs of production rather than on capital advanced. Corporations measure both rates of profit, and useful information can be obtained from the ratio of surplus to costs (the gross margin). Yet the more significant measure, both to individual capitals and to capital at large, is the profit on capital advanced, for this measures the rate at which existing capital is being increased: what was C at the beginning of the period has become $C + T_k c$ at the end.

4.2.3.2 Distributed Inputs

If the production process is point input–point output, all capital C is advanced at day 0 and all output is realized at day t_k. The capital C is tied up for t_k days at a total cost of Ct_k capital-days. Averaged over the t_k days of the production process, the average capital tied up is $Ct_k/t_k = C$ capital-days per day.

Now suppose that inputs are bought throughout the production process. Wages are paid regularly rather than in advance. Furthermore, if some output is sold at t_1 days, some at t_2 days, . . . , and the remainder at t_n days, the process can be divided into n separate processes and later aggregated in the same way as other different processes. Hence if inputs are bought throughout the production process, outputs can be regarded as realized at a date t_k days after production begins.

Let $c(s)$, $0 \geq s \geq t_k$, be the density of capital invested per unit of time at time s. Alternatively, if capital is invested at discrete daily intervals, $c(s)$ can be taken to be the capital invested on day s. Suppose that total capital advanced is C:

$$C = \int_0^{t_k} c(s)ds.$$

The total capital-days for which this capital is invested is

$$\int_0^{t_k} c(s)\,(t-s)ds$$

for a time s there remain $(t-s)$ days in the production process. Therefore the average amount of capital tied up is

$$C^* = \frac{1}{t}\int_0^{t_k} c(s)\,(t-s)ds$$

capital-days per day.

There are two ways by which to analyze this situation. Marx (1967: Vol. II, 257–266) recognized that capital is invested at different stages in the production process. Nevertheless he argued that the entire capital needed in the production process must be available at the beginning of that process. Hence the capital tied up is C. Since Marx's day, however, credit markets have developed widely: even if a capitalist has C capital on hand to begin the production period, the part of capital that is not needed immediately can be lent to a credit institution, which in turn lends it to another capitalist, who does use it immediately. So while C is the cost of production, C^* is the appropriate measure of the capital advanced in production.

The significance of this distinction is clear. If a plant must buy all its inputs at the beginning of the production process, all C of its costs of production are entirely tied up. However, if the purchase of some inputs can be postponed, the capital so released can be used to fund other production processes until needed. Thus the way in which labor is paid is significant to profit calculations. If the pay period can be lengthened, the capital that has to be advanced to pay for given variable costs of production is reduced. Equally, if some of the wage is deferred or paid infrequently as a bonus or in a "profit-sharing" scheme or even as superannuation, the capital cost of that wage is reduced. Postponing the purchase of inputs is equivalent to decreasing the capital needed in production and so to enlarging the capital available for other processes.

As an example, suppose that inputs are bought at a constant rate throughout the production process. If the total cost of production is C, then $c(s) = C/t_k$ per day. Therefore

$$C^* = \frac{1}{t} \int_0^{t_k} \frac{C}{t_k} (t - s)ds = \frac{C}{2}.$$

The capital advanced is only half the cost of production.

The general issue raised by distributed inputs is no different from that raised by variable periods of production. Capital advanced must be distinguished from cost of production. Hence, while the value calculations of equation (4.7) are unaffected by this generalization, measurements of the rate of profit do depend on the way in which inputs are purchased: insofar as inputs are bought over time, usual measures of the rate of profit underestimate actual rates.

4.2.3.3 Measuring Performance

Measures of the performance of a capitalist economy include the composition of capital, the rate of exploitation, the rate of surplus value, and the rate of profit. Each may be measured with respect to costs of production or capital advanced. These performance criteria are now defined.

Let $\mathbf{D}_{N \times 1}$ be a vector that denotes the consumption of each composite commodity by workers per hour of labor power; $\mathbf{D} \geq 0$. Here $\mathbf{D}$ is measured as the sum of each composite commodity consumed by workers and their dependents divided by the total number of hours of labor power sold during the standard period. The value of labor power is

$$\lambda_L = \lambda' D$$

$$= \sum_{k=1}^{N} \lambda_k D_k.$$

The value of labor power measures the value of the inputs that are socially necessary to reproduce the labor force.

Therefore the cost of production rate of exploitation is

$$e = \frac{1 - \lambda_L}{\lambda_L}.$$

Hence

$$1 = \lambda_L + e\lambda_L. \tag{4.10}$$

Now, equation (4.7) defines the values of commodities as

$$\lambda' = \lambda'C + l',$$

which in view of (4.10) may be written

$$\lambda' = \lambda'C + \lambda_L l' + e\lambda_L l'.$$

The three terms on the right-hand side of this equation are, respectively, constant capital input ($\lambda'C$), variable capital input ($\lambda_L l'$), and surplus value ($e\lambda_L l'$) for each industry, all measured in costs of production.

The standard performance measures are now readily derived. The value composition of capital in industry k is the ratio of constant to variable capital:

$$Q_k^* = \frac{\sum_{j=1}^{N} c_{jk}\lambda_j}{\lambda_L l_k.} \tag{4.11}$$

The asterisk designated that this measure is based on costs of production. The cost of production value rate of profit in industry k is the ratio of surplus value to costs of production:

$$\pi_k^* = \frac{e\lambda_L l_k}{\sum_{j=1}^{N} c_{jk}\lambda_j + \lambda_L l_k}. \tag{4.12}$$

Aggregate measures of capital composition and rate of profit are derived from (4.11) and (4.12) as weighted (by output values) averages of Q^* and π^*.

The definitions based on capital advanced are quite different, needing the time structure of production to be treated explicitly. Industry k takes t_k days for production and completes T_k production periods per year. The quantities c_{jk}/T_k and l_k/T_k denote respectively the inputs of constant capital from industry j and of labor power per ton per production period. In a state of simple reproduction these inputs are merely reinvested in each time period, though normally a surplus is extracted each production period, equal over the year to $e\lambda_L l_k$. These distinctions account for variable periods of production that do not last 1 year.

Secondly, cost of production definitions are modified to account for the history of investment during a production period. Recall that

$$c_{jk}/T_k = a_{jk}/T_k + f_{jk}/T_k t_{jk},$$

where a_{jk} denotes the total amount of industry j's output required as circulating constant capital input per ton of output of industry k per production period. Let $a_{jk}(s)$ measure the purchase of industry j's output by industry k per ton of industry k's output on each day s of the production period. Then

$$a_{jk}/T_k = \int_0^{365/T_k} a_{jk}(s)ds.$$

However, only a proportion of this input a_{jk}/T_k has actually to be advanced, for the rest can be invested in the credit market until needed for purchases. Hence the circulating constant capital advanced per unit of output by industry k is

$$h^1_{jk} a_{jk}/T_k = \frac{T_k}{365} \int_0^{365/T_k} a_{jk}(s)\left[\frac{365}{T_k} - s\right]ds,$$

where $0 \le h^1_{jk} \le 1$. Whereas a_{jk}/T_k is capital used up (constant costs of production), $h^1_{jk} a_{jk}/T_k$ is capital advanced.

A similar modification transforms labor inputs to variable capital advanced. The expected quantity of labor power of average skill and intensity purchased by industry k per ton of output per production period is l_k/T_k. We denote by $l_k(s)$ the number of hours of socially necessary abstract labor power per ton of output of industry k purchased (i.e., paid) on day s of the production period. Then

$$l_k/T_k = \int_0^{365/T_k} l_k(s)ds.$$

Only a proportion of this input has actually to be advanced as variable capital, namely,

$$h^2_k l_k/T_k = \frac{T_k}{365} \int_0^{365/T_k} l_k(s)\left[\frac{365}{T_k} - s\right]ds$$

for $0 \le h_k^2 \le 1$. While l_k/T_k is the labor power used, $h_k^2 l_k/T_k$ is the labor power advanced as variable capital.

The third modification to cost of production definitions concerns the treatment of fixed capital. Whereas circulating capital, whether constant or variable, is invested gradually but recouped all at once at the end of the turnover period, fixed capital is advanced in a lump and recouped gradually. The fixed capital returned at the end of a production period can be loaned to other capitalists or used within the business. So the capital advanced as fixed capital declines gradually throughout its service life.

Now f_{jk} is the quantity of type j fixed capital in place in industry k per unit of industry k's output; f_{jk}/t_{jk} is that amount depreciated per year. Depreciation is the amount returned by the production process to pay for fixed capital. Hence $f_{jk}/T_k t_{jk}$ is the depreciation of fixed capital per production period. By definition this is also the return reaped at the end of each production period to pay for the fixed capital used up. At the end of m production periods the fixed capital advanced for the $(m + 1)$th production period is 0 if $m \ge T_k t_{jk}$, for then the capital has been fully repaid; otherwise, it is $f_{jk} - mf_{jk}/T_k t_{jk}$. We denote this quantity by $h_{jk}^3 f_{jk}$, with $0 \le h_{jk}^3 \le 1$. The fixed capital advanced by a plant decreases systematically over the service life of that capital, a fact that provides an important clue for the analysis of technical change.

Performance measures based on capital advanced may now be defined. Constant capital advanced is circulating plus fixed constant capital advanced, namely, for industry k

$$\sum_{j=1}^{N}\left(h_{jk}^1 \frac{a_{jk}}{T_k} + h_{jk}^3 f_{jk}\right)\lambda_j. \tag{4.13}$$

The variable capital advanced is

$$\left(h_k^2 \frac{l_k}{T_k}\right)\lambda_L. \tag{4.14}$$

The organic composition of capital, Q_k, is the ratio of these two quantities. As before, surplus value is $e\lambda_L l_k$ and the rate of profit on capital advanced is the ratio of surplus value to the sum of constant and variable capital:

$$\pi_k = \frac{e\lambda_L l_k}{\displaystyle\sum_{j=1}^{N}\left(h_{jk}^1 \frac{a_{jk}}{T_k} + h_{jk}^3 f_{jk}\right)\lambda_j + \left(h_k^2 \frac{l_k}{T_k}\right)\lambda_L}. \tag{4.15}$$

Dividing the numerator and the denominator of this equation by the variable capital advanced gives

$$\pi_k = \frac{e\lambda_L l_k \left/ \left(h_k^2 \dfrac{l_k}{T_k} \right) \lambda_L \right.}{Q_k + 1} \tag{4.16}$$

$$= \frac{h_k^2}{T_k} \frac{e}{Q_k + 1}$$

Thus the rate of profit can be decomposed into three terms. The first measures the effects of the delay in paying labor and of having several turnover periods per year. The second is the rate of exploitation, the way in which value is extracted from labor without payment. And the third measures the value composition of capital. The last two of these $[e/(Q_k + 1)]$ are found in the usual cost of production measure of the rate of profit, while the quantity h_k^2/T_k measures the ratio by which the rate of profit on capital advanced exceeds the cost of production rate of profit: $(Q_k \neq Q_k^*)$.

The difference between cost of production and capital advanced implies that the rate of exploitation and the rate of surplus value have different magnitudes. The rate of exploitation is the ratio $(1 - \lambda_L)/\lambda_L$. The numerator of this quantity is the difference between the value created by a unit of labor power and the value of that unit; the denominator is the value of labor power. The rate of exploitation measures the ratio of value created but unpaid for to value created and paid for. The rate of surplus value is the ratio of the surplus created to variable capital. In the cost of production calculus the rate of surplus value coincides with the rate of exploitation. However, in the capital advanced calculus the rate of surplus value is

$$\frac{e\lambda_L l_k}{\left(h_k^2 \dfrac{l_k}{T_k} \right) \lambda_L} = \frac{T_k}{h_k^2} e. \tag{4.17}$$

The rate of surplus value exceeds the rate of exploitation by the ratio T_k/h_k^2.

These definitions permit theoretical and empirical analysis of the relations between technical change and the rate of profit. However, statistical agencies publish data in terms of prices rather than values: what is the relation between values and prices?

4.2.4 Value and Price

Value is determined in production. It is the quantity of labor power directly and indirectly required to produce a commodity; the labor power shall be socially necessary and of average intensity and skill. So the expected value of a commodity is the average input of labor power, the average being computed over all the plants in an industry. If two plants produce the same commodity (belong to the same industry), they produce commodities of equal unit value.

Price by contrast is set in the market. As Farjoun and Machover remark (1983: 101–105) prices, like the forms of commodities themselves, are essentially fluctuating phenomena. Prices are different in different shops even within the same city and fluctuate over time, even minute by minute on a stock exchange or in a vegetable market. There is therefore no such thing as the price of a commodity. One can only compute the expected (or average) price of the commodities sold by plants in an industry. It is this claim that most strongly distinguishes Farjoun and Machover (1983) from most existing economic theory: Marxists analyze the price of production of commodities, whereas neo-Ricardians and neoclassicals investigate the properties of equilibrium prices. Yet these concepts are idealizations: they do not exist. All that exist are the individual prices at which individual items of each commodity are sold. An average of the prices can be computed. It is our task in the following subsections to compute that average and examine the relation between price and value rates of profit.

4.2.4.1 The Ratio of Price to Value

We make three assumptions. First, there is no trade with economic systems beyond the borders of the system being analyzed. Therefore the inputs and outputs circulate within the same economic system and are priced and valued according to the same social rules. Secondly, the commodities produced in period t_{-n} but used in period t are repriced in period t's prices. This is a consistent rule of accounting in analyses of value: as equation (4.7) makes clear, all existing instances of a commodity have the same value irrespective of when they were produced. This repricing is effected by replacing the price of an input (produced earlier) by the price of a randomly chosen item of the commodity produced in this period. Thirdly, all commodity sales contribute income to the producer that exceeds constant costs of production. That is, all sales contribute at least some return to the value added in commodities. The argument largely follows Farjoun and Machover (1983: 112–119).

Consider the set of all sales of all commodities produced and sold within the standard period. The set excludes commodities whose production commenced before the standard period opened and commodities that were sold after the standard period ended. There does exist a standard period, equal to the production period of the commodity with the longest turnover time, such that every commodity is represented within this set. Each sale is a trade in one item, a particular unit of one of the composite commodities $c_1, c_2, \ldots, c_N$. We label each item sold $i = 1, 2, \ldots, I$.

The price of the ith item sold in the standard period t is $p_i(t)$. This price is decomposed into three elements: one corresponding to the constant fixed and circulating costs of producing it, namely, $c_i(t)$; one corresponding to the direct labor costs of production, namely, $v_i(t)$; and one corresponding to the surplus, $s_i(t)$. All components are measured in prices rather than values. However, the prices of input commodities, $c_i(t)$, can also be decomposed into three elements: $c_i(t_{-1})$, $v_i(t_{-1})$, and $s_i(t_{-1})$. As this decomposition continues to the nth level the price of the ith item can be expressed as

$$p_i(t) = c_i(t_{-n})$$
$$+ v_i(t) + v_i(t_{-1}) + \cdots + v_i(t_{-n})$$
$$+ s_i(t) + s_i(t_{-1}) + \cdots + s_i(t_{-n}).$$

By assumption the price of items exceeds the constant costs of producing them: $c_i(t_{-k}) > 0$ for all k. Therefore

$$\frac{c_i(t_{-k})}{c_i(t_{-k}) + v_i(t_{-k}) + s_i(t_{-k})} < 1 \qquad \text{for all } k.$$

Let

$$c_i^* = \max_k \left(\frac{c_i(t_{-k})}{c_i(t_{-k}) + v_i(t_{-k}) + s_i(t_{-k})} \right) < 1.$$

It follows that

$$0 < c_i(t_{-n}) < [c_i^*]_n, \qquad c_i(t) \to 0 \quad \text{as} \quad n \to \infty.$$

Thus as the decomposition proceeds indefinitely far into the past, the price of the ith item approaches the price

$$p_i(t) = v_i(t) + v_i(t_{-1}) + \cdots + v_i(t_{-n}) + \cdots$$

$$+ s_i(t) + s_i(t_{-1}) + \cdots + s_i(t_{-n}) + \cdots,$$

which may for convenience be written

$$p_i(t) = v_i + s_i.$$

All prices are measured in terms of commodities produced and sold in the current standard period. Since there is no trade the prices of inputs are the prices of the same output commodities.

The price per unit value of item i is $p_i(t)/\lambda_i$, where λ_i is the expected value of the commodity of which item i is a representative. Section 4.2.2 has defined expected values. Now we define the price per unit value of all commodities produced and sold within the standard period t as the expected value of the random variable p/λ; the expectation is computed over all commodities produced and sold in the standard period, the weights being their value. Thus,

$$E\left[\frac{p}{\lambda}\right] = E\left[\frac{v}{\lambda}\right] + E\left[\frac{s}{\lambda}\right]$$

$$= \sum_i \frac{\lambda_i}{\sum_j \lambda_j} \frac{v_i}{\lambda_i} + \sum_i \frac{\lambda_i}{\sum_j \lambda_j} \frac{s_i}{\lambda_i}$$

$$= \frac{\sum_i v_i}{\sum_i \lambda_i} + \frac{\sum_i s_i}{\sum_i \lambda_i}$$

$$= \frac{\sum_i v_i}{\sum_i \lambda_i} \left[1 + \frac{\sum_i s_i}{\sum_i v_i}\right]$$

Now v_i is the total wage paid (directly and indirectly) to produce all the commodities that were made and sold during the standard period. Equally s_i is the total surplus produced during production. And λ_i is the total quantity of labor power purchased to make the commodities. Thus v_i/λ_i measures the average wage paid per unit of labor power which, by virtue of the definition of λ is the wage per hour of labor. We denote this wage by W. The ratio s_i/v_i is the ratio of the surplus produced to the total wage paid and therefore is the money equivalent of the rate of exploitation. We denote this ratio by e^*.

It follows that

$$E\left[\frac{p}{\lambda}\right] = W(1 + e^*). \qquad (4.18)$$

That is, the expected ratio of prices to values, computed over all the commodities made and sold within the standard period, equals the product of the average wage and 1 plus the money rate of exploitation. This remarkably elegant result is a central conclusion of Farjoun and Machover (1983).

Additional information about sources of profit other than exploitation can be gleaned from this analysis. An individual item i can be sold for a profit s_i, that exceeds e^*v_i if the plant is able to buy inputs more cheaply or sell outputs more dearly than average. One way of doing this is to buy inputs from countries in which the wage is lower than W. Another is to buy inputs sooner than they are needed to profit from inflation if the rate of inflation exceeds the rate of interest.

Finally it is possible to generalize the third assumption: that the price of items at least covers the constant cost of production. Suppose that the condition is met for almost all commodities. Then for a sufficiently large sample of commodities $v_i + s_i > 0$ and equation (4.18) can be derived as the expected value of p/λ over all those samples.

4.2.4.2 Money Rate of Profit

In industry k the price rate of profit is the ratio of the surplus obtained by the plants in the industry to their constant and variable capital. All terms are measured in prices. Using the argument that led to equation (4.16), we can express this ratio as

$$\pi_k^p = \frac{e_k^* l_k \lambda_L \left(W_k/\lambda_L\right)}{\displaystyle\sum_{j=1}^{N}\left(h_{jk}^1 \frac{a_{jk}}{T_k} + h_{jk}^3 f_{jk}\right)\lambda_j \frac{p_j}{\lambda_j} + \left(h_k^2 \frac{l_k}{T_k}\right)\lambda_L \frac{W_k}{\lambda_L}} \, . \tag{4.19}$$

In this equation e_k^* denotes the money equivalent of the rate of exploitation in industry k, the ratio of the surplus to the total wages paid. In contrast to the value rate of exploitation the money equivalent rate varies between industries. Here W_k denotes the money wage per unit of labor power bought by plants in the industry; this too varies between industries, depending on whether they pay labor power above or below its value. Also p_j/λ_j is the expected price per unit value of the products of industry j. Equation (4.19) may be compared to equation (4.16) to establish when industry k's money rate of profit exceeds its value rate of profit.

Recall first that $E[p/\lambda] = W(1 + e^*)$. If commodities that are bought as constant capital are bought at prices below this average, then the industry's money quantity of constant capital is below its value quantity. Thus by buying input commodities at relatively low prices per unit value, plants in an industry can raise their rate of profit.

Secondly, the ratio of the wage in industry k to the value of labor power affects the relative sizes of the price and value variable capitals. If the wage is high, the (price) variable capital is high relative to the (value) variable capital and so the rate of profit is low. Industries in which the wage is low correspondingly reduce their outlays on variable capital.

These two effects are obvious. To eliminate them and simplify analysis, assume that the set of commodities bought as constant capital composes a random sample of all commodities and that the set of commodities bought by labor also composes a random sample of all commodities. The conditions imposed in Section 4.2.1 are assumed to hold. It follows that

$$\pi_k^p = \frac{e_k^* l_k \lambda_L W(1 + e^*)}{W(1 + e^*)\displaystyle\sum_{j=1}^{N}\left(h_{jk}^1 \frac{a_{jk}}{T_k} + h_{kj}^3 f_{jk}\right)\lambda_j + \left(h_k^2 \frac{l_k}{T_k}\right)\lambda_L}$$

$$= \frac{e_k^*}{e}\pi_k.$$

Now the money rate of exploitation equals the surplus divided by the total wage bill and $e = \lambda_L/(1 - \lambda_L)$. So

$$\frac{e_k^*}{e} = \frac{\text{surplus/hour}}{W_k} \frac{\lambda_L}{1 - \lambda_L}$$

$$= \frac{\text{surplus/hour}}{1 - \lambda_L} \frac{\lambda_L}{W_k}$$

$$= \frac{\text{surplus/hour}}{1 - \lambda_L} [W(1 + e^*)]^{-1}.$$

It follows that

$$\pi_k^p = \frac{\text{surplus/hour}}{1 - \lambda_L} [W(1 + e^*)]^{-1} \pi_k, \qquad (4.20)$$

where $W(1 + e^*)$ is the factor that converts values to prices in the economy as a whole. Thus the third factor by which the money rate of profit in an industry deviates from the value rate of profit is the ratio by which the price of the surplus deviates from its value. This factor is an implicit price of the surplus that measures the extent to which industry k is able to acquire surplus produced by other industries. If the implicit price exceeds $W(1 + e^*)$, industry k acquires more surplus than it produces; on the other hand, if the implicit price falls below $W(1 + e^*)$, the industry gives up to other industries some of the surplus that it produces.

A final and important result can be obtained from equation (4.20). Consider the ratio π_k^p/π_k. Suppose that the average of this ratio is computed over all industries:

$$E\left[\frac{\pi^p}{\pi}\right] = [W(1 + e^*)]^{-1} E\left[\frac{\text{surplus/hour}}{1 - \lambda_L}\right],$$

the sum being weighted by the labor power purchased by each industry. The second expectation is the average across all industries of the ratio of the surplus measured in prices to the surplus measured in values. But the surplus is a particular set of commodities and the expectation is thus the expected ratio of the price to value of those commodities. Therefore, if the set of commodities that composes the surplus forms a random sample of all commodities,

$$E\left[\frac{\pi^p}{\pi}\right] = [W(1 + e^*)]^{-1} [W(1 + e^*)] = 1.$$

That is if the set of commodities composing constant capital is a random sample of all commodities, if the set of commodities consumed per unit of labor power is a random sample of all commodities, and if the set of commodities making up the surplus is also a random sample of all commodities, then the expected ratio of the price rate of profit to the value rate of profit is one (provided that there is no trade, that commodities are priced at current prices, and that all prices exceed constant costs of production).

This section has deduced the relations between values and prices and between price and value rates of profit. Since prices are random variables that fluctuate in the market these relations are stated in the form of expected ratios. In a modern economy the sample size over which these ratios are calculated is so large that the variance of the ratios formed over different samples is likely to be small. Under some general conditions the expected price per unit value for a random sample of commodities is $W(1 + e^*)$; the expected ratio of price to value rate of profit is unity. These important results replace what has been known in the past as the transformation problem. [A review of this problem has been provided by Desai (1979); recent debates are aired in Steedman (1981).]

The transformation problem seeks to determine the relationship between the values and prices of commodities, to demonstrate that there is a sense in which values can be said to determine prices. Until the work of Farjoun and Machover (1983: 124–137), the debate had been conducted under the assumptions that every item of commodity sold by industry k has the same price and that the prices to be determined by values are those that hold when there exists an equilibrium in which every industry makes the same money rate of profit. We know that items of the same commodity command different prices in different places and for different purchasers and that there never exists an interindustry equilibrium. The treatment offered in this chapter is thus more general than that offered by the traditional transformation problem.

4.3 CONCLUSION

The point of this chapter has been to demonstrate how to measure commodity values and so to measure the performance of capitalist industries and economies.

We began by defining capital as self-expanding value and value therefore as a measurable category restricted to capitalist production. Value is the only possible universal standard of commodities that permits historical, comparative research of the kind that is needed to evaluate the narratives described in Chapter 3. To be measurable, value must be measured as the quantity of productive labor power invested in an article, under socially normal (average) conditions of production and using labor of average skill and intensity, no matter what the concrete form of that labor.

This definition can be operationalized. Three assumptions are made: economic conditions remain constant within a standard period; each industry buys a random sample of the units of labor power offered for sale during the period; and production periods are not related to the standard period. Then the *expected* unit value of each industry's output is

$$\lambda' = \lambda' (A + [f_{jk}/t_{jk}]) + l'. \tag{4.21}$$

If industries are large, there is virtually no error in assuming that actual values equal their expected value. This provides a precise description of commodity values. The equation has a nonnegative solution provided that the economy is productive.

Finally, we have deduced the relation between values and prices and between price and value rates of profit. Prices are random variables that fluctuate, so the relations are expressed as expected ratios. Under some general conditions the expected price per unit value for a random sample of commodities is $W(1 + e^*)$; the expected ratio of price to value rate of profit is unity. These important results replace the transformation problem.

Essentially this chapter has provided a precise mathematical foundation for measures of values and rates of profit. In practice these definitions give rise to quite straightforward and intuitive methods of measuring. For example, to compute the rate of profit in any given year, one should determine the costs of inputs—raw materials, fuel, semifinished inputs, depreciation, and productive labor. These are the costs of production. Total profit is the difference between sales and costs. Total capital is the sum of net fixed capital and stocks and inventories. The rate of profit in money and in value units is the ratio of the total profit to the total capital. With such definitions in place, we can now examine production, technical change, and interregional investment theoretically and empirically.

Chapter 5

ACCUMULATION, TECHNICAL CHANGE, AND THE FALLING RATE OF PROFIT

Since the mid-eighteenth century, capitalist economies have experienced four major cycles of prolonged growth punctuated by deep and protracted depression. Superimposed upon these long waves of economic fortune, the Kuznets and business cycles run their course, accelerating and retarding growth, providing new jobs, and adding capital stock at some times while also casting thousands out of work and gutting capacity at other times. Between the great depressions of the early 1930s and early 1980s, we have witnessed approximately eight business cycles, periods of inflation, stagnation, rapid growth and job creation, slump, and downsizing. Chapter 2 reviews the postwar history of economic growth and crisis in a number of capitalist countries. The balanced growth and smooth adjustments of conventional neoclassical economic theory seem far removed from the reality of everyday life.

This chapter is concerned with long trends of economic development. In particular, we ask whether a capitalist economy can enjoy continued uninterrupted growth. While the history of capitalist accumulation suggests that growth is limited, the constraints on expansion are unclear. According to the neoclassical view, balanced growth with full employment of resources is an equilibrium state of an unfettered capitalist economy. Short-or long-term crises, from this perspective, are thought to result from external shocks: rapid commodity price changes; wars; and market imperfections, especially government interference. We seek to show instead that economic expansion is checked by forces internal to the capitalist mode of production. We argue that the mechanisms promoting growth are also those that push the economy into protracted periods of decline such as the one presently being experienced by most industrialized nations.

The motivation for this chapter is a central question raised in Chapter 3. For some, such as Mandel (1978) and Gibson and Horvath (1983), the period of more or less sustained growth in the 1950s and 1960s was derailed when contradictions inherent to the capitalist mode of production lowered the rate of profit. For others, such as Lipietz (1986) and Piore and Sabel (1984), growth slowed once certain stability conditions broke down. As we noted in Chapter 3, there does not exist a formal dynamic macroeconomic model that relates capital/output ratios, wage increases, the failure of demand, investment, and technical change to the falling rate of profit. In brief, we seek in this chapter to provide such a model.

Our model of economic growth and crisis rests heavily on the works of the classical school of economics, and in particular on the work of Marx. Since the slowdown of growth in the industrialized nations during the 1970s, Marxist theory of accumulation and crisis has become increasingly prominent in attempts to explain the decline and restructuring of industries (Holmes 1983; Mahon 1984; Massey 1981), regions (Bluestone and Harrison 1982; Carney et al. 1980; Dunford et al. 1981; Massey and Meegan 1982; Webber 1986), and even the global economy (Henderson and Castells 1978; Lipietz 1986; MacEwan and Tabb 1989; Peet 1987). Marx's theory of the falling rate of profit provides the foundation on which many of these accounts rest. Yet the internal consistency of the theory of the falling rate of profit has repeatedly been questioned. Such questions threaten the value of accounts of economic restructuring that posit declines in profitability as the progenitor of change.

Marx offered perhaps the most prescient vision of growth and crisis in the capitalist economy. His theory that the falling rate of profit is the barrier to continuous economic growth has been the subject of considerable debate spanning 100 years. Still today, the main lineaments of this argument are hotly contested (Moseley 1990; Shaikh 1980; van Parijs 1980). We offer a new view of the theory of the falling rate of profit, more general than those that have been developed to date. With this new model we can replicate the findings of previous analysis, reveal the limitations of that analysis, and provide new insights into the theory of the falling rate of profit. We show, under very general conditions, that viable technical changes cause the aggregate rate of profit to fall. This result provides the theoretical foundation upon which many explanations of economic restructuring depend. It also provides the analytical foundation for a claim that growth slowed in the 1970s and 1980s for internal reasons rather than for external reasons associated with the failure of stability conditions.

The chapter is organized in the following manner. Section 5.1 briefly traces the genesis of the theory of economic growth in classical economics. Section 5.2 outlines Marx's model of balanced reproduction and then refines a golden age growth model in the Marxian tradition. In Section 5.3 we begin to investigate crisis theory by examining constraints on accumulation said to derive from profit squeezes, underconsumption, and the falling rate of profit. (An extended discussion of the theory of the falling rate of profit is located in Appendix A5.) Section 5.4 advances a new model of the capitalist economy. This model explicitly rejects traditional notions of equilibrium and thus departs from existing schemes of accumulation. Past accounts of the relationship between economic growth and the falling rate of profit are revealed as special cases of our more general model. We outline the limitations of those earlier arguments and present a new, less restrictive disequilibrium model of the falling rate of profit. This model shows that viable technical changes reduce the aggregate rate of profit and that the capitalist economy cannot enjoy uninterrupted growth. The limits to growth are found within the basic workings of the capitalist economy itself. Section 5.5 concludes the chapter.

5.1 THE CLASSICAL ORIGINS OF THE THEORY OF ECONOMIC GROWTH

The theory of economic growth originated in the writings of the mercantilists. Developed between the Middle Ages and the laissez-faire of the classical period, the overriding concern of mercantilism was growth, the expansion of national wealth. For mercantilists wealth was equated with gold and silver bullion and to a lesser extent other natural resources. Wealth was expanded only by discovery or trade surplus: growth was not yet linked to production. The mercantilists did, however, link the expansion of wealth to the growth of the population, for a larger pool of labor meant lower wages and thus a more competitive export sector (Eagly 1970; Oser and Brue 1988; Reid 1989; Spengler and Allen 1960).

It was not until the emergence of the Physiocrats that a system of growth rooted in production relations appeared. The Physiocrats, in part reacting to the mercantilism of the previous 200 years, regarded trade as "sterile." For them agriculture was the only productive endeavor. Undoubtedly the most significant work of this period was François Quesnay's *Tableau Économique*, which provided the first systematic account of the circulation of goods between different sectors in an economy. Perhaps more important for the theory of economic growth, however, was the notion that a nation's surplus or net product was the real source of national wealth. For the Physiocrats, then, the limits to economic growth were set by the degree to which net agricultural output could be increased. However, the Physiocrats viewed the surplus as a natural phenomenon and did not connect investment and growth.

The classical economists, from Adam Smith to John Stuart Mill, followed the lead of the Physiocrats, though they rejected the notion that the surplus was a natural phenomenon that only arose in agricultural production. For the classical economists growth resulted from productive investment of social surplus. Now the origin of this surplus, the ownership and control of the surplus, and its use all demanded explanation. Thus for the classical economists issues of value, income distribution, and growth were inseparable. The rate of profit occupies a prominent position in these early debates as a category of income, as a source of investment funds, and as a stimulus to further investment (Harris 1983; Hollander 1987).

Whatever their other differences, Smith, David Ricardo, Mill, and their contemporaries shared the belief that the accumulation of capital through investment of part of the social product (profit) was the engine of growth (Harris 1983). Both Smith and Ricardo advanced the notion that growth would reach a "stationary state," although they invoked different mechanisms to explain why accumulation would cease. Smith argued that profits and so further inducements to growth are eroded by competition, whereas Ricardo claimed that diminishing returns guarantee stagnation. It was left to Marx to develop the theory of growth and crises intimated by the classical economists.

5.2 MARXIAN THEORY OF ACCUMULATION AND CRISES

For Marx economic growth or accumulation is defined as an expansion of capitalist forces and relations of production (Wright 1979). Thus accumulation involves an increase in the value of capital employed in productive activity and an expansion and deepening of capitalist relations of production to encompass the provision of a greater variety of goods and services and through that the control of more and more workers. Like his classical predecessors Marx realized that accumulation was driven by productive investment of the social surplus. He set out to show that this surplus was not a natural reward for entrepreneurial ability but rather that it resulted from the exploitation of labor in production. Marx's labor theory of value, the cornerstone of Marxian economy theory, revealed the basis of growth, namely, profit, and also ended the search for a consistent value theory that eluded Ricardo. We outlined the central tenets of Marx's labor theory of value in Chapter 4.

Marx regarded accumulation as a defining feature of the capitalist mode of production. Building on Smith's analysis of competition, Marx recognized that capitalists—owners of the means of production and controllers of the social surplus—had constantly to readvance capital in search of profit. "This is law for capitalist production, imposed by incessant revolutions in the methods of production themselves, by the depreciation of existing capital always bound up with them, by the general competitive struggle, and the need to improve production and expand its scale merely as a means of self-preservation and under penalty of ruin" (Marx 1967: Vol. III, 244–245).

5.2.1 Marx's Reproduction Schemes

The possibility of balanced growth, or accumulation without crisis, was shown by Marx through his reproduction formulas. Marx's model of expanded reproduction is outlined and extended in this section to investigate some of the characteristics of equilibrium growth. These reproduction formulas assume no technical change. One consequence of this, as we shall see, is that accumulation depends on the rate of growth of the labor force. Later technical

change is introduced into the argument. In the terms of Chapter 4, Marx's reproduction schemes assume that production is point input–point output and
that the length of the production period is the same in both sectors of the
economy.

The Marxian model of expanded reproduction is generally formatted in
terms of a two-department scheme: department 1 produces the means of production, and department 2 produces consumption goods. The scheme of accumulation shows the patterns of demand and supply for both commodities
in value terms:

$$C_{1t} + V_{1t} + S_{1t} = C_{1t+1} + C_{2t+1} \tag{5.1}$$

$$C_{2t} + V_{2t} + S_{2t} = V_{1t+1} + V_{2t+1} + (1 - b_t)(S_{1t} + S_{2t}), \tag{5.2}$$

where the subscripts 1 and 2 refer to the department of production:

C represents constant capital, the value of capital advanced to meet
nonlabor costs of production;

V represents variable capital, the value of capital advanced to meet
labor costs of production;

S represents the surplus value produced, the difference between the
value produced per unit of work by labor and the value of the
wage advanced to meet the cost of that labor;

$1 - b$ denotes the proportion of the surplus consumed unproductively.

The accounts cover a period of production of 1 year, say. The subscript t denotes the year.

Equation (5.1) shows that in balanced or equilibrium growth, the value
of output of capital goods in year t must equal the value of capital goods consumed by both departments in the following year. Equation (5.2) shows that
the value of consumption goods produced in year t must equal the value of
goods consumed by laborers in period $t + 1$ and by capitalists in period t.

The Marxian model of accumulation (5.1)–(5.2) has several important
features. First, there is no fixed capital: all capital is fully used up in a single
round of production. Secondly, Marx assumed that the capital advanced in
each department of production has the same rate of turnover. These two assumptions allowed Marx to express performance measures of the economy,
such as the rate of profit, in the terms of equations (5.1) and (5.2). (Chapter 4
shows how to measure performance more generally.) Thirdly, Marx assumed
that sufficient labor power exists to meet the requirements of the economy re-
gardless of the rate of growth and demand for labor. A corollary of this assumption, implicit in the scheme of expanded reproduction, is that the real
wage and the value of labor power are constant. Desai (1979) seems to over-
look this assumption and is at pains to rationalize Marx's model of balanced
accumulation with his more famous statements on crisis. With an unlimited

supply of labor there is no reason to expect the balanced path of accumulation of Marx's reproduction model to falter. Fourthly, the characterization of investment behavior in the model is quite peculiar. Marx argued that the pace of growth is determined by the actions of capitalists in the department producing the means of production. Capitalists in department 1 consume a fixed proportion of their surplus and use the rest for accumulation. Investment by capitalists in department 2 is thus determined by the availability of capital inputs. Morishima (1973) and Desai (1979) have shown that this assumption implies that growth rates in the two departments converge after only one round of production.

5.2.2 Golden Age Growth

To explore equilibrium growth, we now present a Marxian model of accumulation in physical or input–output terms. This growth model retains the flavor of the Marxian reproduction formulas, yet it is more realistic: capital may move between sectors in response to profit rate differences; department 1 does not dictate the pace of aggregate economic growth; and the real wage varies in response to the state of the labor market. The model of expanded reproduction is developed in terms of a two-department scheme: department 1 producing the means of production and department 2 producing consumer goods. In this scheme there is no separate department producing fixed capital inputs, and for simplicity the real wage is assumed equal throughout the economy.

The output of the capital and consumer goods departments is given by equations (5.3) and (5.4), respectively:

$$x_{1t} = a_{11}(1 + g_{1t})x_{1t} + a_{12}(1 + g_{2t})x_{2t} \tag{5.3}$$

and

$$x_{2t} = D_{t+1}L_{t+1} + F_t, \tag{5.4}$$

where $L_{t+1} = l_1(1 + g_{1t})x_{1t} + l_2(1 + g_{2t})x_{2t}$;
  $F_t = (1-b_t)(1-\lambda_2 D_t)L_t$;
  a_{1j}, for $j = 1, 2$, represents the aggregate capital input coefficient in department j;
  λ_i, for $i = 1, 2$, represents the unit value of the aggregate capital good and the aggregate consumer good, respectively;
  D denotes the real wage, equal in both departments;
  L denotes the total labor employed;
  F represents unproductive consumption by capitalists from profit;
  g_i, for $i = 1, 2$, represent the rate of growth in department i.

Equations (5.3) and (5.4) describe the physical flows of the two commodities in the economy. They represent the conditions that must hold for the levels of production in each department to be consistent with the demand for both types of commodities. If the equalities do not hold, there will be overproduction or underproduction of both types of commodities and the process of accumulation will be disrupted.

From equation (5.3), the relative size of the two departments that ensures balanced growth is

$$x_{1t} = \frac{a_{12}(1 + g_{2t})x_{2t}}{1 - a_{11}(1 + g_{1t})} = Wx_{2t}. \tag{5.5}$$

Once the output of department 2 is fixed, the complementary output of capital goods is determined by the capital input coefficients and the growth rates in the two departments. The rate of growth measures the rate of expansion of the inputs to production. The economy-wide growth rate is determined by the average rate of profit and by the proportion of profits used to finance accumulation:

$$g_t = b_t\pi_t.$$

The economy-wide rate of profit is an average of the departmental profit rates:

$$\pi_t = \frac{(1 - \lambda_2 D_t)L_t}{\lambda_1 K_t + \lambda_2 D_t L_t}$$

where $K_t = a_{11}x_{1t} + a_{12}x_{2t}$.
The departmental profit rates are

$$\pi_{jt} = \frac{(1 - \lambda_2 D_t)l_j x_{jt}}{\lambda_1 a_{1j}x_{jt} + \lambda_2 D_t l_j x_{jt}}, \qquad \text{for} \quad j = 1, 2.$$

The rate of profit is defined for a single turnover period. Turnover times are assumed to be equally long in both departments and are constant through time.

There are two adjustment mechanisms. First, the rate of change of the real wage is assumed to be a positive, increasing, and continuous function of changes in the employment rate. That is,

$$dD/D_t = f[d(L_t/N_t)], f' > 0,$$

where N_t denotes the size of the available labor force. Secondly, the total new investment each turnover period, the additional capital advanced in the economy as a whole, is

$$I_t = b_t(1 - \lambda_2 D_t)L_t.$$

The proportion of this new capital invested in each department depends on the relative rates of profit in the two departments

$$u_{1t} = \begin{array}{ll} R(\pi_{1t}/\pi_{2t}) & \text{if} \quad \pi_{1t} > 0, \quad \pi_{2t} > 0 \\ 1 & \text{if} \quad \pi_{2t} < 0, \quad \pi_{1t} > 0 \\ 0 & \text{if} \quad \pi_{1t} < 0, \quad \pi_{2t} > 0 \end{array}$$

and $u_{2t} = 1 - u_{1t}$; R is a positive, increasing and continuous function of the ratio of departmental profit rates. The total new investment in department j in period t is

$$I_{jt} = u_{jt}b_t \, (1 - \lambda_2 D_t)L_t,$$

and the departmental growth rate is

$$g_{jt} = \frac{u_{jt}b_t \, (1 - \lambda_2 D_t)L_t}{C_{jt} + V_{jt}}.$$

This set of equations characterizes the two-department growth model. Some of the properties of this model are now examined.

5.2.3 Characteristics of the Growth Model

The economy is in a state of equilibrium if the departmental rates of profit are constant, that is, if

$$d\pi_j/\pi_{jt} = 0 \quad \text{for} \quad j = 1, 2.$$

If the departmental rates of profit are constant, then the economy-wide profit rate π_t is also constant over time and equal to π_t^*. [If a variable has no department subscript it is economy-wide. The asterisk (*) denotes the value of a variable in equilibrium.] Given $1 - b$, the propensity to consume from profits, the equilibrium growth rate in the economy is

$$g_t^* = b_t\pi_t^*,$$

and if b is constant over time, then

$$g_t^* = b\pi_t^*.$$

The constancy of the rate of profit in the economy also implies that the real wage is fixed, that is,

$$dD/D_t = 0,$$

for without technical change, the rate of profit depends on the real wage. In turn, the constancy of the real wage implies that the rate of employment L_t/N_t does not vary. A constant rate of employment itself implies that

$$L_{t+1}/N_{t+1} = L_t/N_t.$$

Thus,

$$L_{t+1}/L_t = N_{t+1}/N_t,$$

and therefore

$$dL/L_t = dN/N_t.$$

Given that

$$dL_t = (l_1 x_{1t+1} + l_2 x_{2t+1}) - (l_1 x_{1t} + l_2 x_{2t})$$
$$= l_1 dx_{1t} + l_2 dx_{2t}$$

and

$$x_{1t} = W x_{2t},$$

where W is defined in equation (5.5), we have

$$dx_{1t} = W dx_{2t}.$$

From the equations above,

$$dL_t = (l_1 W + l_2)\, dx_{2t},$$

and therefore

$$dL/L_t = \frac{(l_1 W + l_2)\, dx_2}{(l_1 W + l_2)\, x_{2t}}$$
$$= dx_2/x_{2t}.$$

Thus,

$$dN/N_t = g_N = dL/L_t = dx_2/x_{2t} = g_{2t}.$$

If dL/L_t and g_{2t} are constant, then with no technical change

$$g_{1t} = g_{2t} = g_N.$$

Therefore, in the equilibrium defined by constant rates of profit, with fixed production techniques, the growth rates of both departments are equal to one another, constant through time, and equal to the natural rate of growth of the labor supply. Such a pattern of accumulation is termed a "golden age" growth path.

There is little possibility of accelerating or decelerating growth in this model except by shifts in the size of the labor force. Growth depends solely on the level of the real wage, and labor has no basis on which to assert real-wage gains except for changes in the rate of employment. If the speed of economic expansion is tied to the rate of growth of the labor supply, then economic growth is growth in the size of the labor force. This is primitive accumulation in the Marxian sense.

Like Smith and Ricardo, Marx argued that the process of capital accumulation was subject to a series of checks and contradictions, internal barriers to the self-expansion of capital. "Capitalist production seeks continually to overcome these immanent barriers, but overcomes them only by means which again place these barriers in its way and on a more formidable scale . . . . The real barrier of capitalist production is capital itself." (Marx 1967: Vol. III, 250). Three barriers to the accumulation of capital have been identified in the Marxian literature: crises arising from underconsumption, from a squeeze on profits, and from the rising composition of capital. These are now reviewed in turn.

5.3 THEORIES OF CRISIS

We investigate Marxian crisis theory by focusing on the underconsumption, profit squeeze, and falling rate of profit theses. These mechanisms are used to account for secular declines in profitability and economic growth as well as to explain business cycles. Though there is some merit in each argument, each is incomplete as an independent explanation of capitalist crises. In combination the three mechanisms link the relentless drive to accumulate with class struggle, competition in production, and competition in the market.

5.3.1 Underconsumption/Disproportionality Theories

Simply stated, underconsumptionists argue that because workers only receive a portion of the value they create in the form of a wage, supply must exceed demand (Sweezy 1970). Unless capitalists spend the full value of their profits on consumer goods a portion of the value created in production must remain unrealized. Since the propensity to consume out of profits is generally thought to be lower than the propensity to consume out of wages, it is unlikely that capitalists make up the "demand gap." Furthermore, if all profits are spent on consumption, there can be no net investment and no growth. So early under-consumptionists tended to view the capitalist economy as driven by consumption rather than profit and as being incapable of self-sustaining growth (Bleany 1976; Shaikh 1978).

Marx (1967) demonstrated the possibility of balanced accumulation with the reproduction schemes examined in Section 5.2. Effective demand comprises investment as well as consumption expenditure: capitalism is quite capable of generating internal growth. Luxemburg (1951) mistakenly rejects the logic of the reproduction schemes and outlines a theory of imperialism whereby developing nations provide the "missing" effective demand that sustains capitalist expansion. However, she does not make clear how developing nations can sustain net purchases from developed capitalist nations. The most sophisticated attempt to revive the underconsumption argument follows the work of Sweezy (1970).

Sweezy (1970) develops a thesis that disproportionality between the two departments of production will rupture the process of accumulation. As the capital intensity of production increases, Sweezy claims that more capital will have to be directed into the production of capital goods. The growth of the capital goods sector then outstrips the rate of growth of the consumer goods sector; since the rate of growth of output is higher than the rate of growth of consumption, underconsumption must result. Again, it appears that Sweezy ignores the demand for output from the capital goods sector itself. There may be an increasing disparity in the scale of capital and consumer goods production, but it is not clear why this should promote realization crises and a fall in the rate of profit.

Baran and Sweezy (1966) also advance an underconsumption argument to underpin their vision of monopoly capitalism. Under monopolistic conditions a reduction in price competition coupled with continuing cost competition raises the surplus faster than the system's ability to absorb it. While Shaikh (1978) questions why capitalists would persist investing in the face of overcapacity, Wright (1979) correctly observes that the underconsumption position lacks a theory of accumulation to unite the investment behavior of capitalists with profit and effective demand. Wright (1979) himself claims that underconsumption is encouraged by a gap between the rate of profit and the rate of accumulation. He suggests that this gap results from technical changes that reduce production costs, though this too ignores the possibility that demand may be enlarged simply by expanding the scale of production.

Once accumulation falters, the disproportionality thesis might explain a rapid fall in profitability as the economy is burdened with overcapacity. As independent theories of economic crisis, the disproportionality and underconsumption arguments are deficient, however, for they fail to show why reductions in profitability and growth must emanate from a lack of consumer demand. These might be more correctly regarded as consequences of the slowdown. Notwithstanding these charges, the theory of underconsumption has recently been used by Aglietta (1979) to explain reductions in postwar profitability in the USA and elsewhere, and by Devine (1988) to account for the Great Depression of the 1930s.

5.3.2 Profit Squeeze Theory

According to the profit squeeze thesis, crises result from a fall in the rate of profit precipitated by a change in the distribution of income in favor of the working class. The profit squeeze argument is not articulated within a broader framework of accumulation, and for this reason is usually developed independently of other influences on the rate of profit such as technical change. The aggregate rate of profit is

$$\pi = \frac{S}{C + V} = \frac{S/V}{C/V + 1} = \frac{(1 - \lambda_2 D)/\lambda_2 D}{\lambda_1 K/\lambda_2 DL + 1}, \tag{5.6}$$

where the terms are defined as previously. In the absence of technical change, the only factor that can alter the distribution of the value added in production between capital and labor is the real hourly wage (D). If labor is able to increase real wages, then the surplus and rate of profit fall. The profit squeeze thesis has a clear theoretical basis in this abstract sense. The argument focuses directly upon the struggle between capital and labor over the distribution of value added into profits and wages. What is missing in this abstract model is any discussion of how the conditions of accumulation affect the ability of labor to secure real-wage gains. In part, this may be achieved by combining the profit squeeze model with other elements of Marx's broader crisis theory. However, a complete understanding of the profit squeeze can only be addressed when the nature of competition and market relations are given a specific institutional context.

Variants of the profit squeeze argument are used to explain secular reductions in profitability as well as the regular rhythm of the profit rate through the business cycle. In the former camp, Glyn and Sutcliffe (1972) claim that the slowdown of the British economy since the mid-1960s was the result of the rising share of wages in national income because of the rising strength of labor in the class struggle. In the USA, Bowles et al. (1983) provide evidence that the social wage, including wages, benefits, and social security provisions has increased, raising the overall share of national income accruing to labor. As productivity growth has slowed since the early 1970s, increases in the social wage are thought to undermine the rate of profit. Shaikh (1982) is critical of such claims and provides counterexamples.

Interest in the profit squeeze explanation of short-run cycles was stimulated by Boddy and Crotty's (1975) claim that the reserve army of unemployed workers became depleted, so that labor's share of income rose and that of profits fell in the late expansion stages of the US business cycle. Attention has since focused on the precise timing of wage movements, in part as an attempt to understand the forces that influence the ability of labor to secure wage gains. Weisskopf (1979), Sherman (1982, 1990), Hahnel and Sherman (1982), Wolff (1986), Henley (1987), and Moseley (1990) all detail the cyclical swings in the US rate of profit since World War II to evaluate the factors contributing to changes in labor's share of national income. Three variants of the cyclical profit squeeze hypothesis may be recognized. First, underconsumptionists such as Sweezy (1970) favor a wage-lag argument. It asserts that the productivity gains achieved early in the business cycle are captured as profits. Labor is forced to play "catch-up," only realizing its share of growth later in the upswing. Institutional impediments on wage movements, contracts, and state pressure all ensure that wages are sticky, slowing working class responses to the business cycle. Second is the overhead labor hypothesis. It claims that overhead labor does not increase in the early expansion stage of the business cycle; hence productivity measured over all workers increases rapidly, favoring the profit share. As expansion continues, overhead labor is hired, retarding productivity growth and boosting the share of wages in national income. Weisskopf (1979) finds some evidence of this trend. Third and perhaps most favored is the reserve army hypothesis. During the upswing of the business cycle unemployment falls gradually, placing labor in a more advantageous bargaining position. With continued expansion, labor is able to win concessions over the distribution of value added and over conditions of work. In the late expansion stage of the cycle the wage share rises and therefore the cycle subsides.

Perhaps the most sophisticated of recent explanations of the business cycle is Goldstein's (1985) cyclical profit squeeze model. Searching for the microfoundations of the profit squeeze thesis in an oligopolistic market setting, Goldstein shows that capitalists following a mark-up pricing strategy to maximize future profits will not be able to pass on wage gains fully during business cycle upswings because of the threat of competition and erosion of market share. Goldstein frees profit squeeze theorists from assuming away the issue of price determination and from relying on an underconsumption argument to explain the end of the upswing.

The profit squeeze theory explains short-run constraints on accumulation emanating from the growing strength of labor. However, it fails to explain why changes in the rate of accumulation and movements of the real wage do not lead to equilibrium and the golden age growth path captured in Marx's reproduction formulas. Indeed, Rigby (1988) shows that the growth path of Section 5.2.2 is a stable equilibrium. [Morishima (1973) shows that a similar model leads to divergent growth in the two departments and thus a disproportionality crisis, although it is unclear why unequal growth promotes crisis.] The profit squeeze thesis also fails to explain a secular decline in the rate of profit when there is technological change. With a choice of techniques, capitalists may counter rising wage pressures by substituting machinery for labor.

5.3.3 The Theory of the Falling Rate of Profit

The dynamism of the capitalist economy results from the twin processes of class struggle and intercapitalist competition: from the struggle between capitalists and workers over the division of the value added in production by labor and the competition between capitalists over the distribution of surplus value. Technical change plays a central role in both processes. By reorganizing production, the owners of capital attempt to expand the pool of surplus value and their individual dominion over that pool. Marx's (1967) theory of the falling rate of profit asserts that under certain conditions these aims might be contradictory.

Following Marx, in Section 5.3.2 we have defined the aggregate value rate of profit in an economy by equation (5.6). Although Harvey (1982) notes some ambiguity in definitions of the rate of profit, analysis of the effects of technical change on profitability are generally couched in terms of equation (5.6). In essence the theory of the falling rate of profit argues that as an economy expands faster than the rate of growth of the labor force, the wage will be bid up as unemployment falls and workers find themselves in a stronger bargaining position. To restrict the rising strength of labor and shield the rate of profit, capitalists substitute machinery for labor in production, raising the composition of capital (C/V) and increasing the tendency toward overproduction. Unless counteracted by increases in the rate of exploitation (S/V), a rising composition of capital depresses the rate of profit. Thus capitalists face shrinking profits if they allow wages to rise; yet if they introduce more capital-intensive production techniques, they erode the very basis of profit, the exploitation of labor in production.

Marx regarded the theory of the falling rate of profit as a tendency. He claimed that while the logic of capitalist competition produces forces that tend to depress the rate of profit, counteracting forces may operate to raise it. The logical consistency of these claims was the foundation for early debates on the theory of the falling rate of profit (Hodgson 1974; Sweezy 1970; Yaffe 1973). Since the work of Okishio (1961), however, attention has focused on whether cost-reducing technical changes can reduce the rate of profit (Laibman 1982; Roemer 1977, 1978; Shaikh 1978; van Parijs 1980). These arguments are examined in detail in the appendix to this chapter. To date, there is no formal theory that links technical change and the falling rate of profit within a model of accumulation that allows wages to vary with the size of the reserve army of unemployed and that does not assume equilibrium in the supply and demand of produced commodities. We outline such a model in the next section.

5.4 THE RELATIONSHIP BETWEEN ACCUMULATION, TECHNICAL CHANGE, AND THE FALLING RATE OF PROFIT

Existing theory of the relationship between technical change and the rate of profit is deficient. Early discussions suffered from a lack of formalism and failed to link the crucial variables. Wright (1979) extols the traditional Marxian position but does not demonstrate whether labor-saving changes in production techniques can lead to a decline in the economy-wide rate of profit. Okishio (1961) showed that cost-reducing technical changes can not cause the profit rate to fall, at least when prices are in equilibrium. However. Okishio's result holds only under restrictive conditions—when the real wage is constant and markets clear. Models that incorporate fixed capital, that permit joint production, or that maintain the wage share or the rate of exploitation cast doubt on the generality of Okishio's findings; still they do not resolve the issue. While Rigby (1990b) attempts to endogenize wage changes and market clearing, his rate of profit is measured against the capital invested in production rather than the capital available for production. There are also empirical doubts about the long-run tendency of the rate of profit to fall. Marx seems to have held the falling rate of profit to be a long-run tendency, leading to the eventual demise of capitalism. However, there is no evidence of a long-run decline of this sort. Therefore, we are dealing with a tendency that must in some sense by cyclical or wavelike.

Existing analyses of technical change and profitability rely on models of the economy that assume equilibrium in one form or another. No one has yet examined the impact of technical changes on profitability in the context of a disequilibrium model that links input coefficients, output and demand relations, and wages, examining the use of the profits that have been realized. In this section, we develop just such a model. The equilibrium models discussed in Appendix A5 are special cases of our more general approach. Factors other than input coefficients and wages affect the relationship between technology and profitability; these factors cannot be evaluated within equilibrium models.

For simplicity we depart from the traditional two-department format and develop a model with a lineage that dates back to Ricardo's corn economy, with one aggregate commodity that serves as both capital and consumer good. This model differs in other respects from earlier ones. We begin, rather conventionally, by defining total employment as the product of the labor required per unit of output (l) and the quantity of output produced or supplied (x^s):

$$L = lx^s. \tag{5.7}$$

Through equation (5.8) we ensure that the quantity of output supplied (produced) in the economy is greater or equal to that demanded (purchased):

$$x^d \leq x^s, \tag{5.8}$$

where x^d is the quantity of output demanded or purchased. This reflects the fact that purchases are limited by supplies, but it also allows us to depart from equilibrium models that permit no distinction between the volume of demand and supply and thus ensure market clearing. The unit value of the aggregate commodity is defined in terms of the capital and labor input coefficients:

$$\lambda = l(1 - a)^{-1}. \tag{5.9}$$

Since the output produced need not equal that demanded, the profit rate is defined by equation (5.10):

$$\pi = \frac{\lambda x^d - K}{K}. \tag{5.10}$$

Equation (5.10) assumes that production is point input–point output and that all turnover times are one period in length; there is no fixed capital. Through equation (5.10) the rate of profit is calculated against the capital available for production rather than the capital costs of direct production. A capital cost is incurred whether capital is used to finance production or is hoarded or is used to fund unproductive ventures. The rate of profit therefore measures the speed of expansion of the total capital in the economy, not merely the expansion of the capital in productive employment. The rate of profit in equation (5.10) also reflects the possibility of overproduction, the imbalance of supply and demand. Revenue is thus calculated as the volume of the aggregate commodity demanded (purchased) rather than that supplied. For ease of exposition we assume that unsold output cannot be stored; there are no inventories that might add to future supply and profit. (Such output may be given away in the form of foreign aid with no financial loss.)

The remaining equations of our model define rates of growth for a number of variables. Equation (5.11) sets the rate of growth of capital equal to the rate of profit:

$$\hat{K} = \pi. \tag{5.11}$$

We assume that there is no consumption out of the surplus. This implies that all the surplus is counted as capital in the next period and used to calculate the rate of profit, whether it is used productively or not. Equation (5.12) sets the target rate of output growth as a constant proportion of the surplus available:

$$\hat{x}^s = \beta\pi, \qquad 0 < \beta \leq 1, \tag{5.12}$$

$$\text{subject to} \quad x^s \leq \frac{K}{\lambda(a + Dl)}, \tag{5.12a}$$

where K denotes the capital available to finance production;
$\quad$ a denotes the capital input coefficient;
$\quad$ D denotes the real wage.

Thus the rate of output growth is constrained by the value of material inputs per unit of output $[\lambda\,(a + Dl)]$ and by the value of available capital. The rate of growth of demand for output is

$$\hat{x}^d = (a \,\hat{+}\, Dl) + \hat{x}^s, \tag{5.13}$$

$$\text{subject to} \quad x^d \leq x^s.$$

Equation (5.13) sets the rate of growth of demand for output as a function of changes in unit costs of production $(a + Dl)$ and changes in the level of output supplied. It is important to note that the rate of growth of demand may exceed the rate of growth of supply, but only so long as the actual level of output supplied is greater than the level of output demanded. Equation (5.14) defines the rate of change in the value of the aggregate commodity:

$$\hat{\lambda} = \hat{l} + \frac{a}{1 - a}\,\hat{a}. \tag{5.14}$$

Technical change in this economy is any change in the values of the capital or labor input coefficients.

$\quad$ This set of equations implies a social definition of the rate of profit. If, then, the rate of profit by equation (5.10) is falling, there are strategies that one sector—such as manufacturing—may pursue to escape, at least temporarily, the effects of that decline in the social profit rate. Such strategies center on the redirection of capital away from those sectors with a surplus, where some portion of the total capital is unused. It does not matter whether this surplus capital is invested productively or unproductively, as long as it is removed from the pool of capital against which profits are measured.

$\quad$ Using this set of equations, which defines a one-sector capitalist economy, we examine different scenarios of accumulation, technical change, and profitability. The remainder of this section develops a number of simple variants of our model that replicate the results of earlier analyses of technical change and profitability within equilibrium settings. We then move beyond those restrictive accounts and examine technical change and profitability within a context of disequilibrium.

Model 1. Marx's model of equilibrium growth or balanced reproduction

Assumptions. No technical change: $\hat{a} = \hat{l} = 0$.
$\qquad\qquad$ Equilibrium: Equalities in Equations (5.8) and (5.12a) hold.

With these assumptions, the rate of profit [equation (5.10)] may be rewritten as:

$$\pi = \frac{\lambda x^d - K}{K} = \frac{\lambda x^s - \lambda(a + Dl)x^s}{\lambda(a + Dl)x^s} = \frac{1 - (a + Dl)}{a + Dl}. \qquad (5.15)$$

The rate of growth of the rate of profit is

$$\hat{\pi} = \frac{d\pi}{dt}\frac{1}{\pi} = \frac{d\pi}{dD}\frac{dD}{dt}\frac{1}{\pi}, \qquad \text{for } \hat{a} = \hat{l} = 0,$$

$$\hat{\pi} = -\frac{Dl\hat{D}}{[1 - (a + Dl)](a + Dl)}. \qquad (5.16)$$

In a capitalist economy, the value of the real wage for a unit of work, say, 1 day, is less than the value created by labor in a day, or $1 > \lambda D$. If $1 > \lambda D$, then $1 > (a + Dl)$ and, from equation (5.16), $\hat{\pi}$ is positive or negative as D falls or rises. Following Marx, we try to capture the effect of the reserve army of unemployed on the labor market by defining the real wage as a function of the employment rate. Alternative specifications of real wages in theoretical Marxian models are provided by Harris (1983) and Ong (1980). Therefore,

$$D = L/N,$$

so

$$\hat{D} = \hat{L} - \hat{N}$$

$$= \hat{l} + \hat{x}^s - g_N$$

$$= \beta\pi - g_N, \qquad (5.17)$$

where g_N is the rate of growth of the labor force. Combining equations (5.16) and (5.17), we have

$$\hat{\pi} = -\frac{Dl(\beta\pi - g_N)}{[1 - (a + Dl)](a + Dl)}. \qquad (5.18)$$

Equation (5.18) reveals the principal regulatory mechanism of Marx's balanced growth model: the labor market. With no technical change, if the economy expands faster than the rate of growth of the labor supply, then the real wage is bid up. As the real wage rises, the rate of profit falls and economic expansion is checked. If the rate of growth of the labor force exceeds the rate of growth of the economy and thus the demand for labor, then the real wage is bid down and the rate of profit rises, thereby increasing the pace of accumulation. Long-period accumulation at a rate equal to the rate of growth of the labor force is possible in this scenario.

Model 2. Okishio's theorem (in a value-based accounting model)

Assumptions. Constant real wages: $\hat{D} = 0$.
$\qquad\qquad$ Equilibrium: Equalities in equations (5.8) and (5.12a) hold.

Okishio's theorem defines technical change as a shift in the values of the capital and labor input coefficients. Okishio (1961) assumes that in a competitive market firms only adopt technical changes if they are cost reducing at prevailing prices. In a value-based accounting framework this is equivalent to assuming that firms in competitive markets only adopt technical changes if they reduce the value of the capital that must be advanced for production at prevailing commodity values. This condition is

$$(a^* + Dl^*) \leq (a + Dl),$$

where the asterisk indicates a new level of an input coefficient. With the equilibrium assumptions of Okishio's model, the rate of profit is given by equation (5.15). With technical change, the rate of change in the rate of profit is

$$\hat{\pi} = -\frac{a\hat{a} + Dl\hat{l}}{[1 - (a + Dl)](a + Dl)}. \qquad (5.19)$$

Therefore, since $1 > (a + Dl)$

$$\hat{\pi} > 0 \qquad \text{if} \quad (a\hat{a} + Dl\hat{l}) < 0$$
$$\hat{\pi} < 0 \qquad \text{if} \quad (a\hat{a} + Dl\hat{l}) > 0.$$

Coupled with the requirement that technical change reduces the value of capital advanced for production, Okishio's theorem holds in a value-based accounting framework. Viable technical changes increase the rate of profit if wages are constant and markets clear (equilibrium).

Model 3. Viable technical changes with a variable real wage

Assumptions. Equilibrium: Equalities in equations (5.8) and (5.12a) hold.

Here we relax one of the assumptions of Okishio, namely, constant real wages. Once more, with the equilibrium assumption, the rate of profit is defined by equation (5.15). With changes in the real wage and the techniques of production, the rate of change in the profit rate is

$$\hat{\pi} = -\frac{(a \hat{+} Dl)}{1 - (a + Dl)}, \qquad (5.20)$$

where $(a + Dl)$ is the unit cost of production. Therefore,

$$\hat{\pi} > 0 \quad \text{if} \quad (a \hat{+} Dl) < 0$$

$$\hat{\pi} < 0 \quad \text{if} \quad (a \hat{+} Dl) > 0.$$

Thus, profit rates rise if the unit cost of production is reduced, and profit rates fall if the unit cost of production increases. Changes in unit cost depend on technical changes introduced by firms and by the movement of the real wage. Assuming that wages are constant or that labor receives a constant share of the value added in production is critical in determining how technical change impacts the capitalist economy. We consider this issue in more detail in the next model.

Model 4. Viable technical changes with wage adjustments and no assumption of equilibrium.

Assumptions. None.

This is the most general form of the model. No restrictive assumptions are placed on the variables in the system. This model does not assume equilibrium and therefore the rate of profit cannot be simplified as in equation (5.15).

From the equations that define the model of the capitalist economy we know that

$$\pi = \frac{\lambda x^d - K}{K} = \frac{\lambda x^d}{K} - 1.$$

Therefore, $(1 + \pi) = \lambda x^d/K$ and the rate of change of the rate of profit is

$$(1 \hat{+} \pi) = \hat{\lambda} + \hat{x}^d - \hat{K}.$$

Substituting equations (5.11)–(5.13) in the expression above, we obtain

$$(1 \hat{+} \pi) = \hat{\lambda} + (a \hat{+} Dl) + \pi (\beta - 1), \tag{5.21}$$

where $0 < \beta \le 1$.

Firms are conventionally regarded as myopic. This means that they examine the profitability of a technical change under the assumption that other firms are not altering their behavior in response to that technical change. In practice, myopic firms are regarded as choosing only techniques that are cost reducing at current prices, that is, at current wage levels and values. Thus, viable technical changes to myopic firms are those changes such that

$$(a^* + Dl^*) < (a + Dl), \quad \text{or, equivalently} \quad a\hat{a} + Dl\hat{l} < 0. \tag{5.22}$$

If firms are not myopic, they may make a variety of assumptions about the behavior of their competitors. If, however, they have perfect foresight and correctly perceive the reactions of their competitors, then viable technical changes reduce costs of production after prices have altered. Such technical changes meet the following condition:

$$(a \,\hat{+}\, Dl) < 0.$$

The viability condition (5.22) implies that $\hat{l} < -a\,\hat{a}/Dl$, and therefore that $\hat{\lambda} < -a\hat{a}\,(1 - a - Dl)/(1 - a)Dl$, which is negative if $\hat{a} > 0$. Thus, if the real wage remains constant (even after the introduction of new techniques), viable technical changes that reduce both labor and capital input coefficients or that reduce the labor input coefficient while increasing the capital input coefficient cause the rate of profit to fall. It is unclear how viable technical changes that reduce the capital input coefficient and increase the labor input coefficient affect the rate of profit. These results question Okishio's (1961) claims that all viable technical changes must raise the rate of profit. The difference is explained by Okishio's assumption that all commodities produced are sold so that markets clear, even with the assumption of constant wages. Webber (1982a,b) showed that these two assumptions are inconsistent: our analysis confirms this. We have demonstrated above that Okishio's model is not robust, as van Parijs (1980) claims, but rather is sensitive to the assumption of market clearing. Our more general model reveals that if unit costs of production are reduced and real wages fixed, then part of the economy's output remains unsold. Depending on the form of technical change, the unrealized profits may be sufficient to offset the cost saving through technical change and reduce the overall rate of profit.

To this point we have used our disequilibrium model of the capitalist economy to demonstrate the possibility that viable technical changes can reduce the rate of profit with a constant real wage. Next we examine the impact of viable technical change on the rate of profit in an economy where real wages are not fixed. First, we consider the case of technical changes that reduce both input coefficients or that reduce the labor input coefficient (mechanization). Secondly, we examine the case of viable technical change that reduces the capital input coefficient while increasing the labor input to production (demechanization).

From equation (5.21)

$$(1 \,\hat{+}\, \pi) > 0 \qquad \text{if} \quad \hat{\lambda} + (a \,\hat{+}\, Dl) + \pi\,(\beta - 1) > 0,$$

that is, if

$$(a \,\hat{+}\, Dl) > -\,\hat{\lambda} - \pi\,(\beta - 1). \tag{5.23}$$

Viable technical changes that reduce both input coefficients or that reduce the labor input coefficient cause the value of the aggregate commodity to fall. Thus, from inequality (5.23), the rate of profit increases only if the unit cost of production after technical change and real-wage adjustments increases significantly, and where the meaning of significantly is shown by inequality (5.23). In turn, from equation (5.13), the unit cost of production increases significantly only when the rate of growth of demand is significantly greater than the rate of growth of supply, or

$$(a \hat{+} Dl)\, s{>}\, 0 \quad \text{if} \quad \hat{x}^d\, s{>}\, \hat{x}^s,$$

where s> means significantly greater. From equation (5.8) however, the rate of growth of demand cannot permanently exceed the rate of growth of supply, for sooner or later output demanded (purchased) will be constrained by available supply. Once $x^d = x^s$, the real wage may increase to maintain unit costs but continued viable technical change ensures that the unit value of the aggregate commodity will fall and thus that the rate of profit declines. Therefore viable technical change that does not increase the labor input to production must cause the aggregate rate of profit to fall, with or without adjustments in the real wage. This result does not depend upon the precise specification of the real wage. We have attempted to make our model as general as possible.

It may seem counterintuitive that with viable technical change the rate of profit increases only when unit costs of production increase. This relationship is explained when one considers the realization of profits. Unlike most earlier models of technical change and the rate of profit, in our model we have not assumed that markets clear—that all goods produced are automatically sold. In our model, sales of the aggregate commodity are dependent upon the level of working class consumption and on the rate of economic growth. Thus, for instance, if viable technical change is not accompanied by increases in the real wage or the rate of accumulation, a portion of the aggregate commodity produced will remain unsold and profits on that output will remain unrealized. In this model, the rate of profit increases as unit costs increase by raising the proportion of the output produced that is sold. Thus, rising costs are offset by greater sales and by increasing the proportion of potential profits that are realized. However, as we demonstrated above, these circumstances cannot prevent the rate of profit from falling in the long run.

Viable technical change that decreases the capital input coefficient and increases the labor input coefficient, with or without real-wage adjustments, cannot be shown to necessarily reduce the rate of profit. Such technical change may or may not decrease the value of the aggregate commodity and thus, from inequality (5.23), the rate of profit may rise without increases in unit costs of production. Although the inevitability of a fall in the rate of profit cannot be shown in this case, there are reasons why viable technical change that causes demechanization is unlikely to persist. First, technical changes that raise the labor input coefficient are increasingly unlikely to meet the viability constraint $\hat{l}$ $< -a\hat{a}/Dl$ even with constant real wages. If real wages rise as they might be expected to do with the growing demand for labor, the viability constraint becomes even more of a hurdle. Secondly, we show in Chapter 6 that when the costs of searching for new technologies is considered, firms are likely to adopt techniques that save on the most expensive input to production. In this example, labor is becoming relatively more expensive than capital. Finally, although empirical evidence cannot resolve this theoretical question, it is abundantly clear that technical changes in the capitalist economy are predominantly labor saving (see Chapter 8). Empirical evidence, at least, suggests that labor-using technologies are rarely introduced.

The disequilibrium model examined above establishes that most types of viable technical change must eventually cause the rate of profit to fall. In the short run, if the supply of output exceeds demand, viable technical changes may raise profits by increasing the proportion of output that is sold. This strategy can only be employed until demand catches up with supply. Once the rate of growth of demand is constrained by the capacity of the economy, continued viable technical change that is labor saving must cause the aggregate rate of profit to fall. In competitive markets, rational firms will keep introducing such technical changes in an effort to boost their individual rates of profit over the average. These efforts only put further downward pressure on the aggregate rate of profit.

It is instructive to use this model to explore, albeit tentatively, some further issues related to accumulation, technical change, and profitability within the capitalist economy. First, we offer some preliminary ideas about cycles of profitability that seem to follow from our discussion. Secondly, we extend our model to consider the case of more than one region.

While the concept of the falling rate of profit was invoked by Marx to explain the eventual collapse of the capitalist mode of production, it may be more useful as a mechanism to explain the periodic spurts of capitalist growth and recession that characterize the long wave hypothesis (see Berry 1991; Freeman et al. 1982; Kondratieff 1935; Mandel 1981; Mensch 1979; van Duijn 1983). It has proven difficult for long-wave theorists to offer a consistent explanation for the upper and lower turning points of the long-wave that do not depend upon exogenous shocks to the economy or upon unrelated mechanisms to account for the upswing and the downswing. Our general model of the falling rate of profit (Model 4 above), shows that once demand is constrained by supply, viable technical changes that are labor saving necessarily reduce the rate of profit, and that fall in turn provides the impetus for the upper turning point. We also show that technical changes that do not save on labor are increasingly unlikely to meet the viability constraints that meter innovation. The model also suggests the conditions under which profitability may rise and fuel a long-wave upswing. During a long-wave downswing, new capacity is rarely put in place: existing capital is depreciated, and this speeds the way for the introduction of new techniques embodied in new capital. Slow accumulation depresses wages and coupled with the devalorization of capital prompts an increase in the rate of profit. When new fixed capital is installed in an economy, it seems reasonable to suspect that the capacity installed will be greater than current levels of demand. Our model shows that under these conditions viable technical changes coupled with rising wages raise profitability and thus sustain a higher rate of accumulation. The length of the upswing is dependent upon: the level of demand and the capacity of the economy when the new fixed capital is installed; the speed of technical change; the rate of increase in wages; and the rate of growth of demand.

Our general model of the falling rate of profit showed how aggregate demand and supply, technical change, and the profit rate are related. Reductions in the average rate of profit in an economy do not mean that all firms experience a downturn in profitability (see Chapter 4). Indeed, the very act of introducing viable technical changes is one means by which individual firms try to push their profit rates above those of their competitors. Similarly, if the economy comprises more than one region, a reduction in profitability at the level of the economy does not necessarily mean that all regions must experience a decrease in the rate of profit. However, if the economy's profit rate is falling and if the rate of profit is rising in one region, then it must be falling in other regions. Interregional competition thus affords the possibility of some regions escaping the dictates of the falling rate of profit even though firms within those regions are introducing viable technical changes.

We have seen that rational firms will only introduce technical changes that are cost reducing at existing prices. In order to maintain the profit rate, such technical changes must be accompanied by additional restructuring within the economy that raises demand and ensures potential profits are realized. Within an individual region, this restructuring takes the form of an increase in real wages and thus consumption by labor. We have seen that economic restructuring of this sort does not provide a long-term solution to declining profitability. In a multiregional context there are different strategies that may be pursued by the firms within one region to raise consumption of the goods that they produce. The most obvious of these is through export. By exporting output to other regions, firms can raise consumption without having to increase wages in their own region, thus uncoupling the relations of the falling rate of profit, at least temporarily. Firms from one region can also manufacture markets and demand elsewhere by investing capital in other regions.

5.5 CONCLUSION

With the generalization we have introduced it is possible to see the circumstances under which the rate of profit falls and under which the various models of technical change and the rate of profit operate. The generalized model shows that there is no unambiguous tendency for the rate of profit to fall. If wages are fixed, if markets are assumed to clear, and if we confine ourselves to the sectors that use capital (profits) productively, then viable technical changes increase the rate of profit—in equilibrium price terms, in value terms, and (using Chapter 4) in average price terms. However, when we consider the whole capitalist economy and relate wages to the demand for labor, we must recognize that savings in production costs alter the relations between output and demand and between output and the capacity of workers to pay for consumption. Then, when demand is growing faster than supply, viable technical changes may raise the rate of profit. Technical changes that increase the rate of profit raise the rate of growth of demand. This cannot persist, for demand is ultimately limited by supply. Once the growth of demand is constrained by supply viable labor saving technical changes cause the rate of profit to fall. With the rate of accumulation determined by the rate of profit, this model may also be read as a model of accumulation.

The generalized model of technical change and profitability illustrates the wavelike character of profit rates, which seems to correspond to the empirical evidence. So we come back to the questions posed by the evidence of Chapter 2 and the theories examined in Chapter 3. Profitability can alter for reasons internal to the capitalist economy: there do not have to have been reductions in productivity growth or increases in competition from the NICs for the Western economies to have experienced difficulties since the early 1970s. Of course, none of this says that competition from the NICs or changes in rates of productivity growth did not actually force profit rates down; that is an empirical question we address in Chapters 8–10. What we have shown here is that such external mechanisms did not have to be involved.

APPENDIX A5: MARXIAN THEORY OF THE FALLING RATE OF PROFIT

The tendency of the rate of profit to fall was regarded by Marx as the most important law of modern political economy (Marx 1967: 748). This thesis is also the pinnacle of Marx's economic theory, founded on the general laws of capitalist production and circulation outlined in Volumes I and II of *Capital,* and on the analysis of capitalist competition developed in the early parts of Volume III.

Marx spent considerable effort to develop a theory of crisis, or economic breakdown, that was endogenous to capitalist production and accumulation. His law of the tendency of the rate of profit to fall represents this theory. Perhaps the most important aspect of this theory is the logical necessity of the tendency, given the fundamental social relations of capitalist production. To establish the inevitability of crises Marx relied on three claims: first, that competition between capitalists inexorably leads to increases in the technical composition of capital and the productivity of labor; secondly, that the rising productivity of labor leads to an increase in the organic composition of capital; and, thirdly, that increases in the organic composition of capital result in the tendency for the rate of profit to fall. "The progressive tendency of the rate of profit to fall is, therefore, just an expression peculiar to the capitalist mode of production of the progressive development of the social productivity of labour" (Marx 1967: Vol. III, 213).

Marx viewed the law of the tendency of the rate of profit to fall as just that—a *tendency*. He claimed that the logic of accumulation and capitalist competition produces forces that exert a downward pressure on the overall rate of profit. This is not a claim that the rate of profit will necessarily fall, for the same forces that depress the rate of profit give rise to other pressures (*countertendencies*) that tend to raise it. The actual movement of the profit rate depends on the strength of the two sets of influences. If labor-saving technical changes can produce forces that exert a downward pressure on the rate of profit, then Marx's claims are correct. It is another, possibly more important matter to establish whether the countertendencies identified by Marx can permanently offset the tendency of the rate of profit to fall. Early debate on the law of the falling rate of profit, outlined in Section A5.1, focused largely on the logical consistency of Marx's claims. More recent debate, reviewed in Section A5.2, has examined whether reductions in profitability result from technical changes adopted in production.

A5.1 THE EARLY DEBATES

Assuming a two-department economy, we can express the aggregate rate of profit for a single turnover period as

$$\pi = \frac{S}{C + V} = \frac{S/V}{C/V + 1} = \frac{(1 - \lambda_2 D)/\lambda_2 D}{\lambda_1 K/\lambda_2 DL + 1},$$ (A5.1)

where λ_1 = the unit value of the aggregate capital good;

λ_2 = the unit value of the aggregate consumer good;

K = the physical number of units of capital employed in production;

L = the amount of labor employed in production;

D = the real wage, the number of units of the consumer good received by labor as compensation for work.

Early debate about the theory of the falling rate of profit centered on three issues. First, why should technical change be labor saving and not capital saving? Second, while labor-saving technical changes (those that reduce labor input coefficients) raise the technical composition of capital (K/L), they also reduce commodity values (λ_1 and λ_2). It is therefore unclear whether labor-saving technical changes raise the value composition of capital ($C/V = \lambda_1 K/\lambda_2 DL$). Third, reductions in commodity values, resulting from technical change, cause the rate of exploitation (S/V) to rise. Are such increases in the rate of exploitation sufficient to overwhelm the effects of a rising value composition of capital on the rate of profit?

Blaug (1960), Hodgson (1974), and Wright (1979) question whether technical change must be labor saving. Certainly, evidence would suggest that a labor-saving bias has dominated the path of technological change in the capitalist mode of production. But the problem here is theoretical. Are technical changes inevitably labor saving? In general the answer is no. However, Marx noted that without technical change the expansion of the economy is constrained by the rate of growth of the labor supply. Marx termed this "primitive accumulation": it represented an immature form of capitalism where competitive forces were not fully developed. In mature economies that embrace technical change, if the pace of accumulation is lower than the rate of expansion of the labor force, a simple scenario suggests that the real wage is bid down as unemployment increases. Lower wages raise profits and so hasten economic expansion. Accumulation accelerates as long as the rate of growth of the labor supply exceeds the demand for labor. Without labor-saving innovation, the demand for labor must sooner or later meet the constraint imposed by the size of the labor force. To maintain the pace of accumulation therefore requires labor-saving innovation. Of course, the economy could expand more slowly than the supply of labor, but such restraint raises the problem that capitalists must consume ever larger amounts of surplus. In the long-run it seems that while individual capitalists may adopt capital-saving technologies, the general direction of technical change is labor saving if the rate of accumulation is to exceed the rate of growth of the labor force.

Labor-saving technical changes increase the technical composition of capital. Mattick (1969) claimed that such changes must also raise the organic composition of capital, fueling the tendency of the rate of profit to fall. Yaffe (1973) supports this contention and attempts to prove that the organic composition of capital must rise, though Hodgson (1974) berates him for assuming that which he seeks to prove. Hodgson (1974) correctly notes that changes in the methods of production alter the values of commodities as well as the relative size of the aggregate capital and labor inputs. Thus, the impact of labor-saving technical changes on the organic composition of capital cannot readily be determined, let alone the impact of such changes on the rate of profit. Hodgson concludes that, "There seems to be no a priori reason for the organic composition of capital to rise" (1974: 66).

Weeks (1981) provides perhaps the clearest statement of Marx's law of the tendency of the rate of profit to fall. He is critical of the debate for confusing the organic composition of capital with the value composition and for the failure of its combatants to appreciate the concept of a tendency. Weeks argues that the organic composition of capital is a dynamic concept that can only be understood in terms of technological change. Firms advance capital to purchase inputs of capital and labor at their prevailing unit values, λ_1 and $\lambda_L = \lambda_2 D$, respectively. Firms may combine those inputs in novel ways, perhaps lowering the labor time required to produce their output and so reducing commodity values. Before the output from the new techniques is sold, the value of commodities is unchanged. The organic composition of capital measures the ratio of constant to variable capital after technical change, yet prior to the effects of the new techniques on the values of commodities. The organic composition thus represents the value composition insofar as the values of commodities remains unchanged. Seen in this light, any technical change that increases the technical composition of capital increases the organic composition of capital and tends to reduce the rate of profit. This is Marx's law (Weeks 1981: 198–200).

How does technical change affect the value composition of capital after such change has altered commodity values? This was the question Mattick (1969), Yaffe (1973), and Hodgson (1974) debated. However, without formal representation the issue could not be resolved. We use the accounting framework of Chapter 4 to examine the impact of technical changes on the value composition of capital. For simplicity we assume that production is point input–point output and that the length of the turnover period is constant and equal to 1. In a two-department economy, the value composition of capital is

$$C/V = \lambda_1 K/\lambda_2 DL. \tag{A5.2}$$

In turn the value of the two aggregate commodities may be expressed in physical input–output terms as

$$\lambda_1 = \frac{l_1}{1 - a_{11}}$$

$$\lambda_2 = \frac{a_{12}l_1}{1 - a_{11}} + l_2,$$

where a_{ij}, for i, $j = 1$, 2, represents the physical amount of commodity i required on average to produce one unit of commodity j;
   l_j, for $j = 1$, 2, represents the direct labor required on average to produce a unit of commodity j.

Assuming that supply and demand are in equilibrium and that the economy is growing at the rate g (Marx's balanced reproduction), we may express K and L in terms of the physical input–output coefficients of the economy;

$$K = x_1 = a_{11} (1 + g)x_1 + a_{12} (1 + g)x_2$$
$$L = l_1x_1 + l_2x_2.$$

Substituting for K and L yields

$$\frac{C}{V} = \frac{\dfrac{l_1x_1}{1 - a_{11}}}{\left(\dfrac{a_{12}l_1}{1 - a_{11}} + l_2\right) D(l_1x_1 + l_2x_2)}. \tag{A5.3}$$

Labor-saving technical changes are those that reduce labor input coefficients (l_j for $j = 1, 2$). The effects of changes in labor input coefficients on the value composition of capital can be found by differentiating equation (A5.3) with respect to these coefficients:

$$\partial \frac{\dfrac{C}{V}}{\partial l_1} = \frac{Dx_1[(1 - a_{11})l_2^2 x_2 - a_{12}l_1^2 x_1]}{[(a_{12}l_1 + (1 - a_{11})l_2)DL]^2} \tag{A5.4}$$

$$> 0, \quad \text{if } (1 - a_{11})l_2^2 x_2 > a_{12}l_1^2 x_1$$

$$\partial \frac{\dfrac{C}{V}}{\partial l_2} = -\frac{Dl_1 x_1 [a_{12}l_1 x_1 + (1 - a_{11})l_1 x_1 + 2(1 - a_{11})l_2 x_2]}{[(a_{12}l_1 + (1 - a_{11}) l_2)DL]^2} < 0 \tag{A5.5}$$

Equation (A5.4) reveals that a reduction in the labor input coefficient in the capital goods department may increase or decrease the value composition of capital depending upon techniques of production and scale of output. Equation (A5.5) shows that a reduction in the labor input coefficient in department 2 raises the value composition of capital.

While Blaug (1960) and Hodgson (1974) doubt the internal consistency of Marx's tendency of the rate of profit to fall on the grounds that the composition of capital may not increase, Sweezy (1970) questions whether technical change could increase the value composition of capital faster than the rate of exploitation rises and hence reduce the rate of profit. This is not a criticism of Marx's theory of the falling rate of profit; rather it attempts to establish whether certain types of technical change actually cause the rate of profit to fall. Limited to the terms surplus value (S), constant capital (C), and variable capital (V), Sweezy (1970) could not determine how technical changes of various types influence the rate of profit. This issue may be resolved with a more precise definition of the terms of the debate.

From equation (A5.1), assuming balanced reproduction and substituting for the values of capital and consumer goods, the rate of profit is

$$\pi = \frac{\left[1 - \left(\dfrac{a_{12}l_1}{1 - a_{11}} + l_2\right) D\right](l_1 x_1 + l_2 x_2)}{\dfrac{l_1 x_1}{1 - a_{11}} + \left(\dfrac{a_{12}l_1}{1 - a_{11}} + l_2\right) D(l_1 x_1 + l_2 x_2).} \tag{A5.6}$$

Differentiating equation (A5.6) with respect to the labor input coefficients reveals how labor-saving technical change effects the rate of profit, thereby answering Sweezy's (1970) question. If the rate of profit falls as a result of technical change, then such change increases the composition of capital more rapidly than the rate of exploitation. If the rate of profit rises, then technical change causes a greater shift in the rate of exploitation than the value composition.

The partial derivatives of equation (A5.6) with respect to the two labor input coefficients are

$$\frac{\partial \pi}{\partial l_1} = -\frac{(1 - a_{11})\, l_2 x_2 x_1\, (1 - D l_2) + D a_{12} l_1^2 x_1^2 [(1 + (1 - a_{11})] + D a_{12}(1 - a_{11}) l_2 x_2 (2 l_1 x_1 + l_2 x_2)}{[l_1 x_1 + (a_{12} l_1 + (1 - a_{11}) l_2) D L]^2} < 0 \quad (A5.7)$$

$$\frac{\partial \pi}{\partial l_2} = -\frac{(1 - a_{11}) l_1 x_1 x_2 - D(1 - a_{11})^2 L^2 - D l_1 x_1 [a_{12} l_1 x_2 + (1 - a_{11}) l_1 x_1 + 2(1 - a_{11}) l_2 x_2]}{[l_1 x_1 + (a_{12} l_1 + (1 - a_{11}) l_2)\, D L]^2} . \quad (A5.8)$$

Reductions in the labor input coefficient in department 1 cause the rate of exploitation to rise faster than the value composition of capital and hence the rate of profit rises [equation (A5.7)]. From equation (A5.8), reductions in the labor input coefficient to the consumer goods department may increase or decrease the average rate of profit in the economy, depending upon the techniques and scale of production in the two departments.

In the terms of the original discussion, Marx's tendency of the rate of profit to fall derived from the effects of labor-saving technical changes on the rate of profit, assuming that commodity values are unchanged. Labor-saving technical changes are required for long-term economic growth that exceeds the rate of growth of the labor supply. With no change in commodity values, Marx's law of the tendency of the rate of profit to fall is consistent. There are two counters to this tendency: the values of commodities themselves are altered by technical change, which may (i) reduce the value composition of capital and (ii) raise the rate of exploitation (at a constant real wage), thus preventing the rate of profit from falling. Early debate on the theory of the falling rate of profit examined how technical changes affect the value composition of capital, the rate of exploitation, and ultimately the rate of profit. The early theorists lacked the mathematical apparatus to understand how the components of the rate of profit are themselves related because of their mutual dependence on the technical input coefficients. With supply and demand in equilibrium and with constant real wages, we have shown that labor-saving technological change in the capital goods department causes the rate of exploitation to rise faster than the value composition of capital, thereby increasing the rate of profit. Labor-saving technological change in the consumer goods department increases or decreases the rate of profit depending upon techniques of production and scale of output in the two departments.

Profitability depends in a complex way on arbitrary changes in capital as well as labor input coefficients. However, changes in input coefficients are presumably not arbitrary but reflect the desire of capitalists to increase profits. How does this restriction on the forms that technical change might take affect conclusions about the direction in which profitability changes? This was the question that Okishio set out to answer.

A5.2 OKISHIO'S CONTRIBUTION

Okishio (1961) examined the relations between technical change and the rate of profit more formally with an equilibrium price model. He considered the types of technical changes that would be introduced by competitive firms and their effect on the equilibrium price rate of profit. Consider again a two-sector model of the economy, firms in sector 1 producing a homogeneous capital good and firms in sector 2 producing a homogeneous consumer good. The equilibrium prices of the two commodities are

$$p_1 = (1 + \pi_p)(p_1 a_{11} + p_2 D l_1) \tag{A5.9}$$

$$p_2 = (1 + \pi_p)(p_1 a_{12} + p_2 D l_2), \tag{A5.10}$$

where π_p is the equilibrium price rate of profit. The capital and labor input coefficients in the two sectors and the real wage are defined as previously. Okishio assumed that supply and demand are in equilibrium and that the real wage is fixed.

Equations (A5.9) and (A5.10) can be rewritten in matrix notation as

$$\mathbf{p}' = (1 + \pi_p)\mathbf{p}'\mathbf{M}, \tag{A5.11}$$

where $\mathbf{p}'$ is a 2 element row vector of equilibrium prices;
    $\mathbf{M}$ is a 2 × 2 matrix of capital and labor input coefficients augmented by the real wage.

Letting $p_2 D = 1$ be a numéraire, it can be shown that there exists a unique π_p (up to a scalar) and vector $\mathbf{p}'$ that satisfy equation (A5.11). In characteristic form, equation (A5.11) is

$$\frac{1}{1 + \pi_p} \mathbf{p}' = \mathbf{p}'\mathbf{M}.$$

If $\mathbf{M}$ is nonnegative and indecomposable, then there exists a largest $(1 + \pi_p)^{-1}$ associated with a strictly positive vector $\mathbf{p}'$ (Pasinetti 1977). The eigenvalue $(1 + \pi_p)^{-1}$ is a positive and strictly increasing function of the elements of $\mathbf{M}$.

Okishio argued that in a competitive market capitalists only adopt a technical change if it reduces costs at existing prices, that is, if

$$p_1 a^*_{1j} + p_2 D l^*_j < p_1 a_{1j} + p_2 D l_j, \quad \text{for} \quad j = 1, 2,$$

and where the asterisk indicates a new technique of production. In a competitive market (with equilibrium prices) any such viable technical change raises the rate of profit of the innovator. The temporary inequality of rates of profit is then supposed to induce the movement of capital to restore equilibrium by adjusting prices. The question is whether the new equilibrium rate of profit is higher or lower than the old. According to van Parijs (1980), the movement of the equilibrium price rate of profit after technical change constitutes a test of the logical consistency of the theory of the falling rate of profit.

In a world of equilibrium prices, assuming constant real wages and market clearing, Okishio proved that cost-reducing technical changes must increase the equilibrium rate of profit. This is shown below. In equilibrium

$$\frac{\mathbf{p}'\mathbf{m}_j}{p_j} = \frac{1}{1 + \pi_p}, \quad \text{for} \quad j = 1, 2,$$

where $\mathbf{m}_j$ is the jth column of matrix $\mathbf{M}$ and represents the cost of producing commodity j. A new technique for producing a commodity, say commodity 1, is cost reducing at current prices if

$$\frac{\mathbf{p}'\mathbf{m}_1^*}{p_1} < \frac{1}{1 + \pi_p}.$$

Replacing $\mathbf{m}_1$ of the matrix $\mathbf{M}$ with the new technique $\mathbf{m}_1^*$ and renaming the input coefficient matrix $\mathbf{M}^*$, it can be shown that

$$\min_j \frac{\mathbf{p}'\mathbf{m}_j^*}{p_j} < \frac{1}{1 + \pi_p^*} < \max_j \frac{\mathbf{p}'\mathbf{m}_j^*}{p_j}.$$

Then, given that

$$\min_j \frac{\mathbf{p}'\mathbf{m}_j^*}{p_j} = \frac{\mathbf{p}'\mathbf{m}_1^*}{p_1} < \frac{\mathbf{p}'\mathbf{m}_1}{p_1} = \max_j \frac{\mathbf{p}'\mathbf{m}_j^*}{p_j} = \frac{1}{1 + \pi_p},$$

it follows that $(1 + \pi_p^*)^{-1} < (1 + \pi_p)^{-1}$ and therefore $\pi_p^* > \pi_p$. Bowles (1981) offers a simple graphic proof of this theorem.

Although van Parijs (1980) claims that Okishio's theorem settles the relationship between technical change and the profit rate and provides an "obituary" for the Marxist theory of the falling rate of profit, the discovery of Okishio's work seems to have done little save reignite the controversy. Roemer (1977) reviews different types of technical change and their impact on the equilibrium price rate of profit. He demonstrates that there is no ambiguity in Okishio's results and also shows that a reduction in any input coefficient, coupled with constant real wages, must raise the aggregate price rate of profit. Roemer also outlines types of "socially desirable" technical change that may reduce profitability, but he states that these would never be introduced in a competitive market economy. One such "socially desirable" type of technical change, examined by Morishima (1973), is capital using and labor saving but leaves commodity values unaltered. Morishima proves that this type of technical change decreases the rate of profit, but Samuelson (1972) points out that it is not viable and would not be introduced. Roemer (1977), anticipating much of the subsequent debate, correctly argues that the possibility of a fall in the rate of profit depends on the influence of technical change on the real wage.

Roemer (1978) immediately engages this issue. He examines the consequences of relaxing Okishio's assumption of a constant real wage. When labor can maintain a constant relative share of national income—when the profit and wage shares remain constant—viable capital-using and labor-saving technical changes reduce the rate of profit. Laibman (1982) takes this further and shows that with a constant rate of exploitation, reductions in the labor input coefficient in the consumer goods department cause the rate of profit to fall. Laibman's results hold in a pure circulating capital model and in a model with fixed capital. Rigby (1990b) shows that when the real wage is set to clear the market of consumer goods, then capital-saving technical change in the consumer goods department will cause the rate of profit to fall. That Okishio's results seem to depend so heavily on the assumption of constant wages negates van Parijs' (1980) claim of their robustness. Indeed, Salvadori (1981) demonstrates that in a world of joint production, even with constant real wages, viable technical change can reduce the rate of profit.

Okishio's findings have been disputed for other reasons. Alberro and Persky (1979) maintain that the inclusion of fixed capital in Okishio's model will complicate the nature of technical change in situations where existing capital has not been fully depreciated. Roemer (1979) examines Okishio's findings in a model including fixed capital and finds that they still hold, though the fixed capital he employs is rather unusual in that it never wears out. Shaikh (1978) also examines this issue. He claims that without fixed capital, Okishio's definition of the profit rate, as the return on capital actually invested in production, should be construed as the profit margin. He then goes on to show, following Schefold (1976), that increasing the inputs of machinery while saving on materials and labor lowers the maximum rate of profit. Shaikh (1978) claims that in the long run such changes lower the actual profit rate. Shaikh's model of the falling rate of profit and his criticism of Okishio hinges on the choice of technique and on the conceptualization of competition: do capitalists compete to reduce prices or raise the rate of profit? Shaikh contends that two different criteria of competition exist. This is hotly disputed by Steedman (1980) and Nakatani (1980). Reuten (1991) reviews this debate.

Okishio's model can also be questioned on other grounds. First, the relationship between the equilibrium price rate of profit and the aggregate value rate of profit is unclear. In Chapter 4 we showed that commodity values and the value rate of profit are related to average prices and the average price rate of profit. So examining values permits us to say something about average prices. However, equilibrium prices are irrelevant as they never obtain. Whether Okishio's model has any relevance for a theoretical argument based upon the labor theory of value is therefore questionable. Secondly, Okishio has been criticized by Webber (1982a,b) for employing the logically inconsistent assumptions of market clearing and constant wages. It is surprising that this issue of realization has played such a minor role in debates on the falling rate of profit. The issue is assumed away in Okishio (1961) and has rarely since been argued: the equilibrium assumptions are widely accepted. Yet these assumptions are critical in resolving the issue of the falling rate of profit.

Rigby (1988, 1990b) attempts to generalize Okishio's findings by incorporating arguments that fix the level of the real wage and ensure market clearing. He defines a two-department economy as

$$\pi = \frac{S}{C + V}$$

$$S = (1 - \lambda_2 D)L$$

$$C = \lambda_1 x_1$$

$$V = \lambda_2 DL$$

$$x_2 = \frac{(1 - a_{11})x_1}{a_{12}}$$

$$D = \frac{x_2}{L}$$

$$L = l_1 x_1 + l_2 x_2$$

$$\lambda_1 = \frac{l_1}{1 - a_{11}}$$

$$\lambda_2 = \frac{a_{12}l_1}{1 - a_{11}} + l_2.$$

To overcome Okishio's competing assumptions of constant real wages and market clearing, the output of the capital goods department, x_1, is assumed constant and the output of the consumer goods department, x_2, is set by the availability of the capital good and the capital input coefficients in both departments. The output of the consumer goods sector can vary, but only if the capital input requirements in either department change. The real wage is set to ensure that the market for consumer goods is cleared. This is not to say that markets always do clear, but the model illustrates one way in which the impact of unsold commodities on the rate of profit can be evaluated.

The effects of changes in the capital and labor production coefficients are determined using comparative statics. Changes in each of the four input coefficients affect the aggregate value rate of profit as follows:

$$\frac{d\pi}{da_{11}} = -\frac{\pi x_1}{C + V}\left(\frac{l_1}{(1 - a_{11})^2} - \frac{l_2}{a_{12}}\right) \qquad (A5.12)$$

$$\frac{d\pi}{da_{12}} = \frac{\pi l_2 x_2}{(C + V)a_{12}} \qquad (A5.13)$$

$$\frac{d\pi}{dl_1} = -\frac{\pi x_1}{C + V}\left(\frac{1}{1 - a_{11}} + 1\right) \qquad (A5.14)$$

$$\frac{d\pi}{dl_2} = -\frac{\pi x_2}{C + V}. \qquad (A5.15)$$

Equation (A5.12) reveals that a reduction in the capital input coefficient in department 1 increases or decreases the aggregate rate of profit when the real wage adjusts to ensure market clearing. The movement of the rate of profit depends upon the techniques of production in the two departments. The higher the labor intensity of production in the consumer goods sector relative to that in the capital goods sector, the greater the likelihood that reductions in a_{11} cause the overall rate of profit in the economy to fall. Equation (A5.13) shows that reductions in the size of the capital input coefficient in the consumer goods industry decrease the rate of profit. This reduction in profitability results from increases in the real wage needed to buy the expanded consumer goods output. That innovation may alter the real wage is a crucial aspect of the falling rate of profit argument that is assumed away in Okishio's model. Equations (A5.14) and (A5.15) maintain that reductions in the size of the labor input coefficients in either department of production increase the aggregate rate of profit. In this case, the increase in the rate of profit is secured through reductions in the constant and variable capital inputs while the surplus value produced remains constant.

Most technical changes that reduce input coefficients raise the rate of profit. However, reductions in the capital input coefficient in department 2 cause the aggregate rate of profit to fall when real wages adjust to clear the market. In a less restrictive model Okishio's findings are not as robust as van Parijs claimed. However, Rigby's model still suffers from shortcomings. Perhaps most important, there is no growth in this economy: production is set at levels just sufficient to replace the capital consumed in production. Therefore viable technical changes reduce the size of the constant and variable capital inputs to production so the economy contracts. Capitalists are thus forced to hoard a part of their surplus value. Therefore, while the rate of profit might increase on the capital actually invested in production, it is not clear how the rate of profit is affected by technical change if the returns to production are measured against the total capital available for investment.

Chapter 6

THE FORM OF PRODUCTIVITY CHANGE

Technical change is central to competition and capital accumulation. When they invent new products firms seek to create new demands and enter new markets; when they invent new processes firms seek to produce more cheaply or with higher quality than their rivals. When they change the degree of coercion in a plant, reorganize shifts, alter the emphasis on quality of work, or adjust pay relativities between different grades of workers, firms seek to increase the levels of output that are achieved from given quantities of raw materials, machinery, and numbers of workers. By adjusting the composition of inputs and outputs, new techniques alter the relationship between management and the workforce within a firm and reorder the competitive standing of firms, both innovators and noninnovators. In aggregate these changes restructure the relationship between capital and labor and shape the history of development of industries, regions, and labor forces.

Interpretations of changes in the postwar world rely on implicit views about the form, rate, and direction of technical change. Freeman and Perez (1988) and Piore and Sabel (1984) view technology as the primary focus of analysis. To Lipietz (1986) as to Lash and Urry (1987) changes in the nature of technology and in the rate of productivity increase have been crucial in breaking up the Fordist regime of accumulation or organized capitalism. And to both Gibson and Horvath (1983) and Mandel (1978) changes in technique have implied that the rate of profit falls. It is commonly agreed that the growth of productivity has slowed in the 1970s and 1980s; but is the productivity slowdown a cause (as Lipietz and Freeman and Perez maintain) or a consequence (as in the accounts of Piore and Sabel and Mandel) of slower rates of accumulation?

Yet technical change is a poorly understood process of economic change. We lack the concepts to distinguish empirically the accounts of Lipietz and of Freeman and Perez, on the one hand, from those of Mandel and of Piore and Sabel, on the other: there does not exist good theory to explain the pace and direction of technical change. Since we lack good empirical measures of the pace and direction of innovation that do not depend on neoclassical economic theory, there is no empirical basis for distinguishing the different accounts. An understanding of the changes in the postwar world therefore demands a theory of technical change to identify the forces that drive technology and to permit techniques to be measured adequately.

This chapter attempts that task. It advances an evolutionary theory of the rate and direction of technical change due to process innovation. The purpose of this theory is to identify the various forms that changes in techniques of production can take and to provide a means by which the relative magnitude of those forms can be distinguished in the historical record. Since different forms of technical progress are driven by different forces, the theory also identifies the reasons why technologies and technical changes differ geographically and historically. Technical change has been investigated in many different ways (Section 6.2), but rarely is the variety of phenomena that are or appear as technical change adequately understood. Changes in production techniques, or productivity changes, are commonly thought to reflect individual decisions to invest in new technologies—either searching for improvements or copying other plants' practices; yet productivity also changes when individual plants grow or contract and when plants enter or leave the market.

The rate and direction of change of technology depend on decisions by individual plants about investment and appropriate techniques, on capacities to copy, and on the relative rates of growth of plants with different kinds of techniques. If technical change slows—as it apparently did in the 1970s and 1980s—the cause may lie less in the decisions of individual plants and more in the investment and competitive environment that makes some firms grow and others decline. Technical change modifies the future; but it is also grounded in conditions now and in the past. To understand the relations between technical change and the evolution of the global economy is therefore to understand that grounding as well as the modification.

The first part of this chapter, Section 6.1, defines technology, technical change, and productivity change. Section 6.1.1 examines the central role of technical change in capitalist competition, and Section 6.1.2 shows how to measure productivity by using the value theory of Chapter 4. Productivity is output per unit of input. But that definition begs a lot of questions. How are inputs and output to be measured? Is making people work harder a form of productivity change? Are changes in skill levels or average levels of education to be counted as forms of productivity change? And what items are to be counted as capital—plant, machinery, and equipment, as in the orthodox vision, or a broader view of capital? Relations between technical change and changes in productivity, commodity values and profitability are revealed in Section 6.1.3. Section 6.1.4 provides a general description of the components of productivity, returning to such central Marxist categories as the social and technical relations of production and in Section 6.1.5 we briefly review Marxist theory of technical change. In Section 6.2 we broaden the review to encompass models of the nature, direction, and pace of technical change. The main body of the chapter, Section 6.3, presents our theory of productivity change and its central results; the mathematical derivation is consigned to Appendix A6.

6.1 TECHNICAL CHANGE

Technology is defined broadly as the knowledge available to transform raw materials into commodities. In a more limited sense, technology includes the set of products and the techniques of producing those products that are found in an economy at a particular time. The concept of production technique encompasses not only different combinations of inputs but also different ways of organizing the labor force, as well as different institutional arrangements and management practices (Rosenberg 1982). Technological progress is expansion of the wealth of production knowledge. Such progress may take the form of an enlargement in the number of commodities that an economy can produce (product innovation), of improvement in the quality of existing commodities (incremental product innovation), or an expansion of the known techniques for producing existing or new commodities (process innovation).

The technology available to an economy is the sum of the production knowledge held by the firms composing that economy. This knowledge derives in large part from the act of production itself; from the experience of capitalists and workers in processes of competition, bargaining, and exchange; and through the learning and accumulated knowledge of labor in transforming the materials of nature into specific commodity types. Thus, technology should be viewed as much as a cultural product as an economic or scientific product (Nelson 1993). A subset of the economy's technology is typically found within an industry, which is defined as a collection of firms producing an identical commodity (joint production was discussed in Chapter 4). Firms generate technological progress when they introduce techniques of production that are not currently known to other firms in the economy. Firms also produce new technology when they improve the quality of existing products above that currently existing, or when they develop entirely new commodities.

Technical change occurs when firms alter production techniques, when they switch production from one commodity type to another, or do both. Technical change is broader than technological progress. In addition to the development of new production techniques or new products, technical change involves adoption by firms of production techniques already in use or at least known to other firms, or it may involve switching production from one commodity type to another existing commodity type (Gomulka 1990).

Insofar as technical change alters the ratio of inputs to outputs, or changes the quality or type of outputs produced from a set of inputs, productivity is also changed. To a consumer, productivity is seen to improve if some combination of the following occurs: (a) some commodity is produced that could not (for reasons of economy or technology) be produced before; (b) an existing commodity continues to be produced at the same quality but for a lower cost; and/or (c) an existing commodity is sold at the same cost as before, but it embodies quality changes. For a firm, these same changes may constitute the form taken by an improvement in productivity, but the test needs be more direct: revenue per unit of cost rises.

Productivity changes may be carried by innovations in process, in product or by some combination of these. Process changes increase productivity if the same number of workers use the same number of machines as before to produce more output. Product innovations raise productivity by increasing the price of the output produced by the given workers and machines. To a large extent, the distinction between product and process innovations is a tactical one for corporations rather than a theoretical one.

Our focus in this chapter is on changes in production technique rather than product innovation. Our aim is to advance a model of the forms of productivity change induced by changes in the process of production. We limit the model to changes in production techniques for the following reasons. First, we are most concerned with attempting to unravel competing explanations for the demise of the long postwar boom and the relationship between profitability and productivity. We are less interested in trying to identify the key innovations or carrier technologies upon which that boom was predicated (Freeman and Perez 1988; Hall and Preston 1988). Second, although in the past process innovation has received more attention than product innovation (Rosenberg 1982; Sayer 1985), process innovation is still not well understood. However, we also recognize that process and product innovation are often inseparable: distinguishing between types of innovations is dependent on the perspective of the innovator (Kuznets 1972); and innovations of a product or of a process kind perennially, yet in a discontinuous fashion (Schumpeter 1942), spawn innovations of the other kind, giving rise to clusters of interdependent or complementary innovations (Rosenberg 1982). These are variously referred to as growth poles (Perroux 1955), natural trajectories (Nelson and Winter 1982), technological paradigms (Dosi 1982), technological regimes (Hayami and Ruttan 1971), or technological systems (Freeman et al. 1982).

6.1.1 Technical Change and Competition

Competition to sell commodities in a market and to realize profit is a defining feature of the capitalist mode of production. Capitalism is a system of private or isolated production, whereby individual producers advance capital to purchase labor power and the means of production in order to make a commodity for sale in the market. It is in the market that the social nature of commodity valuation is imposed upon the private producer. In the market the individual capitalist learns whether the labor power expended in production is socially necessary and whether the technique of production employed is efficient (Weeks 1981).

Firms compete in both production and in the market. The production environment is highly regulated and tightly controlled. Through the advent of Fordist and Taylorist work practices, the pace of work in an increasing number of manufacturing operations is rhythmically governed and closely coordinated (Burawoy 1979; Edwards 1979). Competition inside the workplace is precise. Unlike the relatively ordered world of production, the market is a chaotic arena where no firm can be guaranteed any price for inputs or outputs. Spatial and temporal fluctuations of supply and demand, special pricing arrangements between suppliers and distributors, discounts on bulk purchases, favorable rates of credit and other perversions of the market place are real phenomena that operate to mask the efficient and regimented nature of production (Farjoun and Machover 1983). In the market, each firm hopes to sell the commodities it produces for a particular price. Although some firms compete by seeking the highest possible price, others may be more concerned with market share and thus discount the price of their output. All firms compete in the market by trying to obtain inputs of a given quality for the lowest price. Production efficiency is not the sole determinant of profitability, however. Good deals and bad deals are struck in the market, and these may regulate the distribution of profits.

Because of the private nature of capitalist production, there is no mechanism regulating the balance of commodity production and consumption. Uncertainty over what to produce and how to produce it is a constant feature of capitalist competition. For firms, the choice of what commodity to manufacture and which technique to use (including locational choice) is not adequately described by models that claim resources are allocated to the branch of production that yields the highest rate of profit or that firms choose a point on a production function to equate the marginal revenue and marginal cost of different factor inputs. This model of "weak competition" fails to do justice to the constraints imposed by information—in particular, knowledge of products, processes, and markets—and to the inertial effects of fixed capital and other indivisibilities in production (Storper and Walker 1989).

Technical change is a central element in the process of capitalist competition in both the sphere of production and the market. Within one industry, firms producing qualitatively identical commodities compete largely on the basis of cost. Each firm seeks to use a production method that minimizes the labor value of the commodity manufactured. However, no firm can be sure that the technique chosen will generate a profit. It is always possible that rival firms will manufacture the same commodity at lower value and thus capture surplus profit or try to force down prices and drive less efficient rivals into bankruptcy. Firms competing in the same commodity market are thus locked in a fierce struggle to continually revolutionize the process of production and to reduce average costs. No firm can afford to ignore this competitive struggle, for the introduction of more productive techniques tends to lower commodity values and thus the rate of profit earned by technological laggards.

Firms may attempt to gain some respite from the unceasing pressure of cost competition by developing new products and new markets. Like all enterprises the firm introducing a product innovation faces an uncertain market, but to some degree it may free itself from constraints on production by temporary monopoly. Once more, however, there is no guarantee that other firms will not crowd into a new market or that qualitatively superior products will not be introduced. In this process of "strong competition" firms do not naturally gravitate toward some market equilibrium; rather, they continually seek competitive advantages and surplus profits and invest in every opportunity to remove their competitors from the market (Storper and Walker 1989).

6.1.2 Labor, Capital, and Output

Chapter 4 has already explained how to measure value. The labor values of commodities are the average labor inputs per unit of output (including, of course, the contribution of plant and equipment). An improvement in productivity is therefore simply a reduction in the labor value of a commodity. The components of the calculation of values—tons of commodities and hours of labor—are, as Chapter 4 indicates, all physical measures from which market valuations have in principle been excluded.

In practice, of course, output is not so simply calculated. The central difficulty is that the output of one commodity is really an aggregation of commodities: products differ and improve. The output of the computer industry includes a huge variety of machines, of different speeds, capacities, and quality of manufacture—a mix that has changed dramatically over time. If it is assumed that the relative price of two versions of the same commodity indexes their relative quality, then it is possible from historic and comparative price data to construct measures of price per unit of quality for that commodity (Griliches 1971). Thus Gordon (1989) calculates that the real price of computers in the USA has declined by 21% a year between 1972 and 1984; Flamm (1988) reflects some consensus when he claims that the price of computing power has fallen by between 20% and 25% a year for the last three decades. From that measure and from data about total sales can be derived a series that indexes the total physical output in constant quality terms of the commodity. While in principle sales data can be adjusted in this manner to take account of quality and price changes, the methods remain contentious (Block 1990: 132–146), so that any interpretation of data about changes in productivity must be cautious.

According to Chapter 4, labor inputs can be measured too. The relevant quantity is the number of hours of productive labor power invested in an article under socially normal conditions of production and using labor of average skill and intensity, no matter what the concrete form of that labor. "Socially normal" means the average of the techniques that actually exist. The value created by 1 hour of labor power of a person of average skill must be the same as that of any other person of average skill no matter what the concrete form of their labor. Skilled laborers produce more value per hour than do unskilled laborers because they produce more commodities per hour. Productive labor power is labor power that creates use values that are in the commodity form, that has the commodity form, and that is exploited. The measure of value, then, is the average productive labor content of an article. The measure of value is inherently statistical, relying on definitions that are the averages of actual instances. Thus a unit of socially necessary labor power of average skill and intensity is a unit that produces the average quantity of value. Then the expected (average) quantity of value created in an industry equals the quantity of productive labor power supplied to that industry.

A cardinal implication of this definition is that social normality is a concept that does not apply to an individual plant. Any one factory employs concrete labor of whatever particular skills, motivations, and effort. In a plant, productivity is altered by changing the skill levels of workers, raising their motivation, altering the lengths of shifts—a whole variety of particular, concrete acts. In the aggregate those acts alter the competitive position of the plant in comparison with other plants in the industry and slightly change the measure of social normality.

Finally, the meaning of "capital" must be clarified. Conventionally, costs of production include: labor costs (of which we include only productive labor); fuel, raw materials, semifinished goods, and other inputs that are bought and used within a single production period); and depreciation of fixed capital (plant, equipment and machinery that lasts more than one production period). Other payments—to unproductive workers, for rent, interest, and profits—are uses of the surplus. In this convention, technology is sometimes equated with the characteristics of the plants and machines that constitute fixed capital. But as we shall see, that is an unduly narrow view of productivity.

Again the accounting systems introduced in Chapter 4 indicate how to measure capital. Capital is the total amount of money that has to be advanced in order to pay for production during a single production period. This includes fixed capital embodied in long-lasting plant and machinery; it also includes the circulating capital that pays for productive labor and such other inputs as fuel and raw materials. A particular form of averaging is needed to account for the fact that capital is not all advanced on the same day nor returned on one particular day later. Capital then is divided into two parts: one (variable capital) is that advanced to pay for labor; the other (constant capital) is that advanced to pay for nonlabor inputs. Variable capital is a portion of circulating capital. Constant capital includes both fixed capital and a part of circulating capital. An important element of the relationship between costs of production and the magnitude of capital is the turnover time of circulating capital.

6.1.3 Productivity, Value, and Profitability

Consider productivity in aggregate—the productivity with which the single, aggregate commodity is produced. (Appendix A6 examines the general case of many commodities.)

From Chapter 4 the value of a commodity, taking into account fixed capital of life t, is

$$\lambda = \lambda(a + f/t) + l. \tag{6.1}$$

Here λ denotes the value of the aggregate commodity; a is the constant (circulating) capital input coefficient; f is the quantity of fixed capital employed in production; and l is the labor input per unit of output (in hours of socially necessary labor time). Similarly, the value of labor power is

$$\lambda_L = \lambda D,$$

where D is the quantity of the aggregate commodity consumed by labor per unit time.

Productivity is thereby improved if there is a reduction in the circulating constant capital input per unit of output, a reduction in the fixed capital input per unit of output, an increase in the service life of fixed capital, or a reduction in the hours of socially necessary labor time. Obviously, though not apparent in the one-commodity equation (6.1), a reduction in the values of these inputs because of productivity changes in other industries will also raise productivity in this industry.

The rate of profit was also defined in Chapter 4. The rate of profit in terms of capital advanced is

$$\pi = \frac{(1 - \lambda D)l}{\lambda\left(h^1\dfrac{a}{T} + h^3 f\right) + \dfrac{h^2}{T}\lambda D l},$$

where h^1, h^2, and h^3 represent the proportions of circulating constant capital, variable capital, and fixed capital costs, respectively, that have to be advanced in the form of capital; T represents the number of turnovers in the period of measure.

Evidently, productivity and the rate of profit move somewhat independently, being influenced to some degree by different variables. Where changes in production coefficients influence productivity and profitability directly, a reduction in one of these measures of performance means a reduction in the other. Several components of the rate of profit do not directly affect productivity, whereas only one component of productivity does not directly influence the rate of profit. These results have an important bearing on theories of economic dynamics. They mean that the trajectory of productivity (changes in the values of commodities) can be different from the trajectory of the rate of profit. Productivity can be stagnant while the rate of profit is rising or falling; conversely, productivity can be improving or deteriorating even though the rate of profit is static.

6.1.4 The Determinants of Productivity

Productivity, we have argued, is indexed by the labor value of a commodity. It is not adequate to understand productivity simply in terms of technology narrowly defined as the characteristics of machines. Productivity is a matter of the social relations of production as well as the technical capacities of the plant and equipment that are installed in a workplace.

Productivity does depend on the technical relations of production. In their concrete forms, the nature of machines, the layout of factories, the quality of the semifinished inputs to production, the technical division of labor within a workplace: all these matters internal to a plant influence the labor value of a commodity. But there are technical matters outside the plant that also influence labor values: the efficiency of a transport system, the geographic structure of production, and the environmental characteristics of plants, for example.

Social controls on productivity are not only internal to plants either. Within a plant, output per unit of effort is obtained by the consent of workers. Plants coerce, at least implicitly, by threatening to fire if people do not work hard enough. Workplaces may offer a degree of security, relatively higher pay, and prospects for promotion in return for greater effort from their workers (Doeringer and Piore 1971). Other employers may induce greater degrees of cooperative behavior from workers in forms of craft production (Sabel and Zeitlin 1985). But it is also true that the efforts of an individual plant or corporation are embedded within the broader framework of social relations outside the plant. Coercion is embedded in the capital–labor relation, for it is the fact that they own no means of production that forces workers to accept at least one plant's conditions of employment. Furthermore, the social division of labor that sees production divided into certain commodities and between certain plants, that sees different social tasks divided into different workplaces and groups of workers—this affects levels of productivity too.

Two conclusions follow from such a view of the determinants of productivity. First, productivity is not simply a matter of the efforts of individual managers. Productivity is not understood just in terms of the behavior of individual plants or firms. There are social controls as well, outside the control of individual plants or firms, such as investments in transport by a government or legal changes to the rights of managers. After all, this is one of the reasons why the state remains so important to the operations of even the largest corporations. Secondly, productivity is not simply a matter of technical arrangements of workers of greater or less skill and of machines of greater or lesser efficiency. Although productivity is measured as a relation between outputs and inputs, it does not follow that it is those inputs that control productivity. Levels of output per person or per machine are determined by a host of factors, as we have seen: productivity measures the effect of those factors.

6.1.5 Marxian Models of Technical Change

For Marxian economists, the dynamic of capitalist production is driven by the struggle between capital and labor over the distribution of the surplus value added in production by labor, and by the competition between capitalists to appropriate as much of that surplus as possible. Technical change plays a critical role in both processes. In competition, the search for surplus profits demands innovation by firms seeking to enter new markets or to reduce costs in existing markets. Firms cannot ignore the force of competition, for cost-reducing technical changes tend to lower commodity prices and thus profits for technological laggards. In the struggle between capitalists and workers over the distribution of the value added, relative shares depend on the bargaining strengths of the two classes. The pressures of competition and the costs of technical change force capitalists to accumulate as fast as possible. However, if the pace of accumulation outstrips the rate of growth of the labor force, real wages are bid up as the labor market tightens. Capitalists may attempt to reduce the strength of labor and exert greater control over production by adopting labor-saving technical changes, and we have seen in Chapter 5 how this affects the rate of profit.

In keeping with Marxian analyses of the relationship between capital and labor, there is an extensive literature on the left that focuses on the impact of new technologies in altering the forms of work organization and the degree of control over the labor process (Braverman 1974; Burawoy 1985; Edwards 1979; Friedman 1977). This work is more sociological than economic, detailing trends in the organization of production such as deskilling and intensification, examining the links between markets, technology, and the division of labor, and more recently focusing on gender and ethnicity as crucial dimensions of workplace restructuring.

Although technical change occupies a central position in Marxian economic theory, the precise determinants of its pace and directional bias have received little attention. For the most part this reflects the lack of formal Marxian analysis, the thorny issue of the relationship between commodity values and their prices, and the difficulty of specifying the microeconomic foundations of behavior in nonequilibrium environments where real time, contingent events, and path dependence are not assumed away. The dynamic style of evolutionary theory and David's (1975) localized learning hypothesis (see below) appear to offer Marxian economists a new approach to the study of technical change, one that might offer an alternative to the neoclassical examination of technical change and economic growth that Nelson and Winter (1982: 205) characterize as a smooth road to a dead end. It is to this literature that we turn to next.

6.2 PROCESS-INDUCED PRODUCTIVITY CHANGE IN THE LITERATURE

Technical change has been studied from many points of view. In this section we examine different approaches to innovation to see how they identify the process of technical change. We concentrate on models that examine the pace, direction, and diffusion of technological change throughout the economy. This review prompts our theory of process innovation, which is outlined in Section 6.3.

Early recognition of the power of technology in transforming human society and propelling economic growth is to be found in the works of nineteenth-century scientists and industrial biographers such as Ure (1845) and Babbage (1846) (see Coombs et al. 1987). Much of this early work was description and not oriented toward an exposition of the links between economic structure and technology. Thus, technical change was regarded as exogenous, a state of affairs that changed little with the ascendancy of the neoclassical vision of economic life over the last 100 years or so. Forced to confront the reality of technical change, after Abramowitz (1956) and Solow (1957) showed that about 85% of per capita output growth in the USA during the first part of the twentieth century was attributable to technical change, the static neoclassical concepts of equilibrium and smooth adjustment have shown themselves particularly unsuited to analyzing the production, rate, direction, and diffusion of new technologies. Our review of the literature on technical change begins in Section 6.2.1 with an examination of the neoclassical model and its deficiencies.

Marx (1967) and later Schumpeter (1939, 1942) and Kuznets (1966) placed much greater emphasis on technical change in their models of economic history. For these theorists technical change was an integral part of the process of production and competition and the disequilibrium created by innovation was regarded as the normal state of the capitalist economy. With cycles of growth and recession linked to the timing of innovation, this work, particularly Schumpeter's (1942) notion of waves of innovation and "gales of creative destruction," has generated great interest in the rate of innovation and its determinants. This literature is reviewed in Section 6.2.2

Whether technical change is propelled by market demand, fueled by the rate of capital investment (Kaldor 1957; Schmookler 1966), or pushed by advances in scientific knowledge (Bush 1947; for a review of competing claims see Mowery and Rosenberg 1979), there is little doubt that changes in market structure and relative input costs influence the direction of technical change. This influence is captured in the theory of induced innovation, providing a useful basis from which to develop accounts of the direction of technical innovation. We highlight the theory of induced innovation in Section 6.2.3.

The induced innovation literature, while a significant improvement over early neoclassical work on technical change, has defects. First, much of this literature ignores the cost of searching for improved techniques and of adopting them. Thus, the spread or diffusion of new techniques is regarded as costless and instantaneous. Second, the theory of induced innovation views technological change as being embodied in new capital equipment and ignores the process of learning in production. Third, induced innovation says little about the trajectories along which technologies sometimes evolve. Each of these deficiencies has generated further streams of academic research. In Section 6.2.4 we review the diffusion of innovations, and in Section 6.2.5 we examine models of localized learning and evolutionary models of technical change.

6.2.1 The Neoclassical Model of Technical Change

According to neoclassical theory, the production techniques available are specified in the form of an aggregate production function such as $Y = F(K, L)$, which states that output (Y) is a function of inputs of capital (K) and labor (L). Adopting the conventional neoclassical assumptions that the function F has positive first-order derivatives with respect to K and L (the marginal products of capital and labor are positive) and negative second-order derivatives (diminishing marginal productivity of factor inputs), the production function may be represented in the form of a smooth curve, an isoquant, which maps the range of technically efficient combinations of capital and labor that can be used to produce a given level of output (Mansfield 1970; Varian 1978).

With the range of technically efficient production methods represented by the isoquant, the firm is expected to choose that technique which is economically efficient: the one that minimizes costs given the prevailing price of inputs. Any change in the ratio of factor prices, with existing techniques, is supposed to induce a movement of the firm along the isoquant in the direction of the input factor whose price has become relatively less expensive. According to neoclassical theory, such movements are regarded merely as factor substitution and do not constitute technical change. Technical change proper is represented by a shift of the isoquant itself, a movement that implies a whole new set of technically more efficient input combinations. In the most general way, technical change is built into the neoclassical model by rewriting the aggregate production function as $Y = F(K, L, t)$, where t represents time. Then it is assumed that the output produced by a fixed combination of capital and labor will increase through time as a result of technological progress.

Within the neoclassical framework considerable effort has been devoted to examining the distinction between factor substitution and technical change (Brozen 1953; Hicks 1932; Kaldor 1957; Salter 1960) and to specifying the bias in the direction of technological change, represented essentially as a shift in the entire production function toward greater labor saving or capital saving (Harrod 1954; Hicks 1932). Relatively simple variants of this neoclassical model have been employed to examine empirically the contribution of technical change to economic growth and the bias in new techniques (Abramowitz 1956; Asher 1972; David and van de Klundert 1965; Denison 1962; Kendrick 1961; Solow 1957). Apart from the conceptual limitations of the neoclassical model that are discussed below, the difficulty of estimating technical change and the problems of separating empirically technical change from economies of scale are examined by Kennedy and Thirlwall (1972), Nadiri (1970), and Stigler (1961). An excellent review of this literature is provided by Thirtle and Ruttan (1987).

A litany of problems with the neoclassical conception of production and technical change can be found in the literature. Perhaps the most well known of these is the controversy over the meaning of capital (Harcourt 1972). In the real world of heterogeneous capital goods the essential issue is whether or not such goods can be aggregated in a meaningful way to explain the level of output and the marginal productivity of capital (Jones 1975). Robinson outlined the tautology involved in attempting to define the price of an aggregate capital good: "we have to begin by taking the interest rate as given, whereas the main purpose of the production function is to show how wages and the rate of interest are determined by technical conditions and the factor ratio" (1953/54: 208). With the neoclassical concept of capital in a multicommodity world threatened, the response, spearheaded by Samuelson (1962), was to show that the central propositions of the neoclassical one good model were the same as those in the n (>1) good case. Crucial to this neoclassical parable is the monotonic relationship between the profit/wage ratio and the capital/labor ratio—a relatively high wage rate and a relatively low profit rate being associated with a high capital/labor ratio, and vice versa, as the assumption of diminishing marginal returns implies. Samuelson's attempted rehabilitation of neoclassical capital theory was effectively denied by Sraffa (1960), who demonstrated that the monotonic relationship between techniques of production and the ratio of factor prices does not necessarily hold. This possibility of "reswitching" invalidates the neoclassical parable (Harcourt 1972; Jones 1975; Sheppard and Barnes 1990), as Samuelson (1966) eventually conceded.

Aside from the issue of measurement, Robinson (1953/54) and Kaldor (1957) also questioned the neoclassical concept of capital as a perfectly malleable input, capable of being freely substituted for labor and of embodying any change in technique instantaneously and at no cost. Although an indispensable part of the frictionless adjustment to market forces that characterize the neoclassical world, this "putty-putty" vision of capital presents a distorted picture of the introduction of new techniques in any real economy. Vintage models that specify investment as the mechanism for transmitting technical change embodied in new capital goods present a more realistic scenario of the cost of innovation and of the relative fixity of capital once installed (Bliss 1968; Johansen 1959; Phelps 1962; Solow 1962).

With the notable exception of Hicks (1932), prior to the late 1950s neo-classical theory remained stubbornly silent on the origin and generation of innovation, leading Robinson (1969) to comment that it supposedly falls like manna from heaven. Perhaps the most serious failing of the aggregate production function is its assumption that the process of technical change is costless and unrelated to the movement of key economic variables. Not until technical change was treated endogenously in the theory of induced innovation did mainstream economists begin to pay attention to the real determinants and impacts of technological progress.

6.2.2 The Rate of Technical Change

Others regard innovations as discrete acts that can be dated and located (Freeman et al. 1982; Mensch 1979; Schumpeter 1939). Technical change is conceived as a means by which firms attempt to gain competitive advantage over their rivals. Since major innovations are a principal driving force of economic growth; this research aims to document the timing of innovations and to display the relationship between the frequency with which innovations are produced and the rate of economic growth (Freeman 1963, 1965, 1974; Hufbauer 1966; Posner 1961).

This tradition believes, following Schumpeter (1939), that innovations cluster in distinct historical periods. Schumpeter thought that innovations swarm because major innovations precipitate further innovation in related products, processes of production and organizational structures. Mensch (1979) presents evidence of such clustering, though he does assume that the innovations examined are all equally significant (see also van Duijn 1983). For Mensch, the lack of profits in existing lines of business forces entrepreneurs to look to innovations as a new source of profits, especially in periods of recession. Freeman et al. (1982) are critical of Mensch's data, finding little correlation between the rate of innovation and the state of economic growth. They claim that it is not the clustering of innovation that propels growth, but rather the complementarities introduced by new technology systems and their rapid diffusion throughout the economy. Rosenberg and Frischtak (1984) offer a similar argument in questioning the "depression-trigger" hypothesis of Mensch. Kleinknecht (1981) suggests that continual incremental innovation may be as important to economic growth as infrequent basic innovation. Clearly there is little convincing theory of the timing of innovations.

The product cycle model (Vernon 1966) and its variants (see Malecki 1991) are commonly used to link innovation and economic growth (Norton and Rees 1979). The product cycle model provides a simple framework that illustrates the importance of endogenous technology development through research and development expenditures; it links product diffusion and market form; and it relates process improvements to technological maturation (Aber-nathy and Utterback 1978). Van Duijn (1983) employs the product cycle in his characterization of economic growth as a series of S-shaped cycles, the amplitude of each extended by the pattern of innovation diffusion. Posner (1961) and later Hirsch (1967) also used the product cycle to argue that a country that initially develops a new product has an advantage in exporting it. Such trade would be maintained by the quality and scale of research and development, the clustering of technical innovations, and dynamic economies of scale. Hufbauer (1966) measured imitation lags in many countries and identified a strong relation between innovation leadership and export perfor-mance. Hufbauer's work has been supported by evidence that firms lead in in-novation if they are committed to research and development (Freeman 1963, 1965). The effects of research expenditure on exports differ by industry: in most capital goods industries exports correlate with spending on research and development, but this is not true of most consumer goods or basic materials industries (Freeman 1978).

The focus of this line of enquiry is creation. Innovation creates new op-portunities that firms (or regions) can exploit, new sources of differences be-tween them. However, there are critics. First, innovation is not simply a mat-ter of adopting a new technology or beginning to produce a new commodity; the first act is merely the prelude to a long series of technical changes (Fishlow 1966; Hollander 1965). Secondly, the product cycle model only crudely repre-sents the market histories of different commodities and therefore links inno-vation and economic growth unconvincingly (Debresson and Lampel 1985; Sayer 1985; Taylor 1986). Industries have different patterns of innovation (Pavitt 1984). These different patterns of innovation and growth depend on industrial structure, on the expectations of firms, and on whether the innova-tion can be appropriated (Dosi 1982; Dosi et al. 1988). The product cycle model is merely one of a range of possible histories. Thirdly, this literature has largely failed to take into account the changing cultural and institutional envi-ronments that at different times retard or accelerate the process of innovation and diffusion (Dosi et al. 1988; Freeman et al. 1982).

6.2.3 Induced Innovation: The Direction of Technical Change

The economic theory of induced innovation has been more concerned with the direction of technical change than its rate. Technical change is biased (rather than neutral) if it saves on one factor of production more than anoth-er. Hicks (1932) suggested that firms seek to economize on more expensive in-puts and so buy technology that is biased by the structure of factor prices. However, Salter (1960) claimed that in a competitive market all factors are equally dear and equally productive at the margin to a profit-maximizing firm: factor substitution is supposed to ensure that no factor is ever relatively expensive. Salter continued to argue that firms are interested in reducing costs in general, not the costs associated with a specific type of input. Yet Abramovitz and David (1973), Asher (1972), David and van de Klundert (1965), and Habakkuk (1962) discovered that British and American technical change did exhibit a significant labor-saving bias.

The existence of a price-induced bias in innovation hinges on the way in which the production function is defined. For example, Salter (1960) defines the production function so broadly as to include all possible technologies that could be developed given the existing state of knowledge. This definition leaves no room for Hicks' (1932) distinction between factor substitution (movement along an existing production function) and technical change (movement of the production function). Still retaining the concept of the production function, Fellner (1961) appealed to the expectations of monopsonist firms and to the relatively scarcity of factors of production to resurrect the theory of induced innovation.

The difficulty of separating factor substitution and technical change led Kennedy (1964) and later Ahmad (1966) to abandon the neoclassical concept of a production function altogether. Kennedy examined the direction of technical change in terms of an innovation possibility frontier (IPF), which describes the trade-offs between rates of capital augmentation and labor augmentation. These frontiers are assumed to be downward sloping, concave, and independent of relative factor proportions and shares. Each period the firm searches for a new technique that maximizes the rate of unit cost reduction. The equilibrium solution occurs when the slope of the IPF equals the ratio of factor shares. Factor shares rather than factor prices therefore fix the bias of technical change. Kennedy's model provides an induced innovation mechanism independent of an explicit production function. [Kaldor (1957) and von Weizsacker (1966) develop growth models embodying induced innovation without using the production function, whereas Dandrakis and Phelps (1966) reunite Kennedy's IPF with a standard neoclassical growth model.]

The notion of an IPF has been widely criticized. Kennedy's conclusions are sensitive to the precise definition of the innovation frontier (Ahmad 1966). Stoneman (1983) questioned whether the IPF represents technological possibilities as yet undeveloped or whether it is a set of blueprints from which the innovating firm can choose. Since Kennedy did not model the resources used in adopting a technique from the IPF, Stoneman concluded that the frontier represents a set of developed techniques. But, then, where does the IPF come from and what decides its form? While Jones (1975) argued that Kennedy's frontier means that neoclassical growth models do not have to assume Harrod-neutral technical change, Nordhaus (1973) claimed that growth models must still assume that the form of the frontier does not change, that it is not influenced by previous technological choices, and that the "natural drift" of invention is to the movement of the frontier over time. David (1975) concluded that Kennedy has simply replaced exogenous technical change with an exogenously determined innovation possibility frontier.

Ahmad (1966) adopted Salter's (1960) broad definition of the production function to specify his innovation possibility curve (IPC). This curve describes the set of technological possibilities open to the firm at any one moment. Each process from this set is supposedly characterized by an isoquant with relatively limited substitution possibilities. The IPC is the envelope of all such isoquants for a given level of output. Ahmad assumes that the firm uses resources to choose a particular isoquant on the IPC. The precise position of the firm on the isoquant is, as usual, given by the factor price ratio. A change in this ratio will induce the firm to move along the isoquant substituting inputs. In time, with technological progress represented by a shift in the IPC, the firm will move to another isoquant on that curve. Ahmad shows that the firm may well choose an isoquant on the more advanced IPC that is characterized by a different set of restricted substitution possibilities than the isoquant chosen on the first IPC. This would constitute a bias in the direction of the firm's technology. Ahmad's (1966) model bolsters the arguments of Hicks (1932) and provides a more solid microeconomic foundation for the theory of price-induced bias in the adoption of new technologies. Like Kennedy's (1964) IPF, however, it is not clear what determines the precise form and the movement of Ahmad's IPC.

Still, the main failing of the above models is their reliance upon an exogenous stream of new technological possibilities. It was not until Kamien and Schwartz (1968) and Evenson and Kislev (1976) began to model explicitly the cost and the productivity of producing new technologies that a solid foundation for induced bias in the direction of innovation was provided. Binswanger and Ruttan (1978) summarize this work by assuming that firms follow different research paths each directed at reducing the input requirements of selected factors. These research paths have varying costs and expected payoff functions measured in terms of efficiency improvements. Thus, research is viewed as an investment problem where the aim of the firm is to maximize profits by choosing optimal levels of inputs and research activity. Within this framework, assuming a fixed research budget and constant productivity in research, it may be shown that firms are most likely to search for new techniques that save the relatively more expensive inputs to production. The relative productivity of alternative research paths, changes in the relative costs of capital-saving and labor-saving research, and the specification of the research budget are all shown to exert a significant influence on the character of innovation. Most importantly, perhaps, by showing that research is a resource using activity, these models effectively refute Salter's (1960) criticism of Hick's (1932) induced innovation hypothesis.

6.2.4 Diffusion

If innovation is the means whereby firms create differences between themselves, then diffusion is a process of imitation whereby the differences between firms are progressively removed. Although innovation is responsible for defining "best practice" techniques and for the introduction of new products, the rate of diffusion plays a key role in determining the pace of aggregate technical change. Soete and Turner (1984), for instance, suggest that the productivity slowdown of the mid-1970s may have been the result of a decrease in the rate of adoption of innovations rather than a decrease in the production of those innovations. Two approaches dominate the study of the diffusion of innovations.

The earlier approach sought empirical regularities in the diffusion of innovations (Mansfield 1961). This work led to the discovery of the S-shaped logistic adoption curve, thought to occur when information about the technical and economic characteristics of an innovation is progressively distributed. Innovation is subject to an information constraint, most explicitly in Hagerstrand's (1967) pioneering study of the adoption of "free" techniques by Swedish farmers. Diffusion is a process in which producers adjust to a new equilibrium state: incomplete adoption is a disequilibrium state. This "epidemic" diffusion model has been widely used to examine the overall rate of product diffusion (Griliches 1957), the spread of technology between firms (Mansfield 1963), and the pattern of international technology transfer (Hayami and Ruttan 1971; Swann 1973). Brown (1981) reviews some spatial extensions of this model.

The epidemic model is not without its critics, however. First, Rogers (1962) has argued that the environment for potential adopters is not homogeneous. For example, the cost of adoption may fall through time as knowledge increases, and the future income stream may decline with time as larger numbers of rivals adopt an innovation (Reinganum 1981). Second, the population of potential adopters is not static: over time technological improvements may increase the pool of potential adopters, or conversely, steeper learning costs may inhibit diffusion (Baldwin and Scott 1987; Coombs et al. 1987). Third, knowledge is not readily disseminated in a "pure form" but is embodied in materials, products, or processes. Vintage or "stock-adjustment" diffusion models remedy this defect (Stoneman 1983). Fourth, the epidemic model says little about the relative costs of innovation, imitation, and knowledge protection. Baldwin and Scott (1987) examine the effects of patent protection, licensing, and joint ventures on diffusion, and Baldwin and Childs (1969) examine the conditions under which imitation is more profitable than innovation.

Diffusion may also be regarded as a sequence of equilibria. Producers are in a state of equilibrium that is determined by their characteristics and the economic environment. As their characteristics or the environment change, so the equilibrium point changes and diffusion goes on. David (1975) has advocated this theory, illustrating how environmental changes and the characteristics of firms interact to produce patterns of innovation. Mansfield (1961, 1963, 1968) used similar arguments to explain patterns of interfirm and intrafirm diffusion in US industries.

In opposition to these equilibrium accounts, it has been objected that firms cannot maximize in complex environments under conditions of uncertainty and that rational behavior may not be defined when "right" and "wrong" depend on the actions of others (Dosi et al. 1988). Rosenberg (1982) has also criticized static diffusion models for failing to recognize crucial differences among the population of adopters, for ignoring postadoption technological improvement, and for failing to recognize institutional changes that influence the pace of adoption. More recently, Gertler (1993) has developed these arguments to account for the difficulty of firms in mature industrial regions to adopt new process technologies. He concludes that the social construction of technology (see also Walker 1985) means that costs of innovation and learning are critically dependent upon differences in the social and political character of regions that produce new technology and those that use it.

6.2.5 Learning, Localized Search, and Evolutionary Models

An alternative to both neoclassical theory of induced innovation and equilibrium analysis of innovation diffusion views technical change as a localized learning process that seeks to reduce production costs at particular points in the spectrum of techniques (Atkinson and Stiglitz 1969). Arrow (1962) introduced the concept of learning by doing, a type of disembodied technical change, to explain how productivity improves as a result of production. Rosenberg (1982) developed the related idea of learning by using. David (1975) developed the notion of learning and localized search to show that the realized factor-saving bias of technical change may reflect factor prices—directly as well as through decisions about choice of technique. David started with Salter's (1960) idea of feasible production processes to explain localized learning by doing (Alchian 1950; Asher 1956; Rapping 1965). Localized learning by doing is locally neutral change that does not alter relative input proportions. Such technical change is visualized as a two-dimensional random walk in which each step is a discrete technical improvement: a viable technical change is one that reduces one input by a fixed proportion and leaves the other input unchanged. Improvements are introduced at a constant rate and are impeded by barriers that retain approximately the initial balance among factor proportions.

David's model of localized learning by doing by firms that have distinct starting technologies is a major contribution to the theory of technical change. The central idea that firms search locally (in technology space) for technical improvements is crucial to understanding technical change. However, the hypothesis that technical change is related to factor proportions rather than to factor levels is an ad hoc assumption made so that change is locally neutral. David has also defined viable technical change in an unnecessarily restrictive way: profitable techniques may increase some inputs provided others are reduced sufficiently (a profitable change may use more machinery but replace much labor). More fundamentally, though, the theory of learning by doing ignores the competition so central to the equilibrium analysis of innovation diffusion. Firms may be learning, but they are also under competitive pressure.

Evolutionary models explicitly recognize that technical change has several distinct sources that were earlier analyzed separately (Metcalfe and Gibbons 1986). Firms are creative as they seek to differentiate themselves from their competitors through major shifts in technology and localized learning by doing. Firms also imitate the technology of others—a diffusion process. And then competition alters the relative market shares and sizes of firms that use different technologies. Evolutionary models also recognize that economic processes are stochastic rather than determinate. Since one firm's decisions alter everyone's economic environment, small events influence the subsequent history of all firms. Nelson and Winter (1982) provide the fullest defense of this approach to the study of economies. Firms are motivated by profit and seek to improve profitability but do not maximize over well-defined and exogenously given choice sets; more profitable firms drive out less profitable ones but cannot drive all out; firms have capabilities and decision rules but are not maximizers; and the market chooses the more profitable firms but in an evolutionary way.

These ideas have been used to study technical change. Dosi et al. (1988) have explored how innovations diffuse. Decision makers face uncertainty about future technical progress, demand, and competitiveness. Decisions are made by rules of thumb depending on orders, backlogs, delivery delays, rates of capacity utilization, and shipments, while aggregate demand is steadily growing. Market shares change with the competitiveness of firms, though a delay reflects brand loyalty and search processes. Innovations diffuse in many different ways. In particular early adopters can be penalized and small early events may dramatically alter the entire history of diffusion because of feedback effects. Metcalfe and Gibbons (1986) analyzed other forms of technical change. In one model there is no technical change within firms. Firms' unit rates of profit depend on the difference between their (constant returns) production costs and the market price. Since a fixed proportion of profit is invested the lowest cost producers grow in comparison with the other producers. Competition (or selection) drives such technical change. In a second model the share of profits invested may vary; the firms with growing market shares now combine high unit profits and high rates of investment. A third model examines the effects of creating new technologies, that is, technical change at the level of the individual firm.

Nelson and Winter (1982) also modeled technical change. One model examines factor substitution (176–184). Firms expand or contract according to profitability. They search for new techniques that, if profitable, are adopted costlessly. Like David (1975), Nelson and Winter assume that the rate of technical improvement depends on the rate of change in input coefficients and that the direction is independent of those coefficients. The sequences of techniques and factor ratios form a Markov chain. For each firm a change in relative prices shifts the probability distribution of factor ratios and so the expected direction of technical progress. Selection effects depend on the covariance of factor ratios and capital shares. Their evolutionary model of growth with technical change (Nelson and Winter 1982: 206–233) generates technical progress with rising output per worker, rising real wages, a rising capital/labor ratio, and a roughly constant rate of return on capital; its rates are not dissimilar to those that occurred in the USA over the last 200 years.

This form of modeling is the most appealing approach to technical change. It recognizes that firms have different technical abilities and policies and allows small, chance events to affect the entire future course of development. It identifies three main means of technical change: (a) innovation, the creation of new technologies; (b) selection or competition by which technically more advanced firms outcompete their rivals; and (c) imitation. The entry of new firms also affects prevailing technology. Still, how can these different effects be identified in practice? Nelson and Winter (1982) have made the only detailed attempt to compare their models to reality. Even so they do not estimate the effects of different parameter values. Again, is it possible to obtain general (analytic) results rather than merely the results of particular simulations with some qualitative conclusions? Both Metcalfe and Gibbons (in simplified circumstances) and Nelson and Winter (by regression analysis on the effects of parameter variations) have made some progress in this direction; yet these results remain far weaker than those obtained from the rigid assumptions of more formal models.

6.2.6 Issues and Evaluation

Nelson (1981) observed that research about the theory and measurement of technical change has essentially asked three kinds of question. Why does growth vary over time? What explains differences between countries in levels and changes in technology? Why do some industries have faster productivity growth than others? As economic growth has apparently slowed in the 1970s and 1980s these have become central questions, answers to which have been examined in Chapter 3. To evaluate theories about these national changes, we must be able to measure technical change accurately and identify its sources.

Equally, though, regions in many countries have experienced changing fortunes over the last 50 years. Increasingly it is recognized that cities and regions are the principal agents of economic development throughout the world (Castells and Hall 1994; Scott and Storper 1990). Thus as high-technology industry has become seen as central to recovery from the slow-growth 1970s and 1980s, so the regional dimensions of technical change have been more closely scrutinized (Amin and Goddard 1986; Aydalot and Keeble 1988; Malecki 1991; Oakey et al. 1982). Two questions are significant.

First, how and why have regions acquired concentrations of high-technology industries? Such regions exhibit a particular constellation of characteristics. Sayer and Morgan (1986) write of Berkshire in the UK as containing a mass of highly skilled people, good international communications, government research institutes, a pleasant living environment, and a lack of trade union traditions. Saxenian (1985) and Oakey (1985) provide similar descriptions of Silicon Valley in California and Route 128 outside Boston. Hall and Markusen (1985) extend this analysis to other high-technology growth regions in the USA, and Castells and Hall (1994) review the development of the world's technopoles, the supposed industrial complexes of the twenty-first century. These descriptions emphasize the importance of the siting of some initial research facilities, around which later cluster smaller establishments that create agglomeration economies of various kinds (Scott 1988a,b). The precise location of such clusters is unpredictable. The emergence of high-technology industrial regions is perhaps best "explained" by the path dependence that follows small, chance events (Storper 1988; Webber 1970). Continued competitive success of the region is then a matter of the creativity of the firms within it.

Secondly, what is the regional structure of innovation behavior (Ewers and Wettman 1980; Gibbs and Edwards 1985; Oakey et al. 1982)? Typical of this form of research, Goddard et al. (1986) distinguish fundamental and incremental product innovations and process innovations. They observe that many firms located in the lagging regions of Britain rate poorly in innovation behavior (for example, they employ few research staff and correspondingly introduce few product innovations). Glasmeier (1986), Malecki (1985) and Oakey et al. (1982) demonstrate that the location of innovation is largely a function of the spatial division of labor within multilocational firms.

Such research begs the question of the effects of other social changes on industrial location. It also relies on particular views of technical change. The idea of major innovations is central: What are the implications of other forms of technical change? To what extent is failure to innovate a consequence or a cause of regional decline? Is it possible to distinguish the causes of technical change? Nelson and Winter (1982) claim that research and development spending predicts industries' rates of innovation, and Goddard et al. (1986) make a similar observation for firms; but what accounts for research and development expenditure? What then are the causes of productivity differences and productivity changes over time?

It is difficult to measure technical change empirically. Calculations of the number of new processes or products invented, patented, or applied for (as by Mensch 1979; Pred 1966) typically assume that each product or process is of equal importance and neglect the many improvements made to products and processes when firms are learning by doing. Measurement of changes in the mix of inputs used per unit of output avoids these problems, but when applied to aggregates of plants the measure confounds several separate processes influenced by different causes. Technical change proper, by which a firm institutes a new production method, changes the mix of inputs used in that plant. This can occur when the firm applies a new method or imitates other firms' methods. The rate at which a new method is applied depends on: the rate of discovery, which reflects the resources invested in research and development and the probability of finding a new technique per dollar expended; and the rate of application of discoveries, which reflects the rate of gross investment and the profit margin that a new technique is expected to achieve. Imitation hinges on the resources available for purchasing new equipment and on barriers to transfers of technologies. The degree of technical change induced by the new method depends on the length and extent of the learning process generated by that new technique. Observed changes in the average techniques used in industries, regions, or nations include other elements that do not embody technical change. Competition, in which the market share of firms with cheaper techniques increases at the expense of the share of those with more expensive techniques (termed *selection* by Metcalfe and Gibbons 1986), induces changes in the average technique even though no plant has changed its methods of production. The rate of change in average techniques caused by competition depends on the severity of competition, the rate of gross investment, and the variations in efficiency among plants. If the production techniques of plants are all equally favored, then competition cannot lead to drift in the average production method. Conscious decisions to innovate have nothing to do with this form of technical change.

The entry and exit of plants into a sector or region can also alter the average production method. The migration of firms into and out of a region may change average techniques without changing production methods in any plant. The increased price of a product allows new and less efficient firms to open or reopen, whereas price decreases force firms out of production, again changing the average technique without technical change. The rate of change due to these processes depends on entry and exit barriers faced by firms (reflecting the concentration of ownership, the expenses of hiring and firing labor, and the quantity of fixed capital) and the rapidity of price changes compared with changes in production costs. The only change like this at all similar to the kinds of behavior that underlie technical change proper is the entry of a new firm applying a technique that is better than the industry or regional average.

So an understanding of the relations between technical change, economic growth, and regional development cannot be achieved by focusing entirely on discrete innovations. There exist additional effects due to imitation, learning, competition, and the entry and exit of plants. Similarly, observation of the change in the average mix of inputs among a sectoral or regional aggregation of firms can mislead. Such observation does not separate innovation from imitation, or either of these from the effects of competition and the entry and exit of plants, which have nothing to do with technical change proper. So analyses that trace intersectoral or interregional differences in the rate of technical change to differences in innovation behavior are potentially deceptive since they misidentify changes in inputs as innovation. Aggregate technical change is in short a "chaotic concept," though we continue to use it, as others do, as shorthand for the aggregate effect of all these processes (Sayer 1984).

To evaluate the causes of observed changes in average production methods and thus rate empirically theories about economic development, sectoral shifts, and regional growth, we must specify the different effects of innovation, imitation, competition, and the entry and exit of plants on the rate and direction of aggregate technical change. Statements about the relationship between innovation and regional economic growth can be accurate only if this separation has been made. In the next section we begin this exercise by summarizing a stochastic model of technical change proper within a plant and the aggregate effect of such change. Competition and the entry and exit of firms are then incorporated into this model.

6.3 THE FORMS OF PRODUCTIVITY CHANGE: A SUMMARY

In this section, we summarize our model of productivity change. Our summary examines a simple one-good economy where production uses only two inputs, capital and labor. A formal presentation of this model, for a multicommodity, multi-input economy, is provided in Appendix A6. We start our summary in Section 6.3.1 by defining technical change and noting the forms that technical change may take. In Section 6.3.2 we outline the conditions under which firms will choose to adopt new techniques. In Section 6.3.3 and 6.3.4 we examine the factors that influence the rate and direction of technical change at the level of the plant and industry.

6.3.1 Types of Technical Change

For an individual plant i producing commodity k the technology employed is defined as $z_k^i = (a_k^i, l_k^i)$, where a_k^i is the capital input and l_k^i is the labor input per unit of output. (We retain this notation for consistency, even though this summary deals with a one-commodity economy.) Technical change in the plant is defined as any change that results in a new vector $z_k^{i+} \neq z_k^i$. Thus, a technical change at the level of the plant is any change that alters the amount of capital or labor input per unit of output of the aggregate commodity.

Observed technical change in a plant can arise from the following sources:

1. Economies or diseconomies of scale that may result from changes in the level of output
2. Learning, whereby producers discover how to combine existing inputs more efficiently

3. Innovation, which arises from research and development; here the plant implements a new technique that has not been adopted by another firm
4. Imitation, which is the adoption of existing technology already in use by other firms
5. Relocation, which results in a change in the transport inputs required per unit of output and therefore a change in technique

An industry is defined as the set of plants that produce the same commodity. We denote by s_i the relative size of plant i in industry k, that is $s_i = a^i/\Sigma a^i$, where a^i denotes output in plant i. Then the industry's technology is $z_k = (a_k, l_k)$, where

$$a_k = \Sigma s_i a_k^i, \qquad l_k = \Sigma s_i l_k^i.$$

Technical change in an industry is any change that results in a new vector $z_k^* \neq z_k$. Technical change at the industry level may be of three basic types. First, there may be technical change within individual plants, of the form analyzed above. Second, the relative sizes of the plants may alter, changing market shares s_i and thus the weight of individual plant technologies. Third, plants may enter or leave the industry, altering the distribution of an industry's technology.

6.3.2 Conditions for Adoption of New Technology in a Plant

Assume that a plant using two inputs (a, l) faces price of output p and an hourly wage w. The unit cost of production for the plant is then $k = pa + wl$.

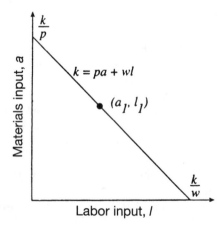

FIGURE 6.1. Cost-reducing technical change.

In $a - l$ space, the equation $k = pa + wl$ maps a straight line along which costs are constant as shown in Figure 6.1. The slope of this line is given by the ratio $-w/p$. All points below the constant cost line denote techniques that are more efficient than those along line k, and all points above the constant cost line denote techniques that are less efficient than those along line k.

Suppose that a firm is considering technical change—changing scale, implementing the discoveries that are learned, innovation, imitation, or relocation. We assume that the firm calculates the benefits of technical change at current prices. In a competitive market, firms adopt techniques that are expected to reduce costs of production. Thus, only those techniques located below the constant cost line k are candidates for adoption. Before the costs of technical change are taken into account, the increased profit expected from technical change is $k - k^+$ per unit of output, where k^+ is the unit cost associated with the new technique.

Technical change involves costs as well as benefits. First are the costs of obtaining information about the new technology and of planning the change, as well as the costs of disrupted production while old plant is scrapped and new plant installed. Second are the costs of learning to use the new technology once it is brought on line. Third is the cost of purchasing the fixed capital that embodies the new technology. This third cost requires a capital outlay, financed from either retained earnings or external borrowing.

The simple criterion that a new technique be cost reducing is not sufficient for technical change to occur. If the costs of disruption and learning can be estimated, and if the size of the investment in new capital and the interest rate are known, then the required cost saving of the new technology can be calculated. The new technology must be such that $k - k^+ > C$, where C is the present value to the firm of the unit cost of changing technology. In the two-

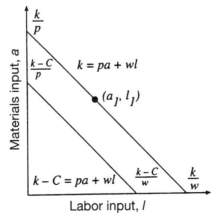

FIGURE 6.2. Cost-reducing technical change with a threshold.

input case, this inequality defines a region as shown in Figure 6.2. The distance from the lower line to the upper line depends on the magnitude of C, but the slopes of these lines are identical because they depend on the same relative prices. Thus a rational firm changes technique if the new technology z^+ satisfies the relation $k^+ \leq k - C$.

6.3.3 The Direction of Technical Change in Plants

In this section we examine the direction of technical change at the level of the plant. First, consider the introduction of new techniques. The plant searches about the vicinity of z for a new technology by learning about the use of existing capital, by engaging in formal research and development, or by looking into existing inventions. There is little evidence that the search is biased (even though revealed technical change may be predominantly labor saving). We assume that—

1. The probability that a new technology z^+ is discovered is a monotonic decreasing function of the distance between z and z^+.
2. The probability that a new technique is discovered is independent of its direction from z.
3. No technology can employ negative amounts of any input.

There are a large number of new techniques available to the plant contemplating technical change. We have shown that viable changes are those that satisfy the condition $k^+ \leq k - C$. The actual direction of technical change taken in a plant is not predictable, but the expected direction of technical change can be shown to be orthogonal to the constant cost line k (Figure 6.3). Thus, technical change is expected to economize on the most expensive factors of production. This bias arises not through the search process but from the constraint on the eligibility of candidate innovations. Appendix A6 provides proof of this claim. It also analyzes the effects of the costs of technical change and boundary constraints on the expected direction of technical change.

Second, consider a plant that is copying technology already in use. Plants do not have to adopt new technologies. Many attempt to copy techniques already being used by other firms, perhaps to save the costs of research. Given a distribution of plants in technology space (Figure 6.4), the possibility of a plant, say P_1, adopting the technology of a more efficient firm, say P_2, is a function of the cost of technical change and the unit cost savings that would accrue to the plant by making such a change. The cost of imitation may include patent and license fees in addition to the usual costs of technical change. With the cost of imitation C, plant P_1, with unit costs

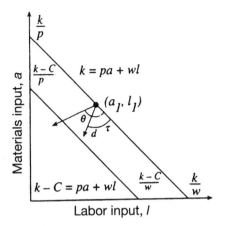

FIGURE 6.3. The expected direction of cost-reducing technical change.

of production k_1, would adopt plant P_2's technology, with unit production costs of k_2, if $k_1 - k_2 > C$. The inducement to imitate should thus be stronger for plants employing the least efficient techniques. The benefit to a plant i of imitating the technology of another plant j is greater the lower the unit costs of production of plant j. So, if the costs of patents and licenses are standard, plants try to imitate techniques that are closest to the southwest corner of the technology space. The precise direction of technical change through im-

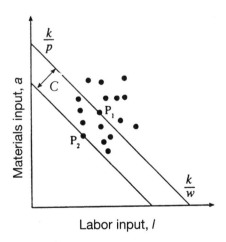

FIGURE 6.4. Technical change by imitation: plant P_1 adopts the technology of the most efficient plant P_2.

itation depends upon the distribution of techniques among the plants that define an industry.

6.3.4 Technical Change in an Industry

Observed technical change in an industry comprises three elements:

1. Real technical change (as discussed in Section 6.3.3)
2. Selection, which is the process whereby the rate of growth of production in a firm varies systematically with the technology used by the firm
3. Entry and exit of firms from an industry, which is the process whereby technologies are added to or removed from the distribution of technologies within an industry

We distinguish real technical change, which is an alteration of technique that follows a deliberate effort by plants, from apparent technical change (selection and entry/exit), which is an alteration of technique that does not result from a deliberate search for superior technologies. This section examines the influence of these three processes on the rate and direction of technical change that would be observed in an industry that contains a variety of techniques and sizes of plants.

6.3.4.1 Real Technical Change in an Industry

The direction of real technical change at the industry level is determined by the direction of technical change within the plants that define an industry (see Section 6.3.3). The expected direction of innovation within an industry is orthogonal to the ratio of input prices. The rate of innovation in an industry, and in a plant, depends on the capital invested in the search for new technology, the productivity of that investment and the fixed cost of innovation. The capital invested in the search for new techniques is higher if more funds are available (from retained earnings or borrowing) or if there is a greater propensity to invest in technical change as opposed to expanded use of current techniques. The productivity of investment in technical change is high if new techniques are cheaply discovered or if research and development is highly effective. If the fixed costs of innovation rise faster than the mean search distance for new technologies, the rate of technical change decreases because the probability of finding techniques that save enough to overcome these costs fall.

The other source of real technical change at the industry level is imitation of superior techniques. In a period of stable technology, when no inventions are being produced, imitation tends to concentrate the technological distribution of the firms within an industry about the most efficient technique used in that industry. The variance of technologies within the industry should also decrease as a result of imitation. The rate of technical change due to imitation depends on the factors influencing the rate of introduction of new technologies, modified by the effects of patent and other restrictions on copying. The expected direction of technical change as a result of imitation lies between the orthogonal to the line of constant cost, k, and the long axis of the ellipse formed by the point distribution of technologies in use. The dynamics of industrial technical change via new techniques and imitation are complex and examined in more detail in Appendix A6.

6.3.4.2 Apparent Technical Change

Selection refers to differences in the rate of growth of output among the plants of an industry that alter the share of output produced by each plant and thus the industry's technology. The direction of apparent technical change due to selection depends on the existing point distribution of techniques within an industry and on the relative rate of growth of each plant's output. In general, the expected direction of technical change due to selection is similar to the expected direction of technical change due to imitation. The rate of technical change from selection depends upon the degree of competition in an industry, on the extent of the variation in efficiency among plants, and on the rate at which profits are reinvested in the same sector.

An industry's technology may also be altered by the entry and exit of plants. In general, if output prices are constant, the techniques of new plants are likely to be similar to those of existing plants, with a bias toward the more efficient end of the market. Thus, the entry of new plants to an industry is likely to alter techniques in a fashion similar to the effects of imitation and selection.

However, if the real price of output rises or falls, there are additional effects to consider. A rise in the price of output within an industry provides a niche of opportunity for new plants. Plants that could not be profitable under the old price can now make a profit and are therefore induced to enter the industry. Conversely, when the real price of output falls, some marginal plants can no longer make a profit and are forced out of the industry. We assume that the degree to which the point distribution of plant technologies expands or contracts with price changes is independent of the mix of inputs used. This implies that the direction of technical change due to the birth and death of plants within an industry is the normal to the constant cost line. The rate of technical change due to the birth and death of plants in an industry is assumed to be a function of the observed change in prices within the industry and the existence of barriers to the entry of plants to the industry and their exit from it.

6.4 CONCLUSION

Existing models of technical change fail to separate the various factors that cause an alteration of technology. Observed levels of technical change in an industry depend on both innovatory behavior at the level of plants and market or competitive effects. Commonly the latter are ignored (except in diffusion studies), though they may be crucial. Thus, the rate of innovation is frequently given too much credit in accounting for fluctuations in the pace of technical change.

Four broad sources of change in technology have been identified. The introduction of new techniques within the plants of an industry causes reductions in the unit costs of production, at a rate that depends on the speed with which unit profits are translated into cost reductions and the average rate of profit. The direction of this technical change depends on the relative prices of capital and labor. This is innovation in the classical sense. A second source of (real) technical change is imitation, whereby plants within an industry copy more efficient technologies already employed by their competitors. The pace of imitation depends on the variance of existing techniques within an industry, on the costs of imitation, including patent and license fees, and on the availability of capital to fund the change. The direction of technical change through imitation depends upon the distribution of techniques among the plants that define an industry. A third source of (apparent) technical change in an industry is selection, the different rates of growth of plants. The rate of cost reduction due to selection depends on the interplant variance in production costs and proceeds in a direction that depends on the covariation between plants in labor and capital inputs. This is a competitive or market-induced effect. Fourthly, technical change also appears when plants are added to or removed from an industry because of changes in the price of the industry's output. The rate of cost reduction caused by the birth and death of plants depends on the level of price changes and is in the same direction as the introduction of new techniques. This is another competitive effect on apparent technology. The challenge now is to identify these different forms of technical change from the empirical record and so to separate the impact of innovation proper from competitive effects and from other (possibly exogenous) influences on technology.

We have argued in this chapter that observed technical change in an industry must be disaggregated into its components: each component is underlain by a different process and some have little relation to the innovative behavior that is generally regarded as the source of technical change. These distinctions are crucial for evaluating empirically the theories of the current transition that were reviewed in Chapter 3. In some theories the productivity slowdown is an external cause of falls in profitability; in others the productivity slowdown was itself a result of slower rates of economic growth. Now we have a theory of the sources of changes in productivity that can be used to identify empirically what appears to have happened.

APPENDIX A6: THE NATURE OF TECHNICAL CHANGE

A6.1 SOME DEFINITIONS

We begin by adapting the main definitions introduced in Section 4.2.2.5 to describe an individual plant. An industry k consists of the set of plants that produce the composite commodity c_k; there are N industries. Suppose that a plant i produces a^i tons of the composite commodity c_k. The plant's input–output coefficients are defined as

$$\mathbf{a}_k^i = (a_{k1}^i, a_{k2}^i, \ldots, a_{kN}^i) = (a_{k1}^{*i}, a_{k2}^{*i}, \ldots, a_{kN}^{*i})/a^i,$$

where a_{kj}^{*i} denotes the total quantity of commodity c_j used in the standard accounting period. One input commodity is transport. Since both a_{kj}^{*i} and a^i are measured in tons the input–output coefficients $\mathbf{a}_k^i$ are dimensionless. Equally, the expected number of hours of socially necessary labor power of average intensity and skill required to produce 1 unit of the commodity c_k is l_k, the quantity of labor power actually supplied to the plants divided by the output of the industry. (Socially necessary labor time is not defined at the level of a single plant.)

The nonnegative vector $\mathbf{f}_k^{*i}$ denotes the total fixed constant capital in place during the year. The elements of $\mathbf{f}_k^{*i}$ are measured in tons. Thus f_{kj}^{*i} denotes the quantity of industry j's products (commodity c_j) that are used as fixed capital by plant i in industry k. Define the entries of $\mathbf{f}_k^i$ by

$$f_{kj}^i = f_{kj}^{*i}/a^i,$$

where f_{kj}^i denotes the fixed constant capital of commodity c_j per unit of output; it is dimensionless. Associated with $\mathbf{f}_k^i$ is a vector $\mathbf{t}_k^i$ that records the service life of each fixed constant capital item; $\mathbf{t}_k^i$ is fixed by social practice in the same manner as the other coefficients. Thus f_{kj}^i/t_{kj}^i is the quantity of fixed constant capital from industry c_j used up (depreciated) per year per unit of output of plant i in industry k.

Thus the technology of plant i that produces the composite commodity c_k is $\mathbf{z}_k^i = (\mathbf{a}_k^i, \mathbf{f}_k^i, l_k^i, \mathbf{t}_k^i)$. So a technical change in the plant is any change that results in a new vector $\mathbf{z}_k^{i+} \neq \mathbf{z}_k^i$: any change that alters the amounts of circulating constant capital, labor power, fixed constant capital, or depreciation times per unit of output of commodity c_k.

A6.1.1 Types of Technical Change Within a Plant

Observed technical change in a plant has several causes.

1. *Change in the capacity utilization rate* spreads fixed constant capital over greater or lesser quantities of output. The effect of such changes may be

calculated. We define f(act) as the vector of fixed capital required per unit produced per production period. Then the fixed capital used per unit produced per year is

$$f = f(act)/RT, \qquad (A6.1)$$

where R is the capacity utilization rate (the ratio of fixed capital in use to total fixed capital), and T is the turnover rate (the number of production periods per year). For a constant technology [f(act)] and a constant turnover time, f is inversely related to R.

This is spurious technical change. It appears as technical change at the level of the plant and is certainly associated with productivity changes but does not follow a deliberate alteration in production methods. Therefore it is necessary to adjust the coefficients of z to account for the effect of variations in the capacity utilization rate in order to figure out the technical composition of capital of capacity that is actually being used. Fortunately, it is usually possible to gauge this effect [by equation (A6.1)] and so remove it from estimates of technical change. The following two effects are different.

2. *Economies or diseconomies of scale* result from changes in the level of output. This form of technical change is distinguished from alterations to the capacity utilization rate because additions to scale involve additions to the plant's fixed capital. These require changes of type 4, below (and will be discussed there).

3. Changes in technology arise as a plant responds to input price changes by moving along its *long-run production possibility frontier*. Such technical change implies that there exists a production function to describe the possible combinations of materials and labor that a plant can use in producing a commodity. A "state of technology" is summarized by a production function—a set of production possibilities from which a plant chooses the most profitable, given input prices. In this vision technical change occurs only when a new production function is introduced, not when a plant moves along an existing production function. It therefore becomes important to distinguish movements along a production function from movements between production functions.

We do not use this distinction. Here any change in the vector z is a technical change. Thus a movement along a production possibility frontier is a movement to a previously existing technology and will be analyzed as such. Furthermore unless one is willing to make heroic assumptions about the form of production functions and factor rewards, changes between production functions are in fact confounded with all the other types of technical change in actual data.

In a strictly neoclassical world changes of types 1, 2, and 3 are not regarded as technical change proper: they are adjustments to an existing technology the boundaries of which are mapped by a production function that defines the range of technically efficient production possibilities now available.

Such changes do alter our description of the technology z, however, and cause observed changes in the input–output coefficients.

4. By contrast, the following are technical changes in both our and the neoclassical view. *Relocation of a plant* results in a change in the transport inputs required per unit of output or in the service life of capital and therefore is also a technical change. The input price changes associated with relocation are not an element of technical change. *Imitation* is the adoption of existing technology, already used by other firms. *Innovation* arises from research and development by a plant that seeks and adopts an existing invention that has not yet been adopted by other firms. Finally, *learning in use* results in technical change as the workers in a plant learn how to use new capital more efficiently.

Clearly, technical change within a plant is a complex phenomenon. The traditional, intuitive view of technical change as the production of inventions and the adoption of innovations is only one of an array of processes that alter input–output coefficients. Very similar, however, are the changes in input coefficients caused by relocation and the learning that takes place within plants after new capital or new organizations have been imported. We call these forms of technical change, described under type 4, "real technical change." Technical changes of types 2 and 3 are alterations in the relative magnitudes of the components of z that can only be identified within an empirical method that employs production function theory. Since such theory is not employed here, these changes cannot be separated from changes of type 4. Thus we call technical changes of types 2, 3, and 4 "apparent technical changes"—changes observed in aggregate data. The "spurious forms of technical change," associated with changes in the capacity utilization rate, can be separately identified and should be removed from data before measuring observed rates of technical change.

A6.1.2 Technical Change at the Level of an Industry

An industry is the set of all plants that produce the same commodity. Denote by s^i the relative size of plant i in the industry:

$$s^i = a^i / \sum_i a^i.$$

Then the industry's technology is $z_k = (a_k, f_k, l_k, t_k)$, where

$$\mathbf{a}_k = \sum_i s^i a^i_k, \qquad \mathbf{f}_k = \sum_i s^i f^i_k, \qquad l_k = \sum_i s^i l^i_k, \qquad \mathbf{t}_k = \sum_i s^i t^i_k.$$

Evidently, technical change in an industry is any change that results in a new vector $z^*_k \neq z_k$. There are two basic sources of technical change at the level of an industry. First, there may be technical change at the level of plants that alters the elements a_k, f_k, l_k, t_k as analyzed in Section A6.1.1. Secondly, the relative sizes of the plants may alter as competition selects some plants and rejects others. Such changes alter the market shares, s^i. An adequate theory of technical change must examine both these forms of change and provide a means of separating them empirically within aggregate industry data.

A6.2 ADOPTION OF A NEW TECHNOLOGY IN A PLANT

Suppose that spurious technical change (type 1) has been removed from the observations. The managers of a plant are considering "apparent" technical change, that is, technical change that results from scale change, relocation, adoption of a technology already in use, invention, adoption of a new, off-the-shelf technology, or learning. Under what conditions will such a new technique be adopted?

Consider a plant that produces commodity c_k with technology z_k^i. The plant faces prices

$$\mathbf{p} = (p_1, \ldots, p_N, p_1^f, \ldots, p_N^f, w, 0, \ldots, 0)$$

for its inputs. If the plant is considering technical change, it is searching for a new technology z_k^{i+} that reduces costs of production. By definition, the current unit costs of production are $K = \mathbf{p} z_k^i{}'$. The point z_k^i lies on a hyperplane in the space of inputs. This hyperplane divides the available technologies into two groups: those that lie "above" the hyperplane and satisfy the relation $\mathbf{p} z_k^{i+}{}' > K$ (the class of cost-increasing technologies) and those that lie "below" the hyperplane and satisfy the relation $\mathbf{p} z_k^{i+}{}' < K$ (the class of cost-decreasing technologies). The second class includes all the viable candidates for adoption.

Consider for example a two-input plant. If the plant uses raw materials and labor, such that $\mathbf{z} = (a, l)$ and $\mathbf{p} = (p, w)$, then its unit cost of production is $K = pa + wl$. In $a - l$ space, the equation $K = pa + wl$ is the straight line shown on Figure 6.1, one of whose points is (a_1, l_1). The slope of this line depends on the relative prices, p and w. All technologies with lower costs of production lie below the line. If capitalists calculate the benefits of technical change at current prices, only technologies below the line are candidates for adoption. Before paying for the costs of technical change, the increased profit expected from the technical change is therefore $K - K^+$ per unit output per annum, where K^+ is the cost of operating the new technique.

This identification of candidate technologies differs from that of David (1975). In his analysis of the direction of technical change by learning, David assumed that candidate technologies are technologies z_k^{i+} for which $z_k^{i+} \leq z_k^i$, that is, in which at least one input coefficient is reduced and none of the input coefficients is increased. However, David's assumption is unnecessarily restrictive.

A technical change also adds to costs. First are the costs of disrupted production while old plant is being scrapped and new plant installed, as well as the costs of obtaining information about the new technology and of planning the change. Second are the costs of learning to use the new technology properly once it is installed; this is learning by using. This element may also include the cost of learning to deal with new suppliers, the cost of labor negotiations required to introduce the new technology, and the cost of labor retraining. Third is the cost of purchasing the new fixed capital that embodies the new technology. The first two are straightforward, but the third requires a capital outlay, financed from either retained earnings or external borrowing.

A firm that uses its own money to finance production makes the following payments out of revenue: payments for labor and raw materials; a payment due to the depreciation of fixed capital; and the remainder is surplus. After the fixed capital is fully depreciated the firm is left with a sum equivalent to its initial capital (obtained from the annual depreciation payments) and may have accumulated some surplus that has not been paid as rent, taxes, unproductive labor, or consumption. If the existing fixed capital is not yet fully depreciated, the capital fund is smaller than it was when the previous round of fixed capital investment was made. What is crucial here is that the capital fund and the accumulated surplus be large enough to purchase the new fixed capital (and perhaps to pay for any losses that accrue because of disruptions and learning). Evidently the longer the existing fixed capital has been depreciating and the larger the past rate of profit, the more likely this condition is to be met. Thus the following are tests that investment in new fixed capital out of retained earnings have to meet:

1. The capital fund and accumulated surplus must be sufficiently large to pay for the investment.
2. The expected rate of profit per annum on the investment, which equals the unit savings ($K - K^+$) multiplied by the volume of output less the costs of change and learning by doing (distributed over the expected lifetime of the fixed capital), divided by the total capital investment in the change, must exceed the rate of return available from alternative investments.

The second source of funding is borrowing. Such borrowing requires that the firm pay interest. It also requires the payment of interest on debt from previous fixed capital investments that have not yet been repaid. So, to the extent that past fixed capital investments have not been depreciated (loans repaid), the cost of new investment rises. Such borrowing may be rationed, too. Now the change must meet the following tests:

1. The firm must be capable of borrowing the required funds.
2. The expected rate of profit per annum on the investment must pay the market rate of interest, the interest and capital repayments of unpaid loans, and a profit on the firm's own capital investment.

   The simple criterion that technical change be cost reducing does not guarantee that change will occur. The firm must have access to funds—either internally generated or borrowed on the financial market—and the profitability of the investment must exceed the current rate of return on financial securities. These requirements suggest some hypotheses about the likelihood that a given firm will adopt a given technical change. (1) If existing fixed capital has not been fully depreciated, the technical change is less likely than if fixed capital has been depreciated. (2) If a firm that uses internal funds has a long history of low profit rates, then technical change is less likely than if the firm has consistently earned high profit rates (since it will have smaller accumulated surplus to invest). A firm that lacks access to the financial market may be unable to afford some kinds of new technology that require large initial fixed capital investments. Thus a firm may become stuck in an old-fashioned technology, in the sense that its rate of profit is insufficient to generate the funds to pay for the technical change or in the sense that its anticipated profit may be insufficient to justify the investment. (3) An addition to capacity is more likely to use the new technology than is replacement of existing capacity, since disruption and the costs of learning must be incurred anyhow when capacity is being added. (4) If the rate of profit in manufacturing is low in relation to profit earned on other investments, then investment in technical change is less likely than when the manufacturing rate of profit is high.

   If the costs of disruption and learning can be estimated, and if the size of the investment and the market rate of interest are known, then the required cost savings from the new technology can be calculated. The new technology must be such that $K - K^+ > C$, where C is the present value to the firm of the unit costs of the change. The size of C may be different for different firms. In the two-input case this inequality defines a region as shown in Figure 6.2. The distance of the lower line from the first depends on the size of C, but the slopes of the lines are identical because they both depend on relative prices. Thus an independent, rational firm changes technique if the new technology z_k^{i+} satisfies the relation

$$\mathbf{p}z_k^{i+}{}' \leq \mathbf{p}z_k^{i}{}' - C = K - C.$$

(A sufficient condition for change is the absence of a technology z_k^{i*} for which $\mathbf{p}z_k^{i*}{}' - C^* \leq \mathbf{p}z_k^{i+}{}'$.)

A6.3 THE DIRECTION OF TECHNICAL CHANGE IN A PLANT

With this background, we now consider the direction of technical change selected by a plant. We examine first a plant that is introducing a new technology and secondly a plant that is copying a technology already in use. This is followed by a discussion of technical change in an industry.

A6.3.1 New Techniques

A plant employs technology z_k^i, represented as a point in $(3N + 1)$ – dimensional space, where N is the number of commodities produced in the economy. (There are three vectors of nonlabor inputs, each of N elements, and one dimension of socially necessary labor time.) The plant searches about z_k^i for a new technology by learning about the use of existing capital, by engaging in formal research and development, or by looking into existing inventions. Some authors claim that plants search for new technologies that are labor saving because they allow greater control over the labor process and because there has arisen a climate of opinion that equates saving labor and reducing costs. There is, though, no evidence that such a *search* is biased to save labor (although revealed technical changes may be labor saving). Therefore we neglect such bias in the search and assume instead that—

1. The probability that a new technology z_k^{i+} is discovered is a monotonic decreasing function of the distance from z_k^i to z_k^{i+}, $d(z_k^i, z_k^{i+})$. That is, plants look for new technologies near their existing technology; because of unfamiliarity they do not look for radically different technologies. Of course radically different technologies do arise from time to time, but they are less likely than less radical inventions. [We make the standard distinction between an invention (the discovery of a new process or technology) and an innovation (the adoption of that invention by a plant). We argue that the probability of finding an invention declines with distance from the existing technology z_k^i.]

2. The probability that a new technology is discovered is independent of its direction from z_k^i. That is, we reject the idea that inventions to save labor are inherently more (or less) likely to be discovered than inventions to save on raw materials or fixed capital. We also reject David's (1975) assumption that the distance from the old to the new technique is proportional to the percentage change in input coefficients between the new technology and the old. (David's assumption ensures that there is an equal proportional reduction in each input coefficient, irrespective of the price of inputs.)

3. No technology can employ negative amounts of any input.

An important issue is concealed in these assumptions and ignored in existing analyses of the direction of technical change. We refer to the "distance" of a technical change and the "direction" of an invention. But the concepts of distance and direction are defined with respect to a particular coordinate system, that is, to a particular set of units of measurement for the input–output coefficients. In everyday life, these units are arbitrary: tons or tonnes, bushels or kilos, gallons or liters. Units of measurement can be ignored only by adopting David's method of modeling percentage changes; but this implies the unnecessarily restrictive result that change always proceeds along a ray linking the old technology to the origin. There is, however, a standard unit of measurement of labor (hours or days of abstract labor) that is a common attribute of all commodities (including labor power) and that we have argued in Section 4.1 is a consistent macroeconomic yardstick (Farjoun and Machover 1983). Empirically labor values are closely correlated with prices of production (Shaikh 1984). The dollar value of heterogeneous capital commodities is not consistent in this sense, as the Cambridge capital controversies showed.

We have previously argued that an invention will only be adopted by a plant if it satisfies the criterion $\mathbf{p}z_k^{i\prime} + < K - C$. There are many such innovations, any one of which may be discovered; thus the actual direction of technical change taken by an individual plant is not predictable but depends on chance discoveries, the preconceptions of research and development personnel, and the abilities of workers and managers to adapt existing machines. But while the actual direction of technical change in any one plant is not predictable, the expected direction is:

Lemma 1. Under assumptions 1 and 2, the expected direction of technical change is normal to the hyperplane defined by $\mathbf{p}z_k^{i\prime} = K - C$ and is proportional to prices.

Proof. It follows from the requirement $\mathbf{p}z_k^{i+\prime} < K - C$ and from assumptions 1 and 2 that in the two input case (Figure 6.3) the expected direction of technical change is

$$E(\theta) = \frac{\int_0^\infty \int_{\tau(d)}^{\pi-\tau(d)} \theta\, Pr(d, \theta)d\theta\, dd}{\int_0^\infty \int_{\tau(d)}^{\pi-\tau(d)} Pr(d, \theta)d\theta\, dd} \cdot \tag{A6.2}$$

The angle θ is measured from the direction of the input price constraint. The integral is taken between the limits τ and $\pi - \tau$, rather than 0 and π, because the technology must pass the $K - C$ test. (The angle τ is defined on Figure 6.3.) By assumption 2, $Pr(d, \theta) = Pr(\theta)\, Pr(d) = r\, Pr(d)$, say. It is a simple matter of integration to prove that $E(\theta) = \pi/2$, the normal to the constraint.

This expected direction is readily calculated. Describe the existing constraint $\mathbf{p}z_k^{i\prime} = K$ as a vector, in terms of the amount each input is increased as labor inputs are decreased. In the diagram, the vector is $[p, -w]$. In general the constraint vector is $\mathbf{b} = [p_1, p_2, \ldots, -w, p_n, \ldots]$. A vector $\mathbf{d}$ is orthogonal to $\mathbf{b}$ if $\mathbf{b}\, \mathbf{d}' = 0$. There are two solutions to this equation but only one is cost reducing, namely,

$$\mathbf{d} = [-w/3Np_1, -w/3Np_2, \ldots, -1, -w/3Np_n, \ldots].$$

It follows that the expected direction of technical change is proportional to prices.   QED

The expected direction of technical change, as defined by Lemma 1, can be interpreted in two ways. First, the expectation can be interpreted as the average of a series of actual technical changes, provided that the direction of successive changes is independent of the direction of changes that precede them and that each change satisfies assumptions 1 and 2. In this sense Lemma 1 purports to describe the actual history of technical change in a plant over a long period if each change is independent of its predecessors and prices are constant (but see Dosi et al. 1988). Secondly, the expectation can be interpreted as a guess about the direction of a single technical change that perhaps has yet to occur; the guess equals the average direction of an (imaginary) indefinitely large sample of single technical changes. In this sense Lemma 1 purports to predict the anticipated direction of individual technical changes.

Lemma 1 has an important implication for factor saving. Consider the two-input case in Figure A6.1. The normal to the vector $[p, -w]$ is the vector $[-w/p, -1]$. That is to say the expected technical change is such that if the labor inputs are reduced by 1, then the material inputs are reduced by p/w. (The acute angle made by the expected direction as it crosses the abscissa equals $\pi/2 - \tan^{-1} p/w$. That is, the higher are wages in relation to material prices, the greater the tendency to reduce labor inputs; the lower are wages, the less the tendency to reduce labor inputs in relation to material inputs.

This is an important result: technical change is expected to economize on the most expensive factors of production (calculated per unit of labor value of a commodity). This does not say that technical changes in all plants have this characteristic—only that the average over a set of independent technical changes has this characteristic. This tendency for technical change to economize most on the most expensive inputs arises not from an assumed bias in the search process but from a constraint on the eligibility of candidate innovations.

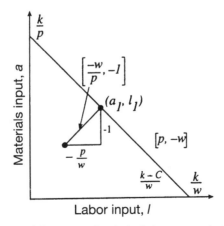

FIGURE A6.1. Expected direction of technical change as relative prices change.

An additional characteristic of technical change can be deduced from this model:

Lemma 2. If assumptions 1 and 2 hold, then the greater is the cost reduction ($C = K - K^+$) that must be effected for the technical change to be profitable, the lower is the variance of the direction of profitable technical changes about the expected direction $E(\theta)$.

Proof. The variance of the direction of profitable technical changes about $E(\theta)$ is

$$V(\theta) = \frac{\int_0^\infty \int_{\tau(d)}^{\pi-\tau(d)} [\theta - \pi\backslash 2]^2 \, Pr(d, \theta)d\theta \, dd}{\int_0^\infty \int_{\tau(d)}^{\pi-\tau(d)} Pr(d, \theta)d\theta \, dd}$$

$$= \int_0^\infty Pr(d) \, [\pi - 2\tau(d)]^2 dd \Big/ \int_0^\infty Pr(d) \, dd.$$

The precise size of the variance evidently depends on the form of the function $Pr(d)$, that is, on the way in which the probability of discovering an innovation declines with distance from the plant's existing technology. However, since $0 \le \tau(d) \le \pi/2$, the variance is an increasing function of the angle $\tau(d)$ at any distance. But

$$\tau(d) = \pi/2 \qquad \text{for} \quad d \le C$$

$$\tau(d) = \sin^{-1}C/d \qquad \text{for} \quad d \ge C.$$

Hence, at any distance d, the greater is C the greater is $\tau(d)$ and so the less is the variance at that distance. That is, the existence of a minimum cost reduction constrains the variety of viable technical changes; and the greater the minimum cost reduction, the less the variety of viable technical changes and the lower the variance in the expected direction of technical change.

A6.3.2 Boundaries and the Direction of Technical Change

These calculations of the expected direction and variance of the direction of technical change have ignored assumption 3—that plants may not use negative quantities of inputs. In the presence of boundaries, the expected direction of technical change generally deviates from the normal to the price constraint:

Lemma 3. The expected direction of technical change is more (less) labor saving than is predicted by the normal to the price constraint if the current constant capital input coefficient is less (more) than the current direct labor input.

Proof. To demonstrate this fact, we again consider equation (A6.2) and let $Pr'(d, \theta)$ denote $Pr(d, \theta)$ normalized by division by the denominator. Then

$$E(\theta) = \int_0^\infty \int_{\tau(d)}^{\pi - \tau(d)} \theta\, Pr'(d, \theta) d\theta\, dd.$$

This expression can be broken into two parts:

$$P[\tau(d), \pi/2: a, l > 0] = \int_0^\infty \int_{\tau(d)}^{\pi/2} \theta\, Pr'(d, \theta) d\theta\, dd \qquad (A6.3)$$

$$P[\pi/2, \pi - \tau(d): a, l > 0] = \int_0^\infty \int_{\pi/2}^{\pi - \tau(d)} \theta\, Pr'(d, \theta) d\theta\, dd. \qquad (A6.4)$$

Expression (A6.3) is the "expected" weight of potential innovations to one side of the plant's current technology; expression (A6.4) is the "expected" weight to the other side. Evidently, the expected direction of technical change is biased away from the normal toward the side that has the largest weight, as defined by expressions (A6.3) and (A6.4). The technical change is more labor saving than expected if (A6.4) exceeds (A6.3), and that is true if at all distances d

$$\int_{\pi/2}^{\pi - \tau/2} Pr(d, \theta) d\theta \geq \int_{\tau(d)}^{\pi/2} Pr(d, \theta) d\theta \qquad \text{for all} \quad a, l > 0 \qquad (A6.5)$$

and if there is at least one distance d for which the inequality holds strictly. Thus it is sufficient to prove that if the material input exceeds the labor input, (A6.5) is true.

Consider Figure A6.2. The proof requires that if $K_1 A_1 < L_1 A_1$, then (A6.5) is true. There are three cases: the plant's technology is represented by A_1, or by A_2, or by A_3. Technology A_1 is located such that the normal to the price constraint at A_1 passes through the origin. We shall examine each in turn.

First, consider the technology A_1. The triangles $\triangle A_1 BO_1$ and $\triangle A_1 O_1 C$ are similar. If $A_1 K_1 < A_1 L_1$, $\triangle A_1 BO_1$ has a smaller area than $\triangle A_1 O_1 C$. Therefore the length of an arc of radius d drawn around A_1 and passing through $\triangle A_1 O_1 C$ is at least as great as that which passes through $\triangle A_1 BO_1$. And this is true for all d. That is,

$$[d_1: \epsilon \triangle A_1 BO_1] \leq [d_1: \epsilon \triangle A_1 O_1 C] \qquad \text{for all} \quad d,$$

where $[d_1: \epsilon X]$ is the length of an arc of radius d drawn about A_1 and lying within the convex hull X. The inequality is strict for $d > A_1 L$.

Next, consider technology A_2. The triangle $\triangle A_2 BO_2$ is similar to and smaller than $\triangle A_1 BO_1$. It follows that

$$[d_2: \epsilon \triangle A_2 BO_2] < [d_2: \epsilon \triangle A_2 O_2 A^*] < [d_2: \epsilon \triangle A_2 O_2 O_1 C] \qquad \text{for all} \quad d.$$

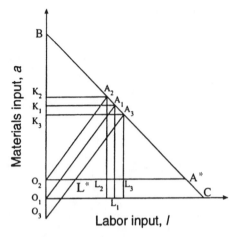

FIGURE A6.2. The effects of boundaries.

Finally, consider the technology A_3, again such that $A_3K_3 < A_3L$. The tri-angle $\triangle A_3BO$ is similar to and smaller than $\triangle A_3L^*C$. Also $A_3BO_1L^*$ is a strict subset of $\triangle A_3BO_3$. Therefore,

$$[d_3: \epsilon\ A_3BO_1L^*] \leq [d_3: \epsilon\ \triangle A_3BO_3]\ [d_3: \epsilon\ \triangle L_2C] \qquad \text{for all}\ d.$$

The inequality is strict for $d > A_3K_3$.   QED

Two aspects of this deviation from the normal to the price constraint are significant. First, the direction of deviation depends only on the relative mag-nitudes of the constant capital and labor input coefficients. It is independent of the price constraint. Secondly, if a technology is located near enough to one boundary (it uses very little labor or very little materials), then the expected deviation from the normal may be associated with an increase in the little-used input. (In contrast the normal to the price constraint always entails a re-duction in all inputs.) Figure A6.3 illustrates this possibility.

A6.3.3 Imitation

Many plants do not adopt new technologies but copy those being used by other plants. Given a distribution of plants in technology space (Figure 6.4), a plant p^i may adopt the technology of the most efficient plant. The most effi-cient plant is on the "lowest" hyperplane parallel to that defined by $\mathbf{p}z_k^{i\prime} = K$: P_2 in the diagram. Evidently the question is merely whether the technology z^2 satisfies the criterion that $\mathbf{p}z^{1\prime} - \mathbf{p}z^{2\prime} > C$.

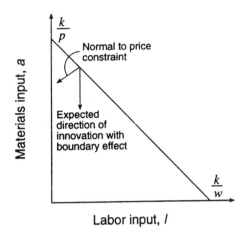

FIGURE A6.3. Analysis of the boundary effect.

This analysis suggests that the best technology, z^2, is most likely to be adopted by the plants with the "worst" technology—those located furthest up and to the right in the diagram—since they have most to gain from adopting technology z^2. Thus in a period when no new inventions are being produced, the distribution of plants in technology hyperspace should become more concentrated around the most efficient technology and the variance of technologies in use should decrease. However, two other considerations weigh against this conclusion.

First, the plants using the least efficient technology are also those making the least profit, unless they have some output price advantage over their rivals. Thus they also have the least resources (retained earnings or ability to attract outside financial support) with which to pay for the capital cost of the new fixed capital. Some of these plants may be trapped in the upper tail of the cost distribution of techniques until they become so unprofitable as to go out of business.

Second, even if no inventions are being produced, selection may alter the average technology in use in industries that supply inputs. Therefore, prices of inputs may change. It follows that the most efficient technology may also change over time.

A6.3.4 Industry-wide Changes

An industry consists of a set of plants. The industry's technology is $z_k = (a_k, f_k, l_k, t_k)$, the average of the technologies used by the individual plants. If by the end of a period the individual plants have changed their technologies, then without competitive effects that change the relative sizes of plants, the industry's technology has become $z_k^i = (a_k^i, f_k^i, l_k^i, t_k^i)$. The expected direction of technical change by innovation (as opposed to imitation) is readily computed when all plants face the same prices:

$$E(\theta_k) = \sum_i s^i \frac{\displaystyle\int_0^\infty \int_{\tau(d^i)}^{\pi-\tau(d^i)} \theta^i \, Pr(d^i, \theta^i) d\theta^i \, dd^i}{\displaystyle\int_0^\infty \int_{\tau(d^i)}^{\pi-\tau(d^i)} Pr(d^i, \theta^i) d\theta^i \, dd^i}.$$

The expected direction of technical change in the industry is

$$E(\theta_k) = \sum_i s^i \pi/2 = \pi/2,$$

the normal to the constraint. Therefore in an industry the expected direction of technical change is

$$\mathbf{d} = [-w/3Np_1, -w/3Np_2, \ldots, -1, -w/3Np_n, \ldots],$$

which is again proportional to prices.

A6.4 TECHNICAL CHANGE IN AN INDUSTRY

This section examines the rate and direction of technical change that would be observed in an industry that contains a variety of techniques and sizes of plants. Figure 6.4 shows an example of the distribution of an industry's plants in the space of technologies when only two inputs are used. Each point represents a technical combination employed by at least one plant in the industry. Observed technical change in the industry as a whole comprises three elements: (i) real technical change, the movement of a point representing a particular plant, as discussed in Section A6.3; (ii) selection, the process by which the rate of growth of production in a firm varies systematically with the technology used by the firm; and (iii) the birth and death of firms, by which technical combinations are added to or subtracted from the point distribution. Any combination of these three processes would change the mean technology observed in an industry, a shift that has typically been ascribed to technical change.

In accounting for such observed aggregate changes, the vector representing the change in the mean technology can be conceptualized as the sum of the vectors representing the mean change due to each of the three components. The size and direction of each of the three vectors is now described before a comprehensive model is presented.

A6.4.1 Real Technical Change

A6.4.1.1 New Techniques

The direction of technical change in individual plants has been described in Section A6.3.1. The rate of technical change depends on the capital invested in technical change, the productivity of investment in technical change, and the fixed costs of innovation. The capital invested is higher if more funds are available (from retained earnings or external sources) or if there is a greater propensity to invest in technical change as opposed to expanded use of current techniques. The productivity of this investment is high if new techniques are cheaply discovered or if research and development is highly effective. If the mean search distance for new technologies does not expand in proportion to increases in the fixed costs of innovation, the rate of technical change decreases as fixed costs increase since the probability of finding techniques that save enough to overcome these costs falls.

For plant i in the industry, the rate of cost reduction due to local search for new techniques, $dh^{(1)i}/dt$, is

$$dh^{(1)i}/dt = -f^{(1)i}(p_k-h^i),\qquad(A6.6)$$

where h^i is the current production cost for plant i; p_k is the price of output of the industry; $(p_k - h^i)$ is thus the profit available for investment per unit produced; and

$$f^{(1)i} = (1 + e^i)k^i\mu^i c^i.\qquad(A6.7)$$

Here e^i is the amount of external funding available to the plant, expressed as a proportion of profits; k^i is the proportion of internal and external funds invested in the search for new techniques; μ^i is the productivity of this investment expressed as the unit reduction in production costs per dollar invested; and c^i is the rate of reduction in the pace of technical change due to the inhibiting effect of fixed costs. Thus $f^{(1)i}$ measures the rate at which profits per unit produced are translated into cost reductions. We assume that $f^{(1)i}$ is a random variable with mean $f^{(1)}$ and constant variance.

The expected industry-wide reduction in production costs due to local technical change, or the rate of technical change, is

$$dh^{(1)}/dt = \sum_i s^i \, dh^{(1)i}/dt,\qquad(A6.8)$$

where s^i is the share of the industry's total output produced in plant i. Taking expectations (after Metcalfe and Gibbons 1986), we have

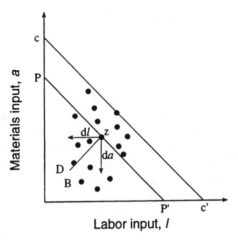

FIGURE A6.4. Technical change via new techniques.

$$dh^{(1)}/dt = -\sum_i s^i f^{(1)i}(p_k - h^i)$$

$$= -E[f^{(1)i}](p_k - h)$$

$$= -f^{(1)}(p_k - h),\qquad\qquad\text{(A6.9)}$$

The dynamics of technical change through new techniques can be seen in Figure A6.4. Here cc' represents the production frontier, or the most expensive techniques that are feasible given the product price; PP' represents the set of techniques at the average production cost; point **z** is the mean technology for the industry, using mean labor input *l* and mean capital input *a*. The slope of these lines is decided by input prices. The line zB represents the vector of technical change, with angle defined by the normal to PP' and length equal to the rate of change. The dynamics of the process defining this vector are

$$dl/dt = \theta(dh^{(1)}/dt)\qquad\qquad\text{(A6.10a)}$$

$$da/dt = \phi(dh^{(1)}/dt),\qquad\qquad\text{(A6.10b)}$$

where *dl/dt* and *da/dt* represent the expected change in mean input coefficients from the new techniques; and

$$\theta = w/(w^2 + p^2)$$

$$\phi = p/(w^2 + p^2),$$

where *p* is the cost of capital per unit (labor) value and *w* is the hourly wage of labor.

A6.4.1.2 Imitation

The other source of real technical change is imitation of superior techniques. The most efficient technique in the industry depicted in Figure A6.4 is that used in plant D, since it is the most efficient at prevailing prices. If other plants imitate plant D, the points representing the individual plants move to the immediate neighborhood of D. This causes a concentration of the point distribution of techniques around the dominant technique, rather than a movement of the entire point distribution down and away from the production frontier. Furthermore, imitation does not improve the dominant technique, since that technique sets the standard for others to imitate.

The rate of technical change due to imitation therefore depends on the factors influencing the rate of introduction of new technologies, modified by the effect of patent and other restrictions on imitation. It is possible to derive the mean direction of technical change due to imitation from the shape of the point distribution and the slope of the input price line. As we shall see, this expected direction is similar to the expected direction of apparent technical change due to selection. However, the variance around this expected direction is likely to be large. The generalized shape of the point distribution with the price input line describes where the dominant technology is likely to be found. Since the point distribution is a probability distribution, however, there is a nonzero probability that the dominant technique is to be found in a quite different direction, such as location C in Figure A6.5. If the dominant technology is at C, imitation concentrates the entire point distribution around C, illustrating how a critical initial event of small probability can affect the subsequent evolution of technical change.

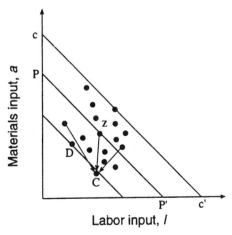

FIGURE A6.5. Variance of technical change due to imitation.

A6.4.2 Apparent Technical Change: Selection

Selection refers to differences in the rate of growth of output among the plants of an industry that alter the share of output produced by each plant. The direction of apparent technical change due to selection depends on the relationship between ds^i/dt and the techniques in use, and on the existing point distribution of techniques. We assume, following Metcalfe and Gibbons (1986), that the rate of change in the share of output is linearly related to the difference between the production costs in a plant and the mean production costs for the industry:

$$ds^i/dt = (f^{(2)}/h)(h - h^i)s^i \qquad (A6.11)$$

Denoting the expected change in production costs in the industry due to selection by $dh^{(2)}/dt$:

$$
\begin{aligned}
dh^{(2)}/dt &= \sum_i h^i ds^i/dt \\
&= \sum_i h^i (f^{(2)}/h)(h - h^i)s^i \\
&= -f^{(2)} Var\{h^i\}/h, \qquad (A6.12)
\end{aligned}
$$

where $Var\{h^i\}$ is the variance in production costs among plants.

It follows (Metcalfe and Gibbons 1986) that apparent technical change due to selection, described by $da^{(2)}/dt$ and $dl^{(2)}/dt$, is

$$dl^{(2)}/dt = -f^{(2)}[w Var\{l^i\} + p Cov\{l^i, a^i\}]/h \qquad (A6.13a)$$

$$da^{(2)}/dt = -f^{(2)}[p Var\{a^i\} + w Cov\{l^i, a^i\}]/h. \qquad (A6.13b)$$

Note that

$$Var\{h^i\} = w^2 Var\{l^i\} + p^2 Var\{a^i\} + pw Cov\{l^i, a^i\}. \qquad (A6.14)$$

The direction of apparent technical change due to selection is therefore given by equations (A6.13), whereas the rate of this change is given by $f^{(2)}$.

The expected direction of apparent technical change due to selection is illustrated in Figure A6.6. The distribution of plants approximates a bivariate normal distribution, with a more gentle slope than the input price line. The general direction of apparent technical change due to selection is labor saving ($dl^{(2)}/dt < 0$; $da^{(2)}/dt \approx 0$) because of the more gentle slope. If the correlation between a^i and l^i is equal to 1 in absolute value, then the direction of change must equal the slope of the point pattern. As the correlation coefficient becomes smaller in absolute value, the direction of technical change becomes less labor saving (i.e., the decrease in labor per unit increase in capital input

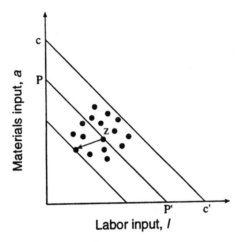

FIGURE A6.6. Apparent technical change due to selection.

falls), until with a correlation of zero the direction of apparent technical change due to selection equals that of real technical change (the normal to the price line). The converse holds if the slope of the ellipse describing the point pattern is steeper than the price line. If the two slopes are equal, the expected direction of technical change is normal to the price line.

Generally, the expected direction of apparent technical change due to selection is close to the expected direction of real technical change due to imitation. The variance around this expected direction is, however, significantly smaller. Selection represents shifts in the quantity produced at—rather than shifts in the location of—the point distribution of techniques and therefore depends heavily on the current point distribution. Alterations in the direction of change occur only slowly under selection, whereas imitation can dramatically restructure the shape of the point distribution and thus can be predicted less easily from the current point pattern.

A6.4.3 Apparent Technical Change: The Birth and Death of Plants

When output prices are constant the point distribution of techniques introduced by new plants or removed by exiting plants is likely to approximate the general distribution of techniques in the industry, biased by a tendency for less efficient plants to go out of business first or for new plants to imitate superior techniques. These processes are already captured by the dynamics described in Sections A6.4.1 and A6.4.2; so the birth and death of plants does not alter the observed direction of technical change in the industry. When the price of output rises or falls, however, there are additional effects. A fall in the commodity price pushes plants with production costs approximately equal to p_k out of business, implying that techniques on the right-hand side of the point distribution in Figure A6.6 disappear. A rise in the commodity price provides a niche of opportunity for less efficient plants, whose production costs approximate the commodity price, to enter profitable production: new points are added to the right-hand side of this distribution close to the price line. Just as a fall in prices puts greatest pressure on plants in the right-hand end of the distribution, so a rise in prices offers the greatest increase in opportunity in the right-hand side of the distribution. For simplicity we assume that the degree to which the distribution expands or contracts on the right-hand side due to the effect of price changes on the birth and death of plants is independent of the mix of inputs used. This implies that the direction of apparent technical change due to births and deaths is the normal to the price line.

The rate of apparent technical change due to births and deaths is assumed to be proportional to the observed change in prices, dp_k/dt. The plants are assumed to make low rates of profit; their production costs are expected to equal approximately the mean of the changing commodity price, $p_k + 0.5dp_k/dt$. Thus the change in production costs due to births and deaths is

$$dh^{(3)}/dt = \alpha dp_k/dt[p_k + 0.5dp_k/dt], \qquad (A6.15)$$

with the direction of change defined by

$$dl^{(3)}/dt = \theta dh^{(3)}/dt \qquad (A6.16a)$$

$$da^{(3)}/dt = \phi dh^{(3)}/dt. \qquad (A6.16b)$$

A6.4.4 The Dynamics of Technical Change in an Industry

The rate of change of production costs in an industry is the sum of real and apparent technical change, plus the effect on costs of changes in the price of inputs. Taking a second-order approximation of the latter effect, we have

$$\begin{aligned} dh/dt &= dh^{(1)}/dt + dh^{(2)}/dt + dh^{(3)}/dt \\ &\quad + adp/dt + ldw/dt + dadp/dt^2 + dldw/dt^2 \end{aligned} \qquad (A6.17)$$

$$\begin{aligned} &= -f^{(1)}(p_k - h) -f^{(2)} Var\{h^i\}/h \\ &\quad + \alpha dp_k/dt[p_k + 0.5dp_k/dt] + G\{w\}, \end{aligned} \qquad (A6.18)$$

where

$$G\{w\} = adp/dt + l\,dw/dt + da\,dp/dt^2 + dl\,dw/dt^2.$$

The aggregate observed technical change is

$$dl/dt = dl^{(1)}/dt + dl^{(2)}/dt + dl^{(3)}/dt$$

$$= -\theta f^{(1)} (p_k - h) - f^{(2)} [w\,Var\{l^i\} + p\,Cov\{l^i, a^i\}]/h$$
$$+ \theta\alpha\, dp_k/dt[p_k + 0.5 dp_k/dt] \qquad (A6.19a)$$

$$da/dt = da^{(1)}/dt + da^{(2)}/dt + da^{(3)}/dt$$

$$= -\phi f^{(1)} (p_k - h) - f^{(2)} [p\,Var\{a^i\} + w\,Cov\{l^i, a^i\}]/h$$
$$+ \phi\alpha\, dp_k/dt[p_k + 0.5 dp_k/dt]. \qquad (A6.19b)$$

If this model is to be economically reasonable, the following conditions must hold:

(i) $Var\{h^i\}$, $Var\{l^i\}$, $Var\{a^i\} > 0$.

(ii) $|Cov\{l^i, a^i\}| \le \sqrt{[Var\{l^i\} Var\{a^i\}]}$,   i.e., $|Corr\{l^i, a^i\}| \le 1$.

(iiia) If the gradient of the point distribution of techniques ($Corr\{l^i, a^i\}/Var\{a^i\}$) is negative and steeper (shallower) than that of the price of inputs ($-p/w$), then the gradient of the direction of selection (g^S) is steeper (shallower) still:

$$-p/w > Corr\{l^i, a^i\}/Var\{a^i\} \Rightarrow Corr\{l^i, a^i\}/Var\{a^i\} < g^S$$
$$-p/w < Corr\{l^i, a^i\}/Var\{a^i\} \Rightarrow Corr\{l^i, a^i\}/Var\{a^i\} < g^S,$$

where

$$g^S = \frac{f^{(2)} [w\,Var\{l^i\} + p\,Cov\{l^i, a^i\}]}{f^{(2)} [p\,Var\{a^i\} + w\,Cov\{l^i, a^i\}]} \;.$$

(iiib) If the gradient of the point distribution of techniques is positive, then the direction of selection lies between this and the gradient of the price line (w/p):

either $w/p > g^S > Corr\{l^i, a^i\}/Var\{a^i\}$

or $w/p < g^S < Corr\{l^i, a^i\}/Var\{a^i\}.$

(iv) The standard deviation of h^i (and thus of l^i and a^i) is significantly smaller than the difference between the cost of production and the price of the commodity produced:

$$\sqrt{Var\{h^i\}} < p_k - h.$$

(v) The slope of the selection gradient points to the place where the ellipse describing the point distribution of techniques is tangential (on the lower side) to the slope of the input price gradient.

A6.4.5 Implications

The processes of technical change and selection have implications for other industry characteristics. These can be briefly spelt out.

The *mass of profits* in an industry, π, is

$$\pi = \sum_i (p_k - h^i)a^i, \tag{A6.20}$$

where a^i is the output of plant i. Therefore

$$d\pi/dt = \sum_i [a^i dp_k/dt - a^i dh^{(1)i}/dt + (p_k - h)da^i/dt].$$

Note that da^i/dt includes changes in production levels due to both selection and to births and deaths. Hence

$$d\pi/dt = A\{dp_k/dt - \sum_i s^i[dh^{(1)i}/dt]\}$$
$$+ \sum_i (p_k - h^i) \{Ads^i/dt + s^i dA/dt\},$$

where A is the total output. Substituting from equations (A6.6) and (A6.11) and taking expectations, we obtain

$$(1/A)d\pi/dt = dp_k/dt + (p_k - h)(1/A)dA/dt + f^{(1)} (p_k - h) + f^{(2)} Var\{h^i\}/h. \tag{A6.21}$$

This equation shows that the change in the level of profit is the sum of four factors. The first element is the change in price at the existing level of output $[Adp_k/dt]$. The second is the rate of increase of output at the existing profit margin $[(p_k - h)dA/dt]$. The third component is the expected fall in production costs caused by introducing new techniques $[Af^{(1)}(p_k - h)]$. And the final element is the expected fall in production costs due to selection $[Af^{(2)}Var\{h^i\}/h]$.

The *productivity* of the industry is defined in physical terms as the number of units of inputs (measured as socially necessary labor) used per unit of output. Thus productivity is

$$P = (l + a)^{-1},$$

whence

$$dP/dt = (l + a)^{-2}[dl/dt + da/dt]$$
$$= -(l + a)^{-2}\{(\theta + \phi) [-f^{(1)}(p_k - h)$$
$$+ \alpha dp_k/dt(p_k + 0.5dp_k/dt)] - f^{(2)} [w Var\{l^i\}$$
$$+ p Var\{a^i\} + (w + p)Cov\{l^i, a^i\}]/h\}. \tag{A6.22}$$

Finally, since $(l + a)$ is the average labor value of all inputs per unit of output, or the labor value of output, λ,

$$d\lambda/dt = dl/dt + da/dt$$

$$= (l + a)^{-2}\{\theta + \phi\}\ [f^{(1)}(p_k - h)$$

$$- \alpha dp_k/dt(p_k + 0.5dp_k/dt)] + f^{(2)}[w\,Var\{l^i\}$$

$$+ p\,Var\{a^i\} + (w + p)Cov\{l^i, a^i\}]/h\}, \qquad (A6.23)$$

whence

$$dP/dt = \lambda^{-2}d\lambda/dt. \qquad (A6.24)$$

Chapter 7

INTERNATIONALIZATION AND GLOBAL CAPITAL FLOWS

S ince the 1960s Japan and some newly industrializing countries (NICs) have outperformed the economies of North America and western Europe. The selective industrialization of countries outside the traditional North Atlantic hub of industrial power has been accompanied by a growth of world trade that is nearly twice as fast as the growth of world production. Chapter 2 recounts these processes. With the expansion of global finance and the rising scope of transnational corporations, selective industrialization and growth of trade have been called collectively globalization. The rise of Japan and the NICs while world trade has grown raises important questions about the reasons why rates of accumulation have slowed in North America and western Europe.

What is the relation between the growth of the NICs and the slowdown? Did the fact that the NICs have been taking an increasing share of the export and domestic markets of western Europe and North America itself act as one cause of that slowdown? Or is the growth of the NICs independent of the slowdown in western Europe and North America, both being caused by separate and possibly different phenomena? Alternatively, did the slowdown give rise in some way to the growth of the NICs? Interpretations of the slowdown in western Europe and North America have proffered particular answers to these questions, commonly referring to the falling rate of profit and relative wage levels. Chapter 3 has argued that these interpretations have not really provided the theoretical and empirical evidence that justifies their answers. And underlying these questions is a more basic one: what is the relationship between the internationalization of production, the rise of the NICs, and costs of production?

This chapter attempts to clarify these issues. It examines theoretically the link between costs of production, profitability, and international change. As in Chapters 5 and 6, we seek to develop theory that is adequate to elucidate the changes that have occurred in the postwar world. Once the theory is provided, the histories of some programs of industrialization are examined in Chapter 10, as an empirical manifestation of our claims. We make two related claims. First, differences in costs of production are not a good basis from which to predict differences in rates of growth. Even in theory rates of profit do not predict rates of growth: low-profit (high-cost) regions may grow more rapidly than high-profit (low-cost) regions. This result corresponds to a fundamental empirical observation: in practice, despite all the claims of low-cost production in the Third World, production and capital flows remain overwhelmingly confined to the First World; what industrialization has occurred in the Third World has been highly selective. Secondly, then, comparative advantage is not a sufficient basis for efficiency; growth is a result not merely of high rates of profit. This claim leaves room for local initiative: the crux of development is, we argue, investment policy not factor costs. This argument has four steps.

International growth theory uses a number of different forms of reasoning to explain locational change. In common use are theories of comparative advantage, competitive advantage, unequal exchange, and the new international division of labor. (The so-called new growth theories associated with the names of G. Grossmann, E. Helpman, P. Krugman, and P. Romer share with the theory of competitive advantage an emphasis upon external economies and differences in efficiency.) Although it derives from a Marxist rather than an orthodox school of thought, the thesis of unequal exchange is actually implied by theories of both comparative and competitive advantage. In fact all these theoretical positions share some common assumptions. Whether they focus on factor abundance (like the theory of comparative advantage), factor abundance, and technical efficiency (the theory of competitive advantage), or on comparative wage costs (as in practice does the theory of the new international division of labor), these contentions all explain growth and location by reference to costs of production: differences in factor costs and the rate of profit are the central variables on which the international location of production is thought to turn. But this explanation is contradicted by a simple empirical observation: most world trade and most international flows of capital occur between countries with similar patterns of factor abundance and similar levels of technical efficiency; only a few low-wage countries are growing rapidly.

One basis of the cost of production view of regional change is the connection between price and equilibrium in economic theory. All branches of economic theory, whether neoclassical, neo-Ricardian, or Marxian, are dominated by attention to an equilibrium state in which rates of profit are equal. Their theories of price, whatever their other differences, derive from the view that in the long run prices are set so as to sustain that equal rate of profit equilibrium. Drawing as they do on their underlying bases in neoclassical, neo-Ricardian, or Marxian thought, theories of comparative and competitive advantage and of the new international division of labor, implicitly derive from this link between price, rate of profit, and equilibrium. Since price and equilibrium have been separated in Chapter 4 our model of international growth does not have to rely on that link; we are free to start by focusing on investment and accumulation rather than price.

The third stage of the argument therefore turns to examine how capital flows and rates of profit are related in a dynamic model of a multinational economy. Given a standard input–output economy and rational investment behavior by central financial institutions and decentralized firms, we ask:

1. What is the relationship between rates of capital accumulation and rates of profit?
2. What is the relationship between profitability and equilibrium?

Three conclusions derive from this model. First, low-profit (high-cost) regions may grow more rapidly than high-profit (low-cost) regions. Secondly, the net flow of capital may point from high-profit to low-profit regions. And, thirdly, rates of profit are not necessarily equal at equilibrium (unless central financial institutions direct all international capital flows and adhere to a particular rule to allocate investment).

One of the central implications of this result is that comparative advantage and profitability do not guarantee efficiency and growth. Rather more generally expressed, prices, outputs, and rates of profit cannot be computed solely from production data but require an understanding of investment policies. Therefore the growth of the NICs may be a matter not simply of differences in factor endowments and efficiencies but also of changes in investment policies by the central financial institutions of the global economy and the decentralized firms of the newly industrializing economies (perhaps aided and abetted by their home governments). The scope for local initiative offered by this conclusion is given empirical foundation in Chapter 10, where specific programs of industrialization in some Third World countries are described.

7.1 INTERNATIONAL GROWTH

The principal theories of the international distribution of economic activity identify relative costs as the central rule governing rates of growth and economic specialization. We assess three of these theories: of international trade and comparative advantage; of competitive advantage; and of the new international division of labor. (The theory of unequal exchange is related to theories of both comparative and competitive advantage.) We seek to demonstrate how the theories understand changes in the geography of production and the scope they provide for local action: by relying on comparative costs they all misspecify geographic changes and leave little scope for local initiative.

7.1.1 Trade and Comparative Advantage

The theory of international trade asks whether countries are better off when trading than when there is no trade. It assumes that technology is the same in all countries and that factors of production do not move between them. Typically such models are neoclassical: they assume neoclassical production functions and markets that clear through price. Here, though, we follow Dutt (1990) to illustrate the theory of international trade in a world of fixed coefficient technologies and cost-plus (neo-Ricardian) prices. Similar models are later used to explain unequal exchange and interregional capital flows. As has been done generally in this book, money and asset markets are ignored. (The models of Section 7.1 are outlined and their central results demonstrated in Appendix A7; Section A7.1.)

The models that are typically used to analyze comparative advantage—and the model that is used here—assume that two commodities are produced: means of production (commodity 1) and a consumption good (commodity 2). The output levels of the two commodities must satisfy materials balance requirements: enough of the consumption good must be produced to feed people, and enough of the means of production must be produced to engage in production. Technologies (input–output coefficients) are the same in both countries. The system has constant returns to scale. Prices are decided by a mark up over the costs of means of production (as in neo-Ricardian price models): the rate of profit and the (money) wage rate are the same in both industries.

We ignore the growth of the labor force and the determination of real wages. Equally, the rate of profit is not calculated. Given the questions we seek to answer, these are not important issues.

The first essential step in the argument about comparative advantage is to understand relative prices. Consider two countries, A and B, that are totally closed. Suppose that in country A the rate of profit exceeds that in B. Then in country A the ratio of price of means of production to the price of consumption goods is lower than in B if the production of means of production is more labor intensive than is the production of consumption goods. In other words, country A, where capital is expensive compared with the price of labor, has a comparative advantage in producing the commodity that uses relatively more labor and little capital to produce.

The second step is to suppose that the two countries interact through and only through trade. Suppose that the countries specialize completely, A producing commodity 1, in which it has a comparative advantage, and B producing commodity 2, in which it has a comparative advantage. Country A sells commodity 1 to B; in return country B sells commodity 2 to A. The rates of profit and rates of growth may differ between the countries, for factors of production do not move even if countries trade.

The question the theory of comparative advantage seeks to answer is whether people in the two countries are better off when the countries trade than when they are isolated. Since the rates of profit in the two economies are regarded as fixed (and so the rates of growth of output are fixed), this question is answered by comparing the real wages of the populations before and after trade. To make this comparison, assume that the relative sizes of real wages in the two countries are the same before and after trade. Then trade does indeed raise real wages—though it remains an open question how those benefits are distributed in practice within and between the two countries. It is also an open question whether some of the gains from trade raise profit rates at the expense of real wages.

The central conclusion of the theory of comparative advantage is that trade benefits the people of the two countries. Whatever the profit rates, if they are unchanged during the move to free trade, specialization raises real wages. To realize these gains, countries should specialize in producing commodities in which they have a comparative advantage, that is, commodities whose price of production is relatively low (compared to other commodities) in comparison with prices in other countries. Such commodities use relatively large amounts of the factors of production that are comparatively cheap. The following section explains the implications of this result.

7.1.2 Implications of Comparative Advantage

The benefits from trade identified in Section 7.1.1 are static economies. They arise from savings in production costs when technologies are fixed and identical. However, if country A specialized in producing commodity 1 and B specializes in producing commodity 2, dynamic economies of trade may be realized. These are economies of specialization, which include economies of scale within plants and economies within industries. Dynamic economies may exceed the static benefits of trade (Garnaut 1989). Economies of scale within a firm arise if average production costs fall as the quantity of output is increased: specialized machines, workers, and managers can be hired; stocks of materials and finished goods can be reduced as a proportion of output. Economies in an industry occur if an increase in the industry's level of output reduces average production costs—when an increase in an industry's output induces new firms to supply components and specialized services to the industry: transport systems, labor training, production of components, managerial services. In addition if an industry expands, more firms may generate heightened competition, forcing prices down. Thus besides the static benefits of trade, countries may anticipate other benefits as well.

The model has ignored transport costs. The benefits of trade are gross, from which must be deducted the costs of transport. In simple versions of the theory of comparative advantage, transport is viewed merely as a cost, rather as if transport services were provided by a third country. [Actually, transport is a produced commodity, so it should be analyzed as an industry within the trading system rather than as an exogenous sector (see Sheppard and Barnes 1990: 66–67).] The conclusion has then to be modified: trade is beneficial if the gains from specialization offset the costs of transporting commodities between countries. For given relative prices of factors, two countries are more likely to benefit from trade the lower are the costs of transport between them.

During the postwar years, the barrier posed by distance has diminished. Transport technologies like jets, containers, and super freighters have increased the scale of transport facilities and reduced their unit cost. Communications technologies now allow information to be transmitted rapidly and cheaply (and, through satellites, to an increasing extent independently of distance): thus production can be coordinated on a global scale. As transport and communications costs have fallen compared with the costs of production, the theory of comparative advantage predicts that countries' production should have become increasingly specialized and that trade in commodities should have grown relative to the production of commodities. This last prediction is certainly born out in practice. So the theory of comparative advantage explains the growth in trade and national specialization (relative to production) as a matter of falling transport and communications costs (compared with the benefits of specialization).

Patterns of growth and development in the postwar world have also been explained by the theory of comparative advantage. For example, the Northeast Asian economies are said to have initially specialized in exporting natural-resource-based products (often food); when they accumulated some capital their export specialization shifted toward labor-intensive manufactured commodities as they traded abundant labor for scarce natural resources and capital; later, production became more capital and knowledge intensive as Northeast Asian wages rose and capital became more abundant (Garnaut 1989: 49–50). The economic problems faced by Western industrial countries are then either the fault of misguided policies (tariffs and other market failures) or the effect of capital migrating to the labor-abundant NICs. The appropriate response is to correct market failures and to shift production into sectors in which industrial countries have a comparative advantage: capital- and knowledge-intensive industries and services.

The theory of comparative advantage provides the ideological foundation for policies of free trade. This is despite the fact that one supporting proposition of the theory of comparative advantage has been proved to be logically wrong (Sheppard and Barnes 1990: 88–103). It is generally supposed by the theory of comparative advantage that the prices of factors of production are inversely proportional to their relative availability: capital is expensive compared with labor where it is relatively scarce. Thus countries should specialize in producing those commodities that use relatively large amounts of the factors of production that are relatively abundant. But this is not true

(Metcalfe and Steedman 1979): capital may be expensive and abundant or expensive and scarce. Therefore, specialization according to factor abundance is not necessarily efficient.

Furthermore the central prediction of the theory of comparative advantage does not stand even casual empirical test. The theory predicts that countries specialize in producing those commodities that use factors of production that are abundant. It follows that trade should consist of exports of commodities that use abundant factors of production and imports of commodities that use scarce factors of production. Trading partners should have unlike factor endowments. Yet, as Chapter 2 shows, the great bulk of world trade flows between Europe, Japan, and North America; the developing economies—with their abundant labor and limited capital—account for less than 10% of world trade; and even the NICs, as they have grabbed larger and larger shares of world trade, have shifted the commodity composition of their exports closer and closer to that of North America, Japan, and Europe. Most trade occurs between countries that have broadly similar factor endowments (Crocombe et al. 1991).

Nevertheless the theory of comparative advantage does offer some insights into the changing geography of world trade and production. It emphasizes how falling transport costs have raised levels of trade in relation to production, though it ignores how the benefits from that trade have been distributed. It stresses the availability of factors of production in fixing the optimal specialization of countries and interprets the economic history of the postwar world in these terms. However, the theory of comparative advantage offers only a limited role for the state: governments have the task of ensuring that the conditions for trade and specialization are in place. There is no scope for industrial policy, for mobilization for development. The state should merely set market conditions. Indeed, it is claimed that this is all the state actually has done effectively in the successful economies of Northeast Asia (Garnaut 1989): some governments may have had industrial policies; but those policies were irrelevant to the success of their countries. In Japan, even, "The conclusion must be . . . that the rapid growth of the 1960s, the modernization of the industrial structure, and the strengthening of export competitiveness were the result not of industrial policy, but rather of the relatively smooth operation of the price mechanism and the ability of firms through their own decisions to adapt" (Tsuruta 1988: 82–83). The scope for local initiative is limited: to optimize is to subject oneself to the market; to grow fast is to have low-cost factors of production.

Growing awareness of the gulf between the trade patterns witnessed throughout the world and those predicted by the theory of comparative advantage has led many economists to question the notion that trade is driven by differences between countries and that the free market is the most efficient way of exploiting those differences (Brander 1986; Helpman and Krugman 1985; Krugman 1986; Porter 1990; Romer 1986). Brander (1986) and Porter (1990) assert that the assumption of perfect competition that underlies the theory of comparative advantage bears little relationship to the actual process of international competition, ignoring many aspects of the real world that are critical when trade policy is considered. Adopting a view increasingly shared by what Howes and Markusen (1993) term "revisionist trade theory," Jacquemin (1991: 13) defines the new international competition and trade as "a sequential game in which the application of new forms of organization, the opening up of new markets and the introduction of new products and production methods continually undermine the possible equilibria and modify the rules of the game."

Strategic trade theory and the concept of competitive advantage have been developed to replace the relatively simple notion of comparative advantage and the inability of perfect competition, on which it rests, to handle strategic interactions between firms, the existence of externalities, and state policy that is driven by market failure. Krugman's (1986) strategic trade theory rests on a particular type of market failure—imperfect competition—driven by economies of scale generated through experience and innovation. The state plays a critical role in this framework, by setting policy to grant first-mover advantages to its own firms (perhaps by protecting domestic markets or granting export subsidies), by targeting key industries that generate externalities, and by pursuing strategies that create other forms of advantage.

Porter (1990) acknowledges the importance of imperfect competition in international trade, although he is critical of strategic trade theory because of its sensitivity to assumptions of firm behavior and its failure to specify patterns of trade. For Porter, success in international markets is a function of productivity advantages and of the ability of the firms in a particular industry to manufacture the skills and technology that sustain productivity growth in constantly changing markets. State policy, firm strategy, the structure of the economy, and a nation's culture and institutional forms are all seen as driving productivity differences, creating and sustaining competitive advantages. It is to Porter's (1990) model of competitive advantage that we now turn.

7.1.3 Competitive Advantages

One reason the theory of comparative advantage leaves so little scope for local action is that in its pure form it ignores all other international relations than trade in produced commodities: there are no factor movements, no differences in the efficiency of production. This is why the theory of comparative advantage cannot explain why most trade takes place between advanced nations with broadly similar factor endowments. Recently Porter (1990) has argued that the essential source of competitive advantage is innovation and change, as nations and firms create and recreate competitive advantages.

In this view companies (and so the countries that are host to them) gain and sustain competitive advantage in international competition through innovation and improvement. The four broad determinants of national competitive advantage in an industry are as follows:

1. *Factor conditions*—these may be basic (inherited like resources and labor) or advanced (produced by investment); factors may be useful for a range of industries, like a road, or specialized and used by a single industry
2. *Demand conditions,* especially within the domestic market—these conditions include the composition of demand (market segments, sophistication, national tastes), the size and pattern of growth of demand (which create economies of scale), and the extent to which demand can be internationalized
3. *Related and supporting industries* that provide inputs to the production process
4. *Firm structure, strategies, and rivalries*—the goals, culture, and domestic competitive conditions of firms

Porter (1990) has in mind a process of continuous dynamic disequilibrium (see also Porter 1985). However, his emphasis on technological advantages can be analyzed by a model that develops the ideas of Section 7.1.1 (the model itself is presented in Appendix A7, Section A7.1).

We modify the model of Section 7.1.1 first by assuming there is perfect international mobility of capital. So the rate of profit in the two countries is the same. If techniques of production are the same in the two countries, this assumption implies that wage rates are also equal even though labor is immobile. Perfect capital mobility implies that wage rates are the same everywhere unless technologies are different in different countries; as we shall see in Section 7.1.6, this is an important conclusion. Thus the second modification to the model of Section 7.1.1 is to assume that the countries produce commodities 1 and 2 with different techniques.

Before trade, if country A is technically more efficient than country B, in the sense that it requires fewer inputs per unit of output than B, then the level of consumption in country A exceeds that in country B. Technical efficiency raises living standards, at least when there is no trade.

To examine the gains from trade suppose that country A has a relative technical advantage in producing commodity 1 so that the relative price of commodity 1 (p_1/p_2) in country A is less than it is in country B. And suppose that country A specializes in producing that commodity in which it has a relative advantage: commodity 1. Again trade is beneficial: if the rate of profit is unaffected by trade, if the real wage in one country is unchanged by trade, the real wage in the other rises. Thus both partners can gain from trade, perhaps by sharing this wage increase in some way.

Such a view of trade and competitive advantage still lies within the framework of competition. Yet it argues that the advantage of nations lies less in their inherited or given factor prices than in the conditions of production that they create. Here there is more scope for local initiative and state action, for now benefits accrue from differences in technique as well as factor prices. Thus, a crucial debate in the interpretation of the growth of Japan and the Northeast Asian NICs concerns the role of the state. Did the state merely provide the market conditions for growth, or did it intervene actively and effectively to create particular competitive advantages? The theory of competitive advantage, like the theory of comparative advantage, presumes that specialization and growth are consequences of cost advantages that stem from processes or characteristics internal to the countries; but the theory of competitive advantage realizes that those cost advantages may have been created by attention to technology rather than simply by reflection of factor endowments. Both theories presume that trade benefits both partners.

7.1.4 Distributing the Benefits of Trade

Yet the distribution of the benefits to the trading countries is not specified. The theory shows that both partners can gain from trade: it does not specify which countries actually will gain. A long literature claims that the benefits from trade flow predominantly to the Western industrialized countries at the expense of Third World raw material producers (Frank 1979; George 1988; Wallerstein 1979). The theory of unequal exchange (Emmanuel 1972) explicitly calculates the flow of the benefits from trade.

Consider the model of competitive advantage. The countries trade. From the conditions of production, the values of the two commodities can be determined. Since specialization is complete, the values of the commodities are also the unit values of the exports of the two countries. The prices can also be calculated and therefore so can the ratio of the prices per unit of value of the two commodities. If the price/value ratio, p_A/λ_A, is high, then country A gains a high price for its commodity exports compared with their value. In fact it can be shown that country A can extract a higher price per unit value of its exports the higher its real wages (and the lower its rate of profit). If, for whatever reason, a country can raise its real-wage rate, it can extract higher prices per unit value from its trading partners. Also, of course, if a country can raise its real wage compared with that of its trading partner, its money terms of trade improve. This is unequal exchange in the narrow sense (Emmanuel 1972; Gibson 1980).

The benefits from trade are not equally distributed among the trading partners. They accrue most to those countries that can raise their real-wage rate—though the causes of such differences in real wages are hardly evident. The conclusion that exchange is unequal is derived from a model of the theory of competitive advantage. It could equally have been derived from a model of comparative advantage (Section 7.1.1). These conclusions of the theory of competitive or comparative advantage are not commonly emphasized. They provide another role for the state—to ensure that the benefits of trade flow to domestic workers rather than workers in another country—without, however, suggesting how that may be done.

7.1.5 The New International Division of Labor

Apparently distinct from theories of competitive or comparative advantage, the thesis of the new international division of labor focuses explicitly on the relations within production between Western industrialized economies and the Third World. The theory of the new international division of labor links several phenomena: slow accumulation in Western industrialized economies; rapid growth in some NICs; and global production. The novelty of the theory lies in its recognition of the significance of global production strategies.

The key distinction is that between global capital and global production (Palloix 1977). Global capital refers to capital that is invested in countries other than its "home." Starting in the mid- to late nineteenth century such capital was invested in infrastructure projects in the Americas and Australia. Later, in Canada, Europe, and Australia, global capital was invested in production units to serve local markets behind tariff walls: an entire production process was replicated behind the tariff. By contrast global production refers to divisions of labor within an industry over international boundaries: a car engine is made in Australia, the interior furnishings in Mexico, the tires in the USA, other parts in Southeast Asia, and the body is stamped and the car assembled in Canada. This form of production has become most evident since the 1960s (Perrons 1981). The unit of this global organization is the transnational corporation (Hymer 1975; Barnet and Muller 1975; Frobel et al. 1980), often with headquarters and research functions in the North Atlantic region or Japan and production functions in parts of the Third World.

The disintegration of production is the effect of several forces. At first glance, the globalization of production could be examined in the same manner as the geography of separate industries: as a matter of comparative or competitive advantage, though with "industries" that are more finely subdivided than in the traditional literature. Falling costs of transport and communications explain why this phenomenon has appeared only recently. However, firms also seek to separate production units to divide their workforces and to prevent worker struggles in one unit from infecting other units (Clark 1981).

Despite Clark's hypothesis, much of the literature on the new international division of labor explains the growth of the NICs as a response to a falling rate of profit in the Western industrialized countries and lower costs of production in the newly industrializing ones. In the 1970s, it is said, global corporations began to deindustrialize in the core and to invest in export-oriented manufacturing in some countries of the periphery. The growth of the NICs is thus both a response to falling profitability in the West and a cause of continuing slow accumulation (and Chapter 3 has examined some theories about this relationship). In practice, therefore, empirical analyses of the growth of global production in particular industries focus on low wages, long working hours, poor working conditions, and rapid rates of labor turnover in the periphery (Jenkins 1984): see, for example, Humphrey (1982) and Kronish and Mericle (1984) on the Latin American car industry, Elson and Pearson (1981) on the textile industry, Perrons (1981) on Ireland, and Fuentes and Ehrenreich (1983) on other industries and countries. According to Peet (1983), whereas hourly wage rates in 1978 in manufacturing were around $6 per hour in the USA and Japan, they ranged from $2 in Spain to less than $0.80 in Singapore, Hong Kong, and Brazil. Of course, there are corresponding, if less pronounced, variations in productivity.

Yet the failing of the theory of the new international division of labor, as of the theory of comparative advantage, is that most capital flows, like most trade, occur between the developed countries. The shift of capital to the developing countries is not nearly as pronounced as the "labor factor" might predict, nor is it as uniform. The transfer of capital is still far greater between developed countries than between developed and developing ones (Grahl 1983; Jenkins 1984): studies of the new international division of labor fail to come to grips with the facts that most international investment is within the developed world (Sayer 1985) and the rest is directed to only a few NICs. Even though rapid industrial growth has emerged in such "new" NICs as Malaysia, it remains true that only a few Third World economies are growing fast.

7.1.6 The Problem of Costs of Production

These different approaches to the theoretical issues posed by the growth of the NICs face significant and interrelated difficulties. The theory of comparative advantage explains specialization, trade, and (implicitly) growth as a matter of relative factor abundance and therefore relative factor prices. However, the assumed relationship between abundance and prices is logically untenable; capital is assumed to be completely immobile; and capital mobility implies wage equalization—destroying the very basis upon which the growth of the NICs is supposed to be founded. Furthermore the theory faces a major empirical hurdle: it predicts that unlike countries trade most; in fact, most world trade is between developed countries, which have similar patterns of factor abundance. The theory of competitive advantage supposes that capital is mobile but not technology. So specialization, trade, and growth are the consequences of technological advantages created and maintained. Specialization is again a matter of relative prices, now decided by techniques rather than simply by factor prices. Capital mobility is supposed to equalize rates of profit. Despite the greater realism of this model, the empirical problem remains: most trade is between countries that have similar technical capacities. The theories of comparative and competitive advantage both imply that exchange is in general unequal: countries in which wages are rising benefit from improved terms of trade, which must tend to offset the comparative advantage induced by low wages. Despite its different theoretical orientation, the theory of the new international division of labor also focuses on factor price differences, particularly wage rates, though within the context of declining rates of profit in the Western industrialized economies. The empirical problem for the theory of the new international division of labor is like that for the theory of comparative advantage: Why do not more low-wage countries grow fast? And why, as wages in the NICs have risen, has growth not passed generally to a much wider range of other developing countries (though see Donaghu and Barff 1990)?

All three approaches thus suffer from a crucial empirical difficulty. The wrong types of countries trade; only a few low-wage countries are growing. Perhaps this defect is related to a common feature of these theories: the assumption that specialization and growth are a matter of exploiting cost of production (or relative cost of production) advantages. In turn, this assumption is linked to the limited role that each theory assigns to local initiative. In the theory of comparative advantage, the state has merely to guarantee market conditions; in the theories of competitive advantage and of the new international division of labor, the state can also establish the conditions for appropriate factor prices and production techniques. If we are to reconstruct theories of trade and growth to remedy these empirical defects and provide theoretical room for local initiative, we must reexamine the relationship between prices and costs of production. This is the task of the following two sections.

7.2 COSTS, PRICES, AND EQUILIBRIUM

Each of the three major branches of economic theory (neoclassical, neo-Ricardian, and Marxian) contains a theory of price. These theories are similar in three respects: short-run changes in prices are ascribed to changes in the relative balance of supply and demand; in the end, prices reflect an equilibrium in which rates of profit are equal; and the prices charged for all representatives of the same commodity are the same. Of course, there are differences between the theories too: neoclassical theory equates price and marginal cost, whereas both neo-Ricardian and Marxian theorists equate price with a (marked up) average cost; and the theory of price plays a smaller role in Marxian economics than in neoclassical or neo-Ricardian theory.

We have already disposed of the third characteristic of received price theory in Chapter 4. Different instances of the same commodity rarely command the same price, a fact that has allowed us to specify exactly the relation between values and prices. Now we turn our attention to the relationship between price and equilibrium. The common assumption that long-run prices support an equilibrium in which rates of profit are equal is the base characteristic that undermines the ability of theories of international location to comprehend the historical geographies of trade, growth, and local initiative.

Notwithstanding the common assumption, profit rates actually differ between plants for many reasons. The abilities of managers, the types of technology, the newness of plant and machinery, the prices of inputs and outputs, and the degree of effort of workers all differ between firms. Accidents can disrupt sources of supply, continuity of operation, and availability of markets. Since profit rates differ between plants they differ between countries and industries too.

Yet it is an assumption of many traditions of economic theory that capital "flows" from less profitable to more profitable plants (and therefore, in aggregate, from less to more profitable countries and industries). Capital "flows" as outside investors choose the most profitable opportunity, as entrepreneurs disinvest from less profitable plants, or simply as plants invest only the profits they themselves generate. When capital flows in this manner, the size of output of the plants, countries, and industries changes: output grows fastest in the most profitable plants or countries or industries. Two effects follow: the growing plants may encounter diseconomies of scale that increase the relative cost of producing each unit of output; and as the output of normal commodities grows, so the price per unit of output falls. These two effects imply that profit rates in more profitable plants or countries or industries tend to fall over time whereas in the less profitable ones profit rates rise over time. As this process continues profit rates tend to converge to an equilibrium state in which all plants and countries and industries earn an equal rate of profit. Despite their other differences, essentially such a story is adopted by Marx (1967) in his theory of prices of production, by Sraffa (1960), and by the neoclassical theory of resource allocation (e.g., Leftwich 1970).

While such flows of capital tend to equalize the rate of profit, economic theory has recognized additional effects. First, barriers hinder the free flow of capital between plants, countries, and industries: a high initial capital investment may deter firms from entering a country or industry; the nominal rate of profit must be balanced against the risk of losing the investment; the costs of obtaining information about countries or industries may cause investors to choose satisfactory rather than optimal investment opportunities; and a lot of capital is tied up in immobile plant (Gertler 1984; Kaldor 1970; Myrdal 1957; Richardson 1978). Secondly, other processes tend to enlarge differences in profit rates: more profitable firms can afford to hire better managers, to invest in new techniques, and to buy off worker discontent; and input prices change and unplanned fluctuations in supply and demand occur.

The actual history of profit rates can thus be regarded as a composite of three kinds of factors: a force that tends to equalize the rate of profit; the search by firms for new kinds of profit advantage, complicated by unplanned fluctuations; and barriers to the free flow of capital. In practice profit rates never attain the equilibrium to which capital flows tend to move them.

Although no one believes that profit rates are actually equal, theoretical economic analysis is dominated by attention to the equilibrium state in which profit rates are equal. Ever since Léon Walras, general equilibrium models have defined equilibrium in part by the criterion that firms cannot reallocate resources to raise their rate of profit (Debreu 1959); if capital flows are not constrained, this criterion requires equal rates of profit. Multisectoral neo-classical growth models presume that each sector makes the same rate of profit (Burmeister 1980); equally, the von Neumann (1945) and "Cam-bridge" (Robinson 1961; Sraffa 1960) growth models demand that all indus-tries make an equal rate of profit. For Marxian economists too the theory of prices is dominated by the idea of prices of production (prices that sustain an equal rate of profit in all industries) and by the transformation between com-modity values and prices of production.

Such an exclusive concern with the equal rate of profit equilibrium has been justified in two ways. It is widely accepted that there does exist a force that tends to equalize rates of profit, and theory thus examines the implica-tions of that force. It is also claimed that even if equilibrium is never attained, the equilibrium state may illuminate the characteristics of other states that are more difficult to analyze. Farjoun and Machover (1983) have questioned both these justifications. They claim that because the search by firms for new sources of profit is endogenous to capitalism (just as the flow of capital is en-dogenous) it is unreasonable to focus attention solely upon the effects of the equalizing force. Farjoun and Machover also observe that there is no basis for claiming that equilibrium analysis helps our understanding of actual, non-equilibrium states; in other branches of science the claim is actually false.

This section demonstrates the link between equilibrium and price (see also Nikaido 1977, 1978). The neo-Ricardian and Marxian theories of price are the vehicles for this demonstration. (As Chapter 4 has already shown, the debate over the transformation problem is irrelevant when real rather than equilibrium prices are examined; so the transformation problem is ignored.) Since the concept of price is strongly linked to the idea of equilibrium, so also are theories of comparative and competitive advantage.

7.2.1 Neo-Ricardian Price Theory

Consider an economy that consists of two countries or industries, each pro-ducing one product. The industries use simple, homogeneous labor and only circulating constant capital. [This is the model of Sraffa (1960: 6–11; on joint production and fixed capital, see 43–73; and on land, see 74–78).] Morishi-ma's (1973) simplifying conditions are assumed (see Chapter 4).

As usual let a_{ij} denote the number of units of commodity j used per unit of output of commodity i and let l_i denote the number of hours of labor pow-er used per unit of commodity i; $a_{ij} \geq 0$. (Commodity i is produced by coun-try or industry i.) The wage rate is denoted by W, and the rate of profit (uni-form for all countries or industries) is denoted by r. Thus Sraffa (1960: 11) writes a prescription for the unit prices of the two commodities:

$$(a_{11}p_1 + a_{12}p_2)\ (1 + r) + Wl_1 = p_1 \tag{7.1}$$

$$(a_{21}p_1 + a_{22}p_2)\ (1 + r) + Wl_2 = p_2. \tag{7.2}$$

In both the equations, the first bracketed terms represent the amount of money needed to buy the commodity inputs into production; to Sraffa, this is capital and prices have to be marked up to cover profits on that capital. In addition, prices must cover wage costs. The system is assumed to be self-replacing, such that the amount of each commodity used up in production does not exceed that produced: $a_{11} + a_{21} \leq 1$ and $a_{12} + a_{22} \leq 1$. Sraffa also assumes that the net national product is known:

$$(1 - a_{11} - a_{21})p_1 + (1 - a_{12} - a_{22})p_2 = 1;$$

it is simpler to replace this condition by the similar

$$p_2 = 1. \tag{7.3}$$

These equations reveal fundamental aspects of the neo-Ricardian theory of prices. First, as Sraffa notes, the rate of profit and the prices of commodities are decided simultaneously. It is therefore inappropriate to call these prices "costs of production," for that implies that the cost of production is somehow independent of price. Sraffa prefers "prices of production," which is the Marxian term. Secondly, the wage is not regarded as advanced from capital [so that profit does not have to be earned on wages in equations (7.1) and (7.2)] but is paid *post factum* as a share of the annual product. Thirdly, it is assumed that the relevant prices are those that hold when industries earn an equal rate of profit (r); all the theoretical development of this model in Sraffa (1960) is based on this assumption.

The three equations (7.1)–(7.3) contain four unknowns (p_1, p_2, r, and W), so the system moves with 1 degree of freedom. Under the conditions, for any wage W there exists a solution to the three equations. It is thought that in reality this degree of freedom (that sets W) is taken up by the struggle between capital and labor for shares of the surplus (and thus for the relative magnitudes of r and W).

This model can be made more complex and realistic in various ways. It is possible to analyze joint production, fixed capital, and the use of natural resources such as land (Abraham-Frois and Berribi 1979; Sraffa 1960; Steedman 1977). The model provides the foundation for an important result: as rates of profit rise, one technique can drop out of use and then at even higher rates of profit become profitable again [Harcourt (1972) and Sheppard and Barnes (1990) review the so-called Cambridge controversy]. Applications of the model to rent theory have challenged assumptions of neoclassical spatial economics (Barnes 1984; Barnes and Sheppard 1984; Scott 1976, 1980). The neo-Ricardian theory of prices has also provided a means of analyzing the nature and effects of technical change.

7.2.2 Marx's Theory of Price

Marx, too, presents a theory of prices of production, though it is relegated to a far less significant role than in neo-Ricardian theory. The theory derives equations for prices that are similar in form to Sraffa's, but the formal similarity hides fundamental differences. Marx starts with notions of value and abstract labor that play no role in neo-Ricardian theory (which recognizes differences between laborers as reflecting heterogeneous labor). And to Marx the value of labor power is decided before production by a social and historical process. The payment of money to laborers to purchase their labor power is therefore an advance of capital rather than a division of the surplus. These differences are easily concealed by the formal similarities of algebra, but are nevertheless important in figuring the consequences of technical change.

As in Section 7.2.1, Morishima's (1973) simplifying conditions are assumed (Chapter 4). The expected unit value of each country's or industry's output is

$$\lambda = A\lambda + l,$$

which modifies equation (4.7) to account for the omission of fixed capital. This can also be written [see equation (4.10)] as

$$\lambda = A\lambda + \lambda_L l + e\lambda_L l. \tag{7.4}$$

The three terms on the right-hand side of this equation are, respectively, constant capital, variable capital, and surplus value.

Suppose that there exists a price system parallel to the value system of equation (7.4). Initially prices are assumed to be proportional to values (and the wage is proportional to the value of labor power) with a coefficient of proportionality that has units of dollars per unit value. Thus

$$p = Ap + Wl + eWl \tag{7.5}$$

(e is the rate of exploitation), from which the rate of profit in industry i is

$$r_i = \frac{eWl_i}{(Ap)_i + Wl_i}. \tag{7.6}$$

Now the two industries' rates of profit, as defined by equation (7.6), are likely to differ; they will differ more the greater the deviations between industries in the ratio $(Ap)_i/Wl_i$ (the value composition of capital). Therefore capital tends to flow from low- to high-profit industries, driving down the price of output in high-profit industries. Eventually equilibrium is established: rates of profit are equal and prices are

$$p = (1 + r)\,(Ap + Wl),\tag{7.7}$$

which, apart from the capitalization of labor costs, is identical to equation (7.1).

The study of the mapping from prices proportional to values (7.5) to equilibrium prices (7.7) is the transformation problem. [Desai (1979) reviews the history of this problem; but see also Steedman (1981).] The problem is this. Equation (7.7) defines a rate of profit that holds when the economy is at an equilibrium in which all firms earn the same rate of profit. Call this the price rate of profit. Equation (7.6) also defines a rate of profit, the value rate of profit (r^v)—the average value of each industry's rate of profit weighted by the quantity of capital employed by that industry. Thus the economy-wide average value rate of profit depends on the relative sizes of industries, whereas the price rate of profit does not depend on the sizes of industries. Therefore the price and value rates of profit do not usually coincide. According to Steedman, this conclusion implies that the value rate of profit is unimportant: it does not coincide with the profit rates that firms actually earn and on the basis of which they make their decisions.

This conclusion rests on an important assumption: that the prices and profit rates existing in the market equal (or nearly equal) those that can be calculated from equation (7.7). In turn, equation (7.7) assumes that there exists an equilibrium in which rates of profit are equal. Both neo-Ricardian and Marxian theories of price assume that the relevant prices are those that obtain when rates of profit are equal (in equilibrium). Thus the equal rate of profit equilibrium is not merely maintained in theories of competitive advantage—it is fundamental to the whole idea of price. It is extremely important therefore that this assumption be investigated, and it is to this task that we now turn.

7.3 CAPITAL FLOWS AND RATES OF PROFIT

Our investigation of capital flows and rates of profit at equilibrium is based on a simple two-country model. Specialization is complete: one country produces means of production, the other food. There is no technical change. Factors are perfectly mobile. The prices of commodities are decided by their relative output levels. A state of dynamic equilibrium is said to exist if the rates of profit in the two countries are unchanging: they are not assumed to be equal in equilibrium (the model seeks to learn whether the rates of profit do indeed equalize in equilibrium). Investment arises out of the surplus produced and is allocated to the two countries either by central financial institutions or by decentralized firms; in either case if the rate of profit in a country rises, so does its share of investment. This system has a unique equilibrium growth path. The central conclusion of the model is this: even if capital does tend to flow from less to more profitable plants or countries, that flow does not in itself guarantee that profit rates tend to equalize. This result casts doubt upon the value of theories that assume an equilibrium in which rates of profit are equal; it also questions the value of an approach (such as that of Richardson 1978) that argues that profit rates do not equalize simply because of immobilities. The model itself is presented in Appendix A7, Section A7.2; here we provide an intuitive account of its characteristics and central conclusions.

7.3.1 The Model

The model constructed in Appendix A7, Section A7.2, is of a two-country economy. It is straightforward to extend the model to encompass n countries, but the additional complexity does not provide additional insights into the nature of equilibrium.

The first country (A) produces means of production, called machinery, and the second (B) produces means of subsistence, called food. There is no fixed capital, and both countries have the same period of production. Processes are point input–point output: all purchases for production are made at the beginning of the production period, and all sales are made at the end of the production period. Workers consume W food per unit of labor time: the real wage is identical in the two countries. All processes are productive.

All complications and all factors other than capital mobility and relative prices are ignored. There are no immobilities, no aggregate shortages of labor, no technical change, and no economies or diseconomies of scale. Transport is free. These factors tend to preserve or to augment differences in profit rates between countries; this model is designed to investigate the relations between capital mobility and the rate of profit even without such "imperfections."

In the models of Section 7.1 prices were assumed to be set at long-run equilibrium levels; there the model was neo-Ricardian, though a Marxian model of prices of production could equally have been used. In a model designed to investigate whether a long-run equilibrium necessarily implies that rates of profit are equal, prices of production are inappropriate, for they assume equal rates of profit (see also Farjoun and Machover 1983). Therefore the neo-Ricardian equations of prices of production, (7.1) and (7.2), are replaced by the assumption that prices clear outputs in the market: output levels determine the relative prices of the two commodities.

It is assumed that the price of food is constant. This simplifying assumption implies that the problems of food overproduction are ignored (or that the price of food is the numéraire). Equally, the fact that the real wage is assumed to be constant implies that labor is supplied in exactly the amount needed for production. We have thus severed the link between accumulation and the growth of the labor force; the model avoids the issues of technical change and the rate of profit that were examined in Chapters 5 and 6.

On the other hand, the price of machinery does respond to the level of output. In models of the von Neumann (1945) type, the price of any commodity that is oversupplied is set to zero. This is a strong assumption, for firms in reality can withhold commodities that are overproduced and can export or import. Instead, we assume that as the output of machinery rises relative to that of food, the price of machinery falls. Machinery is a normal commodity in the sense that as its relative output rises so its price falls.

The total capital investment and total surplus produced in each country are defined conventionally. The total capital advanced in each country is equal to the money required to pay for means of production and for labor power. The total profit is equal to the total revenue less the total capital advanced (since production periods are all of unit length, costs of production equal capital advanced). The rate of profit equals the ratio of total profit to total capital advanced.

In the usual (static) definition of equilibrium, profit rates are required to be equal as well as unchanging. Thus, in Section 7.1.3 we followed tradition in assuming that perfect capital mobility implies that the rate of profit is equal in the two countries. This notion is now generalized: dynamic equilibrium exists if profit rates are unchanging (and positive). It remains to be established whether profit rates are equal in dynamic equilibrium.

Suppose that the output of machinery is growing at a faster rate than the output of food. Then the ratio of the output of country A to the output of country B rises. Therefore, the price of machinery falls. Conversely, if the rate of growth of the output of country B exceeds that of country A, the price of machinery rises.

As machinery and food are produced, the outputs are traded and prices and profits determined. The profits can then be reinvested, yielding added production in which new profit rates are established. (If profits are negative the existing circulating capital must be reduced to cover those losses.) The changes in the rates of profit imply that if the price of machinery rises, the rate of profit in country A rises too, while the rate of profit in country B falls; if the rate of profit in country A is rising, then that in country B is falling.

These results together imply that if the rate of growth of the output of country A exceeds that of country B, then the rate of profit of country A is falling and that of country B is rising.

Hence the state of dynamic equilibrium may be characterized more completely. If the rate of profit in one country is not changing, neither is the profit rate in the other country. Equally, neither the price of machinery nor the ratio of outputs of the two countries changes in a state of dynamic equilibrium.

This section began by defining equilibrium as a state in which rates of profit in both countries are unchanging and positive though not necessarily equal. We conclude that if the rate of profit in one country is unchanging, then: profitability in the other country is constant too; outputs in the two countries are growing at the same rate; and relative prices are constant.

7.3.2 Capital Flows

The path(s) by which the system reaches dynamic equilibrium (or equilibria) and the rates of profit that sustain the equilibrium depend on the manner in which capital flows in response to differences in profit rates between the two countries. It is assumed that capital investment is made out of the surplus that arises during production (or becomes disinvestment if production incurs losses). The importance of retained earnings as a significant source of finance in manufacturing investment is established by Kalecki (1939, 1943) and by Meyer and Kuh (1957); see also Clark et al. (1986). In practice investment arises from the surplus, liquid wealth, and imported capital. In modern capitalist economies, most liquid wealth (which arises from the surplus produced even earlier) is held in banks and other financial institutions, which invest it; so what is liquid wealth to the individual is capital to the economy. Therefore, apart from foreign investment (which is explicitly modelled), capital investment does in practice arise out of the surplus that has been produced.

That surplus is disbursed in several ways. Some is distributed as rent, interest, taxes, and dividends. It is presumed that such a distribution occurs only if there is a positive surplus. (i) Some of this amount is spent on food, including state transfer payments and payments to state employees. (ii) The rest of the rent, interest, taxes, and dividends is reinvested by individuals, governments, banks, and other financial institutions. This is a central pool of capital that is not tied to any particular industry, has no preference for one industry rather than another (apart from a preference caused by differences in profit rates), and is controlled by people and institutions that try to know conditions and opportunities in all sectors. There exists no barrier to the free movement of such capital between countries. (iii) The remaining proportion of the surplus is retained by capitalists as a source of directly invested capital. It is used to finance expansion of their own firms or to invest in other production activities. The two forms of investment—by central financial institutions or by individual firms out of retained earnings—have quite different implications for the evolution of the system.

It is assumed that capital is invested in response to differences in rates of profit: investors are more likely to invest in a country the greater its profitability relative to the rate of profit in the other country. However, the response of capital to profit rate differentials is not perfect, so some capital is invested in the lower profit country. This assumption corresponds to reality.

The central pool of capital is invested in countries in a way that reflects their relative profitability; the steepness of the investment function depends on the elasticity of investment with respect to relative profitability. Capital thus flows in response to actual average profit rates rather than in response to marginal or expected rates of profit. Speculation plays no part in the model.

The remaining investment is directly controlled by the capitalists of each country. Direct investments are allocated to the two countries in proportions that reflect their relative profitability. Somewhat more precisely: if the rate of profit in country A increases over time, firms in both countries (A and B) direct increasing proportions of their investment to country A; but for given rates of profit in the two countries, A's firms direct a higher proportion of their investment to A than do B's firms. That is, firms are rational (higher profitability attracts a higher share of investment) but parochial (they prefer or see more opportunities locally than abroad).

Whereas investment by financial institutions is made out of a central pool of capital, direct investment is made out of the retained earnings of individual firms. This bland assertion hides an important simplification. When capital is international the stock of capital in country A is owned partly by the residents of A and partly by the residents of country B. In the real world the profit made by corporations located in A but controlled by residents of B may be repatriated for consumption or reinvestment. Decisions about the reinvestment of the profits on B's investment in A may be different from those made by A's residents. This difference is ignored here: all profits made in a country are either consumed in that country or reinvested in the same manner as profits on domestic capital.

If these two sources of investment are combined, the rate of capital accumulation in each country can be figured out. If production in one country incurs a loss, the surplus of the other country is invested entirely at home; therefore the rate of growth (decline) of capital advanced in each country is then equal to its rate of profit (or loss). If production in both countries incurs a loss, the rate of decline of capital advanced again equals the rate of loss. If production in both countries are profitable, then there are international flows of capital. Some capital investment flows from A to B; some flows from B to A. These flows must balance: net investment (outflow less inflow) from B to A must equal the net capital inflow received by A.

7.3.3 State of Equilibrium

In a state of dynamic equilibrium the rates of capital accumulation in the two countries are the same. This conclusion follows from the facts that there is no technical change, wages are fixed, and rates of growth of output are equal at equilibrium. Under quite general conditions (that specify the productiveness of the economies and continuity of the equations that describe them) there exists such an equilibrium and it is unique. But what does the equilibrium look like?

Three related propositions dominate thinking about capital flows between countries: (i) at equilibrium, rates of profit in different countries are equal; (ii) capital flows from countries with lower rates of profit toward those with a higher rate of profit; (iii) if there is a net flow of capital between countries, then the system is not in equilibrium. It is possible to show that in this system none of these propositions is generally correct. At equilibrium, rates of profit in countries may differ; net flows of capital may point to low-profit-rate countries; in equilibrium, there is a net flow of capital between countries. These propositions destroy the way in which international capital flows and development are conceived.

This is a central result of the chapter: except in particular circumstances, the two countries generally earn different rates of profit at equilibrium. In general, if investment is controlled partly by financial institutions and partly by individual firms, national rates of profit are not equal at equilibrium, even if the institutions and firms tend to invest more heavily in more profitable countries. The fact that financial markets and firms do respond to differences in profitability when making investment decisions does not by itself guarantee that profit rates are equal at equilibrium. It is important to understand the limits to this conclusion—when and under what circumstances rates of profit are equal at equilibrium—so we now examine some special cases.

7.3.3.1 Special Case 1: Purely Financial Capital

In this special case all investment is controlled from the pool of capital by central financial institutions. Capitalists do not directly invest in their own businesses from their retained earnings. All investment is made through the financial market.

If all capital is invested from the central pool by the financial sector, there exists dynamic equilibrium if and only if the institutions invest in countries in direct proportion to the total capital already accumulated in each country. The equilibrium ratio of profit rates must support this allocation of investment, that is, the equilibrium ratio of profit rates must cause financial markets to invest in proportion to existing capital stocks.

Central financial institutions may follow various rules (Q) in making investment decisions. When the rules satisfy the condition that if the rates of profit in the two countries are equal then capital is invested in proportion to the existing sizes of the countries, this suggests that the state of dynamic equilibrium has equal rates of profit. Some decision rules do satisfy this condition, for example,

$$q_A = \frac{K_A \exp(zr)}{K_A \exp(zr) + K_B \exp(zr)}, \qquad z > 0, \qquad r = r_A/r_B. \qquad (7.8)$$

(Here q_A denotes the proportion of all investment directed to country A; r_A and r_B are the rates of profit in the two countries; K_A and K_B are the sizes of their capital stocks; and the parameter z governs the responsiveness of capital flows to differences in profit rates. If z is large, small differences in profit rates translate into large differences in investment; if z is small, large differences in profit rates translate into small differences in investment.) However, not all decision rules satisfy this condition. For example, suppose that

$$q_A = \frac{\exp(zr)}{\exp(zr) + \exp(z/r)}, \qquad z > 0. \qquad (7.9)$$

This rule simply requires that more capital be invested in the country that is more profitable; if the two countries are equally profitable, the investment is split equally between them. Under decision rule (7.9), when profit rates are equal, $q_A = 0.5$, which is not an equilibrium assignment of investment to countries.

This special case, in which all investment is made by central financial institutions, supports the following conclusions. If institutions allocate capital in a way that depends on both the size of the countries and their relative profitability, then profit rates may be equal at equilibrium. As the second example (7.9) illustrates, however, there are decision rules that do not satisfy this criterion. (Incidentally, the policy of putting all investment in the more profitable country destroys the mathematical assumptions needed to prove the existence of equilibrium.) Since financial institutions may use a rule like (7.8)—invest in relation to the size of a country as well as its profitability—central financial investment may tend to equalize profit rates.

7.3.3.2 Special Case 2: Purely Retained Earnings

In this second case there is no central pool of capital. All investment is made directly by entrepreneurs out of their retained earnings. This case carries some startling implications about the investment decisions of individual firms.

At equilibrium, the firms in both countries must invest more of their capital in their own country than would be warranted simply from the relative sizes of the countries (or both invest less). Thus, whatever the relative rates of profit in the two countries at equilibrium, both sets of firms "prefer" to invest in their own country. This conclusion is quite independent of any specific investment policy; it is rather a requirement that must be imposed on that policy.

Some additional conclusions can be derived by examining a specific investment policy. To fix ideas let us suppose that

$$v_{AA} = \frac{(a + r)K_A}{(a + r)K_A + K_B}, \qquad v_{BB} = \frac{(a + 1/r)K_B}{K_A + (a + 1/r)K_B}, \qquad (7.10)$$

$(a > 0)$. (Here v_{AA} and v_{BB} denote respectively the share of A's firms' earnings that are invested in A and the share of B's firms' earnings that are invested in

B.) These policies mean that firms invest in proportion to the sizes of the two countries, weighted by their relative profitability. As country A becomes more profitable, more of the retained earnings of both countries are invested there. If the rates of profit in the two countries are equal, firms in country A invest more than proportionately in their own country (but some investment is directed to country B) and the firms in country B invest more than proportionately (but not only) in their own country. For example, if $r = 1$, then

$$v_{AA} = \frac{(a + 1)K_A}{(a + 1)K_A + K_B}, \qquad v_{BB} = \frac{(a + 1)K_B}{K_A + (a + 1)K_B}.$$

In other words, a measures the preference that firms have for investing in their own country at a given ratio of profit rates; the larger is a, the greater is that preference.

This investment preference function entails two implications. Dynamic equilibrium is characterized by equal rates of profit if and only if the two countries are the same size. Normally decentralized investment out of retained earnings leads to an equilibrium in which the two countries do not earn the same rate of profit. However, if a becomes indefinitely large (that is if firms invest all their retained earnings in their own countries), the equilibrium rates of profit become equal. In fact, firms do invest some of their retained earnings in other countries, and so this second result is not empirically significant.

This analysis yields an important conclusion about investment. In contrast to investment by central financial institutions, which may tend to equalize profits, investment by decentralized firms out of retained earnings does not normally lead to equal rates of profit at equilibrium. The existence of decentralized investment provides one reason for the central result of Section 7.3.3—that dynamic equilibrium does not mean that rates of profit are equal. The first step in understanding this conclusion is to analyze capital flows at equilibrium.

7.3.3.3 Capital Flows

Sections 7.3.3.1 and 7.3.3.2 have examined the implications of different investment policies for rates of profit at equilibrium. The flows of capital between the countries can now be computed. This investigation does not rely on the specific investment policies introduced in Sections 7.3.3.1 and 7.3.3.2, but rather rests on the general rule that the higher the relative rate of profit in a country, the greater the proportion of all investment that is directed there.

Suppose that country A makes the greater rate of profit in equilibrium. However, at equilibrium the rates of new investment (rates of capital accumulation) are equal. So the rate of net investment in A is less than the rate at which investment funds are produced there. The rate of net investment in B, which makes the lower rate of profit, exceeds the rate at which B produces investment funds. Therefore a net flow of capital occurs from country A to country B. This result thus contradicts received opinion: (i) in dynamic equilibrium there exists a net flow of capital between the countries unless their rates of profit happen to be equal; and (ii) the net flow of capital occurs from the country earning the higher rate of profit toward the country earning the lower rate of profit.

7.3.3.4 An Intuitive Account

We can now provide an intuitive account of these results. The discussion begins by assessing the notion of rationality implied by the model; it next describes the nature of dynamic equilibrium when all investment is directed by central financial institutions; and it then illustrates why decentralized investment policy implies that profit rates are not equal at equilibrium.

There are several views of rationality. Strictly defined, rational firms invest all their capital where the marginal rate of return is highest. This definition suffers three difficulties. First, it predicts wildly fluctuating investment patterns as the marginal rates of return change from being slightly higher in one country to being slightly higher in the other; the existence of dynamic equilibrium is therefore unclear. Secondly, firms have little evidence about marginal (in contrast to actual) rates of profit. Thirdly, firms are uncertain about conditions in other countries and therefore tend to prefer investment in their own country, where conditions are better understood. A more relaxed view of rationality is that as the rate of profit in one country rises in relation to that in the other, so firms and institutions invest increasing proportions of their capital in the country that offers the higher rate of profit. All the investment criteria employed in this chapter satisfy the relaxed definition of rationality, and all the conclusions require only this notion of rationality.

Even if investment behavior is rational in this sense, countries do not generally earn equal rates of profit at equilibrium. Technology may be different or similar in the two countries; wages may or may not differ. However, these are not crucial in determining equilibrium profit rates. The crucial control is investment behavior. The central results reflect investment rules when investment is controlled by central financial institutions and when it is controlled by decentralized firms. It seems that centralized control is more likely to entail an equal rate of profit equilibrium than is decentralized control. In both cases, what matters is how capital is invested in relation to the size of the existing capital stock and the existing rate of profit. Then, if countries do not earn the same rate of profit at equilibrium, capital flows in net from the country earning the higher rate of profit toward the country earning the lower rate of profit. Capital flows depend not only on relative rates of profit as in orthodox accounts but also on the sizes of the existing stocks of capital (and, in the n-country case, on their locations and profitabilities). The aggregate flow of

TABLE 7.1. Numerical illustrations of rates of profit and capital flows

	Capital Flows when Rates of Profit are Equal			
	Investment proportional to profit rate		Investment proportional to size and profits	
	Country A	Country B	Country A	Country B
Capital accumulated K	100.00	60.00	100.00	60.00
Rate of profit r	0.50	0.50	0.50	0.50
Surplus produced	50.00	30.00	50.00	30.00
Share of investment to country A v_{IA}	0.50	0.50	0.77	0.45
Investment in country A	25.00	15.00	38.46	13.64
Investment in country B	25.00	15.00	11.54	16.36
Accumulation $K\dot{K}$	40.00	40.00	52.10	27.90
Rate of accumulation $\dot{K}$	0.40	0.67	0.52	0.46

	Capital Flows at Equilibrium			
	Investment proportional to profit rate		Investment proportional to size and profits	
	Country A	Country B	Country A	Country B
Capital accumulated K	100.00	60.00	100.00	60.00
Rate or profit r	0.40	0.20	0.50	0.58
Surplus produced	40.00	12.00	50.00	34.74
Share of investment to country A v_{IA}	0.63	0.60	0.76	0.44
Investment in country A	25.30	7.20	37.83	15.14
Investment in country B	14.70	4.80	12.17	19.60
Accumulation $K\dot{K}$	32.50	19.50	58.33	31.77
Rate of accumulation $\dot{K}$	0.33	0.33	0.53	0.53

Note: Investment proportional to size and profits follows equation (7.10), with $a = 1$. At dynamic equilibrium, $v_{AA} = 0.7565$, whereas $K_A/(K_A + K_B) = 0.6250$ (the ratio between the two is 1.2104); $v_{BB} = 0.5642$, whereas $K_B/(K_A + K_B) = 0.3750$ (the ratio between the two is 1.5045).

capital from one country to the other is the product of (i) the probability that any one unit of capital is invested in the other and (ii) the quantity of capital that is to be invested.

Table 7.1 illustrates the possibilities. The upper part of the table illustrates a situation in which rates of profit are equal. The left pair of columns illustrate conditions when investment is proportional to profit rates, and the right pair of columns illustrate the circumstance in which investment is proportional to both size and the rate of profit. Consider investment proportional to profit rates first. If the probability of one firm in country A investing in country B is the same as the probability of one firm in country B investing in country B, there must be a net flow of capital toward the smaller country (B). The rate of accumulation in country B therefore exceeds that of country A. This is therefore not equilibrium. The smaller country grows more rapidly. In the other case, investment depends on both size and the rates of profit. Since profit rates are equal, there exists a net flow of capital toward the larger country, which therefore grows more rapidly.

We are led to ask which country grows more rapidly when rates of profit are equal (and therefore to ask which country has the lower rate of profit at equilibrium). This analysis makes perfectly clear that the capital flows when rates of profit are equal depend not only on the propensity of firms to invest in each country but also upon the relative sizes of the countries.

Consequently capital accumulates faster in one country than in the other. Therefore the relative output of one country grows, its price falls, and its rate of profit is reduced. The lower part of Table 7.1 illustrates the equilibrium situation. Rates of profit are not equal. When investment is proportional to the rate of profit, that rate is higher in country A than in country B. Therefore all firms prefer to invest in country A: over 60% of the total surplus is invested there. However, the small amount of earnings that are retained in country B together with the even smaller proportion of the (large) surplus of country A that is invested in country B combine to raise country B's rate of capital accumulation to that of country A. When investment is proportional to size and rate of profit, the larger country earns the higher rate of profit. All firms prefer to invest in their own country, but that preference is stronger (in relation to the sizes of the countries) among the firms of the country making the higher rate of profit. Under both investment rules, the low-probability flow from the country with a large surplus exceeds the magnitude of the high-probability flow from the country with a small surplus; therefore there is a net flow of capital to the country with the lower rate of profit.

7.4 CONCLUSION

The selective industrialization of parts of the world outside the traditional manufacturing core of North Atlantic countries has prompted debate about the relative significance of costs of production and of local state action in determining rates of economic growth. This debate raises two questions. How are internationalization, the growth of the NICs, and costs of production related? And what is the room in theory for local initiative, actions that attempt to alter a country's position in the structure of the world economy? We can now provide theoretical answers to these questions. The answers are theoretical in two senses: they state only what is possible, not whether those possibilities actually occur; and they provide only a logic for actions, not an explanation of them.

Existing theories of industrialization misspecify geographic change and offer little scope for local action. The theory of comparative advantage claims that countries can gain from trade if their factors of production have different relative prices. From these gains must be subtracted transport costs. In this theory the rise of the NICs at the expense of the North Atlantic economies has occurred because of misguided economic policies in the core and because of low wages in the NICs. In the NICs the state has merely set appropriate conditions for the free expression of market forces. The theory of competitive advantage focuses on the technical advantages of producers in different countries: trade provides benefits if countries have different technical conditions of production, but more efficient production always raises living standards and/or wages. In this theory the state may create appropriate conditions for a country's producers to obtain competitive advantages over their competitors. An ignored conclusion of both these theories is that the gains from trade are unequally distributed: higher wages imply improved terms of trade. The theory of the new international division of labor relates the industrialization of the NICs not only to their relatively low costs of production but also to the falling rate of profit in the core manufacturing economies of the North Atlantic region. These three theories suffer a pair of empirical deficiencies: most trade and most capital flows actually occur between developed countries, which have similar factor endowments and factor prices, rather than between developed and developing countries; and the industrialization of the Third World has been selective. The theories have to be respecified.

All these theories suppose that if the NICs are developing faster than the core manufacturing economies, then they must have certain advantages over the core. In particular production in the NICs must be more profitable, that is, lower cost, than production in the North Atlantic region. This view derives from the notion of an equilibrium in which rates of profit in different sectors and countries are equal. This notion is itself centrally bound up with the idea of price: in the accounts of both Sraffa and Marx prices of production are the prices that sustain an equilibrium in which rates of profit are equal.

The first task in reconstructing theories of development is therefore to examine this characteristic of equilibrium. We assembled a simple two-country model of an economy with constant returns to scale. In this model, relative prices respond to relative output levels and rates of investment in each country depend on their relative rates of profit. If the production coefficients are such that positive rates of profit can be earned in both countries, the system has a dynamic equilibrium, characterized by equal and constant rates of growth in the two countries, time-invariant rates of profit, and a constant ratio of output levels. This model enables us to reexamine the links between costs of production and rates of growth.

Three characteristics of the equilibrium state are significant and contrast with intuitive notions about economic equilibria. First, there exists no necessary tendency for rates of profit to be equal in dynamic equilibrium. Secondly, even in dynamic equilibrium there exists a net flow of capital from one country to the other. And, thirdly, that net flow is from the country with the higher rate of profit toward the country with the lower rate of profit. Thus, intuitive conclusions drawn from empirical observations must be questioned: net flows of capital do not imply disequilibrium, nor are flows in the direction of the country offering the greater return. It has been shown that the cause of these results is the different sizes of countries (which are decided by the technical requirements of production): at equilibrium the larger country offers the higher rate of profit, and there exists a net flow of capital toward the smaller (less profitable) country.

There do exist particular kinds of investment functions that lead to equal rates of profit at equilibrium. If all investment is controlled by central financial institutions that allocate capital to countries in proportion to both their size and their rate of profit, then the equilibrium rates of profit may be equal. The inefficient allocation of capital arises from the rational policies of decentralized firms: central financial institutions exist to allocate capital efficiently. Their payment for this function is the additional profit that can be earned by such an investment policy as compared to the profits derived from investments out of retained earnings.

The model casts doubt upon the value of economic models which assume that in equilibrium rates of profit are equal. More generally, the model shows that prices, outputs, and rates of profit cannot be computed solely from production data but need also information on investment policies. The model has an additional, important implication. Suppose that the two countries are not in equilibrium but are approaching it. Then the rate of capital accumulation in one country is greater than in the other. There is a net flow of capital to the country that is growing faster. But the country that is growing faster has a lower rate of profit than the more slowly growing country. Thus, as the countries approach equilibrium, different rates of capital accumulation do not correlate positively with rates of profit: the more rapidly growing country is less profitable.

Therefore, the fact that the NICs have industrialized partly at the expense of the manufacturing countries of the North Atlantic region need not imply that the NICs have been more profitable or lower cost producers than the traditional countries. The NICs may have had cost advantages over the North Atlantic producers, possibly arising from their lower wages, but that fact has to be proved rather than being assumed. Contrary to received wisdom, theory does not imply that faster growing regions have a cost advantage over slower growing regions. The NICs could have industrialized without any cost advantages, as Table 7.1 illustrates. Equally, the NICs could have grown without any improvement in their relative profitability. This model suggests two main ways by which a change in growth rates can occur without any change in relative profitability.

First, some investment might leak from the large and relatively profitable economies of the North Atlantic region. Although these countries are indeed large and profitable and almost all their surplus is invested locally, a few investors may well perceive investment opportunities in the NICs. The NICs are small and relatively unprofitable; their surplus is divided between the traditional manufacturing countries and local opportunities. There is nothing irrational about such policies. The net result is that the NICs grow faster than the North Atlantic economies if the small proportion of investment that leaks to the NICs exceeds the magnitude of the NICs' investment that returns to the traditional manufacturers. If there are static or dynamic economies of scale, the NICs become increasingly profitable as they grow and so gradually account for larger and larger shares of net investment. The rising relative profitability of the NICs is then a consequence not a cause of the initial changes in the pattern of location.

Secondly, after the expansion of the oil rents in the 1970s, the nature of overseas investment changed. In 1970, banks and bonds accounted for 30% of nonconcessional lending to developing countries; direct investment accounted for nearly 35%. By 1978, these proportions had become 46% and 21%, respectively (Hoogvelt 1982: 52). Direct investment by multinational producers has been diminishing compared with investment by financial institutions. If multinational producers and financial institutions have different investment policies, a change in the spatial pattern of investment occurs even if the relative costs of production do not change. Now, manufacturers as a group are probably less likely to invest abroad than are financial institutions. They are usually smaller and so likely to know less about foreign conditions and opportunities than financial institutions. Also manufacturers must, at least initially, maintain a large and profitable base in their "home" country to provide the profits for overseas expansion. If they are capable exporters, manufacturers may regard an overseas plant as competing with domestic production that is already profitable. In the end, the profitability of a manufacturer's new investment depends not only on the profitability of the next individual unit of investment but also on the continuing profitability of the existing profit source. Financial institutions do not suffer these constraints. The different investment rules of financial investors and direct investors are evident in the conclusions of the model. As the share of foreign investment made by financial institutions increases and that made by multinational direct investors falls, so the locational ties on capital diminish. As financial institutions direct a greater share of the surplus, the NICs gain a greater share of investment than they had previously, though the conditions and relative costs of production have not changed. Somewhat more deeply, then, our model is pointing to the possibility that the interests of financial capital and producers' capital may differ.

As a locational change, the growth of the NICs need not be associated with differences in costs of production. But the growth of some NICs is not merely a locational change. It is also one form of the internationalization of capital. Production is increasingly oriented to exports; production is more integrated over national borders: some of this internationally integrated, export-oriented production has located in the NICs. The growth of the NICs consequently also points to the process of globalization. This chapter has raised several reasons for the growth of international production.

The first of these is undoubtedly the fall in relative costs of transport and communications. All theories of location and of trade predict that as transport costs diminish so spatial variations in production costs become more salient in location decisions. Many firms no longer have to locate to minimize costs of transport from raw materials or to markets but can take advantage of special conditions in particular places. Two conclusions follow. On the one hand, low-cost producers can increase their share of production as compared to more favorably located but higher cost producers. On the other hand, firms can increasingly take advantage of spatial variations in production costs to divide production between different places and countries: the stages in a production process no longer have to be agglomerated.

Nevertheless, transport costs are also produced. To some extent at least, innovations in transport and communications are led by demands from users. Bulk ore carriers are produced (i) when someone learns how to make them and (ii) when someone foresees a need for them. Transport costs and international trade have a mutual relation: reductions in transport costs promote world trade; but the potential for profit from new forms and levels of world trade creates a demand for innovations in transport technology. We cannot simply regard transport costs as exogenous but need also to identify why the demand for world trade and international production has risen.

A second reason for the growth of international production is the growth in importance of financial rather than direct investment. Financial firms may invest strictly according to external, objective evaluations of profitability, whereas direct investors have good reasons to prefer investing in their own industry or country (for equivalent rates of profit). If both sets of investors evaluate market opportunities correctly, the financial investors make the greater rate of return because a higher proportion of their investments are made in high-profit countries. Thus, as the capital surplus of the traditional manufacturers was siphoned off to the OPEC countries and thus to banks, a rising proportion of investment became international—not necessarily because of a change in the spatial pattern of returns, but because of a change in the institutional structure of investment. By this reasoning, a cost advantage in different parts of the world became relevant only as new forms of financial control over investment rose in significance.

Thirdly, though, costs of production are not given data. They vary in response to changes in the pattern of production. In particular, wage rates vary in response to changes in the demand for labor. If some capital decamps from the North Atlantic producers to the NICs, a threat is offered to the workers of the traditional manufacturing economies: production in the NICs is profitable, and more relocation is possible unless the profitability of production at home is raised. This argument does not pertain to the particular advantages of one place over another; it concerns the dynamics of costs of production through bargaining between classes in different locations. Freedom of location becomes a strategy in place-specific class bargaining.

The final reason for the growth of international production derives from the relationship between the costs of production and the demand for commodities. In a closed economy wages are both a cost and a source of demand: firms seek to minimize wages to minimize their costs; they also seek to raise (other firms') wage payments to maximize their markets. Since wage rates are generally similar between firms in the same labor market, these twin aims conflict. This is the essential truth identified by regulation theory; and it is embodied in the model of Chapter 5. But if firms can produce for overseas markets, the conflict seems to be deflected: wages are purely a cost, for the market is abroad. (The same strategy can be used in a country in which labor markets are deeply segmented.) Of course, at a global level, the contradiction of the two aspects of labor is not avoided at all; but the available market seems so large as to dilute the problem, at least initially. Furthermore, firms that produce for overseas markets can bargain with their labor force using the argument that prices are given and costs of production must allow competition with firms in other countries. By contrast, firms that produce only for domestic consumption within sheltered boundaries can be forced to adapt to local wage demands.

Production over borders, production in the NICs: these are clearly connected phenomena. But the extent to which they are related to spatial variations in costs of production is unclear. Contrary to much belief, the observed change in the spatial organization of production need not be caused by changes in costs of production (or even differences in costs of production). Elements of strategy and changes in the institutional structure of investment may have been important. Of course, costs of production may have been important. But that is an empirical issue, not one that can be decided a priori.

APPENDIX A7: INTERNATIONALIZATION, CAPITAL FLOWS, AND RATES OF PROFIT

A7.1 INTERNATIONAL GROWTH

Here we follow Dutt (1990) to illustrate the theory of international trade in a world of fixed coefficient technologies and cost-plus (neo-Ricardian) prices. Similar models explain unequal exchange and interregional capital flows. As has been done generally in this book, money and asset markets are ignored.

A7.1.1 A Model of Trade and Comparative Advantage

Consider a single, closed, capitalist economy. Two commodities are produced: means of production (commodity 1) and a consumption good (commodity 2). The output levels (X_1 and X_2) of the two commodities must satisfy

$$X_1 = (1 + g)K \tag{A7.1}$$

$$X_2 = CL, \tag{A7.2}$$

where g is the rate of growth of (circulating) capital; K is the total capital used in production; C is the consumption of commodity 2 per worker per unit time (the real wage); and L is the size of the labor force. Clearly,

$$K = K_1 + K_2 = a_1X_1 + a_2X_2$$

$$L = l_1X_1 + l_2X_2,$$

where a_1, a_2, l_1 and l_2 are, as usual, the input-output coefficients. These equations describe an input–output system with constant returns to scale.

Prices are decided by a markup over the costs of means of production (as in neo-Ricardian price models):

$$P_1X_1 = P_1K_1 (1 + r) + Wl_1X_1 \qquad (A7.3)$$

$$P_2X_2 = P_1K_2 (1 + r) + Wl_2X_2, \qquad (A7.4)$$

where P_1 and P_2 are the prices of the means of production and the consumption good, respectively; r is the rate of profit; and W is the (money) wage rate (the same in both industries). Evidently,

$$W = P_2C, \qquad (A7.5)$$

for the money wage must be sufficient to pay for the real wage.

We ignore the growth of the labor force and the determination of real wages. Equally, the rate of profit is not calculated. Given the questions we seek to answer, these are not important issues.

If we add equations (A7.3) and (A7.4), and note from (A7.2) that $P_2X_2 = P_2CL = WL$ (by A7.5), then

$$P_1X_1 = P_1K(1 + r),$$

whence, using (A7.1), we have

$$P_1X_1 = P_1(1 + r)X_1/(1 + g),$$

so that

$$r = g. \qquad (A7.6)$$

The rate of growth of the means of production equals the rate of profit.

Now we define $k = K_1/K_2$; $p = P_1/P_2$. Also note the input–output coefficients: $a_1 = K_1/X_1$; $a_2 = K_2/X_2$. Then equations (A7.1) through (A7.6) can be written

$$1/a_1 = (1 + r)(1 + k^{-1}) \qquad (A7.7)$$

$$1/a_2 = C(l_1 k/a_1 + l_2/a_2) \tag{A7.8}$$

$$p = pa_1(1 + r) + Cl_1 \tag{A7.9}$$

$$1 = pa_2(1 + r) + Cl_2. \tag{A7.10}$$

These four equations determine the three unknowns C, k, p:

$$k = \frac{a_1(1 + r)}{1 - a_1(1 + r)} \tag{A7.11}$$

$$C = \frac{1 - a_1(1 + r)}{l_2[1 - a_1(1 + r)] + l_1 a_2(1 + r)} \tag{A7.12}$$

$$p = \frac{l_1}{l_2[1 - a_1(1 + r)] + l_1 a_2(1 + r)}. \tag{A7.13}$$

Thus the system is determinate up to the rate of profit, the size of the system (K_1), and the numéraire (P_1).

Suppose that there exist two independent countries, A and B. If the countries do not trade, the system (A7.1) through (A7.6) applies to each country, though possibly with different levels of output, capital, wages, and rates of profit. However, they produce with the same technologies, that is, with the same input–output coefficients. We assume that in country A the rate of profit exceeds that in country B:

$$r_A > r_B. \tag{A7.14}$$

Then

$$p_A = \frac{l_1}{l_2[1 - a_1(1 + r_A)] + l_1 a_2(1 + r_A)}, \tag{A7.15}$$

and similarly for p_B. From equation (A7.15) and the comparable equation for p_B,

$$p_A < p_B$$

if

$$l_1 a_2(r_A - r_B) > l_2 a_1(r_A - r_B),$$

which, given (A7.14), is true if

$$\frac{a_2}{l_2} > \frac{a_1}{l_1}. \tag{A7.16}$$

This is the first essential step in the argument about comparative advantage. Suppose as in (A7.14) that in country A the rate of profit exceeds that in B. Then in country A the price of means of production compared with the price of consumption goods is lower than in B if the production of means of production is more labor intensive than the production of consumption goods. In other words, country A, where capital is expensive compared with the price of labor, has a comparative advantage in producing the commodity that uses relatively more labor and little capital to produce.

To examine the gains from trade, assume that (A7.14) and (A7.16) are true. Suppose that the countries specialize completely, A producing commodity 1, in which it has a comparative advantage, and B producing commodity 2, in which it has a comparative advantage. Country A sells commodity 1 to B; in return country B sells commodity 2 to A. The rates of profit and rates of growth may differ between the countries, for factors of production do not move even if countries trade. The unified trading system can be described by the following equations:

$$X_1 = K_A(1 + g_A) + K_B(1 + g_B), \tag{A7.17}$$

where $K_A = K_1$ and $K_B = K_2$;

$$X_2 = C_A L_A + C_B L_B, \tag{A7.18}$$

where $L_A = l_1 X_1$ and $L_B = l_2 X_2$;

$$P_1 X_1 = P_1 K_1(1 + r_A) + W_A l_1 X_1 \tag{A7.19}$$

$$P_2 X_2 = P_1 K_2(1 + r_B) + W_B l_2 X_2 \tag{A7.20}$$

$$W_A = P_2 C_A \tag{A7.21}$$

$$W_B = P_2 C_B \tag{A7.22}$$

$$P_2 C_A L_A = P_1(1 + g_B) K_B. \tag{A7.23}$$

Equation (A7.23) requires that trade be balanced: country A has to import consumption commodities and country B must import means of production, in amounts and at prices that balance.

By substituting successively (A7.21), (A7.23), and (A7.17) into (A7.19), it can be shown that $g_A = r_A$. By substituting (A7.22), (A7.18), and (A7.23) into (A7.20) it follows that $g_B = r_B$. From these results and using (A7.21) and (A7.22) in (A7.19) and (A7.20), we arrive at the following system:

$$1/a_1 = (1 + r_A) + (1 + r_B)k^{-1} \tag{A7.24}$$

$$1/a_2 = C_A l_1 k/a_1 + C_B l_2/a_2 \tag{A7.25}$$

$$p = pa_1(1 + r_A) + C_A l_1 \tag{A7.26}$$

$$1 = pa_2(1 + r_B) + C_B l_2 \tag{A7.27}$$

$$C_A l_1 = p(1 + r_B)a_1 k^{-1}. \tag{A7.28}$$

However, only three of these equations are independent, whereas four variables need to be determined: k, p, C_A, and C_B. Thus C_A and C_B are only fixed relatively:

$$k = \frac{a_1(1 + r_B)}{1 - a_1(1 + r_A)} \tag{A7.29}$$

$$p = C_A \frac{l_1}{1 - a_1(1 + r_A)} \tag{A7.30}$$

$$[1 - a_1(1 + r_A)] = C_A l_1 a_2(1 + r_B) + C_B l_2[1 - a_1(1 + r_A)]. \tag{A7.31}$$

The relative sizes of C_A and C_B can only be decided by an additional equation.

The question the theory of comparative advantage seeks to answer is whether people in the two countries are better off when the countries trade than when they are isolated. Since the rates of profit in the two economies are regarded as fixed (and so the rates of growth of output are fixed), this question is answered by comparing the real wages of the populations before and after trade. To make this comparison, assume that the relative sizes of real wages in the two countries are the same before and after trade. We denote by C_A^* and C_B^* the real wages in countries A and B before trade. Then the relative real wages are equal before and after trade if

$$C_A/C_B = C_A^*/C_B^*. \tag{A7.32}$$

Clearly, if trade raises the real wage in country B, it also raises the real wage in country A. If, under assumption (A7.32), trade raises real wages, then we have shown that trade is beneficial—though it remains an open question how those benefits are distributed within and between the two countries in practice. It is also an open question whether some of the gains from trade raise profit rates at the expense of real wages.

Now from equation (A7.31) we have

$$C_B = \frac{1}{l_2} - \frac{l_1 a_2(1 + r_B)}{l_2[1 - a_1(1 + r_A)]} C_A$$

$$= \frac{1}{l_2} - \frac{l_1 a_2(1 + r_B)}{l_2[1 - a_1(1 + r_A)]} \frac{C_A^*}{C_B^*} C_B,$$

whence $C_B > C_B^*$ if

$$[1 - a_1(1 + r_A)] > l_2[1 - a_1(1 + r_A)]C_B^* + l_1a_2(1 + r_B)C_A^*. \quad (A7.33)$$

But C_A^* and C_B^* are defined by equation (A7.12), the solution to the model without trade:

$$C_A^* = \frac{1 - a_1(1 + r_A)}{l_2[1 - a_1(1 + r_A)] + l_1a_2(1 + r_A)}$$

and similarly for C_B^*. If these values are substituted in (A7.33), then $C_B > C_B^*$ if

$$r_A > r_B \quad \text{and} \quad a_2/l_2 > a_1/l_1,$$

which are precisely conditions (A7.14) and (A7.16) that were assumed in describing the two countries. This establishes the required result: trade is beneficial in the circumstances.

A7.1.2 Competitive Advantages

We modify the model of Section A7.1.1 by assuming there is perfect international mobility of capital. So the rate of profit in the two countries is the same: $r_A = r_B = r$. If techniques of production are the same in the two countries, this assumption implies that wage rates are also equal (equation A7.12) though labor is immobile. Perfect capital mobility implies that wage rates are the same everywhere unless technologies are different in different countries; this is an important conclusion. Thus the second modification to the model of Section A7.1.1 is to assume that the countries produce commodities 1 and 2 with different techniques.

Before trade the model of equations (A7.1) through (A7.5) needs to be modified merely by adding appropriate subscripts (A or B) to the input–output coefficients to identify the country within which production is taking place. The solution of the model is

$$a_{1I} = \frac{a_{1I}(1 + r)}{1 - a_{1I}(1 + r)} \quad (A7.34)$$

$$C_I = \frac{1 - a_{1I}(1 + r)}{l_{2I}[1 - a_{1I}(1 + r)] + l_{1I}a_{2I}(1 + r)} \quad (A7.35)$$

$$p_1 = \frac{l_{1I}}{l_{2I}[1 - a_{1I}(1 + r)] + l_{1I}a_{2I}(1 + r)} \quad (A7.36)$$

for countries I = A or B. Relative prices and consumption levels are readily found from equations (A7.34)–(A7.36). For example, if country A is technically more efficient than country B, in the sense that at least one of a_{1A}, a_{2A}, l_{1A}, or l_{2A} is below (and none exceeds) the corresponding coefficient in B, then the level of consumption in country A exceeds that in country B: $C_A > C_B$. Technical efficiency raises living standards, at least when there is no trade.

To examine the gains from trade suppose that country A has a competitive technical advantage in producing commodity 1 so that the relative price of commodity 1 in country A is less than it is in country B:

$$p_A < p_B. \tag{A7.37}$$

Now suppose that country A specializes in producing that commodity in which it has a competitive advantage: commodity 1. The basic model is equations (A7.17)–(A7.23), and the solution is equations (A7.29)–(A7.31):

$$k = \frac{a_{1A}(1 + r)}{1 - a_{1A}(1 + r)} \tag{A7.38}$$

$$p = C_A \frac{l_{1A}}{1 - a_{1A}(1 + r)} \tag{A7.39}$$

$$[1 - a_{1A}(1 + r)] = C_A l_{1A} a_{2B}(1 + r) + C_B l_{2B}[1 - a_{1A}(1 + r)]. \tag{A7.40}$$

If the real wage in country A is the same after trade as it was before ($C_A = C_A^*$), then from equation (A7.31) we have

$$C_B = \frac{1}{l_{2B}} - \frac{l_{1A} a_{2B}(1 + r)}{l_{2B}[1 - a_{1A}(1 + r)]} C_A^*,$$

which exceeds C_B^* if, from equation (A7.35),

$$l_{1B}\{l_{2A}[1 - a_{1A}(1 + r)] + l_{1A} a_{2A}(1 + r)\}$$
$$- l_{1A}\{l_{2B}[1 - a_{1B}(1 + r)] + l_{1B} a_{2B}(1 + r)\} > 0,$$

which is precisely condition (A7.37). A similar result holds if the real wage in country B is the same before and after trade. Again trade is beneficial: if the rate of profit is unaffected by trade and if the real wage in one country is unchanged by trade, the real wage in the other rises. Thus both partners can gain from trade.

A7.1.3 Distributing the Benefits of Trade

Consider the model of Section A7.1.2. The countries trade. From the conditions of production, the values of the two commodities are

$$\lambda_A = \lambda_1 = a_{1A}\lambda_1 + l_{1A} \tag{A7.41}$$

$$\lambda_B = \lambda_2 = a_{2B}\lambda_1 + l_{2B}. \tag{A7.42}$$

Since specialization is complete, the values of the commodities are also the unit values of the exports of the two countries. Equations (A7.41) and (A7.42) have the solution

$$\lambda_A = \frac{l_{1A}}{1 - a_{1A}}$$

$$\lambda_B = \frac{a_{2B}l_{1A} + (1 - a_{1A})l_{2B}}{1 - a_{1A}},$$

so that the relative value of the commodities is

$$\lambda = \frac{\lambda_A}{\lambda_B} = \frac{l_{1A}}{a_{2B}l_{1A} + (1 - a_{1A})l_{2B}}. \tag{A7.43}$$

By contrast, from equation (A7.39), the relative price of the two commodities is

$$p = C_A \frac{l_{1A}}{1 - a_{1A}(1 + r)}. \tag{A7.44}$$

Now the ratio p/λ is the ratio of the prices per unit of value of the two commodities:

$$\frac{p}{\lambda} = \frac{p_1/p_2}{\lambda_1/\lambda_2} = \frac{p_1}{\lambda_1} \bigg/ \frac{p_2}{\lambda_2}.$$

If the ratio p/λ is high, country A gains a high price for its commodity exports compared with their value. A comparison of equations (A7.44) and (A7.43) reveals that country A can extract a higher price per unit value of its exports the higher its real wages (and the lower the rate of profit).

A7.2 CAPITAL FLOWS AND RATES OF PROFIT

A7.2.1 The Model

The model that is to be constructed is a model of a two-country economy. The first country (A) produces means of production, called machinery, and the second (B) produces means of subsistence, called food. There is no fixed capital, and both countries have the same period of production. Processes are point input–point output. The production processes are as follows:

a_A machinery + l_A labor yield 1 unit of machinery;
a_B machinery + l_B labor yield 1 unit of food.

Workers consume W food per unit of labor time: the real wage is identical in the two countries. All coefficients are positive and the processes are productive ($0 < a_A < 1; 0 < a_B$).

All complications and all factors other than capital mobility and relative prices are ignored. There are no immobilities, no aggregate shortages of labor, no technical change, and no economies or diseconomies of scale. Transport is free. These factors tend to preserve or to augment differences in profit rates between countries; this model is designed to investigate the relations between capital mobility and the rate of profit even without such "imperfections." These assumptions modify the two-country model of equations (A7.17)–(A7.23).

Let X_A and X_B denote the respective output levels of the two countries. In the models of Section A7.1 prices were assumed to be set at long-run equilibrium levels; there the model was neo-Ricardian, though a Marxian model of prices of production could equally have been used. In a model designed to investigate whether a long-run equilibrium necessarily implies that rates of profit are equal, prices of production are inappropriate, for they assume equal rates of profit (see also Farjoun and Machover 1983). Therefore the neo-Ricardian equations of prices of production, (A7.19)–(A7.20), are replaced by the assumption that prices clear outputs in the market: output levels determine the relative prices of the two commodities.

It is assumed that the price of the food (P_2) is constant:

$$P_2 = 1. \tag{A7.45}$$

This simplifying assumption implies that the problems of overproducing food are ignored (or that the price of food is the numéraire). Equally, the fact that the real wage is assumed to be constant implies that labor is supplied in exactly the amount needed for production. Equation (A7.45) thus severs the link between accumulation and the growth of the labor force; it enables the model to avoid the issues of technical change and the rate of profit that were examined in Chapters 5 and 6.

On the other hand, the price of machinery (P_1) does respond to the level of output. In models of the von Neumann (1945) type, the price of any commodity that is oversupplied is set to zero. This is a strong assumption, for firms in reality can withhold commodities that are overproduced and can export or import. Thus

$$P_1 = P[X_1/X_2]. \tag{A7.46}$$

It is assumed that the function P is continuous (a small change in relative output levels implies a small change in price), is strictly decreasing, and is always positive. Machinery is a normal commodity in the sense that as its relative output rises, its price falls.

A simple function that satisfies these assumptions is

$$P_1 = \alpha[X_1/X_2]\beta,$$

with $\beta < 0 < \alpha$. The first parameter, α, is simply a scale parameter, with dimensions of dollars per ton. The second parameter is a sensitivity parameter that fixes the rate at which prices respond to changes in relative output levels. The larger is the size of β, the greater is the percentage fall in the price of machinery caused by a 1% increase in the ratio of output levels, X_1/X_2. The analysis of the model uses equation (A7.46); no result relies on this example.

The total capital investment and total surplus produced in each country may now be defined. The total capital advanced in country I is

$$K_I = (P_1 a_I + W l_I) X_I, \qquad I = A, B. \tag{A7.47}$$

The total profit produced in country I is

$$R_I = (P_I - P_1 a_I - W l_I) X_I, \qquad I = A, B. \tag{A7.48}$$

Therefore the rate of profit in each industry is

$$r_I = \frac{R_I}{K_I} = \frac{P_I - P_1 a_I - W l_I}{P_1 a_I + W l_I}, \qquad I = A, B. \tag{A7.49}$$

Definition 1. The economy is said to be in a state of dynamic equilibrium at time T if and only if the following conditions hold:

$$dr_A/dt = dr_B/dt = 0 \qquad \text{for all} \quad t > T,$$

where

$$r_A, r_B > 0.$$

Some additional characteristics of the state of dynamic equilibrium can be established readily.

Suppose that the output of machinery is growing at a faster rate than the output of food:

$$\dot{X}_A = \frac{1}{X_A} \frac{dX_A}{dt} > \frac{1}{X_B} \frac{dX_B}{dt} = \dot{X}_B.$$

Then the ratio of the output of country A to the output of country B rises, for

$$d/dt \left[\frac{X_A}{X_B} \right] = \frac{X_A}{X_B} [\dot{X}_A - \dot{X}_B] > 0.$$

Therefore, since P is strictly decreasing, $dP_1/dt < 0$: the price of machinery falls. Conversely, if the rate of growth of the output of country B exceeds that of country A, the price of machinery rises. Thus,

Proposition 1. $dP_1/dt < 0$ if and only if $\dot{X}_A > \dot{X}_B$.

As machinery and food are produced, the outputs are traded and prices and profits determined. The profits can then be reinvested, yielding added production in which new profit rates are established. (If profits are negative, the existing circulating capital must be reduced to cover those losses.) The changes in the rates of profit are

$$\frac{dr_I}{dt} = \frac{d}{dt}\left[\frac{P_1 - P_1 a_I - Wl_I}{P_1 a_I + Wl_I}\right], \qquad I = A, B,$$

so that

$$\frac{dr_A}{dt} = \frac{Wl_A}{(P_1 a_A + Wl_A)^2}\frac{dP_1}{dt} \tag{A7.50}$$

and

$$\frac{dr_B}{dt} = \frac{-a_B}{(P_1 a_B + Wl_B)^2}\frac{dP_1}{dt}. \tag{A7.51}$$

Equations (A7.50) and (A7.51) imply that if the price of machinery rises, the rate of profit in country A rises too, while the rate of profit in country B falls; if the rate of profit in country A is rising, then that in country B is falling. That is,

Proposition 2. (i) $dr_A/dt > 0$ if and only if $dP_1/dt > 0$;

(ii) $dr_A/dt > 0$ if and only if $dr_B/dt < 0$.

Propositions 1 and 2 together imply that if the rate of growth of the output of country A exceeds that of country B, then the rate of profit of country A is falling and that of country B is rising. Thus,

Proposition 3. $dr_A/dt < 0$ (and $dr_B/dt > 0$) if and only if $\dot{X}_1 > \dot{X}_2$.

If these propositions are combined with Definition 1, then the state of dynamic equilibrium may be characterized more completely. From Proposition 2(ii) it follows that if the rate of profit in one country is not changing, neither is the profit rate in the other; that is, to establish whether a state of dynamic equilibrium exists, it suffices to figure out whether one rate of profit is constant. Equally by Propositions 2(i) and 3 in dynamic equilibrium, neither the price of machinery nor the ratio of outputs of the two countries changes. That is,

Proposition 4. The following conditions are equivalent:

    (i) $dr_A/dt = 0$;

    (ii) $dr_B/dt = 0$;

    (iii) $\dot{X}_A = \dot{X}_B$;

    (iv) $dP_1/dt = 0$.

This section began by defining equilibrium as a state in which rates of profit in both countries are unchanging and positive. Rates of profit are not necessarily equal in equilibrium. We conclude, though, that if the rate of profit in one country is unchanging, then: profitability in the other country is constant too; rates of growth of output in the two countries are growing at the same pace; and relative prices are constant.

A7.2.2 Capital Flows

The path(s) by which the system reaches dynamic equilibrium (or equilibria) and the rates of profit that sustain the equilibrium depend on the manner in which capital flows in response to differences in profit rates between the two countries. It is assumed that capital investment is made out of the surplus that arises during production (or becomes disinvestment if production incurs losses).

That surplus is disbursed in several ways. Some is distributed as rent, interest, taxes, and dividends. It is presumed that such a distribution occurs only if there is a positive surplus. (i) Of this amount, some is spent on food, including state transfer payments and payments to state employees. We denote this proportion of the total surplus by s. (ii) The rest of the rent, interest, taxes, and dividends is reinvested by individuals, governments, banks, and other financial institutions. We denote this proportion of the total surplus by u. This is a central pool of capital that is not tied to any particular industry, that has no preference for one industry rather than another, apart from a preference caused by differences in profit rates, and that is controlled by people and institutions which try to know conditions and opportunities in all sectors. Hence there exists no barrier to the free movement of such capital between countries. (iii) The remaining proportion of the surplus $(1 - u - s)$ is retained by capitalists as a source of directly invested capital. It is used to finance expansion of their own firms or to invest in other production activities. The remainder of this section describes the mathematics of these capital flows.

Let the proportion of the central capital pool that is invested in country I be q_I, where

$$q_A = \begin{cases} Q[r_A/r_B] & \text{if} & r_A, r_B > 0 \\ 1 & \text{if} & r_B \leq 0 \\ 0 & \text{if} & r_A \leq 0 \end{cases} \qquad (A7.52)$$

$$q_B = 1 - q_A$$

$$0 \leq q_A, q_B \leq 1.$$

It is required that Q be a continuous and strictly increasing function of the ratio of profit rates, with limit (as r_A tends to 0) of 0 and (as r_B tends to 0) of 1. This formulation claims that the central pool of capital is invested in countries in a way that reflects their relative profitability; the steepness of Q depends on the elasticity of investment with respect to relative profitability. Capital thus flows in response to actual average profit rates rather than in response to marginal or expected rates of profit. Speculation plays no part in the model.

If both countries make a (positive) surplus, the total investment from the central pool of capital to country I is

$$q_I u(R_A + R_B), \qquad I = A, B.$$

If country I makes a loss, it contributes no surplus to the central pool and receives no investment from it either.

The remaining investment is directly controlled by the capitalists of each country. Let v_{IJ} denote the proportion of country I's direct investment that is allocated to country J, where

$$v_{AA} = \begin{cases} V^A[r_B/r_A] & \text{if} & r_B > 0 \\ 1 & \text{if} & r_B = 0 \end{cases} \qquad (A7.53)$$

$$v_{AB} = 1 - v_{AA}$$

$$v_{BB} = \begin{cases} V^B[r_B/r_A] & \text{if} & r_A > 0 \\ 1 & \text{if} & r_A = 0 \end{cases} \qquad (A7.54)$$

$$v_{BA} = 1 - v_{BB}$$

$$0 \leq v_{AA}, v_{BB} \leq 1.$$

The functions V^A and V^B are assumed to be continuous and strictly increasing functions of their respective arguments. Direct investments, then, are allocated to the two countries in proportions that reflect their relative profitability. Whereas investment by financial institutions is made out of a central pool of capital, direct investment is made out of the retained earnings of individual firms. The direct investment in country I is therefore

$$(1 - u - s)(v_{AI}R_A + v_{BI}R_B), \qquad I = A, B.$$

If these two sources of investment are combined, the rate of capital accumulation in each country can be figured out. If r_A or $r_B < 0$, then

$$\dot{K}_I = \frac{1}{K_I} \frac{dK_I}{dt} = r_I, \qquad I = A, B.$$

That is, if production in one country incurs a loss, the surplus of the other country is invested entirely at home; therefore the rate of growth (decline) of capital advanced in each country is equal to its rate of profit (or loss). If production in both countries incurs a loss, the rate of decline of capital advanced again equals the rate of loss. If production in both countries is profitable, r_A and $r_B \geq 0$, then

$$\dot{K}_A = q_A u(r_A + r_B k^{-1}) + (1 - u - s)(v_{AA}r_A + v_{BA}r_B k^{-1})$$

$$\dot{K}_B = q_B u(r_A k + r_B) + (1 - u - s)(v_{AB}r_A k + v_{BB}r_B), \qquad (A7.55)$$

where $k = K_A/K_B$.

Equations (A7.53)–(A7.55) describe international flows of capital. Some capital investment flows from A to B; some flows from B to A. These flows must balance: net investment (outflow less inflow) from B to A must equal the net capital inflow received by A. In each country (I), the level of capital accumulation is $K_I \dot{K}_I$, while the rate of production of capital for investment is $(1 - s)r_I$. Thus the net capital inflow to country I is $K_I[\dot{K}_I - (1 - s)R_I]$. The requirement that investment flows balance is therefore

$$K_A[\dot{K}_A - (1 - s)r_A] = -K_B[\dot{K}_B - (1 - s)r_B],$$

whence

$$k\dot{K}_A + \dot{K}_B = (kr_A + r_B)(1 - s). \qquad (A7.56)$$

Now consider the physical production of commodities in this system. The consumption commodity, made by B, is consumed by the workers in the two countries ($l_A X_A + l_B X_B$ in number) each earning a real wage W. This commodity also feeds capitalists who are consuming out of profits; since the proportion of profits they consume is s, total consumption out of profits is $s(R_A + R_B)$. Production equals this total consumption:

$$X_B = Wl_A X_A + Wl_B X_B + s(R_A + R_B),$$

so that

$$X_B(1 - Wl_B) = Wl_A X_A + s(kr_A + r_B)K_B. \qquad (A7.57)$$

Similarly the total output of the means of production equals total investment in the next period:

$$P_1 X_A = (1 + g_A)K_A + (1 + g_B)K_B. \qquad (A7.58)$$

A7.2.3 State of Equilibrium: Characterization

First we gather the equations that define the model. Then the model is related to the theory of balanced growth paths: in a state of dynamic equilibrium the rates of capital accumulation in the two countries are the same.

Definition 2. The model is the set of equations:

(i) $\dot{K}_I = r_I$, $I = A, B$,   if r_A or $r_B < 0$;

otherwise,

$$\dot{K}_A = q_A u(r_A + r_B k^{-1}) + (1 - u - s)(v_{AA} r_A + v_{BA} r_B k^{-1})$$

$$\dot{K}_B = q_B u(r_A k + r_B) + (1 - u - s)(v_{AB} r_A k + v_{BB} r_B).$$

(ii) $q_A = Q[r_A/r_B]$

$q_B = 1 - q_A$

$v_{AA} = V^A[r_A/r_B]$

$v_{BB} = V^B[r_B/r_A]$,

and the other conditions of (A7.53)–(A7.54)—

(iii) $P_2 = 1$

(iv) $P_1 = P[X_1/X_2]$

(v) $K_I = (P_1 a_I + Wl_I)X_I$, $I = A, B$

(vi) $R_I = (P_1 - P_1 a_I - Wl_I)X_I$, $I = A, B$

(vii) $r_I = R_I/K_I$, $I = A, B$

(viii) $k\dot{K}_A + \dot{K}_B = (kr_A + r_B)(1 - s)$

(ix) $X_B(1 - Wl_B) = Wl_A X_A + s(kr_A + r_B)K_B$

(x) $P_1 X_A = (1 + g_A)K_A + (1 + g_B)K_B.$

In a state of dynamic equilibrium rates of capital accumulation satisfy two relations. First from Definition 2(v)

$$K_I = (P_1 a_I + Wl_I)X_I \qquad I = A, B.$$

However, by Proposition 4(iv), in a state of dynamic equilibrium $dP_1/dt = 0$. Therefore in equilibrium $\dot{K}_I = \dot{X}_I$, $I = A, B$. But, by Proposition 4(iii), in equilibrium $\dot{X}_A = \dot{X}_B$. Therefore, in a state of dynamic equilibrium the rate of accumulation in the two countries is the same:

Proposition 5. In a state of dynamic equilibrium $\dot{K}_A = \dot{K}_B$.

Furthermore, by Propositions 4(i) and 4(ii) the rate of profit is constant in a state of equilibrium. But $dr_A/dt = dr_B/dt$ implies that $d(r_A/r_B)/dt = 0$, which in turn implies that q_A, v_{AA}, and v_{BB} are all constant. Definition 2(i) therefore implies that in a state of dynamic equilibrium the rate of accumulation is constant:

Proposition 6. In a state of dynamic equilibrium, $\dot{K}_A = \dot{K}_B = g$, say, which is constant.

With definition 2(viii), Proposition 6 defines g in relation to k and the rates of profit:

Proposition 7. In a state of dynamic equilibrium

$$g = \frac{kr_A + r_B}{1 + k}(1 - s).$$

It follows from Definition 2(x) that

$$P_1 X_A = (1 + g)(K_A + K_B).$$

A7.2.4 State of Equilibrium: Solution

We turn now to examine the conditions under which there exists a solution to this model. The uniqueness of that solution is also demonstrated.

By substituting Definition 2(x) in 2(ix) and then replacing K_B by Definition 2(v), we find k as a function of g and P_1:

$$k = \frac{P_1(1 - Wl_B) - (P_1a_B + Wl_B)[Wl_A(1 + g) + sP_1g/(1 - s)]}{(P_1a_B + Wl_B)[Wl_A(1 + g) + sP_1g/(1 - s)]}. \quad (A7.59)$$

But, from Definition 2(v),

$$k = \frac{K_A}{K_B} = \left[\frac{P_1a_A + Wl_A}{P_1a_B + Wl_B}\right]\frac{X_A}{X_B},$$

whence using (A7.59) we find X_A/X_B as a function of P_1 and g:

$$\frac{X_A}{X_B} = \frac{P_1(1 - Wl_B) - (P_1a_B + Wl_B)[Wl_A(1 + g) + sP_1g/(1 - s)]}{(P_1a_A + Wl_A)[Wl_A(1 + g) + sP_1g/(1 - s)]}. \quad (A7.60)$$

If we substitute equation (A7.59) and Definition 2(v) in Definition 2(x), we obtain another expression for X_A/X_B:

$$\frac{X_A}{X_B} = \frac{(1 + g)(1 - Wl_B)}{Wl_A(1 + g) + sP_1g/(1 - s)}. \quad (A7.61)$$

Equating (A7.60) and (A7.61) provides an expression for g as a function of P_1:

$$g = \frac{(P_1 - P_1a_A - Wl_A)(1 - Wl_B) - (P_1a_B + Wl_B)Wl_A}{(1 - Wl_B)(P_1a_A + Wl_A) + (P_1a_B + Wl_B)[Wl_A + sP_1/(1 - s)]}. \quad (A7.62)$$

Replacing g in (A7.61) by equation (A7.62) yields a closed expression for X_A/X_B:

$$\frac{X_A}{X_B} = \frac{(1 - Wl_B) + (P_1a_B + Wl_B)s/(1 - s)}{Wl_A + (P_1 - P_1a_A - Wl_A)s/(1 - s)}. \quad (A7.63)$$

This expression is closed since P_1 is itself a function of X_A/X_B, by Definition 2(iv).

Thus the first issue to be resolved about the existence and uniqueness of a solution to this model concerns the existence and uniqueness of a solution to equation (A7.63). To study this issue, we define the function

$$F[X_A/X_B] = \frac{X_A}{X_B} - \frac{(1 - Wl_B) + (P_1a_B + Wl_B)s/(1 - s)}{Wl_A + (P_1 - P_1a_A - Wl_A)s/(1 - s)}. \quad (A7.64)$$

The function F is well defined, for $r_A > 0$, which ensures that $P_1 - P_1a_A - Wl_A > 0$. (This is also the condition that X_A/X_B be positive.) Since P_1 is continuous as a function of X_A/X_B, F is itself continuous as a function of X_A/X_B. But

$$X_A/X_B \to 0 \Rightarrow F \to < 0$$

$$X_A/X_B \to \infty \Rightarrow F \to > 0.$$

With continuity, these facts ensure that there exists a solution to equation
(A7.63). Under the given conditions, F is increasing at $F = 0$, so the solution
to equation (A7.63) is unique. Thus:

Proposition 8. In a state of dynamic equilibrium the relative output levels of
the two countries are given by equation (A7.63). If there exists a P_1 such that
$r_A > 0$, equation (A7.63) has a unique solution with $r_A > 0$. Under these conditions equation (A7.62) determines g, the rate of growth of the capital stock.

If we substitute equation (A7.62) into (A7.59), k is found as a function
of P_1 (itself determined by equation A7.63):

$$k = \frac{(P_1 a_A + W l_A)[1 - W l_B) + (P_1 a_B + W l_B) s/(1 - s)]}{(P_1 a_B + W l_B)[W l_A + (P_1 - P_1 a_A - W l_A) s/(1 - s)]}. \tag{A7.65}$$

This equation decides the relative sizes of the capital stocks in the two countries.

Proposition 5 states that in dynamic equilibrium the rates of growth of
capital in the two countries are equal. From Definition 2(i) this implies that

$$r_A k\{[q_A(1 + k^{-1}) - 1]u + [v_{AA}(k^{-1} + 1) - 1](1 - u - s)\}$$
$$+ r_B\{[q_A(1 + k^{-1}) - 1]u + [v_{BA}(k^{-1} + 1) - 1](1 - u - s)\} = 0.$$

Now we substitute Proposition 7:

$$r_B = \frac{g}{(1 - s)} \frac{(1 + k)[q_A u + v_{AA}(1 - u - s)] - (1 - s)k}{(v_{AA} - v_{BA})(1 - u - s)} \qquad (v_{AA} \neq v_{BA}) \tag{A7.66}$$

$$= k r_A \qquad (v_{AA} = v_{BA}).$$

In equation (A7.66), r_B depends on q_A, v_{AA}, and v_{BA}, which in turn are
functions of r_A/r_B. But, by Proposition 7, r_A depends on r_B once k and g are
fixed. Thus equation (A7.66) provides a solution to the rates of profit that
sustain a dynamic equilibrium. From equation (A7.66), we define the function

$$G[r_B] = r_B(1 - s)(1 - u - s)(v_{AA} - v_{BA}) - g(1 + k)[q_A u + v_{AA}(1 - u - s)] + gK(1 - s)$$

in the region $v_{AA} \neq v_{BA}$; here G is well defined, as is r_B. It is continuous: $G[0]$
$= -g(1 - s) < 0$. As r_B becomes large, q_A, v_{AA}, and v_{BA} all tend to zero, and so g
tends to $gk(1 - s) > 0$. Thus, there exists a solution to equation (A7.66). Since
$dG/dr_B > 0$, that solution is unique.

On a balanced growth path, such as that defined by equations
(A7.62)–(A7.66), the ratio of investment levels is constant. Therefore the
rates of capital accumulation are the same in the two countries. Consequently
their rates of profit are not changing, by Proposition 4. For such a growth

path to be also a state of dynamic equilibrium, these rates of profit must be positive. By Definition 2(vi) rates of profit are positive if

$$P_1(1 - a_A) - Wl_A > 0$$

and

$$1 - P_1 a_B - Wl_B > 0,$$

that is, if

$$\frac{Wl_A}{1 - a_A} < P_1 < \frac{1 - Wl_B}{a_B}.$$

Such an equilibrium price can exist and be positive only if

$$0 < \frac{Wl_A}{1 - a_A} < \frac{1 - Wl_B}{a_B}. \qquad (A7.67)$$

In view of the uniqueness of the ratio of investment levels (k) on a balanced growth path, we need to show that there exists a set of output levels such that $\dot{K}_A = \dot{K}_B$, with P_1 in the interval defined by (A7.67). Suppose first that $P_1 = Wl_A/(1 - a_A)$. Then $r_A = 0$ and $r_B > 0$, whence $\dot{K}_B > \dot{K}_A = 0$. Suppose secondly that $P_1 = (1 - Wl_B)/a_B$. Then $r_A > r_B > 0$, whence $\dot{K}_A > \dot{K}_B$. Since $\dot{K}_A$ and $\dot{K}_B$ are continuous functions of their arguments, it follows that there exists a point in the interval (A7.67) for which $\dot{K}_A = \dot{K}_B$. We have shown:

Proposition 9. If condition (A7.67) holds, there exists a unique dynamic equilibrium that solves the model of Definition 2. It is given by equations (A7.62), (A7.63), (A7.65), (A7.66), and Proposition 7.

A7.2.5 Characteristics of the Equilibrium

A7.2.5.1 The Rate of Profit (General Case)

We denote by an asterisk (*) the value of a variable at equilibrium and by a superscript plus sign (\+) the value of a variable when rates of profit are equal. Under what conditions do the two countries earn the same rate of profit at equilibrium?

Suppose that $r_A = r_B = r^+$. Then prices must satisfy the following equations:

$$P_1 = (1 + r^+)(P_1 a_A + Wl_A)$$

$$1 = (1 + r^+)(P_1 a_B + Wl_B). \qquad (A7.68)$$

Under the given conditions there exists a rate of profit $r^+ \geq 0$ and a price $P_1 > 0$ satisfying equations (A7.68) (Sraffa 1960). We denote this price by P_1^+.

On the other hand, by Proposition 4(iii), in equilibrium the ratio $x^* = X_A^*/X_B^*$ is fixed and its magnitude is found by equation (A7.63). This ratio in turn fixes the equilibrium price P_1^*.

Proposition 10. If P_1^+, as defined by equations (A7.68), equals the equilibrium price P_1^*, as defined by equation (A7.63), then in a state of dynamic equilibrium $r_A = r_B = r^+$. If $P_1^* \neq P_1^+$, then $r_A^* \neq r_B^*$.

Except in particular circumstances, at equilibrium the two countries generally earn different rates of profit.

A7.2.5.2 Special Case I: u = 1 − s

In this special case all investment is controlled from the pool of capital by central financial institutions. Capitalists do not directly invest in their own businesses from their retained earnings. All investment is made through the financial market.

This case requires that the equations of motion, Definition 2(i), become

$$\dot{K} = q_1 u (r_A K_A + r_B K_B) K_I^{-1}, \qquad I = A, B.$$

But in dynamic equilibrium the rates of capital accumulation are equal. The following proposition immediately follows:

Proposition 11. If $u = 1 − s$ then there exists a state of dynamic equilibrium if and only if

$$q_A^* = \frac{K_A}{K_A + K_B}.$$

The equilibrium ratio of profit rates must support this allocation of investment, that is, the equilibrium ratio of profit rates must cause financial markets to invest in proportion to existing capital stocks:

Proposition 12. If $u = 1 − s$, the two countries' rates of profit are equal in a state of dynamic equilibrium if and only if

$$r_A = r_B \Rightarrow q_A = \frac{K_A}{K_A + K_B}.$$

Central financial institutions may follow various rules (Q) in making investment decisions. Rules that satisfy the condition of Proposition 12—that if the rates of profit in the two countries are equal then capital is invested in proportion to the existing sizes of the countries—imply that the state of dynamic equilibrium has equal rates of profit. Some decision rules do satisfy this condition, for example,

$$q_A = \frac{K_A \exp(zr)}{K_A \exp(zr) + K_B \exp(zr)}, \qquad z > 0, \qquad r = r_A/r_B. \quad (A7.69)$$

(The parameter z governs the responsiveness of capital flows to differences in profit rates: if z is large, small differences in profit rates translate into large differences in investment; if z is small, large differences in profit rates translate into small differences in investment.) However, not all decision rules satisfy this condition. For example, suppose that

$$q_A = \frac{\exp(zr)}{\exp(zr) + \exp(z/r)}, \qquad z > 0. \quad (A7.70)$$

This rule simply requires that more capital be invested in the country that is more profitable; if the two countries are equally profitable, the investment is split equally between them. Under decision rule (A7.70), when profit rates are equal, $q_A = 0.5$, which is not an equilibrium assignment of investment to countries.

A7.2.5.3 Special Case 2: u = 0

In this second case there is no central pool of capital. All investment is made directly by entrepreneurs out of their retained earnings. Definition 2 implies that if the rate of profit is positive

$$\dot{K}_A = (1 - s)(v_{AA} r_A + v_{BA} r_B k^{-1})$$
$$\dot{K}_B = (1 - s)(v_{AB} r_A k + v_{BB} r_B)$$

Hence, in dynamic equilibrium, when $\dot{K}_A = \dot{K}_B$

$$r_A[v_{AA}(K_A + K_B) - K_A]K_A = r_B[v_{BB}(K_A + K_B) - K_B]K_B. \quad (A7.71)$$

This equation carries some startling implications about the investment decisions of individual firms.

Clearly both sides of equation (A7.71) must be positive (or both negative). Also, at equilibrium rates of profit and levels of capital accumulation must be positive. It follows that:

Proposition 13. If $u = 0$, in dynamic equilibrium either

$$v_{AA} > K_A/(K_A + K_B) \quad \text{and} \quad v_{BB} > K_B/(K_A + K_B)$$

or

$$v_{AA} < K_A/(K_A + K_B) \quad \text{and} \quad v_{BB} < K_B/(K_A + K_B).$$

That is to say, at equilibrium, the firms in both countries must invest more of their capital in their own country then would be warranted simply from the relative sizes of the countries (or both invest less).

Some additional conclusions can be derived by examining a specific investment policy. To fix ideas suppose that

$$v_{AA} = \frac{(a + r)K_A}{(a + r)K_A + K_B}, \qquad v_{BB} = \frac{(a + 1/r)K_B}{K_A + (a + 1/r)K_B}, \qquad (A7.72)$$

with $a > 0$. These policies mean that firms invest in proportion to the sizes of the two countries, weighted by their relative profitability. For example if $r = 1$, then

$$v_{AA} = \frac{(a + 1)K_A}{(a + 1)K_A + K_B}, \qquad v_{BB} = \frac{(a + 1)K_B}{K_A + (a + 1)K_B}.$$

In other words, a measures the preference that firms have for investing in their own country at a given ratio of profit rates; the larger is a, the greater is that preference. If these policies are substituted in equation (A7.71), then the rates of profit that support dynamic equilibrium must satisfy

$$\frac{r_A}{r_B} = r = \frac{(a - 1)r + 1}{(a - 1) + r} \frac{K_B}{K_A} \frac{(a + r)K_A + K_B}{rK_A + (ar + 1)K_B}.$$

This result entails two implications. Dynamic equilibrium is characterized by equal rates of profit if and only if the two countries are the same size. However, if a becomes indefinitely large (that is, if firms invest all their retained earnings in their own countries), the equilibrium rates of profit become equal.

A7.2.5.4 Capital Flows

The flows of capital between the countries are now investigated. This investigation does not rely on the specific investment policies introduced in Sections A7.2.5.2 and A7.2.5.3, but rests on the generalized functions of Definition 2.

The total investment in the two countries equals the proportion of surplus that is not consumed:

$$\begin{aligned} K_A \dot{K}_A + K_B \dot{K}_B &= (1 - s)(R_A + R_B) \\ &= (1 - s)(r_A K_A + r_B K_B). \end{aligned} \qquad (A7.73)$$

However, at equilibrium the rates of accumulation in the two countries are equal; so equation (A7.73) implies that

$$(K_A + K_B)\dot{K}_A = (1 - s)(r_A K_A + r_B K_B).$$

Now suppose that at equilibrium the rate of profit in country B exceeds that in country A: $r_B > r_A$. It follows that

$$(K_A + K_B)\dot{K}_A > (1 - s)r_A(K_A + K_B),$$

i.e., that $\dot{K}_A > (1 - s)r_A$. Similarly, if the rate of profit in country A exceeds that in country B, then $\dot{K}_B > (1 - s)r_B$. This result is summarized in the following proposition.

Proposition 14. In dynamic equilibrium:

(i) if $r_A > r_B$, then $\dot{K}_A < (1 - s)r_A$ and $\dot{K}_B > (1 - s)r_B$;

(ii) if $r_A < r_B$, then $\dot{K}_A > (1 - s)r_A$ and $\dot{K}_B < (1 - s)r_B$.

Now $\dot{K}_A$ and $\dot{K}_B$ are the rates of net investment in countries A and B, respectively, whereas $(1 - s)r_A$ and $(1 - s)r_B$ are the corresponding rates at which surplus is produced and made available for net investment. Suppose that country A makes the greater rate of profit in equilibrium. Then the rate of net investment in A is less than the rate at which investment funds are produced there. The rate of net investment in B, which makes the lower rate of profit, exceeds the rate at which B produces investment funds. Therefore a net flow of capital occurs from country A to country B. Proposition 14 thus contradicts received opinion: (i) in dynamic equilibrium there exists a net flow of capital between the countries unless their rates of profit happen to be equal; and (ii) the net flow of capital occurs from the country earning the higher rate of profit toward the country earning the lower rate of profit.

A7.2.6 An Intuitive Account

We can now provide an intuitive account of these results. Even if investment behavior is rational in the sense of Definition 2(ii), countries do not generally earn equal rates of profit at equilibrium. This is Proposition 10. Technology may be different or similar in the two countries; wages may or may not differ. However, these are not crucial in determining equilibrium profit rates. The crucial control is investment behavior. The central results are contained in Propositions 12 and 13, which describe investment rules when investment is controlled by central financial institutions and when it is controlled by decentralized firms, respectively. It seems that centralized control is more likely to entail an equal rate of profit equilibrium than is decentralized control. In both cases, what matters is how capital is invested in relation to the size of the existing capital stock and the existing rate of profit. Then, if countries do not earn the same rate of profit at equilibrium, capital flows in net from the country earning the higher rate of profit toward the country earning the lower rate of profit. This is Proposition 14. Capital flows depend not only on relative rates of profit as in orthodox accounts but also on the sizes of the existing stocks of capital (and, in the n-country case, on their sizes, locations, and profitabilities). The aggregate flow of capital from one country to the other is the product of (i) the probability that any one unit of capital is invested in the other and (ii) the quantity of capital that is to be invested.

We are led to ask which country grows more rapidly when rates of profit are equal (and therefore to ask which country has the lower rate of profit at equilibrium). Definition 2(i) identifies the rate of capital accumulation in industries. If rates of profit are equal in the two countries (to r^+), the level of capital accumulation is

$$K_I \dot{K}_I = q_I u r^+ (K_A + K_B) + (1 - u - s) r^+ (v_{AI} K_A + v_{BI} K_B), \qquad I = A, B.$$

Suppose that central investment depends on both size and profit rate (equation A7.72); when rates of profit are equal,

$$q_I = K_I / (K_A + K_B),$$

whence

$$K_I \dot{K}_I = u r^+ K_I + (1 - u - s) r^+ (v_{AI} K_I + v_{BI} K_I), \qquad I = A, B.$$

It follows that the rate of capital accumulation in the two countries when the rates of profit are equal is

$$\dot{K}_I = u r^+ + (1 - u - s) r^+ (v_{AI} K_A + v_{BI} K_B) / K_I, \qquad I = A, B.$$

Therefore, when profit rates are equal, the rate of accumulation in country A is higher than that in country B if (and only if)

$$u r^+ + (1 - u - s) r^+ (v_{AA} K_A + v_{BA} K_B) / K_A > u r^+ + (1 - u - s) r^+ (v_{AB} K_A + v_{BB} K_B) / K_B,$$

that is, if

$$v_{AA} K_A - v_{BB} K_B > K_A - K_B. \tag{A7.74}$$

This result makes perfectly clear that the capital flows when rates of profit are equal depend not only on the propensity of firms to invest in each country but also upon the relative sizes of the countries. Since the country with the higher rate of capital accumulation is also the country in which the rate of profit is falling relatively, condition (A7.74) is also the condition that country A has the lower rate of profit at equilibrium.

Thus we have proved:

Proposition 15. Suppose that when $r_A = r_B = r^+$, $q_A = K_A/(K_A + K_B)$. Then the following conditions are equivalent:

(i) when $r_A = r_B = r^+$, $\dot{K}_A > \dot{K}_B$;

(ii) in dynamic equilibrium, $r_A^* < r_B^*$;

(iii) when $r_A = r_B = r^+$, $v_{AA}K_A - v_{BB}K_B > K_A - K_B$.

Chapter 8

PROFITS AND TECHNICAL CHANGE IN AUSTRALIA, CANADA, JAPAN, AND THE USA

In capitalist economies the rate of profit provides the most accurate barometer of the economic vitality of firms, industries, and regions. It reflects the speed at which capital is expanded through production, trade, and reinvestment as well as regulating several processes that structure competition and economic change. The rate of profit also influences the speed and direction of technological change, governing the need for firms to adopt new techniques (Farjoun and Machover 1983); the ability of firms to finance technical change (Grabowski and Mueller 1978); the set of technologies that are economically viable (Binswanger and Ruttan 1978; see also Chapter 6); and the anticipated returns from innovations (Baldwin and Scott 1987; Binswanger and Ruttan 1978). Broad shifts in economic climate and sudden reversals in industrial fortune ultimately depend on patterns of profitability, investment, and disinvestment (Aglietta 1979; Massey 1978; Storper and Walker 1989; Webber 1982c). The contemporary geography of production and its dynamic hinges on spatial and temporal variations in the rate of profit.

The rate of profit is said to determine the turning points of long waves of economic activity and the attendant rounds of growth, recession and restructuring (Mandel 1978, 1981). As we have seen in Chapter 3, movements in the rate of profit play a crucial role as cause or effect in most theories about the recent slowdown in the pace of accumulation. And we have claimed in Chapter 5 that reductions in the rate of profit are endogenous: when rates of accumulation are rapid the rate of profit eventually falls. So the first task of this chapter is to demonstrate that this theoretical possibility has in fact occurred. The demonstration relies on data about the rate of profit in manufacturing in Australia, Canada, Japan and the USA over the last 40 years or so, supplementing other evidence about the profitability of production in Canada (Webber and Rigby 1986), France (Lipietz 1986), the USA (Dumenil et al. 1987;

Moseley 1991; Wolff 1986), West Germany (Reati 1986), and groups of advanced industrial countries (Armstrong et al. 1991; Weisskopf 1988).

The story is not simple. The rate of profit in Australia, Canada, and the USA fell during the late 1960s and 1970s to a low point in the early 1980s; there has been some recovery in profitability since then. In Japan the rate of profit in manufacturing was rising during the 1960s and 1970s but has fallen during the 1980s. So the rate of profit has fallen in all four countries. But the nature of the downturn, its severity and extent, differs between Australia, Canada, Japan, and the USA. Furthermore there is little evidence that rates of profit were high and stable during the 1950s and 1960s. In this respect the data about rates of profit reinforce the data in Chapter 2 about rates of growth of GDP and capital stock: there is little evidence of a long boom followed by a sharp collapse in the early or mid-1970s. This story of variability is even more marked when data about individual industries or regions are examined.

Changes in profitability themselves reflect the evolution of several features of an economy. One of the driving forces is technique, the adoption of new products and new forms of organizing production. Another is the real wage, influenced by changes in the size of the labor force in relation to the demand for labor and by the ability of workers to purchase the output that is produced. And a third is the supply of capital in relation to the demand for capital to finance expansion of output. A variety of different histories of these variables and of profitability was identified in Chapter 5; so a second task of this chapter is to examine how these variables have changed over time and how they have influenced profitability. Changes in the rate of profit are decomposed into their components, which are then measured.

In Australia, Canada, Japan, and the USA rising wages have prompted firms to adopt techniques that economize on labor. The technical composition of capital has therefore risen and the unit value of commodities fallen: in net the value composition of capital has tended to rise, which in itself tends to depress the rate of profit. Generally the effect of the value composition of capital on profitability has not been offset by increases in the rate of exploitation or in the speed with which capital is turned over. So rates of profit have fallen. However, neither the relative magnitude of these changes nor their timing are common to the four countries. At the level of individual industries or regions these differences are enhanced; indeed they are complemented by differences in the ability of individual industries and regions to compete for the surplus produced by other industries and regions.

Movements and differences in the rate of profit are supposed in economic theory to guide the volume of investment that flows between sectors and regions. Neoclassical, Keynesian, and Marxian theories all contain versions of equilibrium models in which capital tends to flow from less to more profitable activities and places (Borts and Stein 1964; Gertler 1984; Kaldor 1961; Roemer 1981). Yet we have argued in Chapter 7 that this supposition is not true. Even if firms are rational, equilibrium need not be characterized by equal rates of profit; nor need investment flow from less to more profitable activities. This chapter contains evidence about these propositions.

The evidence is drawn from Canada and the USA. It shows that rates of profit in individual industries and individual regions differ; the differences have tended to persist. There is no evidence that competition between industries and regions has forced rates of profit to converge to a common value. The history is consistent with the thesis advanced in Chapter 7 that rates of profit may differ at equilibrium; it implies that rates of capital accumulation are not necessarily determined by rates of profit—capital may accumulate faster in less profitable regions than in more profitable ones. In turn this implication is given empirical bite in Chapter 10, which argues that investment policies are far more important causes of rates of accumulation than are rates of profit.

So this chapter analyzes rates of profit and their changes in the manufacturing industries of Australia, Canada, Japan, and the USA. It uses the definitions and methods of measurement described in Chapter 4. The chapter begins by showing how to decompose rates of profit so as to reveal the interaction of technical changes, wage rates, and prices. It then turns, in Section 8.2, to the task of describing movements in the rate of profit in manufacturing as a whole in the four countries. Section 8.3 decomposes those rates of profit into their components, using the methods of Section 8.1. The next two sections are concerned with changes in profitability and the causes of those changes in the individual industries of Canada and the USA (Section 8.4) and the individual regions of Canada (Section 8.5). The final empirical section of the chapter (8.6) assesses whether interindustry and interregional differences in profitability are tending to persist or to disappear. The implications of these results for the theoretical claims of Chapters 5 through 7 are drawn out at the end of the chapter.

8.1. METHOD: DETERMINANTS OF THE RATE OF PROFIT

This section is methodological. Beginning with the definition of the rate of profit in Chapter 4, it shows how to decompose profitability into its components in order to understand the relations between profitability, on the one hand, and wage rates, exploitation, technical changes, and prices, on the other. The results of the decomposition are applied in Section 8.3.

The rate of profit is

$$\pi_p = \frac{\text{profit}}{\text{capital advanced}}.$$

Firms compete in two arenas to raise their rate of profit. In the market, firms compete by minimizing the costs of inputs and by maximizing the price of their output. If firms obtain inputs below average prices or if they sell output at prices above the market average, they capture additional profit. This profit comes at the expense of firms that are weak in the market, i.e., firms that pay more than market prices for inputs or that sell output below market prices. In production, firms compete by raising productivity—adopting the most efficient production techniques at their disposal. Firms in different industries compete principally in the market arena; firms in the same industry compete both in production and in the market.

This view of competition differs from the neoclassical one. The number of firms in a sector is not the sole dictate of the degree of competition. Furthermore it is not supposed that prices of inputs or of outputs are uniform. The market is a chaotic arena in which no firm is guaranteed prices of inputs or outputs (Farjoun and Machover 1983). Spatial and temporal fluctuations of supply and demand, special pricing arrangements between suppliers and distributors, discounts on bulk purchases, favorable rates of credit, and other institutions in the marketplace all mask the average prices of commodities.

To measure the impact of the two forms of competition on performance, the rate of profit is defined as

$$\pi_p = M\pi_v, \tag{8.1}$$

where M measures the ability of firms to compete in the market and π_v is the value rate of profit.

The value rate of profit measures performance on the assumption that all firms exchange commodities at the same average price. Differences in the value rate of profit therefore depend on differences in the techniques of production rather than in market characteristics. In turn the value rate of profit is defined as

$$\pi_v = \frac{S}{C + V}, \tag{8.2}$$

where S is surplus value or profit; C is constant capital; and V is variable capital.

Dividing equation (8.2) by V, we have

$$\pi_v = \frac{S/V}{C/V + 1} = \frac{e}{(q + 1)t}, \tag{8.3}$$

where e is the rate of exploitation (measuring the distribution of the value added in production to capital and labor); q is the value composition of capital (the ratio of the value of constant capital advanced in production to the value of variable capital advanced); and t measures the turnover time of capital.

In turn equation (8.3) may be expanded to reveal the basic components of the value rate of profit:

$$\pi_v = \frac{(1 - \lambda_2 D)L/\lambda_2 DL}{(\lambda_1 K/\lambda_2 DLt + 1)t}, \tag{8.4}$$

where λ_i for $i = 1, 2$ represents the unit value of means of production and subsistence goods, respectively; D denotes the hourly real wage; L represents the number of labor hours expended in manufacturing; and K measures the physical amount of means of production used to produce.

The influence of the components of the rate of profit is measured by estimating the following differential equations (Webber and Tonkin 1987). First, from equation (8.1) changes in the price rate of profit can be represented by the total differential:

$$d\pi_p = \pi_v dM + M d\pi_v \qquad (8.5)$$

(ignoring second-order interaction terms). Thus changes in the price rate of profit can be decomposed into the effects of changes in market competitiveness ($\pi_v dM$) and changes in production efficiency ($M d\pi_v$).

The value rate of profit can be decomposed and written as

$$d\pi_v = \frac{1}{t(q + 1)} de - \frac{e}{t(q + 1)^2} dq - \frac{e}{t^2(q + 1)} dt. \qquad (8.6)$$

(Again, second-order terms are ignored.) Changes in the value rate of profit are decomposed into the effects of changes in the rate of exploitation ($de/[t(q + 1)]$), changes in the value composition of capital ($-e\, dq/[t(q + 1)^2]$), and changes in the turnover time of capital ($-e\, dt/[t^2(q + 1)]$).

In turn the changes in the rate of exploitation and the value composition of capital can be decomposed. Thus changes in the rate of exploitation can be expressed as

$$de = \frac{1}{\lambda_L \lambda_2} d\lambda_2 - \frac{1}{\lambda_L D} dD \qquad (8.7)$$

(ignoring interactions). Equation (8.7) decomposes changes in the rate of exploitation into the effect of changes in the unit value of consumer goods ($d\lambda_2/\lambda_L \lambda_2$) and the effect of changes in the real wage ($-dD/\lambda_L D$). Changes in the value composition of capital are

$$dq = \frac{P}{\lambda_L} d\lambda_1 + \frac{\lambda_1}{\lambda_L} dP - \frac{\lambda_1 P}{\lambda_L^2} d\lambda_L \qquad (8.8)$$

(ignoring interactions). Equation (8.8) decomposes changes in the value composition of capital into the effects of changes in the unit value of capital goods ($P\, d\lambda_1/\lambda_L$), changes in the unit value of labor power ($-\lambda_1 P\, d\lambda_L/\lambda_L^2$) and changes in the technical composition of capital ($\lambda_1\, dP/\lambda_L$).

The technical composition of capital is

$$P = \frac{K}{Lt}$$

$$= \frac{1}{t}\frac{1}{R}\frac{K_u}{L} + \frac{K_c}{Lt},$$

where R is the capacity utilization rate; K_u/L is the full capacity ratio of fixed capital to labor; and K_c/Lt is the capitalized cost of fuel and raw materials processed per hour of labor. Finally, then, the effects of changes in the capacity utilization rate $(-K_u\, dR/tR^2L)$, the effects of changes in the turnover time of capital $(-K_u\, dt/t^2RL)$, the effects of changes in the ratio of full capacity fixed capital to labor $[d(K_u/L)/tR]$ and the effects of changes in the amount of fuel and materials processed per hour of labor $[d(K_c)/Lt]$ on the technical composition of capital are evaluated. These effects are

$$dP = \frac{-K_u}{t^2RL}\, dt - \frac{K_u}{tR^2L}\, dR + \frac{1}{tR}\, d(K_u/L) + d(K_c/Lt). \qquad (8.9)$$

In sum the differential equations allow industry performance to be decomposed into market and production effects. Variations in market performance show how spatial and sectoral variations in prices influence profitability. Production characteristics reflect the impacts of technical change on the rate of profit. Three particular types of technical change are examined: the substitution of capital for labor; changes in the intensity of the labor process; and changes in the speed of production. In aggregate, at the level of the national economy, value and price rates of profit are equal (Chapter 4). So the effects of price differences on profitability are revealed only at the industry and regional level. Such a decomposition of profit rates is performed in Section 8.3 (national aggregates), Section 8.4 (individual industries), and Section 8.5 (individual regions). First, though, we examine the history of aggregate rates of profit in Australia, Canada, Japan, and the USA.

8.2 PROFITABILITY IN MANUFACTURING

We begin with history. How have rates of profit changed in Australia, Canada, Japan, and the USA, and how are those changes related to the evolution of manufacturing industries there?

8.2.1 Australia

Australia's manufacturing industries are widely perceived as being in a crisis. From different points of view this perception is reflected in Pappas et al. (1990), Garnaut (1989), ACTU (1987), and Stilwell (1980). The best indicator of the crisis is the decline in manufacturing employment from its peak in the early 1970s. Figure 8.1 indicates that total employment in manufacturing has declined from over 1.2 million persons in 1973/74 to only 0.9 million persons in 1986/87 (though the magnitude and precise timing of the fall is measured differently by different sources). The production labor force in manufacturing industry was in 1986/87 only 69% of its 1973/74 peak. Since 1983/84 employment has remained stable.

Figure 8.1 underestimates the decline in employment in Australia. As the

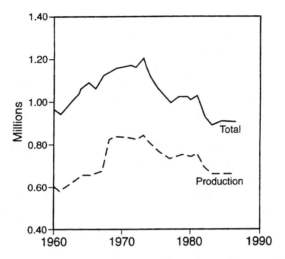

FIGURE 8.1. Employment in Australian manufacturing, 1960/61–1986/87. *Source: Labour Force Survey,* Canberra, Australia: ABS.

numbers employed have fallen, so have the average hours worked by employees: the number of hours worked per year has fallen from 1841 in 1960/61 to 1816 in 1973/74 and to 1629 in 1986/87. The total effort of production workers in manufacturing industry has fallen to only 62% of its 1973/74 level. Equally, as Figure 8.2 indicates, the total capital employed in manufactur-

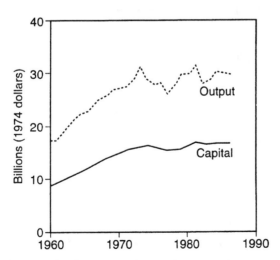

FIGURE 8.2. The growth of output and capital in Australian manufacturing. Fixed capital was estimated using published investment data. Service lives of capital are given by Phillips (1985). Depreciation was calculated using the straight-line method. *Source: Manufacturing Industry Details of Operations Australia,* Canberra, Australia: ABS.

ing industry essentially stopped growing in 1973/74: the capital stock in 1986/87 was only 1.9% greater than in 1974/75.

Figure 8.2 also illustrates the level of output of Australian manufacturing since 1960/61. It shows the same trends as the levels of employment and capital. The 1960s and early 1970s was a period of fairly continuous growth, lasting until 1973/74: average output in the years 1972–1975 was 70% higher than in 1960/61. This was followed by a period in which output was essentially constant: the level of output in 1986 was the same as in 1972–1975.

The history of the rate of profit in Australian manufacturing is illustrated in Figure 8.3. Two measures of profitability are provided. The first measure, π_T, counts all labor as a cost of production. The second, π_P, deducts as a cost of production only the wages of production employees. In both measures, profits must pay for interest, rent, and taxes as well as providing a profit to the capitalist. In the first, profits must also pay for unproductive labor. Both measures indicate the same pattern. Until 1973/74 profitability was relatively high, fluctuating around 0.272 by the second measure. In 1974/75, the rate of profit fell; from then until 1982/83 it averaged only 0.233. In 1983/84 it jumped again and has since been rising, to reach 0.29 in 1986/87.

The relationship between growth and profitability is explored in Figure 8.4. The reduced rates of capital accumulation and GDP growth between the late 1960s and early 1980s seem to reflect falling profitability after the mid-1960s. Indeed, the three variables are positively correlated: the correlation between the rate of capital accumulation and the rate of profit (second measure)

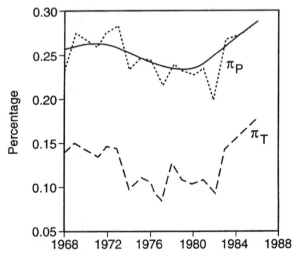

FIGURE 8.3. The rate of profit in Australian manufacturing. The rate of profit was measured as annual profits divided by capital advanced. Annual profits equal the value of shipments (output) less the costs of wages and salaries, raw materials, depreciation, fuel, and electricity. Capital advanced is equal to net fixed capital stock plus owned inventory. *Source:* see Figs. 8.1 and 8.2

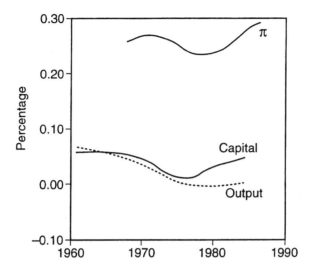

FIGURE 8.4. The rate of profit, π, and the growth rates of output and capital in Australian manufacturing. *Source:* see Figs. 8.1 and 8.2.

is $r = +0.34$; and that between the rate of growth of output and the rate of profit is $r = +0.64$. These data argue for a direct link between profitability and growth. However, it seems unlikely that changes in profitability drive accumulation or growth in a simple way. First, changes in rates of capital accumulation, GDP growth, and profit appear to be contemporaneous rather than lagged: changes in profitability do not drive later changes in rates of accumulation or growth of output. Second, the smoothed estimate of the rate of profit in the late 1960s was about 27.7% per annum whereas the minimum smoothed estimate was 23.5% in 1979—a fall of only 4.2%. This difference appears slight in comparison with the observed reductions in the pace of accumulation and growth. And, third, the rise of profitability in the 1980s to 29% by 1986 has not been reflected in recovery of the pace of accumulation or growth. The linkages between rates of profit, accumulation, and growth are obviously reflected in the data at a crude level; but the nature of the linkages and their details need to be established rather than assumed.

8.2.2 Canada

The development of the crisis in Canada is illustrated in Figures 8.5–8.9. The demand for labor and for plant and equipment has fallen in comparison to supply (Figure 8.5). After fluctuating between 3% and 7% until the mid-1970s the national rate of unemployment began to rise, reaching nearly 12% by 1982. From over 95% in the mid-1950s, the rate of capacity utilization in Canadian manufacturing fell to around 82% through the 1960s. During the

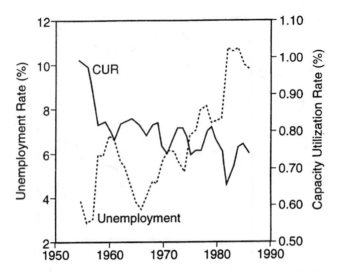

FIGURE 8.5. The unemployment rate and capacity utilization rate (CUR) in Canadian manufacturing. *Source: National Accounts Tables* and *Capacity Utilization Rates in Canadian Manufacturing*, Ottawa, Canada: Statistics Canada.

·1970s the average rate of capacity utilization was less than 80% and through the 1980s has averaged only about 72%. Similarly the input of labor to production has grown less rapidly since the mid-1960s, save for the upturn in hours worked that accompanied the recovery from the recession of 1982/83 (Figure 8.6). As late as 1983 production hours worked in Canadian manufac-

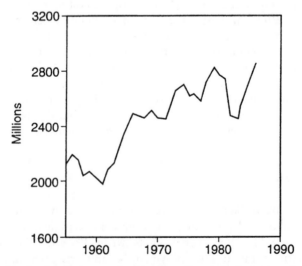

FIGURE 8.6. Production hours worked in Canadian manufacturing. *Source: Manufacturing Industries of Canada: National and Provincial Areas*, Ottawa, Canada: Statistics Canada.

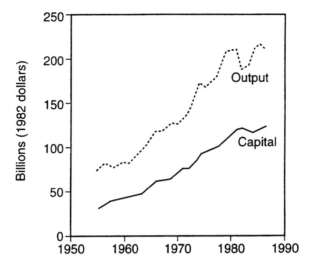

FIGURE 8.7. Output and net fixed capital stocks in Canadian manufacturing. *Source: Manufacturing Industries of Canada: National and Provincial Areas, and Fixed Capital Flows and Stocks,* Ottawa, Canada: Statistics Canada.

turing were lower than they had been in 1966. So increases in both output and capital stock are slowing (Figure 8.7). The average rate of growth of output (in constant dollars), measured from peak to peak of the business cycle, has declined since the late 1960s. After 1979 the volume of manufactured output actually declined in real terms through 1983, since when it has recovered slightly. Figure 8.7 shows also that the rate of growth of the capital stock has slowed since the business cycle of 1965–1973. Whereas the annual rate of growth of the capital stock was about 8.3% before 1975, that rate had fallen to just over 3% between 1975 and 1986.

As the performance of the economy has deteriorated, so has the financial position of the Canadian federal government. From a position of near balance in the 1960s, the federal budget has plunged since 1974 to a series of deficits of several billion dollars. Although this period does not have the dramatic appearance of the Great Depression of the 1930s, since the business cycle peak of 1965 the Canadian manufacturing sector has experienced high levels of unemployment of labor and capacity, limited accumulation of capital, and slow growth of output.

The profitability of production in Canadian manufacturing appears to be correlated with this history (Figure 8.8). From extreme highs in 1955 and 1956, when rates of profit exceeded 40%, profitability tumbled to about 36% in the late 1950s and then slowly declined through the 1960s before declining more sharply in the 1970s to a postwar low of only 24% in 1982. The profit rate had recovered to 33% by 1986. Perhaps the most startling aspect of Figure 8.8—emphasized by the smoothed curve fitted to the data—is the steadiness of the decline in the rate of profit. Such a steady decline casts doubt

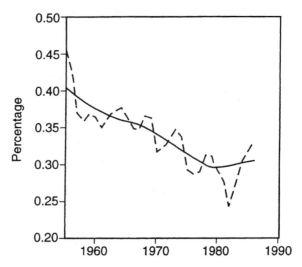

FIGURE 8.8. The rate of profit (see Fig. 8.3) in Canadian manufacturing. *Source:* see Fig. 8.7.

on the generality of accounts of postwar capitalist development that posit a high and stable rate of profit in the 1950s and 1960s, followed by a sharp decline in the early and mid-1970s. In the Canadian case this view is wrong: the rate of profit in Canadian manufacturing was declining through the 1950s and 1960s and, while the fall accelerated in the 1970s, that more recent history is by no means a clean break with the past.

The relationships between profitability, the rate of growth of output, and the rate of capital accumulation in Canadian manufacturing are revealed more precisely in the smoothed data contained in Figure 8.9. There is virtually no correlation between profitability and the rate of growth of output: when profitability was declining between 1956 and 1979, the growth of output first accelerated and then declined; and when profitability began to recover in the 1980s, the rate of growth of output continued to decline. The connection between profitability and the rate of capital accumulation is not direct either. At first the decline of profitability was matched by a decline in the rate of capital accumulation, but then in the 1960s when profitability continued to decline capital accumulation boomed. Between 1969 and 1979 both profitability and the rate of capital accumulation fell, and in the 1980s both have risen. The net effect is a strong correlation between profitability and the rate of capital accumulation ($r = 0.81$ between the two smoothed series with no lag), but the 1960s represents a deviation from this pattern and in the 1980s recovery has been stronger in capital accumulation than in profitability. These data confirm the complexity of the relation between capital accumulation and profitability that was also indicated in the history of profitability and investment in Australian manufacturing.

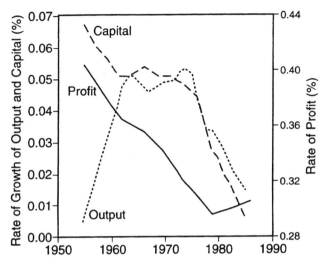

FIGURE 8.9. The rate of profit and the growth rates of output and capital in Canadian manufacturing. *Source:* see Fig. 8.7.

8.2.3 Japan

The Japanese economy has expanded at an unprecedented rate since the early to mid-1950s. Prompted by the Korean War boom and at full speed as early as 1955 (Okawa and Rosovsky 1973), the rate of growth of manufactured output averaged over 13% each year through the 1960s (Figure 8.10). Employment in Japanese manufacturing increased rapidly between 1960 and 1970, then fell during the mid-1970s, and has remained relatively constant since (Figure 8.10). Dramatic gains in manufacturing labor productivity resulted from very high rates of capital accumulation that exceeded 10% each year between 1960 and 1971, except for 1965 and 1966 when the annual rate of growth of net capital stock dropped to 5% (Figure 8.11). The newly installed manufacturing capacity was utilized at increasingly higher rates until the end of the 1970s (Figure 8.11).

Over this same period, between 1960 and the end of the 1970s, the Japanese manufacturing rate of profit exhibited no pronounced tendency to fall. Though profitability declined from about 32% in 1960 to 27% in 1965, it recovered to over 36% by 1970. Through the 1970s the rate of profit fluctuated markedly, rising to a postwar peak of 42.1% in 1978 (Figure 8.12). There was a sharp fall in profitability to 1979 and then a slower drop in profitability through the 1980s. This history differs in two respects from the histories of Australia and Canada: first, the 1960s and 1970s were a period of rising profitability in Japan, in contrast to the falling rates of profit in Australia and Canada; secondly, profitability has not recovered from the deep recession of the early 1980s as it has in Australia and Canada. If the Canadian case

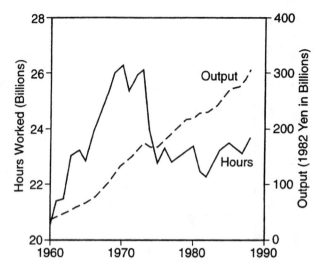

FIGURE 8.10. Manufacturing output and employment in Japan. *Source: Census of Manufacturers* and *Labour Force Survey,* Tokyo: Economic Planning Agency.

raises doubts about the generality of a long boom in profits during the late 1950s and 1960s, the Japanese case indicates that the histories of profitability of manufacturing in different countries have been quite different.

Figure 8.13 presents smoothed data on the rate of profit and the rate of growth of capital and output in Japan's manufacturing sector. The anticipated

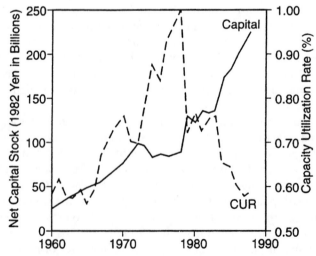

FIGURE 8.11. The net capital stock and capacity utilization rate in Japanese manufacturing. *Source: Japan Statistical Yearbook,* Tokyo: Economic Planning Agency.

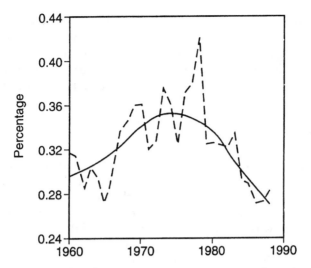

FIGURE 8.12. The rate of profit (see Fig. 8.3) in Japanese manufacturing. *Source:* see Figs. 8.10 and 8.11.

positive relationship between the rate of profit and the growth rates of output and capital does not exist. With no lag, the correlation coefficient between the rates of profit and capital stock growth is –0.375. With capital stock growth lagged by up to 4 years, the correlation coefficient does not improve and the sign is only positive for a lag of 1 year. While the rate of profit and accumulation appear to move together through the 1960s, they move in quite different

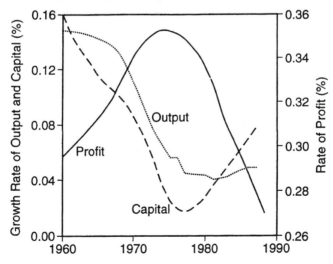

FIGURE 8.13. The rate of profit and the growth rates of output and capital in Japanese manufacturing. *Source:* see Figs. 8.10 and 8.11.

directions from that time onward. The relationship between output growth and profitability is similarly weak, with a correlation coefficient of only 0.073 for no lags. Lagging does not help this relationship either. Slower rates of output growth in the 1980s correspond to the downturn in the rate of profit, but through the 1960s and 1970s output and profitability are unrelated.

8.2.4 The USA

The USA emerged from World War II with an economy that dominated global production. In 1950 manufacturing output in the USA stood at about $90 billion, more than four times greater than that of the second largest manufacturing nation. Total manufacturing employment then numbered close to 15 million, almost twice the size of the workforce of the UK and several times greater than in Japan. In the early postwar period capital investment in manufacturing in the USA was higher than in the rest of the world and American technology and management were second to none (Dertouzos et al. 1989; Dicken 1992; and US Department of Commerce Census of Manufactures various years). With its manufacturing capacity intact, its scale advantages, and its abundant capital, the USA seemed poised to tighten its grip on the global economy.

Postwar expansion was relatively short-lived, however, as the US economy was unable to avoid the global recession that took root in the early 1970s. Indeed, after growing relatively rapidly throughout the 1950s and early 1960s, direct production employment in the US manufacturing sector declined from 14.4 million workers in 1969 to about 11.8 million workers in 1986, less than the number employed in 1950. Over the same period the real rate of growth of US manufactured output, measured between peaks of the business cycle, declined from 5.04% per annum between 1955 and 1965, to 2.94% per annum between 1965 and 1973, to 2.74% per annum from 1973 to 1979, and between 1979 and 1990 manufacturing output actually contracted at a little over 1.0% each year (Figure 8.14). After producing a little over 40% of world manufactured output in 1963, the USA's share of global production fell to less than 30% in 1980 (Dicken 1992). The share of world exports of manufactured goods originating in the USA also declined by 20% between 1963 and 1976 (Watts 1987). As the growth of manufacturing output has slowed, productive resources in the USA have increasingly become obsolescent or idle. Unemployment has risen as the level of capacity utilization has fallen (Figure 8.15); the rate of growth of capital stock has diminished steadily between business cycle peaks (Figure 8.15); and the average age of manufacturing capital has increased (Varaiya and Wiseman 1981).

The rate of profit in the US manufacturing sector has generally declined between 1950 and 1990 (Figure 8.16). The cyclical fluctuations in the rate of profit are obvious in the data for individual years, but the smoothed series indicates the more general trend in profitability. Apart from the cyclical fluctua-

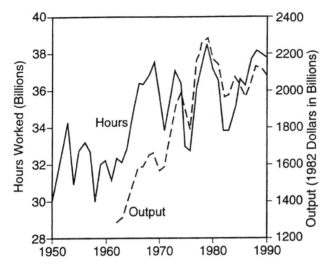

FIGURE 8.14. Manufacturing output and employment in the USA. *Source: Census of Manufactures* and *Annual Survey of Manufactures,* Washington, DC: U.S. Department of Commerce.

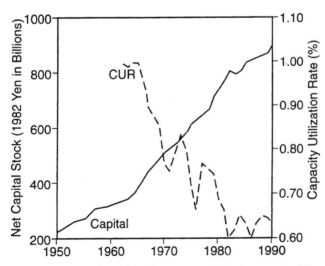

FIGURE 8.15. The net capital stock and capacity utilization rate in US manufacturing. The capacity utilization rate was estimated by dividing annual net capital stocks (capital) by the value of shipments (output). The lowest capital/output ratio over a given period is assumed to represent full capacity. The capacity utilization rate in other years is obtained by dividing the benchmark ratio by the capital/output ratios of the years in question. *Source: Fixed Reproducible Tangible Wealth in the United States, 1925–1989, Census of Manufactures,* and *Annual Survey of Manufactures,* Washington, DC: U.S. Department of Commerce.

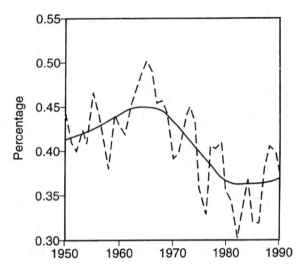

FIGURE 8.16. The rate of profit (see Fig. 8.3) in US manufacturing. *Source:* see Fig. 8.15.

tions, profitability was tending to increase until the mid-1960s. The maximum postwar rate of profit was 50.5%, reached in 1965. Thereafter profitability declined, reaching a postwar low of 30.25 in 1982. The smoothed (trend) data indicate a modest recovery in the rate of profit during the 1980s.

Smoothed series for the rate of profit and the growth rates of output and capital in US manufacturing are displayed in Figure 8.17. With no lag, the correlation coefficient between the rate of profit and rate of growth of the net

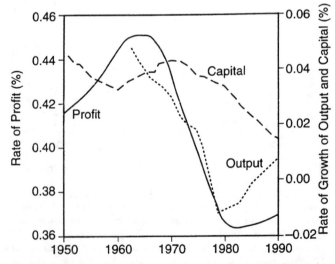

FIGURE 8.17. The rate of profit and the growth rates of output and capital in US manufacturing. *Source:* see Fig. 8.15.

capital stock is 0.493. The correlation coefficient increases to values of 0.73 and 0.703 for lags of 1 and 2 years in the capital stock series, respectively. The rate of growth of output is also positively correlated with the profit rate: the highest correlation coefficient is 0.61 with no lags. The smoothed series in Figure 8.17 shows that the relationship between the rate of profit and the movement of the rate of accumulation and the rate of growth of output endured over the entire period 1965–1990, unlike those relationships in Australia, Canada, and Japan. These data for the USA also exhibit the anticipated lag between movements in the rate of profit and later changes in the pace of accumulation and output growth.

8.2.5 Comparative Conclusion

Table 8.1 shows the real rates of growth of output and net capital stock, the capacity utilization rate, and the unemployment rate in Australia, Canada, Japan, and the USA. The years highlighted correspond to the business cycle turning points of Canada and the USA. These turning points correspond relatively well with those in Australia, but the business cycle is not so apparent in the data for Japan.

In the North American economies, not unexpectedly, the history of economic growth is broadly similar. Annual rates of growth of manufactured output for business cycle upswings averaged about 7% before the mid-1970s and less than half that after. In Canada the net capital stock moved pro-cyclically like output and the rate of growth of capital slowed significantly after the early to mid-1970s. In the USA the rate of growth of the net capital stock was a few percent higher than in Canada and it has not declined quite as dramatically. In Australia the growth of output and capital was also higher on average before 1973/4 than it was after. However, unlike the North American economies, capital stock effectively ceased to grow in Australia after 1973. In Japan the early 1970s do not mark a period of fundamental change in the history of economic growth. While growth was higher in the early 1960s than it was in the mid-1980s, growth rates of output and capital were many times higher throughout this period than in the North American and Australian economies and that growth lasted longer: until 1979 in the case of output and capital stock, although the accumulation of capital halted briefly in the mid-1970s.

Capacity utilization rates decreased in all four countries over the period examined. However, the history of change in the level of capacity used is markedly different from one country to the next. The decline in capacity utilization rates started relatively early in Canada, and by the beginning of the 1960s capacity utilization was already 20% below maximum. In the USA capacity utilization rates were close to 100% at the start of the 1960s. In Australia they were in between those of Canada and the USA, while in Japan they were closer to the Canadian levels. From the mid-1960s, between business cy-

TABLE 8.1. Rates of economic development in Australia, Canada, Japan, and the USA

Country	Year							
	1961^T	1965^P	1970^T	1973^P	1976^T	1979^P	1982^T	1986^P
Australia	-0.4^1	2.1	6.0^5	9.0	1.1	7.4	-14.0	-0.5
	10.9^2	7.0	5.6	1.6	-1.7	-0.6	2.8	1.2
	88.7^3	87.1	81.1	80.2	73.1	77.9	65.3	67.5
	1.4^4	1.3	1.4	1.9	4.8	6.3	7.2	8.0
Canada	-1.5	4.0	-3.5	10.7	3.1	5.2	-10.0	1.1
	2.2	5.8	5.0	3.6	3.9	2.4	3.8	2.0
	77.5	82.4	75.5	81.2	75.0	81.5	66.1	73.8
	5.3	3.9	5.7	5.6	7.1	7.4	11.0	9.6
Japan	19.6	5.3	14.0	9.3	8.3	5.3	0.9	7.8^6
	14.0	11.0	11.3	-3.5	-1.0	31.9	-3.0	6.2
	81.3	68.2	86.8	88.2	97.5	72.7	76.3	54.2
	1.4	1.2	1.2	1.3	2.0	2.1	2.5	2.4
USA	2.2^7	6.6	-6.3	8.3	-5.4	5.4	-5.3	1.4^8
	2.6	6.6	3.8	4.1	2.7	6.9	4.7	4.3
	99.5	99.0	76.7	83.9	66.5	74.8	60.5	63.1
	6.7	4.5	4.9	4.9	7.7	5.8	9.7	5.5

Notes: Superscripts T and P denote trough and peak years of the business cycle in Canada and the USA. These turning points correspond relatively well with those in Australia. In Japan the business cycle is less easy to identify: growth was relatively rapid until the mid-1970s, and from the early 1980s it has declined markedly.

Four variables are measured in the same order for each country. The superscripts 1–4 respectively label the variables: the real rate of growth of output; the real rate of growth of net fixed capital; the capacity utilization rate; and the unemployment rate. Superscript 5: 1970 data are unavailable for Australia and the figures given are 1969 values; 6: the final values of variables for Japan are for 1988; 7: the starting values of all variables for the USA are for 1962; 8: the final values of all variables for the USA are for 1990. *Source:* For Australia, *Labour Force Survey* and *Manufacturing Industry Details of Operations Australia*, Canberra, Australia: ABS; for Canada, *Manufacturing Industries of Canada: National and Provincial Areas* and *Fixed Capital Flows and Stocks*, Ottawa, Canada: Statistics; for Japan, *Census of Manufacturers, Labour Force Survey* and *Japan Statistical Yearbook*, Tokyo, Japan: Economic Planning Agency; for the U.S., *Fixed Reproducible Tangible Wealth in the United States, 1925–1989, Census of Manufactures* and *Annual Survey of Manufactures* Washington DC: U.S. Department of Commerce.

cle peaks, capacity utilization declined very rapidly in the USA, it declined more slowly in Australia, in Canada it remained more or less constant and in Japan it increased strongly until 1978. From the late 1970s through the recession of the early 1980s capacity utilization rates fell in all four countries. The decline in capacity utilization was most pronounced in Japan, and there has been little recovery since 1982.

Table 8.1 also reveals that while unemployment rates increased in all four countries between 1961 and the late 1980s, the level of unemployment and the history of its movement vary considerably from one country to the next. In the mid-1970s unemployment rates increased rapidly in Australia and then continued to rise more slowly through the first half of the 1980s. In Canada the un-employment rate increased more steadily though the 1970s and then jumped sharply in the recession of 1982, since which time it has fallen slightly. Unem-ployment in Japan also increased through the late 1970s, though it still re-mained well below the levels of the other three countries. In the USA unem-ployment rates exhibited much greater cyclical variability than in Australia, Canada, or Japan. Through the 1970s the cyclical swings in unemployment rates in the USA grew larger and unemployment peaked in 1982. Since that re-cession unemployment rates in the USA, unlike those in Australia and Japan, have declined considerably. In aggregate the data in Table 8.1 reveal the com-monality of the experiences of the four countries while also showing that local differences in the history of economic growth and retrenchment have been marked. These differences are just as apparent in profit rate data.

In Australia, Canada, Japan, and the USA the rate of profit tended to fall into the early or mid-1980s. Outside this generalization, however, the details of the history of profitability have been different in the four countries. In Aus-tralia (as far as the data indicate) and the USA profitability climbed until the mid-1960s, then fell until the early 1980s, and has since recovered slightly. In Canada the rate of profit in manufacturing declined consistently from the mid-1950s until the early 1980s. In Japan the rate of profit continued to rise until the mid-1970s; it then fell and has not yet begun to recover.

These data suggest several conclusions. First, only in the USA was there anything like a boom in profit rates that lasted until the mid-1960s, followed by a decline during the 1970s. That generalized history of the rate of profit seems to hold only in some economies; it is certainly not true of manufactur-ing in Canada and Japan. Secondly, the timing and the extent of the decline in profitability are different in the four countries: the decline began earliest in Canada and latest in Japan; and the recovery began in the early 1980s in the three Anglo economies but has hardly appeared in Japan. There is little sense in these data of a common history of profit rates in manufacturing.

Furthermore there is a general sense in the data that the decline in prof-itability has been associated with reduced rates of capital accumulation. In all four countries the rate of growth of capital has fallen during the period of falling profitability. But the association between profitability and accumula-tion is not very close.

8.3 DECOMPOSING CHANGES IN PROFITABILITY

The histories of rates of profit in manufacturing can be decomposed into their elements, following equation (8.3). Are the causes of changes in profitability common to the manufacturing sectors of Australia, Canada, Japan, and the USA? Thus we follow and compare the trajectories of the rate of exploitation, the value composition of capital, and the turnover time in the four economies. Within each of the following subsections the individual components of the three trajectories are also traced.

8.3.1 Rate of Exploitation

The rate of exploitation is directly related to the rate of profit: the higher is exploitation, the higher is the rate of profit. Figure 8.18 tracks the histories of exploitation in Australia, Canada, Japan, and the USA—histories that are quite different.

The average level of exploitation is far higher in Canada and Japan than in Australia and the USA. This partly reflects differences in methods of measurement within national statistical agencies (whether all activities or only the production activities of manufacturers are counted in censuses, for example). But the difference is partly real—and tending to diminish over time. More surprising though are the different trajectories of exploitation. In Australia the rate of exploitation declined only slowly in the 1970s before jumping quickly after 1982/83. Canadian and Japanese rates of exploitation have moved together, falling through the 1960s and early 1970s before rebounding after the mid-1970s. The history of exploitation in the USA is quite different: exploitation has increased consistently throughout the period, though with a sharp drop in 1985/86. Apparently labor in Australia was unable to increase its share of value added in the 1970s and in the 1980s even suffered reductions in its power as the federal government attempted to induce increased in-

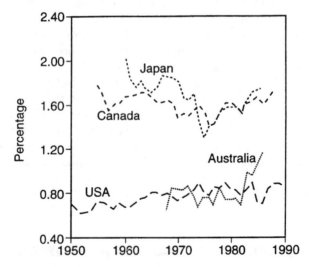

FIGURE 8.18. The rate of exploitation: Australia, Canada, Japan, and the USA. The rate of exploitation was estimated as the ratio of profits to wages and salaries. Profits equal the value of shipments less the costs of materials, wages and salaries, depreciation, fuel, and electricity. *Sources:* for Australia: *Manufacturing Industry Details of Operations,* Canberra: ABS; for Canada: *Manufacturing Industries of Canada: National and Provincial Areas,* Ottawa: Statistics Canada; for Japan: *Census of Manufacturers* and *Labour Force Survey,* Tokyo: Economic Planning Agency; for the USA: *Census of Manufactures* and *Annual Survey of Manufactures,* Washington, DC: U.S. Department of Commerce.

vestment in manufacturing by holding back wage increases. Canadian and Japanese labor gained strength during the 1960s and early 1970s but since then have lost capacity to negotiate increases in their share of value added. American labor has been consistently losing capacity to bargain shares of value added: only in the USA there been anything like a consistent increase in the rate of exploitation. In all four countries labor seems to have lost power vis-à-vis capital during the 1980s, but the earlier histories of the relative strength of labor were different in the 1960s and 1970s. Comparable—but inverse—changes have occurred in the value of labor power.

Changes in the rate of exploitation depend first on changes in the real wage [equation (8.7) and Figure 8.19]. In all four economies the hourly real wage of manufacturing workers has increased. In Australia, where real wages have passed through several phases of rapid increase and greater stability, the real wage in 1986/87 was 2.3 times that of 1960/61, an increase of 3.26% per annum (compound). Canadian real wages grew less strongly; even so they rose on average between 1955 and 1986 by 1.83% per annum (compound). Real wages per hour of production workers in US manufacturing grew even more slowly—by 1.60% per annum (compound) between 1950 and 1990. It was in Japan that workers made the greatest gains in hourly wages: between 1960 and 1988 real wages grew by an average of 5.04% per annum (compound).

Perhaps the most marked feature of real wages in all four economies, though, has been the fact that wage increases have slowed since the early 1970s. Indeed in the USA real wages have stagnated since 1972: by 1990 hourly real wages (in 1982 dollars) were $12.62 compared to $12.06 in 1972, an increase of only 0.25% per annum. Canadian workers fared even worse:

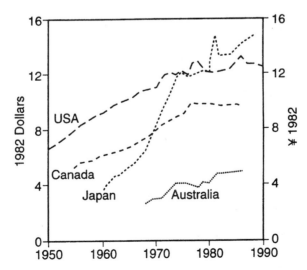

FIGURE 8.19. The hourly real wage: Australia, Canada, Japan, and the USA. *Sources:* see Fig. 8.18.

between 1977 and 1986 real wages fell by an average of 0.34% each year (compound). Even workers in Japan have suffered from the slowdown: between 1960 and 1974 real wages increased on average by 8.64% each year, but between 1974 and 1988 the average increase was only 1.56% each year (compound). Until the mid-1980s Australian workers were the most successful at staving off the effects of the economic slowdown: hourly real wages in manufacturing grew by 4.40% each year between 1960/61 and 1972–1975 and by 2.10% each year between 1972–1975 and 1986/87. As manufacturing has entered the period of slowdown, workers everywhere have had to modify their wage increases, though the degree to which wages have been stabilized does differ between the four countries. In all four countries wage stability after the early 1970s has been associated with an increase in the rate of exploitation; but the relation between wage increases and changes in the rate of exploitation is confused before that.

The second component of the rate of exploitation is the unit value of the means of subsistence, λ_2. As technical change reduces the direct labor time and the value of raw materials and machinery that are needed to produce each item of subsistence, so the unit value of those items has been reduced (Figure 8.20). Such reductions offset the effect of rising real wages on the rate of exploitation: if the unit value of subsistence commodities falls at the same rate as the real wage rises, the rate of exploitation is constant. In this respect the two North American economies have performed significantly worse than those of Australia and Japan. The unit value of subsistence commodities fell

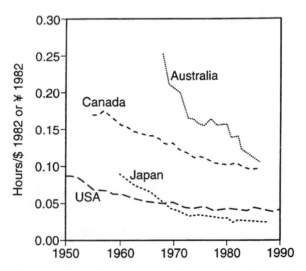

FIGURE 8.20. The unit value of consumer goods: Australia, Canada, Japan, and the USA. The unit value of consumer goods was calculated as the ratio of the unit value of labor power to the hourly real wage. The unit value of labor was measured as $1/(e + 1)$, where e is the rate of exploitation (see Fig. 8.18). *Source:* see Fig. 8.18.

by an average of 1.83% each year in Canada and by 1.77% in the USA (compound). The corresponding rates in Australia and Japan were 4.64% and 4.51% per annum (compound), respectively. The rate of decrease of the value of subsistence commodities has slowed since the early 1970s; the average annual compound rates of change of the unit value of subsistence commodities were as shown:

Australia	−7.99% (1967/68–1973/74)	−3.32% (1973/74–1986/87)
Canada	−2.25% (1955–1974)	−1.16% (1974–1986)
Japan	−7.17% (1960–1973)	−2.15% (1973–1988)
USA	−2.85% (1950–1973)	−0.30% (1973–1990)

This history is summarized in Table 8.2. On average over the entire period, the rate of exploitation rose in Australia and the USA and so tended to raise the rate of profit. In Australia the rapid rise in real wages more than offset technical changes that reduced the unit value of subsistence commodities. In the USA both the real wage and the value of subsistence commodities moved more slowly. In Canada the rate of exploitation was virtually constant as real wage

TABLE 8.2. Determinants of the rate of exploitation

Country	Period	de^1	Effect of $d\lambda_2$	Effect of dD
Australia	Whole[2]	0.5145	1.4533	−1.1390
	Early[2]	0.0256	0.6957	−0.7613
	Late[2]	0.4889	0.7576	− 0.3776
Canada	Whole[3]	0.0253	1.4361	−1.4970
	Early[3]	−0.1505	1.0971	−1.3039
	Late[3]	0.1758	0.3390	−0.1931
Japan	Whole[4]	−0.2435	3.3793	−4.0922
	Early[4]	−0.7233	2.4795	−3.5091
	Late[4]	0.4797	0.8998	−0.5832
USA	Whole[5]	0.1522	0.5324	−0.4653
	Early[5]	0.1946	0.5400	−0.3663
	Late[5]	−0.0424	−0.0076	−0.0990

Notes: [1]The differential de and the effects of $d\lambda_2$ and dD are measured as discrete annual changes, according to equation (8.7), and are summed over the periods indicated.
[2]In Australia (where financial years run from July through June) the entire period is 1968/69 through 1986/87; the early period is 1968/69 through 1974/75; the late period is 1974/75 through 1986/87.
[3]In Canada the entire period is 1955–1986; the early period is 1955 through 1974; the late period is 1974–1986.
[4]In Japan the entire period is 1960–1988; the early period is 1960 through 1975; the late period is 1975–1988.
[5]In the USA the entire period runs from 1962 through 1990; the early period is 1962 through 1974; the late period is 1974–1990.
Source: see Table 8.1.

increases and the changing value of subsistence commodities more or less balanced each other. In Japan the rate of exploitation fell, tending to depress the rate of profit. A very rapid rise in real wages was not counterbalanced even by Japan's rapid reduction in the unit value of subsistence commodities.

In all four countries real wages rose more rapidly before than after the mid-1970s. But the values of subsistence commodities fell more quickly before than after the mid-1970s too. So the change over time in the rate of exploitation has depended on the relative magnitudes of the changes in wages and values of subsistence commodities over time. Thus in Australia, Canada, and Japan the rate of increase of real wages fell to between one-quarter and one-sixth of its earlier level, while reductions in the unit value of subsistence commodities fell to between one-third and one-quarter of their earlier level. Thus the rate of exploitation tended to rise in the later period. By contrast in the USA, even though the rate of increase of real wages fell to one-eighth of its earlier level, the unit value of subsistence commodities essentially stabilized: so the rate of exploitation tended to fall in the later period.

8.3.2 The Value Composition of Capital

The second variable that determines the rate of profit is the value composition of capital: the ratio of the value of constant capital (plant, equipment, and raw materials) to the value of variable capital (labor power). Increases in the value composition tend to depress the rate of profit.

The value composition of capital has risen in all four economies (Figure 8.21). The average annual compound rates of increase in the value composition are as shown:

Australia	+3.18%	(1968/69–1986/87)
Canada	+2.17%	(1955–1986)
Japan	+3.02%	(1960–1988)
USA	+1.59%	(1962–1990)

In Australia and Japan the increasing value composition of capital has put greater pressure on the rate of profit, in Canada less and in the USA less still. Later in this subsection we shall seek to understand these differences.

However, the rates of change in the value composition of capital have themselves altered over time:

Australia	+0.87%	(1967/68–1973/74)	+4.36% (1973/74–1986/87)
Canada	+1.90%	(1955–1974)	+2.60% (1974–1986)
Japan	−1.36%	(1960–1973)	+8.32% (1973–1988)
USA	+1.85%	(1950–1973)	+1.40% (1973–1990)

In Australia, Canada, and Japan the value composition was essentially static in the 1960s and early 1970s and then began to increase more rapidly: in Australia the value composition began to increase after 1975/76, in Canada after

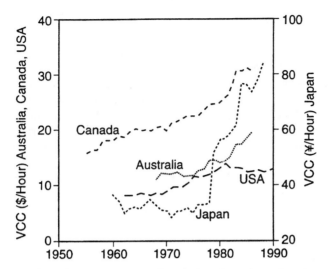

FIGURE 8.21. The value composition of capital (VCC): Australia, Canada, Japan, and the USA. The value composition of capital was calculated as the ratio of constant capital (mid-year net capital stock plus owned inventory) to variable capital (wages and salaries divided by the number of turnover periods each year).

1977, and in Japan after 1978. In these three countries changes in the value composition of capital had little effect on the rate of profit until the mid-1970s. The history of the value composition of capital in the USA is quite different: after a period of relative standstill the value composition rose rapidly between 1969 and 1981 and then has fallen slowly. During the 1970s changes in the value composition of capital were tending to depress the rate of profit in US manufacturing.

According to equation (8.8) changes in the value composition of capital are driven by changes in technique (the physical amount of plant, equipment, and raw materials used per hour of labor power: the technical composition of capital); by changes in the value of plant, equipment, and raw materials; and by changes in the value of labor power. The histories described in Figure 8.21 can be understood in terms of changes in these three variables.

The value of labor power (λ_L) is related to the rate of exploitation (e) through the equation $e = (1 - \lambda_L)/\lambda_L$. Therefore movements in the value of labor power are the inverse of movements in the rate of exploitation that are tracked in Figure 8.18. In Australia the value of labor power changed slowly in the 1970s before falling quickly after 1982/83. Values of labor power in Canada and Japan have risen through the 1960s and early 1970s before falling after the mid 1970s. The value of labor power in the USA has fallen consistently throughout the period, though with a sharp rise in 1985/86. To the extent that the value of labor power has fallen so the value composition of capital has tended to rise, depressing the rate of profit.

By contrast technical changes have tended to reduce the unit value of the means of production (Figure 8.22). The value of plant, equipment, and raw materials has fallen dramatically in Japan—at 6.34% each year (compound). In Canada and the USA the unit value of the means of production has fallen more slowly—by only 1.52% and 1.42% per annum, respectively. In Australia the means of production have been devalued at 2.87% each year (compound): by 1986/87 the unit value of the means of production was only 57% of its level in 1967/68. Such changes tend to hold back the rise in the value composition of capital and so counter any tendency for the value composition to push the rate of profit down.

In all four countries the pace of technical change in industries that produce plant, equipment, and raw materials has slowed in the late 1970s and 1980s. The rates at which the unit value of the means of production falls have themselves fallen:

Australia	−3.81% (1967/68–1973/74)	−2.71% (1973/74–1986/87)
Canada	−1.58% (1955–1974)	−1.42% (1974–1986)
Japan	−9.57% (1960–1973)	−3.45% (1973–1988)
USA	−2.16% (1962–1973)	−0.93% (1973–1990)

In Japan the reduced pace of technical change is especially noticeable, though the rate at which the value of means of production falls has remained relatively high. In Canada and the USA the pace of devaluation of plant, equipment,

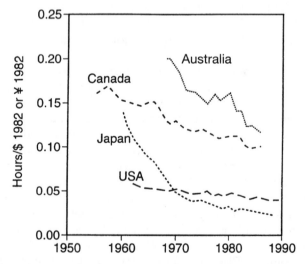

FIGURE 8.22. The unit value of capital goods: Australia, Canada, Japan, and the USA. The unit value of capital goods was calculated as the product of the value composition of capital (see Fig. 8.21) and the unit value of labor power divided by the technical composition of capital (see Fig. 8.23). *Source:* see Fig. 8.18.

and raw materials is similar in the two periods: in both countries the pace of change was slower in the late 1970s and then picked up again in the early 1980s. In Australia the devaluation of the means of production also slowed from the mid-1970s, though it remained considerably higher than in Canada and the USA.

The final element of the value composition of capital is the technical composition of capital. Whereas the value composition measures the ratio of the value of plant, equipment, and raw materials to the value of labor power employed in production, the technical composition measures the ratio of the physical quantity of plant, equipment, and raw materials to the number of hours of labor power employed in production. The unit value of commodities reflects the efficiency with which those commodities are used—they are an input–output ratio, in value units; by contrast the technical composition of capital reflects the quantity of plant, equipment, and raw materials used per unit of labor power. A rise in this ratio implies that labor power is being replaced by plant, equipment, and raw materials. Such a rise may or may not coincide with an increase in efficiency (that is, with a fall in the unit value of commodities).

In all four economies the technical composition of capital has increased (Figure 8.23). As might be expected the rate of increase was far faster in Japan (at 10.33% per annum compound) than in North America (3.71% in Canada and 2.74% in the USA). The rate of increase in the technical compo-

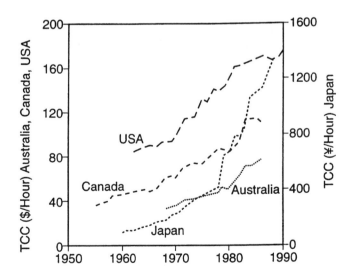

FIGURE 8.23. The technical composition of capital (TCC): Australia, Canada, Japan, and the USA. The technical composition of capital was calculated as the product of the annual number of turnover periods (see Fig. 8.24) and the deflated value of constant capital (see Fig. 8.21) to hours worked. Constant capital data were deflated using ratios of current and constant dollar capital stocks. *Source:* see Fig. 8.18.

sition was 5.20% per annum in Australia. Though there have been short periods in all four economies when the technical composition of capital has grown only slowly, there have been no major long-term fluctuations in the rate of increase:

Australia	+4.24% (1967/68–1973/74)	+5.61% (1973/74–1986/87)
Canada	+3.84% (1955–1974)	+3.51% (1974–1986)
Japan	+10.09% (1960–1973)	+10.53% (1973–1988)
USA	+3.03% (1962–1973)	+2.55% (1973–1990)

The replacement of labor by plant, equipment, and raw materials has been progressing at a fairly steady pace throughout the 1960s, 1970s, and 1980s.

These changes are summarized in Table 8.3. This table illustrates the absolute change in the value composition of capital (dq) and the three effects that have caused that change: the value of plant, equipment, and raw materials $(d\lambda_1)$; the technical composition of capital (dP); and the value of labor power $(d\lambda_L)$. Over the entire period the value composition has risen most

TABLE 8.3. Determinants of the value composition of capital

Country	Period	dq	Effect of $d\lambda_1$	Effect of dP	Effect of $d\lambda_L$
Australia	Whole[1]	8.28	−7.12	12.32	3.51
	Early[1]	0.58	−2.60	3.33	−0.05
	Late[1]	7.70	−4.52	8.99	3.56
Canada	Whole[2]	14.78	−9.91	23.97	0.95
	Early[2]	6.72	−5.71	13.87	−1.01
	Late[2]	8.06	−4.19	10.77	1.96
Japan	Whole[3]	47.39	−67.38	121.74	−1.21
	Early[3]	−6.74	−39.48	45.37	−9.25
	Late[3]	54.13	−27.90	76.37	8.04
USA	Whole[4]	4.51	−4.02	8.11	0.53
	Early[4]	2.00	−1.78	2.88	0.95
	Late[4]	2.51	−2.24	5.23	−0.42

Notes: [1]In Australia (where financial years run from July through June) the entire period is 1968/69 through 1986/87; the early period is 1968/69 through 1974/75; the late period is 1974/75 through 1986/87.
[2]In Canada the entire period is 1955–1986; the early period is 1955 through 1974; the late period is 1974–1986.
[3]In Japan the entire period is 1960–1988; the early period is 1960 through 1975; the late period is 1975–1988.
[4]In the USA the entire period runs from 1962 through 1990; the early period is 1962–1974; the late period is 1974–1990.
Source: see Table 8.1

The differential dq and the effects of $d\lambda_1$, dP, and $d\lambda_L$ are measured as discrete annual changes, according to equation (8.8), and are summed over the periods indicated.

strongly in Japan and least in the USA: in Japan the value of plant, equipment, and raw materials as a ratio of the value of labor power has risen very quickly; in the USA the ratio has hardly risen at all. Australia and Canada occupy intermediate positions between these two extremes. In all four countries the central control over the value composition of capital has been the technical composition (the quantities of plant, equipment, and raw materials used per hour of labor power). Labor power has been replaced by plant, equipment, and raw materials, especially in Japan and to a minor extent in the USA. Partially offsetting the increase in the technical composition have been decreases in the unit value of plant, equipment, and raw materials as production of these commodities has become more efficient. Changes in the value of labor power have been insignificant in altering the value composition of capital. Over the entire period, then, labor power has been replaced by plant, equipment, and raw materials; to some extent this has driven down the unit value of commodities, but not sufficiently to prevent the value composition of capital from rising. The net effect has been a strong tendency for the rate of profit to fall—especially in Japan, to a lesser extent in Australia and Canada, and to a minor extent in the USA.

But these changes have not taken place at a uniform rate in the 1960s, 1970s, and 1980s. In Japan the value composition of capital declined through the 1960s, driven by rapid reductions in the value of the means of production and to a lesser extent a rise in the value of labor power. The value composition of capital changed slowly through the late 1960s and early 1970s in Australia as reductions in the value of capital goods offset the impact of a rising technical composition. Since the mid-1970s (the "late period") the value composition of capital has increased rapidly in Australia and especially Japan as the pace at which labor is replaced by capital has accelerated and the value of labor power has been decreased. In Canada and the USA the increase in the value composition of capital was relatively consistent between the two periods (see Table 8.3), but for different reasons. In the "early period" in Canada the replacement of labor by capital was partially offset by reductions in the value of means of production and by increases in the value of labor power. Later, the pace of labor-saving technical change slowed but gains in the value composition were boosted by the declining strength of labor. In the USA the pace of labor-saving technical change accelerated after the mid-1970s, though the effects of this were dampened by increases in the value of labor power and greater reductions in the value of capital goods.

8.3.3 Turnover Times

The final control over the rate of profit is the time required to turn capital over—the time between the advance of money for production and its return after commodities have been sold. Harvey (1982), after Marx (1967: Vol. II), examines the critical influence of the turnover time of capital on profitability. Recent studies of just-in-time production systems and their reduction of set-up, lead, and cycle times also highlight the importance of time-based competition (Coriot 1980; Linge 1991; Sayer 1986). Surprisingly, given the fact that turnover times have been so commonly ignored, the effects of changes in the time taken for capital to turn over are of the same order of magnitude as changes in the rate of exploitation (Table 8.4).

The turnover time of capital varies markedly between the four countries (Figure 8.24). Capital turned over about 13 times a year in Japan in 1990, about 6 times a year in North America, and only about 5 times a year in Australia. These figures provide one measure of the remarkable success of Japan in reengineering the production process. Furthermore, changes in the turnover time differ between the four countries. The number of turnovers each year has increased by 3.03% per annum in Japan, by 1.08% per annum in Australia, and by 0.97% per annum in Canada (compound). In the USA the number of turnovers a year did not increase between 1962 and 1990: the time series is dominated by year-to-year variations rather than by a trend. There is evidence that in all four countries the number of turnovers has increased particularly rapidly since the mid-1970s:

Australia	+0.48% (1967/68–1973/74)	+1.38% (1973/74–1986/87)
Canada	+0.63% (1955–1974)	+1.52% (1974–1986)
Japan	+1.78% (1960–1973)	+4.48% (1973–1988)
USA	−0.73% (1962–1973)	+0.70% (1973–1990)

These changes have offset any tendency of the rate of profit to fall, especially since the mid-1970s—and most particularly in Japan.

TABLE 8.4. Determinants of changes in the value rate of profit

Country	Period	$d\pi_v$	Effect of de	Effect of dq	Effect of dt
Australia	1969–1979	−0.028	0.011	−0.054	0.021
	1979–1985	0.042	0.085	−0.062	0.033
Canada	1956–1979	−0.111	−0.021	−0.204	0.065
	1979–1985	0.013	0.036	−0.075	0.049
Japan	1961–1974	0.048	−0.061	0.032	0.103
	1974–1987	−0.077	0.050	−0.536	0.251
USA	1963–1965	0.024	0.033	−0.008	−0.000
	1965–1981	−0.159	0.019	−0.262	−0.002
	1981–1989	0.058	0.024	0.020	0.011

Note: The differentials and effects variables are measured as discrete annual changes summed over the periods indicated.
Source: see Table 8.1.

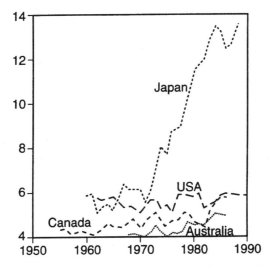

FIGURE 8.24. The annual number of turnovers: Australia, Canada, Japan, and the USA. The annual number of turnover periods was estimated as the ratio of total costs (wages and salaries, raw materials, depreciation, fuel, and electricity) to owned inventory. *Source:* see Fig. 8.18.

8.3.4 Components of the Changing Rate of Profit

The net effect of changes in the rate of exploitation, the value composition of capital, and the turnover time is the rate of profit. Figures 8.3, 8.8, 8.12, and 8.16 contain the actual and smoothed rates of profit; Figure 8.25 compares the histories of profitability in the four countries, using the smoothed series. The series together provide some evidence that profitability in manufacturing initially increased, then entered a long decline, and has begun to rise again. In the USA the rise in profit rates extended from 1950 through the mid-1960s and in Japan from (at least) 1960 until 1974. Even in Australia there is some evidence that profitability in manufacturing was rising until 1971. Only Canada does not exhibit some evidence of such a rise. Thereafter profit rates fell: in Australia the fall was relatively brief (until 1979); in Canada the fall was extended from the 1950s until 1979; in Japan the fall has continued until (at least) 1988; and in the USA the rate of profit fell until 1982. The subsequent rise in profit rates has been strongest in Australia, nonexistent in Japan, and weak in North America.

We interpret the histories of profitability in terms of the changes described in Sections 8.3.1–8.3.3 (Table 8.4). To reduce the effects of year-to-year fluctuations, the data are computed from 3-year moving averages, using the timing of peaks and troughs in profitability from the smoothed series plotted in Figure 8.25. In the table discrepancies between the actual value of $d\pi$

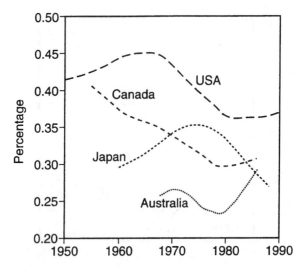

FIGURE 8.25. Smoothed series of the profit rate: Australia, Canada, Japan, and the USA. The data were smoothed using Cleveland's LOWESS smoother. *Source:* see Fig. 8.18.

and the sum of the effects arise because the calculations ignore second- and third-order interactions between the variables.

First, consider the initial periods when rates of profit were rising. Japan's profit boom between 1960 and 1975 derived from reductions in the time taken to turn capital over and to a lesser extent from reductions in the value composition of capital. A fall in the rate of exploitation only partially offset the effects of these two variables. In the USA in the early 1960s profits were rising essentially in line with the rate of exploitation.

The second period witnessed a fall in the rate of profit. In all four economies the dominant control has been the effect of a rising value composition of capital, which has more than accounted for falls in the rate of profit. That is to say, profit rates fell when increases in the technical composition of capital were not offset by improvements in efficiency that could reduce the unit value of plant, equipment, and raw materials. In Japan and the USA the technical composition grew at about the same rate both before and after the rate of profit began to fall, so the shift from a regime in which the value composition of capital fell to one in which the value composition rose occurred when the gains in efficiency slowed down. As Figure 8.22 demonstrates, technical change only slowly reduced the unit value of plant, equipment, and raw materials after 1973 in Japan and the USA. Similarly rises in the value composition of capital, when the technical composition rose faster than efficiency, drove the rate of profit down in Australia and Canada. Only in Canada did a fall in the rate of exploitation also assist the rising value composition of capital in driving down rates of profit. Elsewhere the rate of exploitation and the turnover time of capital have both acted to offset partially the effect of the value composition of capital.

In Australia and North America the latest period has seen profit rates begin to rise again. In Australia this happened because the rate of exploitation and the number of turnovers per year both increased much more rapidly than in the 1970s. In Canada the rate of exploitation grew quickly but the effect of the value composition of capital diminished. In the USA the value composition of capital had little effect in the most recent period and the rate of profit was driven up by increases in the rate of exploitation and (to a lesser extent) in the number of turnovers of capital per year. The real wage has stagnated in all three economies since the early 1980s, so the rate of exploitation has risen as technical changes have reduced the unit value of consumption commodities.

The combination of determinants of profitability within each economy is quite different—even ignoring the different industries within the economies. In each country the rate of profit has a different history and the causes of those histories are themselves different. There is no common history or combination of causes.

The declines in rates of profit in Australia, Canada, Japan, and the USA were driven essentially by increases in the value composition of capital. That is, profit rates fell because increases in the amount of plant, equipment, and raw materials per worker were not offset by improvements in efficiency. When rates of profit were falling, the rate of exploitation and the speed at which capital is turned over were both tending to raise profitability (except in Canada). There is little evidence that labor costs were rising faster than productivity when rates of profit were falling.

In Australia and Canada subsequent increases in the rate of profit have been fuelled by rises in the rate of exploitation—themselves predicated on stagnant real wages rather than by improvements in efficiency. In the USA, by contrast, the value composition of capital has exerted little effect in the most recent period, because the technical composition has changed only slowly. The change in regime in Japan from rising to falling rates of profit depended essentially on a shift from falling to rising value composition of capital once efficiency gains could no longer offset changes in the technical composition of capital. In none of these countries had there appeared by the end of the 1980s a form of development that could yield long-run growth and rising real wages: in Japan profit rates had not started to recover; and in the other economies the recovery was fuelled by deeper exploitation or stagnant technique rather than by high rates of investment that carry new techniques—and as yet the recovery of profit rates has not fuelled high rates of investment.

8.4 INDUSTRIAL AND REGIONAL RATES OF PROFIT

National economies comprise industries and regions. National rates of profit are the averages of rates of profit in industries and regions. Yet there is comparatively little information about the economic performance of industries and regions, especially their profitability. So the industrial and regional extent of the economic crisis is unclear. Industries and regions may exhibit trajectories of development that differ from the national aggregate, they may reveal impediments to accumulation and individual responses to those barriers. Furthermore, the histories of regional and industrial rates of profit may reveal strategies of competition that remain hidden at the aggregate level: as firms in different industries buy and sell commodities they redistribute surplus value among themselves. This transfer of profit through the market may be the dominant form of competition in some sectors, perhaps eclipsing the effects of technical change, exploitation, and turnover time. That is, to understand the capitalist economy in general—and its changing geography—is to understand the economic fortunes of individual industries and regions.

Rates of profit among individual firms and industries have been commonly studied within the orthodox economic tradition. Bain (1951) initiated a series of sectoral studies demonstrating that rates of profit, industry concentration, and collusion are positively correlated (see also Fuchs 1962). However, Brozen (1971) and Demsetz (1973) claimed that the positive correlation between profitability and concentration was caused by economies of scale in production rather than monopoly power. Certainly profitability should be correlated with the characteristics of production, growth, and demand (Mancke 1974; Moseley 1988; Ornstein 1973). Even so, whatever causes these differences in rates of profit between industries, they cannot be sustained unless there exist barriers to the entry of capital to those industries or to the exit of capital from them (Caves and Porter 1977; Qualls 1972). Mueller (1986) and Semmler (1984) summarize this work and address its shortcomings.

Three questions remain unresolved yet are crucial to the interpretations advanced in this book. First, what are the histories of rates of profit in individual industries and regions? Secondly, are there significant differences in regional and industrial profit rates? Thirdly, do those differences persist over time? These questions are addressed in the Sections 8.5 and 8.6. In this section we address the first question: what are the histories of rates of profit in the individual industrial sectors of Canada and the USA and in the various regions of Canada? Furthermore, what are the determinants of changes in industry and regional profit rates? To what extent, then, are the histories traced in Section 8.3 common to the individual industries and regions of the USA and Canada?

8.4.1　Rates of Profit of US Industries

The history of the rate of profit and its components in US industry is contested (contrast Bowles et al. 1983; Moseley 1985, 1988, 1990; Weisskopf 1979,

1985; Wolff 1979, 1986). Yet there is broad consensus that profitability in the USA has declined over the last 40 years or so (Dumenil et al. 1987; compare also Figure 8.16). The same period has seen falling rates of growth of output, investment, and productivity (Dertouzos et al. 1989), stagnant real wages, the deterioration of working conditions, and attempts by capital to redefine the labor contract (Bluestone and Harrison 1990; Goldfield 1987; Moody 1986); capacity utilization has fallen, unemployment has increased, record numbers of plants have closed, and capital has rapidly abandoned manufacturing sectors and regions (Bluestone and Harrison 1982; Clark 1986). The fact of manufacturing decline is clear: To what extent is decline common to all US industries? Is decline specific to certain industries and regions?

Disaggregate studies of the rate of profit in US manufacturing are comparatively rare. Semmler (1984) reviews empirical evidence about rates of profit in industries in relation to the characteristics of their markets. He finds that differences in rates of profit do exist, associated with barriers to the free flow of factors between industries. Rates of profit differ between the 20 two-digit SIC (Standard Industrial Classification) manufacturing industries (Glick 1985) and three-digit SIC industries (Graham et al. 1988) in the USA. Similar differences exist in other countries (Mueller 1990). Graham et al. (1988) describe how industries' rates of profit and economic restructuring are related to the transition between submodes of capitalist production. Industrial rates of profit in regions of the USA have not been estimated largely because regional capital stocks have not been measured.

What is missing is the history of rates of profit in individual industries— and the interpretation of that history through the components of change. At this point we are less interested in the fact of interindustry differences in rates of profit and what that might imply about competition and markets than in differences of history. To what extent is the history described in Section 8.3 common to all 20 two-digit SIC US manufacturing industries between 1962 and 1990? What are the causes of those different histories? A detailed review of the components of profitability in US industries and their change over time is provided in Appendix A8, Section A8.1. In the next subsection we highlight those changes.

8.4.1.1 The Determinants of the Profit Rate in US Industries

Between 1962 and 1990 the average price rate of profit realized by manufacturing firms in the USA declined by almost 16%. Between the trough years of 1962 and 1982 (or between the peaks of 1965 and 1990) the decline in the rate of profit was sharper—about 29%. This crisis in US manufacturing is widespread: profitability fell in 17 of the 20 manufacturing sectors.

Across US manufacturing as a whole labor power has been replaced by plant, equipment, and raw materials. To some extent this has driven down the unit value of commodities, but not sufficiently to prevent the value composition of capital from rising. Profit rates fell when increases in the technical composition of capital were not offset by improvements in efficiency that could reduce the unit value of plant, equipment, and raw materials. Changes in the rate of exploitation and turnover times have been largely irrelevant to the history of rates of profit in US manufacturing as a whole. This aggregate picture is broadly consistent with the claims of the Marxian theory of the falling rate of profit.

Nevertheless this aggregate picture fails to do justice to the diversity of histories of profitability in different industries. This diversity is summarized in Table 8.5. In two industries the price rate of profit rose between the booms of 1965 and 1990: in the food and tobacco industries increases in the price/value ratio more than offset the effect of changes in the value rate of profit. In the petroleum industry the price rate of profit was more or less unchanged between the two booms. So in 17 industries price rates of profit followed aggregate profits down. In two of those 17 industries—rubber & plastics products and stone, clay, & glass products—changes in profitability were dominated by the price/value ratio. These industries were losing market power. In the fabricated metals industries the effects of the price/value ratio and of the value rate of profit were essentially equal. Therefore in 14 industries the price rate of profit fell basically because the value rate of profit fell. In the transport equipment industry changes in the value rate of profit were

TABLE 8.5. Classification of US industries according to history of profitability, 1965–1990

		Industries in which the price rate of profit—			
			Fell mainly because		
Rose	Was constant	π_p/π_v Fell	π_p/π_v and π_v fell	π_v fell	Main cause of π_v fall
FNK	PET	RBP	FBM	TNS	Turnover
TOB		SCG		TEX	VCC
				APP	VCC
				WOD	VCC
				FNT	VCC
				PPR	VCC
				PUB	VCC
				CHM	VCC
				LTH	VCC
				PMT	VCC
				MCH	VCC
				ELC	VCC
				INS	VCC
				MIS	VCC

Note: See Table 8.10 for an explanation of the SIC abbreviations used throughout.
Source: Fixed Reproducible Tangible Wealth in the United States, 1925–1989, *Census of Manufactures* and *Annual Survey of Manufactures* Washington DC: U.S. Department of Commerce.

largely driven by changes in the turnover time of capital. (The transport industry has a history different from all other manufacturing industries, which is ironic since the regulation school identifies transport as the hegemonic industry in the US during the long boom.) The remaining 13 of the 20 industries followed the model of manufacturing as a whole: their price rate of profit fell mainly because the value rate of profit fell and that mainly because the value composition of capital was driven upward by the technical composition of capital.

8.4.2 Rates of Profit in Canadian Industries

The history and causes of the decline in profitability in Canadian manufacturing were reviewed in Section 8.3 (see also Helliwell et al. 1986; Webber and Rigby 1986). To complement this aggregate history there is comparatively little research on the sectoral extent of the crisis. Bradbury (1985) traces the impact of the decline in international demand for raw materials on the Canadian resource sector. Holmes (1983) and Mahon (1984) reveal the structural forces that have prompted the automobile and textile industries to reorganize. Webber and Tonkin (1987, 1988a,b) analyze technical change and profitability in the food, textile and wood industries. Rigby (1990a, 1991a,b) details profit rates and their components by industry and region in Canadian manufacturing.

It remains unclear whether the economic downturn revealed in the aggregate figures of Section 8.3 is a crisis of Canadian manufacturing in general or is limited to particular industries. In this section we trace the history of profitability in individual industries in Canada between 1955 and 1986. What is the sectoral extent of the crisis in manufacturing? Are individual industries driven by the same forces that have driven profitability in manufacturing as a whole? The analysis follows the same logic as that of Section 8.4.1. We examine the components of the rate of profit, their variation, and their impact on profitability in 20 manufacturing sectors. (Once more the detailed analysis is presented in Appendix A8, Section A8.2.) The determinants of changes in manufacturing rates of profit in Canadian industries are summarized below.

8.4.2.1 The Determinants of the Profit Rate in Canadian Industries

In Canadian manufacturing the 1960s and 1970s saw profit rates decline as the value composition of capital rose strongly. The rate of exploitation fell slowly, and shorter turnover times of capital could not offset these two effects. More recently in the 1980s the rate of exploitation has risen and the increase in the value composition of capital has slowed, so profit rates have begun to rise again (Section 8.3).

As in the USA, though, there is a good deal of variation about this story among the individual manufacturing industries of the country (Table 8.6). First, only in 10 industries did the price rate of profit fall between the peaks of 1955 and 1986. In the tobacco, leather, knitting, textile, clothing, furniture, publishing, fabricated metals, and miscellaneous goods industries the price rate of profit rose, and in the petroleum industry it was essentially constant. Of the 10, the price rate of profit fell mainly because of changes in price/value ratios in the rubber and electrical industries. So there are eight industries in which price rates of profit followed the Canadian manufacturing average down during the 1960s and 1970s because their value rates of profit fell. In the primary metals industry, changes in the pace at which capital was turned over was primarily responsible for reductions in the value rate of profit. In seven industries—food & beverage, wood, pulp, machinery, transport, nonmetallic minerals, and chemicals—did price rates of profit fall primarily because of declines in the value rate of profit, which in turn were mainly driven by increases in the value composition of capital. The average has not been especially common. Increases in the value composition were generally driven by increases in the amount of plant, equipment, and raw materials per unit of labor power: technical change has been predominantly to save labor, and changes in commodity values do little to prevent the value composition of capital from rising.

Unequal exchange between industries is not usually considered a counter to declines in rate of profit. These data confirm the findings about US industries: in about one-third of industries the ability of firms to compete in the market has a greater effect on the price rate of profit than does the the value rate of profit.

TABLE 8.6. Classification of Canadian industries according to history of profitability, 1955–1986

		Industries in which the price rate of profit—			
			Fell mainly because		
Rose	Was constant	π_p/π_v fell	π_p/π_v and π_v fell	π_v fell	Main cause of π_v fall
TOB	PET	RBP		PMT	Turnover
LTH		ELC		FNB	VCC
KNT				WOD	VCC
TEX				PPR	VCC
CLO				PMT	VCC
FNT				MCH	VCC
PUB				TNS	VCC
FBM				NMM	VCC
MIS				CHM	VCC

Source: *Manufacturing Industries of Canada: National and Provincial Areas* and *Fixed Capital Flows and Stocks*, Ottawa, Canada: Statistics Canada.

8.4.3 Rates of Profit in Canadian Regions

There is even less information in the literature about regional rates of profit—especially in the USA partly because there is little information about stocks of capital at the regional level. In Canada there are a few recent studies of industrial development in specific areas, such as Grass and Hayter's (1989) work on the British Columbia forest products sector and Bradbury and St. Martin's (1983) analysis of recession in Schefferville, Quebec. Norcliffe (1987) presents a detailed summary of regional unemployment rates but only for the recession of 1981–1984. Gertler (1986, 1987) examines the regional dynamics of manufacturing investment in Canada and the determinants of those capital flows. In this section, the individual terms of equations (8.3)–(8.9) are estimated annually for six regions of Canada: Quebec, Ontario, Alberta, the Atlantic Provinces (Newfoundland, New Brunswick, Nova Scotia, and Prince Edward Island), a Prairie region (Manitoba and Saskatchewan), and British Columbia (including the Yukon and Northwest Territories). We seek to understand how profitability has changed in the regions and the extent to which their histories replicate those of the federation as a whole. (A detailed examination of the components of the profit rate in Canadian regions is relegated to Appendix A8, Section A8.3.) The results of this examination are summarized below.

8.4.3.1 The Determinants of the Profit Rate in Canadian Regions

Between 1955 and 1977 rising real wages mollified the demands of an increasingly strong labor force and provided a ready market for consumer goods throughout Canada. Rising real wages did not themselves squeeze profits, for capitalists introduced technical changes that reduced the unit value of consumer goods. Thus the rate of exploitation remained relatively constant. Technical changes introduced by capital over this period predominantly saved labor, and these pressed the rate of profit downward. In the mid-1970s, in response to declining profits the pace of technical change slowed and capacity utilization rates were reduced. The decrease in capacity utilization rates largely took the place of labor-saving technical changes, causing the technical composition of capital to rise, further reducing the rate of profit. Unlike technical change proper, however, reductions in capacity utilization rates do not tend to decrease the values of commodities; so rates of exploitation fell around 1974 as real wages continued to rise. The rising real cost of labor prompted quick reaction by capital. From 1977 real wages gains were frozen. The rate of profit continued to slide until 1982, as the economy entered the deepest recession of the postwar years.

Table 8.7 presents a summary of the forces that reduced the rate of profit in each region of Canada. In all six regions reductions in the price rate of profit followed the decline of the value rate of profit. In the Prairie region the pace of technical change was relatively slow and thus the value rate of profit

TABLE 8.7. Classification of Canadian regions according to history of profitability, 1955–1986

| | | Industries in which the price rate of profit— | | | |
| | | | Fell mainly because | | |
Rose	Was constant	π_p/π_v fell	π_p/π_v and π_v fell	π_v fell	Main cause of π_v fall
			Prairies	Atlantic	VCC
				Quebec	VCC
				Ontario	VCC
				Alberta	VCC
				BC	VCC

Source: see Table 8.6.

did not decline as quickly as in other regions. However, the failure to innovate as rapidly as did firms in other regions undermined the ability of Prairie manufacturers to compete in the market. In four of the remaining five regions the value rate of profit was driven down by an increasing value composition of capital. Rapid technical change, especially toward the end of the period, caused the value rate of profit to fall very rapidly in Alberta. However, superior technology allowed Albertan firms to boost profits in the market, though this was insufficient to prevent the price rate of profit from falling. Ontario and Quebec performed better than all other regions between 1955 and 1986. In these regions the pace of technical change was below the Canadian average and thus the value rate of profit fell quite slowly. The relatively slow pace of technical change did not severely affect market performance. While firms in Ontario generally gained profits in the market, in Quebec manufacturers tended to lose profits but not at the same rate as in the Atlantic region. In contrast the Atlantic provinces fared badly in both the market and in production. Rapid increases in the value composition of capital through the 1960s severely reduced the value rate of profit. These technological advances did little to improve the competitiveness of the Atlantic Provinces, which consistently performed poorly in the market. In British Columbia (BC) a falling rate of exploitation added considerably to the impact of the rising composition of capital on the rate of profit.

8.4.3.2 Industry in Region Rates of Profit in Canada

In part the differences in histories of profitability between the regions reflect the industries that compose the manufacturing sectors of those regions: the metal-fabricating and auto industries of Ontario; the textile and clothing trades mixed with a resource-processing sector in Quebec; and manufacturing in the other provinces which is dominated by resource processing. Yet industrial composition is not the whole story (Table 8.8).

TABLE 8.8. Industry by region profit rates in Canada

	Atlantic			Quebec			Ontario			Prairies			Alberta			BC		
	1961	1971	1984	1961	1971	1984	1961	1971	1984	1961	1971	198 4	1961	1971	1984	1961	1971	1984
FNB	0.433	0.332	0.284	0.526	0.461	0.451	0.479	0.441	0.476	0.451	0.333	0.299	0.421	0.420	0.348	0.511	0.429	0.420
TOB	—	—	—	0.450	0.525	0.571	0.324	0.507	0.385	—	—	—	—	—	—	—	—	—
RBP	—	0.058	0.402	0.319	0.575	0.443	0.393	0.582	0.494	0.220	0.156	0.302	0.104	0.119	0.211	0.113	0.129	0.219
LTH	0.623	1.014	0.896	0.688	0.727	0.614	0.398	0.406	0.496	0.310	0.600	0.733	0.423	0.636	0.561	0.674	0.791	1.198
TEX	0.589	0.338	0.622	0.302	0.287	0.297	0.231	0.248	0.303	0.295	0.304	0.542	0.398	0.358	0.337	0.469	0.277	0.539
KNT[1]	0.461	0.624	0.666	0.388	0.513	0.401	0.377	0.376	0.504	0.311	0.302	0.345	0.949	0.531	0.653	0.640	0.687	0.277
CLO	0.534	1.054	0.825	0.750	0.878	0.908	0.682	0.973	1.009	0.546	0.831	0.768	0.808	1.127	1.127	0.662	0.969	0.865
WOD	0.362	0.320	0.184	0.444	0.474	0.343	0.301	0.350	0.273	0.367	0.314	0.150	0.304	0.413	0.147	0.184	0.196	0.131
FNT	0.996	0.642	0.570	0.690	0.602	0.685	0.684	0.609	0.834	0.761	0.629	0.617	0.834	0.776	0.635	0.811	0.760	0.685
PPR	0.185	0.002	0.068	0.288	0.181	0.201	0.261	0.223	0.211	0.208	0.077	0.082	0.214	0.085	0.144	0.172	0.057	0.096
PUB	1.222	1.103	1.225	0.716	0.745	1.210	0.731	0.684	0.947	0.933	0.883	1.055	0.867	0.874	1.008	0.813	0.767	0.885
PMT	0.021	−0.01	0.025	0.247	0.217	0.196	0.184	0.169	0.113	0.081	0.105	0.090	0.047	0.060	0.135	0.104	0.131	0.197
MFB	0.461	0.533	0.415	0.431	0.456	0.496	0.419	0.455	0.442	0.495	0.499	0.458	0.462	0.694	0.544	0.453	0.623	0.531
MCH	0.584	0.457	0.378	0.455	0.461	0.408	0.449	0.400	0.387	0.408	0.441	0.479	0.268	0.383	0.551	0.475	0.473	0.509
TNS	0.246	0.505	0.212	0.318	0.466	0.722	0.336	0.411	0.491	0.373	0.897	0.764	0.376	0.520	0.891	0.661	0.501	0.798
ELC	0.616	0.584	0.562	0.483	0.456	0.468	0.518	0.525	0.545	0.670	0.588	0.729	0.708	0.652	0.483	0.549	0.705	0.737
PET	0.153	0.096	0.192	0.195	0.123	0.108	0.185	0.138	0.141	0.161	0.108	0.110	0.176	0.118	0.026	0.134	0.110	0.166
CHM	0.110	0.033	0.040	0.531	0.459	0.390	0.398	0.354	0.230	0.138	0.069	0.054	0.173	0.069	0.036	0.426	0.280	0.200
NMM	0.227	0.282	0.164	0.354	0.354	0.249	0.244	0.266	0.258	0.255	0.285	0.209	0.251	0.412	0.141	0.194	0.232	0.187
MIS	1.479	0.947	0.501	0.983	0.686	0.744	0.748	0.525	0.753	1.278	0.946	0.453	1.422	0.963	0.591	1.129	0.937	0.621

[1]The figures in the 1984 column for this industry are actually from 1982. *Source:* see Table 8.6.

The economic performance of the Canadian space economy has been diverse between 1961 and 1984. There are three dimensions to this diversity. First, within industries and regions, marked differences in rates of profit may be observed over time. Thus in the petroleum industry of Alberta, the profit rate declined by over 85% from 1961 to 1984. By contrast, in the transport sector of Quebec rates of return increased by about 130% after 1961, while in the textile industry of Ontario they remained constant over the period. Second, within a region in any given year, profit rates differ. In the Atlantic Provinces in 1971, for example, the rate of return is negative in the primary metal industry, is close to zero in the paper and chemical industries, and registers over 100% in the leather, clothing, and publishing sectors. These variations are evident throughout the data set. Third, within an industry in a given year profit rates vary between regions. In the chemicals sector, for instance, profit rates vary by several hundred percent between regions in a single year. However, profit rates in the metal-fabricating industry did not differ by more than 10% between any two regions in 1961, and in other years they were remarkably similar over space. Together these dimensions of variation ensure that the history of manufacturing profit rates in the Canadian economy is complex. In some cases profit rates vary markedly between industries, regions, and over time. In other instances industries in one or a number of different regions exhibit broadly similar performance histories.

8.5 SIGNIFICANCE AND PERSISTENCE OF PROFIT RATE DIFFERENTIALS

The previous section has highlighted the manner in which rates of profit differ between industries and regions. The persistence and significance of these differences are now examined more carefully. Two sets of results are presented, one for the USA and one for Canada. The analysis of variance conducted on the US industry data employs only one explanatory factor—the differences of rates of profit between industry groups. Two explanatory factors were employed in the analysis of the Canadian data: differences in industries' profitability holding constant a regional effect, and differences in regions' profitability holding constant the industry effect.

If significant differences exist between the rates of profit of industries and regions, the next question is whether or not the profit rate series converge to an equilibrium. If the series for some industries and regions converge, what are the limits to which they converge? Analysis of this question uses time series techniques. If rates of profit tend to a competitive equilibrium, the profit rates of industries and regions should gravitate to the manufacturing average. Of course spatial and sectoral barriers to mobility and disequilibration forces such as technical change might hinder the movement of individual rates to the average. However, the nature of profit rate deviations may illuminate the relative strength of equilibrating and disequilibrating forces in the US and Canadian economies.

Consider the profit rate series for a single industry or region i: $\{r_i(1),$ $r_i(2), \ldots, r_i(t), \ldots, r_i(n)\}$, where t indexes the year. We subtract from this industry's (or region's) profit rate in year t the average profit rate for all industries (regions) in that year:

$$y_i(t) = r_i(t) - r(t), \qquad \text{for} \quad t = 1, 2, \ldots, n.$$

The subscript denoting the identity of the industry (region) is now dropped. The new series $y = \{y(1), y(2), \ldots, y(n)\}$ is called the profit deviation series.

Suppose that the profit deviation series is autoregressive:

$$y(t + 1) = a + by(t) + e(t), \qquad \text{for} \quad t = 1, 2, \ldots, n - 1.$$

It is assumed that the errors have zero mean, constant variance, and are independent. It follows that

$$\begin{aligned} y(t + 2) &= a + by(t + 1) + e(t + 1) \\ &= a + ab + b^2 y(t) + be(t) + e(t + 1), \end{aligned}$$

and, in general, that

$$\begin{aligned} y(t + n) = {}&a(1 + b + b^2 + \cdots + b^{n-1} + b^n)y(t) \\ &+ e(t + n) + be(t + n - 1) + \cdots + b^n e(t). \end{aligned} \qquad (8.10)$$

This equation has three kinds of terms.

The first term in equation (8.10) is

$$a(1 + b + b^2 + \cdots + b^{n-1}). \qquad (8.11)$$

If $b \geq 1$, the terms inside the parentheses become larger as n increases. If $b \leq -1$, the terms inside the parentheses also become larger in absolute value as n increases and they alternate in sign. But if $-1 < b < 1$, as n becomes larger, the expression (8.11) approaches more and more closely to the limit $a/(1 - b)$.

The second part of equation (8.10) is the term $b^n y(t)$. As n becomes larger, so b^n becomes closer and closer to 0 provided that $-1 < b < 1$. The term b^n alternates in sign if $-1 < b < 0$.

The third part of equation (8.10) is the sum of the error terms:

$$e(t + n) + be(t + n - 1) + \cdots + b^n e(t). \qquad (8.12)$$

This sum is the error term for $y(t + n)$. Each of the errors has zero mean. Hence the mean of the expression (8.12) is also zero. Each of the errors is independent and has constant variance (s, say). Hence the expression (8.12) has variance equal to

$$(1 + b + b^2 + \cdots + b^n)^2 s. \tag{8.13}$$

If $-1 < b < 1$, as n becomes larger and larger, so expression (8.13) tends to approach the value $s/(1 - b)^2$. If b lies outside these limits, the variance of the error term for $y(t + n)$ becomes larger as n becomes larger.

These conclusions may be summarized as follows:

1. If $b \leq -1$ or $b > 1$, the deviation series is not convergent.
2. If $-1 < b < 1$, then

$$\lim_{n \to \infty} y(t + n) = \frac{a}{1 - b} + E(n). \tag{8.14}$$

Here $E(n)$ is the error term; it has mean zero and variance to $s/(1 - b)^2$. Thus the deviation series is convergent (up to an error term of zero mean and constant variance). The series approaches the limit $a/(1 - b)$; if b is negative, the series approaches that limit with alternating sign.

3. Only if $a = 0$ does the deviation series approach the mean profit rate for all industries; if $a > 0$, the series approaches a limit that exceeds the national average profit rate; and if $a < 0$, the industry's profit rate approaches a limit below the national average. These conclusions have guided the empirical work.

For each industry's deviation series an estimate of a and b was obtained from the autoregressive equation:

$$y(t + 1) = a + by(t) + e(t). \tag{8.15}$$

The equation was estimated by ordinary least squares. The 0.95 confidence limits on b are used to determine the probable convergence of the series. The value of $a/(1 - b)$ is the best estimate of the limit to which each series converges. The significance of the difference of this limit from 0 is the significance of the difference of a from 0. All tests are two-tailed.

8.5.1 Differences of Profit Rates between US Industries

On average between 1962 and 1990 differences in profit rates between industries are significant (Table 8.9): industries have different average rates of profit.

The structure of changes in the rates of profit earned by industries are more complex (Table 8.10). The first-order autoregressive time series model

TABLE 8.9. One-way analysis of variance of US industry profit rates, 1962–1990

Source	Sum of squares	Degrees of freedom	Mean square	F-Ratio
Industry	19.880	19	1.046	122.740*
Error	4.944	580	0.009	—
Total	24.824	599	—	—

*Significant at the 0.01 level. *Source*: see Table 8.5.

fits the profit rate deviation data well: the autoregressive equation is significant for all 20 deviation series. The rate of profit in the tobacco industry does not converge (at $p = 0.95$): the tobacco industry's rate of profit is continuing to grow in relation to the manufacturing average. In 9 other industries the series of profit rates may or may not converge: the data are insufficiently precise to allow a certain conclusion. In the other 10 industries the series of profit rates are tending to converge to an equilibrium. Of these 10 industries, the lumber & wood, pulp & paper, stone, clay, & glass, and machinery sectors have rates of profit that trend toward the manufacturing average rate. The rates of profit in the textile, primary metals, and transport industries converge on values that are significantly below the manufacturing average. The rates of profit in the apparel, instruments, and miscellaneous industries converge to values significantly above the manufacturing average.

The long-run growth path of the US manufacturing economy has the following characteristics. In one industry (tobacco), rates of profit are deviating increasingly from the manufacturing average. In another 9 industries, rates of profit may or may not be deviating. Of the 10 industries in which rates of profit are tending to converge to an equilibrium value, only in 4 is that value the average rate for all manufacturing; 3 industries have tended to maintain a rate of profit that is consistently above the manufacturing average, and 3 industries have tended to maintain profits consistently below the manufacturing average. There is no evidence in these data that industries tend to an equilibrium in which their rates of profit are equal; if anything, the evidence is that long-run (equilibrium) rates of profit are not equal to the average in most industries.

8.5.2 Differences of Profit Rates in Canadian Industries and Regions

The analysis of variance of rates of profit in Canadian manufacturing used only 18 industries in each of the six regions. The tobacco and rubber and plastics sectors were included with the miscellaneous sector because data about them were incomplete. The industry, region, and overall group means

TABLE 8.10. First-order autoregressive model of US industry profit rate deviations from the national manufacturing average

Industry	Estimate of a	Estimate of b	95% confidence interval		Convergence of b	$a/(1-b)$
			Lower limit	Upper limit		
FNK	0.0310	0.8617	0.6224	1.1010	Not sure	
TOB	0.0035	1.1604	1.0287	1.2921	Not sure	
TEX	−0.0353	0.6275	0.3121	0.9429	Yes	−0.095
APP	0.1729	0.5563	0.2709	0.8417	Yes	0.390
WOD	−0.0235	0.6679	0.3853	0.9505	Yes	Average
FNT	0.0217	0.8572	0.6577	1.0566	Not sure	
PPR	−0.0254	0.7173	0.4403	0.9943	Yes	Average
PUB	0.0474	0.8954	0.7191	1.0717	Not sure	
CHM	0.0087	0.9337	0.7847	1.0827	Not sure	
PET	−0.0469	0.7442	0.4867	1.0017	Not sure	
RBP	0.0057	0.7932	0.5515	1.0349	Not sure	
LTH	0.0659	0.7480	0.4845	1.0114	Not sure	
SCG	−0.0085	0.7001	0.4171	0.9831	Yes	Average
PMT	−0.1443	0.4121	0.0512	0.7730	Yes	−0.245
FBM	−0.0029	0.8577	0.6115	1.1039	Not sure	
MCH	−0.0002	0.6089	0.3290	0.8892	Yes	Average
ELC	0.0032	0.8995	0.6769	1.1221	Not sure	
TNS	−0.0292	0.6401	0.3366	0.9436	Yes	−0.081
INS	0.0650	0.5695	0.2209	0.9181	Yes	0.151
MIS	0.1033	0.3958	0.0847	0.7069	Yes	0.171

Note: SIC abbreviations—FNK, food & kindred products; TOB, tobacco; TEX, textiles; APP, apparel; WOD, lumber & wood products; FNT, furniture; PPR, pulp & paper; PUB, printing & publishing; CHM, chemicals; PET, petroleum & coal; RBP, rubber & plastics; LTH, leather; SCG, stone, clay, & glass; PMT, primary metals; FBM, fabricated metal products; MCH, machinery; ELC, electrical & electronic equipment; TNS, transportation equipment; INS, instruments; MIS, miscellaneous. *Source*: see Table 8.5.

were weighted by the size of the capital invested in each sector and region. All data were deflated to constant prices. The cost of production, shipments, and owned inventory were deflated using industry-specific selling price indexes; wages were deflated using the consumer price index; and capital stocks were deflated using capital price deflators.

The results of the analysis of variance are displayed in Table 8.11. The rates of profit of different industries are significantly different. The rates of profit of different regions are significantly different. That is, "industry-mix" arguments do not adequately explain regional fortunes. Region-specific determinants of economic vitality must be given greater attention. Since the observations span 24 years the observed differences in rates of profit between industries and regions are not a temporary aberration but a continuing feature of competitive capitalist economies.

The interaction effect in the analysis of variance (Table 8.11) is significant.

TABLE 8.11. Two-way analysis of variance of Canadian industry by region profit rates, 1961–1984

Source	Sum of squares	Degrees of freedom	Mean square	F-Ratio
Industry	118.601	17	6.977	425.396*
Region	17.772	5	3.554	216.396*
Interaction	11.349	85		8.140*
Error	40.735	2484		
Total	188.452	2591		

*Significant at the 0.01 level. *Source*: see Table 8.6.

So different industries are most profitable in different regions: the relative profitability of industries depends on the region in which they are located. However, the interaction effect has a relatively low F-ratio, implying that the ranking of industries by profit rates is relatively stable between regions. Figure 8.26 confirms this implication. The industries are listed along the abscissa in order of their average rate of profit in Canada (that is, the same order in each region). The six regional histograms all exhibit a similar downward trend from left to right: the ranking of industries in terms of average profitability is similar across space. In summary, the relative performance of individual industries is largely but not entirely stable over space; a significant regional influence structures industrial profitability in Canadian manufacturing.

The differences between industries' rates of profit have been modeled by a first-order autoregressive model of deviations from national and regional averages. Table 8.12 describes the characteristics of industrial rates of profit in relation to the Canadian average between 1955 and 1986. All 20 autoregression equations were significant at the 0.05 level: 14 of the series tended to converge; 8 industries—food & beverage, tobacco, leather, metal fabricating, machinery, transport, electrical, and miscellaneous industries—had rates of profit that converged to values higher than the manufacturing average. Profit rates in the pulp & paper, primary metal, nonmetallic minerals, and petroleum & coal sectors converged to values significantly below the manufacturing average. Rates of profit in the textiles and lumber & wood industries converge to the Canadian manufacturing average profit rate.

A second analysis examines differences between regions' rates of profit between 1955 and 1986 (Table 8.13). All six regional autoregression models are significant at the 0.05 level. The average profit rate for the Prairie region converges to the Canadian average. In Quebec and Ontario profit rates converge to values significantly above the national average, and in the Atlantic Provinces profit rates converge to a value significantly below the Canadian average. The profit rate deviation series for Alberta and BC may or may not converge.

It is unlikely that significant differences between the rates of profit

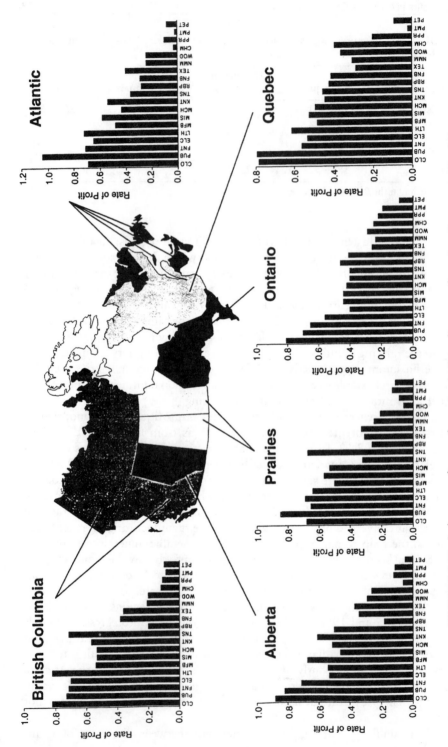

FIGURE 8.26. Industry profit rates by region in Canadian manufacturing. *Source:* see Fig. 8.7.

TABLE 8.12. First-order autoregressive model of Canadian industry profit rate deviations from the national manufacturing average

| Industry | Estimate of a | Estimate of b | 95% confidence interval | | Convergence of b | $a/(1-b)$ |
			Lower limit	Upper limit		
FNB	0.0502	0.5381	0.3062	0.7700	Yes	0.1087
TOB	0.0357	0.7185	0.4786	0.9584	Yes	0.1268
RBP	0.0243	0.7943	0.5728	1.0158	Not sure	
LTH	0.0434	0.7952	0.6367	0.9537	Yes	0.2119
KNT	0.0217	0.8395	0.6743	1.0047	Not sure	
TEX	−0.0089	0.7733	0.6263	0.9203	Yes	Average
CLO	0.0877	0.8344	0.6602	1.0086	Not sure	
WOD	−0.0231	0.4765	0.1423	0.8107	Yes	Average
NT	0.0702	0.8181	0.6248	1.0114	Not sure	
PPR	−0.0514	0.6454	0.3556	0.9352	Yes	−0.1450
PUB	0.0289	0.9544	0.8139	1.0949	Not sure	
PMT	−0.0359	0.7868	0.5950	0.9786	Yes	−0.1684
FBM	0.0471	0.6766	0.4404	0.9128	Yes	0.1456
MCH	0.0455	0.6147	0.3355	0.8959	Yes	0.1181
TNS	0.0447	0.4974	0.1669	0.8279	Yes	0.0889
ELC	0.0847	0.5688	0.2843	0.8553	Yes	0.1964
NMM	−0.0198	0.6657	0.3933	0.9381	Yes	−0.0592
PET	−0.0848	0.5838	0.3611	0.8065	Yes	−0.2037
CHM	0.0045	0.9134	0.7606	1.0662	Not sure	
MIS	0.1361	0.6196	0.3636	0.8256	Yes	0.3578

Source: see Table 8.6.

earned in different regions or industries are caused by a failure of competition throughout the Canadian economy. Rather, differences in rates of profit are a permanent feature of competitive capitalist economies. Without barriers to exit or entry, oligopolies cannot be sustained (Caves and Porter 1977; Semmler 1984). Two barriers to the movement of capital that might prevent rates of profit equalizing are sector-specific knowledge and location-specific knowledge (Harvey 1975; Mueller 1986; Qualls 1972; Semmler 1984). We now try to measure the relative effect of these two forces on profit rates.

Consider first interregional differences in rates of profit. Table 8.14 summarizes 116 first-order autoregression models of interregional differences in the rates of profit of individual industries. This analysis was conducted for the period 1961–1984. For each industry, the deviation is between the industry's rate of profit in the region and the industry's national rate of profit. That is, these are interregional analyses at the industry level. (Data about the tobacco industry refer only to Quebec and Ontario.) So this information about interregional differences in the rates of profit of one industry eliminates the effect of barriers between sectors to equal rates of profit. Table 8.14 reports the significance of the deviation series of each industry in each region; whether the

TABLE 8.13. First-order autoregressive model of Canadian regional profit rate deviations from the national manufacturing average

| Industry | Estimate of a | Estimate of b | 95% confidence interval | | Convergence of b | $a/(1-b)$ |
			Lower limit	Upper limit		
Atlantic	−0.0502	0.6742	0.3949	0.9535	Yes	−0.1541
Quebec	0.0233	0.4360	0.1335	0.7385	Yes	0.0413
Ontario	0.0121	0.6274	0.3374	0.9174	Yes	0.0325
Prairies	−0.0029	0.6803	0.3909	0.9697	Yes	Average
Alberta	−0.0103	0.8690	0.7068	1.0312	Not sure	
BC	−0.0079	0.8847	0.6902	1.0792	Not sure	

Source: see Table 8.6.

series converges at the 0.05 significance level; and to what value the series converges. In total, 35 (or 30%) of the deviation series converges; 24 (or 21%) of these converge to the industry average. Apparently the wood products and machinery industries are the ones in which interregional barriers to equal rates of profit are least; the barriers are strongest in the metal-fabricating industry.

Next consider interindustry differences between rates of profit within each region. Table 8.15 illustrates the effect of sectoral barriers to equal rates of profit. Again 116 deviation series were constructed from data for 1961–1984. The series represent the difference between the rates of profit earned by an industry in one region and that region's average profit rate. Of that 116 time series in the table, 35 (or almost 30%) converge, but only 12 of those (just over 10%) converge to their respective regional averages. BC and to a lesser extent the Atlantic Provinces are the areas within which capital flows most easily between sectors.

These results can be summarized as follows:

Of 20 industries, 14 profit rates converge, 2 to the mean (8.12).
Of   6 regions,   4 profit rates converge, 1 to the mean (8.13).
Of 116 regions, 35 profit rates converge, 24 to the mean (8.14).
Of 116 industries, 35 profit rates converge, 12 to the mean (8.15).

There are both sectoral and spatial barriers to the tendency for rates of profit to converge to equilibrium: in most industries and most regions, profit rates do not converge to the mean. Still the tendency for profit rates to converge is greatest when profit rates of regional industries are examined in relation to national industry averages. Rates of profit in one industry tend to converge to similar levels whatever the region (if they converge at all). By contrast rates of profit in different industries within the one region tend not to converge to

TABLE 8.14. First-order autoregressive model of industry profit Rate deviations within each region from national industry averages

	Atlantic			Quebec			Ontario			Prairies			Alberta			BC		
	1	2	3	1	2	3	1	2	3	1	2	3	1	2	3	1	2	3
FNB	NS			*	C	0.031	**	NC		**	NC		*	C	AVE	**	C	AVE
TOB	NS			NS			NS							NC		**	C	AVE
RBP	NS			**	C	AVE	**	NC		**	NC		**	NC		NS		
LTH	NS			**	NC		**	NC		*	C	AVE	NS	NC		**	NC	
T EX	**	C	AVE	**	NC		**	NC		**	NC		*	C	AVE	NS	NC	
KNT	NS			**	NC		**	NC		**	C	AVE	**	C	AVE	NS		
CLO	NS			**	C	AVE	**	C	AVE	NS	NC		NS	NC		**	C	AVE
WOD	**	C	AVE	**	C	0.126	**	C	AVE	**	C	AVE	**	NC		**	NC	
FNT	NS			**	NC		**	NC		NS	NC		NS	NC		**	C	AVE
PPR	**	C	-0.067	**	C	0.045	**	NC		**	NC		NS	NC		**	NC	
PUB	**	NC		**	NC		**	NC		**	NC		**	NC		**	C	AVE
PMT	NS			NS			*	C	AVE	**	C	AVE	**	NC		*	C	0.071
MFB	NS			NS			**	C	-0.026	NS	NC		**	C	0.196	**	C	0.257
MCH	**	C	AVE	*	C	AVE	**	C	-0.027	NS	NC		*	C	AVE	**	C	0.153
TNS	**	NC		**	NC		**	NC		**	NC		NS	NC		NS	NC	
ELC	NS			NS			NS	NC		NS	NC		**	C	AVE	**	C	AVE
PET	NS			**	NC		**	NC		**	NC		NS	NC		**	NC	
CHM	**	NC		**	NC		**	NC	**	NC	NC	**	NC	NC	**	NC		
NMM	NS			**	NC		**	NC		*	C	AVE	**	NC		**	NC	
MIS	**	NC		**	NC		**	C	-0.275	**	NC		**	NC		**	NC	

Notes: Column 1 reports the significance of the autoregression equations. Column 2 reports whether the deviation series converges at the 0.05 significance level. Column 3 reports the value to which the deviation series converge.

NS   Equation not significant.
 *   Significant at the 0.05 level.
 ** Significant at the 0.01 level.
 C   Converge.
 NC Does not converge.
 AVE Converges to the industry average.
Source: see Table 8.6.

TABLE 8.15. First-order autoregressive model of industry profit rate deviations within each region from the regional average

	Atlantic			Quebec			Ontario			Prairies			Alberta			BC		
	1	2	3	1	2	3	1	2	3	1	2	3	1	2	3	1	2	3
FNB	NS			*	C	0.089	**	NC		**	NC		NS			**	NC	
TOB	**			**	NC		**	C	AVE									
RBP	NS			**	NC		**	NC		NS			**	NC		NS		
LTH	NS			**	NC		**	NC		NX	NC		NS			*	C	0.667
TEX	**	NC		NS			**	NC		**	NC		**	NC		**	NC	
KNT	NS			**	NC		**	NC		NS			*	C	0.389	NS		
CLO	NS			**	NC		**	NC		**	C	0.419	*	C	AVE	**	C	0.626
WOD	**	NC		*	C	AVE	*	C	AVE	**	NC		NS			*	C	AVE
FNT	NS			**	NC		**	NC		**	NS		NS			**	NC	
PPR	**	C	AVE	**	NC	NS	**	NC	**		NC	*		C	-0.085	*	C	-0.117
PUB	**	NC		**	NC		**	NC		**	NC		**	NC		*	NC	
PMT	*	C	-0.173	NS			NS			**	C	-0.177	**	NC		*	C	AVE
MFB	NS			**	C	0.132	**	C	0.108	NS			**	C	0.455	**	C	0.316
MCH	**	C	AVE	NS			**	NC		**	C	0.232	**	C	0.304	NS		
TN S	**	C	AVE	**	NC		NS			**	NC		**	NC		NS		
ELC	NS			*	C	0.117	*	C	0.173	NS			NS			**	NC	
PET	NS			**	C	-0.024	**	C	-0.219	**	C	-0.150	*	C	-0.135	**	C	AVE
CHM	NS			**	NC		**	NC		**	C	-0.221	**	NC		**	NC	
NMM	*	C	0.054	**	NC		NS			**	C	AVE	**	NC		*	C	AVE
MIS	**	NC		**	NC		**	NC		**	NC		**	NC		**	NC	

Notes: Column 1 reports the significance of the autoregression equations. Column 2 reports whether the deviation series converges at the 0.05 significance level. Column 3 reports the value to which the deviation series converge.

NS   Equation not significant.
*   Significant at the 0.05 level.
**   Significant at the 0.01 level.
C   Converge
NC   Does not converge.
AVE Converges to the industry average.
Source: see Table 8.6.

similar levels (even if they converge). Spatial barriers to equilibrium with equal rates of profit are less important than sectoral barriers.

8.5.3 Summary

In both US and Canadian manufacturing industries there are significant sectoral and spatial differences in rates of profit. There was between the mid-1950s and the late 1980s little tendency for either regional or sectoral rates of profit to converge to the national average: the data offer scant support to claims that the rates of profit of industries and regions converge to equilibrium. And even if the rates of profit of industries or regions did converge they were unlikely to converge to a common value: industries and regions exhibited different long-run rates of profit. There is evidence here that long-run (equilibrium) rates of profit in industries and regions differ—markets fail to remove inequalities in rates of profit even over the long run. Finally it seems that sectoral barriers to equal rates of profit are stronger than spatial barriers.

8.6 CONCLUSION

The central fact in this history is that in Australia, Canada, Japan, and the USA the rate of profit in manufacturing tended to fall into the early or mid-1980s. In the USA profitability climbed until the mid-1960s, then fell through the early 1980s, and has since recovered a little. The rate of profit in Australian manufacturing fell from the late 1960s until the early 1980s and then began to recover. In Canada the rate of profit in manufacturing declined from the mid-1950s until the early 1980s. In Japan the rate of profit continued to rise until the mid-1970s and has since fallen. So the slowdown of the late 1970s and 1980s was indeed accompanied by reduced rates of profit. As such the history is compatible with the accounts of Mandel, Lipietz, and Lash and Urry. The fact that rates of profit were falling from at least the late 1960s in Australia, Canada, and the USA seems to argue against the account of Piore and Sabel (in which falling profit rates are a consequence of the slowdown rather than a cause).

In all four economies the main factor causing rates of profit to fall was the rising value composition of capital. Profit rates fell when increases in the technical composition of capital were not offset by improvements in efficiency to reduce the unit value of plant, equipment, and raw materials. In Japan and the USA the shift from a rising to a falling value composition of capital occurred when gains in efficiency slowed. Only in Canada did falling rates of exploitation also assist in driving down rates of profit; everywhere else the rate of exploitation and the turnover time of capital have both tended to raise profit rates. There is little evidence that labor costs were rising faster than productivity when rates of profit were falling. These observations are compatible with Marxian accounts of the falling rate of profit (including that of Mandel), and the apparent role of slowdowns in efficiency accords with the story of Lipietz. It becomes especially important to investigate changes in efficiency more directly (as in Chapter 9). However, the fact that changes in the rate of exploitation have not driven rates of profit down is incompatible with Lipietz' argument.

In Australia and North America profit rates have begun to rise more recently. In Australia the rate of exploitation and the number of turnovers per year both increased more rapidly than in the 1970s. In Canada the rate of exploitation grew quickly but the effect of the value composition of capital diminished. In the USA the rate of profit was driven up by increases in the rate of exploitation and in the number of turnovers of capital per year. The real wage has stagnated since the early 1980s, so the rate of exploitation has risen as technical changes have reduced the unit value of consumption commodities. In none of these countries has there yet appeared development that can yield long-run growth and rising real wages: the recovery was fueled by deeper exploitation or stagnant technique rather than by high rates of investment that carry new techniques. This evidence does not distinguish the possible futures adduced by theorists of economic history.

More disturbing for accounts of the long boom (Lipietz, Piore and Sabel, and Lash and Urry) is the variety of history that has been uncovered. The history of rates of profit is not the same in the four countries: only in the USA was there a boom in profit rates that lasted until the mid-1960s, followed by a decline during the 1970s. Furthermore, while the crisis in US manufacturing has been spread widely over its manufacturing sectors, the histories of profitability in different industries are diverse. In 2 industries the rate of profit rose, and in 2 others it was more or less unchanged. In only 12 of the remaining 16 industries did the rate of profit fall, mainly because of changes in the value rate of profit, and in only 8 of those was that because the value composition of capital was driven upward by the technical composition of capital. (Ironically the history of profitability in the transport industry is different from that of every other industry.) Similarly in Canada, there are wide variations about the aggregate story among the individual industries and regions of the country. Only in 8 industries did rates of profit follow the Canadian manufacturing average down during the 1960s and 1970s because their value rates of profit fell; and in only 6 of those was history driven mainly by increases in the value composition of capital. The average has not been especially common. Variety and difference in timing and cause argue against the concept of an overarching long boom, though they are more in tune with Graham and colleagues' (1988) account of sectoral transitions.

Also problematic for accounts that link profitability and accumulation is evidence about these two rates. Quite clearly rates of profit and accumulation have shifted together: the two rates are certainly correlated. However, the links between them need more scrutiny. Whether profitability drives accumulation or conversely is not obvious from the lag structure of these data. Nor is it clear why changes in profitability are at some times but not at others associated with changes in the rate of accumulation. Models of accumulation must pay attention to this link.

The evidence hardly differentiates conclusively between the various accounts of economic history. However, it does point to some preferred accounts and requires modifications of others to reflect these facts: rates of profit fell; efficiency has been important; rates of exploitation have not driven profits down; and different countries, industries, and regions have different histories. The issue of the timing of changes in efficiency is especially important in the light of this evidence. And the role of the NICs needs to be assessed before the different accounts can be definitely evaluated.

Two additional conclusions have emerged.

The theory of the falling rate of profit is usually explained in terms of the value composition of capital and the rate of exploitation (and their determinants). Yet turnover times of capital and unequal exchange in the market between industries and regions can affect the history of rates of profit. In about one-third of Canadian and US industries the ability of firms to compete in the market has a greater effect on the rate of profit than does the value rate of profit.

In both US and Canadian manufacturing industries there are significant sectoral and spatial differences in rates of profit. Sectoral barriers to equal rates of profit are stronger than spatial barriers. Between the mid-1950s and the late 1980s neither regional or sectoral rates of profit tended to converge to the national average: there is little evidence that the rates of profit of industries and regions converge to equilibrium. And even if rates of profit did converge they were unlikely to converge to a common value: industries and regions exhibited different long-run rates of profit. Long-run (equilibrium) rates of profit in industries and regions differ—markets fail to remove inequalities in rates of profit even over the long run.

APPENDIX A8: COMPONENTS OF THE RATE OF PROFIT

A8.1 COMPONENTS OF THE RATE OF PROFIT IN US INDUSTRIES

A8.1.1 The Rate of Exploitation in US Industries

The rate of exploitation measures the ratio of surplus to variable capital in each industry (in units of value). In the economy as a whole the rate of exploitation is equivalent to the ratio of profits to wages (in prices: see Chapter 4). Within individual industries rates of exploitation differ from the ratios of profits to wages. We are forced (by lack of data) to assume that all workers buy an identical basket of commodities no matter what industry they work in. (Of course, on average workers in a high-wage industry buy more of the basket than do workers in a low-wage industry.) The value of each basket is the same; so the rate of exploitation differs among industries as the real wage. Therefore the difference between the rate of exploitation and the ratio of profits to wages indexes the extent to which firms within an industry obtain labor at a price that differs from the market average. This is one form of competition.

Table A8.1 reports rates of exploitation in all 20 manufacturing sectors. The years are those of peaks and troughs of the most pronounced cycles in the US profit rate series. Differences in the rate of exploitation are wide. Averaged over the business cycle turning points, the rate of exploitation is more than 1 SD above the mean for all manufacturing in the tobacco, apparel, leather, textile, and lumber industries. These are labor-intensive industries. The rate of exploitation is at least 1 SD below the manufacturing average in the petroleum & coal sector and is also relatively low in the transport industry.

Between 1962 and 1990 the rate of exploitation in US manufacturing as a whole increased by about 25%. The rate increased in 19 of the 20 sectors; the exception was the tobacco industry. The fastest growth in the rate of exploitation, more than three times the manufacturing average, occurred in the petroleum, miscellaneous, publishing, rubber & plastics, and primary metals industries. Apart from the tobacco industry, the slowest growth in the rate of exploitation was found in the wood and pulp & paper industries. In addition to this trend the history of rates of exploitation reveals a cycle: rates of exploitation have been higher during peaks than during troughs in all sectors barring apparel (in which the trend dominated the cycle). The fluctuations are especially marked in the petroleum & coal sector. Over the four business cycles, rates of exploitation are positively correlated with rates of profit: if corporations respond to depressed profits by seeking to raise the rate of exploitation, their efforts succeed with a lag of about half a complete business cycle.

Since the unit value of consumer goods (λ_2) is assumed to be the same for all workers, differences in the rate of exploitation between industries reflect differences in the hourly real wage they pay. Table A8.2 reports hourly real wages in manufacturing industries. Hourly real wages are highest, more than 1 SD above the manufacturing mean, in the petroleum, transport, and primary metals sectors. Wages are lowest, at least 1 SD below average, in the labor-intensive apparel, leather, textile, and furniture industries. Wage rates differ markedly between industries: on average between 1962 and 1990 the range of hourly wages (between the best- and the worst-paying industries) almost equaled the manufacturing mean. Furthermore the differences between industries' hourly wages are becoming more acute: standardizing by the mean manufacturing wage, we find that the variance in industry wages increased from 4.97 in 1962 to 9.50 in 1990.

Real wages in individual industries generally followed a common pat-

TABLE A8.1. The rate of exploitation in US industries, 1962–1990

Industry	Year							
	1962	1965	1970	1973	1976	1979	1982	1990
FNK	0.917	1.034	0.915	1.021	0.885	1.130	1.013	1.315
TOB	0.972	1.034	0.793	0.894	0.643	0.610	0.301	0.284
TEX	1.574	1.696	1.597	1.753	1.747	1.977	1.822	2.043
APP	1.542	1.800	1.746	1.950	2.127	2.395	2.335	2.466
WOD	1.476	1.518	1.335	1.315	1.255	1.405	1.344	1.687
FNT	1.255	1.309	1.289	1.400	1.420	1.666	1.480	1.661
PPR	0.764	0.848	0.722	0.823	0.775	0.858	0.721	0.888
PUB	0.613	0.720	0.712	0.752	0.871	1.091	0.998	1.223
CHM	0.437	0.523	0.489	0.616	0.551	0.620	0.499	0.571
PET	0.081	0.122	0.045	0.306	0.170	0.178	0.059	0.280
RBP	0.682	0.828	0.819	0.947	0.979	1.127	1.035	1.273
LTH	1.479	1.619	1.500	1.812	1.878	2.083	1.992	2.093
SCG	0.803	0.883	0.813	0.877	0.889	0.964	0.860	1.382
PMT	0.373	0.460	0.463	0.483	0.387	0.394	0.311	0.674
FBM	0.737	0.825	0.745	0.803	0.770	0.946	0.803	1.042
MCH	0.550	0.634	0.570	0.664	0.686	0.775	0.643	0.838
ELC	0.652	0.742	0.686	0.814	0.777	0.943	0.756	0.913
TNS	0.387	0.394	0.307	0.406	0.391	0.412	0.324	0.474
INS	0.478	0.616	0.615	0.759	0.758	0.933	0.731	0.687
MIS	0.716	1.208	1.153	1.263	1.291	1.580	1.373	1.576
Total	0.715	0.815	0.748	0.838	0.799	0.917	0.802	0.891

Source: *Census of Manufactures* and *Annual Survey of Manufactures* Washington DC: U.S. Department of Commerce.

tern—rising during the 1960s and thereafter showing only slight gains. The most remarkable exception is the tobacco industry, in which real wages grew consistently (by 115% between 1962 and 1990). Higher than average growth of real wages also occurred in the transport, pulp & paper, wood, and chemical industries. In the miscellaneous sector hourly real wages declined by 6.7% between 1962 and 1990 and in the apparel, publishing, rubber & plastics, leather, and stone, clay, & glass industries, real wages increased by less than a quarter of the manufacturing average.

Increases in real wages tend to reduce the rate of exploitation. So in 19 of the 20 industries rising real wages tended to depress the rate of exploitation, particularly in sectors where wages increased most (the exception was the miscellaneous sector). The impact of the wage gains was dampened, however, as the unit value of the basket of consumption commodities fell (Figure 8.20). Reductions in the value of the basket of consumption commodities pushed the value of labor power down and tended to raise the rate of exploitation, especially until 1974. The rate of exploitation increased after 1974, when real wages stagnated while the unit value of consumer goods continued to fall (though more slowly than before).

TABLE A8.2. The hourly real wage in US industries, 1962–1990 ($82)

Industry	Year							
	1962	1965	1970	1973	1976	1979	1982	1990
FNK	8.78	9.34	10.16	11.09	11.45	11.35	11.12	10.18
TOB	8.54	9.24	10.85	11.83	13.14	15.02	17.21	18.35
TEX	6.54	6.97	7.49	8.14	7.86	8.12	7.93	7.74
APP	6.63	6.71	7.08	7.59	6.90	7.12	6.71	6.80
WOD	6.80	7.46	8.33	9.68	9.57	10.06	9.55	8.77
FNT	7.47	8.14	8.50	9.34	8.92	9.07	9.02	8.86
PPR	9.54	10.17	11.30	12.29	12.16	13.01	13.00	12.48
PUB	10.44	10.92	11.36	12.79	11.54	11.57	11.20	11.10
CHM	11.72	12.33	13.06	13.87	13.92	14.93	14.93	15.00
PET	15.57	16.75	18.61	17.16	18.45	20.53	21.13	18.41
RBP	10.01	10.28	10.70	11.51	10.91	11.37	11.00	10.37
LTH	6.79	7.18	7.78	7.97	7.50	7.84	7.48	7.62
SCG	9.34	9.98	10.73	11.94	11.43	12.32	12.04	9.89
PMT	12.26	12.87	13.30	15.11	15.57	17.35	17.08	14.07
FBM	9.69	10.29	11.15	12.43	12.20	12.43	12.41	11.54
MCH	10.86	11.50	12.39	13.47	12.80	13.63	13.62	12.82
ELC	10.19	10.79	11.54	12.35	12.15	12.45	12.75	12.32
TNS	12.14	13.48	14.89	15.93	15.53	17.12	16.91	15.98
INS	11.19	11.63	12.04	12.74	12.28	12.51	12.93	13.97
MIS	9.81	8.51	9.04	9.90	9.42	9.37	9.43	9.15
Total	9.82	10.36	11.13	12.19	12.00	12.62	12.42	12.46

Note: see Figure 8.18 for the method of calculation.
Source: see Table A8.1.

A8.1.2 The Value Composition of Capital in US Industries

Changes in the value composition of capital can be read from Table A8.3. There are wide differences between industries' value compositions. In capital-intensive sectors such as petroleum & coal and pulp & paper, the value compositions are respectively nearly four times and twice the average for all industry. The value composition is also 87% above average in the textile industry, reflecting the low value of labor power in that sector. In these three sectors the value composition of capital is more than 1 SD above the industry norm. In no sector is the value composition at least 1 SD below the manufacturing average, although it is remarkably low in the tobacco, machinery, and electronics industries.

The ratio of constant capital to variable capital increased in the US manufacturing sector by 57% from 1962 to 1990, particularly during the early and mid-1970s. The composition of capital rose in all industries except tobacco, but its history was quite different in different industries. Generally the value composition increased slowly during the 1960s, more rapidly in the 1970s, and only slowly during the 1980s. Clear exceptions to this pattern occur in

TABLE A8.3. The value composition of capital in US industries, 1962–1990

Industry	Year							
	1962	1965	1970	1973	1976	1979	1982	1990
FNK	13.894	15.194	14.487	17.901	17.774	22.183	21.508	22.379
TOB	4.296	4.383	2.836	3.700	3.144	3.258	2.151	1.297
TEX	11.988	12.619	15.147	16.265	22.426	24.564	27.355	26.347
APP	5.106	5.685	5.664	6.679	8.640	9.203	9.631	9.214
WOD	13.782	14.995	14.938	12.693	18.164	19.005	28.952	22.606
FNT	5.718	5.640	5.946	6.484	8.352	9.044	8.951	10.705
PPR	15.998	16.688	17.265	17.813	20.020	24.114	24.732	25.144
PUB	5.426	6.053	6.659	7.333	8.727	9.613	9.550	10.670
CHM	7.400	7.530	8.428	9.980	11.373	14.066	14.755	11.069
PET	29.140	28.447	31.986	43.911	49.406	32.691	47.095	52.287
RBP	7.438	8.000	9.236	9.811	13.323	14.625	14.798	15.109
LTH	5.027	5.312	5.403	6.984	7.856	9.251	9.579	10.323
SCG	10.213	10.715	11.375	12.074	14.265	15.899	17.685	16.266
PMT	10.408	11.086	14.083	15.075	14.154	14.529	22.672	23.313
FBM	6.514	6.215	6.543	6.502	7.266	8.455	9.600	12.296
MCH	4.247	3.954	4.178	4.238	5.178	5.371	5.772	8.635
ELC	3.734	3.781	4.311	4.780	6.189	5.733	6.112	11.116
TNS	6.872	6.631	6.326	7.176	8.412	8.376	8.056	7.809
INS	3.292	3.192	3.391	3.915	4.205	5.364	5.166	4.212
MIS	3.214	5.387	5.171	5.539	6.942	8.310	7.818	8.166
Total	8.111	8.394	8.689	9.498	11.401	12.180	13.000	12.748

Source: see Table 8.5.

the lumber and the petroleum & coal sectors, in which the growth of the value composition was more erratic; the fabricated metals and machinery sectors, which have enjoyed small but steady increases in the value composition through the 1980s; the primary metals industry, which recorded rapid increases in the value composition during late 1960s and early 1980s; and the transport sector, in which the value composition stagnated through the 1980s. The fastest rise in the value composition, more than twice the manufacturing average, occurred in the electronics, miscellaneous, primary metals, and textile industries. In these sectors downward pressure on the rate of profit is largest.

Table A8.4 offers some explanation for the specific industry trends of the value composition of capital. Of the forces acting on the value composition, the direct effect of technical change is dominant. In all industries increases in the technical composition raised the value composition—especially in the petroleum & coal sector and, to a lesser extent, the paper, food, textile, and primary metals industries. Only in the tobacco industry is the effect of the technical composition dominated by the effects of changes in the value of capital goods. Essentially, increases in the technical composition of capital were driving the value composition up; the net offsetting effect of changes in the value

TABLE A8.4. The determinants of the value composition of capital in US industries, 1965–1990

Industry	dq	Effect of the value of capital goods	Effect of the technical composition of capital	Effect of the value of labor power
FNK	7.181	−7.756	12.333	2.003
TOB	−3.086	−4.182	2.616	−1.741
TEX	13.729	−0.300	12.060	2.362
APP	3.530	−0.925	3.018	1.455
WOD	7.612	−0.026	6.450	1.355
FNT	5.065	−0.868	5.082	0.799
PPR	8.457	−7.958	16.645	0.175
PUB	4.617	−1.384	4.767	1.508
CHM	3.540	−4.355	8.740	−0.149
PET	23.841	−21.794	44.891	5.760
RBP	7.109	0.045	4.748	2.385
LTH	5.011	−2.112	6.123	1.055
SCG	5.551	0.426	2.663	3.153
PMT	12.227	−1.538	11.507	4.137
FBM	6.081	−0.367	5.549	0.968
MCH	9.466	−1.748	10.639	0.714
ELC	7.335	−1.853	8.648	0.409
TNS	1.177	−1.514	3.003	0.349
INS	0.448	−1.557	2.012	−0.186
MIS	2.779	−1.551	3.612	0.821
Total	4.354	−3.027	7.239	0.229

Note: Calculated using equation (8.8).
Source: see Table 8.5.

of means of production and in the value of labor power were relatively small in virtually all industries.

There are significant differences in the ratio of constant capital per hour of labor power between industries (Table A8.5). In every year between 1962 and 1990 the technical composition in the petroleum & coal sector was more than an order of magnitude greater than in manufacturing as a whole. It is also two to three times the manufacturing average in the pulp & paper and chemical sectors, and about twice the manufacturing average in the food and primary metals sectors. In the apparel, furniture, leather, and miscellaneous sectors the technical composition is well below half the manufacturing average.

Even though the magnitude of the technical composition varies widely across industries, it increased strongly throughout manufacturing. In most industries recorded the technical composition rose most steeply during the late 1960s and the early 1970s. Through the 1980s the technical composition has generally risen more slowly; however, in the tobacco, electronics, and machinery industries it rose more quickly; and in the lumber, petroleum & coal, rub-

TABLE A8.5. The technical composition of capital in US industries, 1962–1990

Industry	Year							
	1962	1965	1970	1973	1976	1979	1982	1990
FNK	145.784	167.479	195.751	246.649	252.500	290.081	305.463	332.060
TOB	76.000	82.111	75.525	97.943	105.781	123.761	133.446	215.895
TEX	54.560	60.275	76.002	87.407	97.478	109.831	118.398	119.605
APP	21.741	23.213	25.391	29.785	31.258	32.534	34.382	35.644
WOD	61.585	74.083	88.825	105.458	118.702	136.478	151.041	122.483
FNT	32.590	34.724	38.310	43.220	48.652	50.022	54.672	65.996
PPR	161.820	179.008	217.694	238.889	263.090	319.049	345.596	405.327
PUB	65.532	72.849	82.521	102.356	95.310	102.155	104.045	129.259
CHM	171.863	193.571	217.774	275.762	301.620	406.607	388.960	439.463
PET	894.210	1071.150	1305.490	1833.640	2226.600	2905.020	2632.020	2929.810
RBP	79.554	84.369	101.387	115.944	129.783	134.910	138.256	135.083
LTH	23.506	24.975	29.074	32.250	32.605	38.420	41.578	52.840
SCG	104.325	114.834	129.263	150.432	153.201	184.603	182.274	144.421
PMT	144.861	169.806	201.551	251.519	227.561	274.149	295.889	333.357
FBM	58.957	59.841	73.509	78.799	84.901	95.329	105.035	120.837
MCH	46.672	46.863	52.821	59.050	63.550	72.596	81.198	127.901
ELC	36.713	40.104	49.114	56.161	65.619	65.640	76.772	152.215
TNS	98.349	113.391	107.040	131.771	134.659	155.801	151.328	159.637
INS	42.514	45.060	53.225	61.125	64.887	73.019	80.566	81.815
MIS	30.255	37.332	40.011	45.777	51.471	57.865	61.840	63.469
Total	83.219	89.557	97.902	113.430	129.190	143.024	161.424	173.690

Note: Calculated using equation (8.9).
Source: see Table 8.5.

ber & plastics, and stone, clay, & glass sectors it declined. The most rapid rates of increase in the ratio of capital to labor, more than 1 SD above the manufacturing standard, were recorded by the electronics (315%), petroleum & coal (228%), tobacco (184%), and machinery (174%) sectors. Sluggish rates of increase in the technical composition of capital were recorded by the stone, clay, & glass (38%), transport (62%), apparel (64%), and rubber & plastics (70%) sectors.

Different forms of technological change have affected the technical composition of capital in each industry differently (Table A8.6). Technical change proper, increases in the intensity of labor, and reductions in capacity utilization rates have generally tended to increase the technical composition, but changes in turnover times had a more variable impact. The direct impact of technical change proper (that is, increases in the capital/labor ratio at full capacity) dominated the movement of the technical composition of capital in 7 industries; the direct impact of reductions in capacity utilization dominated the movement of the technical composition in 11 industries; and changes in the speed of production dominated the technical composition in 2 industries. Increases in turnover times exerted about the same effect on the technical composition as did changes in the throughput of fuel and materials per hour

Table A8.6. The determinants of the technical composition of capital in US industries, 1965–1990

Industry	dP	Effect of turnover times	Effect of capacity utilization	Effect of technical change	Effect of labor intensity
FNK	164.580	13.123	87.069	43.768	13.829
TOB	133.780	–6.145	6.451	98.075	13.055
TEX	59.330	9.689	28.717	7.218	3.205
APP	12.431	–3.025	13.212	0.875	–0.689
WOD	48.400	4.760	–20.288	20.117	9.045
FNT	31.272	–0.197	18.376	5.438	2.989
PPR	226.320	–13.804	84.691	115.850	18.213
PUB	56.410	–6.842	33.690	18.747	3.026
CHM	245.890	–16.600	51.113	152.760	29.707
PET	1858.700	–1112.100	–551.550	1931.600	291.640
RBP	50.714	5.816	11.414	10.997	4.027
LTH	27.869	–8.836	16.207	9.038	6.969
SCG	29.587	–13.510	3.402	17.668	4.792
PMT	163.550	–22.338	26.315	71.096	17.047
FBM	60.996	11.638	25.524	9.251	5.099
MCH	151.930	48.679	21.060	27.623	12.619
ELC	112.110	8.845	49.324	28.771	10.879
TNS	46.246	–67.742	26.622	33.199	15.197
INS	28.683	–10.316	–18.226	19.300	4.420
MIS	26.137	–2.632	10.463	8.566	4.672
Total	84.133	–0.253	34.695	30.181	9.237

Note: Calculated using equation (8.9).
Source: see Table 8.5.

of labor. Reductions in turnover times tended to raise the technical composition of capital in manufacturing as a whole, though in most industries the speed at which capital is turned over declined between 1962 and 1990 and this dampened the rising technical composition. In all but 3 industries—the instruments, lumber, and petroleum & coal sectors—capacity utilization rates declined steeply.

The turnover time of capital indicates the average time between advancing capital to fund production and recouping that investment through sale. The turnover time measures the speed of production. A reduction in turnover time tends to raise the rate of profit. Changes in turnover times are linked to the business cycle (Table A8.7). In manufacturing as a whole the speed of production increased only slightly after 1962, though most reductions in turnover time are linked to business cycle upswings, for reductions in inventories mean a faster throughput of commodities into the market. The speed of production increased in 13 of 20 industries—but cyclically. Changes in the speed of production have exerted little consistent pressure on the movement of the rate of profit.

TABLE A8.7. The annual number of turnovers in US industries, 1962–1990

Industry	Year							
	1962	1965	1970	1973	1976	1979	1982	1990
FNK	8.806	9.207	8.992	9.526	9.333	9.641	9.767	10.006
TOB	1.341	1.413	1.475	1.644	1.581	1.837	1.291	1.641
TEX	5.235	5.591	5.532	5.872	5.447	6.510	6.331	6.618
APP	7.009	6.474	5.762	5.692	5.455	5.688	5.864	5.443
WOD	5.832	6.617	6.089	7.326	5.775	7.277	6.928	7.826
FNT	6.168	6.052	4.988	4.803	4.395	5.044	4.779	5.642
PPR	7.802	7.794	7.381	7.956	6.575	7.871	7.465	7.611
PUB	8.821	9.334	8.445	8.681	7.696	8.427	8.609	8.871
CHM	5.494	5.517	4.907	5.566	4.772	6.066	5.352	5.574
PET	8.685	9.471	9.829	11.915	12.261	16.842	11.372	12.031
RBP	6.204	6.262	5.692	6.278	5.475	6.479	6.215	6.798
LTH	6.199	6.320	5.802	5.544	5.227	5.319	5.086	4.591
SCG	6.000	6.273	5.766	6.527	5.403	6.770	5.621	6.090
PMT	4.894	5.843	5.121	6.287	4.162	5.468	4.277	5.797
FBM	5.005	4.587	4.517	4.869	4.025	4.870	4.623	5.584
MCH	3.610	3.587	3.225	3.405	3.142	3.556	3.101	4.146
ELC	4.632	4.430	3.837	4.086	3.757	4.015	3.804	4.656
TNS	6.733	6.777	4.265	5.815	4.922	5.760	4.260	4.173
INS	3.921	3.773	3.362	3.167	2.933	3.352	3.180	3.302
MIS	5.368	4.751	4.038	3.855	3.554	4.110	3.870	4.347
Total	5.746	5.827	5.075	5.668	5.078	5.903	5.264	5.858

Note: see Figure 8.24 for the method of calculation.
Source: see Table 8.5.

A8.1.3 The Value Rate of Profit in US Industries

The value rate of profit measures the return on capital advanced when all commodities exchange in the market at their respective values. Changes in the value rate of profit reflect changes in the rate of exploitation, the value composition of capital, and the turnover time of capital. Now we examine how the value rate of profit has been influenced by these components.

Table A8.8 reports the value rate of profit through the business cycles between 1962 and 1990 in the 20 manufacturing industries. The level of profitability is somewhat higher than other estimates (Dumenil et al. 1987) because we used census estimates of value added to measure the labor time expended in production. Estimates of value added tend to be inflated because the shipments of intermediate goods between firms are double counted. However, the trends in our estimates accord well with those of Dumenil et al. (1987), and it is these trends and their determinants that are important here.

The value rate of profit differs widely between industries. Value rates of profit are inversely related to labor intensity. Between 1962 and 1990 the value rate of profit was more than 1 SD above the manufacturing average in the

TABLE A8.8. The value rate of profit in US industries, 1962–1990

Industry	Year							
	1962	1965	1970	1973	1976	1979	1982	1990
FNK	0.542	0.575	0.518	0.514	0.440	0.470	0.440	0.563
TOB	0.246	0.271	0.305	0.313	0.425	0.263	0.123	0.203
TEX	0.634	0.696	0.547	0.596	0.406	0.504	0.407	0.494
APP	1.771	1.743	1.510	1.455	1.203	1.335	1.283	1.314
WOD	0.582	0.628	0.510	0.704	0.378	0.511	0.311	0.559
FNT	1.152	1.193	0.926	0.898	0.667	0.836	0.710	0.801
PPR	0.351	0.373	0.292	0.348	0.243	0.269	0.209	0.259
PUB	0.842	0.953	0.795	0.783	0.689	0.866	0.814	0.853
CHM	0.286	0.339	0.255	0.312	0.212	0.250	0.170	0.264
PET	0.023	0.039	0.014	0.081	0.041	0.089	0.014	0.0 63
RBP	0.502	0.576	0.455	0.550	0.374	0.467	0.407	0.537
LTH	1.522	1.621	1.360	1.258	1.108	1.081	0.958	0.848
SCG	0.430	0.473	0.379	0.438	0.315	0.386	0.259	0.487
PMT	0.160	0.222	0.157	0.189	0.106	0.139	0.056	0.161
FBM	0.491	0.525	0.446	0.521	0.375	0.487	0.350	0.437
MCH	0.380	0.459	0.355	0.431	0.349	0.432	0.295	0.361
ELC	0.637	0.688	0.495	0.575	0.406	0.559	0.404	0.351
TNS	0.331	0.350	0.179	0.289	0.204	0.253	0.152	0.225
INS	0.437	0.554	0.471	0.489	0.390	0.492	0.377	0.435
MIS	0.912	0.899	0.755	0.745	0.578	0.698	0.602	0.747
Total	0.451	0.505	0.392	0.454	0.327	0.411	0.302	0.380

Note: see Figure A8.6 for the method of calculation.
Source: see Table 8.5.

labor-intensive apparel, leather, and furniture industries. It was marginally less than 1 SD above average in the miscellaneous sector. As one might expect, the value profit rate was at least 1 SD below average in the most capital-intensive sector, petroleum & coal. It was also relatively low in the primary metals sector.

Between 1962 and 1990 the value rate of profit in US manufacturing as a whole declined by 15.7%. Of the 20 individual sectors the value rate of profit fell in 14. Between the peaks of 1965 and 1990 the value rate of profit fell in 18 of the 20 industries. The greatest reductions in the value rate of profit occurred in the apparel and leather industries, both of which suffered profit rate declines nearly three times greater than the manufacturing average. The electronics and furniture industries also performed poorly, losing profits twice as fast as the industry norm. The food, textiles, and miscellaneous sectors also lost profits faster than the manufacturing average. The only sectors to register gains in the value rate of profit between 1965 and 1990 were the petroleum & coal and the stone, clay, & glass sectors.

In manufacturing as a whole, increases in the value composition of capital tended to depress the rate of profit; increased turnover times had the same effect; increases in the rate of exploitation only partially offset the effect of

TABLE A8.9. The determinants of the value rate of profit in US industries, 1965–1990

Industry	$d\pi_v$	Effect of the rate of exploitation	Effect of the value composition of capital	Effect of turnover times
FNK	−0.130	0.158	−0.209	0.032
TOB	−0.068	−0.262	0.141	0.021
TEX	−0.202	0.092	−0.429	0.053
APP	−0.429	0.463	−0.696	−0.300
WOD	−0.069	0.066	−0.356	−0.001
FNT	−0.393	0.224	−0.541	−0.161
PPR	−0.115	0.013	−0.144	−0.031
PUB	−0.100	0.407	−0.445	−0.086
CHM	−0.075	0.031	−0.124	−0.024
PET	0.024	0.001	−0.040	0.010
RBP	−0.038	0.223	−0.343	−0.002
LTH	−0.772	0.326	−0.784	−0.416
SCG	0.015	0.206	−0.183	−0.054
PMT	−0.061	0.012	−0.106	−0.056
FBM	−0.087	0.106	−0.284	0.041
MCH	−0.046	0.102	−0.452	0.158
ELC	−0.337	0.113	−0.468	−0.052
TNS	−0.125	0.046	−0.029	−0.223
INS	−0.053	0.084	−0.127	−0.096
MIS	−0.151	0.200	−0.268	−0.152
Total	−0.126	0.039	−0.167	−0.035

Note: Calculated using equation (8.6).
Source: see Table 8.5.

these two variables (Table A8.9). Individual industries reveal quite different patterns. In two sectors—tobacco and stone, clay, & glass—movements in the rate of exploitation had the greatest effect on the value rate of profit: increases in the rate of exploitation tended to raise profitability (except in the tobacco industry). In the transport sector changes in turnover time dominate reductions in the rate of profit. In the remaining 17 sectors, the largest single effect on the value rate of profit is the value composition of capital. In 13 of those 17 sectors, increases in the value composition were too large to be compensated by increases in the rate of exploitation and the speed of production; in the other 4 sectors changes in the rate of exploitation and the turnover time of capital more than compensated for increases in the value composition of capital.

A8.1.4 Price–Value Profit Rate Deviations in US Industries

Firms compete for profits in the market as well as in production. In the market firms can gain profits by purchasing inputs below their value as well as by selling outputs at prices above their value. Firms can realize profits in the market to boost the price rate of profit above the value rate. Such market competition is the process of unequal exchange. Thus an hour of labor power in one sector may command a higher or lower market price than an hour of labor power in another sector.

The deviations of value and price rates of profit by industry are revealed in Table A8.10. The numbers in this table are the ratio of the price rate of profit to the value rate in each industry each year. Values greater (less) than unity indicate a price rate of profit higher (lower) than the value rate.

Three broad groups of industries may be identified (by a k-means classification of industries on the data in Table A8.10). Industries that consistently gain a lot of profit in the market are the tobacco, chemicals, and petroleum & coal sectors; these are the market-efficient group. Within this group the tobacco sector improved its ability to compete in the market: the price/value profit rate ratio increased from about 1.6 in the 1960s to 2.1 in the 1970s, and over 5 in the 1980s. The petroleum & coal sector is noteworthy for large fluctuations in its market performance over the business cycle. During upswings the price/value ratio falls in the petroleum & coal sector, only to rise again during

TABLE A8.10. Price–value profit rate deviations in US industries, 1962–1990

Industry	Year							
	1962	1965	1970	1973	1976	1979	1982	1990
FNK	1.103	1.087	1.200	1.153	1.266	1.126	1.225	1.177
TOB	1.665	1.630	2.006	1.799	2.294	2.330	4.417	6.653
TEX	0.565	0.601	0.562	0.591	0.493	0.554	0.528	0.616
APP	0.518	0.517	0.563	0.537	0.517	0.535	0.575	0.614
WOD	0.492	0.523	0.579	0.799	0.583	0.692	0.372	0.564
FNT	0.611	0.621	0.630	0.623	0.577	0.599	0.646	0.641
PPR	1.008	0.986	1.033	1.009	1.098	1.001	1.099	1.211
PUB	1.064	1.008	1.027	1.026	0.918	0.923	0.969	1.004
CHM	2.231	2.087	2.045	1.849	1.959	1.847	1.922	2.148
PET	6.504	5.278	12.264	2.916	4.532	5.470	11.660	3.362
RBP	0.931	0.900	0.909	0.921	0.835	0.767	0.820	0.811
LTH	0.519	0.514	0.590	0.525	0.538	0.549	0.596	0.676
SCG	1.002	0.981	0.955	0.955	0.904	0.935	0.799	0.805
PMT	1.223	1.261	1.002	1.059	1.063	1.178	0.007	0.919
FBM	0.850	0.871	0.918	0.864	0.906	0.865	0.822	0.723
MCH	0.991	1.050	1.050	1.048	0.924	1.026	1.055	0.995
ELC	0.952	0.971	0.930	0.894	0.820	0.902	0.978	1.009
TNS	1.322	1.480	1.210	1.285	1.126	1.183	1.333	1.335
INS	1.218	1.313	1.378	1.282	1.168	1.125	1.269	1.333
MIS	0.856	0.764	0.781	0.776	0.755	0.761	0.841	0.813

Note: see Figure A8.7 for the method of calculation.
Source: see Table 8.5.

downswings. Industries that consistently lose a lot of profit in the market are the textiles, apparel, wood, furniture, rubber & plastics, leather, fabricated metals, and miscellaneous sectors. In the remaining group of industries the price rate of profit is equal to or slightly above the value rate of profit. The primary metals industry belongs to this last group: its relatively strong market performance prior to the recession of 1979–1982 has been succeeded by more recent losses in the market. Apart from the primary metals industry, industries have remained consistently within the same group: the Spearman correlation between the rank of an industry's price/value ratio in one year and that in another exceeds +0.91 for all pairs of years. The capacity to capture profits in the market seems to be a relatively long-run structural characteristic of most industries.

Industries that lose profits in the market are characterized by relatively low real wages, high rates of exploitation, and a low technical composition of capital. A dollar's worth of output in these sectors embodies more labor time than the average; when this output is traded, surplus value is lost to other sectors whose output embodies below-average quantities of socially necessary labor time. This transfer of value between sectors (and regions) is a form of unequal exchange.

A8.1.5 The Price Rate of Profit in US Industries

There are wide variations in profitability between US industries (Table A8.11). The highest levels of profitability are recorded by the apparel and publishing industries, both of which recorded rates of profit of over 0.70 in 1982. The other industries with above-average levels of profitability are the food, tobacco, furniture, leather, electrical, instruments, and miscellaneous sectors. At the other extreme are the wood products, petroleum & coal, and primary metals industries, in which profit rates were less than 0.17 in 1982. (This classification was obtained by a k-means procedure that sought four groups from 1982 rates of profit; $F = 61.41$; df = 3, 16; $p < 0.001$.) Price/value profit rate ratios are not correlated with price rates of profit: some industries with high price/value profit rate ratios have high rates of profit (tobacco, transport), but others have low rates of profit (petroleum & coal and primary metals).

Between 1962 and 1990 in US manufacturing the price rate of profit fell by almost 16%. The price rate of profit declined in 15 of 20 manufacturing industries. Between the peak of 1965 and that of 1990 the price rate of profit declined in 18 of the 20 industries and was static in just one; the rate decreased by a little over 25% in manufacturing as a whole. The economic crisis appears to be spread wide across manufacturing: only the food, tobacco, and petroleum & coal sectors have escaped. Though the crisis of profitability has been general, some industries have suffered far more than others. Since 1962

TABLE A8.11. The price rate of profit in US industries, 1962–1990

				Year				
Industry	1962	1965	1970	1973	1976	1979	1982	1990
FNK	0.597	0.625	0.662	0.594	0.557	0.529	0.589	0.686
TOB	0.410	0.442	0.612	0.562	0.562	0.614	0.544	1.350
TEX	0.359	0.419	0.308	0.352	0.200	0.279	0.215	0.305
APP	0.917	0.901	0.849	0.776	0.623	0.715	0.741	0.806
WOD	0.287	0.329	0.295	0.562	0.221	0.354	0.116	0.315
FNT	0.704	0.741	0.583	0.559	0.385	0.501	0.459	0.513
PPR	0.353	0.368	0.301	0.351	0.266	0.269	0.230	0.313
PUB	0.896	0.955	0.817	0.804	0.633	0.799	0.789	0.857
CHM	0.637	0.707	0.521	0.577	0.416	0.461	0.326	0.566
PET	0.152	0.206	0.166	0.237	0.188	0.487	0.163	0.212
RBP	0.467	0.518	0.414	0.506	0.312	0.359	0.334	0.436
LTH	0.790	0.833	0.802	0.661	0.596	0.593	0.571	0.573
SCG	0.431	0.464	0.361	0.418	0.284	0.361	0.207	0.392
PMT	0.196	0.280	0.157	0.200	0.113	0.164	0.000	0.148
FBM	0.417	0.457	0.409	0.450	0.340	0.421	0.288	0.316
MCH	0.376	0.482	0.373	0.452	0.340	0.421	0.311	0.354
ELC	0.606	0.667	0.461	0.514	0.333	0.504	0.396	0.354
TNS	0.437	0.517	0.216	0.371	0.230	0.300	0.203	0.300
INS	0.532	0.731	0.654	0.627	0.455	0.553	0.478	0.580
MIS	0.800	0.687	0.589	0.578	0.436	0.531	0.507	0.608
Total	0.451	0.505	0.392	0.459	0.327	0.411	0.302	0.380

Note: see Figure 8.3 for the method of calculation.
Source: see Table 8.5.

the largest reductions in profitability were recorded by the electronics and transport sectors (their reductions in profitability were twice the manufacturing average). In the furniture, leather, miscellaneous, and metalworking industries profitability declined over 50% faster than in manufacturing as a whole.

The effect of production and market efficiency on the price rate of profit between 1965 and 1990 is illustrated in Table A8.12. In 15 of the 20 sectors competition in production exerted the largest influence on the price rate of profit realized by firms. In the other 5 sectors competition in the market dominated changes in price rates of profit. The tobacco and petroleum & coal sectors exhibit the strongest gains in market performance over the period examined. Improvements in market performance also gave a significant boost to profitability in the leather and apparel industries. Deteriorating market performance compounded the effects of reduced value rates of profit in the metalworking, transport, textiles, and lumber industries. Weakening market performance was directly responsible for reducing the price rate of profit in the rubber & plastic and the stone, clay, & glass sectors.

TABLE A8.12. The determinants of the price rate of profit in US industries, 1965–1990

Industry	$d\pi_p$	Effect of deviation between price and value	Effect of value rate of profit
FNK	0.061	0.071	0.007
TOB	0.907	0.980	0.139
TEX	–0.114	–0.013	–0.129
APP	–0.095	0.115	–0.233
WOD	–0.013	–0.026	–0.111
FNT	–0.228	0.015	–0.249
PPR	–0.055	0.070	–0.125
PUB	–0.099	0.008	–0.099
CHM	–0.141	0.010	–0.107
PET	0.006	0.795	0.321
RBP	–0.082	–0.054	–0.033
LTH	–0.260	0.170	–0.447
SCG	–0.071	–0.090	0.008
PMT	–0.132	–0.084	–0.163
FBM	–0.141	–0.054	–0.077
MCH	–0.071	–0.022	–0.060
ELC	–0.313	0.003	–0.325
TNS	–0.217	–0.084	–0.124
INS	–0.060	0.011	–0.044
MIS	–0.079	0.027	–0.114

Note: Calculated using equation (8.5).
Source: see Table 8.5.

A8.2 COMPONENTS OF THE RATE OF PROFIT IN CANADIAN INDUSTRIES

A8.2.1 The Rate of Exploitation in Canadian Industries

The rate of exploitation varies between Canadian industries (Table A8.13). In manufacturing as a whole, the rate of exploitation averaged 1.63, implying that for every dollar advanced to cover wages, $1.63 was realized as profits. On average between 1955 and 1986 the rate of exploitation ranged from a low of 0.79 in the petroleum & coal sector to over 3.0 in the knitting and clothing industries. The rate of exploitation was also greater than 1 SD above average in the leather, textiles, and furniture industries. These differences reflect variations in real wages since workers in all sectors are assumed to purchase the same basket of consumption commodities (though in different amounts).

The rate of exploitation moves pro-cyclically (it is higher in peaks than in troughs, as in US industries). Overall from 1955 to 1986 it increased by only 1.4%. However, the history of the rate of exploitation differs across industries. In 8 of the 20 industries the rate of exploitation fell between 1955 and

TABLE A8.13. The rate of exploitation in Canadian industries, 1955–1986

Industry	Year								
	1955	1961	1964	1970	1973	1976	1979	1982	1986
FNB	2.260	2.145	2.140	1.842	1.832	1.553	1.789	1.725	1.964
TOB	1.903	1.657	1.539	1.139	1.130	0.970	1.086	0.956	0.712
RBP	1.760	1.578	1.611	1.656	1.722	1.685	1.919	1.864	2.119
LTH	2.964	2.845	2.797	2.636	2.767	2.517	2.753	3.038	3.345
KNT	3.155	3.224	3.247	2.922	3.145	2.758	2.930	3.191	*
TEX	2.641	2.494	2.457	2.150	2.257	2.105	2.224	2.320	2.689
CLO	3.005	3.006	3.013	2.826	2.880	2.656	2.801	3.072	3.740
WOD	2.058	1.955	2.022	1.603	1.525	1.286	1.383	1.344	1.767
FNT	2.036	2.340	2.360	2.100	2.261	2.142	2.501	2.554	2.885
PPR	1.342	1.251	1.325	1.108	1.156	0.971	1.113	1.069	1.104
PUB	1.349	1.236	1.267	1.211	1.261	1.227	1.418	1.428	1.535
PMT	1.374	1.018	1.126	1.011	1.051	0.960	1.164	0.952	1.052
FBM	1.322	1.440	1.537	1.328	1.411	1.375	1.565	1.531	1.960
MCH	1.403	1.356	1.354	1.203	1.287	1.309	1.474	1.411	1.914
TNS	1.392	1.243	1.205	1.079	1.154	1.060	1.242	1.211	1.511
ELC	1.585	1.586	1.684	1.564	1.759	1.598	1.682	1.706	1.843
NMM	1.725	1.601	1.635	1.360	1.351	1.197	1.333	1.324	1.557
PET	1.099	0.867	0.893	0.693	0.745	0.600	0.844	0.696	0.732
CHM	1.621	1.395	1.435	1.253	1.341	1.230	1.397	1.237	1.416
MIS	2.250	2.124	2.209	1.941	2.124	2.156	2.255	2.269	2.545
Total	1.779	1.696	1.724	1.499	1.556	1.421	1.584	1.543	1.804

Note: see Figure 8.18 for the method of calculation.
Source:*Manufacturing Industries of Canada: National and Provincial Areas*, Ottawa, Canada: Statistics Canada..

1986. The rate declined most rapidly in the tobacco and petroleum & coal sectors, fueled by hourly real wages that grew at 2.5 times and 1.5 times the overall manufacturing rate, respectively. In the remaining 12 sectors the rate of exploitation increased. Sluggish real-wage gains in the fabricated metals and machinery sectors underlie faster than average gains in the rate of exploitation in these industries.

Hourly wage rates differ between industries (Table A8.14). Hourly real wages in manufacturing as a whole averaged $8.30 between 1955 and 1986. Hourly wages are more than 1 SD above the average in the petroleum & coal, primary metals, and pulp & paper sectors. Hourly wages are at least 1 SD less than the norm in the knitting, clothing, leather, and furniture industries. Interindustry differences in wages have increased since 1955. In most industries the growth in hourly real wages was concentrated in the 1960s and early 1970s. Between 1976 and 1986 hourly real wages declined or were stagnant in most industries (the exceptions are the industries that already paid high wages—the tobacco, pulp & paper, primary metals, electrical, petroleum & coal, and chemicals sectors). Correspondingly the rate of ex-

TABLE A8.14. The hourly real wage in Canadian industries, 1955–1986 ($82)

Industry	\-	\-	\-	\-	Year	\-	\-	\-	\-
	1955	1961	1964	1970	1973	1976	1979	1982	1986
FNB	4.713	5.383	5.771	7.011	7.930	9.232	9.143	9.154	9.188
TOB	5.292	6.371	7.137	9.313	10.544	11.967	12.220	12.757	15.905
RBP	5.566	6.567	6.940	7.501	8.253	8.778	8.735	8.710	8.731
LTH	3.876	4.403	4.772	5.479	5.963	6.702	6.794	6.178	6.268
KNT	3.698	4.008	4.267	5.080	5.419	6.272	6.488	5.952	*
TEX	4.220	4.485	5.242	6.324	6.896	7.591	7.909	7.515	7.382
CLO	3.836	4.226	4.515	5.207	5.788	6.447	6.707	6.126	5.745
WOD	5.025	5.730	5.995	7.654	8.895	10.312	10.700	10.641	9.841
FNT	4.648	5.069	5.393	6.427	6.887	7.501	7.282	7.020	7.010
PPR	6.560	7.520	7.794	9.449	10.419	11.960	12.068	12.059	12.941
PUB	6.540	7.571	7.992	9.009	9.932	10.583	10.543	10.277	10.743
PMT	6.472	8.388	8.524	9.909	10.954	12.027	11.780	12.782	13.271
FBM	6.616	6.939	7.143	8.557	9.315	9.923	9.939	9.857	9.198
MCH	6.395	7.187	7.699	9.042	9.823	10.205	10.304	10.347	9.345
TNS	6.423	7.548	8.217	9.584	10.428	11.446	11.373	11.285	10.846
ELC	5.944	6.547	6.752	7.769	8.140	9.072	9.505	9.220	9.577
NMM	5.637	6.510	6.877	8.441	9.553	10.726	10.928	10.734	10.651
PET	7.318	9.066	9.570	11.771	12.874	14.761	13.830	14.714	15.721
CHM	5.861	7.070	7.443	8.843	9.595	10.568	10.637	11.153	11.272
MIS	4.727	5.419	5.646	6.774	7.189	7.468	7.833	7.631	7.683
Total	5.528	6.280	6.652	7.972	8.786	9.737	9.868	9.810	9.710

Source: see Table A8.13.

ploitation fell in every industry (except furniture, fabricated metals, electrical, and machinery) from the mid-1960s to the mid-1970s as wage gains outstripped reductions in the unit value of consumer goods, so tending to reduce the rate of profit. Since the late 1970s, as real wages have declined, reductions in the value of consumer goods have begun to boost the rate of exploitation.

A8.2.2 The Value Composition of Capital in Canadian Industries

Both the value composition of capital and its history differ between industries (Table A8.15). The value of plant, equipment, and raw materials used per hour of labor power is now more than 100 times as great in the petroleum & coal sector as in the clothing industry. The value composition in Canadian manufacturing more than doubled after 1955. In every industry except clothing the value composition of capital rose between 1955 and 1986: such changes tended to depress profitability. The largest increases in the value composition, over twice the overall growth rate, are found in the petroleum &

TABLE A8.15. The value composition of capital in Canadian industries, 1955–1986

Industry	Year								
	1955	1961	1964	1970	1973	1976	1979	1982	1986
FNB	22.8	31.7	35.8	33.7	37.0	33.7	37.4	40.0	41.5
TOB	10.0	11.2	10.9	12.2	11.7	13.9	11.6	12.2	13.3
RBP	9.4	12.5	12.3	16.1	13.6	14.8	14.6	17.1	17.4
L TH	5.5	5.5	5.2	5.3	6.3	5.7	6.8	5.9	5.8
KNT	7.1	8.3	8.9	8.1	8.0	7.3	7.9	8.2	*
TEX	13.6	15.9	16.1	16.1	16.9	17.4	19.1	19.7	24.9
CLO	5.0	4.5	4.3	3.7	3.7	3.6	3.5	3.4	3.4
WOD	10.5	12.7	13.5	13.0	15.0	15.7	15.5	18.0	19.8
F NT	4.8	6.5	6.3	5.9	6.1	6.3	6.1	6.5	6.4
PPR	24.9	29.1	36.2	40.3	50.8	40.2	50.3	52.9	60.9
PUB	15.2	18.2	20.5	20.0	19.8	18.7	18.2	19.7	16.9
PMT	27.4	23.4	28.0	27.0	29.0	26.7	33.9	29.7	37.4
FBM	8.8	9.8	10.2	9.2	10.2	9.3	10.7	11.0	13.6
MCH	6.9	7.9	9.1	7.3	7.7	7.9	8.8	9.2	10.8
TNS	14.1	17.3	18.8	10.2	19.5	21.6	18.2	20.9	35.2
ELC	7.6	8.5	8.7	8.4	9.2	9.0	9.6	8.2	11.2
NMM	20.1	23.9	26.1	26.4	27.3	26.7	33.0	35.0	34.5
PET	94.1	133.9	157.0	166.4	254.1	281.4	313.5	299.1	350.5
CHM	24.5	35.2	41.0	39.3	46.9	53.8	77.2	92.1	87.3
MIS	5.7	6.1	6.1	5.8	6.4	6.3	6.4	6.9	7.5
Total	15.7	18.7	20.1	19.7	21.8	22.3	24.5	27.0	30.5

Note: see Figure 8.21 for the method of calculation.
Source: see Table 8.6.

coal and chemical sectors. Increases in the value composition of capital were relatively low in the printing & publishing and leather sectors. Industries whose value composition was relatively high in 1955 have increased their value compositions more than other industries (the correlation between the logarithms of the value compositions in 1986 and 1961 is $r = +0.98$). So differences between industries in the value composition of capital increased between 1955 and 1986. Thus the greatest pressure on profitability occurred in industries where the value composition already pressed profit rates the most.

Table A8.16 identifies the components of changes in the value composition of capital between 1955 and 1986. In all 20 industries reductions in the value of capital goods acted to reduce the value composition. Similarly in all 20 sectors gains in the technical composition led to increases in the value composition of capital, though these gains were small in the leather, knitting, clothing, furniture, and miscellaneous industries. Changes in the value of labor power exerted a more uneven influence on industries, tending to reduce the value composition in 9 industries and increase it in the remaining 11. In

TABLE A8.16. The determinants of the value composition of capital in Canadian industry, 1955–1986

Industry	dq	Effect of the value of capital goods	Effect of the technical composition of capital	Effect of the value of labor power
FNB	18.687	−17.750	40.291	−3.223
TOB	3.332	−6.397	16.540	−7.142
RBP	8.026	−6.279	12.881	1.698
LTH	0.298	−3.186	3.036	0.544
KNT	1.095	−4.420	5.667	−0.079
TEX	11.317	−6.684	17.813	0.466
CLO	−1.550	−2.931	1.002	0.457
WOD	9.351	−7.382	17.956	−0.736
FNT	1.562	−3.375	4.177	0.947
PPR	36.010	−15.989	58.073	−4.699
PUB	1.720	−7.957	8.566	1.719
PMT	9.975	−11.621	26.904	−5.696
FBM	4.753	−3.932	6.437	2.282
MCH	3.900	−4.061	6.377	1.813
TNS	21.065	−9.031	29.204	1.857
ELC	3.621	−4.074	7.230	0.615
NMM	14.401	−11.078	27.074	−0.849
PET	256.490	−64.379	358.420	−25.663
CHM	62.743	−23.061	90.411	−1.066
MIS	1.768	−3.077	5.064	0.552
Total	14.784	−9.316	23.969	0.948

Note: Calculated using equation (8.8).
Source: see Table 8.6.

all except the leather and clothing industries the effect of changes in the technical composition made the largest single contribution to changes in the value composition of capital, and in all except the leather, clothing, furniture, and printing & publishing sectors the effect of changes in the technical composition exceed the combined weight of the two other effects.

The average technical composition of capital in Canadian manufacturing between 1955 and 1986 is about 212 (Table A8.17). The variance in the technical composition between industries is large. In 1986 the technical composition in the petroleum & coal sector was more than 200 times that in the clothing industry. The technical composition of capital is also relatively high, more than twice the manufacturing average, in the chemicals and paper industries. The technical composition is less than one-quarter of the average in the clothing, leather, knitting, furniture, and miscellaneous goods sectors.

In all 20 industries the technical composition increased after 1955. In most industries, the fastest gains in this variable occurred before the mid-1970s. The industries experiencing well above average increases in the techni-

TABLE A8.17. The technical composition of capital in Canadian industries, 1955–1986

Industry	1955	1961	1964	1970	1973	1976	1979	1982	1986
FNB	115.6	178.5	203.9	233.3	298.2	311.9	342.9	375.2	399.9
TOB	61.0	81.1	84.6	126.6	133.9	174.7	152.4	168.8	230.4
RBP	68.6	101.6	100.4	145.7	135.1	150.1	134.0	157.8	169.2
LTH	26.0	29.8	29.9	35.2	42.6	43.9	50.3	42.7	44.8
KNT	27.0	31.9	33.0	41.7	45.1	50.9	54.9	54.9	*
TEX	72.6	82.7	82.3	107.7	123.5	138.6	152.7	155.5	193.2
CLO	21.0	21.2	20.0	22.5	24.8	28.4	29.0	26.9	26.8
WOD	59.3	80.3	83.4	111.2	144.1	173.9	173.3	201.6	208.8
FNT	27.3	38.8	38.1	45.9	48.4	53.1	51.2	53.2	53.7
PPR	196.0	256.5	317.8	446.7	583.6	494.6	622.4	649.9	815.7
PUB	128.7	167.0	187.2	215.4	231.5	225.5	198.9	212.6	196.3
PMT	220.5	238.4	273.2	321.0	371.0	352.8	407.8	392.8	535.9
FBM	74.2	83.3	84.0	93.1	109.7	103.1	113.8	118.8	138.6
MCH	52.2	64.7	73.4	72.1	82.6	86.8	96.9	105.5	113.9
TNS	106.4	146.7	160.7	205.4	217.7	255.2	213.6	247.5	404.6
ELC	54.1	63.7	62.9	73.3	83.0	89.0	97.8	84.6	119.6
NMM	138.3	183.6	199.4	258.3	300.8	315.3	376.9	386.8	386.5
PET	901.3	1587.4	1934.0	2489.7	3785.6	4221.4	4395.1	4415.7	5686.1
CHM	165.4	281.1	328.6	390.1	496.4	582.1	830.8	1038.7	1023.3
MIS	31.0	37.2	37.2	43.9	49.9	51.4	56.3	60.0	68.5
Total	104.9	136.1	146.6	178.9	212.6	229.3	248.8	275.0	315.1

Note: see Figure 8.23 for the method of calculation.
Source: see Table 8.6.

cal composition include the petroleum & coal, chemicals, and pulp & paper sectors. In the leather, clothing, furniture, printing & publishing, and fabricated metals industries the technical composition increased less than half as quickly as in manufacturing in general. The technical composition increased more rapidly in industries in which it was already relatively high (the correlation between 1986 and 1961 technical compositions is $r = +0.98$)—industries are becoming technically more different.

Table A8.18 shows the determinants of the technical composition of capital in Canadian industries. The components of the technical composition have different impacts on the performance of industries. Technical change proper—changes in the amount of capital employed in production per unit of labor power—has tended to save labor in all industries. The effect of changes in technique has exceeded the combined weight of all three other effects in 9 industries and has been the largest single effect in 8 other sectors. In the tobacco industry increases in the intensity of labor have exerted the largest effect on the technical composition of capital; in the clothing industry the effects of changes in capacity utilization and labor intensity have both been

TABLE A8.18. The determinants of the technical composition of capital in Canadian industry, 1955–1986

Industry	dP	Effect of turnover times	Effect of capacity utilization	Effect of technical change	Effect of labor intensity
FNB	284.270	50.702	43.674	134.510	40.831
TOB	169.380	−36.514	21.773	66.612	68.052
RBP	100.570	−0.337	−2.129	32.834	13.838
LTH	18.810	−1.927	−4.212	11.525	6.886
KNT	27.850	1.164	−5.637	16.706	9.029
TEX	120.570	28.974	−0.049	54.438	13.935
CLO	5.790	−1.669	−5.546	4.104	4.598
WOD	149.520	10.987	−19.459	85.526	18.325
FNT	23.390	6.398	−9.143	13.083	6.967
PPR	619.630	96.335	35.073	305.120	31.504
PUB	67.580	−10.625	−51.805	89.831	10.621
PMT	315.340	−104.030	114.110	138.270	23.600
FBM	64.480	24.713	−11.539	20.084	10.351
MCH	61.700	−7.744	3.911	23.252	16.898
TNS	298.140	61.552	−71.604	129.310	47.875
ELC	65.510	3.012	5.282	23.770	16.236
NMM	248.190	60.614	−36.878	143.610	19.746
PET	4784.600	215.330	−50.309	3287.500	653.980
CHM	857.860	116.500	111.700	423.010	65.175
MIS	37.511	4.281	−6.699	14.843	13.059
Total	210.240	51.915	19.467	87.353	25.146

Note: Calculated using equation (8.9).
Source: see Table 8.6.

important; and in the fabricated metals industry changes in turnover times have had the largest effect on the technical composition. Labor has also been used more intensively in all industries. However, changes in turnover times and capacity utilization rates have had a more variable impact on technical compositions. Increases in capacity utilization rates since 1955 have tended to lower the technical composition in 13 industries. Reductions in turnover times have tended to depress the technical composition in 7 industries.

Table A8.19 highlights the annual number of turnovers in Canadian manufacturing. Capital was turned over about 10 times a year in the transport industry in 1986, but only about 1.7 times a year in the tobacco industry. Outside these two industries turnover times of capital range from about 4 through 7. The annual number of turnovers is about 10% higher in a peak year than in a trough. Even so production has speeded up more uniformly in Canadian industries than in their US counterparts: the annual number of turnovers increased in 17 Canadian manufacturing sectors. It decreased in the clothing, primary metals, and machinery industries.

TABLE A8.19. The annual number of turnovers in Canadian industries, 1955–1986

Industry	\multicolumn{9}{c}{Year}
	1955	1961	1964	1970	1973	1976	1979	1982	1986
FNB	5.172	5.723	5.995	6.022	6.692	6.552	7.238	7.171	7.228
TOB	1.657	1.601	1.642	1.843	1.877	2.347	1.404	1.656	1.761
RBP	3.065	2.751	3.057	5.228	4.178	4.096	4.097	4.170	5.465
LTH	3.305	3.849	3.805	3.590	4.060	3.816	4.226	3.293	3.631
KNT	2.806	3.353	3.678	3.719	3.860	3.981	4.150	3.636	*
TEX	3.309	3.451	3.813	3.533	4.292	3.772	4.470	3.773	4.844
CLO	4.004	3.904	3.870	4.206	4.172	4.418	3.673	2.960	3.985
WOD	4.322	4.574	5.306	4.715	5.918	5.541	5.428	4.361	5.787
FNT	3.064	4.644	4.536	3.887	4.266	4.195	4.411	3.894	5.010
PPR	4.518	4.408	5.502	5.722	6.916	5.603	7.031	5.934	7.301
PUB	7.119	7.406	7.516	8.017	7.881	7.737	7.338	7.606	7.853
PMT	5.458	3.663	4.420	4.381	4.743	3.625	4.588	3.392	4.737
FBM	3.150	3.406	4.229	3.848	4.368	3.695	4.223	3.691	5.252
MCH	2.903	2.390	3.329	2.408	2.951	2.730	3.198	2.598	2.822
TNS	6.396	5.185	6.637	5.704	7.165	6.991	5.740	4.270	10.265
ELC	2.697	2.606	2.949	2.673	3.042	2.963	3.125	2.170	3.329
NMM	5.044	4.208	4.871	4.335	5.312	4.774	5.387	4.273	6.181
PET	4.713	4.956	5.576	5.755	7.263	6.131	7.069	5.879	6.558
CHM	2.939	3.398	3.855	3.503	4.075	3.786	4.318	4.566	4.692
MIS	2.630	3.599	3.524	2.387	3.006	3.164	2.898	2.897	3.825
Total	4.303	4.073	4.640	4.377	5.113	4.738	5.044	4.382	5.808

Note: see Figure 8.24 for the method of calculation.
Source: see Table 8.6.

A8.2.3 The Value Rate of Profit in Canadian Industries

There are wide differences in the value rate of profit between industries (Table A8.20). On average between 1955 and 1986 the value rate of profit in Canadian manufacturing was approximately 0.34. Profitability was more than 1 SD above the manufacturing norm in the labor-intensive clothing, knitting, leather, and furniture industries. The value rate of profit was less than half the manufacturing average in the petroleum & coal, chemicals, pulp & paper, and primary metals sectors.

Between 1955 and 1986 the rate of profit in Canadian manufacturing fell 27.5% (see Section 8.3). Over the same period the value rate of profit fell in 11 of the 20 industries (Table A8.20). Between the business cycle troughs of 1961 and 1982 the value rate of profit declined in 16 sectors: the rubber, knitting, publishing, and fabricated metals industries escaped. (By comparison the value rate of profit fell in 17 US industries.) Since 1955 the petroleum & coal, tobacco, and chemical sectors have suffered the largest reductions in the value rate of profit, more than twice the industry average.

TABLE A8.20. The value rate of profit in Canadian industries, 1955–1986

					Year				
Industry	1955	1961	1964	1970	1973	1976	1979	1982	1986
FNB	0.492	0.375	0.348	0.320	0.323	0.293	0.337	0.302	0.334
TOB	0.288	0.218	0.213	0.159	0.167	0.153	0.121	0.120	0.088
RBP	0.518	0.322	0.371	0.507	0.492	0.436	0.503	0.429	0.628
LTH	1.504	1.690	1.726	1.505	1.539	1.434	1.501	1.449	1.783
KNT	1.090	1.164	1.200	1.195	1.346	1.319	1.362	1.259	*
TEX	0.600	0.510	0.549	0.445	0.542	0.431	0.494	0.423	0.504
CLO	2.017	2.125	2.196	2.534	2.580	2.560	2.271	2.074	3.375
WOD	0.775	0.655	0.739	0.538	0.564	0.427	0.454	0.309	0.491
FNT	1.215	1.452	1.476	1.177	1.351	1.227	1.552	1.327	1.960
PPR	0.234	0.183	0.196	0.154	0.154	0.132	0.152	0.118	0.130
PUB	0.592	0.477	0.443	0.462	0.478	0.481	0.541	0.525	0.672
PMT	0.264	0.153	0.172	0.158	0.166	0.126	0.153	0.105	0.130
FBM	0.424	0.455	0.581	0.501	0.553	0.495	0.565	0.469	0.707
MCH	0.517	0.363	0.446	0.350	0.434	0.400	0.481	0.360	0.459
TNS	0.588	0.351	0.404	0.290	0.404	0.328	0.371	0.236	0.428
ELC	0.496	0.433	0.512	0.444	0.523	0.473	0.497	0.403	0.502
NMM	0.412	0.270	0.294	0.215	0.254	0.207	0.211	0.157	0.271
PET	0.055	0.032	0.032	0.024	0.021	0.013	0.019	0.014	0.014
CHM	0.187	0.131	0.132	0.109	0.114	0.085	0.077	0.061	0.075
MIS	0.881	1.082	1.097	0.681	0.868	0.939	0.885	0.835	1.147
Total	0.459	0.350	0.378	0.317	0.348	0.288	0.313	0.241	0.333

Note: see Figure A8.6 for the method of calculation.
Source: see Table 8.6.

Value rates of profit are generally lower in business cycle troughs than in peaks, even though rates of exploitation shift pro-cyclically. These swings with the business cycle have persisted since 1955 rather than occurring only since the early 1970s.

The value rate of profit has several components (Table A8.21). The value composition of capital generally exerts the most consistent and the largest effect on the value rate of profit. The value composition of capital has increased in 19 of the 20 industries since 1955, tending to depress the value rate of profit. (The clothing industry is the exception.) In 13 industries the speed of production has increased, thereby countering the effect of rises in the value composition of capital. The rate of exploitation increased in 12 industries, also tending to raise the rate of profit. Even so, in 11 industries the effect of changes in the value composition of capital exceeded the effects of both other components combined, and in another 4 industries the effect of the value composition was the largest single effect. In the tobacco and publishing industries the rate of exploitation exerted the largest single pressure on the value rate of profit (in tobacco downward; in publishing upward); in the furniture

TABLE A8.21. The determinants of the value rate of profit in Canadian industry, 1955–1986

Industry	$d\pi_v$	Effect of the rate of exploitation	Effect of the value composition of capital	Effect of turnover times
FNB	−0.157	−0.048	−0.258	0.115
TOB	−0.200	−0.164	−0.079	−0.045
RBP	0.110	0.096	−0.348	0.145
LTH	0.279	0.192	−0.115	−0.039
KNT	0.169	0.029	−0.170	0.155
TEX	−0.097	0.005	−0.292	0.099
CLO	1.358	0.542	0.647	−0.347
WOD	−0.284	−0.136	−0.323	0.011
FNT	0.745	0.332	−0.333	0.487
PPR	−0.104	−0.035	−0.157	0.042
PUB	0.080	0.067	−0.062	0.016
PMT	−0.134	−0.062	−0.054	−0.085
FBM	0.282	0.208	−0.219	0.164
MCH	−0.058	0.117	−0.171	−0.139
TNS	−0.160	0.007	−0.325	−0.071
ELC	0.005	0.067	−0.174	0.032
NMM	−0.141	−0.051	−0.137	−0.017
PET	−0.041	−0.016	−0.039	0.007
CHM	−0.111	−0.026	−0.148	0.041
MIS	0.266	0.099	−0.222	0.018
Total	−0.126	−0.013	−0.209	0.057

Note: see Figure 8.24 for the method of calculation.
Source: see Table 8.6.

and primary metals industries the largest single component of changes in the value rate of profit was the effect of turnover times (in furniture upward; in primary metals downward).

A8.2.4 Price–Value Profit Rate Deviations in Canadian Industries

Five sectors—petroleum & coal, chemicals, tobacco, publishing, and the food & beverage industries—consistently gain surplus in the market, raising their price rates of profit above their value rates (Table A8.22). These industries are more competitive than most in the market—able to pay less than the average market price for inputs of a given labor value and to sell output of a given value for above the market average price. These profits are captured in the market at the expense of such labor-intensive industries as leather, knitting, clothing, textiles, wood, furniture, and the miscellaneous goods sector. The price

TABLE A8.22. Price–value profit rate deviations in Canadian industries, 1955–1986

Industry	Year								
	1955	1961	1964	1970	1973	1976	1979	1982	1986
FNB	0.930	1.294	1.385	1.333	1.354	1.378	1.203	1.312	1.329
TOB	1.286	1.825	1.644	2.071	3.184	3.307	3.247	3.963	5.763
RBP	1.258	1.020	0.879	1.016	0.817	0.798	0.733	0.729	0.749
LTH	0.316	0.306	0.317	0.349	0.311	0.316	0.355	0.358	0.313
KNT	0.289	0.336	0.305	0.361	0.357	0.308	0.331	0.348	*
TEX	0.395	0.535	0.553	0.602	0.606	0.540	0.595	0.631	0.588
CLO	0.335	0.337	0.321	0.327	0.299	0.316	0.362	0.371	0.280
WOD	0.490	0.394	0.434	0.362	0.822	0.601	0.750	0.340	0.653
FNT	0.475	0.484	0.466	0.547	0.506	0.449	0.412	0.457	0.423
PPR	1.421	1.288	1.252	1.017	1.125	1.191	1.490	0.931	1.349
PUB	1.377	1.586	1.557	1.582	1.724	1.678	1.453	1.554	1.407
PMT	1.490	1.118	1.103	1.122	1.127	0.857	1.031	0.651	1.139
FBM	1.135	0.939	0.906	0.912	0.903	0.928	0.835	0.913	0.699
MCH	0.917	1.234	1.216	1.214	0.896	1.045	1.060	1.249	0.844
TNS	0.842	0.963	1.084	1.190	1.031	1.177	1.032	1.100	1.097
ELC	1.518	1.182	1.160	1.105	0.982	1.045	1.028	1.236	1.132
NMM	0.857	0.991	1.103	1.150	1.267	1.297	1.168	1.065	1.096
PET	2.388	5.430	5.042	4.710	4.570	7.933	5.233	7.624	9.344
CHM	1.858	2.858	2.597	2.595	2.678	2.408	2.616	2.480	2.972
MIS	0.689	0.763	0.761	0.807	0.724	0.674	0.695	0.753	0.554
Total	0.689	0.763	0.761	0.807	0.724	0.674	0.695	0.753	0.554

Note: see Figure A8.7 for the method of calculation.
Source: see Table 8.6.

per unit value of the petroleum & coal sector is some 20 times that of the leather, knitting, and clothing industries. Most other industries have similar value and price rates of profit, neither gaining or losing significant surplus through unequal exchange in the market.

In many industries the ratio of price to value rates of profit has been quite constant between 1955 and 1986. As in the USA, market power seems a structural characteristic of industries. Even so the petroleum & coal and to-bacco sectors have improved their ability to compete in the market since 1955, the price/value ratios increasing markedly in these industries. Conversely the rubber & plastics and fabricated metals industries have lost their competitive edge in the market. In the wood products industry large swings in market performance are positively correlated with phases of the business cycle.

A8.2.5 The Price Rate of Profit in Canadian Industries

Price rates of profit differ between industries much less than value rates. Whereas industries' value rates of profit (averaged over the 31 years) have an

SD of 0.59, the SD of the price rates of profit is only 0.19 (Table A8.23). Five industries enjoyed price rates of profit more than 1 SD above the average: clothing, furniture, publishing, electrical equipment, and the miscellaneous goods sectors. Only one sector—petroleum & coal—has a price rate of profit at least 1 SD below the manufacturing average, but price rates of profit are also low in the primary metals and the pulp & paper industries.

The price rate of profit fell in 10 industries between 1955 and 1986 and rose in the other 10. Between the business cycle troughs of 1961 and 1982, the profit rate fell in 13 of the 20 industries; most—but by no means all—industries have experienced the effects of the postwar downturn in Canada's economic performance. The largest losses in the price rate of profit since 1955 were recorded by the primary metals, pulp & paper, and chemicals industries; the largest gains, by the furniture, clothing, and tobacco industries. Superimposed on the trend and sometimes concealing it are business cycle effects.

The price rate of profit depends on both the value rate and the price/value ratio (Table A8.24). The ability of firms to compete in the market affects the rate of profit. Indeed in seven industries changes in the price/value ratio

TABLE A8.23. The price rate of profit in Canadian industries, 1955–1986

Industry	1955	1961	1964	1970	1973	1976	1979	1982	1986
FNB	0.457	0.485	0.483	0.465	0.437	0.404	0.406	0.396	0.444
TOB	0.370	0.398	0.349	0.329	0.531	0.505	0.392	0.474	0.506
RBP	0.651	0.354	0.316	0.515	0.445	0.348	0.369	0.313	0.470
LTH	0.475	0.517	0.547	0.525	0.463	0.453	0.533	0.519	0.559
KNT	0.315	0.391	0.367	0.432	0.434	0.407	0.451	0.438	*
TEX	0.237	0.273	0.303	0.267	0.328	0.233	0.294	0.267	0.296
CLO	0.676	0.716	0.706	0.830	0.773	0.808	0.822	0.770	0.946
WOD	0.379	0.258	0.321	0.195	0.464	0.256	0.340	0.105	0.321
FNT	0.577	0.702	0.688	0.643	0.684	0.551	0.639	0.606	0.830
PPR	0.333	0.236	0.246	0.156	0.174	0.157	0.227	0.110	0.176
PUB	0.816	0.756	0.690	0.731	0.824	0.808	0.786	0.816	0.945
PMT	0.393	0.171	0.189	0.177	0.187	0.108	0.158	0.068	0.148
FBM	0.481	0.414	0.526	0.457	0.499	0.459	0.472	0.428	0.494
MCH	0.474	0.448	0.543	0.424	0.389	0.418	0.509	0.449	0.387
TNS	0.495	0.338	0.438	0.346	0.416	0.386	0.382	0.259	0.470
ELC	0.753	0.512	0.594	0.491	0.514	0.495	0.511	0.498	0.568
NMM	0.353	0.268	0.324	0.248	0.322	0.268	0.246	0.167	0.296
PET	0.127	0.175	0.159	0.112	0.096	0.103	0.099	0.104	0.128
CHM	0.347	0.374	0.389	0.283	0.305	0.205	0.202	0.150	0.224
MIS	0.607	0.826	0.835	0.550	0.628	0.633	0.615	0.629	0.635
Total	0.459	0.350	0.378	0.317	0.348	0.288	0.313	0.241	0.333

Note: see Figure 8.3 for the method of calculation.
Source: see Table 8.6.

TABLE A8.24. The determinants of the price rate of profit in Canadian industry, 1955–1986

Industry	$d\pi_p$	Effect of deviation between price and value	Effect of value rate of profit
FNB	−0.013	0.179	−0.162
TOB	0.136	0.729	−0.470
RBP	−0.181	−0.244	0.067
LTH	0.084	0.004	0.112
KNT	0.123	0.064	0.061
TEX	0.059	0.098	−0.037
CLO	0.270	−0.131	0.494
WOD	−0.059	0.028	−0.202
FNT	0.253	−0.069	0.350
PPR	−0.157	−0.029	−0.165
PUB	0.130	0.013	0.141
PMT	−0.245	−0.040	−0.213
FBM	0.013	−0.170	0.249
MCH	−0.087	0.038	−0.070
TNS	−0.025	0.070	−0.119
ELC	−0.186	−0.120	0.033
NMM	−0.056	0.088	−0.131
PET	0.000	0.187	−0.144
CHM	−0.123	0.149	−0.256
MIS	0.028	−0.124	0.194

Note: Calculated using equation (8.5).
Source: see Table 8.6.

were the main cause of movements in the price rate of profit. In three sectors—tobacco, textiles, and petroleum & coal—changes in the ability of firms to compete in the market offset the tendency for the value rate of profit to fall. In another two—rubber & plastics and electrical products—changes in the price/value ratio forced the price rate of profit down even though the value rate of profit was rising.

A8.3 COMPONENTS OF THE RATE OF PROFIT IN CANADIAN REGIONS

A8.3.1 The Rate of Exploitation in Canadian Regions

It is assumed that the wages of all workers, whatever region they live in, are spent on an identical basket of goods (though they may buy different quantities of that basket). The value of each of basket is the same, and thus the rate of exploitation varies between regions as the real wage differs between them.

While the rate of exploitation in Canadian manufacturing remained relatively constant between 1955 and 1986, at the regional level the picture was quite different (Figure A8.1). In British Columbia (BC) the rate of exploitation declined by more than 21% after 1955, the largest reduction of any region. In Alberta too the reduction in the rate of exploitation was relatively large (16%). In Quebec and the Atlantic Provinces the rate of exploitation declined more slowly, whereas in Ontario and the Prairie region it increased. Perhaps the most striking feature of Figure A8.1 is the marked spatial variation in the rate of exploitation. In the Atlantic Provinces this rate is on average about 90% greater than in BC. Thus for every dollar of value added, labor in BC receives about 45% more in wages than does labor in the Atlantic Provinces. Regional differences in exploitation are increasing.

The determinants of changes in the rate of exploitation are shown in Table A8.25. From the late 1950s the unit value of the aggregate consumer basket steadily decreased as technical changes reduced the capital and labor inputs required to produce consumer goods, reducing the value of labor power and so raising the rate of exploitation. This tendency was strongest between 1958 and 1974. Hourly real wages increased strongly in all regions until the mid-1970s (Figure A8.2), tending to raise the value of labor power and reduce the rate of exploitation. Figure A8.2 also reveals the marked regional disparity in hourly real wages in Canadian manufacturing, which accounts for regional differences in the rate of exploitation. After 1977, the rate of exploitation increased sharply in most regions, fueled by continued reductions

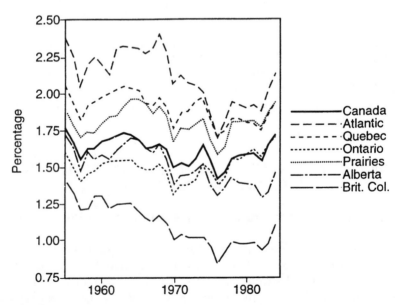

FIGURE A8.1. The rate of exploitation (see Fig. 8.6) in Canadian regions. *Source:* see Fig. 8.18.

TABLE A8.25. The determinants of the rate of exploitation in Canadian regions, 1955–1986

Industry	de	Effect of the value of consumer goods	Effect of the real wage
Atlantic	−0.315	1.729	−2.200
Quebec	−0.158	1.612	−1.869
Ontario	0.098	1.373	−1.360
Prairies	0.116	1.553	−1.537
Alberta	−0.253	1.382	−1.748
BC	−0.311	1.161	−1.566

Note: Calculated using equation (8.7).
Source: see Table 8.6.

in the value of consumer goods and by stabilization of the real wage. Only in Alberta did real wages continue to rise in the 1980s.

A8.3.2 The Value Composition of Capital in Canadian Regions

The value composition of capital increased in all regions (Figure A8.3). Nevertheless the history of the value composition is quite dissimilar across Canada. In the Prairie region the value composition increased most rapidly around 1960; in the Atlantic Provinces it increased quickest in the 1970s; and in Al-

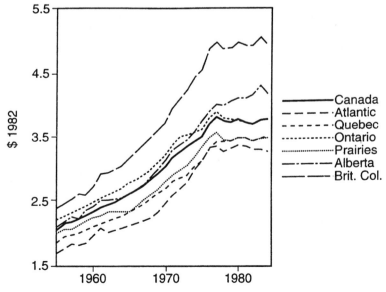

FIGURE A8.2. The hourly real wage (see Fig. 8.6) in Canadian regions. *Source:* see Fig. 8.18.

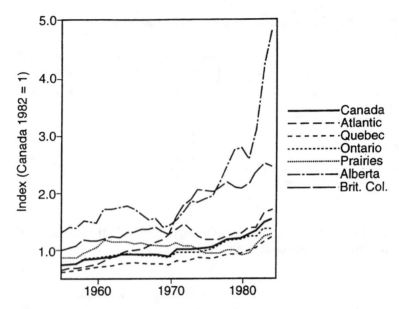

FIGURE A8.3. The value composition of capital (see Fig. 8.6) in Canadian regions. *Source:* see Fig. 8.21.

berta it rose fastest after 1981. Alberta recorded the largest absolute increase in the value composition of capital between 1955 and 1986, though in relative terms the composition of capital rose most rapidly in the Atlantic Provinces. The Prairie region lagged behind all others in adopting new technologies, its value composition increasing by only 39%.

The increases in the value composition of capital were dominated by the direct effects of technical change, measured as changes in the technical composition of capital (Table A8.26). In all regions the effects of the technical

TABLE A8.26. The determinants of the value composition of capital in Canadian regions, 1955–1986

Industry	dq	Effect of the value of capital goods	Effect of the technical composition of capital	Effect of the value of labor power
Atlantic	34.582	−13.698	50.724	−0.990
Quebec	13.760	−7.431	22.136	−0.388
Ontario	11.499	−9.306	20.064	1.646
Prairies	7.117	−10.099	16.898	1.143
Alberta	39.715	−18.679	61.111	1.828
BC	10.197	−12.711	27.320	−3.023

Note: Calculated using equation (8.9).
Source: see Table 8.6.

composition on the value composition of capital were significantly larger than the effects of all other variables. Technical changes also cause the unit value of capital goods to fall. The unit value of the means of production declined by 37% in Canada after 1955—especially in the 1960s and after 1982. The regional strength of this counter to increases in the value composition vary. In the Prairie region reductions in the value of capital goods suppress over 50% of the impact of the technical composition, whereas in Alberta they suppress only about 30%. Finally, between 1955 and 1986 reductions in the unit value of labor power had a negligible effect on the value composition of capital, though after 1977 they contributed to the general increase in the value composition (chiefly the result of reductions in the real wage).

A8.3.3 The Technical Composition of Capital in Canadian Regions

The technical composition of capital increased in all regions between 1955 and 1986 (Figure A8.4). The growth of the technical composition was most rapid in the Atlantic Provinces, which in 1955 had the lowest technical composition in Canada. By 1986 the technical composition in the Atlantic Provinces was second only to Alberta. The technical composition of capital

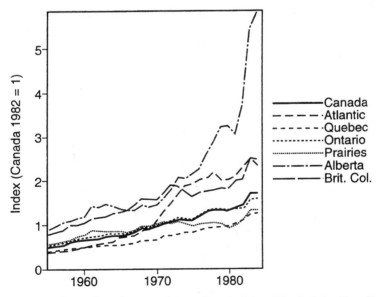

FIGURE A8.4. The technical composition of capital (see Fig. 8.6) in Canadian regions. *Source:* see Fig. 8.23.

also increased rapidly (by over 315%) in Alberta. In Quebec the technical composition grew at a faster rate than in the nation as a whole. In all other regions the technical composition increased more slowly than in Canada as a whole. Figure A8.4 also reveals significant regional variations in the technical composition of capital: in Alberta the technical composition is 1.5–3 times its level in other regions.

In general between 1955 and 1986 changes in turnover times, capacity utilization rates, labor intensity, and "pure" technical change all tended to increase the technical composition of capital (Table A8.27). Even so the most important effect has been that of the full capacity ratio of fixed capital to labor. This variable represents the impact on industries of "pure" technical changes as new techniques of production are embodied in additions to the capital stock. Increases in the capacity-adjusted capital/labor ratio account for about 50% of the rise in the technical composition in most regions after 1955. This type of technical change was sluggish in the Prairie region and Quebec and faster in Alberta, BC, and the Atlantic Provinces.

Increases in the amount of energy and materials processed per hour of labor (labor intensity) were responsible for about 13% of the increase in the technical composition in Canada from 1955 to 1986. Regional and temporal variations in the intensity of the labor process were not as great as variations in the capital/labor ratio.

Changes in the length of the turnover period account for about 20% of the changes in the technical composition of capital between 1955 and 1986. The turnover time of capital is closely related to the business cycle, decreasing in upswings and lengthening during downswings. So in Alberta the pace of production has slowed since the late 1970s, tending to depress the technical composition. In BC too reductions in the speed of production since 1979 have tended to slow the growth of the technical composition of capital.

Changes in the capacity utilization rate have exerted an uneven influence

TABLE A8.27. The determinants of the technical composition of capital in Canadian regions, 1955–1986

Industry	dP	Effect of turnover times	Effect of capacity utilization	Effect of technical change	Effect of labor intensity
Atlantic	362.530	115.100	−20.333	180.430	30.311
Quebec	181.660	49.265	32.465	59.396	20.904
Ontario	176.440	41.503	−8.197	85.472	25.650
Prairies	127.080	24.082	2.719	55.289	15.172
Alberta	572.340	−181.620	95.979	281.970	53.195
BC	263.190	1.524	−49.045	190.640	27.247

Note: Calculated using equation (8.9).
Source: see Table 8.6.

on the technical composition of capital. In all regions capacity utilization
rates fell during the downswing of the late 1950s: changes in capacity utilization were dominating the movement of the technical composition as the pace
of technical change was slow. Between 1974 and 1982 reductions in capacity
utilization rates once more dominated the movement of the technical composition in all regions except Quebec and BC. Investment in new technology is
not always the most significant influence on the technical composition: in Ontario throughout the second half of the 1970s, lower rates of capacity utilization caused over 90% of the increase in the technical composition; in the Atlantic Provinces, Alberta, and the Prairie region, reductions in the use of
existing fixed capital were also the main reason why the technical composition rose in the 1970s.

Figure A8.5 shows the history of the number of turnovers in manufacturing in the six regions of Canada between 1955 and 1986. The annual number
of turnovers increased in all regions over the 30 years, though with wide fluctuations over the business cycle. The increase in the speed of production has
been most rapid in the Atlantic Provinces and in Alberta, regions that experienced the greatest increase in the value composition of capital. In both these
regions, as well as BC, the speed of production declined markedly after 1979,
though this was the time of greatest increase in the number of turnovers per
year in Quebec and the Prairie region.

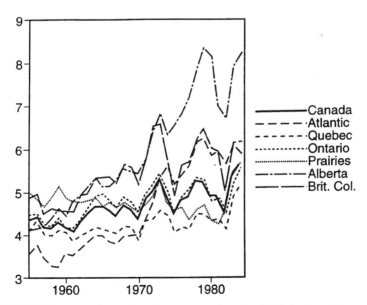

FIGURE A8.5. The annual number of turnovers (see Fig. 8.6) in Canadian regions.
Source: see Fig. 8.24.

A8.3.4 The Value Rate of Profit in Canadian Regions

The value rate of profit decreased in all regions between 1955 and 1986 (Figure A8.6). In the Atlantic Provinces the reduction in profitability was more severe than elsewhere, falling by almost 54%. In Alberta, BC, and to a lesser extent Quebec, the decline in profitability was also greater than average. In Ontario and the Prairie region the rate of profit declined at a slower pace than the Canadian average. Figure A8.6 shows the marked differences in the pattern of profitability between regions. On average between 1955 and 1986 the value rate of profit was more than twice as high in Quebec as in Alberta. Through the 1950s and 1960s the value rate of profit was significantly above average in the Atlantic Provinces, though from 1970 it has fallen below average. In BC the value rate of profit appears susceptible to business cycle swings, testament to the resource orientation of this region's manufacturing sector.

The history of the value rate of profit in Canada's regions has been controlled by changes in the rate of exploitation, the value composition of capital, and the number of turnovers per year (Table A8.28). Increases in the value composition have dominated the movements of the profit rate in all regions. Reductions in turnover times tended to bolster the rate of profit everywhere except BC, though these effects were overwhelmed in all regions by the rising value composition. Only in Ontario and the Prairie region did the rate of exploitation increase between 1955 and 1984, tending to raise the

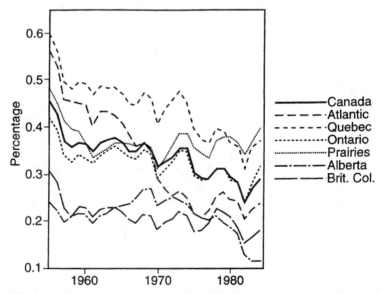

FIGURE A8.6. The value rate of profit in Canadian regions. The value rate of profit is calculated as the product of the rate of exploitation and the annual number of turnover periods divided by the value composition of capital plus 1. *Source:* see Fig. 8.7.

TABLE A8.28. The determinants of the value rate of profit in Canadian regions, 1955–1986

Industry	$d\pi_v$	Effect of the rate of exploitation	Effect of the value composition of capital	Effect of turnover times
Atlantic	–0.318	–0.074	–0.444	0.141
Quebec	–0.218	–0.057	–0.299	0.090
Ontario	–0.079	0.003	–0.163	0.035
Prairies	–0.050	0.014	–0.131	0.023
Alberta	–0.115	–0.055	–0.211	0.091
BC	–0.118	–0.066	–0.093	–0.012

Note: Calculated using equation (8.6).
Source: see Table 8.6.

rate of profit; everywhere else the rate of exploitation decreased, exacerbating the reduction in profitability.

A8.3.5 Price–Value Profit Rate Deviations in Canadian Regions

The ability of firms to capture profit in the market varies widely between regions (Figure A8.7). Between 1955 and 1986 all regions except the Prairies

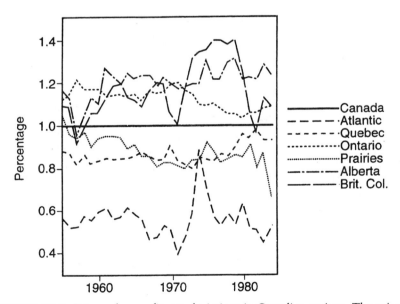

FIGURE A8.7. Price–value profit rate deviations in Canadian regions. The price–value profit rate deviation is calculated as the ratio of the (price) rate of profit (see Fig. A8.8) and the value rate of profit (see Fig. A8.6). *Source*: see Fig. 8.7.

were consistently either net winners or net losers in the market. The Prairie region suffered the worst decline in market performance over the 30 or so years. Ontario has also suffered a deterioration in market performance since the late 1960s and early 1970s, while the remaining regions, with the exception of the Atlantic Provinces, improved their market standing. The strong market performance of BC through the 1970s is especially notable.

A8.3.6 The Price Rate of Profit in Canadian Regions

The net effect of all these influences has been that the price rate of profit declined in all regions of Canada between 1955 and 1986 (Figure A8.8). Regional variations in profitability are significant, however. In absolute terms Quebec has performed best over the 30 years, posting an average rate of profit of 38.1%. Ontario ranks second, with an average rate of profit between 1955 and 1986 of almost 37%. The Atlantic Provinces fared worse, with an average profit rate of only 18.6%. BC, Alberta, and the Prairie region all performed worse than the Canadian average. In terms of changing performance levels the Atlantic Provinces again fared worse over the 30 years, experiencing a decline in the annual price rate of profit of nearly 42%. The reduction in levels of profitability was also severe in Alberta (–34%) and in Quebec (–29%). Both BC and Ontario performed better than average, suffering a decline in manufacturing profitability of only 11.6% and 20.9%, respectively.

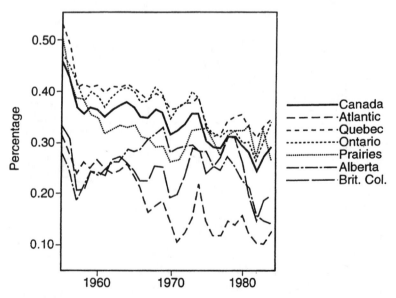

FIGURE A8.8. The price rate of profit (see Fig. 8.3) in Canadian regions. *Source:* see Fig. 8.7.

TABLE A8.29. The determinants of the price rate of profit in Canadian regions, 1955–1986

Industry	$d\pi_p$	Effect of deviation between price and value	Effect of value rate of profit
Atlantic	−0.133	0.042	−0.183
Quebec	−0.154	0.033	−0.176
Ontario	−0.099	−0.006	−0.085
Prairies	−0.111	−0.052	−0.066
Alberta	−0.097	0.032	−0.132
BC	−0.038	0.061	−0.129

Note: Calculated using equation (8.5).
Source: see Table 8.6.

(The relatively strong showing of BC is largely an artifact of its strong rebound since the deep recession of 1982. Between 1955 and 1982 the downturn in profitability in BC was second only to that of the Atlantic Provinces.)

Table A8.29 shows how the price rate of profit has been affected by production and market performance in each region between 1955 and 1986. In the Prairie region poor market performance was as much to blame for the reduction in profits as growing inefficiencies in production. In other regions market performance was more variable and had less effect on profitability than did the value rate of profit.

Chapter 9

THE RATE AND DIRECTION OF TECHNICAL CHANGE IN US MANUFACTURING

The history of changes in technology is central to the way in which many people understand postwar economic history. Long-wave theorists such as Berry (1991; Berry et al 1993) and Freeman and Perez (1988) regard prices and economic growth as determined by the timing of clusters of innovations. Similarly Mensch (1979), following Schumpeter (1942), explains periods of slow growth by stalemates in technology. Increasingly, the performance of industries (Dosi 1982; Holmes 1983; Utterback 1987), regions (Markusen 1985; Morgan and Sayer 1988; Oakey et al. 1982; Scott 1988b), and nations (Freeman 1987; Porter 1985) is linked to the their ability to innovate, and the changing fortunes of industries and regions are commonly explained by reference to the way that they restructure or reorganize the technology of production (Massey and Meegan 1982; Noponen et al. 1993; Saxenian 1994; Scott and Storper 1986).

The fall in the rate of productivity and economic growth in many of the advanced industrial economies since the mid-1970s has generated numerous visions of the decline of postwar capitalism. Several of the most influential of these visions were reviewed in Chapter 3. Four of those accounts characterize the slowdown by reductions in the rate of profit and the rate of growth of productivity. However, the accounts offer different views of the relationship between profitability and productivity and thus competing explanations of economic crisis. The aim now is to use the theory of Chapter 6 to examine the links between profitability and productivity in US manufacturing so as to arbitrate between the competing accounts of the slowdown.

The main contenders are Freeman and Perez (1988) and Lipietz (1986), who regard the slowdown in productivity growth as one of the causes of the failure of Fordism as a regime of accumulation, and Mandel (1978) and Piore and Sabel (1984), who claim that the observed slowdown in aggregate productivity is a consequence rather than a cause of the slower rate of accumulation. There are of course others who engage in this debate, but their claims will not be explicitly addressed here (see Berndt 1980; Clark 1979; Denison 1979; Filer 1980; Griliches 1980; Kendrick 1980; Thurow 1979). Wolff (1985) provides a detailed review of these contributions to the discussion.

In Chapter 6 we outlined a theoretical framework to measure and decompose the determinants of productivity change. This framework explicitly links the rate of profit to productivity changes through the medium of investment and embodied technical change. With this framework we can distinguish the hypotheses of Freeman and Perez and Lipietz, on one side, and Mandel and Piore and Sabel, on the other. Now we seek to evaluate them by examining the pace and direction of productivity change in manufacturing industries within the USA. To what extent do changes in technique depend on rates of profit and investment, the degree of competition, and the supply of innovations? How does the direction of productivity change respond to changes in the price of inputs? We seek then to provide an empirical basis for distinguishing the different accounts of profitability and productivity changes.

We begin in Section 9.1 by outlining a method of measuring the components of technical change identified in Chapter 6. Section 9.2 applies this method to examine the nature and determinants of observed technical change in the US manufacturing sector as a whole. In Section 9.3 we examine the characteristics of productivity change in US industries. Finally, Section 9.4 summarizes the relationship between the rate of profit and productivity.

9.1 ESTIMATING THE COMPONENTS OF PRODUCTIVITY CHANGE

Chapter 6 argued that the level of productivity in an economy is indexed by the value of commodities:

$$\lambda = \lambda(a + f/t) + l,$$

where a denotes the input of constant circulating capital commodities per unit of output; f is the level of fixed capital input per unit of output; t denotes the service life of fixed capital; and l is the labor input per unit of output. Since f/t is the level of depreciation in any one interval, the level of productivity depends on the two coefficients:

$$a_l = \frac{\text{(hours of labor by production workers)}}{\text{(market value of shipments)/ISPI}}$$

$$a_k = \lambda_1 \frac{\text{(depreciation + fuel + raw materials)/MSPI}}{\text{(market value of shipments)/ISPI}},$$

where MSPI is the all-manufactures' selling price index and ISPI is the individual industry's selling price index; λ_1 is the unit labor value of constant capital commodities employed in the economy. Thus the coefficient a_k measures the values of constant circulating capital used up and of depreciation per "ton" of output; a_l measures the number of hours of productive labor used to produce 1 "ton" of output. The two coefficients a_k and a_l are thus measured in the same units: hours of labor per 1982 dollar's worth of shipments. (Output is valued in constant dollars in order to measure physical productivity.) These are the basic data from which productivity can be calculated.

The price of constant capital, $w_k = \text{MSPI}/\lambda_1$, is the price index per hour's worth of constant capital and the price of labor, w_l, is measured as the hourly wage: total wages paid to production workers divided by the total number of production hours worked.

Productivity change is measured as a change in the capital input coefficient (da_k) or a change in the labor input coefficient (da_l). Production costs change when input prices change or when productivity changes. Price changes must therefore be abstracted from measures of production costs in order to measure observed changes in productivity. Therefore the change in production costs, when prices are constant, is taken to identify productivity changes and is itself measured as

$$dh^T = w_k\, da_k + w_l\, da_l.$$

The history of productivity in an economy may be described by the movement of input coefficients and production costs.

The task in this chapter is to interpret the movements of these variables in the light of the theory of productivity change developed in Chapter 6 by identifying the components into which observed productivity change may be divided. In Chapter 6 the central equation deduced for this task is

$$dh^T = -f_1\pi - f_2\pi(h - h_m) - f_3\text{Var}(h)/h + f_4 q \qquad (9.1)$$

Here, π is the rate of profit; h is the average unit cost of production; h_m is the minimum unit cost of production in any plant; $q = dp/dt(p + 0.5dp/dt)$ is the effect of price changes on the entry and exit of firms; f_1, f_2, f_3, and f_4 are parameters to be estimated.

This equation identifies the four components of productivity change and the variables that determine them. The first term, $-f_1\pi$, states that the rate of unit cost reduction from innovation by individual plants depends on the rate of profit of those plants (π) and the rate at which profits are converted into cost-reducing innovations (f_1). Secondly, the term $-f_2\pi(h - h_m)$ identifies the effects of imitation on productivity change: these effects depend on profitability and on the difference between average and best practice costs of production. These two terms represent productivity increases due to actual changes in the technical and social relations within plants. The latter two terms represent productivity changes due to changes in the division of labor between plants. The third component, $-f_3\text{Var}(h)/h$, measures the expected change in production costs due to selection (i.e., different rates of growth of output between plants), which depends on the variance in plants' cost structures (in relation to the average level of costs) and on the rate at which differences in costs between plants translate into different rates of growth. The fourth term, f_4q, identifies the effects of the entry and exit of plants upon productivity, depending on the rate at which prices rise and the rate at which those rises cause new, less productive plants to enter the market. Equation (9.1) thus provides a means of assessing the sources of changes in productivity. In order to estimate the parameters of the equation and so to measure the sources of change in the rate of productivity improvement, we have modified this model in three ways.

First, the theory of Chapter 6 was derived for a closed deterministic world. In reality there are imports of technology, chance discoveries, and other sources of technological variability for which we simply cannot account. We therefore supplement equation (9.1) by a term, e, representing unaccounted sources of productivity change; e is assumed to be a random variable with zero mean and constant variance.

Second, our theory made the convenient but unrealistic assumption that the technologies embodied in new investment had a single, lump impact on input–output coefficients. In practice, the effect of a new technology may become apparent over several years (Binswanger and Rutttan 1978; Mansfield 1961; Stoneman 1980). So, for example, the rate of unit cost reduction from innovation by individual plants depends on current levels of profitability, $-f_{10}\pi_t$, on profitability last year, $-f_{11}\pi_{t-1}$, on profitability the year before that, $-f_{12}\pi_{t-2}$, and so forth. Equally, the effect of imitation depends on cost structures now, $-f_{20}\pi(h - h_m)_t$, and cost structures in the previous years, $-f_{21}\pi(h - h_m)_{t-1}, -f_{22}\pi(h - h_m)_{t-2}, \ldots$. In empirical work we have taken the current values of these variables and values for lags over two time periods.

Third, equation (9.1) is embedded in an economic system in which such variables as the rate of profit and the rate of productivity change mutually determine each other. That is, changes in productivity influence rates of profit, which in turn influence the next period's changes in productivity. In order to estimate accurately the parameters of the model of productivity change, that interdependence must be modeled explicitly. A model of profitability is used in this empirical work not because of a renewed interest in profitability (this was discussed in the previous chapter) but because such a model is necessary if equation (9.1) is to be estimated accurately. The equation is conventional, representing the rate of profit as dependent on current and lagged values of the capacity utilization rate (CUR), the level of shipments (O), and the rate of change in the level of shipments from one year to the next (o).

In Appendix A9, Section A9.1 describes the system of structural equations used and the way in which it was linearized for estimation. The variables in the system of equations have been estimated in the manner shown below. All intervals are 1 year and the data are collected for calendar years.

The mean cost of production per unit of output, h, is measured as

$$h = \frac{\text{wages + fuel + raw materials + depreciation}^*\text{CUR}}{(\text{market value of shipments})/\text{ISPI}}.$$

This is a conventional measure of cost per physical unit of output (physical units are approximated by output in constant dollars). Unlike the measure h^T, the mean cost of production is measured in current prices (in the same way as p reflects current prices). The only unusual feature in this definition is that the annual cost of fixed capital (depreciation) has been corrected for the CUR. As argued in Chapter 6, this correction is needed in order to remove spurious productivity change.

The CUR is conventionally measured as the capital/output ratio in a given year divided by the benchmark capital/output ratio. The benchmark is the lowest capital/output ratio found over the period examined and is assumed to represent full capacity utilization.

It has proved difficult to measure Var(h), the variance of production costs among all the plants of an industry (or economy). We know that virtually all plants in an industry are profitable. That is, we know that for virtually all plants, i,

$$(p - h_i) > 0.$$

If h is normally distributed, virtually all plants have a cost h_i in the range

$$h \pm Vs_h,$$

where s_h represents the standard deviation of h_i and V represents the strength of "virtually." For example, $V = 2$ implies that "virtually" means 95%. That is,

$$p - (h \pm Vs_h) > 0,$$

or, more particularly, that

$$p - h - Vs_h > 0,$$

whence

$$\text{Var}(h) = s_h^2 < [(p - h)/V]^2.$$

Of course this is only an upper limit on Var(h); we denote it by U[Var(h)] and suppose that there is a constant W such that

$$\text{Var}(h) = WU[\text{Var}(h)].$$

Then

$$\text{Var}(h) = (p - h)^2 (W/V^2).$$

In the empirical work we have taken W/V^2 to be a parameter to be estimated.

It has proved equally difficult to measure $h - h_m$, the difference between average and best practice unit costs of production. We have had to assume that the range from average to best $(h - h_m)$ is related to the range from worst to average $(p - h)$: $h - h_m = m(p - h)$. Thus, equation (9.1) becomes

$$dh^T = -f_{10}\pi_t - f_{11}\pi_{t-1} - f_{12}\pi_{t-2} - f_{20}\pi_t m(p - h)_t - f_{21}\pi_{t-1} m(p - h)_{t-1}$$

$$-f_{22}\pi_{t-2} m(p - h)_{t-2} - f_3(W/V^2)(p - h)^2/h + f_4 q + e_1, \tag{9.2}$$

in which $(p - h)^2$ is an observable variable and $f_2 m$ and $f_3(W/V^2)$ are parameters to be estimated. In summary, this equation states that measured rates of unit cost reduction (excluding input price changes) depend on the following:

1. The rate at which innovations cause cost reductions (which rate depends on levels of profitability over the last 3 years)
2. The rate at which imitation reduces costs of production (depending on the difference between average and best practice costs of production; but estimated as proportional to the difference between worst and average practice costs of production—and depending on costs over the past 3 years)
3. The rate at which selection reduces costs of production (depending on the current variance of production costs, but estimated as proportional to a function of the rate of profit)
4. The effect of the entry and exit of firms (estimated directly from price changes)
5. The effect of random or chance events on productivity

This equation and the estimates derived by using it (in Table 9.1) relate changes in costs of production to levels of such other variables as profitability, the spread of costs, the variability of costs, and price changes. These levels of profitability, costs, and variability are sometimes similar to each other; but the measures (and so the similarity) have all been derived from the theory explained in Chapter 6, modified to account for data availability.

The two simultaneous equations [(A9.2) and (A9.3) in Appendix A9] have been estimated by two-stage least squares. In estimating the structural equation on dh^T, collinearity prevented separation of the effects of innovation and imitation. The estimated structural equation on dh^T therefore combines these effects. (See Appendix A9, Section A9.1, for details.)

9.2 THE PACE AND DIRECTION OF PRODUCTIVITY CHANGE IN US MANUFACTURING

The method of Section 9.1 was used to estimate the pace and direction of productivity change in the manufacturing sectors of the USA. The results of our investigation are presented below.

9.2.1 Productivity Change in US Manufacturing

We begin by examining the history of productivity change in the US manufacturing sector as a whole. The history is summarized in Figures 9.1 and 9.2. Figure 9.1 shows for each year the inputs of capital and labor used per unit of output (a_k and a_l). This figure also shows the average ratio of input prices (w_l/w_k) for the intervals 1962–1973 (0.4297), 1974–1981 (0.3846), and 1982–1990 (0.3654). Figure 9.2 reveals the shift in costs of production (dh^T) over time caused by changes in productivity. On the basis of these measures, the history of productivity change in US manufacturing since 1962 can be separated into three distinct periods.

Between 1962 and 1973 there was steady improvement in productivity. Both input-output coefficients, a_k and a_l, declined regularly: on average the capital input coefficient decreased by 2.12% of its mean value in the period; the labor input coefficient by 1.68%. If we regard progress normal to the

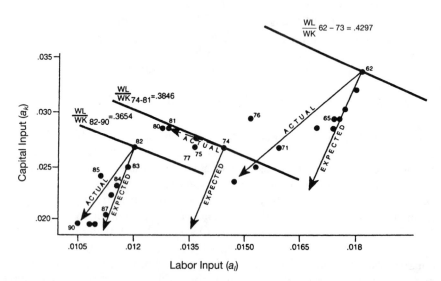

FIGURE 9.1. Input coefficients in US manufacturing. *Source: Fixed Reproducible Tangible Wealth in the United States, 1925–1989, Census of Manufactures* and *Annual Survey of Manufactures*, Washington, DC: U.S. Department of Commerce.

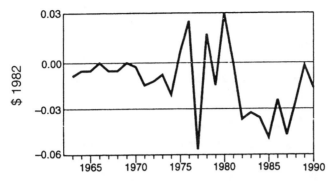

FIGURE 9.2. Unit production cost changes in US manufacturing. *Source*: see Figure 9.1.

price ratio as neutral, as it would be if innovation was the only source of pro-ductivity change, then before 1967 productivity change was neutral. From the late 1960s until 1971 productivity change exhibited a pronounced labor-sav-ing bias: labor was being replaced somewhat faster than relative prices war-ranted. Between 1971 and 1973 the labor-saving bias of new techniques was dampened. The steady technological progress of the period 1962 to 1973 was interrupted by slight increases in the labor input coefficient between 1965 and 1966 and in the capital input coefficient between 1969 and 1970. These anomalies to the steady productivity improvements prior to 1974 are appar-ent in the cost of production (Figure 9.2). As a result of productivity progress before 1974, costs of production (at constant prices) declined at an average annual rate of 2.07%.

After 1973 productivity improvements in the US manufacturing sector slowed as technical change ceased to reduce costs of production. Between 1974 and 1981 capital was substituted for labor. On average the capital input coefficient rose by 0.61% each year while the labor input coefficient fell by 1.56%. This was a period of a very strong bias against labor in production methods: relatively large amounts of capital were being substituted for labor inputs. In part, this is probably evidence of the search by firms for more ener-gy efficient technologies in the face of the dramatic oil price increases in 1973 (Berndt and Wood 1981; Lakshmanan et al. 1984; Stpindyck and Rotemberg 1983): corporations bought new plant and equipment that was more energy efficient but more expensive and of higher value than the old equipment. The net effect of productivity change was a steady rise in costs of production by an average of 0.8% each year. Only in three years in this interval did changes in social and technical relations reduce production costs: 1976/77, 1978/79, and 1980/81.

Through the 1980s productivity change resumed a more stable path of reducing input coefficients. Between 1982 and 1990 both capital and labor inputs per unit of output have fallen, by 2.53% and 1.46% each year, respectively. The net effect has been to decrease production costs by 2.96% per annum. Apart from a significant increase in unit capital costs in 1984/85, productivity change prior to 1988 was approximately neutral. After 1988 productivity change resumed its labor-saving bias: annual reductions in the labor input coefficient averaged about 1.84%, while the capital input coefficient remained quite stable.

The net result over the 29 years has been an average reduction in costs of production of about 1.61% each year. The capital input coefficient on average declined by 1.41% each year, and the labor input coefficient declined at an average annual rate of 1.85%. Although relative prices have fluctuated in the 29 years, the history of productivity change reveals a bias: labor input coefficients have been reduced faster and capital input coefficients more slowly than relative prices would warrant. Such bias is sometimes interpreted as reflecting corporations' use of new techniques and investment in plant and machinery in the continuing struggle to control labor [the sources of technical change and their relation to the labor process are well summarised in Harvey (1982: 106–136)]. Evidently, it could be argued, corporations are replacing labor faster than price ratios would warrant: so there must be some other dynamic, such as control over or replacement of labor. There may be truth in the observation about the sources of technological change: we have no evidence about the proposition. However, the observed tendency to replace labor faster than relative prices would warrant requires two comments. First, only innovation and imitation are expected to proceed in a direction neutral to the relative price line; other sources of productivity change, including selection of more profitable plants and the entry and exit of plants, occur in different directions. The observed bias, then, may just as simply reflect the shape of the distribution of plants within the technology space. Secondly, changes in relative prices within the categories we have lumped together as capital or as labor may also influence choice of techniques. The clearest example of this was the rise in energy prices after 1973. This rise in prices contributed to a rise in the relative price of capital, but it also induced additional capital investment as corporations sought to install new plant and equipment that were more energy efficient or to produce commodities that were more energy efficient (the obvious example was new models of car). Paradoxically, then, the rise in the price of capital could induce new investments in capital.

Figure 9.2 indicates that the variability of year-to-year changes in production costs seems to have increased over time. This is partly an artifact of the way in which cost changes are measured. Since the weights used to combine da_k and da_l into db^T are the prices per unit of capital and labor, the gradual rise in those prices over time translates a given change in input—output coefficients into a greater and greater change in production costs. We must now interpret these data using the theory of Chapter 6 and the methodology of Section 9.1, above.

Table 9.1 displays the results of the two-stage least squares estimation of the structural equation (A9.3) that describes the sources of changes in productivity. [Since this chapter concerns productivity changes, that equation as well as our discussion of the estimation of the rate of profit—Appendix equation (A9.2)—are consigned to Section A9.2 of Appendix A9.] Statistical support for our model of cost changes induced by productivity change appears to be relatively good with an r^2 value of 0.77. In general, the signs on the coefficients of the model are of the anticipated direction. The only exception is the positive sign on the rate or profit with one time lag. This may be due partly to collinearity between the rate of profit and lagged values of that rate. However, the collinearity does not bias the estimators and the t-scores on the joint effect of innovation and imitation are generally good. The t-scores on the remaining variables also suggest that the model is statistically significant.

The effects of innovation and imitation on unit cost reductions are captured in the coefficients on

$$E[(1 + (p - h)_t)\pi_t],$$

$$E[(1 + (p - h)_{t-1})\pi_{t-1}],$$

and

$$E[(1 + (p - h)_{t-2})\pi_{t-2}].$$

In theory these coefficients reflect the impact of both the rate of profit (which influences innovation) and the range of costs of production (which influences imitation) on the introduction of new techniques. The sum of the coefficients for the effects of innovation and imitation is –0.0045, confirming our hypothesis about the relationship between profitability and the pace of innovation and imitation. The rate of profit influences a firm's ability to raise investment capital through retained earnings or borrowing, and the range of costs is a positive indication of the potential benefits of imitation. The foregoing coefficients measure these influences as well as the significance of innovation and

TABLE 9.1. Two-stage least squares estimation of dh^T

Variable	Coefficient	SE	t-Score
$E([1 + (p - h)_t]\pi_t)$	–0.3130	0.0568	–5.51
$E([1 + (p - h)_{t-1}]\pi_{t-1})$	0.4009	0.0802	5.00
$E([1 + (p - h)_{t-2}]\pi_{t-2})$	–0.0924	0.0557	–1.66
$(p - h)^2/h$	–0.1402	0.0438	–3.20
q	0.2903	0.1143	2.54

Note: $n = 26$; $r^2 = 0.77$; F-ratio = 12.27; SEE = 0.0120.
Source: *Census of Manufactures* and *Annual Survey of Manufactures*, Washington, DC: U.S. Department of Commerce.

imitation in capital investment and the cost reduction induced by the new techniques that are embodied in the invested capital. The coefficient on the current rate of profit and the range of techniques is negative. Therefore, increases in the rate of profit or the range of costs in a given year lead to reductions in production costs in the same year. With a lag of 1 year, profitability and the range of costs appear to lower productivity, though there are again positive benefits with a lag of 2 years. Using the coefficients from Table 9.1 and the product of the average annual profit rate and range of costs in US manufacturing between 1965 and 1990, we find that innovation and imitation cause unit costs to decrease by about 0.0020 each year. This is equivalent to about 26% of the average annual change in costs of production over the period.

Selection refers to the effects of competitive pressures that cause less efficient firms to lose market share to more efficient firms. The effects of selection are measured in the coefficient on $Var(h)/h$; it is hypothesized that this coefficient should be negative, for the greater is its variability the greater is the pressure of selection on productivity. Here we have been forced to measure the variable $(p - h)^2/h$, so that the coefficient -0.1402 measures not only the effects of selection on costs but also the ratio of $(p - h)^2$ to $Var(h)$. This mixture inhibits a direct interpretation of the coefficient as a measure of selection. In any event the coefficient is negative, implying that the wider the spread of costs among the firms in US manufacturing the greater the pressure of selection to reduce costs. This result is also consistent with our theoretical expectations.

The final source of productivity change is the entry and exit of firms induced by changes in prices. This effect is measured by the coefficient on q. The coefficient is positive as anticipated, indicating that as prices rise new firms enter the US manufacturing sector and that, on average, these firms are less efficient than existing producers and so tend to raise average production costs.

These results can now be used to interpret the history of productivity change in US manufacturing reported in Figures 9.1 and 9.2. The effects of

TABLE 9.2. Sources of technical change in US manufacturing

Period	Total dh^T	Innovation and imitation	Selection	Entry/exit	Drift and error
1965–1973	−0.0054	−0.0021	−0.0068	0.0020	0.0015
1974–1981	0.0037	0.0005	−0.0118	0.0148	0.0003
1982–1990	−0.0222	−0.0042	−0.0252	0.0099	−0.0026
1965–1990	−0.0084	−0.0020	−0.0147	0.0087	−0.0003

Note: The data are average annual changes in dh^T and its components. A negative sign implies that the source tended to reduce costs.
Source: see Table 9.1.

the four sources of productivity change are revealed in Table 9.2. The effect of innovation and imitation is computed as

$$-f_{10}[1 + (p - b)_t]\pi_t - f_{11}[1 + (p - b)_{t-1}]\pi_{t-1} - f_{12}[1 + (p - b)_{t-2}]\pi_{t-2},$$

using actual rather than estimated values of the rate of profit. The effect of selection is $-f_3(W/V^2)[(p - b)^2/b]$, and the effect of the entry and exit of new firms is captured as f_4q. Random drift and error are measured as e_1. Because lagged values of independent variables are used in the estimation, the calculations start in 1965.

Figures 9.1 and 9.2 confirm that prior to 1974 there was no slowdown in aggregate productivity growth (measured by changes in unit costs of production). In the late 1960s productivity change was reducing costs of production by 0.0027 (1.1%) on average each year. After a temporary halt in 1970, productivity gains accelerated during the first three years of the 1970s, reducing average costs of production by about 0.0149 (4.9%) a year. The slowdown in productivity growth occurred after 1973 when significant increases in the capital input coefficient tended to raise costs of production. It was not until 1982 that productivity changes once more began consistently to lower costs of production.

Aggregate productivity changes reflect variations in labor productivity and the capital/output ratio. Figure 9.3 shows the annual rate of change of labor productivity in US manufacturing between 1962 and 1990. Apart from significant fluctuations through the mid-1970s, the rate of growth of labor productivity has changed only slightly since 1962. Over the three subperiods identified from Figure 9.2, the annual rate of labor productivity growth averaged 1.93% between 1962 and 1973, 2.12% per annum between 1974 and 1981, and 2.13% per annum after 1982. The rate of growth of productivity of production workers within the US manufacturing sector did not decline

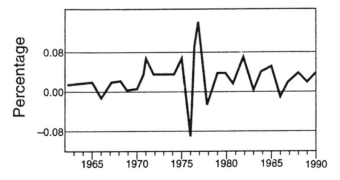

FIGURE 9.3. The annual rate of change of labor productivity in the USA. *Source: Census of Manufactures* and *Annual Survey of Manufactures*, Washington, DC: U.S. Department of Commerce.

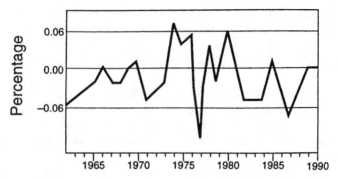

FIGURE 9.4. The annual rate of change of the capital/output ratio in US manufacturing. *Source*: see Figure 9.1.

through the 1970s. This result contradicts the claims of the regulationists who maintain that a productivity slowdown was responsible for the fall of the rate of profit in US manufacturing. Figure 9.4 shows the annual rate of change of the capital/output ratio in the US manufacturing sector. The slowdown in aggregate productivity growth (the rate of unit cost reduction) after 1973 is largely explained by the annual rate of change in the capital/output ratio. Between 1962 and 1973 and between 1982 and 1990 the capital/output ratio decreased at an annual average rate of 2.02% and 2.52%, respectively. However, the period 1974 to 1981 saw the capital/output ratio rise by an average of 0.73% each year.

   The timing of the slowdown in aggregate productivity growth is crucial to understand the relationship between the rate of profit, productivity, and economic crisis in the USA. The rate of profit for the US manufacturing sector as a whole began to fall rapidly after 1965 (Figure 9.5), well before the downturn in the pace of aggregate productivity improvements. These data suggest

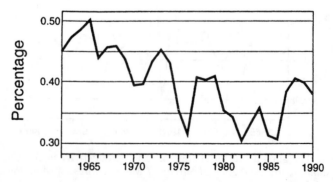

FIGURE 9.5. The rate of profit in US manufacturing. *Source*: see Figure 9.1.

that the slowdown in productivity cannot be used to explain the downturn of the US economy as measured by the aggregate manufacturing rate of profit. In fact it would appear that supporters of the productivity slowdown explanation of the recent US economic crisis have mistakenly reversed the relationship between the rate of profit and productivity. Table 9.2 allows us to understand how the changes in productivity were produced.

Between 1965 and 1990 the pace of innovation and imitation mirrored the pattern of unit cost changes (Table 9.2). Together these two sources of real productivity change reduced costs by an average of 0.0021 a year from 1965 to 1973. These were years when rates of profit and investment were relatively high, although they were beginning their downward slide. In 1965 the rate of profit in the US manufacturing sector as a whole peaked at 50.5% and the rate of gross investment in manufacturing peaked at just under 10% a year later. The rate of investment, the medium through which new techniques are introduced to the economy, shadows the rate of profit with a lag of about 1 year (Figure 9.6). Between 1965 and 1973 the rate of profit averaged 44.7% and the rate of investment averaged 7.7%. While profitability and the pace of investment remained relatively high, the speed at which embodied productivity changes were introduced to the economy also remained relatively high.

By the business cycle peak of 1973 the rate of profit had dropped to about 43%, and in the following year the rate of gross investment was below 8%. From 1974 to 1981 the rates of profit and investment averaged 38% and 7.2% a year, respectively. The pace of embodied productivity change and aggregate productivity growth slowed as the rate of investment slackened. Table 9.2 shows that between 1974 and 1981 innovation and imitation *increased* unit costs of production by an average of 0.0005 each year. These cost increases measure the rise in the capital/output ratio induced by the capital-using bias of new techniques introduced to the manufacturing sector in the latter half of the 1970s.

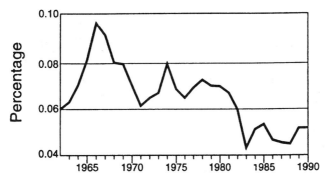

FIGURE 9.6. The rate of gross investment in US manufacturing. *Source: Fixed Reproducible Tangible Wealth in the United States, 1925–1989*, Washington, DC: U.S. Department of Commerce.

After 1982, innovation and imitation once more improved techniques of production, raising the rate of growth of productivity and causing unit costs to fall by an average of 0.0042 each year. The strong rise in productivity in part reflects the emergence of the manufacturing sector from the deep recession of 1982. While the rate of profit improved considerably between 1982 and 1984, and again between 1986 and 1988, the rate of investment increased to only about 5.5% in 1985 and then averaged about 5% through the latter half of the 1980s.

Countering the decline in the rate of investment over the latter part of the period examined, the pace of imitation has accelerated as the range of costs widened notably after 1972 (Figure 9.7). Using the difference between price and average cost as a proxy for the range of costs, we note that the pressure to imitate more efficient technologies remained largely unchanged until the early 1970s. Between 1972 and 1973 and again between 1974 and 1975, the pressure to imitate increased sharply and then climbed at a relatively consistent rate between 1977 and 1981. Slowing through the recession years of 1981/82, the range of costs widened further between 1984 and 1986 and again between 1987 and 1989, helping to explain the acceleration of aggregate productivity growth through the 1980s.

Table 9.2 also shows how selection has affected changes in unit costs of production between 1965 and 1990. Selection is another aspect of competition that captures the tendency for more profitable firms to grow at the expense of less profitable ones. Selection depends on the variance of unit production costs between firms. While we do not know what that variance is, Figure 9.8 illustrates the history of $(p - h)^2/h$, which is likely to be proportional to the variance. Since the mid 1970s, the variance of unit production costs has increased steadily, save for slight reductions in 1983/84 and in 1987/88, as rising prices of inputs have driven up costs of production. Therefore, selection has played a consistently larger role in reducing costs of production, a role that was not interrupted by the slowdown after 1974. Our measure of this competitive process in Table 9.2 shows that the average annual impact of

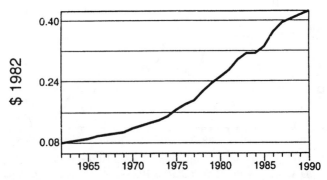

FIGURE 9.7. The range of costs in US manufacturing. *Source*: see Figure 9.1.

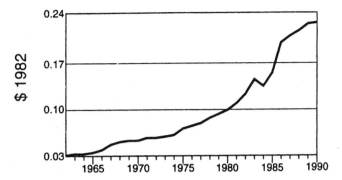

FIGURE 9.8. Estimate of the variance in costs in US manufacturing. *Source*: see Figure 9.1.

selection on costs of production doubled between 1965–1973 and 1974–1981 and doubled again between 1974–1981 and 1982–1990.

The second source of unit cost changes that reflects competition and market conditions is the impact of the entry and exit of new firms. As real prices rise or fall, marginal firms enter or leave manufacturing, driving average costs up or down in the process. The measure of cost changes induced by the entry and exit of firms is illustrated in Figure 9.9. Until 1973 this variable was both relatively low and stable. Between 1973 and 1981 price changes increased sharply and fluctuated wildly. Through the 1980s prices changes decreased although they still exhibited considerable instability. The entry and exit of firms has played an increasing role in raising costs of production since the early 1960s and in causing those costs to fluctuate from one year to the next. Here indeed is to be seen the variable that more than any other source of productivity change has driven the slowdown in cost reductions that occurred between

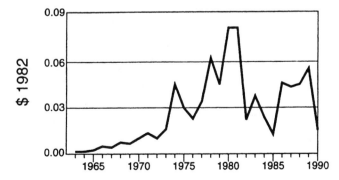

FIGURE 9.9. Estimate of the effect of the entry and exit of firms in US manufacturing. *Source*: see Figure 9.1.

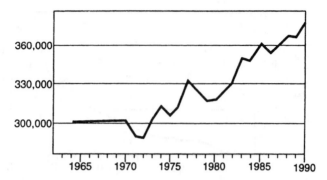

FIGURE 9.10. The number of establishments in US manufacturing. *Source*: see Figure 9.3.

1974 and 1981. Through this period prices rose rapidly, inducing less efficient firms to enter the economy and causing unit costs to increase. Figure 9.10 shows the number of manufacturing establishments in the US between 1965 and 1990. These data generally support the above claims, showing that the number of manufacturing establishments increased over the period and that the speed of this increase accelerated sharply after the early 1970s.

The sum of all these effects is summarized in Figures 9.11 and 9.12. The first figure illustrates the values of dh^T and the estimates of that variable derived from the regression results of Table 9.1. The regression equation is able to predict the general level and the fluctuations in the rate of cost reduction relatively well. Figure 9.12 illustrates the annual values of the three effects that were summarized in Table 9.2. The figure reveals clearly the steady increase in significance of selection, particularly after the mid-1970s. The increasing role of entry and exit of plants in slowing productivity change is also obvious.

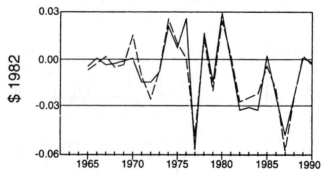

FIGURE 9.11. The change in unit production costs and its estimate. *Source*: see Figure 9.1.

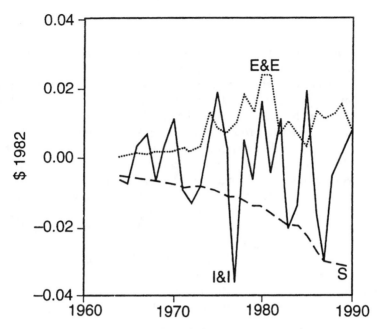

FIGURE 9.12. Components of technical change in US manufacturing. I&I, innovation and imitation; E&E, entry and exit; S, selection. *Source*: see Figure 9.1.

9.2.2 Summary

Figure 9.12 and Table 9.2 suggest the following interpretation of changes in the pace at which productivity changes have tended to reduce unit costs of production. Before 1974, there were fluctuations in the rate of innovation and imitation but no trend for the pace of cost reduction to fall. From 1974 until 1981 innovation and imitation acted to raise unit costs, though at a relatively insignificant rate. After 1981, innovation and imitation pushed unit costs of production down faster than at any other time since the early 1960s. More important in explaining the shifts in unit production costs between 1965 and 1990 were the rapid cost reductions introduced by selection and, especially, the cost increases introduced by new, marginal plants. The slowdown in aggregate productivity improvements in US manufacturing and the rise in unit production costs through the second half of the 1970s appears to have resulted from a sevenfold jump in the effect of the entry and exit of firms on production costs. Since 1981, as prices have stabilized, new plants are causing smaller increases in costs and their effect has been swamped by the selection of relatively efficient firms. This history suggests that changes in the rate of unit cost reduction have been driven far more by changes in the structure of the market within which manufacturing firms operate, that is, by the selection of profitable firms and by the entry and exit of marginal firms, than by changes in the pace of real productivity change caused by innovation or imitation.

The results also clarify the relationship between changes in productivity and the rate of profit within the manufacturing sector of the USA. The rate of growth of productivity of production workers in manufacturing increased slightly from the period 1965–1973 to 1974–1981 and then increased marginally again through the 1980s. With the growth of labor productivity effectively constant, aggregate productivity growth was dominated by the capital/output ratio, which declined at a relatively stable rate until 1973. It was not until 1974 that the capital/output ratio increased dramatically, leading to a marked reduction in the rate of aggregate productivity growth. From Chapter 8 we know that the rate of profit in the US manufacturing sector started to fall in 1965. Thus the decline in the rate of profit cannot be attributed to a slowdown in the rate of growth of productivity as Freeman and Perez (1988) and Lipietz (1986) have suggested. Rather, the data for the USA supports the vision of capitalist crisis offered by Mandel (1978)—that the productivity slowdown resulted from the decline in profitability. Piore and Sabel (1984) are also correct in claiming that the productivity slowdown is a consequence rather than a cause of the end of the mass production phase of capitalist accumulation.

9.3 PRODUCTIVITY CHANGE IN US INDUSTRIES

This section examines the nature of productivity change in all 20 (two-digit SIC) manufacturing industries in the USA using the framework outlined in Section 9.1. The industry survey is conducted to remove the possibility of aggregation bias that may be present in the study of the manufacturing sector as a whole and to determine whether individual industries exhibit significantly different histories of technological change and productivity growth between 1962 and 1990.

The two-stage least squares procedure of Section 9.1 was used to estimate the structural equation on dh^T [equation (A9.3)] for each industry. The results of this procedure are presented in Table 9.3. In all 20 cases an F-test revealed that the regression equation was significantly different from zero. The goodness of fit of the regression line varied from an r^2 value of 0.44 for the food & kindred products industry to an r^2 value of 0.94 for the fabricated metals industry. The coefficients on the five independent variables from equation (A9.3) are given in Table 9.3 along with the corresponding t-scores. Summing the lagged coefficients on the rate of profit and range of techniques, we note that 18 of 20 industries show the anticipated negative relationship between innovation and imitation and the change in unit costs. Sixteen sectors show the hypothesized negative relationship between selection (the variance in unit costs) and unit cost changes, and the anticipated positive association between the effects of entry and exit and the movement of unit production

TABLE 9.3. Two-stage least squares estimation of dh^T

Industry r^2		Coefficients on:				
		π_t	π_{t-1}	π_{t-2}	$(p-h)^2/h$	q
FNK	0.44	−0.2752	−0.0418	0.2805	0.0159	0.6507
		(−0.98)	(−0.09)	(0.94)	(0.08)	(2.83)
TOB	0.79	−0.3091	0.2338	0.0787	0.0232	−0.7595
		(−2.60)	(1.70)	(0.62)	(0.60)	(−2.55)
TEX	0.83	−0.6254	0.3689	0.2080	−0.1844	0.7670
		(−6.53)	(2.76)	(2.14)	(−0.82)	(3.85)
APP	0.81	−0.3157	0.1792	0.1162	−0.0872	0.8459
		(−6.07)	(2.75)	(2.40)	(−1.05)	(4.58)
WOD	0.82	−0.4230	0.4350	−0.0127	−0.7268	1.1686
		(−5.47)	(4.13)	(−0.17)	(−1.80)	(3.55)
FNT	0.61	−0.2411	0.1722	0.0485	−0.0517	0.5641
		(−3.86)	(2.07)	(0.81)	(−0.75)	(3.50)
PPR	0.91	−0.9113	0.6796	0.1694	0.0251	0.4387
		(−11.05)	(5.21)	(1.78)	(0.23)	(2.73)
PUB	0.78	−0.2145	0.2109	−0.0039	−0.0455	0.7737
		(−6.02)	(4.04)	(−0.11)	(−2.16)	(6.29)
CHM	0.85	−0.5021	0.5403	−0.0422	−0.1453	0.7463
		(−6.14)	(4.97)	(−0.53)	(−1.97)	(3.76)
PET	0.84	−1.3444	1.0819	0.3767	−5.7130	0.8064
		(−60.4)	(5.26)	(1.88)	(−2.90)	(1.20)
RBP	0.71	−0.2596	0.2569	−0.0099	−0.1412	0.7515
		(−3.88)	(2.94)	(−0.16)	(−1.50)	(5.23)
LTH	0.84	−0.4127	0.4015	−0.0008	−0.2953	0.9547
		(−6.87)	(5.44)	(−0.01)	(−3.31)	(4.92)
SCG	0.71	−0.5625	0.5181	0.0195	−0.0142	0.4559
		(−4.78)	(3.33)	(0.19)	(−0.11)	(1.86)
PMT	0.88	−1.3189	1.1675	0.0319	−0.4285	0.8489
		(−6.88)	(5.70)	(0.24)	(−0.94)	(2.30)
FBM	0.94	−0.3910	0.2513	0.1082	−0.0439	0.6209
		(−3.97)	(2.08)	(1.19)	(−0.53)	(3.41)
MCH	0.58	−0.2716	0.1546	0.0891	−0.0631	0.6067
		(−3.28)	(1.43)	(1.15)	(−0.98)	(2.58)
ELC	0.55	−0.1579	−0.0265	0.1524	−0.0639	0.7128
		(−1.93)	(−0.23)	(1.89)	(−1.36)	(3.26)
TNS	0.62	−0.3358	0.4088	−0.0951	−0.3441	0.8291
		(−3.37)	(3.17)	(−1.11)	(−1.56)	(3.17)
INS	0.74	−0.2215	0.2454	−0.0348	−0.0194	0.3142
		(−5.35)	(4.79)	(−0.87)	(−1.23)	(2.60)
MIS	0.61	−0.2421	0.2827	−0.0647	−0.0349	0.5946
		(−3.33)	(3.90)	(−0.93)	(−0.58)	(3.25)

Note: t-scores are shown in parentheses.
Source: see Table 9.1.

TABLE 9.4. Sources of technical change in US manufacturing industries

Industry	db^T	Innovation and imitation	Selection	Entry/exit	Drift and error
FNK	−0.0085	−0.0314	0.0010	0.0215	0.0004
TOB	−0.0426	−0.0271	0.0119	−0.0243	−0.0032
TEX	0.0011	−0.0178	−0.0092	0.0552	−0.0271
APP	−0.0024	−0.0227	−0.0095	0.0293	0.0006
WOD	0.0029	−0.0004	−0.0343	0.0395	−0.0022
FNT	−0.0016	−0.0140	−0.0064	0.0182	0.0006
PPR	−0.0078	−0.0259	0.0021	0.0270	−0.0110
PUB	−0.0034	−0.0116	−0.0159	0.0245	−0.0005
CHM	−0.0105	−0.0039	−0.0304	0.0241	−0.0003
PET	−0.0199	0.0223	−0.0779	0.0266	0.0090
RBP	0.0022	−0.0075	−0.0166	0.0254	0.0009
LTH	−0.0046	−0.0072	−0.0297	0.0309	0.0014
SCG	0.0003	−0.0121	0.0017	0.0134	−0.0027
PMT	−0.0029	−0.0168	−0.0172	0.0277	0.0034
FBM	0.0008	−0.0144	−0.0048	0.0196	0.0003
MCH	−0.0068	−0.0150	−0.0104	0.0998	−0.0813
ELC	−0.0061	−0.0175	−0.0134	0.0216	0.0032
TNS	−0.0059	−0.0071	−0.0232	0.0260	−0.0016
INS	−0.0081	−0.0103	−0.0080	0.0092	0.0009
MIS	−0.0040	−0.0181	−0.0061	0.0193	0.0009

Note: The data are average annual changes.
Source: see Table 9.1.

costs is found in 19 industries. In general, therefore, the model of unit cost reduction appears to fit the data very well, with 15 of the 20 industrial sectors displaying the anticipated signs on all independent variables.

Table 9.4 reports the average annual effect of the components of productivity change on unit production costs in US manufacturing industries between 1965 and 1990. Negative signs in the table imply a reduction in production costs. The lagged values of innovation and imitation are summed in the table to reveal the overall impact of these variables on unit costs.

The significance of the different components of productivity change varies markedly between industries. For the US manufacturing sector as a whole selection exerted the largest impact on production costs between 1965 and 1990. At the industry level, selection dominates the other sources of productivity change in the chemicals and petroleum & coal sectors only. Innovation and imitation exert the largest effect on production costs in only 3 sectors—food & kindred products, tobacco, and instruments. In the remaining 15 industries the entry and exit of firms is the most important determinant of changes in technique, although in the pulp & paper, stone, clay, & glass, and miscellaneous sectors, the effect of entry and exit on unit costs of production is only marginally higher than the effects of innovation and imitation. Figures 9.13 through 9.16 examine the impact of the different forms of productivity change on production costs over the three subperiods 1965–1973, 1974–1981, and 1982–1990.

Figure 9.13 reveals average annual changes in unit costs of production in the 20 industrial sectors for the three periods 1965–1973, 1974–1981, and 1982–1990. The slowdown in the rate of aggregate productivity change that characterizes the US manufacturing sector as a whole is evident in 15 industries. The tobacco industry experiences virtually no change in the rate of aggregate productivity growth over the first two periods, and in the petroleum & coal, leather, machinery, and electrical & electronics sectors aggregate productivity growth accelerates after 1974. In 13 industries unit cost reductions accelerate dramatically through the 1980s. Over the period as a whole, unit cost reductions are more than 3 SDs above average in the tobacco industry and more than 1 SD above average in the petroleum & coal sector. In all other sectors, the pace of unit cost change is within 1 SD of the manufacturing average, although in the lumber industry unit costs increase by almost 1 SD above the average rate of cost change.

The impact of innovation and imitation on the rate of change of industry production costs over the three periods is shown in Figure 9.14. Between 1965 and 1990 as a whole, innovation and imitation exerted the smallest influence on production costs of all three sources of productivity change. Before 1974, however, innovation and imitation exerted a larger impact on costs than either selection or the effect of entry and exit in the majority of industries. Figure 9.14 shows that only in about half the sectors did the pace of innovation and imitation slow from the period 1965–1973 to the period 1974–1981. Indeed, in the food & kindred products, furniture, petroleum & coal, machinery, and electrical & electronics sectors the effect of innovation and imitation on unit costs remained more or less constant over the first two subperiods, whereas in the apparel, printing & publishing, leather, and miscellaneous goods sectors the pace of unit cost reduction resulting from real productivity change increased after 1973. After 1981 productivity gains resulting from innovation and imitation increased in 15 industries. The largest gains were recorded by the tobacco, food & kindred products, and printing & publishing sectors. In four additional sectors the pace of innovation and imitation was largely unchanged through the 1970s and 1980s, and in the petroleum & coal sector real productivity change slowed markedly after 1981.

The sectoral and temporal variation in the effect of innovation and imitation reported in Figure 9.14 corresponds closely with the levels and the movement of the profit rate within individual industries (see Table 8.14). In the majority of industries, a higher rate of profit during the early to mid-1960s was responsible for the faster pace of real productivity change. In the food & kindred products and tobacco sectors, though, higher rates of profit in the 1980s were associated with significant reductions in unit production costs resulting from innovation and imitation. Between the second and third subperiods profit rate increases in the pulp & paper, chemicals, and stone, clay, &

Figure 9.13   Figure 9.14

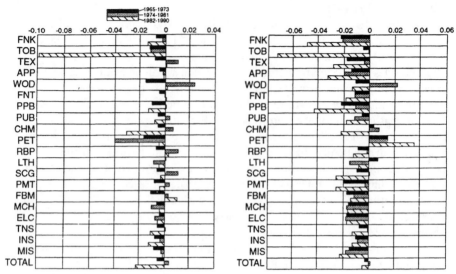

FIGURE 9.13. Average annual changes in unit costs of production in US manufacturing industries. *Source*: see Figure 9.1.
FIGURE 9.14. Effects of innovation and imitation on unit production costs in US manufacturing industries. *Source*: see Figure 9.1.

glass sectors are correlated with significant upswings in the pace of innovation and imitation. The downturn in the rate of innovation and imitation in the lumber industry during the late 1970s and in the petroleum & coal sector in the 1980s also appear due to significant reductions in industry profitability and the rate of investment.

Figure 9.15 reveals the impact of selection on unit costs of production in the manufacturing sectors. In all industries save for the petroleum & coal sector, the effect of selection on production costs has increased steadily between the three periods. In the majority of sectors, the impact of selection roughly doubled between the first and second subperiods and then doubled again between the second and third subperiods. In 16 of 20 industries selection lowered average costs of production. In the food & kindred products, tobacco, pulp & paper, and stone, clay, & glass sectors selection raised production costs.

The impact of the entry and exit of firms on production costs by industry is illustrated in Figure 9.16. The significance of the entry and exit of firms, especially in the second and third subperiods is clear from the table. In all industries except tobacco the entry of less efficient firms has raised unit production costs, and this effect dominated the movement of unit costs of

Figure 9.15   Figure 9.16

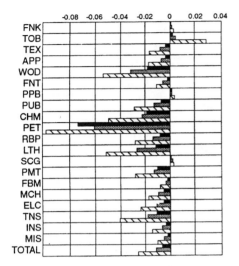 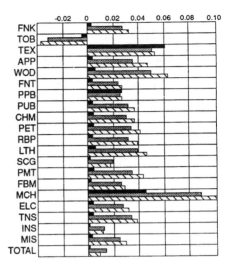

FIGURE 9.15. Effect of selection on unit production costs in US manufacturing industries. *Source*: see Figure 9.1.
FIGURE 9.16. Effect of entry and exit of firms on unit production costs in US manufacturing industries. *Source*: see Figure 9.1.

production after 1973. In part the increase in the significance of entry and exit results from our measurement of this effect through price changes that were inflated after the early 1970s. However, data on the number of establishments in US manufacturing provides additional support for the growing role of the entry and exit of firms on production costs since the mid-1970s. In 15 US manufacturing sectors the number of establishments increased between 1965 and 1990 and the speed of this increase accelerated sharply after 1973. The machinery, rubber & plastics, electrical & electronics, and instruments industries experienced the fastest growth in the number of establishments. In the food & kindred products, tobacco, textile, apparel, and leather industries the number of establishments declined after 1965. In the tobacco industry a rate of establishment closure of about 65% exceeded that of any other sector, giving rise to the production cost reductions shown in Figure 9.16.

Table 9.5 provides a summary of the main forces acting on unit costs of production in each industry and indicates when those forces were strongest over the three periods examined. The entry and exit of firms exerted the largest single influence on industry production cost changes between 1965 and 1990. In most sectors the entry of new firms tended to raise average pro-

TABLE 9.5. The causes and timing of unit cost changes in US manufacturing industries

	Increasing unit costs			Decreasing unit costs	
Industry	Main cause of change[1]	Timing of change[2]	Industry	Main cause of change[1]	Timing of change[2]
TEX	E/E	Throughout	FNK	I&I	Late
WOD	E/E	Middle & late	TOB	I&I; E/E	Late, Middle & late
RBP	E/E	Middle & late	APP	I&I	Late
SCG	E/E	Middle & late	FNT	I&I	Late
FBM	E/E	Middle & late	PPR	I&I	Late
			PUB	S	Late
			CHM	S	Late
			PET	S	Throughout
			LTH	S	Late
			PMT	I&I; S	Early & late; Late
			MCH	D&E	NA
			ELC	I&I; S	Throughout; Late
			TNS	S	Late
			INS	I&I	Throughout
			MIS	I&I	Throughout

Notes:
[1]The main causes correspond with the determinants of unit costs changes: E/E is entry or exit; I&I is innovation and imitation; S is selection; and D&E is drift and error.
[2]The timing indicates the period when the effect was greatest: *early* is the period 1965–1973; *middle* is 1974–1981; and *late* is 1982–1990.
Source: see Table 9.1.

duction costs. However, this effect was generally dominated by the combined impact of innovation and imitation, selection, and random drift, such that 15 of 20 industries experienced a net reduction in unit costs between 1965 and 1990. In 5 industries the entry of new firms caused unit costs to increase after 1965. The influence of selection dominated the movement of unit costs changes in only 2 industries, though it was chiefly responsible for unit cost reductions in 3 others. The effects of selection and the entry and exit of firms tended to increase in most industries over the three subperiods examined. Indeed, the rapid increase in new firm entry during the mid-1970s was the single most important factor that tended to reduce aggregate productivity growth. The effect of innovation and imitation on cost changes was more varied by sector. In only 11 industries the impact of innovation and imitation on unit costs slowed through the mid 1970s, in 5 other sectors it remained constant, and in the remaining 4 sectors it accelerated. The aggregate productivity slowdown in the 1970s was not primarily a result of a reduction in the pace of real productivity change.

9.4 CONCLUSION

Prior to 1974, the pace of real productivity change (innovation and imitation) fluctuated but there was no trend for the pace of unit cost reduction to fall. Between 1965 and 1974 innovation and imitation together were responsible for about 20% of the annual average change in unit costs, outweighing the impact of the entry and exit of marginal firms. Selection, the tendency for more profitable firms to grow at the expense of less profitable ones, exerted the strongest influence on the costs of production—more than three times that of innovation and imitation. Between 1974 and 1981, capital-using and labor-saving productivity change increased unit costs slightly. The impacts of selection and the entry and exit of firms on production costs increased sharply through this period: a sevenfold increase in the effect of the entry of new, less efficient firms caused the slowdown in the speed of unit cost reduction. After 1981, innovation and imitation decreased unit costs of production faster than at any other time since the early 1960s. Selection resumed its role as the principal determinant of unit cost changes after 1981, when fewer new firms entered the economy.

Within individual manufacturing industries the history of technological change is more varied and complex. In 5 sectors unit costs increased after 1965 as the impact of new firm entry overwhelmed the combined influence of innovation, imitation, and selection. In 15 industries unit costs of production declined between 1965 and 1990. In these cases real productivity change and selection have been the chief determinants of the cost savings in about the same number of industries. The effects of selection and the entry and exit of firms increased in most industries over the three subperiods examined. The timing of the impact of real productivity change was more varied by sector. In 11 industries the effects of innovation and imitation on unit costs slowed through the mid-1970s, in 5 others it remained constant, and in the remaining 4 sectors it accelerated.

The postwar history of productivity change in the manufacturing sector of the USA reveals that the pace of unit cost reduction has been dominated by the effects of selection and by the entry and exit of marginal firms rather than by innovation and imitation. Thus, changes in production costs have been driven more by changes in the structure of the market within which manufacturing firms operate than by changes in the pace of real productivity change. Most accounts of technological change, at least in the case of the US manufacturing sector, exaggerate the impact of innovation and imitation on unit costs.

Armed with these findings we are now able to combine the results of Chapter 8 with the model of accumulation developed in Chapter 5 to arbitrate between the competing theories of crisis outlined in Chapter 3 and to provide an alternative account of the relationship between the rate of profit, investment, and productivity in the US manufacturing sector between 1965 and 1990. In understanding this relationship it is crucial to remember that changes in productivity and in profitability have quite different causes. As Chapter 6 emphasized, improvements in productivity result from technical and social changes within plants, the relative growth and decline of plants, and the entry and exit of plants. Productivity changes then are at heart reflections of the attempt by some plants to gain advantages over others. The rate of profit, as we have defined and measured it, is an aggregate, industry-wide measure, reflecting quite different forces: technical composition of capital and the real wage, among others. Therefore the movements in the two, productivity and profitability, can be quite different.

There was no slowdown in the rate of growth of labor productivity in US manufacturing after 1974. Aggregate productivity growth slowed after 1974 because of the overaccumulation of capital that could not be profitably invested. The rate of profit started to fall in 1965, almost a decade prior to any slowdown in the rate of productivity growth. These facts strongly suggest that changes in the rate of growth of productivity follow movements in the rate of profit. We therefore conclude that the accounts of capitalist crisis offered by Mandel (1978) and, to a lesser extent, Piore and Sabel (1984) appear consistent with the postwar history of accumulation in the USA; the accounts of Freeman and Perez (1988) and Lipietz (1986) do not. We now offer a revised version of the history of profitability and productivity in the USA after 1965.

High rates of profit in the early 1960s encouraged investment that led to relatively large unit cost savings through innovation and imitation. These productivity changes exhibited a labor-saving bias that increased the value composition of capital and tended to push down the rate of profit especially after 1965. The rate of profit was not pushed lower as a result of the growing strength of labor: real-wage increases were effectively countered by consistent gains in labor productivity that resulted from the rise in the technical composition of capital. There appears to have been no breakdown in the relationship between wages and productivity until the mid-1970s, when the wage share began to decline. Aggregate productivity growth also remained relatively stable as strong gains in the rate of growth of output maintained the capital/output ratio.

By the middle to late 1960s things had begun to unravel. By 1970 the rate of profit had fallen by more than 22% from its postwar high in 1965 following the dramatic growth of the value composition of capital. Consequently, the pace of investment and productivity change proper (innovation and imitation) slowed. The productivity changes that were introduced were even more heavily biased toward saving labor, part of a reaction to the scramble to substitute capital for energy after the oil shock of 1973. The value composition of capital increased more rapidly, driving down the rate of profit once again. As the rate of growth of output slowed from the business cycle peak of 1973 the capital/output ratio also increased sharply, pushed higher by the capital-for-labor substitution of productivity change. Falling rates of capacity utilization compounded the decline in the rate of profit and also led to a steep reduction in the rate of growth of aggregate productivity. The rate of growth of labor productivity increased by a few percentage points after 1974 buoyed by the same increases in capital intensity that caused aggregate productivity growth to falter. Rising energy costs also led input prices higher after 1973 and costs of production increased. The variance of unit costs of production followed the rise in prices. Therefore, the impact of selection on changes in unit costs increased significantly after 1974 along with the effects of the entry and exit of firms. Indeed, the entry of new firms through the late 1970s contributed more to the aggregate productivity slowdown than any other form of productivity change.

Although modified by business cycle swings through the late 1970s and into the early 1980s the story remained essentially the same: innovation continued to be biased against labor; the value composition of capital continued to climb; labor productivity growth remained largely unchanged while aggregate productivity slumped with the rise in the capital/output ratio; and the rate of profit fell even further.

Since 1982 a recovery has been underway. The rate of profit has increased, though somewhat shakily, but the rate of investment has not improved much. The impact of innovation and imitation on unit costs has increased due largely to the continued growth in the range of costs. For the same reason the importance of market forces, notably selection, on the rate of unit cost reductions has increased. The labor-saving bias of productivity change has been less extreme through the 1980s, and the rate of increase of the value composition of capital has slowed. Labor-saving productivity changes have increased labor productivity, and with real wages essentially constant the wage share has diminished. Improvements in capacity utilization that typically follow a recession have also reduced the capital/output ratio and raised aggregate productivity. However, the sluggish pace of investment and productivity gains do not bode well for the future, especially with the growth in trade and global competition. In Chapter 10 we examine the growth of the NICs, global competition, and the pattern of international capital flows in more detail.

APPENDIX A9: ESTIMATION

A9.1 STRUCTURAL EQUATIONS AND ESTIMATION

The system of structural equations employed for the task is

$$dh^T = -f_{10}\pi_t - f_{11}\pi_{t-1} - f_{12}\pi_{t-2} - f_{20}\pi_t(h - h_m)_t - f_{21}\pi_{t-1}(h - h_m)_{t-1} \\ - f_{22}\pi_{t-2}(h - h_m)_{t-2} - f_3\text{Var}(h)/h + f_4q + e_1 \tag{A9.1}$$

$$\pi = b_1 dh^T + b_{20}\text{CUR}_t + b_{21}\text{CUR}_{t-1} + b_{22}\text{CUR}_{t-2} + b_{30}O_t + b_{31}O_{t-1} \\ + b_{32}O_{t-2} + b_{40}o_t + b_{41}o_{t-1} + b_{42}o_{t-2} + e_2. \tag{A9.2}$$

Equation (A9.1) generalizes equation (9.1) by adding a random error term and by distributing the effects of profits and costs on innovation over 3 years. Equation (A9.2) is a conventional addition to the model, representing the rate of profit as dependent on current and lagged values of the capacity utilization rate (CUR), the level of shipments (O), and the rate of change in the level of shipments from one year to the next (o).

Given the difficulties in estimating Var(h) and ($h - h_m$), equation (A9.1) has been replaced by

$$dh^T = -f_{10}\pi_t - f_{11}\pi_{t-1} - f_{12}\pi_{t-2} - f_{20}\pi_t m(p - h)_t - f_{21}\pi_{t-1}m(p - h)_{t-1}$$
$$-f_{22}\pi_{t-2}m(p - h)_{t-2} - f_3(W/V^2)(p - h)^2/h + f_4 q + e_1. \tag{A9.3}$$

The two simultaneous equations (A9.2) and (A9.3) have been estimated by two-stage least squares. If we substitute equation (A9.2) in (A9.3) to obtain the reduced-form equation, we obtain a quadratic expression in dh^T. Rather than attempt to estimate quadratic expressions of the independent variables, we have estimated linearised forms of them:

$$E(dh^T) = c_{10} + c_{11}\text{CUR}_t + c_{12}\text{CUR}_{t-1} + c_{13}\text{CUR}_{t-2} + c_{14}O_t + c_{15}O_{t-1} + c_{16}O_{t-2}$$
$$+ c_{17}o_t + c_{18}o_{t-1} + c_{19}o_{t-2} + c_{20}q_t + c_{21}q_{t-1} + c_{22}q_{t-2} + e_{10}$$

$$E(\pi) = c_{30} + c_{31}\text{CUR}_t + c_{32}\text{CUR}_{t-1} + c_{33}\text{CUR}_{t-2} + c_{34}O_t + c_{35}O_{t-1} + c_{36}O_{t-2}$$
$$+ c_{37}o_t + c_{38}o_{t-1} + c_{39}o_{t-2} + c_{40}q_t + c_{41}q_{t-1} + c_{42}q_{t-2} + e_{20}.$$

Given the lags, there are 26 observations and 12 independent variables. Both regression equations are highly significant, with r^2 values of 0.84 and 0.99, respectively. The two reduced form equations provide estimates of the dependent variables $E(dh^T)$ and $E(\pi)$, which in turn are used to estimate the structural equations (A9.2) and (A9.3).

In estimating the structural equation on dh^T, collinearity prevented separation of the effects of innovation and imitation. Since the theory of Chapter 6 establishes the significance of these as separate processes, we have chosen not to drop one of the terms but to combine them. The complex term (innovation + imitation) thus measures in combined form the effects of real forms of productivity change that reflect alterations to the technical and social relations within plants.

The estimated structural equation on dh^T was therefore

$$E(dh^T) = -f_{10}[(1 + (p - h)_t)E(\pi_t)]$$
$$-f_{11}[(1 + (p - h)_{t-1})E(\pi_{t-1})]$$
$$-f_{12}[(1 + (p - h)_{t-2})E(\pi_{t-2})] \tag{A9.4}$$
$$-f_3(W/V^2)[(p - h)^2/h] + f_4 q + e_1.$$

The two output measures are both shipments, that is, actual sales, rather than production. The one, O, measures the level of shipments in the given

TABLE A9.1. Two-stage least squares estimation of π

Variable	Coefficient	SE	t-Score
Constant	−0.4999	0.1190	−4.20
CUR_t	1.6964	0.2547	6.66
CUR_{t-1}	−0.5558	0.2787	−1.94
CUR_{t-2}	−0.2204	0.1811	−1.22
O_t	0.00000097	0.0000002	4.82
O_{t-1}	−0.00000033	0.00000028	−1.16
O_{t-2}	−0.00000051	0.00000071	−2.46
o_t	−2.3096	0.4094	−5.64
o_{t-1}	−1.2117	0.4060	−2.98
o_{t-1}	−0.0621	0.0549	−1.13
dh^T	−0.4466	0.1947	−2.29

Note: $n = 26$; $r^2 = 0.98$; F-ratio = 73.71; SEE = 0.0098.

year. The other, o, measures the rate of change in the level of shipments over the previous year. Shipments are measured in constant 1982 dollars.

A9.2 PRODUCTIVITY IN US MANUFACTURING

Table A9.1 contains the results of the two-stage least squares estimates of the structural equation for rate of profit. The prediction of the rate of profit appears sound, with $r^2 = 0.98$. Capacity utilization and levels of output in the current period affect the rate of profit in the anticipated positive direction. However, lagged values of both variables tend to depress profitability, though statistically the lagged values are not as significant. Most surprisingly, current and lagged values of the rate of change in shipments are negatively related to the rate of profit. These are not expected results and may in part be explained by the collinearity between measures of output. Productivity changes that reduce the unit cost of production raise the rate of profit. This is generally quite standard and used solely to improve estimates of the model for productivity change (which is why we are not concerned with the collinearity between measures of output).

Chapter 10

THE GROWTH OF THE NICs

In the early 1950s none of the NICs was rich or industrially powerful. In Brazil, South Korea, and Taiwan average levels of GNP per person were less than $US 900 per person (1986 dollars); production was predominantly rural as only 10% of the GDP of South Korea and Taiwan originated in manufacturing; and exports were largely traditional food and raw material commodities. Only 40 years later all this had changed: Brazil's GDP was 8 times larger than it had been, and those of South Korea and Taiwan more than 15 times larger; more than 30% of GDP originated in manufacturing; and at least 80% of exports were manufactured. Meanwhile the countries in the OECD that had been rich and growing at the end of the war—the USA, Australia, and Canada among them—are now languishing. In contrast to average rates of growth of GNP of 6.2% in Brazil and over 8% in South Korea and Taiwan, the OECD has been growing at less than 4% each year. This chapter seeks the links between these two histories.

Development theorists study the growth of the NICs and the lack of growth in other countries. They examine whether and why growth has occurred. Can peripheral countries grow in a world dominated by a center, and if so how? The focus is NICs; the context is advanced capitalist countries. Those who study the advanced capitalist countries examine the effect on economic history of the evolution of the NICs. Their focus is advanced capitalist countries; their context is NICs. This chapter takes the second focus but uses evidence accumulated by those who adopt the first. We do not seek to know why Brazil, South Korea, or Taiwan are growing—indeed, this may be a nonquestion (Kim 1990)—but rather, how they are growing and the relations between their growth and the economic histories of advanced capitalist countries. What is the relation between the growth of NICs and the rate of profit in advanced capitalist countries?

Chapter 7 has examined theoretical answers to this question. The theory of comparative advantage argues that growth depends on relative cost advantages derived from patterns of factor abundance. The theory of competitive advantage observes that relative cost advantages also derive from conditions other than factor abundance. In both views the NICs faced lower costs of production than did traditional countries and therefore outcompeted them in world markets. The slowdown in advanced capitalist countries was therefore caused, or at least exacerbated, by the growth of NICs. Flows of capital from advanced capitalist economies to NICs reflected cost—and so profitability—differences and were the means by which NICs achieved high rates of economic growth. The theory of the new international division of labor explains the growth of NICs as a response to falling rates of profit in advanced industrialized countries and low costs of production in newly industrializing ones. In the 1970s corporations began to deindustrialize in the core and to invest in export-oriented manufacturing in some countries of the periphery. The growth of the NICs is both a response to falling profitability in the West and a reason why accumulation continues slowly.

Many political economic histories rely on these theories to interpret economic change (see Chapter 3). The thesis of the new international division of labor is especially popular. Piore and Sabel (1984), Lash and Urry (1987), and Lipietz (1986) claim that capital flight from advanced capitalist countries has reduced domestic rates of accumulation and—invested in the NICs—increased competition for domestic industries. The flight of capital is ascribed to differences in wage levels between advanced capitalist countries and NICs. So the growth of the NICs is a (proximate) cause of the slowdown in advanced capitalist countries and is itself an effect of wage differences and forces of internationalization that emanate from the center.

Other accounts question the significance of cost advantages in the growth of NICs. Chapter 7 argued that capital flows do not necessarily point to lower cost countries: the growth of NICs was not necessarily a matter of costs of production. Among political economic histories, Mandel's study (1978), like that of Harvey (1982), regards the slowdown in the advanced capitalist economies as intrinsic. NICs have grown in part because of the slowdown in advanced capitalist countries, employing capital that is produced but cannot be profitably invested there.

This chapter evaluates these arguments with data. It illustrates empirically the theoretical arguments of Chapter 7. After a brief historical introduction to Brazil, South Korea, and Taiwan (Section 10.1), three main claims are made and substantiated.

First, growth in NICs has not been determined by cost advantages—neither in its rate nor in its direction (Section 10.2). Orthodox accounts emphasize how the East Asian NICs have opened their economies to world trade and so profited from their abundance of cheap, skilled labor. Piore and Sabel (1984) and Lipietz (1987) argue in the same vein. By contrast, the competitiveness of NICs was irrelevant to their growth; industries were set up independently of competitiveness. Evidence directly contradicts the emphasis placed on cost advantages by theories of comparative advantage, competitive advantage and the new international division of labor (Section 10.3).

Secondly, Section 10.4 observes flows of capital into NICs. The largest in-flows of financial capital into NICs occurred after 1974, well after rates of profit had begun to fall in advanced capitalist economies and rates of accu-mulation had slowed. The policies and power of transnational corporations have been of little general significance in Brazil, South Korea, and Taiwan. In any case, the strategies of the transnational corporations have been com-plex: it is a parody to rate them as merely seeking low wages. The image of rapacious transnational corporations scrambling around the Third World for sites where labor is cheap and governments compliant is true of some in-dustries, but not most. In many countries foreign direct investment is of small consequence and controlled by states to foster their programs of in-dustrialization. The most important form of foreign capital in South Korea and Taiwan is financial; and even in Brazil many industries have relied on fi-nancial rather than direct productive investment. These observations rebut the argument of the theory of the new international division of labor that the flow of capital to NICs caused slower rates of accumulation in the ad-vanced capitalist economies and was controlled by transnational corpora-tions.

Thirdly, the chapter observes that productive development in NICs has been a matter of investment and learning. Growth has been a principal means to competitiveness. In South Korea especially exports have been a means to competitiveness; in Brazil they have often been an accidental by-product of import-substituting policies. Section 10.3 provides evidence consistent with this proposition. The crucial control over growth has been national accumu-lation strategies and nationally directed investment policies—within the con-text of a global economy awash with overaccumulated (finance) capital (Sec-tions 10.5 and 10.6). In Brazil, South Korea, and Taiwan the state has exercized a political will to develop. This will reflects local class structures and perceptions of geopolitical forces. Certainly these states have used the ex-cess capital produced in the center to finance their development programs, commonly to permit national, productive capitals to grow. But the programs were indigenous, not driven by foreign, direct investment; they were assisted by the need of central, financial capital to find profitable investment outlets. The central role of investment strategies in determining rates of growth re-flects the theory of Chapter 7 and explains why capital has flowed to only some Third World countries.

10.1 BACKGROUND

By almost any measure recent rates of economic growth in South Korea and Taiwan have been spectacular. The economic performance of Brazil has been less obtrusive only in comparison with the superstars of development: its economy has still grown much more rapidly than most of those in the OECD. This section reviews the growth of these three NICs.

In the 1950s and early 1960s real GDP was growing at 5.9% per annum in Brazil, 4.2% in South Korea, and 7.3% in Taiwan (Figure 10.1). While the mid-1960s was a period of slow growth in Brazil (GDP was growing at 3.5% per year), growth rates in South Korea, and Taiwan accelerated to more than 9% per year. In 1968–1973 GDP grew at more than 10% each year in all three countries. More recently growth rates have faltered: the 1974/75 recession hit Brazil and Taiwan especially hard, and the early 1980s were difficult for both Brazil and South Korea. Between 1984 and 1989, though, growth rates recovered to 7.1% per annum in Brazil, 10.1% in South Korea and 9.2% in Taiwan. By 1990 the Brazilian economy was about 8 times larger than in 1953; and the South Korean and Taiwanese economies about 16 times larger (Figure 10.2).

This rapid growth was accompanied by rapid industrialization. In the 1950s the economies of South Korea and Taiwan were still largely rural; even in Brazil only 20% of GDP originated in industry (Figure 10.3). By 1987 nearly 40% of Brazil's GDP originated in industry and more than that in South Korea and Taiwan. Manufacturing accounted for 30% of GDP in Brazil and South Korea and nearly 40% in Taiwan. These are now three of the most industrialized countries in the world.

In all three countries exports have provided one of the engines of growth

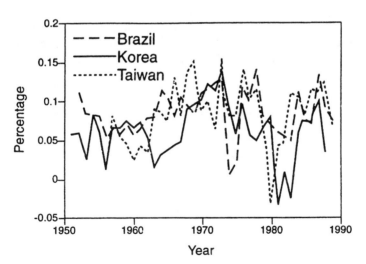

FIGURE 10.1. Rates of growth of GDP: Brazil, Korea, and Taiwan, 1950–1990. Data are calculated in local currencies, standardized to 1986 prices. Source: For Brazil and Korea data are drawn from *Yearbook of National Accounts Statistics* (annual), New York: United Nations, *National Accounts Statistics* (annual), New York: United Nations, *Statistical Yearbook* (annual), New York: United Nations; for Taiwan data come from the Economic Yearbook of the Republic of China (annual), Taipei: Economic Daily News, and from *Statistical Yearbook of the Republic of China* (annual)Taipei: Directorate General of Budget, Accounting and Statistics.

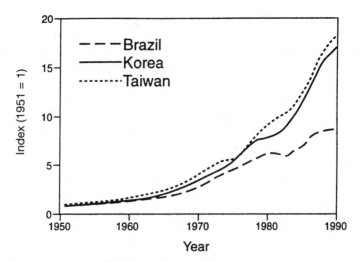

FIGURE 10.2. Levels of GDP: Brazil, South Korea, and Taiwan, 1950–1990. Data are standardized such that GDP in 1951 = 1 in all three countries. *Source*: see Figure 10.1.

(Figure 10.4). They are among the most successful exporters in recent history. By the early 1960s in South Korea and Taiwan and the late 1960s in Brazil merchandise export earnings were increasing at rates well above the world average. By 1970 South Korea's exports were 20 times larger than they had been 10 years earlier. Since 1973 exports from all three countries have grown more slowly; even so, they have grown 3–5 times faster than world trade as a whole.

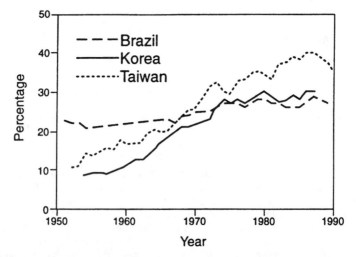

FIGURE 10.3. Proportion of GDP arising in manufacturing: Brazil, South Korea, and Taiwan, 1950–1990. *Source*: see Figure 10.1.

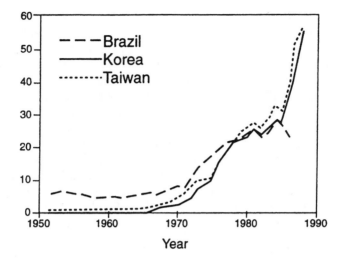

FIGURE 10.4. Merchandise exports: Brazil, South Korea, and Taiwan, 1950–1990. Data are in constant 1986 $US billion. *Source*: see Figure 10.1.

Exports of manufactures from Brazil, South Korea, and Taiwan have grown even more rapidly (Figure 10.5). In the 1950s all three NICs exported mainly agricultural and mineral commodities. Even in the late 1950s less than 15% of their merchandise exports were manufactured. In South Korea and Taiwan, which are densely populated countries with few natural resources, manufacturing provided over 75% of merchandise exports by 1970; now

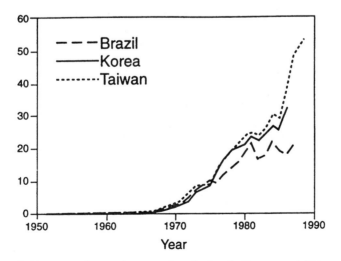

FIGURE 10.5. Exports of manufactures: Brazil, South Korea, and Taiwan, 1950–1990. Data are in constant 1986 $US billion. *Source*: see Figure 10.1.

more than 90% of exports are manufactured. In Brazil, where natural resources are more plentiful, the transition has been less remarkable; still manufactured commodities furnished 50% of merchandise export earnings by 1972 and now afford more than 80%. (Data are from Figures 10.4 and 10.5.) Little wonder that political elites in advanced capitalist countries view exports from NICs as a cause of their trade imbalance and economic slowdown.

Rates of fixed capital accumulation have been correspondingly high (Figure 10.6). After hovering about 7% per annum in Brazil and Taiwan and 10% in South Korea, rates of fixed capital accumulation jumped in the mid 1960s to about 15% per annum (and over 20% for a while in South Korea), before starting to fall about 1974/75. In Brazil, after a period in the late 1970s and early 1980s when they gradually fell to 4.4%, rates of fixed capital accumulation have now recovered to 7–8% per year. In South Korea rates of accumula-

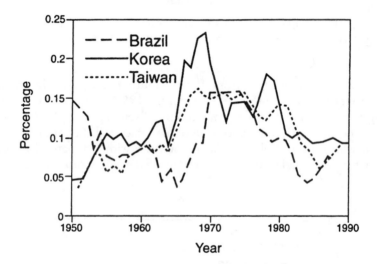

FIGURE 10.6. Rates of fixed capital accumulation: Brazil, South Korea, and Taiwan, 1950–1990. These data are constructed from levels of gross fixed capital formation (GFCF) and allowances for consumption of fixed capital, expressed in 1986 prices in local currency. The life of fixed capital (n) was estimated by comparing estimated levels of depreciation (as $1/n$ of the sum of the last n years GFCF) with allowances for consumption of fixed capital; data were sufficient to compare estimated depreciation and actual allowances for 1980–1990 in Taiwan and with $n = 23$ years, average differences were 3.2% of the actual allowances per year; data were sufficient to compare estimated depreciation and actual allowances for 1984–1988 in Korea and with $n = 31$ years, average differences were 2.89 of the actual allowances per year; data were insufficient to permit this comparison in Brazil, so it has been assumed that $n = 30$ years. Data on consumption allowances then permit GFCF to be estimated back to the 1920s (and in the case of Brazil, data on GFCF permit consumption allowances to be estimated for 1980–1990). It was assumed that the fixed capital accumulation is calculated as GFCF less (actual or estimated) consumption of fixed capital. *Source:* see Figure 10.1.

tion have fallen back to nearly 9.9% per year in the 1980s. Taiwan's rates of capital accumulation fell to 5.7% in 1986 but have since averaged 8.5% per annum.

Conditions in all three NICs, and especially in South Korea and Taiwan, have been conducive to rapid capital accumulation, industrialization and growth of output. Even real wages have grown in Brazil, South Korea, and Taiwan (Figure 10.7): by 1985 real wages in manufacturing were 1.4 times their 1970 level in Brazil and about 2.5 times in South Korea and Taiwan (van Liemt 1988: 74). But there has been a price: popular groups have been largely excluded from political power (Deyo 1990). In Taiwan policy has been economically exclusionary: wages have been held down; there has been no countercyclical public expenditure in recessions; social welfare expenditures are low [see Chiou (1986) on opposition and conflict in Taiwan; and Deyo et al. (1987) on manipulation of trade unions]. According to Deyo, South Korea is characterized by conflict and opposition, not exclusion. Generally wages have been controlled, legislation protects foreign firms against strikes, social welfare is limited, and laws protecting workers are not enforced (Deyo et al. 1987; Launius 1984; Park 1987). Following the 1930 revolution in Brazil, a populist alliance of the national bourgeoisie, workers, and middle class was installed. Even so, populist groups have been unable to resist cuts in living

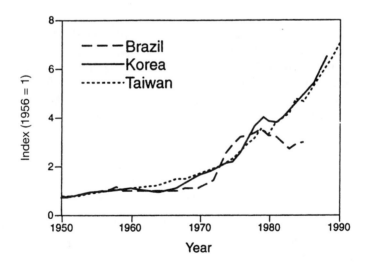

FIGURE 10.7. Real monthly earnings in manufacturing: Brazil, South Korea, and Taiwan, 1950–1990. Data are monthly earnings of male and female workers in manufacturing, expressed in constant 1986 prices in local currency and then standardized to 1956 = 1. *Source*: For Brazil and Korea, *Statistical Yearbook* (annual), New York: United Nations, supplemented in the case of Brazil for 1976–1985 by Deyo 1990:191; for Taiwan data come from *Economic Yearbook of the Republic of China* (annual), Taipei: Economic Daily News, and from the *Statistical Yearbook of the Republic of China* (annual) Taipei: Directorate General of Budget, Accounting and Statistics.

standards during periods of economic crisis and were especially impotent after the 1964 coup: thus the 1.4-fold rise in real wages between 1970 and 1985 compares with a 1.7-fold increase in GDP per person. Some of the monetary benefits of economic growth have trickled down to the workers, especially in South Korea and Taiwan, but few of the political benefits.

10.2 COST ADVANTAGES

The theories of comparative and competitive advantage claim that a country's production becomes efficient if it adopts free trade policies and specializes in producing only commodities in which it has a comparative advantage or has created a competitive advantage. Even the theory of the new international division of labor argues that low-cost production explains the growth of the NICs. It is a small step to argue that countries that open their economies to international competition and encourage their companies to export internationally competitive commodities can hasten their industrialization and economic growth. Krueger (1981) makes just such a claim. Similarly, Balassa (1985) maintains that outward-oriented policies benefit productivity and economic growth, contributing comparative advantages, higher rates of capacity utilization, economies of scale, and rapid technical progress in response to competition abroad (Little 1982). Opponents of this orthodox view argue that even in theory trade liberalization merely offers a once and for all gain in efficiency rather than continuing higher rates of growth (Bienefeld 1988; Krueger 1981; Wade 1990a: 14), that comparative or competitive advantage are not a sufficient basis for efficiency, and that growth is a result not merely of low-cost production (Chapter 7).

In view of this dispute, this section examines growth in Brazil, South Korea, and Taiwan in terms of costs of production and comparative or competitive advantage. This seems a straightforward task: compare degrees of trade liberalization with rates of growth over many countries. Indeed the World Bank (1987) has made such a comparison, though its conclusions are hardly robust statistically (Wade 1990a: 17–20); we shall later examine similar data. The problem concerns measures of liberalization: what are the policies applied by NICs, and how are they related to the categories of comparative or competitive advantage? Disagreement about the facts forces a more limited but detailed study of trade policies in the three countries. So after we describe how the orthodox interpret development sequences (Section 10.2.1), Section 10.2.2 surveys price distortions and trade policies and Section 10.2.3 recounts evidence about export success and growth rates. Price distortions imply that domestic prices are not international prices, contrary to the claims of the orthodox. Protection and export enhancement indicate that domestic producers in NICs were shielded against foreign competition by means other than cost competitiveness—contrary to the claims of comparative or competitive advantage and the theory of the new international division of labor.

10.2.1 The Argument

One of the great debates about policies for economic development argues the relative merits of import substitution and export orientation. It is asserted that the continuing success of South Korea and Taiwan owes much to their switch from import substitution to export orientation in the 1960s, which permitted them to exploit their cost advantages. By implication, Brazil's slower rates of growth in the 1970s and 1980s derive from its failure to convert from import substitution to export orientation.

Five accumulation strategies have been identified (Gereffi 1990). They may be linked in different historical sequences (Figure 10.8).

Initially commodities are exported. According to Gereffi this phase lasted until 1930 in Brazil and until the end of the Japanese occupation of South Korea and Taiwan. Capital is limited, so according to the Heckscher–Ohlin theory resource-based products must be exported with little additional processing. This accumulation strategy offers little long-term potential for growth (Hamilton 1987): most resources, especially agricultural ones, have a low income elasticity of demand; natural resource constraints limit long-term development; and there are technical limits on large-scale production and advanced division of labor. Long-term capital accumulation depends on industrialization.

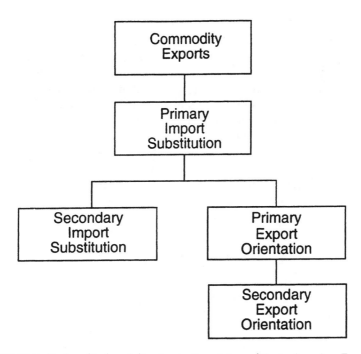

FIGURE 10.8. Paths of industrialization in East Asia and Latin America. From Gereffi (1990: 18). *Source*: Gereffi 1990.

A second strategy is primary import substitution. According to Gereffi, Brazil followed this strategy between 1930 and 1955, South Korea between 1953 and 1960, and Taiwan between 1950 and 1959. Countries progressively replace imports of basic consumer goods, commonly textiles, clothing, footwear, and food processing. In substituting for imports a technologically backward country tries to accelerate investment primarily for the home market by manipulating market prices, barriers to entry, and access to imports and finance so as to improve profit–risk trade-offs (Felix 1989). The state intervenes on infant industry grounds, "getting the prices wrong"; such intervention raises production costs above world market prices because the domestic currency is overvalued and intermediate inputs overpriced (Hirata 1988). In Heckscher–Ohlin terms capital can be accumulated in manufacturing to exploit reserves of unskilled or semiskilled workers in labor-intensive production (Gunasekera 1989).

Primary import substitution is commonly nationalistic: an attempt to assert political independence. However, the domestic market for consumer nondurables is limited by income (and perhaps population), so the scope for continuing to substitute for imports is restricted. Once the scope is exhausted there lies an important choice: continued import substitution in capital goods, durable consumer goods, and intermediate products (the usual choice) or primary export substitution (the East Asian choice)—in which the labor-intensive manufactures previously supplied to domestic markets are exported (Ranis 1989).

By orthodox accounts Brazil embraced secondary import substitution between 1955 and 1968 whereas South Korea and Taiwan adopted primary export orientation until 1972. In Heckscher–Ohlin terms such exports merely confirm the comparative advantages of unskilled or semiskilled labor-intensive manufacturing in countries poor in resources and capital (Gunasekera 1989).

Since 1968 Brazil has supplemented secondary import substitution with diversified export promotion. In 1973 South Korea and Taiwan joined Brazil in secondary import substitution but combined with secondary export orientation: they began a heavy and chemical industrialization, which is import substituting and export oriented (Gereffi 1990). All three—Brazil since 1955, South Korea and Taiwan since 1973—have programs of heavy industrialization to produce capital and intermediate and durable consumer goods. In Heckscher–Ohlin terms surplus produced in labor-intensive industries is invested in machinery and equipment to raise labor productivity; the benefits of investment flow more to heavy than to light industries, shifting comparative and competitive advantages away from labor-intensive toward capital-intensive industries (Dollar and Sokoloff 1990). The shift of advantage was confirmed when the domestic labor surplus was eliminated and wages started to rise relative to capital prices (Ranis 1989; Garnaut 1989).

According to orthodoxy East Asian dragons like South Korea and Taiwan constructed their success by devising free, open economies in which prices reflect real (international) as opposed to induced scarcities (Wade 1990b). Exchange rates are realistic; production is not protected, or at least specific sectors are not indulged; factor market policies promote intersectoral mobility (Laird and Nogues 1988). Resources are therefore used efficiently (in sectors with comparative or competitive advantage), and manufacturers are induced to overcome the constraints of small domestic markets by exporting goods at competitive prices (see also Bienefeld 1988). Markets have adjusted themselves: governments had to shift policy from import substitution, but once the dials were correctly set governments merely provided infrastructure and prevented politics from interfering with the market. Brazil never embraced such export-oriented policies. Its policies remain oriented inward and therefore perform poorly (Laird and Nogues 1988): competition is impeded; economies of scale are restricted; rent-seeking and unproductive activities are encouraged; and nontariff barriers obstruct macropolicy.

Yet the contrast between import substitution and export orientation is oversimplified. It conflates several distinctions: import–export orientation, government–market direction, and discriminatory–liberal policies (Bradford 1990). More care is taken in Table 10.1. There are degrees of inward and outward orientation, of liberality, and of government intervention. An open economy is only one type of outward orientation. Openness is not necessarily indexed by the proportion of imports and exports in GDP. An economy may be closed—with exports or imports being small compared to GDP—because of size or geography rather than policy. The theories of comparative and competitive advantage claim benefits for open, liberal, market economies over autarchic, import-substituting, or export-push economies, over discriminatory policies, and over government-directed economies.

TABLE 10.1. Distinctions: Trade, discrimination, and direction

Import–export orientation	Discrimination–liberal policies	Government–market direction
Autarky	No trade delinking and self-reliance	Dirigisme
Import substitution	Discriminates against imports by exchange rate OR selective discrimination OR mild discrimination	↑↓
Inward orientation	Priority to the domestic economy	Markets
Outward orientation	Priority to exports	Markets
Open economy	Internal liberalization via exchange rate for tradable goods OR tradable and nontradable goods	↑↓
Export push	Uniform subsidies for all exports OR selective subsidies, industrial policy, import substitution	Dirigisme

Source: Bradford (1990: 33).

Superimposed on debates over import substitution and export orientation is an argument about discrimination and government intervention. Orthodox theorists argue either that East Asian economies were open (liberal and market directed) after 1960 or that selective industrial policies were retained after 1960 but the government followed the market and so made no difference (Wade 1990b). To show that governments have actively and selectively intervened in all three countries is only the first step in demonstrating that growth and export success have not originated in cost advantages; we need also to show that prices are wrong.

10.2.2 Government intervention

Early in their drives to industrialize all three NICs lacked capital. Their major asset in competing internationally was an ample supply of low-wage labor power. Yet the governments of all three NICs believed (or acted as though they believed) that these factor endowments could not drive industrialization in the right direction or fast enough. Governments have intervened to promote selected industries by economic, financial, and industrial policies (Section 10.2.2.1). These are not market economies. In turn policies have distorted prices (Section 10.2.2.2): in Amsden's (1989) words, governments have deliberately got the prices wrong.

10.2.2.1 Degrees of Liberalization

Between 1910 and 1945 all of Korea (North and South) was a colony of Japan. Initially its role was to export rice, fish, silk, and minerals. Some heavy industries were developed later, mostly in the North; little heavy industry remained in the South after the World War II and the Korean War. At first policy was import substituting, with overvalued and multiple exchange rates and payments balanced through foreign aid (Balassa 1985). The exchange rate was overvalued to avoid inflation, to maximize the won value of sales to the US armed services, and to increase the domestic purchasing power of aid (Koo and Park 1990). Import substitution contributed 24% of industrial growth in the second half of the 1950s; exports—mainly primary commodities—only 5% (Balassa 1985: 143). After 1957 the economy stagnated as the possibilities for primary import substitution were exhausted.

In the orthodox account South Korea was transformed in the 1960s and 1970s after it adopted an outward-oriented strategy that exploited comparative and competitive advantages (Balassa 1985). Policy was reversed between 1960 and 1963. The value of the won was halved; exchange rates unified; import controls liberalized; a 50% tax reduction granted on profits from exports; and exporters exempted from indirect taxes on inputs. After 1961 the balance of payments deteriorated, so imports were again restricted and another multiple exchange rate system imposed. The trend toward openness and exports picked up in 1964 when President Chung Hee Park again halved the value of the won (Koo and Park 1990), reunified exchange rates and provided more incentives for exports. The same rules applied to all nontraditional exporters and incentives for domestic and foreign production were uniform: policy discriminated neither by sector nor by market. Whereas earlier import licences had been automatically refused except for specified goods, after 1967 imports were automatically approved except for specified commodities (Balassa 1985). By 1968 tariffs, export subsidies, and import restrictions were raising domestic prices for manufactured goods 16% above international prices (Argentina's domestic prices were 70% above international prices in 1969); subsidies to producers for domestic markets were 0.95 of those for export markets, whereas in Argentina the ratio of subsidies was 3.4:1 (Balassa 1985: 151).

This story about South Korea overemphasizes trade liberalization (Ohno 1989). The liberalization of the 1960s was only nominal. Export promotion, not free trade, replaced import substitution. South Korea's selective industrial policies included tax treatments, tariffs, and interest rate policies.

Preferential tax rates have been applied to specific industries including iron and steel, chemicals and electronics (Rhee 1988). Until 1980 these included investment tax credits, income tax deductions, and corporate tax exemptions. In 1975 the industries were granted preferential depreciation rates and allowed to keep tax-free reserves for investment. Since 1981 income tax deductions and corporate tax exemptions have been removed from the list of preferential tax allowances and functional tax concessions on research and development have exceeded selective, direct incentives (Rhee 1988: 238): incomes, facility investments, training expenses all receive tax credits or preferential depreciation allowances.

Tariff rates have remained high and selective. Imports have been liberalized, but really only after 1978 and then slowly. According to Rhee (1988: 240–241) by 1978 some 65% of items were liberalized; and by 1984, 85%. Yet in 1978 the liberalized items accounted for only 18% of imports; and only 32% by 1984. Tariff rates did not begin to fall substantially until 1978. The average rate of legal tariffs was 27.4% in 1955/56; 35.4% in 1957–1961; 49.5% in 1962–1967; 56.7% in 1968–1972; 48.1% in 1973–1976; 41.3% in 1977; 34.4% in 1979; 26.7% in 1984; and 26.4% in 1985 (Kim 1990). Typically tariffs have been higher in import-competing industries than in other (Hamilton 1987); and over the 1970s tariffs began to discriminate more effectively between different sectors (van Liemt 1988). In 1978 effective rates of protection were 135% in transport equipment, 131% in consumer durables, and 47% in machinery production (Bienefeld 1988); on all capital-intensive manufactures they were 72.5% (Hong 1990: 116; Luedde-Neurath 1986: 140–144). Quantitative restrictions are still imposed to protect infant industries: as late as 1982 28.8% of (four-digit) commodities were restricted quantitatively (some were subject to tariffs too); they amounted to 41% of imports by value (Luedde-Neurath 1986: 136–138). Specific industries are exempt from import tariffs or pay reduced rates so that duties do not disadvantage exporters. For key industries (especially facility equipment and machinery) these deductions were 80–100% until 1974, 70–90% in 1975–1983, and 55–65% since 1984 (Rhee 1988).

The government provides capital at subsidized interest rates to favored borrowers (Table 10.2). Firms with such loans enjoyed negative real-interest rates during much of the 1970s, especially for export financing. The Bank of Korea has imposed quantitative credit controls—over interest rates, reserve requirements, and security sales—and qualitative or selective controls that favor heavy and chemical industries, particular regions and firm types (Ito 1984; Vos 1982). The margin between official and actual interest rates has not fallen since 1984, though other areas of financial life have been liberalized (Kohsaka 1987).

Central to South Korea's economic performance has been the Foreign Exchange Demand and Supply Plan. Foreign exchange holdings must be surrendered to or deposited with the Bank of Korea: the government controls the rate at which firms earn and spend foreign currency. Since the late 1960s this Plan has set detailed sectoral requirements for earning foreign currency and allowances for spending it. Industry associations use the Plan to prepare production targets and import quotas for each corporation. In particular consumer goods imports have been severely restricted (C. Hamilton 1986:

TABLE 10.2. Real price of capital: South Korea, 1971–1984

Year	Wholesale price index	Rate of interest		Real rate of interest	
		Investment	Export	Investment	Export
1971	8.7	12.0	6.0	3.3	−2.7
1972	13.8	11.0	6.0	−2.8	−7.8
1973	6.0	10. 0	6.5	4.0	0.5
1974	42.1	10.0	9.0	−31.1	−33.1
1975	26. 5	12.0	8.0	−14.5	−18.5
1976	12.2	12.5	7.5	0.3	−4.7
1977	9.0	13.0	8.0	4.0	−1.0
1978	11.6	14.0	8.5	2.4	−3. 1
1979	18.8	15.0	9.0	−3.8	−9.8
1980	38.9	21.0	15.0	−17.9	−23.9
1981	20.4	18.5	15.0	−1.9	−5.4
1982	4.7	13 .0	11.0	8.3	6.3
1983	0.2	10.0	10.0	9.8	9.8
1984	0.7	10.0	10.0	9.3	9.3

Note: The rate of interest on investment is the rate for Facility Investment Loans from the Korean Development Bank; the export rate is the rate of interest on export financing; the real rate of interest is the rate of interest less the wholesale price index.
Source: Rhee (1988: 231).

119–127). The Plan seems to be binding: between 1972 and 1979 foreign exchange receipts exceeded planned receipts every year (except 1975 when actual receipts were 99.7% of planned) and payments have never exceeded planned payments by more than 10%, except in 1973 when oil prices rose (Luedde-Neurath 1986: 118). The Plan directly contradicts the notion that South Korea followed its comparative and competitive advantage after 1963-1965.

There is little basis for claiming that South Korea liberalized significantly in the 1960s: quantitative controls, the Foreign Exchange and Supply Plan, and voluntary self-regulation by industry associations all remain. In Taiwan things have been little different. Even so, the orthodox claim that the expansion of foreign trade was decisive among the factors that contributed to Taiwan's economic growth and attribute that expansion to comparative or competitive advantage (lower costs).

Initially Taiwanese policy was to substitute local goods for imports. There was a trade deficit and costs of production were relatively high (especially in comparison with Japan). Imports were restricted quantitatively and by tariffs; the exchange rate was overvalued (a lower rate applied to imports of capital goods) (Lin 1973). As in South Korea much of the burden of paying for industrialization fell on farmers: the price of rice was halved in relation to the price of cotton textiles between 1949 and 1952 (Kuo and Frei 1985: 49). But easy import substitution came to an end as the limit of the domestic market was reached.

So export promotion emerged between 1956 and 1960. Economic life in Taiwan was liberalized: tax, foreign exchange, and financial preferences were offered to private business; taxes were modified to encourage capital formation; a unitary exchange rate was established; and exports stimulated. The basic data on exchange rates are contained in Table 10.3. The response from industry was slow until 1965, when the Kaohsiung Export Processing Zone was set up, marking a definite end to import substitution. Rebates compensated exporters for the tariffs they paid on imports. The nominal rate of protection on manufacturing, weighted by domestic sales, fell from 53.5% in 1961 to 39.1% in 1966 and to 36.0% in 1971 (Kuo and Frei 1985: 53). During the 1960s the expansion of exports accounted for over half the growth of output in manufacturing, and in the early 1970s over 80%; the expansion of domestic demand accounted in the 1960s for less than 40% of the growth of output, and in the early 1970s for less than 20% (Kuo and Frei 1985: 66-68). Since 1955 import substitution has accounted for less than 15% of the growth of output of manufacturing industry in Taiwan.

Yet Taiwan, like South Korea, did not replace import substitution with an open economy but with a policy that promoted exports in some industries and encouraged import substitution behind barriers in others (Wade 1990b: 115–117). In the 1960s and 1970s measurable export incentives averaged 11% of gross receipts (Scitovsky 1986: 160; Wade 1990: 139–148). In 1969 tariffs, subsidies, and import restrictions still encouraged manufacturers to

TABLE 10.3. Exchange rates: Taiwan, 1950–1969

Date	Rates for exports					Rates for imports					Official rate	Market rate
	Government			Private		Government				Private		
11 04 1951	10.25			14.73		10.30				15.69		
21 05 1951										15.69		
21 05 1952				14.49							15.65	23.07
	Sugar, rice	Salt	Other									
01 09 1952	10.25	12.37	10.25									
01 08 1952		14.49										
04 01 1953	14.49	15.55	15.55	15.55		15.65					15.65	26.50
						RM(+3)	Other					
16 09 1953						15.65	18.78					
04 04 1954	15.55					18.78				18.78	18.78	30.10
	(+1)			Banana	Other	C(+4)	NC(+5)					
01 05 1955	15.55	15.55	20.35	18.60	20.43	18.78	24.78			24.78 24.88	24.78	40.20
10 09 1955	20.35	18.55				24.78	24.78			24.78		
01 06 1956		20.35									24.78	38.50
27 10 1956				23.55								
01 07 1957										32.28	24.78	38.3
08 06 1958				26.35	26.35						36.38	46.90
	Sugar, salt, rice			Others (+2)		RMtl (+6)	Wheat + bean	Raw cotton	Other (+2)			
14 04 1958	24.58			36.08		24.78	24.78	24.78	36.38			
05 07 1958				38.03					38.23			
21 11 1958	36.08			37.13		36.38	36.38	36.38	37.33			
01 01 1959				39.73					39.93		36.38	45.11
10 08 1959				38.90		36.38	36.38	40.03	38.90			
01 03 1960				40.02		36.38	40.03	40.03	40.92		36.38	42.26
01 04 1960				39.98		40.03	40.03	40.03	39.82			
01 07 1960	40.03			38.82								
1961											40.03	43.98
1962											40.03	46.99
30 09 1964		40.00					40.01				40.03	42.48
1964											40.10	45.88
1965											40.10	41.63
1966											40.10	41.00
1967											40.10	41.61
1968											40.10	41.12
1969											40.10	41.44

Notes: Rates are $NT per $US. Rates are for exports or imports by government or government enterprises as compared to exports or imports by private enterprises.

+1: Sugar, salt, petroleum, and aluminum.

+2: Average of a range.

+3: Raw materials and equipment.

+4: Imports by government enterprises whose prices are controlled.

+5: Imports by government enterprises whose prices are not controlled.

+6: Essential machinery, fertilizers, and oil for domestic use.

Sources: On the multiple rates, Directorate General of Budget, Accounting and Statistics (1976) *Statistical Yearbook of the Republic of China* Taipei; on official and market rates, Council for International Economic Cooperation and Development (1970) *Taiwan Statistical Data Book* Taipei.

produce for the domestic market: incentives for the domestic market were 1.34 times those for overseas markets (Balassa 1985: 151). Average legal tariffs were 31% in 1981 (Tsiang and Chen 1984), compared to the average among all developing countries in 1985 of 34% (Erzan et al. 1988). Legal tariffs may even have increased between 1966 and the early 1970s (when more than a quarter of all items paid duty of over 60%) before falling somewhat (Tsiang and Chen 1984). And while many nontariff barriers to imports have been eliminated, "permissible" items can often be imported only by specific firms or from specific countries that do not compete with Taiwanese firms (e.g., clothing from the USA and Europe) (Wade 1990b: 128–129); in 1984 over half of all imports by value had to be approved (Tu and Wang 1988). In effect Taiwan has operated a "cascading" structure of protection, with greater tariff and nontariff protection on final demand goods than on raw materials or intermediates (Wade 1990b: 136–137). Exporters pay little or no duty on imports of raw materials and intermediate goods. Imports of machinery and equipment to be used in producing specific items (including iron and steel, electronics, machinery, and chemicals) do not pay duty provided that the goods are not manufactured in Taiwan (Wade 1990b: 127). Right through to the 1980s, though with declining emphasis as trade surpluses have mounted, Taiwan has operated export promotion schemes: export processing zones, tariff rebates, easing of nontariff barriers, export tax incentives, export credits, cartels to limit competition in international markets, quality inspection systems, government marketing assistance, and an undervalued currency (Wade 1990b: 139–148).

Taiwan has operated selective industrial policies and applied them with discretion. Over and above tariff and nontariff barriers, the government has encouraged industrial reorganization, given administrative guidance, controlled entry to many industries, and imposed local content requirements to build infant industries (Wade 1990b: 159–194). For example, the Taiwanese government provides subsidized inputs of technology to the machine tool industry (Fransman 1986). It offers fiscal incentives for in-house research and development and subsidizes the research of the Mechanical Industrial Research Laboratories. Other forms of state assistance to the machine tool industry include cheap loans from the Bank of Communication, import controls, and export help. According to producers, the most valuable form of assistance is subsidized credit, followed by technical assistance; market protection and export assistance rank third (Fransman 1986: 1388).

The extent to which the government directs the economy is indexed by the level of public ownership. In 1987 four of Taiwan's largest companies were state owned (Gereffi 1990). From 1951 through 1980 public enterprises formed over 30% of gross fixed capital in Taiwan and contributed over 11% of GDP; in South Korea public enterprises also formed 30% of gross fixed capital in 1963, but that share fell to 22% by 1978–1980; in Brazil the share rose from 14% in 1968 to 23% by 1980; the share in Europe was 23% in 1974–1977 (Wade 1990b: 177). Public enterprises are concentrated in refining, petrochemicals, steel, shipbuilding, heavy machinery, and transport equipment, as well as utilities—industries in which both the benefit and the entry costs are high and which are intimately linked to Taiwan's defence industry. Public enterprises substitute for imports in industries often dominated by multinationals and do so without high levels of protection (Wade 1990b: 176–182). The gains from public enterprises flow to professional and capitalist classes, helping to secure their support for the state (Davis and Ward 1990; Chan et al. 1990).

There is general agreement that the Brazilian government has been interventionist and substituted for imports rather than promoted exports. In 1984 tariff rates in Brazil were 51% on (unweighted) average and all imports were still controlled by licenses (Laird and Nogues 1988). The "Law of Similars"' restricts imports of goods similar to local products (do Lago 1988). Much growth of production in Brazil has been ascribed to local demand, enhanced by government procurement policies. In 1974 capital projects had to contain 44% local equipment to be approved; in 1978 the requirement was raised to 76% (Teubal 1984). The state owns many enterprises in heavy and infrastructural industries, often controlling their prices: such state companies as Telebras (telecommunications), Eletrobras (electricity generation), Petrobras (petroleum refining), and Siderbras (steel) absorbed more than 60% of fixed investment in 1969 (Baer et al. 1973: 30; van Liemt 1988).

Yet this story of Brazil as an import substituting country understates the changes that took place in the mid 1960s (Clements 1988: 13–15). Imports were liberalized (at least until the oil crisis in 1974); and exports promoted by fiscal incentives, credit incentives and bureaucratic simplification. Fiscal incentives exempted exports from tariffs, industrial products taxes, state value added taxes and business income taxes. Credit incentives included subsidized loans for export financing. Export incentives were 43% of the free-on-board value of manufactured exports in 1969, rising to 63% in 1978 and 69% in 1982, before falling under international pressure to 43% in 1985 (Clements 1988: 15). Like South Korea and Taiwan, Brazil promoted exports after the mid-1960s; in the mid-1970s the export push was combined with renewed heavy industrialization under import-substituting policies when balance of payments problems emerged in the wake of the first oil price shock (van Liemt 1988).

These subsidies compensated for losses on exports when domestic costs of production exceeded international prices. South Korea's exports were often not profitable (and so did not reflect cost advantages). In 1966 it cost 600 won (then $2.21) to produce a dollar's worth of radio exports. Similar costs applied to plywood and knitted products. Together the three products constituted a third of South Korea's manufactured exports (C. Hamilton 1986: 119–127). Brazil became the world's third largest exporter of ships even though they cost 40% more to produce than foreign equivalents (van Liemt 1988: 41).

10.2.2.2 Price Distortions

This government intervention implies that prices are wrong: domestic prices do not reflect international prices. If prices are distorted, costs of production may be below international market prices not simply because of comparative or competitive advantage but also because of government manipulation.

One of the most distorted prices is the price of capital, the rate of interest.

In Brazil after 1964 subsidized loans were provided to exporters. The loans were given before export so that production costs could be financed at rates below the market; and they were given after export so that money could be borrowed at international rates for long-term projects. Clements (1988: 15) estimates that credit subsidies to exporters were worth 4% of the free-on-board value of manufactured exports in 1969, rising to nearly 20% in 1977 and 22% in 1982, before falling sharply in the mid-1980s. Nominal export subsidies were more than five times as great in machinery, electrical equipment, furniture, plastics, textiles, and apparel industries as in food products (Tyler 1981).

The financial system in South Korea consists of a regulated formal sector (deposit money banks and nonbank financial institutions) and an unorganized sector (the curb market). The government imposes ceilings on bank loan and deposit rates in the formal sector, while selective credit controls direct funds to designated sectors. Despite attempts to integrate the two sectors and the growth of nonbanks, there still exists a dual structure: credit demands that cannot be met in the formal sector—because of interest rate ceilings or credit allocation policies—are satisfied in the curb market (Kim 1988; Ito 1984; Vos 1982). Prices in the two sectors are quite different (Table 10.4; compare Table 10.2).

Firms with access to domestic banks have a considerable privilege, for the

TABLE 10.4. Costs of capital: South Korea, 1966–1986

Interest rates	1966–1970	1971–1975	1976–1980	1981–1983	1984/85	1986
1 Domestic banks	24.2	17.4	18.0	13.8	10.0	10.0
Curb market	54.2	40.1	41.4	30.5	24.4	23.2
2 90-day Eurodollar	7.2	7.9	9.5	13.0	9.5	6.7
3 Exchange rate depreciation percent	3.1	9.3	4.7	8.5	5.9	1.3
4 GDP deflator percent	15.4	18.8	20.9	8.5	4.0	1.4
5 Differential: 1–2–3	14.1	0.2	3.8	−7.7	−5.4	2.0
6 Real cost of foreign capital: 2+3–4	−5.1	−1.6	−6.7	13.0	11.4	6.6

Source: Koo and Park (1990: 87).

real cost of capital in South Korea is far higher than the interest rate charged by domestic banks. Curb market rates are commonly two to three times bank rates. Approved firms have a second advantage: access to the even cheaper loans of the Korean Development Bank. Loans from the Development Bank were far cheaper than ordinary bank loans until the mid-1970s: between 1971 and 1976, for example, ordinary bank loans cost 17.4% on average, whereas Development Bank loans cost 10–12% (Tables 10.2 and 10.4). A third advantage for such firms is that domestic interest rates are distorted in relation to international ones: firms permitted access to international capital markets paid negative real interest rates throughout the 1960s and 1970s (line 6 of Table 10.4). On average the interest subsidy on domestic bank loans exceeded 10% from 1954 through 1979 and in both the early 1960s and early 1970s was over 20% (Hong 1990: 118). These subsidies equaled 3% of GNP until 1971 but in the 1970s were about 10% of GNP. Hong (1990: 119) goes on to show that loans (domestic and foreign) averaged about 90% of value added in labor-intensive manufacturing sectors, about 150% in intermediate sectors, and over 200% in capital-intensive sectors. So the interest subsidy went disproportionately to the capital-intensive producers. South Korea has been operating rationed, segmented markets in capital.

Similar conditions apply in Taiwan. Interest rates for export financing have been below those for other secured loans (Figure 10.9). The differential ex-

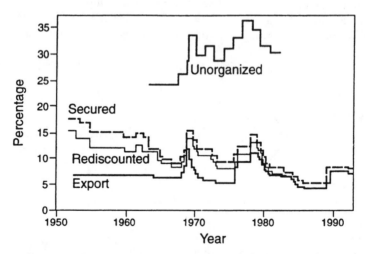

FIGURE 10.9. Interest rates: Taiwan, 1961–1992. The various interest rates are: "rediscount" is the rediscount rate of the Central Bank; "secured" is the rate of discount of the Central Bank on secured loans; "export" is the rate of discount of the Central Bank on export financing; "unorganized" is the annual average interest rate in the unorganized market in Taipei on unsecured loans. *Source: Statistical Yearbook of the Republic of China* (annual) Taipei: Directorate General of Budget, Accounting and Statistics.

ceeded 10 percentage points in the early 1960s, fell to 3 percentage points in 1973, before rising to 5.5 percentage points under policies to counter the effects of the oil price rise. The differential remains but has been only 1 percentage point since 1985. Between 1956 and 1970 the value of export incentives gradually increased; the export credit interest subsidy (and some other rebates, but not industry-specific export bonuses) was equivalent to a 14% devaluation (Lin 1989: 18). Figure 10.9 also illustrates the advantage gained by those with access to the formal financial market: interest rates are 20 percentage points higher in the unorganized ("curb") market in Taipei. Capital markets are segmented in Taiwan too. Financial liberalization in the 1980s has been even slower than in South Korea (Kohsaka 1987).

Wages have also been manipulated.

Taiwan has neither effective minimum wage legislation nor labor codes; unions are weak; public sector wages are low. There are company unions; strikes are outlawed; the minimum wage is so low as to be irrelevant. Prior to 1945, as in Korea, workers' organizations were suppressed by the Japanese; later, they were discouraged by the USA and weakened by the supply of agricultural labor (Deyo et al. 1987). The Kuomintang (KMT) did encourage the formation of unions but then penetrated them: union leaders need to be approved by the party, for example. Deyo et al. conclude that the Taiwanese state has weakened the position of unions and buttressed the position of management rather than formally controlling them. This may, they think, partly reflect the important role played by small firms in the Taiwan economy.

The South Korean state has been far more interventionist (Park 1987). The Labor Union Law permits unions to represent workers only if recognized by the state, prevents unions linking with political parties, and limits unions to a plant or enterprise level (Launius 1984). The Labor Dispute Adjustment Law effectively makes strikes illegal: disputes are subject to a long procedure of conciliation and arbitration, and third parties are not allowed to interfere in disputes. The police and South Korean CIA have regularly purged unions of their leadership (Launius 1984). Since 1981 the government has held wages down by restricting credit to high-wage companies and by jawboning (Fields and Wan 1989). So, between 1970 and 1980 the inequality of official household incomes rose dramatically: the top 20% of households earned 2.1 times as much as the bottom 40% of households combined in 1970 but 2.8 times in 1980 (Choo and Kim 1981; Economic Planning Board 1981). Urban–rural and regional income disparities are wide: in 1981 per capita income in Seoul was 2.2 times that in Cholla (Steinberg 1988). In the 1970s labor productivity rose 11.1% per annum but real wages only 7.8% (Launius 1984: 9).

In both South Korea and Taiwan weekly hours of work in manufacturing remain high. In South Korea weekly hours averaged 52 from 1970 to 1988. In Taiwan they fell from 52 in the mid-1970s to 48 in 1987. The discrepancy between the wages of men and women is huge. In South Korea in 1985 female wages were only 47% of male wages (Steinberg 1988; van Liemt 1988), a discrepancy that Deyo (1989) ascribes to the difficulty of organizing class action among a group that turns over rapidly and often lives in company dormitories. Little is spent on social services in South Korea: two-thirds of education expenses and over 85% of health costs are met by households (Steinberg 1988).

It is often supposed that workers' organizations have been stronger in Latin America than in East Asia (Deyo et al. 1987; Jenkins 1991). Yet Brazilian workers have managed to secure a smaller share of per capita GDP rises than their East Asian colleagues: while GDP per capita rose 1.7 times between 1970 and 1985, real wages rose only 1.4 times. And Brazil's income distribution is far more uneven than that of East Asia: in 1970 the upper 5% of individuals in Brazil earned 3.6 times the combined income of the lowest 40% of individuals, compared to 2.4 times in 1960 (van Liemt 1988: 122; see also Mahler 1989; Meir 1976).

Subsidies, capital price distortions, and wage manipulation distort prices from equilibrium. C. Hamilton (1986: 73–105) reports the most detailed attempt to measure price distortions in South Korea. He estimates an economic model from Brody to calculate equilibrium outputs and prices. These are the outputs and prices of a balanced growth path, when rates of growth are as high as possible given the input–output coefficients.

In 1966 prices of agricultural and other food sectors in South Korea were mostly below their prices of production. Prices of manufactures and services—especially exports—usually exceeded their prices of production. However, export prices were commonly lower than domestic prices: subsidies compensated. Actual prices of government utilities (such as power and transport) were below prices of production: capitalists were also subsidized through utility charges. Actual outputs exceeded model outputs in textiles and clothing, wood products, and other manufacturing—all export sectors—which were growing faster than expected. Sectors growing more slowly than expected were metal production, machinery, and building: foreign exchange limits may have created bottlenecks that restrained these sectors. Foreign exchange was undervalued by 37%.

By 1978 in South Korea the average percentage deviation of prices from production prices had increased from 7.8% to 11.8%; the average deviation of modeled from actual outputs had fallen from 9.1% to 5.4%. No longer was underpriced agriculture subsidizing overpriced industry. Sectors that exported tended still to earn higher rates of profit than average. The exchange rate was underpriced by only 1%. Some of the capital goods industries, especially machinery, were now producing close to their expected levels as the foreign exchange constraint was eased. Still overproducers tended to be export sectors and underproducers to be import dependent (for either inputs or supply). Unfortunately such calculations do not appear to have been made for Brazil or Taiwan.

The implicit tariff indexes how domestic prices deviate from international prices. In Brazil in 1980/81 domestic prices in nonmetallic minerals, transport equipment, paper, rubber, and food products industries were less than 85% of international prices; by contrast prices in the electrical equipment and chemicals industries were at least 40% above world levels and in the pharmaceuticals industry 79% (Tyler 1981).

Bradford (1987, 1990) has examined price distortions in NICs. He computes the prices of commodities in individual countries relative to international prices [from the international price comparison data of Kravis et al. (1982)]. The ratio is

$$\frac{\text{price of commodity (in thousands, say)}}{\text{international price of commodity}} : \frac{\text{price of GDP (in thousands)}}{\text{international price of GDP}}.$$

If the ratio exceeds 1, then the commodity is more expensive in domestic than on international markets. Generally consumer goods are priced at about world market levels and government commodities underpriced (Table 10.5). What distinguishes NICs is that they, like advanced capitalist countries, underprice investment goods whereas other countries overprice investment goods.

In South Korea and Brazil a given rate of investment, as a proportion of GDP, translates into a higher rate when calculated in international prices. In South Korea in 1975 20.2% of GDP was invested (in won), equivalent to 22.0% of GDP in international prices. Similarly Brazil's 21.4% of GDP invested (in cruzeiros) becomes 23.0% in international prices (Bradford 1987: 308). In everyone else's terms South Korea and Brazil were investing 22% or 23% of GDP rather than the 20% or 21% they figured. Bradford argues that NIC governments have intervened to reduce prices of investment goods relative to consumption goods (compared to other economies), raising investment levels and inducing structural changes that provoke a supply-side export push. The overall effect is a bias toward exports.

TABLE 10.5. Relative commodity prices in developing countries

Country or group	Relative price ratios of types of good			
	Consumer	Investment	Government	GDP
"Hungarian group"	0.97	1.05	1.04	1
"Romanian group"	0.96	1.13	0.93	1
NICs	1.01	0.96	0.86	1
Low income nations	1.04	1.19	0.66	1
South Korea	1.05	0.92	0.86	1
Brazil	1.06	0.93	0.73	1

Note: The "Hungarian group" includes Hungary, Poland, Italy, and Spain; the "Romanian group" includes Romania, Mexico, the former Yugoslavia, Iran, Uruguay, and Iceland; the NICs are South Korea, Malaysia, Colombia, Brazil, Jamaica, and Syria.
Source: Bradford (1987: 307).

All told, prices are "wrong": governments have affected the market by tariff and nontariff protection, subsidies, and direct price policies. Export competitiveness has not been simply a matter of factor proportions and market prices as predicted by the theories of comparative and competitive advantage. Nor has the growth of NICs merely reflected low wages as claimed by the theory of the new international division of labor.

10.2.3 Exports and Growth

In none of the three NICs has there been a free market for imports. Import substitution has continued in Brazil, supplemented by an export drive to pay off foreign debts. In South Korea and Taiwan export promotion has been combined with selected import substitution. In all three countries prices have been distorted. These are not open, liberal economies but government-led ones. Government distortion may have impeded or accelerated growth (according to the theory of comparative advantage, it must have impeded growth). We turn now to assess whether export promotion policies have contributed to growth rates: the focus on exports in orthodox theories is not justified by evidence about the relations between exports and growth.

In theory trade orientation, comparative advantage, exports, and economic growth are interrelated (Figure 10.10). Generally export-oriented policies augment exports; in turn, exports raise productivity and assist growth rates by extending economies of scale or forcing firms to international standards. According to the theory of comparative advantage, open and liberal policies boost exports of some commodities and cheapen imports of others. Cheaper imports reduce costs of production for domestic and export producers. Again exports benefit growth through productivity increases caused by scale increases and international competition. (More sophisticated versions model the feedback from export success to economic and political conditions in export markets.) Evidence allows these models to be evaluated partially.

The World Bank (1987) has classified 41 less developed countries (LDCs) by degree of outward orientation. Outward-oriented countries had low effective rates of protection; made little use of direct controls such as licenses and quotas; provided net incentives to export; and under- rather than overvalued their currency. This classification measures export or import orientation; it does not scale countries according to openness and liberality. Alam (1991) employed the classification to study the relationship between trade orientation and the growth of exports and output. Outward orientation is positively correlated with both export growth rates and output growth rates in 1965–1973 and 1973–1984. However, outward orientation is poorly correlated with levels of savings and investment. The first relationship of the general model seems to be substantiated: trade orientation is associated with the performance of exports.

The second issue concerns export performance and productivity. Chen and

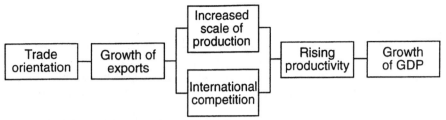

A. Trade orientation, exports and growth

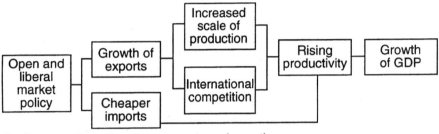

B. Comparative advantage, exports and growth

FIGURE 10.10. The potential links between comparative advantage, trade orientation, exports, and growth.

Tang (1990) analyze changes in total factor productivity in 16 two-digit Taiwanese manufacturing industries between 1968 and 1982. Across the industries export growth is correlated with output growth ($r = 0.63$), as in Alam's (1991) sample of countries; growth in total factor productivity is correlated with export growth ($r = 0.47$) and output growth ($r = 0.79$). Chen and Tang regress changes in total factor productivity on increases in output and exports for each of the 16 industries. Changes in scale positively affect productivity in every industry, significantly in 10 of them. Export growth has a weak and ambiguous relation to productivity: its effect varies in sign and is significant in only one industry. The data are longitudinal rather than cross sectional and refer to one country only; nevertheless they indicate that exports affect productivity by influencing scale rather than through other mechanisms.

Thirdly, exports and growth have been directly related. Krueger (1981) declared that success in export markets is a main determinant of rapid growth: high rates of growth of exports boost rates of economic growth. There is evidence in favor of this claim. Both Michaely (1977) and Balassa (1978) observed positive correlations between rates of export growth and rates of GDP growth across samples of developing countries. Unfortunately their samples were small.

Kavoussi (1985) has related exports to growth over 52 countries. He collected data for two periods: 1967–1973, when world market conditions were favorable, and 1973–1977, when world markets were growing more slowly. Kavoussi's study was updated by Singer and Gray (1988), who provided data for 1977–1983, when world market conditions were more unfavorable still. During favorable market conditions export performance and growth rates were strongly correlated. In 1973–1977, when world market conditions were unfavorable, the correlation was weak and of doubtful significance. In 1977–1983, both inward- and outward-oriented countries experienced a decrease of export earnings; the Spearman rank correlation between export performance and GNP growth rates was even weaker than before. Apparently successful exporters grow faster only when circumstances favor trade: if markets are tight, exports do not help growth. The relationship between export growth and GDP growth depends on market conditions.

Furthermore exports are a component of GDP, so exports and GDP are related by accounting even if they are not causally related (Goncalves and Richtering 1987). Since GDP equals exports plus domestic consumption plus investment less imports, an increase in exports means that GDP rises even if exports do not affect domestic consumption and investment. Goncalves and Richetering try to separate the accounting relation from the effect of exports on other components of GDP. Using data for 70 developing countries over 1960–1981 Goncalves and Richtering (1987: 7–8) measured the following:

Y/N GDP per capita in $US 1970 (Brazil 837; South Korea 416)

Y Compound annual rate of growth—GDP 1960–1981 (Brazil 6.9%; South Korea 8.5%)

YD Compound annual rate of growth—GDP less exports 1960–1981 (Brazil 6.9%; South Korea 5.1%)

X Compound annual rate of growth—exports 1960–1981 (Brazil 8.0%; South Korea 27.8%)

X/Y Exports as a percentage of GDP, average 1960–1981 (Brazil 6.6%; South Korea 14.8)

XC Average annual percentage change in X/Y, 1960–1981 (Brazil 0.0%; South Korea 1.5)

Goncalves and Richtering (1987: 9) report Spearman rank correlation coefficients between these variables for all 70 countries and for a subset of 10 high-income developing countries (with per capita incomes exceeding $US 1000). Some of the coefficients are as follows (significance levels in parentheses):

	All 70 countries	10 countries
Y and X	0.494 (0.0001)	0.721 (0.018)
YD and X	0.006 (0.957)	0.357 (0.310)
Y and X/Y	0.024 (0.838)	0.284 (0.425)
Y and XC	0.299 (0.011)	0.345 (0.328)

Export growth and GDP growth (X and Y) are indeed correlated; the correlation is even higher among the 10 high-income developing countries. But the correlation between the growth of exports (X) and the growth of GDP less exports (YD) is virtually zero for the whole sample and insignificant in the subsample of high-income developing countries. It seems that the correlation between export growth and GDP growth derives from the accounting relationship between them, for export growth does not affect the growth of non-exported GDP. Growth of exports does contribute to growth of GDP; the contribution is, however, only direct and does not extend to indirect effects.

Certainly more study of trade and growth is needed; yet the evidence so far supports several conclusions. Outward-oriented countries experience faster rates of growth of exports than inward-oriented countries (and faster rates of growth of output). Outward-oriented countries are not, however, necessarily open, liberal, market economies. Increases in output afford economies of scale. Increases in exports do not independently influence productivity, so the chill winds of international competition do not raise productivity. Countries with rapidly growing exports do grow faster than countries with stagnating exports—but only when markets are expanding and only because exports are a component of GDP. These data are consistent with the proposition that outward-oriented countries have a successful growth strategy; it does not follow that export growth is that successful growth strategy, for it may be growth that generates exports (Dodaro 1991; Jung and Marshall 1985).

10.2.4 Conclusion

In the orthodox view the trade regimes of South Korea and Taiwan were switched in the 1960s from import substitution to liberal export promotion. Promoting exports, the two countries have used their comparative and competitive advantages in labor costs to increase their exports of labor-intensive manufactured products, supported by the expansion in world trade. By contrast Brazil continued to substitute for imports and only more recently has promoted exports. Not being able to pursue comparative advantages, Brazil's industries have been less successful than those of South Korea and Taiwan, especially in the 1980s.

Yet this story is so simplified as to mislead. The export-oriented policies of South Korea and Taiwan are not liberal, open-market ones. All three states have protected domestic industries by tariffs, import restrictions, and subsidies and have intervened in capital and labor markets. So prices of capital, labor, and commodities are distorted; the prices of investment commodities are particularly low.

In any event export success is less obviously related to growth than is assumed in orthodoxy. When world trade grew fast high rates of export growth fostered high rates of GDP growth; but at other times export success has been unrelated to GDP growth. Indeed the growth of exports contributed to the growth of GDP only directly: since the growth of exports and of nonexport GDP are not correlated, exports do not stimulate other sectors of the economy. Still, export-oriented economies do seem to have coined a successful growth strategy, even if export expansion is not that strategy. There is evidence too that some export commodities have been subsidized. International prices are commonly lower than the domestic prices of South Korea's export industries even when the prices of export industries exceed equilibrium prices. Continued success in international markets has not been a matter of price competitiveness.

This evidence contradicts the importance placed on relative costs in theories of competitive or comparative advantage and of the new international division of labor. Low costs of production were not the important factor.

10.3 DEVELOPING FORCES OF PRODUCTION

The theory of comparative or competitive advantage claims that countries should produce commodities that require large amounts of their abundant factors of production. South Korea and Taiwan have done just that, it is said: exporting first resource- based commodities, then labor-intensive manufactures, and—after the labor surplus was used up by the late 1960s—more capital-intensive manufactures. Even Brazil followed the same path, though trends in exports lag 30 years behind trends in production (Teitel and Thoumi 1986). In fact none of the economies was open (as assumed by theory): price distortions and export subsidies destroy the link between cost competitiveness and successful exporting. Many export industries were not competitive on international markets when first established. Some industries have since become competitive as learning and economies of scale have reduced costs: Ohno and Imaoka (1987) testify to economies of scale in South Korean manufacturing; productivity growth in Taiwan has been dominated by economies of scale (Chen and Tang 1990). The competitiveness of industries in the three countries is caused by growth, not a cause of it. In NICs efficiency is an effect of production not its cause. Inefficiencies and subsidies have been displayed; now we illustrate the learning that occurred in Brazil, South Korea, and Taiwan.

Teubal (1984) interviewed Brazilian producers of capital goods to discover what they learnt. Some learning is related to manufacturing: the capability to manufacture; operating experience and practice on similar equipment; and experience in quality control. Secondly, firms stated that they were learning design: mechanical design capacity, process design capacity and skills in project management. Finally, there were other types of learning: building a reputation; acquiring the capacity to plan and execute investments; gaining a knowledge of markets. These types of learning have been important in the steel industries of Brazil and South Korea.

The Brazilian state-owned integrated steel producer Usiminas has raised the productivity of investment planning, project design and management, and manufacturing capability (Dahlman et al. 1987). Usiminas was set up in the late 1950s. Before building its first plant Usiminas commissioned feasibility studies, sent study teams abroad, and solicited offers to build. The plant was constructed as a joint venture with a consortium of 30 Japanese companies that provided foreign technology and experience. Export credits were granted on the equipment, too. The Japanese did the engineering and project management, but the Brazilians worked closely with them to learn design, equipment selection, installation, construction, and operation.

There were many problems. The source of ore had to be changed. Usiminas had to adapt the planned administrative structure to suit a small, Brazilian plant. Severe world steel overcapacity had developed. Yet in 6 years Usiminas doubled the capacity of its furnace and steelmaking operations—not by investing in equipment but by learning how to select ores, extend service lives, change operations, and raise quality. Studying recipes and comparing its performance with that of overseas plants, Usiminas developed greater engineering and technical support, eventually generating a research and development (R&D) center in the firm.

Despite these increments to capacity Usiminas had to invest in additional plant and equipment, tripling its capacity to make steel. In the first stage of this investment, foreign technical advisers taught design, choice of equipment, selection of technology, specification of equipment, calling bids, choosing from bidders, negotiating details, and controlling the work. Usiminas' own staff performed about one-third of the engineering for this stage. Then Usiminas engineered all the next phase of the expansion (though it was checked by overseas firms).

A similar story can be told about the South Korean state-owned steel maker, Pohang Steel Company (POSCO) (Enos and Park 1988). Construction began on the first integrated iron and steel mill in 1970. Its initial capacity was 1.03 million tonnes (metric tons) of crude steel per year. This was increased to 2.6 million tonnes in May 1976, in a first expansion; second and third expansions occurred in 1978 and 1981 (Enos and Park 1988: 56–58), taking capacity to 5.5 million tonnes and 8.5 million tonnes, respectively (Enos and Park 1988: 176–177).

The South Korean government had tried several times to create an integrated steel mill but failed to obtain foreign loans. In the event Japan provided loans as well as technology and facilities [Japanese government banks provided 70% of the finance, Japanese commercial loans 15% and other sources the remainder (Enos and Park 1988: 178)]. All the technology was imported from NKK Corp. and Nippon Steel. The contract specified training for construction engineers and on-site assistance in start up and operation.

Like Usiminas, POSCO learned how to build such plants and to install equipment. In the initial plant and the first expansion, foreign engineers did the general engineering planning, the material balancing and the inspection of drawings; the South Koreans participated in inspecting specifications. In the second expansion the South Korean engineers took over all tasks except general engineering planning; and in the third expansion they did that too (Enos and Park 1988: 189). So POSCO paid royalties of $US6.13 per tonne of installed capacity for the initial plant; $3.81 for the first expansion; $0.13 for the second expansion; and nothing for the third (Enos and Park 1988: 180, 189). Construction times for all stages were less than those for similar plants in France and only half those of Usiminas. Construction costs per tonne of capacity were below those in Japan and the European Community (EC) and only half those in the USA (Enos and Park 1988: 187–188).

POSCO has rapidly absorbed the technology it imported. The first blast furnace was operating normally 107 days after burning in; the Japanese companies had expected this to take 12 months (Enos and Park 1988: 183–189). Average costs of production (deflated by the wholesale price index) fell from 14,000–16,000 won per metric ton in 1974–1978 to 11,000–12,000 won per metric ton in 1979–1983 (Enos and Park 1988: 205). The average annual compound rate of cost reduction has been 5.1%. Of this 0.3–0.7% was contributed by the increased efficiency of the larger blast furnaces installed later. So operating performance has contributed an annual rate of cost reduction of between 4.4% and 4.8% (Enos and Park 1988: 207). Since 1980 POSCO has earned a greater rate of return on sales than the average of the five largest Japanese steelmakers and a far larger return than the largest US steelmakers (Enos and Park 1988: 214).

Such gains have improved the productivity of manufacturing in NICs. In South Korea value added per worker in all manufacturing rose from 0.37 of the West German level in 1966 to 0.58 in 1978; in steelmaking the corresponding ratios were 0.52 and 1.08 (Dollar 1991: 265–266). Total factor productivity in South Korean manufacturing rose from 0.49 of the West German level in 1966 to 0.83 in 1978 though relative total factor productivity levels in steelmaking fell.

Improvements in productivity arise from many sources. In Brazil, South Korea, and Taiwan productivity gains partly derive from increases in scale—sometimes sustained by exports. To that extent exports cause productivity rather than being its effect. Productivity gains are also learnt, as practice makes better. Both kinds of gain are possible only after investments have been made. The learning described in this section illustrates that competitiveness is a consequence of investment and growth, not its cause. As we shall see, state institutions directed and supported investment so that production could become profitable.

10.4 CAPITAL FLOWS AND TRANSNATIONAL CORPORATIONS

The growth of NICs such as Brazil, South Korea, and Taiwan was apparently favored during the 1950s and 1960s by global economic conditions (Fishlow

1989). Trade was growing rapidly, the North American and European markets were expanding, and trade barriers were falling. After 1974 conditions deteriorated, as oil price rises ate into current account balances, external debt constrained policy, economic growth slowed in North America and Europe, and the advanced capitalist countries protected themselves from imports from developing countries. It is easy to exaggerate the contrast between the periods before and after 1974 (Chapter 2) and how the relations between the OECD nations and NICs changed. We now seek to sort out more precisely the relationship between the slowdown in the advanced capitalist countries and the growth of NICs. In particular this section examines the flows of capital to NICs. We demonstrate that the growth of NICs has generally depended on foreign capital inflows, but that these inflows became particularly significant after the profitability of investments had begun to decline in North America and western Europe. Much of the impetus to growth in the 1970s and 1980s in NICs derived from the slowdown in the advanced countries, rather than being a major cause of that slowdown. This evidence contradicts the thesis of the new international division of labor.

Furthermore, contrary to popular perception and to the story told by regulation theorists, the history of foreign capital in the NICs is not one of footloose transnational corporations that use low-wage labor as a platform from which to export standardized products to advanced capitalist countries. Foreign direct investment has been relatively large in Brazil, where transnationals have historically dominated the economy. Here, though, the incentives for those firms to produce in Brazil are tariff barriers and much of their production is for the Brazilian (or Latin American) market. In South Korea and Taiwan foreign direct investment has been of little general significance and closely controlled by the government.

The issue of the relation between foreign capital inflows and growth is debated. To some foreign capital represents an addition to productive resources; to others foreign capital merely depresses local savings rates. Others claim that the relationship is a matter of empirical evidence. Gupta and Islam (1983) have proposed and estimated a simultaneous equation model that allows not only the direct effect of foreign investment on savings and growth to be estimated but also its indirect effect (via other variables). This model is estimated for the period 1965–1973 over a sample of 52 countries. The direct effects of aid, foreign private investment and other inflows on the savings rate are negative; the direct and indirect effects are also negative (or insubstantial). Nevertheless, all three forms of capital inflow stimulate rates of GNP growth. In general, savings has a greater effect on growth than does foreign capital. Aid directly spurs growth more than does foreign private capital; but aid also depresses savings more than foreign private capital; so the total positive effect of foreign private investment on growth is greater than the effect of aid. That is, growth rates seem to respond positively to capital inflows, even though those inflows do depress local savings rates.

10.4.1 Total Capital Inflows

Capital leaking from the industrialized world to NICs might reduce rates of growth of output and capital accumulation in industrialized countries in two ways. Directly, if capital leaves the industrialized countries, less capital is available to be invested and the demand for capital and wage goods is reduced (since fewer people are employed in constructing the investments than previously). Indirectly, if the capital that flows to NICs stimulates production there, then the markets of established producers are eroded: producers in NICs may use their access to low wages to exclude imports from the industrialized countries; producers in NICs may undercut traditional producers in the markets of the industrialized countries. It is widely supposed that both effects have occurred and that the growth of NICs therefore influenced the slow-down in the industrialized countries.

The evidence in favor of this hypothesis is not strong. Total capital inflows into NICs remained relatively small until the early 1970s: not until the economies of industrialized countries had already slowed did capital exports to NICs really take off. Furthermore most of the capital flow has not taken the form of direct investment: relatively little of the growth of NICs can be attributed to multinational corporations leaving industrialized countries in search of cheap labor. It is also important to clarify the way imports affect the industrialized countries: imports to the USA from Latin American and East Asian NICs substitute for American capital but complement American labor (Aw and Roberts 1985).

The data on capital inflows into Brazil, South Korea, and Taiwan (Table 10.6) do not include aid. Particularly in South Korea and Taiwan but also in Brazil the significance of aid in relation to other capital inflows has varied. In Taiwan in the 1950s the inflow of aid was 4.48 times that of long-term capital; in the 1960s aid comprised only 0.68 of long-term capital (Ranis and Schive 1985). The US provided South Korea with $US12.6 billion in economic and military aid between 1946 and 1976; other sources provided another $US3 billion (Woo 1991). The average inflow exceeded average annual net borrowing until the early 1970s: the total inflow of aid plus net foreign capital averaged $1032 million in 1961–1965; $1284 million in 1966–1970; $1325 million in 1971; $998 million in 1971; $981 million in 1972; $1423 million in 1973; and $2101 million in 1974 (1986 dollars; annual inflows of aid from Economist Intelligence Unit, *Quarterly Economic Review of Japan and South Korea*). Much of the increase in capital inflows between 1961–1965 and 1966–1970 reflects the replacement of aid by commercial capital flows; indeed, one reason why Taiwan adopted an export oriented strategy in the late 1950s was to substitute foreign direct investment for declining US aid (Huang 1989).

The inflow of foreign capital to all three countries sharply increased in the early 1970s. By 1975 net capital flows to Brazil were more than five times larger than in 1966–1970; in South Korea and Taiwan, more than twice as

TABLE 10.6. Long-term net foreign capital inflows: Brazil, South Korea, and Taiwan, 1961–1986

Year(s)	Brazil	South Korea	Taiwan
1961–1965	471.1	387.0	146.2
1966–1970	1367.4	929.9	347.0
1971	2865.5	1195.4	225.1
1972	6550.2	985.6	215.1
1973	4993.5	976.3	424.5
1974	8237.5	1421.2	846.9
1975	7142.0	2100.6	1267.5
1976–1980	8393.5	3093.7	767.2
1981–1982	8670.2	3143.3	790.8
1983–1985	–4944.9	1902.0	—
1986–1988	–9986.5	–5006.1	—

Note: Data are in millions of constant $US of 1986.
Source: For Brazil and South Korea the data for 1961–1965 are from Stallings (1990: 62) using conversion factors obtained by comparing data for Taiwan in Stallings and *Economic Yearbook of the Republic of China* and *Statistical Yearbook of the Republic of China*. For Taiwan for 1976–1982 data are from Stallings using conversion factors obtained by comparing data for Brazil and South Korea in Stallings and United Nations *Statistical Yearbook*. All other data are from United Nations *Statistical Yearbook*.

large. In Brazil the year of sharpest break in levels was 1972: the average annual capital inflow in 1961–1971 was $US1568 million per year, whereas in 1972–1982 it was $US7331 million per year. In South Korea the sharp break occurred in 1975: the average annual inflow in 1961–1974 was $US983 million, compared to $US2779 million between 1975 and 1982. The break in Taiwan occurred in 1974: average annual inflows were $US272 million in 1961–1973, compared to $US918 million in 1974–1982. The years of sharpest increase in capital inflows to the three NICs were the early to mid-1970s: 1972 in Brazil, 1975 in South Korea, and 1974 in Taiwan. Nor were capital flows to these NICs exceptional: in 1970 the net flow of foreign capital to all developing countries was 1.71 times the 1961 level; by 1980 the net flow was 3.20 times as large as a decade earlier (data from Stallings 1990: 66). To the extent that there has been an increase in outflows of capital from developed to developing countries, it has occurred at the same time or after the slowdown rather than before it. These data are consistent with the view that the increase in foreign capital inflows to developing countries was a response to rather than a cause of the slowdown in the industrialized countries.

The significance of foreign capital inflows differs between countries. In the 1960s and 1970s foreign capital provided the equivalent of 15.0% of gross fixed capital formation in Brazil, 19.6% in South Korea, and 9.9% in Taiwan. However, its importance has changed over time. Table 10.7 reveals two quite different patterns. Brazil's program of industrialization in the 1960s and 1970s relied heavily on foreign capital. So foreign capital came to comprise a quarter

TABLE 10.7. Net foreign capital inflows as a proportion of gross fixed capital formation: Brazil, South Korea, and Taiwan, 1961–1988

Year(s)	Brazil	South Korea	Taiwan
1961–1965	8.3	24.3	11.5
1966–1970	11.9	18.9	11.6
1971	12.4	18.8	4.9
1972	25.1	15.7	4.0
1973	16.4	11.6	7.1
1974	23.5	14.7	12.9
1975	18.4	19.9	16.7
1976–1980	20.5	19.2	7.5
1981–1982	−10.3	17.5	5.5
1983–1985	−27.0	8.2	
1986–1988		−16.4	

Note: Levels of capital formation have been expressed in constant 1986 values of the national currency and then converted to $US using the 1986 exchange rate.

Source: For foreign capital inflows, Table 10.6; for gross fixed capital formation, *Economic Yearbook of the Republic of China* (Taipei: Economic Daily News) and *Yearbook of National Accounts Statistics* (New York: United Nations).

of gross fixed capital formation by 1972. In South Korea and Taiwan foreign capital has played a diminishing role in capital formation: in both countries foreign capital was less than half as important in 1972 as in the early 1960s. The increase in the availability of foreign capital after the early 1970s led to a temporary reversal of that trend in 1974 and 1975. Only in South Korea (where it comprised 21.6% of fixed capital formation) did foreign capital provide much more than 10% of gross fixed capital formation in the 1960s.

10.4.2 Foreign Direct Investment

Long-term foreign capital inflows are divided into two categories. In direct foreign investment a foreigner takes a controlling interest in a local plant; "controlling interest" is usually defined as at least 50% [in South Korea foreign firms are those not wholly owned by Koreans (Luedde-Neurath 1986)]. Other forms of long-term capital inflows do not imply control of local production facilities. Inaccurately, direct foreign investment is sometimes equated with investment of production capital while other inflows are of financial capital; slightly more accurately, direct foreign investment is regarded as conferring control while portfolio and other forms of foreign investment do not confer control over production. Certainly support for domestic corporations in both South Korea and Taiwan has assumed that such corporations can be controlled in the national interest more easily than transnational corporations; when capital is scarce this has led South Korea and Taiwan to rely on finance rather than production capital.

Stallings (1990) has classified net foreign capital inflows into those that are between countries, either bilateral or multilateral; those that derive from private banks; and those that represent direct foreign investment (see Table 10.8).

Transnational corporations do not dominate production in the three countries. In Brazil foreign direct investment has been declining as a proportion of foreign capital inflows. In the 1960s direct investment comprised nearly 40% of all inflows, but it is now less than a quarter. In Taiwan direct investment has until recently comprised a smaller proportion of total inflow than in Brazil—about 20%—but by the mid-1980s that proportion has risen to 44%. In South Korea, while total inflows have been larger than in Taiwan, the proportion that is direct investment is smaller—generally less than 10%. The three countries have relied on direct foreign investment to a smaller degree than have developing countries as a whole: direct foreign investment comprised more than 40% of all foreign capital inflows to all developing countries in the early 1960s though less than 20% by the early 1980s (Stallings 1990: 66). Foreign direct investment has comprised less than 2% of gross fixed capital formation in every period in South Korea, less than 3% in Taiwan, and less than 6.5% in Brazil (calculations from Tables 10.7 and 10.8). In Brazil in 1987 three of the largest ten companies were transnationals, but they were all oil companies (Gereffi 1990). However, in 1977 almost half of Brazil's exports to the USA came from US affiliates, that is, firms in which US companies have at least 10% ownership (Alger 1991: 900). None of South Korea's ten largest companies are foreign owned (Gereffi 1990), only 5.7% of its exports to the USA were derived from US affiliates in 1977 (Alger 1991: 900), and over 77% of its exports in 1978 came from companies wholly owned by South Koreans (Luedde-Neurath 1986: 19). In 1987 none of Taiwan's ten largest companies were overseas owned (Gereffi 1990) and less than 15% of Taiwan's exports to the US derived from USA affiliates in 1977 (Alger 1991: 900).

TABLE 10.8. Forms of long-term net foreign capital inflows: Brazil, South Korea, and Taiwan, 1961–1986

	Brazil		South Korea		Taiwan	
Period	Private bank	Direct FI	Private bank	Direct FI	Private bank	Direct FI
1961–1965	−3.2	38.3	12.6	1.6	8.9	12.8
1966–1970	29.0	39.6	55.1	3.5	39.4	25.8
1971–1975	52.0	34.6	38.7	11.5	30.2	18.0
1976	66.7	25.9	60.4	5.2	47.2	18.2
1981–1982	61.2	27.5	59.3	3.1	61.3	22.8
1983–1986	54.9	23.0	67.6	11.8	−97.3	43.8

Note: Data are expressed as a percentage of total capital inflows. Bilateral and multilateral flows represent the proportion of inflow that is missing. (FI = foreign investment.)
Source: Stallings (1990: 62).

All three countries have controlled foreign companies. While the South Korean government has advertised its liberal investment laws, the Foreign Capital Inducement Law screens applications to invest in South Korea according to their balance of payments effect; gives preference to joint ventures; and prohibits investment unless specified (Luedde-Neurath 1986; Koo 1985). The government interferes and requires many reports; it demands local participation, local managerial control, an export policy, and transfers of technology. In Taiwan foreign direct investment has been restricted by: the need to seek approval from the Investment Commission for investment and changes in company operations; the prohibition of foreign activity in some sectors and the condition in others that foreign capital enter joint ventures with local capital; exchange controls; local content and export requirements; and the need to obtain licenses to import (Huang 1989). Taiwan has become more selective about foreign direct investment since the 1970s. In Brazil fear that sovereignty over resources would be lost and that domestic capital would be swept aside by the superior financial strength and organization of transnational corporations has prompted attempts to limit the role of the transnationals in the economy—tempered by the need to hasten investment and growth (Baer 1989; Coffey and do Lago 1988; Fritsch and Franco 1991).

Multilateral and bilateral flows have been of declining significance at least until recently. In Brazil in the early 1960s bilateral and multilateral flows comprised over 65% of all long-term capital inflows; in South Korea, and Taiwan more than 75%. Those proportions had fallen to less than 20% by the early 1980s except in South Korea. In the mid-1980s such intergovernmental arrangements became more important again, as developing countries sought to pay of the debts accumulated in the 1970s. These proportions are higher than those of developing countries as a whole (Stallings 1990: 66), perhaps reflecting the strategic significance of the three NICs to the US alliance.

The place of bilateral and multilateral flows and of direct foreign investment has been taken by private bank lending: the long-term movement of finance capital. In the early 1960s private banks provided less than 15% of the long-term capital inflow into developing countries; the proportion rose to 35% by the mid-1970s and over 50% by the early 1980s (Stallings 1990: 66). In Brazil, South Korea, and Taiwan the proportion of long-term foreign capital provided by banks rose sharply in the 1970s: to over 50% in Brazil and South Korea and nearly 40% in Taiwan. Thus the inflows of finance capital to the three NICs increased dramatically in the early 1970s: as the total inflow of capital rose sharply, so did the proportion of that capital that was provided by private banks.

These data convey several overwhelming impressions. The economies are not dominated by foreign transnationals and direct foreign investment. Capital inflows increased in the early 1970s, but most of that increase was finance capital offered by private banks rather than intergovernmental loans or direct investment. These impressions are consistent with the view that capital inflows have been dominated—at least since the late 1960s—by considerations of capital availability rather than of least cost location by footloose transnationals.

This statistical evidence is confirmed by studies of individual industries in particular countries. Consider for example the Brazilian iron and steel industry (Foot and Webber 1990b; Webber and Foot 1988). While international capital has made limited direct investment in the Brazilian steel industry, it provides a lot of finance and technology. Funding for small private mills is mostly domestic, though some private firms do obtain foreign loans (Table 10.9). However, the capital required to construct an integrated, flat-producing mill is large, and much of it has come from international financial institutions.

Methods of financing public steel plants have changed as the scale of operations has increased. For example, Companhia Siderúrgica Nacional (CSN; Naional Steel Corporation) was begun in 1942 with the help of a loan of $20 million from the Export–Import Bank of America. The Brazilian federal government contributed the equivalent of $25 million (Braga 1984: 197; Teixeira 1981: 72). Cosipa was inaugurated in 1953 with private interests of $50,000, though the state of São Paulo became directly involved as well as the federal government through the Banco Nacional de Desenvolvimento Econômico (BNDE; National Bank for Economic Development). Foreign finance in the form of suppliers' credits was guaranteed by the national treasury (Braga 1984: 199). Usiminas also began with local capital of $50,000 but quickly obtained technical support and 40% equity from Nippon Usiminas K.K. (the remaining capital came from BNDE, the state of Minas Gerais, and CSN).

Governments have subsequently financed the steel industry almost entirely through BNDE and the Fundo de Financiamento para Aquisição de Máquinas e Equipamentos Indústriais (FINAME; Fund to Finance the Acquisition of Industrial Machinery and Equipment). This has been either direct equity involvement or loans to the companies (or the holding company, Siderbras). Loans from BNDE or FINAME are not necessarily domestic. BNDE and FINAME themselves acquire finance from abroad (*BOLSA Review* January 1965: 6). International financial institutions have also loaned money directly for steel expansion projects in Brazil. Table 10.9 lists loans reported mainly by the *BOLSA Review* and some other minor sources. (The list is not exhaustive.) In addition, Table 10.10 lists all outstanding loans to CSN, Cosipa, and Usiminas in 1984; 42% of their total debt was owed directly to international financial institutions.

Over 20% of loans were linked to the purchase of equipment overseas. Technical ability has been developed by the established Brazilian companies, in particular CSN (through its subsidiary Cobrapi) and Usiminas. Cobrapi handles most of the engineering and construction work. In addition Usiminas Mecânica is involved in machinery production (*BOLSA Review* September, 1976). But most equipment must still come from foreign sources. For example, the Conselho de Não-Ferrosos e de Siderurgia (Consider; Council for Non-Ferrous and Steel Industries, a part of the Ministry of Trade and Indus-

TABLE 10.9. Selected foreign loans to Brazilian steel companies, 1962–1979

Year	Lending sources	Quantity (1980 $US Millions)	Debtor (purpose)
1962	Japanese Govt & Eximbank	90.2	Usiminas, through BNDE
1963	US & Europe consortium; IADB	110.7	Cofavi (expansion to 380,000 tonnes by 1967[1]
1965	US Eximbank; Japanese Govt; IFC	26.1 + 64 Yen	CSN (stage II); Usiminas (pay off earlier loan); Aco Villares
1968	US Eximbank; Nippon Usiminas	119.1	CSN (steel-finishing equipment); Usiminas (equity injection); Siderama
1970	French consortium; other	10.1FFr + 129.5	Usiba; Cosipa, Usiminas through BNDE
1971	British bank; BOLSA; Japanese consortium; IDB; IBRD; US Eximbank; US consortium	1209.6	CSN (sintering plant); Piratini (construction); Usiminas stage (II)[2]; CSN (electrolytic tinning line); Cosigua (Construction equipment from US)
1972	IDB; IBRD; US Eximbank	1344.5[3]	CSN (stage II); Cosipa; Usiminas
1974	IDB	172.0[4]	Cosipa; CSN
1975	IBRD; British consortium	345.3 + 67.9stg	CSN; Cosipa; Acesita (UK, US equipment)
1976	British consortium; Japanese Eximbank	130.7 stg	Siderbras (stage III contracts in UK)
1976	Ferrostaal (GDR); International consortium	312.6 + 192.5 Yen 28.9SWFr + 350.0DM	CSN; Cosipa (Japanese equipment); Acominas (export credit); Siderbras; Acesita 1977
	IBRD; IBD; French, GDR, Japanese, UK, US, International consortiums; Thyssen Hutte; IFC; Japanese, US Eximbank; Nippon Usiminas; Banco Exterior de España	1223.3 +414.65Fr +149.2DM +823.6Yen +474.3Stg	CSN ; Cosipa; Usiminas; Consigua (Thyssen Purofer equipment); Acominas (blast furnace from UK); Siderbras; Cimetal (expansion)
1978	Japanese consortium; UK bank	441.9 +33.2stg	Tubarao (50% spent in Brazil); Acominas (Davy Ashmore contracts)
1979	Japanese, International consortium	82.8Y + 510.8	Tubarao; Siderbras; CSN 1980
	Japanese consortium	100.0	Tubarao

Year	CSN	Cosipa	Usiminas
Due dates on long-term loans, 1984 (CR$ 1000):			
1986	697,013,282	779,313,465	462,238,848
1987	714,537,084	730,092,555	461,730,669
1988	579,914,380	620,739,319	383,884,867
1989	602,047,953	541,083,567	328,52 4,477
1990	536,385,851	384,502,246	239,417,237
1981–1999	854,850,618	926,461,719	2,219,796,913

Notes:
[1]This project was never completed.
[2]Estimated cost of project $235m—the balance to be obtained from IDB, IBRD, and local sources.
[3]At this stage the government was seeking external credits of $690m for financing stage II expansion.
[4]*Source*: Federal Trade Commission (1977).
LIBOR = London Interbank Offering Rate.
All loans are denominated in $US. Loans in other currencies are identified; they are exchanged to (then) current $US using average market exchange rates for the relevant year from International Monetary Fund (annual) *International Financial Statistics,* Washington: IMF. Current $US are deflated to 1980 $US by the consumer price index, also from *International Financial Statistics.*
Source: Foot and Webber (1990a,b), who used *BOLSA, Review,* various issues, except note 4; data on loans from company reports, 1984.

try) estimated in 1965 that steel expansion projects up to 1970 would require $1.5 billion, 40% of which would be spent abroad. For the stage II expansion at Usiminas 46% of total costs (estimated in 1972) were contracted abroad and 76% of equipment was purchased abroad [Usiminas stage II appraisal, 1972, International Bank for Reconstruction and Development (IBRD)]. IBRD loans went toward blast furnace, coke plant, basic oxygen furnace (BOF) shop, and continuous casting, slabbing, plate and hot and cold strip mills, equipment for water and energy systems, mobile equipment, and rolling stock—all purchased abroad. The plate mill, new port facilities, steel plant, oxygen plant, and blast furnace renovation for Cosipa's stage III expansion were all contracted abroad (Cosipa, Stage III progress report, April 1985). CSN's new hot rolling mill came from Mitsubishi in Japan.

Most international interest in Brazil's steel development has been in the circuits of commodity and finance capital. The expansion of markets for steel industry technology has provided an outlet for engineering firms in developed countries. These outlets have been financed largely through the cooperation of financial capital. Profit has been extracted from Brazil by international banks as interest, an appropriation of surplus produced under the control of domestic and state capital in the productive circuit.

Tables 10.6 through 10.8 suggest that such a history is not unusual in Brazil, South Korea, and Taiwan. Productive capital has largely remained under the control of local corporations; most foreign capital has entered countries either as bilateral or multilateral aid or as financial capital. Production in all three countries is implicated in global capital. While it is financing production the capital is controlled domestically rather than by foreign transnational corporations. The distinction between foreign finance and foreign productive capital has political and economic significance in all three countries.

This evidence directly contradicts two central claims of the thesis of the new international division of labor. Capital flowed into NICs most rapidly after the onset of the slowdown in advanced capitalist economies in the mid-1970s. The inflows were a consequence of the slowdown—overaccumulated capital—rather than its cause. Furthermore the capital inflows have largely taken the form of financial capital rather than direct investment controlled by multinational corporations. Capital inflows have been strongly controlled by national forces in all three countries.

10.5 ACCUMULATION AND NATIONAL POLICY

The theories of comparative advantage, competitive advantage, and the new international division of labor suffer crucial empirical defects. They cannot account adequately for the history of development in Brazil, South Korea, and Taiwan. Subsidies, tariffs, and other price distortions destroy the basis for comparative advantage and reveal that industries could not be established simply on the ground of their cost competitiveness in international markets.

Instead, industries were established which then became internationally competitive. Equally, capital inflows accelerated after the slowdown in advanced capitalist economies rather than before it.

The crucial determinant of rates of growth is not profitability but investment policy (Chapter 7). Rates of profit guide investment certainly; but the forms taken by investment and the guiding principles of investors play a leading role in determining paths and rates of development. We now take two more steps in this argument. Different forms of capital are subject to different constraints and so must be controlled in different ways. International flows of capital now comprise a variety of forms. Furthermore the nature of capital inflows helps determine export policy. The rate of growth of exports is not simply a matter of cost competitiveness but depends also on national development strategies and the form of international capital movements.

10.5.1 Circuits of Capital

The thesis of the new international division of labor—images of corporations seeking a least cost location for each function across a global space and then marketing products globally—relies on a single concept of capital: global industrial capital. The image overemphasizes the role of global industrial capital in the economies of NICs, including Brazil, South Korea, and Taiwan. We therefore distinguish different forms of capital, in two ways.

First, different capitals engage in different stages of the circuit of capital (Figure 10.11). The circuit of industrial capital begins and ends with production. Commodities are produced and sold so that more labor power and means of production can be bought and the scale of production enlarged: buying and selling are for production. A concrete expression of productive capital is the industrial corporation. In the commercial or commodity circuit produced commodities are bought (from a producer) and resold as means of production or consumption in a cycle that begins and ends with commodities. Trading companies exemplify commodity capital. Finance capital is the form of capital that trades money—lending money to producers and traders and re-

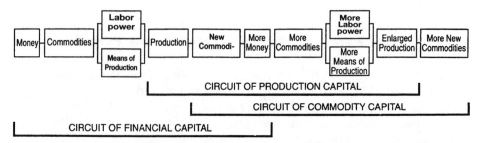

FIGURE 10.11. Organizations of the circuits of capital. *Source*: Desai 1979.

covering it after production or trade. Finance capital appears as banks and nonbank financial institutions (Daly and Logan 1989).

Different corporations act out the stages in the circuit of capital. While the surplus is produced within the productive circuit, traders and financiers extract some surplus from the producers; they conflict over the distribution of surplus. Furthermore the three circuits are anchored differently. Production facilities are difficult to move, for they have a physical reality on the ground; production within them has to be organized socially, which also fixes production in place. Commodities can be moved; though they weigh, commodities are not physically or socially embedded in the same way as production facilities. Money can be shifted more easily still. The differences between the forms of capital are manifest in the degree to which they are shackled to place and so to which they are concerned with the social relations of their place.

Secondly, production has three phases. During production itself labor power and means of production are assembled to produce new commodities. The value of the new commodities is realized when they are sold. The profit from production is reinvested when capital is reproduced, completing the circuit. Each phase can be accomplished within a single nation or internationally (Bryan 1987). A commodity can be produced over several countries—when components from overseas plants of the corporation are assembled—or within a single country. If a commodity is not exported, realization is national; but realization is international if some production is for export. If capital is local and is reinvested locally, reproduction is national; if profits may be reinvested in other countries, reproduction is international.

If a single corporation organizes production internationally, realization and reproduction must be international too. The fact that a plant assembles components made in other plants of the same corporation in other countries implies that the corporation is engaged in international trade and in international investment. Such capital is global: production, realization, and reproduction are all international. It is this form of capital to which the thesis of the new international division of labor largely refers. This form of capital is not especially important in Brazil, South Korea, or Taiwan, though some of their largest corporations are becoming global in scope.

More significant in all three countries are nationally constrained capitals. In the market-constrained form, realization is national (the commodity is not traded) but reproduction is international. This circuit is created by import-substitution policies that rely on transnational corporations: production behind tariff barriers for domestic markets. However, it is also induced by high transport costs: oil refining and some food processing have been market constrained. In the investment-constrained circuit realization is international (the commodity is traded) but reproduction is national. In this circuit local capitalists seek to export commodities but their investment space is purely national. Textile, clothing, and footwear producers have typically been investment constrained, and so for a while were domestic steel and automobile producers. The final category of capital is the national circuit: production, realization, and reproduction are all national. This circuit contains on average smaller capitals than the other circuits because realization and reproduction are both limited by domestic market size and domestic investment opportunities. Many of the smaller firms in the nontradable sectors of the service industry fall into this category.

This classification points to another set of competing interests. If realization is national, capitals compete within the domestic market and protect their position within that market; that protection may involve tariff policies, for example. If realization is international, capitals compete in the global marketplace and seek domestic production costs that are as low as possible. If reproduction is international, capitals are served by the free flow of capital and deregulated international transfers; by contrast nationally reproduced capitals may seek to protect themselves against international capital inflows. Nationalist policies thus may derive from market-constrained capitals seeking to protect their local market from importers or from investment-constrained capitals seeking to protect their local investment opportunities. Once capitals come to influence state policies; the relative size of the different circuits in a country can affect state policies for example, South Korea is deregulating now that its chaebol (large business groups; see Section 10.6.3) have become global or internationally reproduced corporations.

Empirical categories are different. Many countries' policies distinguish foreign from domestic capitals. This distinction refers to the location of the headquarters of a company or the nationality of its shareholders rather than to the source of its fixed and working capital or the location of its markets. Foreign capital is either global or market constrained (if reproduction is constrained to the nation, the capital must be domestic), though domestic transnationals can be global or market constrained capitals too. Still until the development of domestic transnationals in the three NICs during the 1980s, the empirical category of foreign corporations generally has coincided with the theoretical categories of global and market-constrained capitals. Domestic corporations are not investment constrained though: in all three countries domestic corporations have borrowed on global financial markets. The one corporation may embody both nationally and internationally reproduced capital.

Figure 10.12 summarizes the forms of corporations, capital sources, and circuits.

10.5.2 Foreign Capital and the Growth of Exports

The level of foreign capital inflows to the three NICs increased rapidly after the early 1970s (Table 10.6). The history of exports is different (Figures 10.4 and 10.5). After a period of negligible growth, exports grew rapidly in the years 1968–1974 in Brazil and 1960–1974 in South Korea and Taiwan. The decade following the first oil crisis was a period of slow growth of exports, especially in Brazil; but exports have grown briskly again in the years since

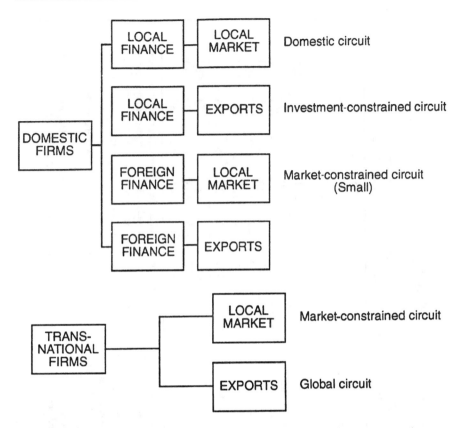

FIGURE 10.12. Classification of firms and of capital. The market-constrained circuit of domestic firms is likely to be small since repayment of foreign finance requires at the national level an equivalent trade surplus. It is not yet clear from the recent history of Brazil, South Korea, and Taiwan whether behavioral differences mean that the category of transnational firms should be subdivided into domestic and foreign firms.

1985 (1986 in Brazil). In these statistics the relation between capital inflows and export activity is not obvious; however, the export booms up to 1974 may have helped slow the industrial market economies. How are capital inflows, exports, and the slowdown related? We begin by reconsidering the development of the Brazilian steel industry.

Despite relying on international finance, development of the Brazilian steel industry was not imposed by international capital. Development was the result of a contradictory partnership between international and domestic factions of the capitalist class. The virtual exclusion of international capital from the productive circuit in Brazil's steel industry suggests either that it has been controlled for nationalist reasons or that the major steel companies were not interested in making direct investments there. The Brazilian government made

TABLE 10.10. Costs of producing steel: Brazil, South Korea, USA, and developing countries

Input	USA 1981	Developed Country 1975	Developing Country 1975	POSCO 1982	Brazil 1979	1980	1981	1982	1983	1984
Labor	186	178	138	16	73	68	108	108	59	50
Iron ore & scrap	102				32	34	35	33	27	35
Energy	139				80	94	123	128	92	91
Other	107				78	72	103	115	99	99
All material	348	223	306	227	190	200	261	276	218	225
All variable costs	534	401	444	243	263	268	369	384	277	275
Depreciation	23				29	30	55	51	31	43
Interest	9				49	47	102	150	117	109
All capital costs	32	237–355	394	87	78	77	157	201	148	152
All costs (1)	566	638–756	838	330	341	345	526	585	425	427
(1) add taxes (2)	574				409	415	611	666	474	483
(2) with yield < 80% (3)					432	445	638	708	500	514
(3) + $84 to ship to US					516	529	722	792	584	598

Note: All data are expressed in $US of 1986 (using the CPI as deflator) and are per tonne of cold rolled sheet. Row (3) at the bottom recalculates the data in row (2) under the assumption that yields are only 80%, since it is thought that yields above this figure in Brazil reflect differences in accounting methods rather than operations (see Webber and Foot 1988 for details). The last row adds $84 to the costs in row (3) to allow for the costs of landing steel in the USA (Barnett and Schorsch 1983). These cost comparisons are subject to differences in quality of inputs, accounting methods, mix of output, and exchange rates.

Sources: US 1981 data from Barnett and Schorsch (1983: 61). The three 1975 estimates are from Benbouali (1980: 37) and are from calculations, not operating experience; the Developing Country column is Benbouali's estimate for a new plant in a NIC similar in scale and efficiency to the new plant for which calculations are presented in the *Developed country* column. POSCO data are from Hogan (1985: 33). Brazil data are from Foot (1986), but see also Webber and Foot (1988) and refer to the three integrated plants in the Siderbras group (CSN, Cosipa, Usiminas). All data have been recalculated.

repeated attempts to induce foreign direct investment in steel production; this implies that steel companies were not interested in producing in Brazil.

If foreign corporations were not interested in Brazil as a location for steel production, was Brazil a cost-effective place in which to produce steel? The evidence is not clear (Webber and Foot 1988; see also Table 10.10). The variable costs of producing steel in Brazil are lower than in the USA because labor is cheaper and materials costs are lower. Although wages in American steel were five times those in Brazil in 1981, the cost of production in the Brazilian companies was only 13% lower than if they had paid the Americans' wages bill: low wages were largely offset by lower labor productivity (compare the Brazilian wage bill with POSCO's). Brazil's advantage in variable costs was balanced by its disadvantage in capital costs: high construction costs, expensive loans, new equipment, and a depreciating currency all contributed to this disadvantage. In 1981 and 1982, when capacity utilization rates were similar in the two countries the costs of production were similar too; adjusted for differences in measuring yields and for shipping steel to the USA, Brazil could not export steel to the USA in the 1980s any more cheaply than the Americans could produce it themselves. Yet Brazil's exports of steel rose from 21% of production in 1982 to 41% in 1983; and in 1984 Brazil was the world's fourth largest net exporter of steel (van Liemt 1988: 97). The results of this comparison are broadly comparable to those of Benbouali (1980). Equally, China Steel exports more steel to Japan than any other country except South Korea; yet imports of steel to Taiwan are still restricted and the internal price of steel is 20% greater than the price of steel landed from Japan (Wade 1990b: 131).

It is unlikely that costs of production justified a major steelmaker investing in Brazil, given uncertainty about exchange rates. [Even the Koreans found it difficult to attract the capital needed to build POSCO (D'Mello 1985).] Direct foreign investors needed Brazil to be an especially profitable place in which to produce steel—or offered a large protected market. But international financial capital did not need Brazil to be one of the most profitable places to produce steel, so the development of the industry did not depend on cost advantages. All that was required was that the government guarantee to repay: that Brazilian industry in general (not just the steel industry) could compete within its expected market. Furthermore substantial government involvement indicates that domestic interests in the growth of the industry were partly political rather than purely economic. This is a direct example of capital failing to seek a maximum profit location, the kind to which Chapter 7 points; it illustrates a difference in the behavior of financial and production capital.

The development of the Brazilian steel industry illustrates another lesson. Growth of exports depends as much on the need for foreign currency as on capacity to undercut prices. When interest rates were high and the cruzeiro depreciating, Brazilian steel producers faced huge capital costs: 22% of total costs in 1980 when capacity utilization rates were high, and 36% in 1982 when utilization rates had fallen (Table 10.10). In a depressed domestic market when interest rates were high, the Brazilian steelmakers had to export: the share of exports in output doubled between 1982 and 1983, when Siderbras exported more than half a billion dollars worth of steel (Clements 1988: 132). If the Brazilians undercut American steel prices by 10% in 1983, each tonne of steel sold in the USA would have contributed more than $200 to capital costs. So long as the Brazilians' variable costs were covered by the US selling price, exports helped pay the steel companies' debts and depreciation. The debt of the steel producers and their depressed domestic markets has forced them to export, possibly at less than their average costs of production: borrowing has compelled exports rather than financed efficient production.

This argument has been generalized. Brazil's public and private debt rose after the first oil shock as it responded to low real-interest rates and rising export prices: debt service payments on public debt rose from 12.5% of exports in 1970 to 17.9% in 1975 and then to 34.5% in 1980 (Preusse and Schinke 1988: 150). Most of the new debt arose from accumulated interest payments on earlier debt: the combination of a slowdown in world trade and a rise in interest rates after the mid-1970s (the London InterBank Offered rate rose from 6.1% in 1976 to 16.7% in 1981). In order to pay off some of the debt the Brazilian state has tried to expand exports: if foreign exchange is constrained by lack of new foreign capital, the net worth of a dollar of foreign exchange exceeds that of a dollar earned in domestic savings (Preusse and Schinke 1988). Yet even when exports were expanded, the pressure of debt payments has forced savings rates down and reduced rates of gross capital formation from 28% of GDP in the late 1970s to 17% in the early 1980s (Preusse and Schinke 1988: 153). If Brazil continues to raise exports without investing, there will be few opportunities to embody technical changes in new capital, so Brazilian companies will have to compete on the basis of low wages rather than advanced technology (Fishlow 1989): then competition from NICs on the basis of wage differences may become a reality.

The sources of the growth of Brazil's exports have also been measured statistically. Carvalho and Haddad (1980) regressed the real value of manufactured exports from 1955 through 1974 on measures of incentives and market conditions. The most significant determinant of the level of Brazil's exports was the quantity of manufactures imported by the main industrial countries; second in significance was the ratio of the real exchange rate to an index of fiscal incentives; and third (negatively) was an index of industrial capacity use in Brazil. The growth of world trade accounted for 33% of the growth of Brazil's manufactured exports in 1971–1974; 60% in 1974–1978; and 32% in 1978–1981 (Martone and Braga 1987). Competitiveness, incentives, and the pressures of idle capacity caused the remaining growth of exports.

Furthermore, some of the expansion of exports from NICs in the 1970s was destined less for the industrial market economies than to other developing countries. Whereas 76% of Brazil's exports were sent to industrial market economies in 1970, only 54% were sent there in 1980; for South Korea the proportions were 87% and 63%, respectively (van Liemt 1988: 122). Even so, exports from the three NICs accounted in the mid-1980s for only 4.8% of world exports; and while Taiwan has run a positive balance of trade since 1975, South Korea has always imported more than it has exported and Brazil's balance of trade turned positive only in 1981 under the pressure of debt repayments. The combined balance of all three has been positive only since 1982 (Lin 1989: 106–108): until the debt crisis, these NICs have demanded more than they supplied.

10.5.3 Interpretations

Several questions arise from the history of capital flows. What are the relations between local and international capital? What differences are caused by relying on financial rather than industrial capital as a source of funds? What is the relationship between capital inflows and export growth?

Brazil has relied heavily on debt, particularly after the first oil shock. It has encouraged and discouraged foreign direct investment at different times. Direct investors have provided foreign exchange to pay for investment and brought advanced production and organizational techniques. Still the foreign exchange benefit is offset by later remittances of profits and their new techniques pose a threat to domestic capitals (Baer 1989: 218–226). The costs and benefits have been evaluated differently at separate times.

South Korea has relied on foreign capital too (Iqbal 1988). Its external finance in the past has hinged on internationally syndicated bank loans: foreign direct investment has formed less than 2% of gross fixed capital formation; of the external debt in 1983, the stock of foreign direct investment accounted for 4.4% (Iqbal 1988: 141). This pattern has been the result of several factors. First, the innovation of syndicated credits has permitted banks to pool assets to make larger loans than any one could justify itself. Secondly, like Brazil, South Korea has taken tactical advantage of the low or negative interest rates charged for petrodollars in the 1970s, an especially cheap source of finance since inflation was high and the won undervalued (Park 1986). Thirdly, direct foreign investment has been discouraged: the Japanese are feared; and internal subsidies and incentives are provided for South Korean firms, not foreign ones. Presumably this policy views large, capable corporations as a national asset or seeks to retain profits within the domestic economy. However, the South Korean government has not entirely eschewed foreign direct investment.

Limiting direct foreign investment has created problems though. For example, overseas construction, shipping, and shipbuilding expanded in a period of great demand (the 1970s) with cheap loans and without any effective brake: between 1965 and 1975 South Korea's gross foreign debt rose from 6% of GNP to over 40% and by 1985 was over 55% (Corbo and Nam 1988: 41; Park 1986; Woo 1991). Since the government typically imports capital and lends it to individual chaebol, it is the government's capacity to repay that is relevant and that depends on South Korea's aggregate economic performance rather than on the performance of individual industries. As the markets for these commodities crashed in the early 1980s firms could not generate the output with which to pay the debts, which are now accruing high interest rates. South Korea depends on its rapidly growing exports to pay these obligations (Bradford 1990).

Taiwan has engaged in a third form of policy about foreign capital and direct foreign investment (Wade 1990b: 148–157). Brazil, like South Korea, has actively sought foreign investment. But unlike South Korea, Brazil has controlled foreign direct investment in some industries, steel for one. Like Brazil, Taiwan has generally been relaxed about foreign direct investment; unlike Brazil, it has sought to control foreign capital's involvement in its economy. Taiwan has tried to balance conflicting needs: investment, technology, and control of local capital against national development objectives and space for local capital.

The international geography of production has been affected by the extent to which NICs have relied on financial rather than production capital. Financial capital was commonly lent to governments or their banks during the heyday of cheap money, after the onset of the slowdown in 1974. It was lent under government guarantees to repay that relied upon the continued expansion of the economy as a whole, not on the profitability of individual industries. The industries financed in this way did not have to be competitive with their international rivals even in domestic markets. To the extent that industries in NICs were financed by international banks, NICs were not necessarily least cost locations for those industries. They may have later become least cost locations, by learning, exporting, and economizing with scale. By contrast direct foreign investors required NICs to be maximum profit locations. International financial capital offered the NICs freedom to plan industrial growth without the constraints of competitiveness; long-term success has depended on acquiring competitiveness, not starting with it.

The distinction between financial and productive capital has modified the relations between capital inflows and growth of exports. Long-run production costs in the USA may be below those in other countries even while US markets are being invaded by imports. When interest rates are high and domestic markets depressed, debt forces exports: so long as variable costs are paid, even small contributions to fixed costs raise capacity utilization rates and reduce the burden of debt. In this sense financial inflows have contributed to the growth of exports from the NICs, but only because the global economy has stagnated during a period of high interest rates. It is less the financial inflows after the mid-1970s than the failure of international capital flows to continue in the 1980s that has spurred the NICs to ever greater feats of exporting. This is another sense in which the growth of the NICs and their exports has been a response to rather than a cause of the slowdown in the industrial market economies.

10.6 LOCAL ACCUMULATION

The growth of NICs has been a response to the slowdown in advanced capitalist countries. Capital inflows postdated rather than preceded the slowdown. Exports have been partially in response to the slowdown too. NICs have been using excess capital that has been accumulated in advanced industrial economies but that cannot find profitable uses there. What is remarkable about this history is that only some Third World countries became NICs: capital that ranged over the world for productive and profitable investment was particularly selective in its choice of roosting spots. Using that capital, NICs were able to forge a local accumulation strategy by which cost competitiveness was achieved. In most NICs the state has been the institution that articulated local accumulation strategies.

Industrialization in the NICs exemplifies various forms of local initiative. What happened in one country differs from what happened in others; but each history demonstrates a local power to act. The state is in social context: where does it acquire the will and the strength to create industrial policy? Successful NICs have acted in ways different from the prescriptions of orthodox economics by creating local policies. The fact that industrialization of the third world has been selective implies that the traits of individual places influence economic change. Development is not purely structural; nor is it decided solely by relative wage levels and capital prices. Whereas Frank (1982) ascribes a common, uncertain, and dependent role to Hong Kong, Singapore, Taiwan, and South Korea, others have examined the individuality of development in NICs (Ho 1978), emphasizing the inherited social structure and the state's attempts to shape the pace and pattern of industrialization. States have a variety of powers to influence industry and investment: national industrial policy includes investment incentives, employment and labor policies, state ownership of assets, government procurement policies, institutional structures, and environmental and health regulations; national financial policy may control foreign direct investment, either outward investment by domestic firms or inward investment by foreign firms; national trade policy affects costs and prices through tariff and nontariff barriers, and export policies (Donges 1976).

The stylized fact of East Asian success and Latin American failure has been ascribed to internal differences. Felix (1989) points to the strong indigenous artisanal sector in East Asia as compared to Latin America and to demands from the Latin American middle class for imported consumer goods. Ranis (1989) emphasizes differences in resources. South Korea and Taiwan were endowed with few natural resources; surplus labor; cultures that emphasize the here and now; egalitarian attitudes to opportunity; and nationalism. In the early 1950s South Korea and Taiwan were the two developing countries with lowest ratio of income to sociocultural development (Adelman and Morris 1967: 168–171). Whereas South Korea and Taiwan were forced by lack of resources to become export oriented, many Latin American countries were encouraged to continue substituting for imports (Ranis 1990). Traditional, resource-based exports from Latin America are subject to terms of trade fluctuations. Policies that stress export orientation and liberalization when terms-of-trade are high are forced to retreat to import substitution when terms of trade fall. To Ranis part of the problem is that natural resource wealth is shared among the population, for example, in the form of minimum wage legislation. Whitehead (1990) has constructed a typology of political explanations of macroeconomic policies: historical traditions (of informal consultation and consensus); social structure (class, ethnicity, religious distinctions); self-interest of powerful groups; entrenched characteristics of political systems; formal properties of political institutions; economic ideologies; vicious or virtuous circles of policies and events; and unpredictable political events.

The individuality of state action is sometimes indexed by the concept of strong (or hard) and weak states (Wade 1990b). Strong states give priority to industrialization; delegate to technocrats the tasks of targeting and designing policy; subordinate private and regional pressures to long-term national goals; and fashion an effective bureaucracy. Weak states cannot perform these tasks. A comparable distinction rates state autonomy (Jenkins 1991). Relatively autonomous states act in the long-run interests of capital as a whole even if they conflict with the interests of particular fractions: policy making is insulated from political pressure by vested interests. Cumings (1984) similarly writes of internationalist mercantilist states that believe in a strong state guiding an organic society toward effective competition in the world economy in order to increase the wealth and power of the state and society. These definitions are tautological and fail to distinguish the successes from the failures (Felix 1989).

Such explanations are too general. Strong and weak states, degrees of state autonomy, resource endowments: these are background to the economic history of Brazil, South Korea, and Taiwan. Why do such states emerge? Why are certain policies chosen at particular times? How do relations between the state and other cultural characteristics shift during development? The differences between South Korea and Taiwan and between Brazil and other countries in Latin America are glossed over. In any event the question of national success and failure is misspecified: "success" means rapid rates of capital accumulation; other classes in Brazil, South Korea, and Taiwan might interpret the economic history of the last 40 years quite differently. This section begins by reviewing briefly the roles that states can play in capitalist societies according to the theories advanced in this book. It continues by describing the internal class characteristics of Brazil, South Korea, and Taiwan and the perceptions of the global environment that have led the state to particular policies about capital accumulation. Policies about electronics production provide an example.

10.6.1 Roles for the State

The state plays many roles in capitalist societies. Some states directly assist production—constructing infrastructure and supporting basic industries that are not profitable, for instance. The state also helps to reproduce capitalist societies, especially the labor force. So states commonly organize education, welfare, and health services and offer an ideological foundation for capitalist society. These are tasks that individual corporations cannot perform because they are valuable to all corporations but hard to charge for. As we saw in Chapter 4 the reproduction of a labor force is unlike most production processes in being largely outside capitalist control. These functions have been recognized by many writers; they apply to a greater or lesser degree to all capitalist states. But what roles do our refashioned models assign the state that might illuminate the rise of the NICs?

Chapter 5 described a closed capitalist economy. Technical change leads an economy to overproduce or, if production is limited to demand, to overaccumulate capital. Overproduction and overaccumulation reflect the way in which technical change reduces the demand for labor and other inputs as it enlarges potential output. As a result the rate of profit falls. Thus capital must find other outlets for expansion: either intensively (within existing capitalist social formations) or extensively (by expanding the regions under capitalist social relations). In practice the state aids both these changes. Ideological support for private capital accumulation and privatization of previously state-provided services are intensive responses to the falling rate of profit. Aid, imperialism, and efforts to stabilize international relations are means to extend capitalism that have been employed at one time or another.

The theory of technical change (Chapter 6) suggests a second role for the state. Technical change is the movement of a plant (or industry or group of industries) in technology space, generally toward the technical frontier. Some plants are near the frontier, others more distant. If the techniques of the advanced plants are common knowledge, backward plants adopt new techniques only if the returns on the investment in new techniques exceed the cost of making the change. Backward plants enjoy higher returns on the technical change than do advanced plants; some costs of technical change (e.g., disruption) may be no greater in backward plants than in less backward ones. But backward plants are making lower rates of profit than advanced plants. Thus backward plants may never invest in new techniques because, although the investment is highly profitable, they lack the surplus to invest.

Suppose that backward plants are mainly in one country and advanced plants mainly overseas. A second role for the state is to provide the funds that encourage technical changes by backward plants. In this way the plants are saved from eventual creeping bankruptcy through ever less efficient production and the state has provided an investment that offers profitable returns to the adoption of known, more advanced technology. This is restructuring by the state.

The backward plants generate little surplus. Therefore, even though the change itself is profitable, the plants cannot afford it. But why cannot the plants borrow the funds to pay to invest in technical change? In a world of perfect information such borrowing would be easy, for lenders would also know that it is profitable to invest in technical change. But when information is imperfect and the future uncertain lenders pay at least as much attention to the current performance of laggards (which is poor) as to the potential for improved performance. A role for the state in restructuring requires not only that investment in the laggards be profitable but that the capital market does not respond perfectly to that profit potential.

A third role for the state arises from economies of scale and learning by doing. Most trade theory, like most models of growth, assumes that there are constant or decreasing returns to scale. This assumption is important in neoclassical economics, for it guarantees the reasonableness of the rule that prices equal marginal costs and ensures that market outcomes are determinate: initial conditions matter less than costs of production. But when returns to scale increase or there is learning by doing, market outcomes depend essentially on initial conditions: long-run cost conditions matter less than an early start. If returns increase or firms learn, the pattern of specialization of countries and of comparative advantage is essentially random.

Individual corporations learn by doing: Chapter 6 and Section 10.3 provide evidence. Equally there may be some scales of production that are subject to increasing returns. A state might accordingly intervene to provide support for a corporation to learn or grow enough to compete on a world scale. This is the argument that the state ought to support infant industries. It has been countered by arguments that state support may encourage inefficiency and be politically difficult to remove when industries are no longer infants. Nevertheless, if industries do achieve international competitiveness, state support will have raised national levels of welfare as well as supporting the expansion of (domestic) capital.

The issue for the theory of development also concerns the existence of these conditions at the level of the nation. It is not simply individual producers but the whole society that learns by doing: suppliers, workers, and marketers all learn (or are forced to learn) their roles by practising them. Equally, costs of production depend not only on the expansion of output of a single corporation but on the level of output of the entire society: transport systems need to be organized, labor training put in place, subcontractors developed, downstream industries expanded, and domestic markets expanded. These developments need to be coordinated in some fashion so that investors in one industry understand investments and planned investments in other related sectors. State support for the expansion of production across a wide range of industries permits such national economies of scale to be achieved.

State promotion of domestic industries appears to support domestic capital. Indeed the capitalists who organize individual production units may be domestic nationals. Nevertheless, state support for domestic development is not necessarily at odds with the interests of international capital. Finance for domestic expansion may be borrowed on the international capital market: Brazil and Mexico provide classic examples of this process. In this sense development also extends the scope of capitalist accumulation. Still if individual domestic producers do become internationally competitive, they will undermine the market position of established producers in other countries. This is the sense in which domestic and international interests conflict. Yet other overseas producers benefit from domestic industrialization—those who buy from the new producers or sell to the enlarged domestic market.

There is ample scope for states to affect industrialization. The state may support the expansion of capitalist accumulation. States may help in restructuring industries. And states may support domestic capital while it learns and acquires the scale to compete in world markets. This role seems particularly important in the growth of NICs.

10.6.2 State, Class, and Policy in Brazil

The end of land-based federalism in Brazil in the 1930s and the Estado Novo (new state) created institutions that could frame explicit industrial policies. After the war, cycles of nationalist and internationalist policies eventually gave way to military dictatorship in 1964. Military rule ended in 1985 under the cloud of the debt crisis, with the military leaders unable to solve the conflicts that had driven contradictory policies. Though influenced by external economic events, development has not been externally imposed: in Brazil international capital has been unfettered for brief periods. The discussion relies on Foot and Webber (1990a).

In the early twentieth century Brazil supplied raw materials: coffee, beef, cotton, tobacco, iron ore, hides, rubber, and timber. Until 1930 power was held by agricultural fazendeiros (planters and cattlemen) of the southern states who controlled trade policy, exchange rates, and agricultural marketing policies (Dean 1969: 4–5; Erickson 1977: 12). The power of the fazendeiros was undermined by the growth of local industry, which spawned a capitalist class opposed to the landowners' interests but without a voice in the decentralized political structure (Dean 1969), and by the collapse of coffee prices in 1929 (Wirth 1970: 19), which upset the planters' economic power.

The revolution of 1930 was not in direct support of one ruling class nor against a threat from dominated classes. President Getulio Vargas (1930–1945) maintained a populist platform (Quartim 1971: 24) formalized as a corporatist state that assimilated a wider variety of interests than the federalism of the Old Republic, including the interests of a growing working class (Deyo 1990). The wages and conditions of workers were improved, broadening the government's legitimacy with workers. Labor relations were institutionalized, preempting a revolutionary threat to urban industrial expansion (Quartim 1971: 24). Militant unionism was succeeded by bureaucratic unionism (Erickson 1977: 14) ruled by laws that as yet remain in force. *Sindicatos* (state-run unions) were organized by municipality and industrial sector. They were to deal with workplace grievances, wage demands, and welfare services, but only if recognized by the Ministry of Labor (Erickson 1977:

32). Conflicts between employers and employees were to be resolved through labor courts, strikes without court approval being illegal.

The Estado Novo signaled that Brazil was to industrialize. Continued stagnation of export prices and expansion of imports drove Brazil to begin substituting local products for foreign (Dean 1969: 208–209). The state would "supply the deficiencies of individual initiative and coordinate the factors of production so that conflicts may be avoided or resolved and a consideration of the interests of the Nation, represented by the State, may be introduced" [from the 1937 constitution, quoted in Dean (1969: 210)]. The exchange rate was raised and tariffs imposed on consumer goods but relaxed on industrial machinery. Industrial growth by import substitution was a nationalist policy designed to extract Brazil from its stifled position as a supplier of raw materials (Baer 1989: 51; van Liemt 1988: 24). The state became directly involved in enterprise. It consolidated shipping lines, formed an airline, and began to manage ports. In 1938 the National Petroleum Council was formed (a predecessor of Petrobras); Fábrica Nacional de Motores (FNM) and Companhia Siderúrgica Nacional (CSN) soon followed (Evans 1979: 87–90). Some companies were intended to exclude foreign capital, but other attempts to induce foreign direct investment failed. State involvement was motivated by nationalist policy and by the need to develop industries in which domestic capital was incompetent and international capital not interested. This was a nationalist and populist policy from which all classes should benefit. Internal class forces dominated the course of development in the context of the global Great Depression.

The ideology of populism could not maintain cohesion. The forces seeking to suppress authority were those that had been suppressed by authority. Industrial capitalists sought to gain an influence over policy that they were denied by the relatively autonomous Vargas government. State industrial enterprises were seen to intrude upon the arena of private accumulation (Quartim 1971: 29). Opposed by industrial capitalists, Vargas was driven to depend on the left for support, threatening the centralized control of labor and upsetting the fazendeiros as well as the industrialists. United, they were able to make Vargas legalize political parties and call elections for the end of 1945; he was forcibly removed before the elections.

Four governments were elected in the following years. President Enrico Gaspar Dutra (1946–1951) and again Vargas (1951–1954) controlled foreign direct investment (Leff 1968: 60): until 1954, foreign direct investment net of profits and remittances was negative (do Lago 1988: 59). As the terms of trade declined the government was obliged to rely on labor for support, but in 1954 widespread strikes caused the military to intervene briefly. Vargas was forced to resign and committed suicide. Protection and nationalism had proved unacceptable to the bourgeoisie, and the 1955 election was won by Juscelino Kubitschek, who inaugurated "a regime of economic euphoria and imperialist take-over" (Quartim 1971: 40; see also Leff 1968: 61). Under the Kubitschek government between 1957 and 1961, foreign direct investment exceeded $400 million per year and net of profits and remittances exceeded $300 million (1986 dollars: do Lago 1988: 59). By the late 1950s the open policy was producing its own problems: competition from companies with technical and financial resources that domestic industrialists could not equal; international financial pressure to balance payments and repay debts; and use of foreign currency to remit profits and pay interest [25% of foreign exchange payments (Leff 1968: 72)]. João Goulart became president in 1961 and abandoned foreign-driven development: by 1964 net foreign direct investment was less than $100 million (do Lago 1988: 59). Growth was to be financed by restricting consumer imports. Social reforms and wage increases were to balance the benefits of industrialization but proved inflationary. Goulart was forced to the left. In 1962 unions called a general strike (Quartim 1971: 45) and independent political leaders united all workers' organizations (illegally). The situation worsened through 1963, with more strikes, political violence, and the rise of an agrarian reform movement (Deyo 1990). The army intervened as it had in 1945 and 1954. Goulart was forced into exile.

Each government faced similar contradictions [Evans (1979) calls them contradictions of dependent development]: repeated military interventions index failure to solve the contradictions. The interests of industrialists lay in rapid industrial growth. Growth depended on foreign technology and money which imperiled the independence of domestic capital from international business. So international influence did not last long. But governments that restricted foreign influence came to depend on the left. Means of controlling labor on the shop floor relied upon the literal application of the labor laws (Humphrey 1982). Whenever the government leaned toward labor for support, the system of labor control, smooth accumulation, and industrial growth were threatened. So policies aimed at encouraging indigenous capital accumulation in Brazil themselves produced the conditions under which this growth was threatened, either increasing foreign influence or losing control over labor. The reversals in policy between 1945 and 1964 derive from the struggle of domestic capital to secure its conditions of reproduction within the Brazilian state against the interests of workers and international capital.

The military now strengthened the means to suppress political resistance. Independent political parties were banned. The constitution was rewritten so that Congress could be suspended. The labor laws of the Estado Novo were more effectively used. Insurances on job security were withdrawn (Humphrey 1982: 45; TIE 1984). The scale that kept wages in line with inflation was abolished. The government purged the leaders of the active unions (Erickson 1977: 158). Strikes in 1968 were put down with force (TIE 1984: 13). The political stabilization was also intended to attract foreign investment. In its early stages the new government actively courted investment from abroad. The state-run FNM was sold to Alfa Romeo, and Thyssen Steel was allowed to purchase equity in Cosigua (Evans 1979: 217; *Business Latin America* 1968: 232).

Antinationalist policy did not last long. The military was not proforeign but reacting to the inability of nationalist democratic governments to control workers. A policy of joint development sought to attract foreign capital without compromising local interests. The state participated in industries that required resources beyond the means of domestic capital, that could not attract foreign interest, or that were protected against foreign capital for national reasons. The prices of state telecommunications, electricity, petroleum, and steel companies were controlled; these companies presented limited prospects for profit and induced little interest abroad. The government partnered private capital to restrict the autonomy of international capital and ensure the participation of local capital. When Fiat began producing in the early 1970s, it had to invest jointly with the state of Minas Gerais (Evans 1979: 228); petrochemicals projects often had to be shared with Petroquisa, a subsidiary of Petrobras. Private indigenous capital was sometimes a partner (Evans 1979: 231–232). Some multinational corporations were dissuaded from investing in Brazil by government involvement (Evans 1979: 267–274; *Business Latin America* 1977: 193–307). The 1964 coup allowed development to be driven by foreign investment while protecting national interests and suppressing populist and communist reactions. The military state came "to restrict international capital to a degree almost unthinkable during the initial orthodox stage, making economic space for itself and for the national bourgeoisie" (O'Donnell 1978: 21).

Nevertheless foreign investment grew rapidly. Net foreign direct investment ran at $515 million (1986 dollars) per year from 1969 through 1972 (do Lago 1988: 59). Growth was stimulated by stabilization: working class activity was suppressed and inflation was below 20%; the state had alleviated bottlenecks especially in the supply of steel and electricity (Wirth 1970). Large corporations were finding it easier to internationalize their operations. Between 1973 and 1982, net direct foreign investment in Brazil exceeded $1.75 billion per year (1986 dollars; do Lago 1988: 59). Foreign capital drove development by its focus on key manufacturing sectors, yet local interests were actively involved. Direct foreign investment never accounted for more that 6.7% of total fixed capital formation and 27% of that was reinvestment (IMF various years; UN various years).

The conflicts within Brazil that encouraged the imposition of authority were not eliminated by it. The military government appealed to the success of its policies (Alves 1985: 141). But after 1974 rising oil prices, falling terms of trade, increasing trade deficits and foreign debt, rising interest rates, and another bout of inflation called that success into question, even among the ruling classes (Deyo 1990). The official union apparatus was circumvented as workers called for change and authoritarian rule was slightly relaxed (Deyo 1990). A series of strikes began (TIE 1984). In 1978, 24 strikes involved 539,000 workers; in 1979, 119 strikes involved 3.2 million workers. The strikes were organized outside the *sindicatos*, threatening the structure of labor control, and offering workers hope for independent organization. Brazil defaulted on loan repayments in 1982. The IMF had to provide short-term loans to service debts. After 1983, foreign direct investment plummeted and net of profits and remittances was negative (do Lago 1988: 59). Inflation ran out of control. Of 2 million industrial workers in São Paulo in 1980, 437,000 were laid off in the next 2 years (Alves 1985: 232–233). The changes in policy needed to solve these problems could not be made by the military. Foreign-driven development and direct political suppression, built into the constitution of the authoritarian state, now intensified the crisis. Military government ended in early 1985.

Brazilian development has not been imposed by international capital following the dictates of comparative advantage. Only in short intervals have the interests of domestic capital been suppressed. The interests of local capital are different from those of international capital: they compete for domestic markets, political power, and surplus. So the problem for the Brazilian state has been to use international capital to foster domestic capital accumulation but in the context of a militant workforce. Shifts from expansionary to restrictive state strategies alter the balance of strength of workers and the domestic bourgeoisie as well as between international and local capital. In regulating the conditions of capital accumulation the state has to control labor and delimit the role of international capital. This is a different problem from that faced by the state in South Korea and Taiwan: the problem of relative success and failure is mis-stated.

10.6.3 State, Class, and Policy in South Korea

In 1910 South Korea was annexed by Japan. The colony provided an agricultural surplus, immigrant workers to Japan (and other colonies), and mineral exports. The Japanese privatized land, nationalized common and royal land and ended up owning perhaps a half of South Korea's land. The occupation saw a breakdown in village self-sufficiency and an increase in production to supply Japan. Industrial development was limited and South Koreans were restricted from owning industrial facilities, though by 1938 more than a million of them worked as wage earners (C. Hamilton 1986: 9–20). By the end of World War II the Japanese had abolished the Korean monarchy and nobility; weakened the traditional landed aristocracy; greatly increased tenancy and exchange relations; prompted the development of a proletarian class within South Korea and among emigrants; and permitted a small industrial class and a few managers in Japanese enterprises to emerge (Amsden 1989: 32–36).

After Japan was defeated in 1945, Korea was divided into military occupation zones at the 38th parallel: the Americans controlled the southern zone; the Russians, the northern zone. A People's Republic was declared illegal in the South by the US government, which instead organized elections won by Syngman Rhee. President Rhee's support came from the US military, bureaucrats, and police (to whom Rhee was the best guarantee against reprisals from nationalists). Popular support for land redistribution in the North and the experience of land reform in Japan prompted Rhee's government to distribute Japanese and landlords' land to the peasantry, even though landlords dominated the National Assembly (C. Hamilton 1986: 20–28). Agriculture was destroyed as an arena of asset holding, investment and accumulation (Hamilton 1987). Rhee's regime had no local social foundation, though land reform permitted him to neutralize opposition (Steinberg 1988).

Economic issues were neglected: growth depended on aid. Capital was accumulated as huge volumes of aid were used to provide infrastructure and to stimulate local demand (Hamilton 1987). Between 1946 and 1976 the USA provided $12 billion in economic and military aid, Japan $1 billion, and international financial institutions $2 billion (Woo 1991: 43–72). Since the Japanese had left a strong bureaucratic apparatus and there were few local capitalists, the state led development. Import substitution was prompted by foreign exchange shortages (Cheng 1990) and by the fear that comparative advantage would merely subordinate South Korea to Japan once again (Woo 1991: 43–72). In effect the state began to create a capitalist class as capitalist social relations came to dominate politically and economically (C. Hamilton 1986: 29–38). Rentier capital was transformed into commercial capital: landlords had been expelled from the land and were attracted into commerce by the need to distribute US aid and by the profits that could be made through access to scarce foreign exchange. Industrial growth was derived from US aid; it did not deliver material gains to the people (a fact reflected in the revolt of 1960).

Import substitution degenerated into rent seeking: the rewards from import permits were guaranteed (Steinberg 1988; Cheng 1990; Woo 1991). The USA became disenchanted with Rhee's fanaticism and repression. After a student revolt a new government was elected in July 1960 (Hamilton 1987). The government devalued the won—which deepened the recession and was highly unpopular—and could not control streets and villages. The military intervened in a coup in May 1961, and the head of the junta, Gen. Chung Hee Park was elected president in 1963. The junta was composed of middle-ranking officers from rural and peasant backgrounds, nationalist and against corruption.

This was the first successful military coup in South Korea since the fourteenth century. It overthrew an elected government and was unpopular among traditional elites (Steinberg 1988): economic performance became the test of legitimacy (Cheng 1990; Benjamin 1982). Independence from the USA was sought by industrializing and promoting agricultural self-sufficiency in cooperation with local capital. Continued balance of payments problems, inflation, poor harvests, US advice, anxiety about Japan and North Korea—all inspired a more export-oriented policy (Cheng 1990; Benjamin 1982). The new US policy of encouraging economic development in client states led it to reduce aid and increase pressure to industrialize (Woo 1991: 73–117). Crucially, access to capital was linked to production: foreign exchange became available to producers. The US helped by procuring over a billion dollars of new industrial products for its war effort in Vietnam between 1966 and 1970

(Woo 1991: 73–117). This phase saw commercial capital transformed into industrial capital (C. Hamilton 1986: 26–38).

C. Hamilton (1986: 39–49) has emphasized four aspects of the relationship between the state and emerging class structures in South Korea in the 1960s. First, agricultural incomes were squeezed to provide a surplus to finance industrial development. By 1974 owner cultivators formed 70% of the agricultural population (Hamilton 1987: 50): the destruction of landlord power permitted industry to exploit agriculture through taxes and prices. Farmer's terms of trade fell from 93 in 1963 to 78–79 in 1966–1968 (C. Hamilton 1986: 40). Low output was offset by PL480 imports [until they fell too, when rice production was stimulated by higher prices that improved agriculture's terms of trade (C. Hamilton 1986: 107–111)]. Urban rice prices have been held stable and low, providing low wages and off-farm migrants to industry. Secondly, wages were suppressed and the working class repressed politically. Between 1967 and 1972 a million people left the countryside for cities (Hamilton 1987: 52), forming a labor force that kept real (as opposed to official) unemployment over 15% in the early 1970s (C. Hamilton 1986: 42) and restricted wage rises to skilled workers, of whom a shortage developed. The high and rising female labor force participation rate (over 40% by 1984) assisted in this process (Lin 1989: 44–47). Thirdly, a specific form of industrial capital has emerged, closely connected to the state: the large business group, or chaebol. The state has induced import substitution and coerced export growth using subsidies, tax concessions, import rights, tax penalties, and threatened loss of import licenses to offset the unprofitability of exports. Fourthly, the state has subordinated financial to industrial capital (Ito 1984). The state controls commercial banks, special banks, and development institutions and instituted low interest rates, though it has no power over the unorganized ("curb") money market. The South Korean state has positioned itself between foreign capital and local, developing capitalists, funding new industries, creating large firms, and buttressing social support (Woo 1991: 1–18): it has thus produced a particular form of capitalist social relations.

Industrial policy has prodded heavy and chemical industry since the early 1970s. The main stimulants to renewed import substitution were the request to curb exports of textiles to the US and the apparent waning of Pax Americana after the Vietnam War (Woo 1991: 118–147). The policy sought to capitalize on backward linkages as domestic demand had become sufficient to support heavy industries; self-defense was becoming more important, implying that steel and machinery should be produced locally; some advanced capitalist countries were losing competitiveness in shipbuilding and worried about pollution; competition from the next NICs was threatening established industries (Cheng 1990). The neglect of the rural sector and the growth of urban wage labor was pushing the state closer to the chaebol, who were offered finance, new investment funds, and relief from their debts.

The Chun period (1979–1987) has witnessed continued centralization and export promotion. The problem of legitimation had become more profound since there had been a short democratic period between President Park's assassination and Gen. Doo Hwan Chun's coup. After the Kwangju uprising was suppressed in May 1980, the government relied to an even greater extent than previously on economic performance for legitimacy. Electoral reforms since 1986 have partially accommodated middle class and student demands for presidential elections (Deyo 1990): the new vigor of the elective process implies more public control over economic decision making (Steinberg 1988). Electoral liberalization has been accompanied by some economic and financial liberalization as national capitals have entered the global sphere, increasingly able to survive without state support and interference (Woo 1991: 176–203).

The close alliance between industrial capital and government has rapidly raised business concentration (Kwon 1990). Access to cheap funds has meant that chaebol are highly leveraged: average equity ratios of nonfinancial firms on South Korea's stock exchange are less than half the ratios in Japan and the USA. Size provides the chaebol power over government: the bankruptcy of a large corporation could threaten South Korea's stability (Woo 1991: 148–175). But the formation of large firms has allowed the state to exert pressure on them (for example, during heavy and chemical industrialization) and has provided the financial power that allows South Korean firms (such as automobile firms) to internationalize their production (Gereffi 1990).

The South Korean state has faced a problem different from the Brazilian. With weak traditional and agrarian elites, the South Korean state has created a new form of industrial capital that depended on state support. Access to international capital and to finance has been controlled to a degree impossible in Brazil. Direct military suppression of labor has provided room for policy to shift. But as in Brazil, policy is nationalist. Fear of comparative advantage and of Japan, the loneliness after Pax Americana broke down, the threat from the North—all have prompted the state to seek to build a South Korea that is industrially powerful. Now that the chaebol comprise a second source of power in South Korea, the form of policy and its effectiveness may have to change.

10.6.4 State, Class, and Policy in Taiwan

Like South Korea, Taiwan was occupied by the Japanese in the first half of the twentieth century (1895–1945). In Taiwan the Japanese did not own much agricultural land but they weakened the traditional governing class and landed aristocracy, appropriating much of their material base (Hamilton 1987). Rising productivity was funneled into rice exports. No merchant class or indigenous manufacturing was permitted, though trade and production grew. No indigenous leadership stratum survived (Wade 1990b: 74–75). As in South Korea, Japan's attack on rural power was completed by Chiang Kai-shek's incoming Nationalist [Kuomintang (KMT)] government, which reformed landholding between 1949 and 1953: by 1965 owner cultivators were

67% of the agricultural population of Taiwan (Hamilton 1987: 50). The redistribution of land destroyed agriculture as an arena of investment and accumulation and allowed it to be exploited through taxes and pricing policies (Hamilton 1987) and an overvalued exchange rate (Wade 1990b: 76).

The new KMT government took control of former Japanese property, soon owning 90% of all capital (Hamilton 1987). Heavy industry was to be developed with US aid and light industry sold off to the monied classes and dispossessed landlords. The state was intimately involved at all levels in the process of transforming capital from agricultural/merchant forms to the industrial form.

Despite land reform—or by it—the state squeezed agriculture to provide a surplus for industrialization (Cheng 1990). The government forced farmers to grow rice, (withholding fertilizer from those who did not comply), demanded taxes in rice and compulsorily acquired a portion of each harvest at low prices (sometimes only 70% of market prices) (Hamilton 1987: 50; Wade 1990b). Annual grain procurements of 400,000 tons in the early 1950s had risen to 600,000 tons by the end of the decade (Ka and Seldon 1986), feeding the urban population and providing export income. Cultivators received less than 63% of the harvest in 1953–1955, less than their share under the Japanese. The other source of early capital was US aid, which paid for infrastructure and local demand: between 1951 and 1965 Taiwan received $US 1.5 billion in aid, of which the bulk was directed to infrastructure, including education and housing (Hamilton 1987: 54; Wade 1990b: 82–84).

Japanese colonial rulers were replaced by another immigrant group: the defeated KMT forces from mainland China. The new occupation of Taiwan brought more than a million urban and middle class immigrants (Ka and Seldon 1986): capitalists, managers, and professionals from the mainland. The Nationalist government had no long-term class basis in Taiwan (except among immigrants from the Mainland). The local population largely comprised rural and landowning peasants without local leaders (Wade 1990b: 231–232). In effect the KMT immigrants extracted a surplus from local farmers and used it to pursue an import-substituting industrial policy that promoted industrial capital accumulation (Cheng 1990). Until virtually the end of the 1980s the state was isolated from popular groups (Deyo 1990). Economic policy was also exclusionary: wages were low; public expenditures were never countercyclical; social welfare expenditures were low. A small elite of mainlanders controlled policy in a quasi-corporatist fashion with a large public sector. While political power remained in the hands of the mainlanders (Wade 1990b: 237), economic power was developed by local Taiwanese; this ethnic cleavage is partly responsible for the state's preference for weak businesses (Cheng 1990; Gereffi 1990).

Import-substituting industrialization reflected local economic and social circumstances. The landlords lacked the power to defeat industrial policies. Indigenous capitalists were few and the state controlled former Japanese businesses; so the state was itself producing and sought to protect its capital. A shortage of foreign exchange implied that imports must be limited (Cheng 1990; Wade 1990b: 77–82). The state apparatus that had migrated from mainland China proved easily capable of managing this process (Wade 1990b: 195–227 describes the economic bureaucracy). Unlike the South Korean state, the state in Taiwan was financially autonomous and did not rely on budding capitalists for political dues; and not having been paid dues, it owed no favors (Cheng 1990).

The push to export began in 1958–1960. Agrarian interests and small, local capitalists were too weak to oppose a policy of export promotion that derived from the apparent exhaustion of the domestic market and consequent charges of anticompetitive collusion (Cheng 1990). In contrast to the methods employed in South Korea, the Taiwanese state persuaded and pressed rather than forced firms to implement the program; retained state ownership of major enterprises; decentralized light industry around the island; and successfully encouraged direct foreign investment (which brought new entrants). The KMT's links to the masses and to small and medium enterprises precluded an explicit alliance between state and capital of the kind that emerged in South Korea: small and medium enterprises were fostered as a means of restraining the political power of capital and of decentralizing industry (to the regime's rural support).

Similarly distinct policies were developed in Taiwan during secondary import substitution in the mid-1970s [a development that had been planned as far back as 1961 but reinforced by the experience of international price fluctuations in the early 1970s (Wade 1990b: 87, 97)]. Facing the same economic challenges as South Korea, the Taiwanese state moved to develop backward linkages, but gradually rather than in a big push. A broad coalition of interests—farmers, state employees, workers, savers—were favored by such a policy: a development coalition with business remained impossible. The state sector was redeveloped in steel, shipbuilding, and petrochemicals, partly for economic reasons but also to crowd out private capital. The state is thus a party in, not just a mediator of conflicts between, upstream import-substituting firms and downstream exporters. However, private firms remain free of debt—fragmented and unconcentrated but uncaptured by the state (Cheng 1990; Gereffi 1990). The Taiwanese state implements through its own state enterprises and persuasion rather than direct pressure. This reflects the ethnic cleavage between political leaders (mainlanders) and many capitalists who are Taiwanese: the state cannot count on the unqualified support of capitalists.

In Taiwan, the new KMT government was pushed toward rapid economic growth and industrialization by several factors (Wade 1990b: 256–296). If the Nationalists were driven by a desire to regain China's greatness, aspects of their situation on Taiwan enhanced that desire: the need for military security, especially after the USA recognized the People's Republic of China (PRC) in 1978; the desire to maintain a state independent of the economic power of the local Taiwanese; and the irrelevance of landlords. Unproductive routes to wealth have been systematically closed off to raise the domestic demand for labor and so buttress local support. While the external threats to Taiwan and changes in the global economy seem similar to those that have agitated the South Korean state, the internal political economy is quite different, prompting a different route to both import-substituting and export oriented industrialization.

10.6.5 Electronics Industries

Industrial policies for the electronics sector exemplify the details of local influences on development. Macroeconomic policies affect overall demand and do not aim to affect different industries differently (though they may do so); industrial policies seek to influence the decisions of firms to produce and invest. Industrial policies may be either functional, affecting one function in many industries (promoting R&D, for example), or industry specific, targeting an industry. Industry-specific policies either follow the market (assisting firms to do what they would do anyway) or lead the market (inducing firms to do what they would otherwise not do). Industrial policies may lead without state control (Wade 1990b).

The evolution of Brazil's computer industry reflects the interaction of class and state and of local and international capital as well as bureaucratic finesse (Evans 1986). In 1970 Brazil's demand for computers was being met by imports, sales by transnational corporations (notably IBM and Burroughs), and some local assembly by transnational corporations (Evans and Tigre 1989). No local capital was involved. The state had no explicit policies for the industry.

Several conditions provoked policies to foster the computer industry (Evans 1986). Universities had begun to graduate computer and electronics engineers who were restricted to selling for transnational producers: a group of nationalist technicians was being formed. BNDE, the entrepreneurially oriented state development bank, was trying to develop a more diversified and integrated local industrial structure. The bureaucracy needed more data processing equipment and were frustrated since the importers were first satisfying the tremendous growth of the US market. And there was happenstance: the Brazilian Navy bought frigates at the end of the 1960s containing electronic equipment that had to be maintained.

Initial moves were modest (Evans 1986). A working group, GTEIII, was formed in 1971 under BNDE leadership. In 1972 the Commission to Coordinate Electronic Processing Activities (CAPRE) began to survey and rationalize purchases. GTEIII developed a plan in 1973/74 to set up an industry to produce minicomputers using an association of local and foreign firms with the government [tripé (tripod) companies]. A prototype research program was established at the University of São Paulo. However, the major transnational corporations did not want to share their technology and local capital was not interested, so the initial entrants were small, inexperienced local firms and

Ferranti (which had provided the electronic equipment for the frigates). Cobra started in 1974 to produce minis. The start-up costs were huge and the computer hard to sell: Cobra needed heavy injections of funds from BNDE. State initiative had to replace the disinterest of local capital.

As Cobra got into difficulties, rising imports of computers began to exacerbate the balance of payments problem induced by the oil price rise of 1974 (Evans 1986). CAPRE, set up to rationalize purchases, was now used to regulate imports. CAPRE's actions were supported by the nationalist, import substituting policies of the government of President Ernesto Geisel. Opposed to them was IBM, which could offer low-cost, quality computers with local manufacture. To resolve the balance of payments issue and Cobra's difficulties, the government called a competition to decide which firms could produce minis, in Brazil. By 1976 the banks had discovered data processing and more local capitalists had become interested in producing minis so there were more submissions than in the earlier competition. The entrants included local firms and proposals in association with small transnational producers; but the large transnational companies submitted proposals for wholly owned subsidiaries. The proposals from the large transnational producers were rejected in June 1977 in favor of local and joint production.

This policy of fostering local production of minicomputers without the transnationals was initially successful. Between 1979 and 1983 sales by local producers rose from $US 190 million to $687 million whereas sales by transnationals in Brazil rose from $640 million to $800 million (Evans 1986: 796). Local companies employed many more engineers than did the transnational producers and performed more R&D: in 1983 local companies employed 1353 university trained personnel in R&D; the transnational producers, only 121 (Evans 1986: 797). The industry had become large and organized enough to persuade the government to exclude IBM from producing a mainframe in Brazil that would compete with the local minis. Success did not depend only on political battles within Brazil though. In the mid-1970s minicomputers were of little interest to the majors. Specialized miniproducers like DEC and Hewlett Packard did not have a network of local subsidiaries and found it difficult just to keep up with US demand; they were not in a position to compete in Brazil. A space was available for Brazil to enter.

Then along came microcomputers (Evans 1986). These are based on microprocessors produced by independent firms and sold as commodities. The rest of the technology is simple. Local Brazilian companies quickly began to produce micros behind tariff walls: by 1982, 50 Brazilian firms were making clones and local designs. They found it easy to move to 16-bit machines and have become cost competitive in old machines (Apple IIs were at first two to three times the US price but by mid-1984 were being sold below the US price). This development, though not state-led, did take advantage of the space created by the minicomputer market and the preexisting training and state apparatus that had been created for that market.

This spontaneous and competitive growth contrasts with developments in the mini market (Evans 1986). Local mini technology has not been able to keep up with international advances. By 1984 sales of minicomputers were declining and the local producers were losing money. In spring 1984 a new round of licensing technology was to begin: the mini policy had not worked as a means of developing indigenous R&D. Brazil's computer industry needs continued access to international technology—either through licensing (minis) or processors (macros) and through imports of mainframes. Still there is local product innovation in micros now and exports are rising.

In 1984 CAPRE's successor the SEI (Special Secretariat for Informatics) decided that licenses of foreign technology were needed to reduce the technology gap (Evans and Tigre 1989). The 1977 agreement could not underpin local development of superminis. Some, including Cobra, believed that superminis could be developed using off-the-shelf 32-bit microprocessors. However, licensing offered a quick fix without risk and even proprietary technology was allowed. By 1985 there were seven supermini licenses. However, market demand was not up to predictions: by mid-1988 only 250 superminis had been sold compared to the expected 1200–1800, because of slow economic growth and competition from small mainframes. There remains the question of how Brazilians will be able to absorb the technology. Some R&D staff have ignored licensed technology that was not fully compatible with the products that the company had itself engineered. The state did not attend sufficiently to the problem of promoting success once the entrants had been secured: state-supported research and manpower training were neglected. In Wade's (1990b) terms the state has followed in the micro market, has led developments in the mini market in particular periods (early 1970s, 1976/77, 1984), but has failed to provide continuous leadership. Still there has been some commercial success, rapid growth of installed base, and some indigenous innovation (Fritsch and Franco 1991: 96–98).

The history of the Brazilian computer industry does not simply reflect the balance of forces in the early 1970s but has altered that balance. The first initiatives were taken by the state when local capitalists were not interested. After financial capital perceived opportunities in the mini market by the mid-1970s the banks entered production. Financial capital, not concerned about local–transnational distinctions, could profit from a close association with the transnational producers. Local, smaller capitals have focused on the micro market using owners' knowledge and technology; to these firms the local–transnational distinction is vital. Local gains from the policy so far are questionable: other firms pay more for computing power than if entry had been free to the mini market (Fritsch and Franco 1991: 105); but these losses may be compensated by the long-term development of Brazil's technical capacity—Brazil's non-micro output was three times that of South Korea in 1985 (Evans and Tigre 1989). In the short term, international productive capital has suffered a loss in the mini market though it profits from sales of micro processors to micro producers; international financial capital profits from capital accumulation within Brazil.

The South Korean state has long promoted electronics production (Wade 1990b). In the 1960s the government assisted transnationals like Fairchild and Motorola to produce semiconductors. When in the mid-1970s it was decided that the electronics sector should grow, the government entered a phase of industrial leadership. The government offered credit, R&D subsidies, protection, and public procurement policies to develop electronics. Later in the 1980s the state has followed (and facilitated) the initiatives of the chaebol.

The early 1970s witnessed a big push to establish capacity to produce semiconductors (Wade 1990b). Research institutes, training, and licensed imports of technology were all provided. The Korea Institute of Electronics Technology (KIET) was set up in 1976, and in 1979 it began to build South Korea's first wafer fabrication facility. By the late 1970s, though, there had been little spillover to core processes and few local firms had established fabrication facilities. Huge investments were needed for large-capacity chips and for R&D.

The size and financial power of the chaebol proved important now (Wade 1990b). Two took over small local semiconductor firms in the late 1970s, and a third started production from scratch. The government assigned monopoly segments of the market and renegotiated technology agreements to secure profitable sections of the protected telecommunications industry for Samsung, Goldstar, and Daewoo (Hyundai entered later). Joint ventures were signed with multinational producers for technology in return for access to risk-free telecommunications business. The 1982–1986 plan offered $US 346 million of cheap credit to the four firms. When the chaebol speeded R&D the government began to withdraw. KIET discovered by 1984 that the chaebol had better R&D facilities and fabrication, so it sold off its fabrication facilities and reoriented itself to provide more basic R&D functions.

The semiconductor industry began to produce very-large-scale integrated circuits in 1983 (Schive 1990). Between 1983 and 1984 the four companies invested about $US 1 billion, and exports were expected to exceed $2 billion by 1987 (placing South Korea third after the US and Japan). Competition forces the prices of established products down, putting pressure on companies that are not quite at the technical frontier: losses were reported by Hyundai in 1985. In contrast with Taiwan the South Korean industry has emphasized production at the expense of R&D, perhaps because the chaebol can buy access to technology and afford the investments needed to produce very cheaply.

The size of the chaebol has influenced South Korean policy toward the computer industry (Evans and Tigre 1989). Infant industry protection was important in the early 1980s, but the chaebol used their experience as producers of consumer electronics to shift into local computer production and penetrate the US clone market for personal computers. Sales increased by more than 100% between 1980 and 1986. Confident of the capacity of the chaebol, the government removed barriers to imports and investment, preempting protectionism in the USA. Much export from South Korea has taken the form of monitors (which are not sophisticated) and computers that are not brand named. These forms of production are a way of learning to get into more design-intensive, higher value added products. As in the semiconductor market the central strategy for diversifying output has been to form alliances with foreign producers: Goldstar with AT&T, Honeywell, and Hitachi; Samsung with Hewlett Packard and NEC. But these moves have not led to many super-minis or even supermicros being produced; to this extent the Brazilians are producing more sophisticated machines.

In South Korea attention has been paid to ensuring success (Enos 1984; Evans and Tigre 1989). A National Administrative Information System was set up to computerize the civil service using local area networks, to boost both administrative efficiency and the computer industry. The plan called for 10,000 workstations to be installed around 100 superminis. Support for the proposal came from the central leadership. The Ministry of Communications allocated 3% of its revenues to research and offered future procurement. Research was conducted in ETRI (the Electronics and Telecommunications Research Institute) and its predecessors (like KIET), which had a long history of electronics research. In 1982 DACOM, a subsidiary of the Ministry of Communication's operating company, was designated the prime contractor for the NAIS system. The hardware to implement the system was to be built under license from a small US producer of Unix machines, Tolerant. The technology needed to produce whole machines was quickly learnt. However, the initial installation faced problems, weakening the commitment of potential users in the bureaucracy. So whether the NAIS can be built around the Tolerant machine is an open question. The chaebol have also to be convinced to make the risky investments that are required if the machine is to be a commercial success when they are tempted to stay with proven overseas successes. Yet the project has cultivated enormous design and engineering learning, which may be important as it becomes increasingly difficult for South Korean firms to buy technology abroad (Arnold 1988).

The South Korean state's policies for the electronics industry have been different from those of Brazil. The Brazilian state led the mini market at times since the early 1970s but has merely facilitated the micro producers. In South Korea the state led the semiconductor industry in the 1970s and the mini industry in the 1980s; it largely followed the initiatives of the chaebol in semiconductor and micro production in the 1980s. Whereas in Brazil local finance capital is involved in the mini market and small local capitals in the micro market, in South Korea all markets are dominated by the chaebol. In South Korea the financially powerful chaebol have been able to build a large-scale competitive industry that exports standard components and machines. Brazil's firms, lacking power and systematic state support, have developed more slowly and over a broader range of products—but are more self-reliant (Clarke and Cable 1982).

Until the early 1970s electronics firms in Taiwan were transnational subsidiaries producing standard components with low-cost labor (Wade 1990b): a classic penetration of a dependent economy by international capital. The Taiwanese government has intervened directly in specific sectors, leading at times. Since the 1950s the state has itself established new industries and then handed them over or run them itself: glass, plastics, cement, and chemicals production were all established in this manner. When the state withdrew from one industry, new industries were taken up. A similar process has been followed in electronics as the state exercised leadership since the mid-1970s.

The state was crucial in shifting the labor-intensive industry into acquiring and mastering advanced semiconductor and computer technology (Wade 1990b). In 1973/74 the Taiwanese state formed the publicly owned Electronics Research and Service Organization (ERSO) to find foreign partners to develop and commercialize technology. An industrial park for science was set up in 1980; the state has funded and promoted software development, particularly in 1979–1983; ERSO has spun off companies to commercialize its research. Integrated circuit design began in 1977, when ERSO signed a technology transfer agreement with RCA (Schive 1990). United Microelectronics was formed in 1979 to commercialize some of the innovations flowing from ERSO. In 1983 ERSO signed an agreement for a research project with Vitelic, a company from Silicon Valley. In general the Taiwanese industry has been strikingly successful at research: it was third in the world after Intel and Hitachi to develop a 256KB (kilobyte) complementary metal oxide surface (cmos) dynamic random access memory chip. The problem in Taiwan has been manufacturing the products of this research: only in 1985 was the government able to orchestrate an agreement with Philips to begin producing very-large-scale integrated circuits. In that agreement Philips provided 27.5% of the capital, the government 48.3%, and private local companies 24.2% (Schive 1990: 279).

The state has been more directly involved in research and production in Taiwan than in South Korea (Wade 1990b; but see Arnold 1988). Such involvement included public enterprises and state research organizations, import controls, domestic content requirements, entry restrictions, and tax incentives. A similar policy has been followed in promoting the production of computer numerically controlled lathes (Jacobsson 1985). The availability of subsidized loans induced one traditional lathe manufacturer to enter this more advanced field. But a major state initiative has been to design numerically controlled lathes in a research institute for smaller producers; such development supplements small firms' own design teams when they are trying to raise product quality or reduce costs. Supply the technology and other changes will follow (Arnold 1988).

As in South Korea, the Taiwanese state has led at times (1973–1987 in semiconductors, 1979–1983 in software) and has spun off new firms that have evolved from its direct activities. But, more open to foreign capital than either Brazil or South Korea and more afraid of the power of local capital, the Taiwanese state has continued to promote activities that introduce new competitors and rely on small local firms: in electronics, strong research and relatively weak manufacturing sectors reflect this pattern of development.

10.7 CONCLUSION

In orthodox accounts the NICs are implicated in the slowdown in the industrial market economies. Theories of comparative and competitive advantage and of the new international division of labor have been marshaled to argue that capital has left the industrial market economies in search of the locations where labor power is cheap. The flight of capital slowed accumulation in the industrial market economies while fueling the growth of industries in NICs to compete with established firms. Encouraged by new technologies that ease the international movement of capital, such capital flight induced by wage differences has been a cause of the slowdown in the advanced industrial economies.

This story paints a picture of growth in NICs that is far too deterministic. The growth of Brazil, South Korea, and Taiwan had little to do with wage costs; and its relation to the slowdown in the industrial market economies is less cause than consequence.

The first steps to growth in all three countries were independent of cost advantages. Brazil started industrializing when world trade was interrupted by the Great Depression and World War II. In South Korea and Taiwan infusions of US aid—related to geopolitical strategy, not to costs—provided the first growth impulses. Growth began when it was widely believed that the prices of primary commodities were in long-term decline. Thereafter all three NICs took advantage of world conditions but for domestic political and strategic reasons. The goal in Brazil was domestic capital accumulation, subject to the constraints of the power of landowners and workers. In South Korea and Taiwan capital accumulation has been a means to achieve independence and economic power in the face of perceived threats. These are domestic goals; development has not been imposed by international capital following the dictates of costs of production.

The problems to be overcome in achieving those goals differ in the three countries. The Brazilian state has used international capital to foster domestic capital accumulation, in the context of a militant workforce. Shifts from expansionary to restrictive state strategies alter the relative strength of workers and the domestic bourgeoisie as well as that of international and local capital. In regulating the conditions of capital accumulation the state has to control labor and delimit the role of international capital. The South Korean state has faced a quite different problem. It has created a form of industrial capital highly dependent on state support; having created capital, the state is able to control it (and labor) to a degree impossible in Brazil. In Taiwan the state has sought to remain independent of the economic power of local Taiwanese, using state and foreign capital. This independence has provided room for policy shifts in Taiwan.

Since industrialization began, the three states have been deeply involved in directing it. The state affects prices and determines market conditions. Protection of domestic markets and support for exporters have figured largely.

Prices have been manipulated and are not international; cost advantage does not determine outcomes. The three countries had choices which they have exercised in a way that depends on local class forces and their perceptions of the global environment.

In the long run, continued growth depends on ability to repay debts and reinvest large surpluses. That ability is enhanced by exploiting noncapitalist sectors, particularly agriculture and households. Even so, many of the industries in Brazil, South Korea, and Taiwan are now internationally competitive. But not all. Some industries did not need to be competitive when they were first established: as they were financed by loans, it was necessary only that the state guarantee loan repayments, depending on the profitability of the economy as a whole. Some industries have even exported successfully without long-run cost competitiveness. The present competitiveness of the NICs is not a result of their initial advantage of lower wages but has been acquired: corporations have learnt and reaped economies of scale. Exports have helped develop competitiveness. In some cases exporting has been forced by the conditions under which loans have to be repaid rather than being the natural by-product of low costs.

In all three countries the state has exercized a political will to develop. This will reflects local class structures and perceptions of geopolitical forces. Brazil, South Korea, and Taiwan have used excess capital produced in the center to finance their development, to permit national, productive capitals to grow. The programs were indigenous, not driven by foreign, direct investment; but they were assisted by the need of central, financial capital to find profitable investment outlets.

Labor has largely been excluded from the process of setting goals in all three countries. Brazil, South Korea, and Taiwan are unequal societies and, in the last 30 years, have become increasingly so. It is unclear whether inequality is correlated empirically with strategies to industrialize (Clements 1988). Nevertheless, even if wage levels do not sufficiently explain development, they are connected to development. If industrialization substitutes for imports, then domestic demand provides the only market for industry: wages become a source of demand as well as a cost. This closed model of development is analyzed in Chapter 5. If industrialization promotes exports, wages are purely cost: demand can grow by wage rises in other countries. In this sense export promotion permits firms to avoid paying sufficient wages to absorb supply. Here lies the threat of globalization.

Chapter 11

CONCLUSION

The world economy has grown and changed since 1950. It is six times larger and more integrated than then. Growth has been uneven through time and over space. Rates of profit, GDP growth, capital formation, and world trade were greater before 1973 than since. As rates of growth have slowed, so has the global economy become more organized. Some features of the global economy have remained constant—poverty and famine at one end of the scale, and at the other end the dominance of the industrial market economies. Other features have changed—financial markets have become global, and multinational corporations have entangled more and more countries ever tighter into a network of intracorporate links. The countries of the world have become increasingly integrated: trade has grown faster than output. The other central change in the structure of the global economy has been the emergence of Japan and the NICs as economic powers. Japan's emergence was essentially confirmed before 1973, while growth was still rapid. NICs have grown differently: their output grew fast before 1973, but their exports have grown relatively faster still since 1973. Changes in the pattern of world trade have been consistent with the emergence of the NICs: the pattern of world trade has been changing faster since 1973 than in the 1950s and 1960s. Labor markets have altered too. Unemployment has risen, especially in the industrialized economies, as rates of profit and growth have fallen. The globalization of the economy has been paced by its feminization: more and more women have entered the paid labor force, though still in segmented labor markets as in the past. Nonstandard forms of employment are becoming more common, particularly for women.

Though rates of profit and growth were higher before the mid-1970s than after, the OPEC price rises at the end of 1973 do not separate postwar history into distinct periods. The phases merge. Rates of growth of output and capital formation were not everywhere significantly higher than they are now. Different places have different experiences: the experiences of individual

485

regions and industries diverge. So interpretations of economic history and geography must not overemphasize either the internal homogeneity of the phases or the differences between phases. Furthermore changes that have become obvious since 1973 can be traced to earlier characteristics, for example, the technical changes and the emerging trade surpluses that made global finance possible. The acceleration in the pace of change originates in part in the slowdown of growth. Observation also contests the notion of a "long boom": the periods of rising and sustained rates of growth of output lasted little more than 10 years and were generally over by the mid-1960s. The phases may be more readily interpreted as (weak) waves or cycles than as periods.

Many theorists and commentators more or less concur with this general history—with perhaps some differences in emphasis. The difficult question is that of interpretation. There has been insufficient evidence with which to distinguish the explanations adduced by different theories. Nor has there been an appropriate body of theory to demonstrate how various factors are related to the rate of profit and to identify measures that can distinguish between the accounts. Existing economic and geographic theory has been inadequate to make comprehensible postwar political economic history. So having started with the quest to understand the postwar historical geography of capitalism, we have been driven to develop appropriate theory. The first task has been to rectify theory. Nevertheless new theory gives rise to different evidence that permits us to reinterpret what has happened to the industrial and industrializing economies of the world since World War II. In this final chapter we first emphasize what we regard as the important theoretical innovations of this book. Second, we review the empirical record and assess how existing interpretations stack up against it. Finally, we sketch our reinterpretation of postwar historical geography.

11.1 NEW THEORY

There are three central issues of postwar historical geography that theory has been unable to disentangle.

How are capital/output ratios, wage increases, the failure of demand, and productivity change related to the history of the rate of profit? And how, conversely, does a fall in the rate of profit translate into a failure of demand? This is a classic problem of macroeconomic dynamics. Early writers, including Marx, identified three barriers to the accumulation of capital—crises arising from underconsumption, from a squeeze on profits and from the rising composition of capital—but their analyses were qualitative and could not specify the relative magnitudes of the forces tending to increase and the forces tending to decrease the rate of profit. The technical apparatus of theory has not been able to characterize the problem well, for despite all the effort that has been put into the theory of the falling rate of profit, formal models simply have not specified how all these variables are related. So, for example, Okishio relied on the assumptions that prices are at equilibrium, that real wages are constant, that markets clear, and that all capital is productively employed to prove that cost-reducing technical changes increase the equilibrium rate of profit. Roemer, Laibman, Rigby, and Salvadori have all adjusted Okishio's assumptions and question the generality of his conclusions. But there still does not exist a formal, dynamic, macroeconomic model in which capital/output ratios, wage changes, demand, and technical change are all internally connected—to each other and to the rate of accumulation.

Is the productivity slowdown of the 1970s and 1980s a cause or a consequence of slower rates of accumulation? We have lacked the conceptual apparatus to answer this question, for there has been no good theory to explain the pace and direction of productivity change. To what extent do changes in technique depend on the rate of investment, the degree of competition, and the supply of innovations? How does the direction of productivity change respond to changing prices of inputs? Existing theory of productivity change has analyzed the rates at which major innovations are produced; the process by which they are produced; the diffusion of innovations; learning; the evolution of innovation; and technical change within the Marxian tradition. Yet there has been little progress toward integrating these traditions of research. We have also lacked good empirical measures of the pace and direction of productivity change that do not depend on neoclassical economic theory: the number of new processes or products invented or patented ignores smaller scale changes, while input–output coefficients confound several separate processes (innovation within a plant, imitation, changes in market share, and the entry and exit of plants). So there has been little effort devoted to measuring the importance of the determinants of productivity change. There has consequently existed no empirical basis for distinguishing the different accounts of the role of productivity change.

What has been the role in recent capitalist history of the internationalization of production? This process has several components: increasing trade between "Western" (advanced industrial) economies; increasing rates of international investment and a change in the form of that investment to finance rather than direct forms; and the rise of NICs. Only recently have attempts been made to theorize international capital. To what extent is the rise of NICs autonomous: is the profitability crisis of the advanced industrialized economies the result of increased foreign competition, especially the growth of NICs, or is the rise of NICs explained by a falling rate of profit in the "West" and relative wage levels? And what was the effect of the accident of the OPEC surplus and the policy "mistake" of deregulating exchange rates and international capital movements? Again, theories of regional growth and development have not been able to answer these questions adequately, for existing theories of international location and growth—whether from the right (comparative advantage and competitive advantage) or the left (regulation and the new international division of labor)—all revolve around costs of production. Factor costs and the rate of profit are the central variables on which the international location of production is thought to turn despite the selectivity of industrialization in the Third World and the continuing concentration of activity in the established centers of economic production.

The flaws in existing theories of accumulation, profitability, productivity change, and internationalization have two sources.

First, existing theories rely overly on the notion of equilibrium. Even dynamics is commonly conceived as change from one equilibrium position to another. So prices of production are prices that support equal rates of profit. Indeed, the entire idea of "the price" clearly reflects the equilibrium concept that all instances of a commodity are offered for sale at the same price. Chapter 4 explicates this relation between price and equilibrium. In addition the effects of technical change on profitability are usually calculated under the assumptions that demand and supply are equal, the wage rate is fixed exogenously, and all capital is employed in production. Chapter 5 demonstrates this fact. The rate and direction of technical change itself are studied by methods that suppose that change takes place between two successive equilibrium states. See Chapter 6. Equally theories of location and international growth are dominated by the comparison of factor costs in models where payments balance and factors are paid according to their productivity. Chapter 7 makes this clear. All the sources of theory that are employed to understand postwar historical geography depend on the concept of equilibrium.

Actually all economies are off equilibrium. Change is intrinsically non-equilibrium and is not generally well understood as a shift between a pair of equilibria. So instances of a commodity do not normally command the same price. The demand and supply of commodities differ geographically and vary historically; wages depend on the demand and supply of labor but also on historical and geographic conditioning; capital is under- or oversupplied. Equally productivity change is an inherently probabilistic process in which marginal adjustments and learning reflect imperfect attempts to find better technical conditions rather than optimal states: firms innovate, learn, imitate, compete. And location is dominated by history and by local attempts to overcome history. The East Asian dragons and other NICs have demonstrated just how powerful local struggle can be in escaping structural traps. It simply will not do for models—however many time subscripts they contain—to reflect equilibrium thinking.

Secondly, equilibrium thinking, even in the context of dynamic models, derives from static concepts. The basic thesis assumes that if underlying conditions remain the same, so will the investments, technologies, and location patterns that we observe. Economic momentum is conserved. Conversely, if investments, technologies, and location patterns alter, so must underlying conditions be changing. Existing theories consequently identify alterations and differences in the underlying structure of costs as the forces that drive changes in observable variables. For example, when relative prices change, firms are induced to change techniques to economize on the input that has become more expensive. Or when relative prices differ, firms are induced to change locations to take advantage of new, lower costs of production.

This will not do either. The driving force of accumulation is not comparative cost but investment policy. Of course, prices and costs affect the bottom line; but firms' investment policies control the long run. If firms learn and production is subject to dynamic returns to scale, investment policies are in the longer run of far more importance than static comparisons of costs. For prices are not independent variables. Investment policies, technologies, and location patterns have an underlying dynamic of their own, a dynamic that does reflect costs but that has its own, independent force, which in turn determines costs. Models of productivity change, accumulation, and profitability in different locations need to reemphasize accumulation policies and to eschew equilibrium. The consequences are startling.

The first victim is the concept of prices of production. These are equilibrium prices when all firms earn the same rate of return on capital. If we abandon the notion that firms all earn the same rate of profit and that all instances of a commodity are sold at the same price, the tools of probability theory can be used to investigate the average and variance of the prices at which a commodity is sold. We move to *the concepts of expected prices* and *expected rates of profit*. The transformation problem can be ignored altogether, for values and expected prices are related in a simple fashion while aggregate rates of profit are the same in the value and the expected price calculus. Models, whether written in terms of values or expected prices, can be directly related to empirical observations that are made in the price sphere.

It is not necessary to redefine value in the same way. Value is the only universal standard of commodities that permits historical, comparative research of the kind that is needed to evaluate economic and historical geographies of the postwar world. To be measurable, value must be defined as the quantity of productive labor power invested in an article under socially normal conditions of production and using labor of average skill and intensity, no matter what the concrete form of that labor. This definition is operationalized by taking "socially normal" to mean the average of the techniques that actually exist. Value is inherently an average of conditions in different plants and so does not assume that all plants are in some sense equal. By contrast "the price" supposes that all plants are equal.

The second victim is debate about appropriate models of the falling rate of profit. Many models of the falling rate of profit are special instances—with different equilibrium conditions—of a more general nonequilibrium model. Okishio's theorem and Roemer's modifications reflect equilibria in which prices are prices of production, wages are fixed exogenously, demand can absorb all the commodities that are produced, and profits are calculated only on the capital employed in production. These conditions never hold in reality. The essence of macroeconomic dynamics turns on the relations between the demand for labor, wages, the demand for commodities, and the supply and demand for capital—and the way these relations change over time. Equilibrium thinking assumes this problematic away.

The central relations that determine the history of profitability are these. Rapid rates of accumulation raise the demand for labor faster than the labor force grows and therefore tend to press wages upward or induce firms to economize on labor. The demand and supply of commodities are linked through wages and investment policies. The aggregate profitability of capital depends not simply on the return on capital that is actually used in production but also on the amount of capital that can find no productive use. That is, the history of profitability depends on the relations between accumulation and the rate of growth of the labor force; between wages and the demand for commodities; between investment policies and supply; and between capacity and demand. None of these conditions are found in conventional models of the falling rate of profit.

In abstract the rate of profit may fall or may rise if cost-reducing technical changes are introduced—this is by now the conventional view about the history of profitability. We can go further. Cost-reducing technical changes tend to raise the rate of profit if supply is growing faster than the capital stock (if unused capacity is being used to supply) or if demand is growing faster than supply. In the long run, however, the rate of growth of supply is constrained by the rate of growth of the capital stock and the rate of growth of demand is limited by supply: supply cannot grow faster than the capital stock nor demand faster than supply in the long run. If that pair of constraints hold (supply–capital, demand–supply), cost-reducing technical changes cause the rate of profit to fall. The limits to growth are to be found within the basic workings of the capitalist economy itself; the search for the origins of capitalist crises need go no further than the basic relations of capitalist production. In particular the slowdown of growth since the early 1970s need not have an exogenous cause. (It is an empirical matter to decide whether the slowdown actually did have an exogenous cause.)

Whether or not the rate of profit falls does not depend solely on technology and the profitability of production within individual plants. Changes in the rate of profit depend on the manner in which technical change and accumulation interact with the demand for and supply of labor, commodities, and capital. These interactions differ from one country to another. In Japan, for example, significant off-farm migration continued until the 1970s to provide a rapidly growing industrial labor force; the state encouraged investment that carried new technologies and supported enlarged economies of scale; as costs continued to fall, the huge expansion of exports severed the link between the demand for commodities and the wages of workers. These conditions are quite different from those in the USA, where off-farm migration provided only a small portion of the industrial labor force, investment was growing quite slowly, and manufactured exports were growing only sluggishly. Quite reasonably the history of profitability in the two countries is quite different.

The third victim is deterministic and unicausal models of productivity change. The technologies of plants are instances of a random variable, and the technology of an industry is an *expected technology*. Technologies change for all sorts of reasons, though three broad sources can be identified. New techniques within plants cause reductions in the unit costs of production, at a rate that depends on the average unit rate of profit and the speed with which unit profits are translated into cost reductions. The direction of this productivity change depends on the relative prices of capital and labor. This is innovation (and imitation) in the classical sense. A second source of productivity change in an industry is selection, when plants that embody different technologies grow at different rates. The rate at which costs are reduced by selection depends on the interplant variance in production costs, and its direction depends on the covariation between plants in labor and capital inputs. These are competitive or market-induced effects. Thirdly, productivity changes when plants are induced by price changes to enter or to leave an industry. The rate of cost reduction caused by the birth and death of plants depends on the level of price changes and is in the same direction as the introduction of new techniques. This is another effect of competition on apparent technology. These different forms of productivity change can be identified from the empirical record, thus separating competitive effects from those induced by investment and other (possibly exogenous) effects.

The fourth victim is theories of international industrial location that rely on static comparisons of costs. Theories of comparative or competitive advantage and of the new international division of labor claim that the international relocation of industry depends fundamentally on the relative or absolute cost advantages of countries. If NICs are developing faster than the core economies, it is said, they must have certain advantages over the core. In particular production in NICs must be more profitable, that is, lower cost, than production in the North Atlantic region. This view derives from a notion of equilibrium in which rates of profit in different sectors and countries are equal, a notion that is itself centrally bound up with the idea of price of production. These theories suffer a pair of empirical deficiencies: most trade and most capital flows actually occur between developed countries that have similar factor endowments and factor prices, rather than between developed and developing countries; and the industrialization of the Third World has been selective. Prices, outputs and rates of profit cannot be computed solely from production data but rely also on investment policies.

In fact there exists no necessary tendency for rates of profit to be equal in dynamic equilibrium. Even in dynamic equilibrium, there is a net flow of capital from some countries (with a higher rate of profit) to others (with a lower rate of profit). The allocation of capital arises from the rational policies of decentralized firms and centralized financial institutions. Thus different rates of capital accumulation do not correlate positively with rates of profit: more rapidly growing countries are less profitable. Therefore the fact that NICs have industrialized partly at the expense of the manufacturing countries of the North Atlantic region need not imply that NICs have been more profitable or lower cost producers than the traditional countries. Theory does not imply that faster growing regions have a cost advantage over slower growing regions. NICs could have industrialized without any cost advantages and could have grown without any improvement in their relative profitability.

We think that these theories enable us to interrogate the real world more effectively and encourage a more convincing interpretation of recent historical geography.

11.2 THE EMPIRICAL RECORD

We have measured profitability, productivity change, and location, for these are the variables that put empirical bite on the theoretical innovations of Chapters 4 through 7. They also provide the strongest tests of existing interpretations of postwar historical geography.

The first issue concerned the manner in which capital/output ratios, wage increases, changes in demand, and productivity change are related to the rate of profit and how variations in profitability are themselves translated into changes in demand.

In Australia, Canada, Japan, and the USA the rate of profit tended to fall into the early or mid-1980s. The details of the history of profitability have been different in the four countries. In the USA (and perhaps Australia) profitability climbed until the mid-1960s, then fell until the early 1980s, and has since recovered slightly. Only in the USA was there anything like a boom in profit rates that lasted until the mid-1960s, to be followed by a decline during the 1970s. In Canada the rate of profit in manufacturing declined consistently from the mid-1950s until the early 1980s. In Japan the rate of profit continued to rise until the mid-1970s; it then declined and has not yet begun to recover. The timing and the extent of the decline in profitability are different in the four countries: the decline began earliest in Canada and latest in Japan; and the recovery began in the early 1980s in the three Anglo economies but has hardly appeared in Japan.

The decline in profitability was loosely associated with reduced rates of capital accumulation. In all four countries the rate of growth of capital has fallen during the period of falling profitability, but both the mechanism and the strength of this relationship need to be examined more closely. So the slowdown of the late 1970s and 1980s was indeed accompanied by reduced rates of profit. As such the history is compatible with the accounts of Freeman and Perez, Mandel, Lipietz, and Lash and Urry. The fact that rates of profit were falling from at least the mid-1960s in Australia, Canada, and the USA seems to argue against the account of Piore and Sabel (in which falling profit rates are a consequence of the slowdown rather than a cause).

The declines in rates of profit in Australia, Canada, Japan, and the USA were driven essentially by increases in the value composition of capital. That is, profit rates fell because increases in the amount of plant, equipment, and raw materials per worker were not offset by improvements in efficiency. When rates of profit were falling, the rate of exploitation and the speed at which capital is turned over were both tending to raise profitability (except in Canada). There is little evidence that labor costs were rising faster than productivity when rates of profit were falling. These observations are compatible with Marxian accounts of the falling rate of profit (including that of Mandel). While the apparent role of slower gains in efficiency accords with the story of Lipietz, the fact that changes in the rate of exploitation have not driven rates of profit down is incompatible with his argument.

In Australia and Canada subsequent increases in the rate of profit have been fueled by rises in the rate of exploitation—themselves predicated on stagnant real wages rather than on improvements in efficiency. In the USA, by contrast, the value composition of capital has exerted little effect in the most recent period, because the technical composition has changed only slowly. The change in regime in Japan from rising to falling rates of profit depended essentially on a shift from falling to rising value composition of capital once efficiency gains could no longer offset changes in the technical composition of capital. In none of these countries had there appeared by the end of the 1980s a form of development that could yield long-run growth and rising real wages: in Japan profit rates had not started to recover; and in the other economies the recovery was fueled by deeper exploitation or stagnant technique rather than by high rates of investment that carry new techniques. As yet the recovery of profit rates has not fueled high rates of investment. This evidence does not distinguish the possible futures adduced by theorists of economic history.

The aggregate picture fails to do justice to the diversity of histories of profitability in different industries. In Canada and the USA some industries' price rates of profit rose despite the aggregate decline in profitability: increases in the price/value ratio more than offset the effect of changes in the value rate of profit. In other industries the price rate of profit was more or less unchanged during the aggregate decline. In most industries price rates of profit followed aggregate profits down. But in only about a half or less of the industries did the price rate of profit fall basically because the value rate of profit fell. Fewer than half of all industries followed the model of manufacturing as a whole: in most industries, either (i) their value rate of profit was not the primary cause of falls in their price rate of profit or (ii) their value rate of profit did not fall, because the value composition of capital was driven upward by the technical composition of capital. (The transport industry has a history all of its own, which is ironic since the regulation school identifies transport as the hegemonic industry in the USA during the long boom.) Similar diversity is apparent in the history of profitability in Canada's regions.

The variety of history that has been uncovered is disturbing for accounts of the long boom (Lipietz, Piore and Sabel, and Lash and Urry). The history of rates of profit is not the same in the four countries: only in the USA was there a boom in profit rates that lasted until the mid-1960s to be followed by a decline during the 1970s. Furthermore, while the crisis in US manufacturing has been spread widely over its manufacturing sectors, the histories of profitability in different industries are diverse. Similarly in Canada, there are wide variations about the aggregate story among the individual industries and regions of the country. The average has not been especially common. Variety and difference in timing and cause argue against the concept of an overarching long boom, though they are more in tune with Graham and colleagues' account of sectoral transitions.

Also problematic for accounts that link profitability and accumulation is evidence about these two rates. Quite clearly rates of profit and accumulation have shifted together: the two rates are certainly correlated. However, the links between them need more scrutiny. Whether profitability drives accumulation or conversely is not obvious from the lag structure of these data. Nor is it clear why changes in profitability are at some times but not at others associated with changes in the rate of accumulation. Models of accumulation must pay attention to this link.

An additional limitation of existing theory has emerged. The theory of the falling rate of profit is usually explained in terms of the value composition of capital and the rate of exploitation (and their determinants). Yet turnover times of capital and unequal exchange in the market between industries and regions can affect the history of their rates of profit. In about one-third of Canadian and US industries the ability of firms to compete in the market has a greater effect on the rate of profit than does the value rate of profit. Clearly theories of the rate of profit need not only to be couched in terms of a formal, dynamic model (like that of Chapter 5) but must also examine controls and changes in controls over turnover times and market power.

Secondly, we have examined the history and sources of productivity change in US manufacturing. The central issue concerns the relations between profitability, rates of economic growth, and productivity change. Was there a slowdown, and if so when? What forms of productivity change have altered most over the interval? What can be deduced about the determinants of any slowdown? And is the aggregate history common to individual industries?

Between 1962 and 1973 there was steady productivity progress in US manufacturing. This progress was largely neutral (that is, normal to the ratio of prices), though with occasional bouts of labor-saving bias. Then until 1981 capital was substituted for labor and costs of production were increased rather than reduced. Since then technical change has returned to its role of reducing costs of production. Labor-saving technical change is sometimes interpreted, particularly within the Marxian tradition, as evidence of the bias of corporations to prefer investment in plant and equipment rather than in labor power. Plant and equipment can be used to control labor and to reduce the demand for labor. However, the data we have provided is not direct evidence of that effect, for neutral technical progress would be expected only if all productivity change occurred through innovation: selection of more profitable plants and the entry and exit of plants both drive productivity change away from neutrality. Furthermore, the period between 1973 and 1981 was also one in which energy price increases prompted at least some firms to invest in new, energy-efficient plant and equipment; paradoxically, that period was therefore one of increases in both the prices of and the investment in fixed capital.

Nevertheless the history of rates of productivity change is significant. Productivity change was consistently reducing costs of production until the onset of the slowdown in growth and investment in the early 1970s. The slowdown in productivity progress must therefore have been a consequence rather than a cause of the slowdown in growth and of the falling rate of profit. What is more, when the slowdown in productivity change did occur it was not caused by a failure of labor productivity: rather the capital/output ratio rose between 1973 and 1981. These results contradict the claims that slower productivity progress caused by a failure of labor productivity was one of the causes of the falling rate of profit. Actually capital was oversubstituted for labor.

The causes of the slowdown in productivity progress are better understood as consequences of changes in rates of profit and investment. When profitability and investment fell in the 1970s, so innovation and imitation both fell too—because it is investment that carries the new technologies that are central to these forms of productivity change. Since 1981 the rate of investment has remained low but imitation has been spurred by widening cost differences between best and worst practice firms. By contrast, the effects of selection on productivity change have grown gradually stronger as the variance of production costs has grown wider. Finally the inflation of the middle and late 1970s induced many new firms to enter US manufacturing; these firms tended to raise costs. In the 1960s and 1980s, when prices have been more stable, fewer firms have entered US manufacturing industry and their effect on costs of production has been correspondingly weaker. In other words the slowdown in productivity change after 1973 was caused as (i) reduced rates of investment cut both innovation and imitation; and (ii) rapid price increases induced new, marginal firms to enter manufacturing. Since 1981 the pace of productivity change has recovered as (i) imitation has picked up because intraindustry cost differences have widened; and (ii) stable prices have deterred additional marginal firms from entering manufacturing. That is, changes in the structure of markets have been far more important than changes in the pace of real productivity change.

Again, though, the history of individual industries has been varied. Only the history of the effects of the entry and exit of firms has been common to virtually all industries. A quarter of the industries experienced no slowdown in productivity growth after 1974. Selection has tended to raise production costs in some sectors. In only about half the sectors did the pace of innovation and imitation slow after 1974. Furthermore, both the history of innovation and imitation and its difference between sectors is correlated with intersectoral differences in profitability. The aggregate story cannot be read into the histories of particular industries.

These results carry powerful implications for theories of global economic history. The accounts described in Chapter 3 provide three different interpretations of the relations between productivity growth and accumulation. Gibson and Horvath (1983) and also Lash and Urry (1987) are agnostic about the relation since they do not specify why profitability has fallen. Freeman and Perez as well as Lipietz regard lower rates of productivity growth as a cause of lower profitability and slower accumulation. Mandel and also Piore and Sabel, by contrast, regard the history of productivity change as a consequence rather than a cause of changes in profitability and accumulation. The evidence in Chapter 9 broadly accords with the views of Mandel and of Piore and Sabel: (i) productivity slowed in the 1970s, after profitability had already begun to fall and after rates of accumulation had tumbled; (ii) the productivity slowdown originated in lower rates of investment (which slowed innovation and imitation) and in inflation (which spurred the entry of inefficient firms); (iii) productivity and innovation or imitation are positively correlated across different industries; (iv) faster gains in productivity since 1981 have not been reflected in rates of profit. Freeman and Perez and Lipietz seem to have their pattern of causation wrong and so their timing.

The third empirical issue concerns the international location of production—specifically the growth of NICs. When did they grow? What were the forces underlying growth? Was growth a matter of comparative costs, or did local conditions and agency have more effect? The crucial question is then, how is the growth of the NICs related to the history of growth and profitability in the advanced industrial countries?

To start we observe that in both the USA and Canada there are significant differences between the rates of profit earned in different manufacturing industries and regions. Sectoral barriers to equal rates of profit are stronger than spatial barriers. Neither regional or sectoral rates of profit tended to converge to the national average: there is little evidence that the rates of profit of industries and regions converge to equilibrium. And even when rates of profit did converge they were unlikely to converge to a common value: industries and regions exhibited different long-run rates of profit. Long-run (equilibrium) rates of profit in industries and regions differ because markets fail to remove inequalities in rates of profit even over the long run. These results are consistent with the model of interregional dynamics of Chapter 7. That is, they are consistent with a model that predicts that capital tends to flow from regions in which profit rates are high to regions in which profit rates are low. This background observation makes plausible the argument that flows of capital do not necessarily point to regions where costs of production are lowest.

The growth of Brazil, South Korea, and Taiwan had little to do with wage costs; and its relation to the slowdown in the industrial market economies is less cause than consequence. The first steps to growth in all three NICs were independent of cost advantages. Brazil started industrializing when world trade was interrupted by the Great Depression of the 1930s and then World War II. In South Korea and Taiwan infusions of US aid—related to geopolitical strategy not to costs—provided the first growth impulses. All three took advantage of world conditions but for domestic political and strategic reasons. The goal in Brazil was domestic capital accumulation, subject to the constraints of the power of landowners and workers. In South Korea and Taiwan capital accumulation has been a means to achieve independence and economic power in the face of perceived threats. Since industrialization began, the states have been deeply involved in directing it. The state affects prices and determines market conditions. Protection of domestic markets and support for exporters have figured largely. Prices have been manipulated and are not international; cost advantage does not determine outcomes. The countries had choices which they have exercised in a way that depended on local class forces and their perceptions of the global environment.

In the long run, continued growth depends on ability to repay debts and reinvest large surpluses. That ability is enhanced by exploiting noncapitalist sectors, particularly agriculture and households. Even so, many of the industries in Brazil, South Korea, and Taiwan are now internationally competitive. But not all. Some industries did not need to be competitive when they were first established: financed by loans, it was necessary only that the state guarantee loan repayments, depending on the profitability of the economy as a whole. Some industries have even exported successfully without long-run cost competitiveness. The present competitiveness of these NICs is not a result of their initial advantage of lower wages but has been acquired: corporations have learnt and reaped economies of scale as they have continued to invest and grow. Exports have helped develop competitiveness. In some cases exporting has been forced by the conditions under which loans have to be repaid rather than being the natural by-product of low costs.

Labor has largely been excluded from the process of setting goals in all three countries. Brazil, South Korea, and Taiwan are unequal societies and, in the last 30 years, increasingly so. It is unclear whether inequality is correlated empirically with strategies to industrialize (Clements 1988). Nevertheless, even if wage levels do not sufficiently explain development, they are connected to development. If industrialization substitutes for imports, then domestic demand provides the only market for industry: wages become a source of demand as well as a cost. This closed model of development is analyzed in Chapter 5. If industrialization promotes exports, wages are purely cost: demand can grow by wage rises in other countries. In this sense export promotion permits firms to avoid paying sufficient wages to absorb supply.

The growth of NICs is not merely a locational change. It is also a form of the internationalization of capital. Production is increasingly oriented to exports; production is more integrated over national borders: some of this internationally integrated, export-oriented production has located in the NICs. The growth of the NICs consequently also points to the process of globalization. There are several reasons for the growth of international production: the fall in relative costs of transport and communications (though also a product of the growth of trade); the growth in importance of financial rather than direct investment; the use of freedom of location as a strategy in place-specific class bargaining; and the fact that trade forces local labor to compete with workers in other countries.

Interpretations of postwar economic history offer two accounts of the relations between the internationalization of production (including the growth of NICs) and profitability and accumulation in the industrially mature economies. (The agnostics are Freeman and Perez and Mandel.) Piore and Sabel regard the internationalization of the world's economies as a deep cause of the instability that eventually wrought the end of the long boom and specifically competition from NICs as an immediate reason why demand failed in Europe and North America. The evidence seems to favor the other camp (of Gibson and Horvath, Lash and Urry, and Lipietz), who maintain that internationalization and growth of the NICs has been mainly consequence rather than cause of the slowdown in advanced capitalist economies: export-oriented industrialization really began in NICs in the 1970s; and capital flowed most strongly into NICs after profit rates had fallen in Europe and North America. However, the argument from the theories of regulation and of the new international division of labor do seem to overemphasize the significance of low wages and other production costs in stimulating growth and exports—growth in NICs was not merely structural but reflected their strategic exploitation of global economic conditions.

11.3 SO WHAT DID HAPPEN?

Most existing accounts of the slowdown in the world economy have not described or explained this history well. Theorists of the long boom (Piore and Sabel, Lash and Urry, and Lipietz) have overemphasized the homogeneity of the 1960s and early 1970s and erred in seeking external reasons for the falling rates of profit. Freeman and Perez as well as Lipietz have mistakenly sought to explain falling rates of profit by referring to slower rates of growth of productivity rather than regarding productivity changes as driven by investment and profitability. Piore and Sabel have misread the NICs as a cause of slower rates of accumulation in advanced capitalist economies rather than as exploiting the new global conditions. The error of interpreting the locational changes in the light of costs of production has been common. While the accounts of Gibson and Horvath and of Mandel are broadly compatible with the evidence, they remain incomplete.

Our theoretical innovations permit us to interpret the changes that we have described in the global economy since 1950. A complete account of the historical geography of the postwar years requires a far deeper investigation of the political economy of individual countries and a more concrete history of the global political economy than we can provide. As our data about individual countries, regions, and industries makes clear, history is different in different places and is driven by different imperatives: history is geographic. But a sketch is possible.

The underlying change was a fall in profitability in the advanced industrial economies. The declines in rates of profit were driven by increases in the value composition of capital. That is, profit rates fell because increases in the amount of plant, equipment, and raw materials per worker were not offset by improvements in efficiency even though the rate of exploitation and the speed at which capital is turned over were both tending to raise profitability. This fall was underway by the mid-1960s in Australia and North America and by the mid-1970s in Japan. Investment subsequently slowed—much more than profitability—and by the early 1970s rates of growth of output had faltered too.

This much is clear even though we have measured rates of profit in manufacturing rather than in the economy at large (and certainly not over all capital). Once rates of profit had risen sufficiently the rate of capital accumulation began to exceed the rate of growth of the labor force, putting pressure on wages. Furthermore, in a largely closed economy the market into which firms could sell itself depended on the wages paid to workers, and corporations at large had an incentive to raise wages (even if individual corporations sought advantages by paying less than their competitors). For both these reasons the real wage was bid up and the rate of capacity utilization approached its effective upper bound. Under these circumstances demand and supply grow at the same pace and the rate of profit is subject to the classic constraints. Productivity change raises the capital/labor ratio. But if all the output that is produced is to be sold the real wage must rise, for otherwise some capital has to shift into unproductive uses. In practice, both effects occurred: real wages continued to rise, limiting corporations' capacity to raise the rate of exploitation, and some capital became surplus. For both these reasons rates of profit began to fall under the impetus of rises in the technical composition of capital. (In Japan exports provided a means by which demand could be raised even though real wages grew only slowly, and it was not until the mid-1970s that the links between productivity change, real wages, and excess capital forced rates of profit down.)

The history of profitability differs between places and sectors. The fall in rates of profit was delayed in Japan because of particular conditions there; was delayed or hastened in some industries and regions and was subject to particular influences; and never appeared in a few industries. Market power, the ability to exclude competitors, policies toward labor, investment in process innovations, and the capacity to capture consumers' dollars have all modified the history of profits in individual industries and regions. That is, at the level of individual industries and regions, external influences on rates of profit can prove important. But at the level of the aggregate economy the rate of profit is driven largely by internal effects.

Two effects followed the aggregate fall in rates of profit.

First, in the advanced industrial economies productivity change slowed.

The pace of productivity change in US manufacturing has been slower in the period 1974–1981 than before or since. There have been two reasons for this slowdown. As investment slowed, there were fewer new plants and machines to carry innovations and to permit firms to imitate. Furthermore, as inflation got underway in the aftermath of the oil shock of 1974, new, relatively inefficient firms were induced to enter manufacturing—and they dragged productivity down too. More recently, as inflation has fallen, fewer firms have been entering the market; and as the differences between firms have grown, imitation has once more emerged. In general productivity seems to follow investment and therefore profits rather than to initiate a virtuous cycle of productivity and investment.

Secondly, since rates of investment had fallen far more than rates of profit there was a sea of surplus capital by the early 1970s that was seeking profitable avenues for investment. Some of it was creamed off by the OPEC countries after 1974, but most of that was eventually invested by the banks of the advanced industrial economies. Both the internal and the OPEC surpluses have contributed much to the capacity of banks and other financial institutions to range over the globe seeking new outlets for locally unproductive capital. Much of this surplus capital was invested in the NICs—commonly as financial capital rather than as direct investment—spurring their very rapid growth. The locational pattern of investment had little to do with relative cost differences and a lot to do with the availability of capital, the development of global financial markets, and the strategies of the newly industrialized states.

The NICs were investing in new plant and equipment during an interval when productivity change in the advanced industrial economies had slowed. They were also learning and achieving economies of scale. The companies in the NICs were therefore gradually reducing the technological lag between themselves and more established corporations. So their capacity to compete in global markets was improved and exports from the NICs could grow faster than their imports from advanced market economies. The export boom from the NICs was a matter of their gradual relative improvement in technology, not of any absolute advantage in production costs.

So far the NICs—at least the East Asian ones that have escaped the demands of international monetarists—have avoided the constraint on profitability that has ensnared the more advanced economies. In Australia, Canada, Japan, and the USA rates of profit have eventually been driven down as the pace of accumulation has exceeded the rate of growth of supply and the capacity to produce has exceeded the capacity of workers' incomes to pay for additional consumption. In the NICs, export-led growth has so far severed the link between the growth of output and the growth of workers' consumption. There is recent evidence that this link has been reestablished even in the East Asian NICs. Protectionism in European and North American markets and stronger working and middle classes in South Korea and Taiwan have combined since the mid-1980s to bring the rate of growth of exports back to the rate of growth of imports. Under these conditions output is constrained by internal demand unless rates of offshore investment can remedy the deficiency. Complaints about wage levels, protectionism, and currency revaluations in all four dragons—South Korea, Taiwan, Hong Kong, and Singapore—evidence the power of this new political economy.

The past 45 years has witnessed the expansion of industrial capitalism to a new set of countries. The major impetus for this spread has been the existence of a capital surplus since the mid 1970s. In the last decade eastern Europe, China, and the ASEAN-4 (Indonesia, Malaysia, the Philippines, and Thailand) have shown evidence that they are about to enter this realm too—again using surplus capital from Japan, Europe, North America, and to some extent the four dragons. However or wherever the industrially mature economies discover a new source of growth, they now include the former NICs. This is a larger group than formerly of industrial capitalist countries to which the constraint on capital accumulation applies. As capital has sought to unbind itself from the constraints of labor and demand in industrial capitalist countries, it has brought additional economies into the bounds of those constraints.

BIBLIOGRAPHY

ABD [Australian Bureau of Statistics] *Labour Force Survey*. Canberra: Australian Government Publishing Service, Cat. 6203.0 (various years).

Abernathy W J and Utterback J M (1978) Patterns of industrial innovation. *Technology Review* 80: 40–47.

Abraham-Frois G and Berribi E (1979) *Theory of Values, Prices and Accumulation: A Mathematical Integration of Marx, von Neumann and Sraffa*. Cambridge, UK: Cambridge University Press.

Abramowitz M (1956) Resource and output trends in the United States since 1870. *Papers and Proceedings of the American Economic Association* 76: 5–23.

Abramowitz M and David P A (1973) Economic growth in America: Historical parables and realities. *De Economist* 121: 251 –272.

Acordino J J (1992) *The United States in the Global Economy: Challenges and Policy Choices* Chicago: American Library Association.

ACTU [Australian Council of Trade Unions] (1987) *Australia Reconstructed*. Canberra: Australian Government Publishing Service.

Adelman I and Morris C (1967) *Society, Politics and Economic Development: A Quantitative Approach*. Baltimore: Johns Hopkins University Press.

Aglietta M (1979) *A Theory of Capitalist Regulation*. London: New Left Books.

Ahmad S (1966) On the theory of induced innovation. *Economic Journal* 76: 344–357.

Alam M S (1991) Trade orientation and macroeconomic performance in LDCs: an empirical study. *Economic Development and Cultural Change* 39: 839–848.

Alberro J and Persky J (1979) The simple analytics of falling profit rates, Okishio's theorem and fixed capital. *Review of Radical Political Economics* 11: 37–41.

Alchian (1950) Uncertainty, evolution and economic theory. *Journal of Political Economy* 58: 211–222.

Alger K (1991) Newly and late industrializing exporters: LDC manufactured exports to the United States 1977–84. *World Development* 19: 885–901.

Alves M (1985) *State and Opposition in Military Brazil* Austin: University of Texas Press.

American Iron and Steel Institute, *Statistical Yearbook* (various years).

Amin A and Goddard J B, eds. (1986) *Technological Change, Industrial Restructuring and Regional Development*. London: Allen and Unwin.

Amsden A H (1989) *Asia's Next Giant: South Korea and Late Industrialization*. New York: Oxford University Press.

Armstrong P Glyn A and Harrison J (1991) *Capitalism Since 1945*. Oxford: Blackwell.

Arnold W (1988) Science and technology development in Taiwan and South Korea. *Asian Survey* 28: 437–450.

Arrow K (1962) The economic implications of learning by doing. *Review of Economic Studies* 29: 155–173.

Asher E (1972) Industrial efficiency and biased technical change in American and British manufacturing: the case of textiles in the nineteenth century. *Journal of Economic History* 32: 431–442.

Asher H (1956) Cost–quantity relations in the airframe industry. Report No. R-291, RAND Corporation, Santa Monica, CA.

Atkinson A B and Stiglitz J E (1969) A new view of technological change. *Economic Journal* 79: 573–578.

Aw B Y and Roberts M J (1985) The role of imports from the newly industrializing countries in US production. *Review of Economics and Statistics* 67: 108–117.

Aydalot P and Keeble D (1988) *High Technology Industry and Innovative Environments*. London: Routledge.

Babbage C (1846) *On the Economy of Machinery and Manufactures*, 4th ed. London: J Murray.

Baer W (1989) *The Brazilian Economy*. New York: Praeger.

Baer W Kerstenetsky I and Villela A (1973) The changing role of the state in the Brazilian economy. *World Development* 1: 23–24.

Bain J (1951) Relation of profit rate to industry concentration: American manufacturing 1936–40. *Quarterly Journal of Economics* 65: 293–324.

Bakker I (1988) Women's employment in comparative perspective. In Jensen J Hagen E and Reddy C, eds., *Feminization of the Labour Force: Paradoxes and Promises*. Cambridge, UK: Polity, pp. 17–44.

Balassa B (1978) *The Newly Industrializing Countries in the World Economy*. New York: Pergamon.

Balassa B (1985) The role of foreign trade in the economic development of Korea. In Galenson W, ed., *Foreign Trade and Investment: Economic Development in the Newly Industrializing Asian Countries*. Madison: University of Wisconsin Press, pp. 141–175.

Baldwin W L and Childs G L (1969) The fast second and rivalry in research and development. *Southern Economic Journal* 70: 294–298.

Baldwin W L and Scott J T (1987) *Market Structure and Technological Change*. Chur, Switzerland: Harwood Academic Press.

Bank of England, *Quarterly Bulletin* (various years).

Baran P (1957) *The Political Economy of Growth*. New York: Prometheus.

Baran P and Sweezy P (1966) *Monopoly Capital*. New York: Monthly Review Press.

Barnes T J (1984) Theories of agricultural rent within the surplus approach. *International Regional Science Review* 9: 125–140.

Barnes T J and Sheppard E (1984) Technical choice and reswitching in space economies. *Regional Science and Urban Economics* 14: 345–362.

Barnet R J and Muller R E (1975) *Global Reach: The Power of the Multinational Corporation*. London: Cape.

Barnett D F and Schorsch L (1983) *Steel: Upheaval in a Basic Industry*. Cambridge, MA: Ballinger.

Beechey V and Perkins T (1987) *A Matter of Hours: Women, Part-time Work and the Labour Market.* Cambridge, UK: Polity.

Beenstock M (1984) *The World Economy in Transition,* 2nd ed. London: Allen and Unwin.

Beetham D (1984) The future of the nation state. In McLennan G Held D and Hall S, eds., *The Idea of the Modern State.* Milton Keynes, UK: Open University Press, pp. 208–222.

Benbouali B (1980) Long term contractual arrangements for setting up capital goods in the iron and steel industry. UNIDO ID/WG 324/6.

Benjamin R (1982) The political economy of Korea. *Asian Survey* 22: 1105–1116.

Berlage L and Terweduwe D (1988) The classification of countries by cluster and by factor analysis. *World Development* 16: 1527–1545.

Berndt E S (1980) Energy price increases and the productivity slowdown in United States manufacturing. In *The Decline in Productivity Growth.* Federal Reserve Bank of Boston, Conference Series No.22, pp. 60–89.

Berndt E S and Wood D O (1981) Interpretations of energy capital complementarity— reply and further results. *American Economic Review* 71: 1105–1110.

Berry B J L (1991) *Long-Wave Rhythms in Economic Development and Political Behavior.* Baltimore: Johns Hopkins University Press.

Berry B J L Kim H and Kim H-M (1993) Are long waves driven by techno-economic transformations? Evidence for the US and the UK. *Technological Forecasting and Social Change* 44: 111–135.

BIE [Bureau of Industry Economics] (1985) *Productivity Growth in Australian Industry: 1954–55 to 1981–82.* Canberra: Australian Government Publishing Service.

Bienefeld M (1988) The significance of the newly industrializing countries for the development debate. *Studies in Political Economy* 25: 7–39.

Bingham T (1985) *Banking and Monetary Policy.* Paris: OECD.

Binswanger H and Ruttan V, eds. (1978) *Induced Innovation: Technology, Institutions, and Development.* Baltimore: John Hopkins University Press.

BIS (1990) Bank for International Settlements Economic Papers (Basel) August.

Blaug M (1960) Technical change and Marxian economics. *Kyklos* 13: 495–509.

Bleany M (1976) *Underconsumption Theories.* London: International.

Bliss C J (1968) On putty-clay. *Review of Economic Studies* 35: 105–132.

Block F (1990) *Postindustrial Possibilities: A Critique of Economic Discourse.* Berkeley: University of California Press.

Blomström M and Persson H (1983) Foreign investment and spillover efficiency in an underdeveloped country: evidence from Mexican manufacturing industry. *World Development* 11: 493–501.

Bluestone B and Harrison B (1982) *The Deindustrialization of America.* New York: Basic Books.

Bluestone B and Harrison B (1990) Wage polarization in the United States and the "flexibility" debate. *Cambridge Journal of Economics* 14: 351–373.

Boddy R and Crotty J (1975) Class conflict and macro-policy: the political business cycle. *Review of Radical Political Economics* 7: 1–19.

Bohm–Bawerk E von (1975) *Karl Marx and the Close of His System.* Clifton, NJ: Kelley.

BOLSA Review (various years).

Booth D (1985) Marxism and development sociology: interpreting the impasse. *World Development* 13: 761–787.

Borts G H and Stein J L (1964) *Economic Growth in a Free Market.* New York: Columbia University Press.

Bowles S and Boyer R (1990) A wage-led employment regime: income distribution, labour discipline and aggregate demand in welfare capitalism. In Marglin S A and Schor J B, eds., *The Golden Age of Capitalism.* Oxford: Clarendon Press, pp. 187–217.

Bowles S Gordon D M and Weisskopf T (1983) *Beyond the Wasteland.* New York: Anchor Press.

Bowles S Gordon D M and Weisskopf T (1986) Power and profits: the social structure of accumulation and the profitability of the postwar US economy. *Review of Radical Political Economics* 18: 132–167.

Boyer R and Mistral J (1978) *Accumulation, Inflation, Crises.* Paris: Presses Universitaires de France.

Bradbury J H (1985) Regional and industrial restructuring processes in the new international division of labour. *Progress in Human Geography* 9: 39–63.

Bradbury J H and St. Martin I (1983) Winding down in a Quebec mining town: a case study of Schefferville. *Canadian Geographer* 27: 128–144.

Bradford C I (1987) Trade and structural change: NICs and next tier NICs as transitional economies. *World Development* 15: 299–316.

Bradford C I (1990) Policy interventions and markets: development strategy typologies and policy options. In Gereffi G and Wyman D L, eds., *Manufacturing Miracles: Paths of Industrialization in Latin America and East Asia.* Princeton, NJ: Princeton University Press, pp. 34–51.

Braga C A (1984) Steel, trade, and development: a comparative advantage analysis with special reference to the case of Brazil. Unpublished PhD. thesis, University of Illinois, Urbana–Champaign.

Bramble T (1988) The flexibility debate: industrial relations and new management production practices. *Labour and Industry* 1: 187–209.

Brander J A (1986) Rationales for strategic trade and industrial policy. In Krugman P, ed., *Strategic Trade Policy and the New International Economics.* Cambridge, MA: MIT Press, pp. 23–46.

Braverman H (1974) *Labor and Monopoly Capital: The Degradation of Work in the Twentieth Century.* New York: Monthly Review Press.

Brown L A (1981) *Innovation Diffusion.* New York: Methuen.

Brozen Y (1953) Determinants of the direction of technical change. *American Economic Review, Papers and Proceedings* 65: 288–302.

Brozen Y (1971) Bain's concentration and rates of return revisited. *Journal of Law and Economics* 14: 351–369.

Bryan R (1987) The state and the internationalization of capital: an approach to analysis. *Journal of Contemporary Asia* 17: 253–275.

Burawoy M (1979) *Manufacturing Consent: Changes in the Labor Process under Monopoly Capitalism.* Chicago: Chicago University Press.

Burawoy M (1985) *The Politics of Production.* London: Verso.

Burgess J and Campbell I (1992) Atypical employment and unemployment. Paper presented to the Conference on Responding to Unemployment, University of Wollongong, New South Wales, Australia.

Burmeister E (1980) *Capital Theory and Dynamics.* Cambridge, UK: Cambridge University Press.

Bush V (1947) *Endless Horizons.* Washington, DC: Public Affairs Press.

Business Latin America (various years).

Callenicos A (1989) *Against Postmodernism*. Cambridge, UK: Polity.

Carchedi G (1975) The reproduction of social classes at the level of production relations. *Economy and Society* 4: 1–86.

Carney J Hudson R and Lewis J, eds. (1980) *Regions in Crisis: New Perspectives in European Regional Theory*. London: Croom Helm.

Carvalho J L and Haddad C L S (1980) *Estratégias Comerciais e Absorção de Mão Obra no Brasil*. Rio de Janeiro: Fundação Getulio Vargas.

Castells M and Hall P (1994) *Technopoles of the World: The Making of 21st Century Industrial Complexes*. London: Routledge.

Caves R and Porter M E (1977) From entry barriers to mobility barriers: conjectural decisions and contrived deference to new competition. *Quarterly Journal of Economics* 91: 241–261.

Chan S Clark C and Davis D R (1990) State entrepreneurship, foreign investment, export expansion, and economic growth: Granger causality in Taiwan's development. *Journal of Conflict Resolution* 34: 102–129.

Chen T J and Tang D P (1990) Export performance and productivity growth: the case of Taiwan. *Economic Development and Cultural Change* 38: 577–585.

Cheng T J (1990) Political regimes and development strategies: South Korea and Taiwan. In Gereffi G and Wyman D L, eds., *Manufacturing Miracles: Paths of Industrialization in Latin America and East Asia*. Princeton, NJ: Princeton University Press, pp. 139–178.

Chiou C L (1986) Politics of alienation and polarisation: Taiwan's Tangwai in the 1980s. *Bulletin of Concerned Asian Scholars* 18: 16–28.

Choo H and Kim D (1981) *Probable Size Distribution of Income in Korea Over Time and by Sectors*. Seoul: Korean Development Institute.

Christopherson S (1990) Emerging patterns of work. In Noyelle T, ed., *Skills, Wages and Productivity in the Service Sector*. Boulder, CO: Westview Press, pp. 11–30.

Christopherson S (1993) Market rules and territorial outcomes: the case of the United States. *International Journal of Urban and Regional Research* 17: 274–288.

Clark G L (1981) The employment relation and spatial division of employment. *Annals of the Association of American Geographers* 71: 412–424.

Clark G L (1986) The crisis of the midwest auto industry. In Scott A J and Storper M, eds., *Production, Work, Territory: The Geographical Anatomy of Industrial Capitalism*. London: Allen and Unwin, pp. 127–148.

Clark G L Gertler M S and Wiseman J (1986) *Regional Dynamics*. Boston: Allen and Unwin.

Clark P K (1979) Issues in the analysis of capital formation and productivity growth. *Brookings Papers on Economic Activity* 2: 423–431.

Clarke J and Cable V (1982) The Asian electronics industry looks to the future. *Bulletin of Concerned Asian Scholars* 13: 24–34.

Cleary M N and Hobbs G D (1984) The fifty year cycle: a look at the empirical evidence. In Freeman C, ed., *Long Waves in the World Economy*. London: Pinter, pp. 164–182.

Clements B J (1988) *Foreign Trade Strategies, Employment, and Income Distribution in Brazil*. New York: Praeger.

Coffey P and do Lago L A C, eds. (1988) *The EEC and Brazil: Trade, Capital Investment and the Debt Problem*. London: Pinter.

Cole K Cameron J and Edwards C (1983) *Why Economists Disagree: The Political Economy of Economics.* London: Longman.

Coombs R Savioti P and Walsh V (1987) *Economics and Technological Change.* Totawa, NJ: Rowman and Littlefield.

Corbo J and Nam S W (1988) Korea's macroeconomic prospects and policy issues for the next decade. *World Development* 16: 35–45.

Corbridge S (1986) *Capitalist World Development.* London: Macmillan.

Corbridge S (1990) Post-Marxism and development studies: beyond the impasse. *World Development* 18: 623–639.

Coriot B (1980) The restructuring of the assembly line: a new economy of time and control. *Capital and Class* 6: 34–43.

Crocombe G T Enright M J and Porter M E (1991) *Upgrading New Zealand's Competitive Advantage.* Auckland, New Zealand: Oxford University Press.

Cumings B (1984) The origins and development of the Northeast Asian political economy: industrial sectors, product cycles, and political consequences. *International Organization* 38: 1–40.

Dahlman C J Ross-Larson B and Westphal L E (1987) Managing technological development: lessons from the newly industrializing countries. *World Development* 15: 759–775.

Dale R (1984) Nation state and international system: The world-system perspective. In McLennan G Held D and Hall S, eds., *The Idea of the Modern State.* Milton Keynes, UK: Open University Press, pp. 183–207.

Daly M T and Logan M I (1989) *The Brittle Rim.* Melbourne: Penguin.

Dandrakis E M and Phelps E S (1966) A model of induced invention, growth and distribution. *Economic Journal* 76: 823–840.

Dassbach C H A (1989) *Global Enterprises and the World Economy.* New York: Garland.

David P A (1975) *Technical Choice, Innovation and Economic Growth.* Cambridge, UK: Cambridge University Press.

David P A and van de Klundert T (1965) Biased efficiency growth and capital–labor substitution in the U.S., 1899–1960. *American Economic Review* 55: 357–394.

Davis R D and Ward M D (1990) The entrepreneurial state: evidence from Taiwan. *Comparative Political Studies* 23: 314–333.

Dean W (1969) *The Industrialization of Sao Paulo 1880–1945.* Austin: University of Texas Press.

Debresson C and Lampel J (1985) Beyond the life-cycle-organizational and technological design. 1. An alternative perspective. *Journal of Product Innovation and Management* 2: 170–187.

Debreu G (1959) *Theory of Value.* New Haven, CT: Yale University Press.

Demsetz H (1973) Industry structure, market rivalry and public policy. *Journal of Law and Economics* 16: 1–9.

Denison E F (1962) *The Sources of Economic Growth in the United States and the Alternatives Before Us.* New York: Committee for Economic Development.

Denison E F (1979) Explanations of declining productivity growth. *Survey of Current Business* 59: 1–24.

Department of Foreign Affairs and Trade (1992) *Australia and Northeast Asia in the 1990s: Accelerating Change.* Canberra: Australian Government Publishing Service.

Dertouzos M L Lester R K and Solow R M (1989) *Made in America: Regaining the Productivie Edge.* Cambridge, MA: MIT Press.

Desai M (1979) *Marxian Economics.* Totowa, NJ: Littlefield, Adams.

Destler I M and Henning C R (1990) *Dollar Politics: Exchange Rate Policymaking in the United States.* Washington, DC: Institute for International Economics.

Devine J N (1983) Underconsumption, over-investment and the origins of the Great Depression. *Review of Radical Political Economics* 15: 1–28.

Devine J N (1988) Falling profit rates and the causes of the 1929-33 collapse: towards a synthesis. *Review of Radical Political Economics* 20: 87–93.

Deyo F C (1989) Labor and development policy in East Asia. *Annals of the American Academy of Political and Social Science* 505: 152–161.

Deyo F C (1990) Economic policy and the popular sector. In Gereffi G and Wyman D L, eds., *Manufacturing Miracles: Paths of Industrialization in Latin America and East Asia.* Princeton, NJ: Princeton University Press, pp. 179–204.

Deyo F C Haggard S and Koo H (1987) Labor in the political economy of East Asian industrialization. *Bulletin of Concerned Asian Scholars* 19: 42–53.

Dicken P (1992) *Global Shift,* 2nd ed. London: Chapman.

D'Mello B (1985) South Korea: pointers to a new international division of labour. *Economic and Political Weekly* 20: 1592–1594.

Doeringer P B and Piore M J (1971) *Internal Labor Markets and Manpower Analysis.* Lexington, MA: DC Heath.

Dollar D (1991) Convergence of South Korean productivity on West German levels 1966–78. *World Development* 19: 263–273.

Dollar D and Sokoloff K (1990) Changing comparative advantage and productivity growth in manufacturing industries. In Kwon J K, ed., *Korean Economic Development.* New York: Greenwood, pp. 129–142.

Donaghu M T and Barff R (1990) Nike just did it: international subcontracting and flexibility in athletic footwear production. *Regional Studies* 24: 537–552.

Donges J B (1976) A comparative survey of industrialization policies in fifteen semi-industrial countries. *Weltwirtschaftliches Archiv* 112: 636–657.

Dosi G (1982) Technological paradigms and technological trajectories: a suggested interpretation of the determinants and directions of technical change. *Research Policy* 3: 147–162.

Dosi G Freeman C Nelson R Silverberg G and Soete L, eds. (1988) *Technical Change and Economic Theory.* London: Pinter.

Dreze J and Sen A (1979) *The Political Economy of Hunger.* Oxford: Clarendon.

Drucker P F (1986) The changed world economy. *Foreign Affairs* Spring: 768–791.

van Duijn J J (1977) The long wave in economic life. *De Economist* 125: 544–576.

van Duijn J J (1983) *The Long Wave in Economic Life.* London: Allen and Unwin.

Dumenil G Rangel G and Glick M (1987) The rate of profit in the United States. *Cambridge Journal of Economics* 11: 331–359.

Dunford M (1990) Theories of regulation. *Society and Space* 8: 297–321.

Dunford M Geddes M and Perrons D (1981) Regional policy and the crisis in the U.K.: a long-run perspective. *International Journal of Urban and Regional Research* 5: 337–410.

Dunleavy P and O'Leary B (1987) *Theories of the State: The Politics of Liberal Democracy.* London: Macmillan.

Dunning J H (1983) Changes in the level and structure of international production: the last 100 years. In Casson M, ed., *The Growth of International Business.* London: Allen and Unwin, pp. 84–139.

Dunning J H and Cantwell J (1987) *IRM Directory of Statistics of International Investment and Production.* New York: New York University Press.

Dutt A K (1990) *Growth, Distribution and Uneven Development.* Cambridge: Cambridge University Press.

Eagly (1970) *The Structure of Classical Economic Theory.* New York: Oxford University Press.

Economic Planning Agency annual, *Economic Survey of Japan.* Tokyo: Japan Times.

Economic Planning Board (1981) *Social Indicators of Korea.* Seoul: Economic Planning Board.

Edwards R (1979) *Contested Terrain: The Transformation of the Workplace in the Twentieth Century.* London: Heinemann.

Elson D, ed. (1979) *Value: The Representation of Labour in Capitalism.* London: CSE Books.

Elson D (1984) Imperialism. In McLennan G Held D and Hall S, eds., *The Idea of the Modern State.* Milton Keynes, UK: Open University Press, pp. 154–182.

Elson D and Pearson R (1981) Nimble fingers make cheap workers: analysis of women's employment in Third World export manufacturing, *Feminist Review* 7: 87–107.

Emmanuel A (1972) *Unequal Exchange: A Study of the Imperialism of Trade.* New York: Monthly Review Press.

Enos J L (1984) Government intervention in the transfer of technology: the case of South Korea. *Institute of Development Studies Bulletin* 15: 26–31.

Enos J L and Park W H (1988) *The Adoption and Diffusion of Imported Technology.* London: Croom Helm.

Erickson K P (1977) *The Brazilian State and Working-Class Politics.* Berkeley: University of California Press.

Erzan R et al. (1988) The profile of protection in developing countries. Discussion Paper 21, UNCTAD, Geneva.

Evans P B (1979) *Dependent Development: The Alliance of Multinational, State and Local Capital in Brazil.* Princeton, NJ: Princeton University Press.

Evans P B (1986) State, capital and the transformation of dependence: the Brazilian computer case. *World Development* 14: 791–808.

Evans P B and Tigre P B (1989) Going beyond clones in Brazil and Korea: a comparative analysis of NIC strategies in the computer industry. *World Development* 17: 1751–1768.

Evenson R and Kislev Y (1976) A stochastic model of applied research. *Journal of Political Economy* 84: 265–281.

Ewers H J and Wettman R W (1980) Innovation-oriented regional policy. *Regional Studies* 14: 161–179.

Fagan RH and Rich DC (1990) Industrial restructuring in the Australian food industry: corporate strategy and the gloal economy. In Hayter R and Wilde PD, eds., *Industrial Transformation and Challenge in Australia and Canada.* Ottawa: Carleton University Press, pp. 175–194.

Farjoun E and Machover M (1983) *Laws of Chaos: A Probabilistic Account of Political Economy* London: Verso.

Federal Trade Commission, US (1977) *The United States Steel Industry and Its International Rivals: Trends and Factors Determining International Competitiveness* (Bureau of Economics staff report). Washington, DC: US Government Printing Office.

Feldstein M (1988) The United States in the world economy: introduction. In Feldstein

M, ed., *The United States in the World Economy*. Chicago: University of Chicago Press, pp. 1–8.

Felix D (1989) Import substitution and late industrialization: Latin America and Asia compared. *World Development* 17: 1455–1469.

Fellner W (1961) Two propositions in the theory of induced innovations. *Economic Journal* 71: 305–308.

Fields G S and Wan H (1989) Wage-setting institutions and economic growth. *World Development* 17: 1471–1483.

Filer R K (1980) The downturn in productivity growth: a new look at its nature and causes. In Maital S and Meltz N M, eds., *Lagging Productivity Growth*. Cambridge, MA: Ballinger, pp. 109–128.

Fine B and Harris L (1979) *Rereading Capital*. London: Macmillan.

Fishlow A (1966) Productivity and technological change in the railroad sector, 1840–1910. In *Output, Employment and Productivity in the US after 1800* (Studies in Income and Wealth No. 30). New York: National Bureau of Economic Research.

Fishlow A (1989) Latin American failure against the backdrop of Asian success. *Annals of the American Academy of Political and Social Science* 505: 117–128.

Flamm K (1988) *Creating the Computer: Government, Industry and High Technology*. Washington, DC: Brookings Institution.

Foot S P H (1986) *International relocation of steel production*: USA and Brazil. Unpublished Ph.D. thesis, McMaster University, Hamilton, Canada.

Foot S P H and Webber M J (1990a) State, class and international capital 1: Background to the Brazilian steel industry. *Antipode* 22: 93–120.

Foot S P H and Webber M J (1990b) State, class and international capital 2: The development of the Brazilian steel industry. *Antipode* 22: 233–251.

Frank A G (1979) *Dependent Accumulation and Underdevelopment*. New York: Monthly Review Press.

Frank A G (1982) Asia's exclusive models. *Far Eastern Economic Review* 25: June 22–23.

Fransman M (1986) International competitiveness, technical change and the state: the machine tool industry in Taiwan and Japan. *World Development* 14: 1375–1396.

Fraser R (1987) *The World Financial System*. Harlow, Essex, UK: Longman.

Freeman C (1963) The plastics industry: a comparative study of research and innovation. *National Institute Economic Review* 26: 22–62.

Freeman C (1965) Research and development in electronic capital goods. *National Institute Economic Review* 34: 40–91.

Freeman C (1974) *The Economics of Industrial Innovation*. Harmondsworth: Penguin.

Freeman C (1978) *Technology Policy and Economic Performance: Lessons from Japan*. London: Pinter.

Freeman C, ed. (1984) *Long Waves in the World Economy*. London: Pinter.

Freeman C and Perez C (1988) Structural crises of adjustment: business cycles and investment behaviour. In Dosi G et al., eds., *Technical Change and Economic Theory*. London: Pinter, pp. 38–66.

Freeman C Clark J A and Soete L (1982) *Unemployment and Technical Innovation: A Study of Long Waves and Economic Development*. London: Pinter.

Frieden J A (1987) *Banking on the World: the Politics of American International Finance*. New York: Harper and Row.

Friedman A L (1977) *Industry and Labour: Class Struggle at Work and Monopoly Capitalism.* London: Macmillan.

Fritsch W and Franco G (1991) *Foreign Direct Investment in Brazil: Its Impact on Industrial Restructuring.* Paris: OECD.

Frobel F Heinrichs J and Kreye O (1980) *The New International Division of Labour.* Cambridge, UK: Cambridge University Press.

Fryer D D (1987) The political geography of international lending by private banks. *Transactions of the Institute of British Geographers* 12: 413–432.

Fuchs V R (1962) Integration, concentration, and profits in manufacturing industries. *Quarterly Journal of Economics* 75: 278–291.

Fuentes A and Ehrenreich B (1983) *Women in the Global Factory.* Boston: South End Press.

Garnaut R (1989) *Australia and the Northeast Asian Ascendancy.* Canberra: Australian Government Publishing Service.

GATT (1993) *International Trade.* Geneva: General Agreement on Tariffs and Trade.

George S (1988) *A Fate Worse than Debt.* London: Penguin.

Gereffi G (1990) Paths of industrialization: an overview. In Gereffi G and Wyman D L, eds., *Manufacturing Miracles: Paths of Industrialization in Latin America and East Asia.* Princeton, NJ: Princeton University Press, pp. 3–31.

Gerster H J (1989) Econometric tests on long waves in price and volume series from sixteen countries. Paper presented at the International Conference on the Long Waves of the Economic Conjuncture, Vrije Universiteit, Brussels, January 12–14.

Gertler M S (1984) Regional capital theory. *Progress in Human Geography* 8: 50–81.

Gertler M S (1986) Regional dynamics of manufacturing and non-manufacturing investment in Canada. *Regional Studies* 20: 523–534.

Gertler M S (1987) Economic and political determinants of regional investment and technical change in Canada. *Papers of the Regional Science Association* 62: 27–44.

Gertler M S (1992) Flexibility revisited: districts, nation-states, and the forces of production. *Transactions of the Institute of British Geographers* NS17: 259–278.

Gertler M S (1993) Implementing advanced manufacturing technologies in mature industrial regions: towards a social model of technology production. *Regional Studies* 27: 665–680.

Gibbs D C and Edwards A (1985) The diffusion of new production innovations in British industry. In Thwaites A T and Oakey R P, eds., *The Regional Impact of Technological Change* London: Pinter, pp. 132–163.

Gibson B (1980) Unequal exchange: theoretical issues and empirical findings. *Review of Radical Political Economics* 12: 15–35.

Gibson K D and Horvath R J (1983) Aspects of a theory of transition within the capitalist mode of production. *Society and Space* 1: 121–138.

Glasmeier A K (1986) High-tech industries and the regional division of labor. *Industrial Relations* 25: 197–211.

Glick M (1985) Monopoly or competition in the U.S. economy? *Review of Radical Political Economics* 17: 121–127.

Glismann H H Rodemer H and Wolter F (1984) Long waves in economic development. In Freeman C, ed., *Long Waves in the World Economy.* London: Pinter, pp. 135–163.

Glyn A and Sutcliffe B (1972) *British Capitalism, Workers and the Profit Squeeze.* Harmondsworth: Penguin.

Glyn A Hughes A Lipietz A and Singh A (1990) The rise and fall of the golden age. In Marglin S A and Schor J B, eds., *The Golden Age of Capitalism*. Oxford: Clarendon Press, pp. 39–122.

Goddard J B Thwaites A and Gibbs D (1986) The regional dimension to technological change in Great Britain. In Amin A and Goddard J B, eds., *Technological Change, Industrial Restructuring and Regional Development*. London: Allen and Unwin, pp. 140–156.

Goldfield M (1987) *The Decline of Organized Labor in the United States*. Chicago: Chicago University Press.

Goldstein J P (1985) The cyclical profit squeeze: a Marxian microfoundation. *Review of Radical Political Economics* 17: 103–128.

Gomulka S (1990) *The Theory of Technological Change and Economic Growth*. New York: Routledge.

Goncalves R and Richtering J (1987) Intercountry comparison of export performance and output growth. *The Developing Economies* 25: 3–18.

Gordon D M Edwards R and Reich M (1982) *Segmented Work, Divided Workers*. New York: Cambridge University Press.

Gordon R (1989) The postwar evolution of computer prices. In Jorgenson D W and Landau R, eds., *Technology and Capital Formation*. Cambridge, MA: MIT Press, pp. 77–125.

Gough I (1972) Marx's theory of productivie and unproductive labor. *New Left Review* 76: 47–72.

Grabowski H G and Mueller D C (1978) Industrial research and development, intangible capital stocks, and firm profit rates. *Bell Journal of Economics* 9: 328–343.

Graham J Gibson K Horvath R and Shakow D M (1988) Restructuring in US manufacturing: the decline of monopoly capitalism. *Annals, Association of American Geographers* 78: 473–490.

Grahl J (1983) Restructuring in West European industry. *Capital and Class* 19: 118–142.

Grass E and Hayter R (1989) Employment change during recession: the experience of forest product manufacturing plants in British Columbia, 1981–1985. *The Canadian Geographer* 33: 240–252.

de Grazia R (1984) *Clandestine Employment*. Geneva: ILO.

Grigg D B (1986) *World Food Problem, 1950–1980* New York: Blackwell.

Griliches Z (1957) Hybrid corn: an exploration in the economics of technological change. *Econometrica* 25: 501–522.

Griliches Z, ed. (1971) *Price Indexes and Quality Change: Studies in New Methods of Measurement*. Cambridge, MA: Harvard University Press.

Griliches Z (1980) R&D and the productivity slowdown. *American Economic Review* 70: 343–347.

Grimwade N (1989) *International Trade: New Patterns of Trade, Production and Investment*. London: Routledge.

Gunasekera H D B H (1989) Intraindustry specialization in production and trade in newly industrializing countries: a conceptual framework and some empirical evidence from East Asia. *World Development* 17: 1279–1287.

Gupta K L and Islam M A (1983) *Foreign Capital, Savings and Growth*. Dordrecht, Netherlands: Reidel.

Habakkuk HJ (1962) *American and British Technology in the Nineteenth Century*. Cambridge, UK: Cambridge University Press.

Hagen E and Jensen J (1988) Paradoxes and promises. In Jensen J Hagen E and Reddy C, eds., *Feminization of the Labour Force: Paradoxes and Promises*. Cambridge, UK: Polity pp. 3–16.

Hagerstrand T (1967) *Innovation Diffusion as a Spatial Process*. Chicago: University of Chicago Press.

Hahnel R and Sherman H (1982) Note: the rate of profit over the business cycle. *Cambridge Journal of Economics* 6: 185–194.

Haig B D (1982) Sex discrimination in the reward for skills and experience in the Australian labour force. *Economic Record* 5: 1–10.

Hall P and Markusen A R, eds. (1985) *Silicon Landscapes*. Boston: Allen and Unwin.

Hall P and Preston P (1988) *The Carrier Wave: New Information Technology and the Geography of Innovation, 1846–2003*. London: Unwin Hyman.

Hallwood P and MacDonald R (1986) *International Money: Theory, Evidence and Institutions* New York: Blackwell.

Hamilton A (1986) *The Financial Revolution*. Harmondsworth: Penguin.

Hamilton C (1983) Capitalist industrialization in East Asia's four little tigers. *Journal of Contemporary Asia* 13: 35–73.

Hamilton C (1986) *Capitalist Industrialization in Korea*. Boulder, CO: Westview Press.

Hamilton C (1987) Price formation and class relations in the development process. *Journal of Contemporary Asia* 17: 2–18.

Harcourt G (1972) *Some Cambridge Controversies in the Theory of Capital*. Cambridge, UK: Cambridge University Press.

Harris D J (1977) *Capital Accumulation and Income Distribution*. Stanford, CA: Stanford University Press.

Harris D J (1983) Accumulation of capital and the rate of profit in Marxian theory. *Cambridge Journal of Economics* 7: 311–330.

Harris R G (1985) *Trade, Industrial Policy, and International Competition*. Toronto: University of Toronto Press.

Harris R G (1992) *Exchange Rate and International Competitiveness of the Canadian Economy*. Ottawa: Economic Council of Canada.

Harrod R (1954) *Towards a Dynamic Economics*. London: Macmillan.

Harvey D (1975) The geography of capitalist accumulation: a reconstruction of the Marxist theory. *Antipode* 7: 9–21.

Harvey D (1982) *The Limits to Capital*. Chicago: Chicago University Press.

Harvey D (1988) *The Condition of Postmodernity*. Oxford: Blackwell.

Harvey P (1985) The value creating capacity of skilled labor in Marxian economics. *Review of Radical Political Economics* 11: 83–102.

Hayami Y and Ruttan V (1971) *Agricultural Development: An International Perspective*. Baltimore: Johns Hopkins University Press.

Helleiner G K and Lavergne R (1979) Intrafirm trade and industrial exports to the US. *Oxford Bulletin of Economics and Statistics* 41: 297–311.

Helliwell J F MacGregor M E and Padmore T (1986) Economic growth and productivity in Canada, 1955–90. In Sargent J, ed., *Economic Growth: Prospects and Determinants*. Toronto: University of Toronto Press, pp. 27–64.

Helpman E and Krugman P (1985) *Market Structure and Foreign Trade*. Cambridge, MA: MIT Press.

Henderson J and Castells M, eds. (1987) *Global Restructuring and Territorial Development*. London: Sage.

Henley A (1987) Labour's Shares and Profitability Crisis in the United States. *Cambridge Journal of Economics* 315–330.

Hicks J (1932) *The Theory of Wages*, 1st ed. London: Macmillan.

Hilferding R (1919) *Bohm-Bawerk's Criticism of Marx*. Glasgow: Socialist Labour Press.

Himmelweit S and Mohun S (1981) Real abstractions and anomalous assumptions. In Steedman I et al., eds., *The Value Controversy*. London: Verso, pp. 224–265.

Hirata A (1988) Promotion of manufactured exports in developing countries. *The Developing Economies* 26: 422–437.

Hirsch F and Oppenheimer P (1977) The triad of managed money: currency, credit, and prices 1920–'70. In Cippola C, ed., *Fontana Economic History of Europe: The Twentieth Century, Part 2*. London: Fontana, pp. 603–697.

Hirsch S (1967) *Location of Industry and International Competitiveness*. Oxford: Clarendon Press.

Ho S P S (1978) Decentralized industrialization and rural development: evidence from Taiwan. *Economic Development and Cultural Change* 28: 321–343.

Hodgson G (1974) The theory of the falling rate of profit. *New Left Review* 84: 55–82.

Hodgson G (1981) On exploitation and labor value.*Science and Society* 45: 228–233.

Hodgson G (1982) *Capitalism, Value and Exploitation*. Oxford: Oxford University Press.

Hollander S (1965) *The Sources of Increased Efficiency: The Study of Du Pont Rayon Plants*. Cambridge, MA: MIT Press.

Hollander S (1987) *Classical Economics*. Oxford: Basil Blackwell.

Holmes J (1983) Industrial reorganization, capital restructuring and locational change: an analysis of the Canadian automobile industry in the 1960s. *Economic Geography* 59: 251–271.

Hong W (1990) Market distortions and polarization of trade patterns: the Korean experience. In Kwon J K, ed., *Korean Economic Development*. New York: Greenwood, pp. 115–128.

Hoogvelt A M M (1982) *The Third World in Global Development*. London: Macmillan.

Howes C and Markusen A R (1993) Trade, industry and economic development. In Noponen H Graham J and Markusen A R, eds., *Trading Industries, Trading Regions*. New York: Guilford, pp. 1–44.

Huang C (1989) The state and foreign investment: the cases of Taiwan and Singapore. *Comparative Political Studies* 22: 93–121.

Hudson R (1989) Labour market changes and new forms of work in old industrial regions: maybe flexibility for some but not flexible accumulation. *Environment and Planning D: Society and Space* 7: 5–30.

Huertas T F (1990) US multinational banking: history and prospects. In Jones G, ed., *Banks as Multinationals*. London: Routledge, pp. 248–267.

Hufbauer G C (1966) *Synthetic Materials and the Theory of International Trade*. Cambridge, MA: Harvard University Press.

Humphrey J (1982) *Capitalist Control and Workers' Struggle in the Brazilian Auto Industry*. Princeton, NJ: Princeton University Press.

Hunt E K (1979) Categories of productive and unproductive labor in Marxist economic theory. *Science and Society* 43: 303–325.

Hunt I (1983) An obituary or a new life for the tendency of the rate of profit to fall? *Review of Radical Political Economics* 15: 131–148.

Hyman R (1988) Flexible specialization: miracle or myth? In Hyman R and Streek W, eds., *New Technology and Industrial Relations*. Oxford: Blackwell, pp. 48–60.

Hymer S (1975) The multinational corporation and the law of uneven development. In Radice H, ed., *International Firms and Modern Imperialism*. Harmondsworth: Penguin, pp. 37–62.

International Labor Organization (1981a) *Employment Effects of Multinational Enterprises in Developing Countries*. Geneva: ILO.

International Labor Organization (1981b) *Employment Effects of Multinational Enterprises in Industrialized Countries*. Geneva: ILO.

International Labor Organization (1984) *World Labour Report*, Vol. 1. Geneva: ILO.

International Labor Organization (1985) *World Labour Report*, Vol. 2. Geneva: ILO.

International Monetary Fund annual, *International Financial Statistics*.

Iqbal F (1988) External financing for Korea: the next phase. *World Development* 16: 137–155.

Ito K (1984) Development finance and commercial banks in Korea. *The Developing Economies* 22: 453–475.

Itoh M (1980) *Value and Crisis*. New York: Monthly Review Press.

Itoh M (1990) *The World Economic Crisis and Japanese Capitalism*. London: Macmillan.

Jacobsson S (1985) Technical change and industrial policy: the case of computer numerically controlled lathes in Argentina, Korea and Taiwan. *World Development* 13: 353–370.

Jacquemin (1991) *The New Industrial Organization*. Cambridge, MA: MIT Press.

Jamieson N and Webber M (1991) Flexibility and part-time employment in retailing. *Labour and Industry* 4: 55–70.

Jenkins R (1984) *Transnational Corporations and the Latin American Automobile Industry*. London: Macmillan.

Jenkins R (1991) The political economy of industrialization: a comparison of Latin American and East Asian industrializing countries. *Development and Change* 22: 197–231.

Jessop B (1982) *The Capitalist State*. Oxford: Martin Robertson.

Jessop B (1990) *State Theory: Putting the Capitalist State in its Place*. Cambridge, UK: Polity.

Johansen L (1959) Substitution versus fixed production coefficients in the theory of economic growth. *Econometrica* 11: 157–177.

Johnson C (1982) *MITI and the Japanese Miracle: The Growth of Industrial Policy, 1925–1975* Stanford, CA: Stanford University Press.

Jones G, ed. (1990) *Banks as Multinationals*. London: Routledge.

Jones H G (1975) *An Introduction to Modern Theories of Economic Growth*. New York: McGraw-Hill.

Jorgenson D W and Landau R, eds. (1989) *Technology and Capital Formation*. Cambridge, MA: MIT Press.

Jung W S and Marshall P J (1985) Exports growth and causality in developing countries. *Journal of Development Economics* 18: 1–12.

Ka G M and Seldon M (1986) Original accumulation, equity and late industrialization: the case of socialist China and capitalist Taiwan. *World Development* 14: 1293–1310.

Kaldor N (1957) A model of economic growth. *Economic Journal* 67: 591–624.

Kaldor N (1961) Capital accumulation and economic growth. In Lutz F A and Hague D C, eds., *The Theory of Capital*. London: Macmillan, pp. 93–107.

Kaldor N (1970) The case for regional policies. *Scottish Journal of Political Economy* 17: 337–347.

Kalecki M (1939) *Essays in the Theory of Economic Fluctuations.* New York: Farrar and Rinehart.

Kalecki M (1943) *Studies in Economic Dynamics.* London: Allen and Unwin.

Kamien M and Schwartz N (1968) Optimal induced technical change. *Econometrica* 36: 1–17.

Kavoussi R (1985) International trade and economic development: the recent experience of developing countries. *Journal of Developing Areas* 19: 379–392.

Kay G B (1979) *The Economic Theory of the Working Class.* New York: St. Martin's Press.

Kendrick J W (1961) *Productivity Trends in the United States.* Princeton, NJ: National Bureau of Economic Research.

Kendrick J W (1980) Productivity trends in the United States. In Maital S and Maltz N M, eds., *Lagging Productivity Growth.* Cambridge, MA: Ballinger, pp. 9–30.

Kennedy C (1964) Induced bias in innovation and the theory of distribution. *Economic Journal* 74: 541–547.

Kennedy C and Thirlwall A (1972) Technical progress: a survey. *Economic Journal* 82: 11–72.

Khoury S J (1990) *The Deregulation of the World Financial Markets: Myths, Realities, and Impact.* New York: Quorum.

Kim K S (1990) Import liberalization and its impact in Korea. In Kwon J K, ed., *Korean Economic Development.* New York: Greenwood, pp. 99–113.

Kim Y S (1988) Financial market behavior and balance of payments during the periods of partial financial reform in Korea, 1976–81. *The Developing Economies* 26: 247–263.

Kleinknecht A (1981) Observations on the Schumpeterian swarming of innovations. *Futures* 13: 293–307.

Kleinknecht A (1987) *Innovation Patterns in Crisis and Prosperity.* London: Macmillan.

Kohsaka A (1987) Financial liberalization in Asian NICs: a comparative study of Korea and Taiwan in the 1980s. *The Developing Economies* 25: 325–345.

Kondratieff N (1935) The long waves in economic life. *Review of Economics and Statistics* 17: 105–115 (translated by W F Stolper).

Koo B H and Park W A (1990) Exchange rate policy in Korea. In Kwon J K, ed., *Korean Economic Development.* New York: Greenwood, pp. 79–98.

Koo B Y (1985) The role of direct foreign investment in Korea's recent economic growth. In Galenson W, ed., *Foreign Trade and Investment: Economic Development in the Newly Industrializing Asian Countries.* Madison: University of Wisconsin Press, pp. 176–216.

Krause E A (1982) *Division of Labor, a Political Perspective.* Westport, CT: Greenwood.

Kravis I Heston A and Summers R (1982) *World Product and Income: International Comparison of Real Gross Product.* Baltimore: Johns Hopkins University Press for the World Bank.

Kronish R and Mericle M J (1984) *The Political Economy of the Latin American Motor Vehicle Industry.* Cambridge, MA: MIT Press.

Krueger A (1981) Export-led industrial growth reconsidered. In Hong W and Krause L B, eds., *Trade and Growth of the Advanced Developing Countries in the Pacific Basin.* Seoul: Korean Development Institute, pp. 3–27.

Krugman P, ed. (1986) *Strategic Trade Policy and the New International Economics.* Cambridge, MA: MIT Press.

Kuo S W Y and Frei J C H (1985) Causes and roles of export expansion in the Republic of China. In Galenson W, ed., *Foreign Trade and Investment: Economic Development in the Newly Industrializing Asian Countries*. Madison: University of Wisconsin Press, pp. 45–84.

Kuznets S (1930) *Secular Movements in Production and Prices*. Boston: Houghton Mifflin.

Kuznets S (1966) *Modern Economic Growth: Rate, Structure and Spread*. New Haven, CT: Yale University Press.

Kuznets S (1972) Innovations and adjustments in modern economic growth. *Swedish Journal of Economics* 74: 431–451.

Kwon J K (1990) The uncommon characteristics of Korea's economic development. In Kwon J K, ed., *Korean Economic Development*. New York: Greenwood, pp. 33–49.

do Lago L A C (1988) In Coffey P and do Lago L A C, eds., *The EEC and Brazil: Trade, Capital Investment and the Debt Problem*. London: Pinter.

Laibman D (1982) Technical change, the real wage and the rate of exploitation: the falling rate of profit reconsidered. *Review of Radical Political Economics* 14: 95–105.

Laird S and Nogues J (1988) Manufactured export performance of the highly indebted countries. *The Developing Economies* 26: 403–421.

Lakshmanan T R Anderson W P and Jourabchi M (1984) Regional dimensions of factor and fuel substitution in U.S. manufacturing. *Regional Science and Urban Economics* 14: 381–398.

Lall S (1978) The pattern of intrafirm exports by US multinationals. *Oxford Bulletin of Economics and Statistics* 40: 209–222.

Lall S (1980) *The Multinational Corporation*. London: Macmillan.

Lash S and Urry J (1987) *The End of Organized Capitalism*. Cambridge, UK: Polity.

Launius M A (1984) The state and industrial labour in South Korea. *Bulletin of Concerned Asian Scholars* 16(4): 2–10.

Leborgne D and Lipietz A (1988) New technologies, new modes of regulation: some spatial implications. *Environment and Planning D: Society and Space* 6: 263–280.

Leff N H (1968) *Economic Policy Making and Development in Brazil, 1947–1964*. New York: Wiley.

Leftwich R H (1970) *The Price System and Resource Allocation*. Hinsdale, IL: Dryden Press.

Lever-Tracy C (1988) The flexibility debate: part-time work. *Labour and Industry* 1: 210–241.

Levich R M (1988) Financial innovations in international financial markets. In Feldstein M, ed., *The United States in the World Economy*. Chicago: University of Chicago Press, pp. 215–257.

Lewis W A (1978) *Growth and Fluctuations 1870–1913*. London: Allen and Unwin.

van Liemt G (1988) *Bridging the Gap: Four Newly Industrializing Countries and the Changing International Division of Labour*. Geneva: International Labor Organization.

Lin C Y (1973) *Industrialization in Taiwan 1946–1972*. New York: Praeger.

Lin C Y (1989) *Latin America vs East Asia: A Comparative Development Perspective*. New York: M. E. Sharpe.

Linge G J R (1991) Just-in-time: more or less flexible. *Economic Geography* 67: 316–332.

Lipietz A (1979) *Crise et Inflation: Pourqoui* Paris: Maspero.

Lipietz A (1986) Behind the crisis: the exhaustion of a regime of accumulation. A "regulation school" perspective on some French empirical work. *Review of Radical Political Economics* 18: 13–32.

Lipietz A (1987) *Mirages and Miracles: The Crisis of Global Fordism.* London: Verso.

Little I M D (1982) *Economic Development: Theory, Policy, and International Relations.* New York: Basic Books.

Llewellyn D I (1980) *International Financial Integration: The Limits of Sovereignty.* New York: Wiley.

Luedde-Neurath R (1986) *Import Controls and Export-Oriented Development: A Reassessment of the South Korean Case.* Boulder, CO: Westview Press.

Lukerman F (1965) The "Calcul des Probabilités" and the École Française de Géographie. *The Canadian Geographer* 9: 128–137.

Luxemburg R (1951) *The Accumulation of Capital.* London: Routledge and Kegan Paul.

MacEwan A and Tabb W K, eds. (1989) *Instability and Change in the Global Economy.* New York: Monthly Review Press.

Maekawa H (1986) *Report of the Advisory Group on Economic Structural Adjustment for International Harmony.* Tokyo: Department of the Prime Minister.

Mahler V A (1989) Income distribution within nations: problems of cross national comparison. *Comparative Political Studies* 22: 3–32.

Mahon R (1984) *The Politics of Industrial Restructuring: Canadian Textiles.* Toronto: University of Toronto Press.

Malecki E J (1985) Industrial location and corporate organization in high technology industries. *Economic Geography* 61: 345–369.

Malecki E J (1991) *Technology and Economic Development: The Dynamics of Local, Regional and National Change.* Harlow, UK: Longman.

Mancke R B (1974) Causes of interfirm profitability differences: a new interpretation of the evidence. *Quarterly Journal of Economics* 88: 181–193.

Mandel E (1978) *Late Capitalism.* London: Verso.

Mandel E (1981) Explaining long waves of capitalist development. *Futures* 13: 332–338.

Mansfield E (1961) Technical change and the rate of imitation. *Econometrica* 2: 741–766.

Mansfield E (1963) Intrafirm rates of diffusion. *Review of Economics and Statistics* 45: 348–359.

Mansfield E (1968) *Industrial Research and Technological Innovation.* New York: Norton.

Mansfield E (1970) *Microeconomics: Theory and Applications,* 1st ed. New York: Norton.

Markusen A R (1985) *Profit Cycles, Oligopoly, and Regional Development.* Cambridge, MA: MIT Press.

Martone C L and Braga C A P (1987) *Trade Policies and the Performance of the Export Sector.* (Unpublished manuscript.).

Marx K (1967) *Capital,* 3 vols. New York: International.

Massey D (1978) Regionalism: some current issues. *Capital and Class* 6: 106–125.

Massey D (1981) The U.K. electrical engineering and electronics industries: the implications of the crisis for the restructuring of capital and locational change. In Dear M J and Scott A J, eds., *Urbanization and Urban Planning in Capitalist Society.* London and New York: Methuen, pp. 199–230.

Massey D (1984) *Spatial Divisions of Labour, Social Structures and the Geography of Production*. London: Macmillan.

Massey D and Meegan R (1982) *The Anatomy of Job Loss*. London: Metheun.

Mattick P (1969) *Marx and Keynes: The Limits of the Mixed Economy*. Boston: Peter Sargent.

McDowell L (1991) Life without father and Ford: the new gender order of post-Fordism. *Transactions of the Instititute of British Geographers* NS16: 400–419.

McFetridge D G, ed. (1986) *Canadian Industry in Transition*. Toronto: University of Toronto Press.

McLennan G (1984) Capitalist state or democratic polity? Recent developments in Marxist and pluralist theory. In McLennan G Held D and Hall S, eds., *The Idea of the Modern State*. Milton Keynes, UK: Open University Press, pp. 80–109.

McLennan G Held D and Hall S, eds. (1984) *The Idea of the Modern State*. Milton Keynes, UK: Open University Press.

Meiksins P (1981) Productive and unproductive labor and Marx's theory of class. *Review of Radical Political Economics* 13: 32–42.

Meir G (1976) *Leading Issues in Economic Development*. New York: Oxford University Press.

Mensch G (1979) *Stalemate in Technology*. Cambridge, MA: Ballinger.

Metcalfe J S and Gibbons M (1986) Technological variety and the process of competition. *Économie Apliquée* 39: 493–520.

Metcalfe J S and Steedman I (1979) Heterogeneous capital and the Hekscher-Ohlin-Samuelson theory of trade. In Steedman I, ed., *Fundamental Issues in Trade Theory*. New York: St. Martin's Press, pp. 64–76.

Meyer J R and Kuh E (1957) *The Investment Decision: An Empirical Study*. Cambridge, MA: Harvard University Press.

Michaely M (1977) Exports and growth: an empirical investigation. *Journal of Development Economics* 4: 49–53.

Millward A S (1977) *War, Economy and Society 1939–45*. London: Allen Lane.

Ministry of International Trade and Industry (annual), *International Trade*. Tokyo: MITI.

Miyazaki I (1987) The Maekawa plan for structural adjustment. In Miyazaki I Tsujimura K Nakatani I Takeuchi H Terao Y Honma M and Otsuka K, eds. *Opinions on Japan's Economic Restructuring*. Tokyo: Foreign Press Center, pp. 1–9.

Moffitt M (1983) *The World's Money: International Banking from Bretton Woods to the Brink of Insolvency*. New York: Simon and Schuster.

Moody K (1986) *An Injury to All*. London: Verso.

Morgan K and Sayer A (1988) *Microcircuits of Capital: Sunrise Industry and Uneven Development*. Boulder, CO: Westview Press.

Morishima M (1973) *Marx's Economics: A Dual Theory of Value and Growth*. Cambridge, UK: Cambridge University Press.

Morishima M and Catephores G (1978) *Value, Exploitation and Growth*. London: McGraw-Hill.

Moselely F (1985) The rate of surplus-value in the postwar U.S. economy: a critique of Weisskopf's estimates. *Cambridge Journal of Economics* 9: 57–79.

Moseley F (1988) The rate of surplus value, the organic composition, and the general rate of profit in the United States economy, 1947–1967—a critique and update of Wolff's estimates. *American Economic Review* 78: 298–303.

Moseley F (1990) The decline in the rate of profit in the postwar United States economy. *Review of Radical Political Economics* 22: 17–37.

Moseley F (1991) *The Falling Rate of Profit in the Postwar U.S. Economy*. London: Macmillan.

Mowery D C and Rosenberg N (1979) The influence of market demand upon innovation: a critical review of some recent studies. *Research Policy* 8: 102–153.

Mueller D C (1986) *Profits in the Long Run*. Cambridge, UK: Cambridge University Press.

Mueller D C, ed. (1990) *The Dynamics of Company Profits: An International Comparison*. Cambridge, UK: Cambridge University Press.

Murray F (1987) Flexible specialization in the 'Third Italy.' *Capital and Class* 33: 84–95.

Myrdal G (1957) *Economic Theory and Underdeveloped Regions*. London: Duckworth.

Nadiri M I (1970) Some approaches to the theory and measurement of total factor productivity. *Journal of Economic Literature* 8: 1137–1177.

Nakatani T (1980) The law of the falling rate of profit and the competitive battle: comment on Shaikh. *Cambridge Journal of Economics* 4: 65–68.

Nelson R (1981) Research on productivity growth and differences: dead ends and new departures. *Journal of Economic Literature* 19: 1029–1064.

Nelson R (1993) Technological change as cultural evolution. In Thomson R, ed., *Learning and Technological Change*. New York: St. Martin's Press.

Nelson R and Winter S (1982) *An Evolutionary Theory of Economic Change*. Cambridge, MA: Belknap Press of Harvard University.

von Neumann J (1945) A model and general economic equilibrium. *Review of Economic Studies* 13: 1–19.

Nikaido H (1977) Refutation of the dynamic equalization of profit rates in Marx's scheme of reproduction. Working Paper No. 7722, Modeling Research Group, Department of Economics, University of Southern California, Los Angeles.

Nikaido H (1978) Do profit rates equalize by movement of money capital in Marx's scheme of reproduction? Working Paper No. 7812, Modeling Research Group, Department of Economics, University of Southern California, Los Angeles.

Noponen H Graham J and Markusen A R, eds. (1993) *Trading Industries, Trading Regions*. New York: Guilford.

Norcliffe G (1987) Regional unemployment in Canada in the 1981-84 recession. *Canadian Geographer* 31: 150–159.

Nordhaus W D (1973) Some skeptical thoughts on the theory of induced innovation. *Quarterly Journal of Economics* 87: 209–219.

Norton R D and Rees J R (1979) The product cycle and the spatial decentralization of American manufacturing. *Regional Studies* 13: 141–151.

Oakey R P (1985) High technology industry and agglomeration economies. In Hall P and Markusen A R, eds., *Silicon Landscapes*. Boston: Allen & Unwin, pp. 94–117.

Oakey R P Thwaites A T and Nash P A (1982) Technological change and regional development: some evidence on regional variations in product and process innovation. *Environment and Planning A* 14: 1073–1086.

O'Connor J (1973) *The Fiscal Crisis of the State*. New York: St. Martin's Press.

O'Donnell J (1978) Reflections on the pattern of change in the bureaucratic-authoritarian state. *Latin American Research Review* 13: 3–38.

Ohno K (1989) A note on the dual-industrial growth and learning effects. *The Developing Economies* 27: 350–358.

Ohno K and Imaoka H (1987a) The experience of dual-industrial growth: Korea and Taiwan. *The Developing Economies* 25: 310–324.

Okawa K and Rosovsky H (1973) *Japanese Economic Growth, Trend Acceleration in the Twentieth Century*. Stanford, CA: Stanford University Press.

Okishio N (1961) Technical changes and the rate of profit. *Kobe University Economic Review* 7: 86–96.

Ong N (1980) Marx's classical and post-classical conceptions of the wage. *Australian Economic Papers* 19: 264–277.

Organization for Economic Cooperation and Development (1979a) *Report of the Secretary-General*. Paris: OECD.

Organization for Economic Cooperation and Development (1979b) *1979 DAC Review*. Paris: OECD.

Organization for Economic Cooperation and Development (1980) *National Accounts Statistics 1: Aggregates 1950–1978*. Paris: OECD.

Organization for Economic Cooperation and Development (1985) *External Debt of Developing Countries in 1984*. Paris: OECD.

Organization for Economic Cooperation and Development (1987a) *Bank Profitability 1980–1984*. Paris: OECD.

Organization for Economic Cooperation and Development (1987b) *Employment Outlook*. Paris: OECD.

Organization for Economic Cooperation and Development (1989a) *Employment Outlook*. Paris: OECD.

Organization for Economic Cooperation and Development (1989b) *Historical Statistics 1960–1987*. Paris: OECD.

Organization for Economic Cooperation and Development (1990) *National Accounts Statistics 1: Aggregates 1976–1988*. Paris: OECD.

Organization for Economic Cooperation and Development (1991) *Employment Outlook*. Paris: OECD.

Organization for Economic Cooperation and Development (1993a) *Economic Surveys 1992–1993*. Paris: OECD.

Organization for Economic Cooperation and Development (1993b) *Labour Force Statistics 1971–1991*. Paris: OECD.

Ornstein S I (1973) Concentration and profits. In Weston J F and Ornstein S I, eds., *The Impact of Large Firms on the US Economy*. Lexington, MA: Lexington Books, pp. 87–102.

Oser J and Brue S C (1988) *The Evolution of Economic Thought*, 4th ed. New York: Harcourt Brace Jovanovich.

Palloix C (1977) The self-expansion of capitalism on a world scale. *Review of Radical Political Economics* 9: 1–28.

Pappas Carter Evans and Koop/Telesis (1990) *The Global Challenge: Australian Manufacturing in the 1990s*. Melbourne: Australian Manufacturing Council.

van Parijs P (1980) The falling rate of profit theory of crisis: a rational reconstruction by way of obituary. *Review of Radical Political Economics* 12: 1–16.

Park M K (1987) Interest representation in South Korea. *Asian Survey* 27: 903–917.

Park Y C (1986) Foreign debt, balance of payments and growth prospects: the case of the Republic of Korea, 1965-88. *World Development* 14: 1019–1058.

Park Y S and Zwick J (1985) *International Banking in Theory and Practice*. Reading, MA: Addison-Wesley.

Pasinetti LL (1977) *Lectures on the Theory of Production*. New York: Columbia University Press.

Pavitt K (1984) Sectoral patterns of technical change: towards a taxonomy and a theory. *Research Policy* 13: 343–373.

Pearce R D (1983) Industrial diversification amongst the world's leading multinational enterprises. In Casson M, ed., *The Growth of International Business*. London: Allen and Unwin, pp. 140–179.

Peet R (1983) Relations of production and the relocation of United States manufacturing industry since 1960. *Economic Geography* 59: 112–143.

Peet R (1986) The destruction of regional cultures. In Johnston R and Taylor P J, eds., *A World in Crisis? Geographical Perspectives*. Oxford: Blackwell, pp. 150–172.

Peet R, ed. (1987) *International Capitalism and Industrial Restructuring*. London: Allen and Unwin.

Perrons D (1981) The role of Ireland in the new international division of labour: a proposed framework for analysis. *Regional Studies* 15: 81–100.

Perroux F (1955) Note sur la notion de pole de croissance. *Économie Appliqué* 8, [translated in McKee D L Dean R D and Leahy W H, eds. (1970) *Regional Economics*. New York: Free Press, pp. 93–103].

Phelps E S (1962) The new view of investment: a neoclassical analysis. *Quarterly Journal of Economics* 76: 548–567.

Piore M J and Sabel C F (1984) *The Second Industrial Divide: Possibilities for Prosperity*. New York: Basic Books.

Porter M E (1985) *Competitive Advantage*. New York: Free Press.

Porter M E (1990) *The Competitive Advantage of Nations*. New York: Free Press.

Posner M V (1961) International trade and technical change. *Oxford Economic Papers* 13: 323–341.

Poulantzas N (1975) *Classes in Contemporary Capitalism*. London: New Left Books.

Pred A R (1966) *The Spatial Dynamics of U.S. Urban-Industrial Growth 1800–1914*. Cambridge, MA: MIT Press.

Preusse H G and Schinke R (1988) Debt-equity swaps: foreign direct investment and the Brazilian debt crisis. In Coffey P and do Lago L A C, eds., *The EEC and Brazil: Trade, Capital Investment and the Debt Problem*. London: Pinter, pp. 148–170.

Qualls D (1972) Concentration, barriers to entry, and long run economic profit margins. *Journal of Industrial Economics* 20: 231–242.

Quartim J (1971) *Dictatorship and Armed Struggle in Brazil*. London: New Left Books.

Ranis G (1989) The role of institutions in transition growth: the East Asian newly industrializing countries. *World Development* 17: 1443–1453.

Ranis G (1990) Contrasts in the political economy of development policy change. In Gereffi G and Wyman D L, eds., *Manufacturing Miracles: Paths of Industrialization in Latin America and East Asia*. Princeton, NJ: Princeton University Press, pp. 207–230.

Ranis G and Schive C (1985) Direct foreign investment in Taiwan's development. In Galenson W, ed., *Foreign Trade and Investment: Economic Development in the Newly Industrializing Asian Countries*. Madison: University of Wisconsin Press, pp. 85–137.

Rapping L (1965) Learning and World War II production functions. *Review of Economics and Statistics* 47: 81–86.

Reati A (1986) The rate of profit and the organic composition of capital in West German industry from 1960 to 1981. *Review of Radical Political Economics* 18: 56–86.

Reid G C (1989) *Classical Economic Growth: An Analysis in the Tradition of Adam Smith*. New York: Blackwell.

Reinganum J F (1981) Market structure and the diffusion of new technology. *Bell Journal of Economics* 12: 618–624.

Reuten G (1991) Accumulation of capital and the foundation of the tendency of the rate of profit to fall. *Cambridge Journal of Economics* 15: 79–93.

Rhee S (1988) Recent industrial adjustments of the Korean economy and underlying policy reforms. *The Developing Economies* 26: 222–246.

Richardson H (1978) *Regional Economics*. Urbana: University of Illinois Press.

Rigby D L (1988) Technical change in Canadian manufacturing: a regional analysis. Unpublished Ph.D. thesis, McMaster University Hamilton, Canada.

Rigby D L (1990a) Regional differences in manufacturing performance: the case of the Canadian food and beverage industry, 1961–1984. *Environment and Planning A* 22: 79–100.

Rigby D L (1990b) Technical change and the rate of profit: an obituary for Okishio's theorem. *Environment and Planning A* 22: 1039–1050.

Rigby D L (1991a) The existence, significance and persistence of profit rate differentials. *Economic Geography* 67: 210–222.

Rigby D L (1991b) Technical change and profits in Canadian manufacturing: a regional analysis. *The Canadian Geographer* 35: 353–366.

Robinson J (1953/54) The production function and the theory of capital. *Review of Economic Studies* 21: 81–106.

Robinson J (1961) Equilibrium growth models. *American Economic Review* 51: 360–369.

Robinson J (1969) *The Accumulation of Capital*, 3rd ed. London: Macmillan.

Rodwin L and Sazanami H, eds. (1989) *Deindustrialization and Regional Economic Transformation*. Boston: Unwin Hyman.

Roemer J E (1977) Technical change and the 'tendency of the rate of profit to fall.' *Journal of Economic Theory* 16: 403–425.

Roemer J E (1978) The effect of technological change on the real wage and Marx's falling rate of profit. *Australian Economic Papers* 17: 152–166.

Roemer J E (1979) Continuing controversy on the falling rate of profit: fixed capital and other issues. *Cambridge Journal of Economics* 3: 379–398.

Roemer J E (1981) *Analytical Foundations of Marxian Economic Theory*. Cambridge, UK: Cambridge University Press.

Rogers E M (1962) *Diffusion of Innovations*. New York: Free Press.

Romer P (1986) Increasing returns and long-run growth. *Journal of Political Economy* 94: 1002–1038.

Rosenberg N (1982) *Inside the Black Box: Technology and Economics*. Cambridge, UK: Cambridge University Press.

Rosenberg N and Frischtak C (1984) Technological innovation and long waves. *Cambridge Journal of Economics* 8: 7–25.

Rothacher A (1984) The Green Party in German politics. *West European Politics* 7: 109–116.

Rowthorn R (1974) Neoclassicism, neo-Ricardianism and Marxism. *New Left Review* 86: 63–87.

Rubin I I (1972) *Essays on Marx's Theory of Value* (translated by M Samardzija and F Perlman). Detroit, MI: Black and Red.

Sabel C F and Zeitlin J (1985) Historical alternatives to mass production: politics, markets and technology in nineteenth-century industrialization. *Past and Present* 108: 133–176.

Salter W E G (1960) *Productivity and Technical Change*, 1st ed. Cambridge, UK: Cambridge University Press.

Salvadori N (1981) Falling rate of profit with a constant real wage. An example. *Cambridge Journal of Economics* 5: 59–66.

Samuelson P (1957) Wages and interest: a modern dissection of Marxian economic models. *American Economic Review* 47: 884–912.

Samuelson P (1962) Parable and realism in capital theory: the surrogate production function. *Review of Economic Studies* 29: 193–206.

Samuelson P (1965) A theory of induced innovation along Kennedy-Weisacker lines. *Review of Economics and Statistics* 47: 343–356.

Samuelson P (1966) A summing up. *Quarterly Journal of Economics* 80: 568–583.

Samuelson P (1972) The economics of Marx: an ecumenical reply. *Journal of Economic Literature* 51: 51–55.

Saso M (1990) *Women in the Japanese Workplace*. London: Hilary Shipman.

Saxenian A L (1985) The genesis of Silicon Valley. In Hall P and Markusen A R, eds., *Silicon Landscapes* London: Allen and Unwin, pp. 20–34.

Saxenian A L (1994). *Regional Advantage: Culture and Competition in Silicon Valley and Route 128* Cambridge, MA: Harvard University Press.

Sayer A (1984) *Method in Social Science: A Realist Approach*. London: Hutchinson.

Sayer A (1985) Industry and space: a sympathetic critique of radical research. *Environment and Planning D: Society and Space* 3: 3–29.

Sayer A (1986) New developments in manufacturing: the just-in-time system. *Capital and Class* 30: 43–72.

Sayer A and Morgan K (1986) The electronics industry and regional development in Britain. In Amin A and Goddard J R, eds., *Technological Change, Industrial Restructuring and Regional Development*. London: Allen and Unwin, pp. 157–187.

Sayer A and Walker R (1992) *The New Social Economy: Reworking the Division of Labor*. Cambridge, MA: Blackwell.

Schefold B (1976) Different forms of technical progress. *Economic Journal* 86: 806–819.

Schive C (1990) The next stage of industrialisation in Taiwan and Korea. In Gereffi G and Wyman D L, eds., *Manufacturing Miracles: Paths of Industrialization in Latin America and East Asia*. Princeton, NJ: Princeton University Press, pp. 267–291.

Schmookler J (1966) *Invention and Economic Growth*. Cambridge, MA: Harvard University Press.

Schoenberger E (1988) From Fordism to flexible accumulation: technology, competitive strategies and international location. *Environment and Planning D: Society and Space* 6: 245–262.

Schumpeter J (1939) *Business Cycles*, 2 vols. New York: McGraw-Hill.

Schumpeter J (1942) *Capitalism, Socialism and Democracy*. New York: Harper.

Scitovsky T (1986) Economic development in Taiwan and South Korea 1965-1981. In Lau L, ed., *Models of Development: A Comparative Study of Economic Growth in South Korea and Taiwan*. San Francisco: Institute for Contemporary Studies.

Scott A J (1976) Land and land-rent: an interpretive review of the French literature. *Progress in Human Geography* 9: 101–146.

Scott A J (1980) *The Urban Land Nexus and the State*. London: Pion.

Scott A J (1988a) *Metropolis: From the Division of Labor to Urban Form*. Berkeley: University of California Press.

Scott A J (1988b) *New Industrial Spaces*. London: Pion.

Scott A J and Cooke P (1988) The new geography and sociology of production. *Environment and Planning D: Society and Space* 6: 241–244.

Scott A J and Storper M, eds., (1986) *Production, Work, Territory: The Geographical Anatomy of Industrial Capitalism*. Boston: Allen and Unwin.

Scott A J and Storper M (1987) High technology industry and regional development: a theoretical critique and reconstruction. *International Social Science Journal* 1: 215–232.

Scott A J and Storper M (1990) Regional development reconsidered Lewis Center for Regional Policy Studies. Working Paper No. 1, University of California, Los Angeles.

Semmler W (1984) *Competition, Monopoly, and Differential Profit Rates*. New York: Columbia University Press.

Shaikh A (1978) Political economy and capitalism: notes on Dobb's theory of crisis. *Cambridge Journal of Economics* 2: 92–99.

Shaikh A (1980) Marxian competition versus perfect competition: further comments on the so-called choice of technique. *Cambridge Journal of Economics* 4: 75–83.

Shaikh A (1982) Neo-Ricardian economics—a wealth of algebra, a poverty of theory. *Review of Radical Political Economics* 14: 67–83.

Shaikh A (1984) The transformation from Marx to Sraffam. In Mandel E and Freeman A, eds., *Ricardo, Marx, Sraffa*. London: Verso, pp. 43–84.

Sharpe A (1982) A survey of empirical Marxian economics. Paper presented at the annual meeting of the Union for Radical Political Economy, Allied Social Science Association, New York.

Sheppard E and Barnes T J (1990) *The Capitalist Space Economy*. London: Unwin Hyman.

Sherman H J (1982) Monopoly power and profit rates. *Review of Radical Political Economics* 15: 125–133.

Sherman H J (1990) Cyclical behavior of the labor share. *Review of Radical Political Economics* 22: 92–112.

Singer H W and Gray P (1988) Trade policy and growth of developing countries: some new data. *World Development* 16: 395–403.

Soete L and Turner R (1984) Technology diffusion and the rate of technical change. *Economic Journal* 94: 612–623.

Soja E W (1989) *Postmodern Geographies*. London: Verso.

Solomou S (1989) Long waves in national and world economic growth, 1850-1973. Paper presented at the International Colloquium on the Long Waves of the Economic Conjuncture, Vrije Universiteit, Brussels, January 12–14.

Solow R M (1957) Technical change and the aggregate production function. *Review of Economics and Statistics* 39: 312–320.

Solow R M (1962) Substitution and fixed proportions in the theory of capital. *Review of Economic Studies* 24: 207–218.

Spengler J J and Allen W R, eds., (1960) *Essays in Economic Thought: Aristotle to Marshall*. Chicago: Rand McNally.

Sraffa P (1960) *The Production of Commodities by Means of Commodities*. Cambridge, UK: Cambridge University Press.

Stallings B (1990) The role of foreign capital in economic development. In Gereffi G and Wyman D L, eds., *Manufacturing Miracles: Paths of Industrialization in Latin America and East Asia*. Princeton, NJ: Princeton University Press, pp. 55–89.

Statistical Yearbook of the Republic of China. Taipei (annual).

Statistics Canada, *Inventories, Shipments and Orders in Manufacturing Industries.* Ottawa: Government Printer, Cat. 31-003 (various years).

Statistics Canada, *General Review of the Manufacturing Industries of Canada* Ottawa: Government Printer, Cat. 31-201 (various years).

Statistics Canada, *Consumer Price Index.* Ottawa: Government Printer, Cat. 62-001 (various years).

Statistics Canada, *Industry Selling Price Indexes.* Ottawa: Government Printer, Cat. 62-011 (various years).

Statistics Canada, *Historical Labour Force Statistics.* Ottawa: Government Printer, Cat. 71-201.

Statistics Canada, *Fixed Capital Flows and Stocks.* Unpublished regional series.

Steedman I (1975) Positive profits with negative surplus values. *Economic Journal* 85: 114–123.

Steedman I (1977) *Marx after Sraffa.* London: New Left Books.

Steedman I (1980) A note on the 'choice of technique' under capitalism. *Cambridge Journal of Economics* 4: 61–64.

Steedman I (1981) Ricardo, Marx, Sraffa. In Steedman I et al., eds., *The Value Controversy.* London: Verso, pp. 11–19.

Steinberg D I (1988) Sociopolitical factors and Korea's future economic policies. *World Development* 16: 19–34.

Stigler G (1961) Economic problems in measuring changes in productivity. In *Output, Input and Productivity Measurement* (Studies in Income and Wealth Vol. 25). Princeton, NJ: National Bureau of Economic Research.

Stilwell F J B (1980) *Economic Crisis, Cities and Regions: An Analysis of Current Urban and Regional Problems in Australia.* Oxford: Pergamon.

Stoneman P (1980) The rate of imitation, learning and profitability. *Economic Letters* 6: 179–183.

Stoneman P (1983) *The Economic Analysis of Technological Change.* London: Oxford University Press.

Stopford J M Dunning J H and Haberich K O (1981) *The World Directory of Multinational Enterprises.* London: Macmillan.

Storper M (1985) Oligopoly and the product cycle: essentialism and economic geography. *Economic Geography* 61: 260–282.

Storper M (1988) Big structures, small events, and large processes in economic geography. *Environment and Planning A* 20: 165–185.

Storper M and Scott A J (1988) The geographical foundations and social regulation of flexible production complexes. In Wolch J and Dear M, eds., *The Power of Geography: How Territory Shapes Social Life.* Boston: Unwin Hyman, pp. 21–40.

Storper M and Walker R (1989) *The Capitalist Imperative.* Oxford: Blackwell.

Stpindyck R S and Rotemberg J J (1983) Dynamic factor demands and the effects of energy price shocks. *American Economic Review* 73: 1066–1079.

Suzuki D (1990) *Inventing the Future.* Sydney: Allen and Unwin.

Swann P L (1973) The international diffusion of an innovation. *Journal of Industrial Economics* 22: 61–69.

Sweezy P M (1970) *The Theory of Capitalist Development.* New York: Modern Reader.

Tarbuck K J (1984) Marx, productive and unproductive labour. *Studies in Political Economy* 12: 81–102.

Taylor M J (1986) The product-cycle theory: a critique. *Environment and Planning A* 18: 751–761.

Teitel S and Thoumi F E (1986) From import substitution to exports: the manufacturing exports experience of Argentina and Brazil. *Economic Development and Cultural Change* 34: 455–490.

Teixeira M J (1981) Development of Brazil's iron and steel industry: state entry and competition. Unpublished Ph.D. thesis, Columbia University, New York.

Teubal M (1984) The role of technological learning in the exports of manufactured goods: the case of selected capital goods in Brazil. *World Development* 12: 849–865.

Tew B (1985) *The Evolution of the International Monetary System*, 3rd ed. London: Hutchinson.

Tharakan P K M (1979) *The International Division of Labour and Multinational Companies*. European Centre for Study and Information on Multinational Corporations.

Thirtle C G and Ruttan V W (1987) *The Role of Demand and Supply in the Generation and Diffusion of Technical Change*. Chur, Switzerland: Harwood Academic Press.

Thrift N and Leyshon A (1988) The gambling propensity: banks, developing country debt exposures and the new international financial system. *Geoforum* 19: 55–69.

Thurow L (1979) The U.S. productivity problem. *Data Resources Review*.

TIE (Transnationals Information Exchange) (1984) *Brazil: The New Militancy*. Amsterdam: TIE, Report No. 17.

Tsiang S C and Chen W L (1984) *Developments towards Trade Liberalization in Taiwan*. Taipei: Chung-hua Institution for Economic Research.

Tsuruta T (1988) The rapid growth era. In Komiya R Okuno M and Suzumura K, eds., *Industrial Policy of Japan*. Tokyo: Academic Press, pp. 49–87.

Tu C H and Wang W T (1988) *Trade Liberalization in the Republic of China and the Economic Effects of Tariff Reductions on Taiwan*. Seoul: Korea Development Institute.

Tukey J W (1977) *Exploratory Data Analysis*. Reading, MA: Addison-Wesley.

Tyler W G (1981) *Trade Policies and Industrial Incentives in Brazil, 1980-1981*. Rio de Janeiro: IPEA/INPES.

UNCTNC (UN Commission on Transnational Corporations) (1983) *Transnational Corporations in World Development: Third Survey*. New York: United Nations.

Union for Radical Political Economics (1978) *Crisis Reader*.

Ure A (1845) *Recent Improvements in Arts, Manufactures and Mines*. New York: Appleton.

US Congress: Joint Economic Committee (various years).

US Department of Commerce Bureau of Economic Analysis: Census of Manufactures (various years).

US Department of Commerce Bureau of Economic Analysis: Annual Survey of Manufactures (various years).

Utterback J M (1987) Innovation and industrial evolution in manufacturing industries. In Guile B R Brooks H, eds., *Technology and Global Industry: Companies and Nations in the World Economy*. Washington, DC: National Academy Press, pp. 16–48.

Varaiya P and Wiseman M (1981) Investment and employment in manufacturing in US metropolitan areas. *Regional Science and Urban Economics* 11: 431–469.

Varian H R (1978) *Microeconomic Analysis*. New York: Norton.

Vaupel J W and Curhan J P (1973) *The World's Multinational Enterprises*. Cambridge, MA: Harvard University Press.

Velleman P F and Hoaglin D C (1981) *Applications, Basics and Computing of Exploratory Data Analysis*. Belmont, CA: Duxbury.

Vernon R (1966) International investment and international trade in the product cycle. *Quarterly Journal of Economics* 80: 190–207.

Vos R (1982) External dependence, capital accumulation, and the role of the state: South Korea 1960-77 *Development and Change* 13: 91–121.

de Vries R (1990) Adam Smith: managing the global wealth of nations. *World Financial Markets* 2: 1–15.

de Vroey M (1981) Value, production and exchange. In Steedman I et al. *The Value Controversy*. London: Verso, pp. 173–201.

Wade R (1990a) *Governing the Market*. Princeton, NJ: Princeton University Press.

Wade R (1990b) Industrial policy in East Asia: does it lead or follow the market? In Gereffi G and Wyman D L, eds., *Manufacturing Miracles: Paths of Industrialization in Latin America and East Asia*. Princeton, NJ: Princeton University Press, pp. 231–266.

Walker R (1981) A theory of suburbanisation. In Dear M and Scott A J, eds., *Urbanization and Urban Planning in Capitalist Society*. London: Methuen, pp. 383–429.

Walker R (1985) Technological determination and determinism: industrial growth and location. In Castells M, ed., *High Technology, Space and Society*. Beverly Hills, CA: Sage, pp. 226–264.

Walker R (1989) Regulation, flexible specialization and the forces of production in capitalist society. Paper presented to the Cardiff Symposium on Regulation, Innovation and Spatial Development, September.

Wallerstein I M (1979) *The Capitalist World Economy: Essays*. New York: Cambridge University Press.

Walmsley J (1991) *Global Investing: Eurobonds and Alternatives*. New York: St. Martin's Press.

Walter A (1991) *World Power and World Money: The Role of Hegemony and International Monetary Order*. New York: St. Martin's Press.

Watts H D (1987) *Industrial Geography*. Harlow, Essex, UK: Longman.

Webber M J (1970) *Impact of Uncertainty on Location*. Canberra: Australian National University Press and Cambridge, MA: MIT Press.

Webber M J (1982a) The tendency of the rate of profit to fall: 1. Values. Unpublished manuscript, Department of Geography, McMaster University, Hamilton, Ontario, Canada.

Webber M J (1982b) The tendency of the rate of profit to fall: 2. Prices, Unpublished manuscript, Department of Geography, McMaster University, Hamilton, Ontario, Canada.

Webber MJ (1982c) Agglomeration and the regional question. *Antipode* 14: 1–11.

Webber M J (1986) Regional production and the production of regions: the case of steeltown. In Scott A J and Storper M, eds., *Production, Work, Territory: The Geographical Anatomy of Industrial Capitalism*. Boston: Allen and Unwin, pp. 195–224.

Webber M J (1987) Quantitative measurement of some Marxist categories. *Environment and Planning A* 19: 1303–1322.

Webber M J and Foot S P H (1984) The measurement of unequal exchange. *Environment and Planning A* 16: 927–947.

Webber M J and Foot S P H (1988) Profitability and accumulation. *Economic Geography* 64: 335–351.

Webber M J and Jamieson N (forthcoming) Labour supply: female employment in retailing. *Labour and Industry*.

Webber M J and Rigby D L (1986) The rate of profit in Canadian Manufacturing, 1950–1981. *Review of Radical Political Economics* 18: 33–55.

Webber M J and Tonkin S (1987) Technical changes and the rate of profit in the Canadian food industry. *Environment and Planning A* 19: 1579–1596.

Webber M J and Tonkin S (1988a) Technical changes and the rate of profit in the Canadian textile, knitting and clothing industries. *Environment and Planning A* 20: 1487–1506.

Webber M J and Tonkin S (1988b) Technical changes and the rate of profit in the Canadian wood, furniture and paper industries. *Environment and Planning A* 20: 1623–1643.

Webber M J Campbell I and Fincher R (1990) Ethnicity, gender and industrial restructuring in Australia, 1971–1986. *Journal of Intercultural Studies* 11: 1–48.

Webber M J Clark G L McKay J and Missen G (1992) Industrial restructuring. Working Paper No. 92-2, Universities of Monash and Melbourne Joint Project on Comparative Australian–Asian Development.

Weeks J (1981) *Capital and Exploitation*. Princeton, NJ: Princeton University Press.

Weisskopf T E (1979) Marxian crisis theory and the rate of profit in the postwar US economy. *Cambridge Journal of Economics* 3: 341–378.

Weisskopf T E (1985) The rate of surplus value in the postwar US economy: a reply to Moseley's critique. *Cambridge Journal of Economics* 9: 81–84.

Weisskopf T E (1988) An analysis of profitability changes in eight capitalist countries. *Review of Radical Political Economics* 20: 68–79.

von Weizsacker C C (1966) Tentative notes on a two sector model with induced technical progress. *Review of Economic Studies* 33: 245–251.

Whitehead L (1990) Political explanations of macroeconomic management: a survey. *World Development* 18: 1133–1146.

Williams K Cutler T Williams J and Haslam C (1987) The end of mass production? *Economy and Society* 16: 405–439.

Wirth J D (1970) *The Politics of Brazilian Development: 1930-1954*. Stanford, CA: Stanford University Press.

Wolff E N (1975) The rate of surplus value in Puerto Rico. *Journal of Political Economy* 83: 935–949.

Wolff E N (1979) The rate of surplus value, the organic composition and the general rate of profit in the U.S. economy. *American Economic Review* 69: 329–341.

Wolff E N (1985) The magnitude and causes of the recent productivity changes in the United States: a survey of recent studies. In Baumol W J and McLennan K, eds., *Productivity Growth and U.S. Competitiveness*. New York: Oxford University Press, pp. 29–57.

Wolff E N (1986) The productivity slowdown and the fall in the US rate of profit 1947-1976. *Review of Radical Political Economics* 18: 87–110.

Woo J E (1991) *Race to the Swift: State and Finance in Korean Industrialization*. New York: Columbia University Press.

World Bank (1977) *Prospects for the Developing Countries 1978-1985*. New York: Oxford University Press.

World Bank (1981) *World Development Report 1981*. New York: Oxford University Press.

World Bank (1985) *World Development Report 1985*. New York: Oxford University Press.

World Bank (1987) *World Development Report 1987*. New York: Oxford University Press.

World Bank (1989) *World Development Report 1989*. New York: Oxford University Press.

World Bank (1992) *World Development Report 1992*. New York: Oxford University Press.

World Commission on Environment and Development (1987) *Our Common Future*. Melbourne: Oxford University Press.

Wright E O (1979) *Class, Crisis and the State*. London: Verso.

Wright E O (1981) Reconsiderations. In Steedman I et al., eds., *The Value Controversy*. London: Verso, pp. 130–162.

Wrigley N (1992) Antitrust regulation and the restructuring of grocery retailing in Britain and the USA. *Environment and Planning A* 24: 727–749.

Yaffe D (1973) The Marxian theory of crisis, capital and the state. *Economy and Society* 2: 186–232.

INDEX